Lecture Notes in Computer Science 9458

Commenced Publication in 1973
Founding and Former Series Editors:
Gerhard Goos, Juris Hartmanis, and Jan van Leeuwen

More information about this series at http://www.springer.com/series/7408

Xinyu Feng · Sungwoo Park (Eds.)

Programming Languages and Systems

13th Asian Symposium, APLAS 2015
Pohang, South Korea, November 30 – December 2, 2015
Proceedings

Springer

Editors
Xinyu Feng
University of Science and Technology of China
Hefei, Anhui
China

Sungwoo Park
Pohang University of Science and Technology
Pohang
Korea (Republic of)

ISSN 0302-9743 ISSN 1611-3349 (electronic)
Lecture Notes in Computer Science
ISBN 978-3-319-26528-5 ISBN 978-3-319-26529-2 (eBook)
DOI 10.1007/978-3-319-26529-2

Library of Congress Control Number: 2015954608

LNCS Sublibrary: SL2 – Programming and Software Engineering

Springer Cham Heidelberg New York Dordrecht London

Printed on acid-free paper

Springer International Publishing AG Switzerland is part of Springer Science+Business Media (www.springer.com)

Preface

This volume contains the proceedings of the 13th Asian Symposium on Programming Languages and Systems (APLAS 2015), held in Pohang, Korea, from November 30 to December 2, 2015. APLAS aims to stimulate programming language research by providing a forum for the presentation of latest results and the exchange of ideas in programming languages and systems. APLAS is based in Asia, but is an international forum that serves the worldwide programming language community. Past APLAS symposiums were successfully held in Singapore (2014), Melbourne (2013), Kyoto (2012), Kenting (2011), Shanghai (2010), Seoul (2009), Bangalore (2008), Singapore (2007), Sydney (2006), Tsukuba (2005), Taipei (2004), and Beijing (2003) after three informal workshops.

APLAS 2015 solicited submissions in two categories, regular research papers and system and tool presentations. The topics covered in the conference include, but are not limited to, semantics, logics, and foundational theory; design of languages and foundational calculi; domain-specific languages; type systems; compilers, interpreters, and abstract machines; program derivation, synthesis, and transformation; program analysis, constraints, verification, and model-checking; software security; concurrency and parallelism; and tools for programming, verification, and implementation.

This year 74 papers were submitted to APLAS. Each submission was reviewed by three or more Program Committee members with the help of external reviewers. After thoroughly evaluating the relevance and quality of each paper, the Program Committee decided to accept 24 regular research papers and one system and tool presentation. This year's program also continues the APLAS tradition of invited talks by distinguished researchers: Peter O'Hearn (Facebook), Sukyoung Ryu (KAIST), Eran Yahav (Technion), and Hongseok Yang (University of Oxford).

This program would not have been possible without the unstinting efforts of several people, whom we would like to thank. First, the Program Committee and additional reviewers for the hard work put in toward ensuring the high quality of the proceedings. Our thanks also go to the Asian Association for Foundation of Software (AAFS), founded by Asian researchers in cooperation with many researchers from Europe and the USA, for sponsoring and supporting APLAS. We would like to warmly thank the Steering Committee in general and Gyesik Lee and Hyeonseung Im for their support in the local organization and for organizing the poster session. Finally, we are grateful to Andrei Voronkov whose EasyChair system eased the processes of submission, paper selection, and proceedings compilation.

September 2015

Xinyu Feng
Sungwoo Park

Preface

Organization

General Chair

Sungwoo Park	Pohang University of Science and Technology (POSTECH), Korea

Program Chair

Xinyu Feng	University of Science and Technology of China, China

Program Committee

James Brotherston	University College London, UK
James Cheney	University of Edinburgh, UK
Huimin Cui	Institute of Computing Technology, CAS, China
Mike Dodds	University of York, UK
Xinyu Feng	University of Science and Technology of China, China
Nate Foster	Cornell University, USA
Alexey Gotsman	IMDEA Software Institute, Spain
Aquinas Hobor	School of Computing, National University of Singapore/Yale-NUS College, Singapore
Chung-Kil Hur	Seoul National University, Korea
Radha Jagadeesan	DePaul University, USA
Annie Liu	Stony Brook University, USA
Andreas Lochbihler	ETH Zurich, Switzerland
Santosh Nagarakatte	Rutgers University, USA
David Naumann	Stevens Institute of Technology, USA
Michael Norrish	NICTA, Australia
Hakjoo Oh	Korea University, Korea
Murali Krishna Ramanathan	Indian Institute of Science, India
Xavier Rival	CNRS/ENS/Inria, France
Kohei Suenaga	Kyoto University, Japan
Gang Tan	Lehigh University, USA
Alwen Tiu	Nanyang Technological University, Singapore
Martin Vechev	ETH Zurich, Switzerland
Bow-Yaw Wang	Academia Sinica, Taiwan
Nobuko Yoshida	Imperial College London, UK
Lijun Zhang	Institute of Software, CAS, China

Poster Chair

Hyeonseung Im — Kangwon National University, Korea

Local Arrangements Chair

Gyesik Lee — Hankyong National University, Korea

Additional Reviewers

Abate, Pietro
Anderson, Gabrielle
Berger, Martin
Bielik, Pavol
Boyland, John
Brandt, Steven
Brandvein, Jon
Cerone, Andrea
Chand, Saksham
Dahlqvist, Fredrik
Deng, Yuxin
Dhok, Monika
Dietl, Werner
Feret, Jerome
Fernandez, Maribel
Franco, Juliana
Gay, Simon
Gorogiannis, Nikos
Hasuo, Ichiro
He, Chaodong
Hou, Zhe
Igarashi, Atsushi
Kane, Christopher
Kanovich, Max
Lee, Woosuk
Li, Feng
Lin, Bo
Mariño, Julio
Morihata, Akimasa
Mostrous, Dimitris
Mudduluru, Rashmi
Murawski, Andrzej
Padovani, Luca
Paige, Richard
Poluri, Sri Varun
Pérez, Jorge A.
Reich, Jason S.
Rowe, Reuben
Russo, Claudio
Schöpp, Ulrich
Sezgin, Ali
Simon, Axel
Singh, Gagandeep
Song, Lei
Spitters, Bas
Terauchi, Tachio
Turrini, Andrea
Weng, Xuetian
Ying, Mingsheng

Invited Talks

Programming with "Big Code"

Eran Yahav

Technion, Haifa, Israel
yahave@cs.technion.ac.il

Abstract. The vast amount of code available on the web is increasing on a daily basis. Open-source hosting sites such as GitHub contain billions of lines of code. Community question-answering sites provide millions of code snippets with corresponding text and metadata. The amount of code available in executable binaries is even greater. In this talk, I will cover recent research trends on leveraging such "big code" for program analysis, program synthesis and reverse engineering. We will consider a range of semantic representations based on symbolic automata [11, 15], tracelets [3], numerical abstractions [13, 14], and textual descriptions [1, 22], as well as different notions of code similarity based on these representations.

To leverage these semantic representations, we will consider a number of prediction techniques, including statistical language models [19, 20], variable order Markov models [2], and other distance-based and model-based sequence classification techniques.

Finally, I will show applications of these techniques including semantic code search in both source code and stripped binaries, code completion and reverse engineering.

Analyzing JavaScript Web Applications in the Wild (Mostly) Statically

Sukyoung Ryu

School of Computing, KAIST, Daejeon, Republic of Korea
sryu.cs@kaist.ac.kr

Analyzing real-world JavaScript web applications is a challenging task. On top of understanding the semantics of JavaScript [4], it requires modeling of web documents [20, 21], platform objects [5], and interactions between them. Not only JavaScript itself but also its usage patterns are extremely dynamic [15, 16]. Most of web applications load JavaScript code dynamically, which makes pure static analysis approaches inapplicable.

In this talk, we present our attempts to analyze JavaScript web applications in the wild mostly statically using various approaches. From pure JavaScript programs to JavaScript web applications using platform-specific libraries, we explain technical challenges in analyzing each of them and how we built an open-source analysis framework for JavaScript, SAFE [7, 17], that addresses the challenges incrementally.

First, we describe quirky language features and semantics of JavaScript that make static analysis difficult and our first design of SAFE [10] designed to be scalable for growth. SAFE transforms a JavaScript source program to an Abstract Syntax Tree (AST), an Intermediate Representation (IR), and a Control Flow Graph (CFG) to enable various analyses on different levels of representations. Its default static analyzer on CFGs is based on the abstract interpretation framework, and it supports flow-sensitive and context-sensitive analyses of stand-alone JavaScript programs by faithfully modeling the semantics of ECMAScript 5. The pluggable and scalable design of the framework allowed experiments with JavaScript variants like adding a module system [8], eliminating the with statement [12], and detecting code clones [3].

We then describe how we extended SAFE to model web application execution environments of various browsers [14] and platform-specific library functions. To provide a faithful (partial) model of browsers, we support the configurability of HTML/DOM tree abstraction levels so that users can adjust a trade-off between analysis performance and precision depending on their applications. To analyze interactions between applications and platform-specific libraries specified in Web APIs, we develop automatic modeling of library functions from Web APIs and detect possible misuses of Web APIs by web applications [2]. Analyzing real-world web applications requires more scalable analysis than analyzing stand-alone JavaScript programs [9, 13].

In spite of active research accomplishments in JavaScript web applications [1, 6, 11, 18, 19], many issues still remain to be resolved such as events, callback functions, and hybrid web applications. We discuss possible future research directions with open challenges.

References

1. Andreasen, E., Møller, A.: Determinacy in static analysis for jQuery. In: Proceedings of the 29th Annual Object-Oriented Programming Systems, Languages, and Applications (2014)
2. Bae, S., Cho, H., Lim, I., Ryu, S.: SAFE$_{\mathsf{WAPI}}$: Web API misuse detector for web applications. In: Proceedings of the 22nd ACM SIGSOFT Symposium and the 13th European Conference on Foundations of Software Engineering. ACM (2014)
3. Cheung, W., Ryu, S., Kim, S.: Development nature matters: an empirical study of code clones in JavaScript applications. Empir. Softw. Eng. (2015)
4. ECMA. ECMA-262: ECMAScript Language Specification. Edition 5.1 (2011)
5. Linux Foundation. Tizen. http://tizen.org
6. Jensen, S.H., Madsen, M., Møller, A.: Modeling the HTML DOM and browser API in static analysis of JavaScript web applications. In: Proceedings of the 19th ACM SIGSOFT Symposium and the 13th European Conference on Foundations of Software Engineering. ACM (2011)
7. KAIST PLRG. SAFE: JavaScript analysis framework (2013). http://safe.kaist.ac.kr
8. Kang, S., Ryu, S.: Formal specification of a JavaScript module system. In: Proceedings of the ACM International Conference on Object Oriented Programming Systems Languages and Applications, pp. 621–638 (2012)
9. Ko, Y., Lee, H., Dolby, J., Ryu, S.: Practically tunable static analysis framework for large-scale JavaScript applications. In: Proceedings of the 30th ACM/IEEE International Conference on Automated Software Engineering (2015)
10. Lee, H., Won, S., Jin, J., Cho, J., Ryu, S.: SAFE: formal specification and implementation of a scalable analysis framework for ECMAScript. In: International Workshop on Foundations of Object Oriented Languages (2012)
11. Madsen, M., Livshits, B., Fanning, M.: Practical static analysis of JavaScript applications in the presence of frameworks and libraries. In: Proceedings of the 2013 9th Joint Meeting on Foundations of Software Engineering. ACM (2013)
12. Park, C., Lee, H., Ryu, S.: All about the `with` statement in JavaScript: removing `with` statements in JavaScript applications. In: Proceedings of the 9th Symposium on Dynamic Languages (2013)
13. Park, C., Ryu, S.: Scalable and precise static analysis of JavaScript applications via loop-sensitivity. In: Proceedings of the European Conference on Object-Oriented Programming. LNCS, Springer (2015)
14. Park, C., Won, S., Jin, J., Ryu, S.; Static analysis of JavaScript web applications in the wild via practical DOM modeling. In: Proceedings of the 30th ACM/IEEE International Conference on Automated Software Engineering (2015)
15. Richards, G., Hammer, C., Burg, B., Vitek, J.: The eval that men do: a large-scale study of the use of eval in JavaScript applications. In: Proceedings of the 25th European Conference on Object-Oriented Programming (2011)
16. Richards, G., Lebresne, S., Burg, B., Vitek, J.: An analysis of the dynamic behavior of JavaScript programs. In: Proceedings of the 2010 ACM SIGPLAN Conference on Programming Language Design and Implementation (2010)
17. Ryu, S., Choi, J., Choi, W., Ko, Y., Lee, H., Park, C.: The SAFE specification (2015). https://github.com/sukyoung/safe/blob/master/doc/manual/safe.pdf
18. Schäfer, M., Sridharan, M., Dolby, J., Tip, F.: Dynamic determinacy analysis. In: Proceedings of the ACM SIGPLAN Conference on Programming Language Design and Implementation (2013)

19. Sridharan, M., Dolby, J., Chandra, S., Schäfer, M., Tip, F.: Correlation tracking for points-to analysis of JavaScript. In: Noble, J. (ed.) ECOOP 2012. LNCS, vol. 7313, pp. 435–458. Springer, Heidelberg (2012)
20. W3C. Document Object Model Activity Statement. http://www.w3.org/DOM/Activity
21. WHATWG. HTML Living Standard. http://www.whatwg.org/specs/web-apps/current-work/multipage/

Probabilistic Programming

Hongseok Yang

University of Oxford, Oxford, UK

Probabilistic programming refers to the idea of using standard programming constructs for specifying probabilistic models and employing generic inference algorithms for answering various queries on these models. Although this idea itself is not new and was, in fact, explored by several programming-language researchers in the early 2000, it is only in the last few years that probabilistic programming has gained a large amount of attention among researchers in machine learning and programming languages, and that serious probabilistic programming languages (such as Anglican, Church, Infer.net, PyMC, Stan, and Venture) started to appear and have been taken up by a nontrivial number of users.

My talk has two goals. One is to introduce probabilistic programming to the programming-language audience. The other is to explain a few lessons that I learnt about probabilistic programming from my machine learning colleagues in Oxford. They have been developing a high-order call-by-value probabilistic programming language called Anglican, and through many discussions and close collaborations, they taught me why people in machine learning cared about probabilistic programming and pointed out new interesting research directions. These lessons had huge influence on how I think about probabilistic programming. I will try to explain the lessons through their influence on my ongoing projects, which aim at optimising probabilistic programs using techniques from programming languages and providing denotational semantics of high-order probabilistic programs. These projects are jointly pursued with Sam Staton, Jan-Willem van de Meent, Frank Wood (Oxford), Diane Gallois-Wong (ENS), Chris Heunen (Edinburgh), Ohad Kammar (Cambridge) and David Tolpin (Paypal).

Contents

Hoare Logic and Types

Functional Programming and Semantics

Model Checking

Program Analysis - I

Medley

Invited Talk

Programming with "Big Code"

Eran Yahav(✉)

Technion, Haifa, Israel
yahave@cs.technion.ac.il

Abstract. The vast amount of code available on the web is increasing on a daily basis. Open-source hosting sites such as GitHub contain billions of lines of code. Community question-answering sites provide millions of code snippets with corresponding text and metadata. The amount of code available in executable binaries is even greater. In this talk, I will cover recent research trends on leveraging such "big code" for program analysis, program synthesis and reverse engineering. We will consider a range of semantic representations based on symbolic automata [11,15], tracelets [3], numerical abstractions [13,14], and textual descriptions [1,22], as well as different notions of code similarity based on these representations.

To leverage these semantic representations, we will consider a number of prediction techniques, including statistical language models [19,20], variable order Markov models [2], and other distance-based and model-based sequence classification techniques.

Finally, I will show applications of these techniques including semantic code search in both source code and stripped binaries, code completion and reverse engineering.

As of August 2015, the GitHub open-source hosting site hosts over 26 million public repositories. The popular question-answering site Stackoverflow holds over 16 million answers, many of them containing code. Both of these sites, as well as other similar sites, are growing rapidly. Furthermore, there are millions of binary executables of mobile applications hosted on the Apple App Store, Google Play, and others. The number of binaries of desktop applications is larger by at least an order of magnitude.

The availability of these massive amounts of code and meta-data has the potential to revolutionize the way software is being developed, taught, debugged, analyzed, and reverse-engineered. In this talk, and this short paper, I will give a brief description of some of the main challenges in leveraging "big code" and how we address them in our work.

The Unreasonable Effectiveness of Data. In recent years, statistical techniques have revolutionized many areas [5]. Problems that have been considered extremely difficult saw tremendous progress through the use of statistical machine learning and huge amounts of training data. These include problems from language processing such as speech recognition and machine translation, problems from machine vision such as scene completion [6], object identification [9], and others [4]. Applying similar techniques to software can unlock a new world of opportunities.

X. Feng and S. Park (Eds.): APLAS 2015, LNCS 9458, pp. 3–8, 2015.
DOI: 10.1007/978-3-319-26529-2_1

Challenges

Big Code vs. Big Data. A program is a *data transformer*, not just data. A single program may represent an unbounded number of behaviors, depending on its inputs. The analysis of "big code" therefore includes not only the challenges associated with big data (see [8]), but also a host of additional challenges, those that stem from the difficulty of modeling (and extracting) semantic properties of programs.

The ability to extract precise semantic information from a program is a critical aspect of learning from "big code". The semantic information extracted from the program allows us to reason about a program as a data transformer, and not only on the surface properties of the program itself. The importance of the precision of static analysis for effective learning from "big code" is supported by experimental evidence [11,18,19].

Semantic Representation. To learn from "big code", we need to define the semantic representation that we extract from each program, and the model that we use to represent the aggregate knowledge. The semantic representation can range from surface properties of the program (based on program syntax), through tracelets [3] that capture partial information about possible execution traces, symbolic automata [11,15] that summarize possible execution using regular approximations, numerical abstractions [13,14] that capture possible numerical runtime values, textual descriptions [1,22] correlated with a program, and more.

Program Similarity. Similarity is a central notion in many machine learning algorithms. Even for algorithms that are not based on similarity, understanding the similarity between objects can help in the design of the model. While there has been a lot of work on various notions of program equivalence [12,16,17], and qualitative notions of program differencing [7,13,14], the problem of *quantitative* program similarity remains largely unexplored.

Applications

Program Synthesis. Program synthesis techniques generate procedural code from declarative specifications. Existing techniques apply synthesis at such a fine grain that they can never hope to generate code of the richness and complexity required by application-level programmers. In contrast, synthesis algorithms using "big code" may leverage the collective programming knowledge captured in millions of open-source projects [11,15,19].

While synthesis of an entire realistic program from a declarative specification remains a somewhat distant vision, there are forms of synthesis that are already of practical value. In some cases, the problem of synthesis can be reduced to the problem of *semantic code search.* That is, trying to synthesize code for which a solution already exists, the problem is finding that solution (and verifying that it satisfies the desired specification) rather than synthesizing the solution from scratch.

In other cases, part of the program is already known, and the programmer only needs the synthesizer to synthesize a certain *code completion*, filling the missing parts. For example, Fig. 1 shows a partial program using the `FTPClient` API. This program has two "holes" (`H1`, `H2`) left by the programmer who did not know which operations should be invoked. Automatic code completion techniques (such as [11,19]) use aggregate models to compute the most likely completions for a partial program. For this example, one of the results may be that `H1` should be completed with a call to `login` and `H2` should be completed by a call to `logout`.

```
FTPClient ftp = new FTPClient();
ftp.connect(server);
ftp.?; //H1
ftp.storeFile(rem, in);
ftp.?; //H2
ftp.disconnect();
```

Fig. 1. Partial code using `FTPClient` API. Code completion technique can compute the most likely completions for the holes `H1`, `H2` based on how other programs are using the API.

Reverse Engineering of Binaries. New software is released daily. Most of the software that reaches users is delivered in binary form without sources. The only way to make sure that software is free from vulnerabilities and back-doors is to understand how it works. To gain such understanding, experts usually go through the difficult and tedious process of reverse engineering binaries.

Reverse Engineering Dynamic Dispatch: When reverse engineering a binary, the main goal is to understand the control and data flow of the program. Indirect calls to dynamically computed targets, such as when virtual tables are in play, make this task more difficult by hiding the real target of a call [21].

Analysis of "big code" can assist reverse engineering by automatically recovering types of objects in binaries. Specifically, given a stripped (no debug information) optimized binary which uses dynamic dispatch, one can use "big code" to *statically* infer the likely types for objects in the binary, and thus the likely targets of each indirect method call. One approach by Katz et al. [10] is to infer the likely type of an object based on usage patterns of the object. Katz et al. use Variable-order Markov Models (VMMs) as a classification mechanism to determine the most likely types for each object.

Finding Similar Code Fragments: One of the goals of reverse engineering is detecting software vulnerabilities. When a new vulnerability is discovered, it is challenging to find all of its occurrences in different binaries. The code of a single vulnerable function may have been stripped from the original library, slightly patched, and statically linked, leaving a ticking time-bomb in an application without an effective way of identifying it.

An effective technique for searching in executables can help find such vulnerabilities in a given code base. Given a function f in binary form, and a large code base, the goal is to statically find functions that are similar to f in the code base. The main challenge is to define a notion of *similarity* that goes beyond

```python
def p (head, tail=''):
  if len(head) == 0:
    print tail
  else:
    for i in range(len(head)):
      p(head[0:i]+head[i+1:], tail+head[i])
p("abc")
```

(a)

```java
public static Set<String> generateP(String input) {
  Set<String> set = new HashSet<String>();
  if (input == "") return set;
  Character a = input.charAt(0);
  if (input.length() > 1) {
    input = input.substring(1);
    Set<String> permSet = generateP(input);
    for (String x : permSet)
      for (int i = 0; i <= x.length(); i++)
        set.add(x.substring(0, i) + a + x.substring(i));
  } else {
    set.add(a + "");
  }
  return set;
}
```

(b)

Fig. 2. Semantically related fragments for generating permutations of a given string. (a) in Python and (b) in Java.

direct syntactic matching. One approach, used by David et al. [3] is to define a notion of *similarity by decomposition* based on decomposing each function to a set of *control tracelets* and defining similarity between sets of tracelets.

Similarity Across Different Programming Languages and Libraries. Consider the two code fragments in Fig. 2. Both of these fragments generate permutations of a given string. The code fragment in Fig. 2(a) is written in Python and the code in Fig. 2(b) is written in Java. Despite their considerable syntactic difference, and the fact that they are written in two completely different programming languages, we would like to say that the two are similar, as they have similar functionality (there is a slight difference as Fig. 2(a) prints the permutations and Fig. 2(b) just generates them).

	Snippet (a)
Title	How to generate all permutations of a list in Python?
Content	How do you generate all the permutations of a list in Python, independently of the type of elements in that list? For example: <*some code*>
Tags	python, algorithm, permutation, combinatorics, python-2.5

	Snippet (b)
Title	Generating all permutations of a given string.
Content	What is an elegant way to find all the permutations of a string. E.g. *ba*, would be *ba* and *ab*, but what about *abcdefgh*? Is there any example Java implementation?
Tags	java, algorithm

Fig. 3. Example textual descriptions associated with the code fragments in Fig. 2

Efforts to capture this similarity via syntactic approaches, such as strings or ASTs comparison will fail due to the significant differences in the language syntax and the fact that the two use different computation structure. Even semantic approaches based on input-output relations will have difficulty to establish the connection between the snippets because Fig. 2(a) holds concrete values and Fig. 2(b) expects to get them as input. Moreover, the usage in language specific operations (e.g., `range` in Python, `chatAt` in Java), adds another layer of difficulty. One approach to address these challenges is to bypass them using external source of information - textual descriptions associated with the code fragments (as shown in Fig. 3). This approach leverages "big code" together with its corresponding textual metadata [22].

Acknowledgement. The research leading to these results has received funding from the European Union's - Seventh Framework Programme (FP7) under grant agreement no. 615688 ERC- COG-PRIME.

References

1. http://like2drops.com
2. Begleiter, R., El-Yaniv, R., Yona, G.: On prediction using variable order Markov models. J. Artif. Intell. Res. **22**, 385–421 (2004)
3. David, Y., Yahav, E.: Tracelet-based code search in executables. In: Proceedings of the 35th ACM SIGPLAN Conference on Programming Language Design and Implementation, PLDI '14, pp. 349–360 (2014)
4. Faktor, A., Irani, M.: Clustering by composition: unsupervised discovery of image categories. IEEE Trans. Pattern Anal. Mach. Intell. **36**(6), 1092–1106 (2014)
5. Halevy, A., Norvig, P., Pereira, F.: The unreasonable effectiveness of data. IEEE Intell. Syst. **24**(2), 8–12 (2009)
6. Hays, J., Efros, A.A.: Scene completion using millions of photographs. In: ACM SIGGRAPH 2007 Papers, SIGGRAPH '07, New York, NY, USA (2007)
7. Horwitz, S.: Identifying the semantic and textual differences between two versions of a program, vol. 25. ACM (1990)
8. Jagadish, H.V., Gehrke, J., Labrinidis, A., Papakonstantinou, Y., Patel, J.M., Ramakrishnan, R., Shahabi, C.: Big data and its technical challenges. Commun. ACM **57**(7), 86–94 (2014)
9. Kang, H., Hebert, M., Efros, A.A., Kanade, T.: Data-driven objectness. IEEE Trans. Pattern Anal. Mach. Intell. **37**(1), 189–195 (2015)
10. Katz, O.: Type prediction using variable order Markov models. Master's thesis, Technion (2015)
11. Mishne, A., Shoham, S., Yahav, E.: Typestate-based semantic code search over partial programs. In: OOPSLA '12 (2012)
12. Necula, G.C.: Translation validation for an optimizing compiler. In: Proceedings of the ACM SIGPLAN 2000 Conference on Programming Language Design and Implementation, PLDI '00, pp. 83–94, New York, NY, USA (2000)
13. Partush, N., Yahav, E.: Abstract semantic differencing for numerical programs. In: Logozzo, F., Fähndrich, M. (eds.) Static Analysis. LNCS, vol. 7935, pp. 238–258. Springer, Heidelberg (2013)
14. Partush, N., Yahav, E.: Abstract semantic differencing via speculative correlation. In: Proceedings of the ACM SIGPLAN Conference on Object-Oriented Programming, Systems, Languages and Applications, OOPSLA'14 (2014)
15. Peleg, H., Shoham, S., Yahav, E., Yang, H.: Symbolic automata for represnting big code. In: International journal on Software Tools for Technology Transfer, STTT'15 (2015)
16. Pnueli, A., Siegel, M.D., Singerman, E.: Translation validation. In: Steffen, B. (ed.) TACAS 1998. LNCS, vol. 1384, pp. 151–166. Springer, Heidelberg (1998)

17. Ramos, D.A., Engler, D.R.: Practical, low-effort equivalence verification of real code. In: Gopalakrishnan, G., Qadeer, S. (eds.) CAV 2011. LNCS, vol. 6806, pp. 669–685. Springer, Heidelberg (2011)
18. Raychev, V., Vechev, M., Krause, A.: Predicting program properties from "big code". In: Proceedings of the 42nd Annual ACM SIGPLAN-SIGACT Symposium on Principles of Programming Languages, POPL '15, pp. 111–124 (2015)
19. Raychev, V., Vechev, M., Yahav, E.: Code completion with statistical language models. In: Proceedings of the 35th ACM SIGPLAN Conference on Programming Language Design and Implementation, PLDI'14, p. 44 (2014)
20. Rosenfeld, R.: Two decades of statistical language modeling: where do we go from here? Proc. IEEE **88**, 1270–1278 (2000)
21. Sabanal, P.V., Yason, M.V.: Reversing C++. https://www.blackhat.com/presentations/bh-dc-07/Sabanal_Yason/Paper/bh-dc-07-Sabanal_Yason-WP.pdf
22. Sinai, M.B., Yahav, E.: Code similarity via natural language descriptions. In: POPL Off the Beaten Track, OBT'15 (2014)

Compilers

Memory-Efficient Tail Calls in the JVM with Imperative Functional Objects

Tomáš Tauber[1](✉), Xuan Bi[1], Zhiyuan Shi[1], Weixin Zhang[1], Huang Li[2], Zhenrui Zhang[2], and Bruno C.D.S. Oliveira[1]

[1] The University of Hong Kong, Pok Fu Lam Road, Hong Kong, China
{ttauber,xbi,zyshi,wxzhang2,bruno}@cs.hku.hk
[2] Zhejiang University, 38 Zheda Road, Hangzhou, China
{lihuanglx,jerryzh168}@gmail.com

Abstract. This paper presents **FCore**: a JVM implementation of System F with support for full *tail-call elimination* (TCE). Our compilation technique for **FCore** is innovative in two respects: it uses a new representation for first-class functions called *imperative functional objects*; and it provides a way to do TCE on the JVM using constant space.

Unlike conventional TCE techniques on the JVM, allocated function objects are reused in chains of tail calls. Thus, programs written in **FCore** can use idiomatic functional programming styles, relying on TCE, and perform well without worrying about the JVM limitations. Our empirical results show that programs which use tail calls can run in constant space and with low execution time overhead when compiled with **FCore**.

1 Introduction

A runtime environment, such as the JVM, attracts both functional programming (FP) languages' compiler writers and users: it enables cross-platform development and comes with a large collection of libraries and tools. Moreover, FP languages give programmers on the JVM other benefits: simple, concise and elegant ways to write different algorithms; high code reuse via higher-order functions; and more opportunities for parallelism, by avoiding the overuse of side-effects (and shared mutable state) [2]. Unfortunately, compilers for functional languages are hard to implement efficiently in the JVM. FP promotes a programming style where *functions are first-class values* and *recursion* is used instead of mutable state and loops to define algorithms. The JVM is not designed to deal with such programs.

The difficulty in optimizing FP in the JVM means that: *while FP in the JVM is possible today, some compromises are still necessary for writing efficient programs.* Existing JVM functional languages, including Scala [16] and Clojure [10], usually work around the challenges imposed by the JVM. Those languages give programmers alternatives to a FP style. Therefore, performance-aware programmers avoid certain idiomatic FP styles, which may be costly in those languages, and use the available alternatives instead.

X. Feng and S. Park (Eds.): APLAS 2015, LNCS 9458, pp. 11–28, 2015.
DOI: 10.1007/978-3-319-26529-2_2

In particular, one infamous challenge when writing a compiler for a functional language targeting the JVM is: How to eliminate and/or optimize tail calls? Before tackling that, one needs to decide how to represent functions in the JVM. There are two standard options: *JVM methods* and *functions as objects* (FAOs). Encoding first-class functions using only JVM methods directly is limiting: JVM methods cannot encode currying and partial function application directly. To support these features, the majority of functional languages or extensions (including Scala, Clojure, and Java 8) adopt variants of the functions-as-objects approach:

```
interface FAO {Object apply(Object arg);}
```

With this representation, we can encode curried functions, partial application and pass functions as arguments. However, neither FAOs nor JVM methods offer a good solution to deal with *general tail-call elimination* (TCE) [22]. The JVM does not support proper tail calls. In particular scenarios, such as single, tail-recursive calls, we can easily achieve an optimal solution in the JVM. Both Scala and Clojure provide some support for tail-recursion [11,16]. However, for more general tail calls (such as mutually recursive functions or non-recursive tail calls), existing solutions can worsen the overall performance. For example, JVM-style trampolines [19] (which provide a general solution for tail calls) are significantly slower than normal calls and consume heap memory for every tail call.

Contributions. This paper presents a new JVM compilation technique for functional programs, and creates an implementation of System F [9,18] using the new technique. The compilation technique builds on a new representation of first-class functions in the JVM: *imperative functional objects* (IFOs). *With IFOs it is possible to use a single representation of functions in the JVM and still achieve memory-efficient TCE.* As a first-class function representation, IFOs also support currying and partial function applications.

We represent an IFO by the following abstract class:

```
abstract class Function {
  Object arg, res;
  abstract void apply();
}
```

With IFOs, we encode both the argument (`arg`) and the result of the functions (`res`) as mutable fields. We set the argument field before invoking the `apply()` method. At the end of the `apply()` method, we set the result field. An important difference between the IFOs and FAOs encoding of first-class functions is that, in IFOs, *function application is divided in two parts*: *setting the argument field*; and *invoking the apply method*. For example, if we have a function call `factorial 10`, the corresponding Java code using IFOs is:

```
factorial.arg = 10; // setting argument
factorial.apply(); // invoking function
```

The fact that we can split function application into two parts is key to enable new optimizations related to functions in the JVM. In particular, the TCE approach with IFOs does not require memory allocation for each tail call and has less execution time overhead than the JVM-style trampolines used in languages such as Clojure and Scala. Essentially, with IFOs, it is possible to provide a straightforward TCE implementation, resembling Steele's "UUO handler" [23], in the JVM.

Using IFOs and the TCE technique, we created **FCore**: a JVM implementation of an extension of *System F*. **FCore** aims to serve as an intermediate functional layer on top of the JVM, which ML-style languages can target. According to our experimental results, **FCore** programs perform competitively against programs using regular JVM methods, while still supporting TCE. Programs in **FCore** tend to have less execution time overhead and use less memory than programs using conventional JVM trampolines.

In summary, the contributions of this paper are:

- **Imperative Functional Objects:** A new representation of first-class functions in the JVM, offering new ways to optimize functional programs.
- **A memory-efficient approach to tail-call elimination:** A way to implement TCE in the JVM using IFOs without allocating memory per each tail call.
- **FCore**: An implementation of a System F-based intermediate language that can be used to target the JVM by FP compilers.
- **Formalization and empirical results:** Our basic compilation method from a subset of **FCore** into Java is formalized. Our empirical results indicate that **FCore** allows general TCE in constant memory space and with execution time comparable to regular JVM methods.

2 FCore and IFOs, Informally

This section informally presents **FCore** programs and their IFO-based encoding and how to deal with tail-call elimination. Sections 3 and 4 present a formalized compilation method for a subset of **FCore** (System F) into Java, based on the ideas from this section. Note that, for purposes of presentation, we show slightly simplified encodings in this section compared to the formal compilation method.

2.1 Encoding Functions with IFOs

In **FCore**, we compile all functions to classes extending the `Function` class presented in Sect. 1. For example, consider a simple identity function on integers. In **FCore** or System F (extended with integers), we represent it as follows:

$$id \equiv \lambda(x : Int).\ x$$

We can manually encode this definition with an IFO in Java as follows:

```
class Id extends Function {
   public void apply () {
      final Integer x = (Integer) this.arg;
      res = x;
   }
}
```

The arg field encodes the argument of the function, whereas the res field encodes the result. Thus, to create the identity function, all we need to do is to copy the argument to the result. A function invocation such as *id* 3 is encoded as follows:

```
Function id = new Id();
id.arg = 3; // setting argument
id.apply(); // invoking apply()
```

The function application goes in two steps: it first sets the arg field to 3 and then invokes the apply() method.

Curried Functions. IFOs can naturally define curried functions, such as:
$constant \equiv \lambda(x : Int).\ \lambda(y : Int).\ x$
Given two integer arguments, this function will always return the first one. Using IFOs, we can encode *constant* in Java as follows:

```
class Constant extends Function {
   public void apply () {
      final Integer x = (Integer) this.arg;
      class IConstant extends Function {
         public void apply() {
            final Integer y = (Integer) this.arg;
            res = x;
         }
      }
      res = new IConstant();
   }
}
```

Here, the first lambda function sets the second one as its result. The definition of the second apply method sets the result of the function to the argument of the first lambda function. The use of inner classes enforces the lexical scoping of functions. We encode an application such as *constant* 3 4 as:

```
Function constant = new Constant();
constant.arg = 3;
constant.apply();
Function f = (Function) constant.res;
f.arg = 4;
f.apply();
```

We first set the argument of the constant function to 3. Then, we invoke the apply method and store the resulting function to a variable f. Finally, we set the argument of f to 4 and invoke f's apply method. Note that the alias x for **this**.arg is needed to prevent accidental overwriting of arguments in partial applications. For example in *constant* 3 (*constant* 4 5), the inner application *constant* 4 5 would overwrite 3 to 4 and the outer one would incorrectly return 4.

Partial Function Application. With curried functions, we can encode partial application easily. For example, consider the following expression: $three \equiv constant\ 3$. The code for this partial application is simply:

```
// tail-call elimination
class Mutual {
  Function teven;
  Function todd;
  class TEven extends Function {
    public void apply () {
      final Integer n =
        (Integer) this.arg;
      if (n == 0) {
        res = true;
      }
      else {
        todd.arg = n - 1;
        // tail call
        Next.next = todd;
      }
    }
  }
  class TOdd extends Function {
    public void apply () {
      final Integer n =
        (Integer) this.arg;
      if (n == 0) {
        res = false;
      }
      else {
        teven.arg = n - 1;
        // tail call
        Next.next = teven;
      }
    }
  }
  { // initialization block
    todd = new TOdd();
    teven = new TEven();
  }
}
```

Fig. 1. Functions even and odd using IFOs with tail-call elimination

```
Function constant = new Constant();
constant.arg = 3;
constant.apply();
```

Recursion. FCore supports simple recursion, as well as mutual recursion. For example, consider the functions *even* and *odd* defined to be mutually recursive:

$$even \equiv \lambda(n : Int).\ \textbf{if}\ (n = 0)\ \textbf{then}\ true\ \textbf{else}\ odd(n - 1)$$
$$odd \equiv \lambda(n : Int).\ \textbf{if}\ (n = 0)\ \textbf{then}\ false\ \textbf{else}\ even(n - 1)$$

These two functions define a naive algorithm for detecting whether a number is even or odd. We can encode recursion using Java's own recursion: the Java references even and odd are themselves mutually recursive (Fig. 1).

2.2 Tail-Call Elimination

The recursive calls in *even* and *odd* are tail calls. IFOs present new ways for doing tail-call elimination in the JVM. The key idea, inspired by Steele's work on encoding tail-call elimination [23], is to use a simple auxiliary structure

```
class Next {static Function next = null;}
```

that keeps track of the next call to be executed. Figure 1 illustrates the use of the `Next` structure. This is where we make a fundamental use of the fact that function application is divided into two parts with IFOs. In tail calls, we set the arguments of the function, but we delay the `apply` method calls. Instead, the `next` field of `Next` is set to the function with the `apply` method. The `apply` method is then invoked at the call-site of the functions. The code in Fig. 2 illustrates the call `even 10`. In JVM-style trampolines, each (method) call creates a Thunk. IFOs,

```
// TCE with JVM-style trampolines
interface Thunk {
 Object apply();
}
...
  static Object teven(final int n) {
    if(n == 0) return true;
    else return new Thunk() {
      public Object apply() {
        return todd(n-1);
      }
    };
  }
  static Object todd(final int n) {
    if(n == 0) return false;
    else return new Thunk() {
      public Object apply() {
        return teven(n-1);
      }
    };
...
Object trampoline = even(10);
while(trampoline instanceof Thunk)
      trampoline =
      ((Thunk) trampoline).apply();
return (Boolean) trampoline;
```

```
// TCE with IFOs + Next
Mutual m = new Mutual();
Function teven = m.teven;
...
teven.arg = 10;
Next.next = teven;
Function c;
Boolean res;
do {
  c = Next.next;
  Next.next = null;
  c.apply();
} while (Next.next != null);
res = (Boolean) c.res;
```

Fig. 2. This figure contrasts the TCE approach with JVM-style trampolines (left, custom implementation) and with IFOs and the Next handler (right, see Fig. 1 for implementation).

however, are reused throughout the execution. The idea is that a function call (which is not a tail-call) has a loop that jumps back-and-forth into functions. The technique is similar to some trampoline approaches in C-like languages. However, an important difference to JVM-style trampolines is that utilization of heap space is not growing. In other words, tail-calls do not create new objects for their execution, which improves memory and time performance. Note that this method is *general*: it works for *simple recursive tail calls*, *mutually recursive tail calls*, and *non-recursive tail calls*.

3 Compiling FCore

This section formally presents **FCore** and its compilation to Java. **FCore** is an extension of System F (the polymorphic λ-calculus) [9,18] that can serve as a target for compiler writers.

Syntax. In this section, for space reasons, we cover only the **FCore** constructs that correspond exactly to System F. Nevertheless, the constructs in System F represent the most relevant parts of the compilation process. As discussed in Sect. 5.1, our implementation of **FCore** includes other constructs that are needed to create a practical programming language.

System F. The basic syntax of System F is:

$$\begin{array}{ll}\textbf{Types} & \tau ::= \alpha \mid \tau_1 \to \tau_2 \mid \forall\alpha.\tau \\ \textbf{Expressions} & e ::= x \mid \lambda(x:\tau).e \mid e_1\ e_2 \mid \Lambda\alpha.e \mid e\ \tau\end{array}$$

Types τ consist of type variables α, function types $\tau_1 \to \tau_2$, and type abstraction $\forall\alpha.\tau$. A lambda binder $\lambda(x:\tau).e$ abstracts expressions e over values (bound by a variable x of type τ) and is eliminated by function application $e_1\ e_2$. An expression $\Lambda\alpha.e$ abstracts an expression e over some type variable α and is eliminated by a type application $e\ \tau$.

From System F to Java. Figure 3 shows the type-directed translation rules that generate Java code from given System F expressions. We exploit the fact that System F has an erasure semantics in the translation. This means that type abstractions and type applications do not generate any code or have any overhead at run-time.

We use two sets of rules in our translation. The first one is translating System F expressions. The second set of rules, the function $\langle\tau\rangle$, describes how we translate System F types into Java types.

In order to do the translation, we need *translation environments*:

$$\Gamma ::= \epsilon \mid \Gamma\ (x_1 : \tau \mapsto x_2) \mid \Gamma\alpha$$

Translation environments have two purposes: (1) to keep track of the type and value bindings for type-checking purposes; (2) to establish the mapping between System F variables and Java variables in the generated code.

The translation judgment in the first set of rules adapts the typing judgment of System F:

$\Gamma \vdash e : \tau \rightsquigarrow J$ **in** S

It states that System F expression e with type τ results in Java expression J created after executing a block of statements S with respect to translation environments Γ. `FJ-Var` checks whether a given value-type binding is present in an environment and generates a corresponding, previously initialized, Java variable. `FJ-TApp` resolves the type of an abstraction and substitutes the applied type in it. `FJ-TAbs` translates the body of type abstractions – note that, in the extended language, type abstractions would need to generate suspensions. `FJ-Abs` translates term abstractions. For translating term abstractions, we need evidence for resolving the body e and a bound variable x of type τ_1. We then wrap the generated expression J and its deriving statements S as follows. We create a class with a fresh name *FC*, extending the *Function* class. In the body of `apply`, we first create an alias for the function argument with a fresh name y, then execute all statements S_1 deriving its resulting Java expression J that we assign as the output of this function. Following that, we create a fresh alias f

$\boxed{\Gamma \vdash e : \tau \rightsquigarrow J \textbf{ in } S}$

$$(\text{FJ-VAR})\ \frac{(x_1 : \tau \mapsto x_2) \in \Gamma}{\Gamma \vdash x_1 : \tau \rightsquigarrow x_2 \textbf{ in } \{\}} \qquad (\text{FJ-TAPP})\ \frac{\Gamma \vdash e : \forall\alpha.\tau_2 \rightsquigarrow J \textbf{ in } S}{\Gamma \vdash e\,\tau_1 : \tau_2[\tau_1/\alpha] \rightsquigarrow J \textbf{ in } S}$$

$$(\text{FJ-TABS})\ \frac{\Gamma, \alpha \vdash e : \tau \rightsquigarrow J \textbf{ in } S}{\Gamma \vdash \Lambda\alpha.e : \forall\alpha.\tau \rightsquigarrow J \textbf{ in } S}$$

$$(\text{FJ-ABS})\ \frac{\Gamma, x : \tau_1 \mapsto y \vdash e : \tau_2 \rightsquigarrow J \textbf{ in } S_1 \quad f,\ y\ ,\ FC\ fresh}{\Gamma \vdash \lambda(x : \tau_1).e : \tau_1 \to \tau_2 \rightsquigarrow f \textbf{ in } S_2}$$

```
S2 := {
  class FC extends Function {
    void apply() {
      ⟨T1⟩ y = (⟨T1⟩) this.arg;
      S1;
      res = J;
    }
  };
  Function f = new FC();}
```

$$(\text{FJ-APP})\ \frac{\Gamma \vdash e_1 : \tau_2 \to \tau_1 \rightsquigarrow J_1 \textbf{ in } S_1 \quad \Gamma \vdash e_2 : \tau_2 \rightsquigarrow J_2 \textbf{ in } S_2 \quad f,\ x_f\ fresh}{\Gamma \vdash e_1\, e_2 : \tau_1 \rightsquigarrow x_f \textbf{ in } S_1 \uplus S_2 \uplus S_3}$$

```
S3 := {
  Function f = J1;
  f.arg = J2;
  f.apply();
  ⟨T1⟩ xf = (⟨T1⟩) f.res;}
```

Translation of System F types to Java types:

$\langle\alpha\rangle = \texttt{Object}$
$\langle\forall\alpha.\tau\rangle = \langle\tau\rangle$
$\langle\tau_2 \to \tau_1\rangle = \texttt{Function}$

Fig. 3. Type-directed translation from system F to Java

for the instance of the mentioned function, representing the class *FC*. `FJ-App` is the most vital rule. Given the evidence that e_1 is a function type, we generate a fresh alias f for its corresponding Java expression J_1. The S_3 block contains statements to derive the result of the application. As described in Sect. 2, we split applications into two parts in IFOs. We first set the argument of f to the Java expression J_2, given the evidence resulting from e_2. Then, we call f's `apply` method and store the output in a fresh variable x_f. Before executing statements in S_3, we need to execute statements S_1 and S_2 deriving J_1 and J_2 respectively. To derive x_f, we need to execute all dependent statements: $S_1 \uplus S_2 \uplus S_3$.

Properties of the Translation. Two fundamental properties are worthwhile proving for this translation: *translation generates well-typed (cast-safe) Java programs*; and *semantic preservation.* Proving these two properties requires the static and dynamic semantics (as well as the soundness proof) of the target language (an imperative subset of Java with inner classes in our case). Unfortunately, as far as we know, the exact subset of Java that we use has not been completely formalized yet. Three possibilities exist: (1) choosing an existing Java subset formalization and emulating its missing features in the translation, (2) developing our own formalized Java subset, (3) relating the translation to complete Java semantics within matching logic [5]. Each option would require complex changes beyond this paper's scope, hence it is a part of future work.

4 Tail-Call Elimination

In this section, we show how we can augment the basic translation in Sect. 3 to support tail-call elimination.

As shown in Fig. 1, we can do TCE with IFOs. To capture this formally, we augment the `apply` method call generation, in rule `FJ-App`, with two possibilities:

1. The `apply` method is in a tail position. This means we can immediately return by setting the `next` field of the controlling auxiliary `Next` class to the current `Function` object, without calling the apply method.
2. The `apply` method is not in a tail position. This means we need to evaluate the corresponding chain of calls, starting with the current call, followed by any apply calls within it.

We need to make two changes to achieve this goal: (1) add a tail call detection mechanism; and (2) use a different way of compiling function applications.

Detecting Tail Calls. We base the detection mechanism on the tail call context from the Revised Report on Scheme [1]. When we translate a value application $e_1\ e_2$, we know that e_2 is not in a tail position, whereas e_1 may be if the current context is a tail context. In type applications and abstractions, we know they only affect types: they do not affect the tail call context. Thus, they preserve the state we entered with for translating the apply calls. In λ abstractions, we enter a new tail call context. This detection mechanism is integrated in our translation and used when compiling function applications.

Compiling Function Applications. We augment the `apply` method call generation as follows. We extend the premise of `FJ-App` to include one extra freshly generated variable c:

$$\frac{\begin{array}{c}\Gamma \vdash e_1 : \tau_2 \to \tau_1 \rightsquigarrow J_1 \ \textbf{in}\ S_1 \\ \Gamma \vdash e_2 : \tau_2 \rightsquigarrow J_2 \ \textbf{in}\ S_2 \qquad f,\ x_f,\ c\ \mathit{fresh}\end{array}}{\Gamma \vdash e_1\, e_2 : \tau_1 \rightsquigarrow x_f \ \textbf{in}\ S_1 \uplus S_2 \uplus S_3}$$

In the conclusion, we change S_3. For tail calls, we define it as follows:

```
S3 := {
    Function f = J1;
    f.arg = J2;
    Next.next = f;
}
```

Note that x_f is not bound in S_3 here. Because the result of a tail call is delayed, the result of the tail call is still not available at this point. However, this does not matter: since we are on a tail call, the variable would be immediately out of its scope anyway and cannot be used.

For non-tail calls, we initialize x_f in S_3 as the final result:

```
S3 := {
    Function f = J1;
    f.arg = J2;
    Next.next = f;
    Function c;
    Object xf;
    do {
      c = Next.next;
      Next.next = null;
      c.apply();
    } while (Next.next != null);
    xf = c.res;
}
```

This generated code resembles the example in Sect. 2, except for the general `Object` x_f being in place of the specialized `Boolean res`. The idea of looping through a chain of function calls remains the same.

5 Implementation and Evaluation

5.1 Implementation

We implemented[1] a compiler for **FCore** based on the representation and type-directed translation we described in Sects. 3 and 4. Our actual implementation has extra constructs, such as primitive operations, types and literals, let bindings, conditional expressions, tuples, and fixpoints. It also contains constructs for a basic Java interoperability. The compiler performs other common forms of optimizations, such as optimizing multi-argument function applications, partial evaluation, inlining, and unboxing. We wrote the compiler in Haskell and the code repository contains several example programs as well as a large test suite.

5.2 Evaluation

We evaluate two questions with the respect to IFOs:

1. Do IFOs support general TCE in constant memory space?
2. What is the execution time overhead of IFOs?

[1] **FCore** code repository: https://github.com/hkuplg/fcore.

The first question is assessed through measuring total allocated objects on heap in an implementation of DFA. The second question is evaluated in two parts. Firstly, we use microbenchmarks to isolate different simple call behaviors. Secondly, we come back to the DFA implementation's time performance.

# of Objects	Min	Max
IFO	5451	5451
Java (T)	4665	104879
Java (M)	4128	4128
Java (FAO)	18102	24082

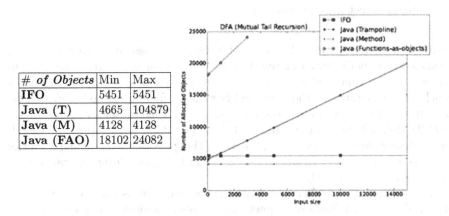

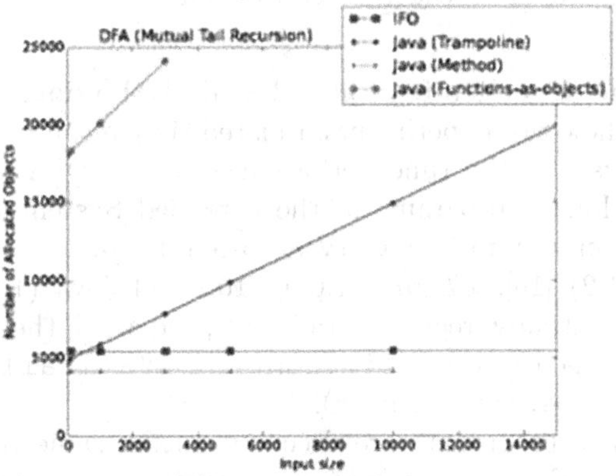

Fig. 4. The DFA encoding: the two columns show the minimum and maximum numbers of total allocated objects on heap from isolated profiled runs with all input lengths. Due to space limitations, the x-axes of plots are cropped at 15000 for clarity.

General TCE in Constant Memory. One common idiom in functional programming is encoding finite states as tail recursive functions and state transitions as mutual calls among these functions. One trivial example of this is the naive even-odd program which switches between two states. A more useful application is in the implementation of finite state automata [13]. Normally, functional language programmers seek this idiom for its conciseness. However in JVM-hosted functional languages, programmers tend to avoid this idiom, because they either lose correctness (`StackOverflow` exceptions in a method-based representation) or performance (in a trampoline-based one). In this experiment, we implemented a DFA recognizing a regular expression $(AAB^*|A^*B)^+$ and measured the performance on randomly generated Strings with different lengths.

We implemented it in **FCore** to assess IFOs (with all the optimizations mentioned in Sects. 4 and 5.1) and in Java (1.8.0_25) to assess different closure representations: method calls, Java 8's lambdas (functions-as-objects), and custom trampolines. We chose plain Java implementation, because we can examine the runtime behavior of different representations without potential compiler overheads. All implementations used primitive **`char`** variables and did not allocated any new objects on heap when reading from the input Strings. We report the total number of allocated objects on heap in the isolated application runs, as measured by HPROF [17], the JDK's profiling tool.

We executed all benchmarks on the following platform with the HotSpot™VM (1.8.0_25): Intel®Core™i5 3570 CPU, 1600MHz DDR3 4GB RAM, Ubuntu 14.04.1.

We show the result of this experiment in Fig. 4. The IFO- and trampoline-based implementations continued executing after method-based and FAO-based ones threw a `StackOverflow` exception. IFOs, similarly to the method-based implementation, allocated a constant number of objects on heap. The trampoline one, however, increased its object allocation with the input, because it needed to create an object for each tail call.

Time Overhead: Isolated Call Behavior. For measuring time overhead, we show two experiments: isolated simple call behavior in different microbenchmarks and the time performance of the DFA implementation. We wrote the benchmark programs in the extended System F for our compilation process and in the following JVM-hosted languages in their stable versions: *Scala* (2.11.2) [16], *Clojure* (1.6.0) [10], and Java (1.8.0_25, as before). For encoding mutually recursive tail calls, we used the provided trampoline facilities in Scala (`scala.util.control .TailCalls`) and Clojure (`tramp` from `clojure.core.logic`).

The programs were executed on the same platform as the memory experiment. For the automation of performance measurement, we used the Java Microbenchmark Harness (JMH) tool which is a part of OpenJDK [8]. Based on the provided annotations, JMH measures execution of given programs. In addition to that, it takes necessary steps to gain stable results. They include non-measured warm-up iterations for JITC, forcing garbage collection before each benchmark, and running benchmarks in isolated VM instances. We configured JMH for 10 warm-up runs and 10 measured runs from which we compute averages.

We chose four programs to represent the following behaviors:

- *Non-tail recursive calls*: Computing the factorial and Fibonacci numbers using naive algorithms.
- *Single method tail recursive calls*: Computing factorial using a tail recursive implementation.
- *Mutually recursive tail calls*: Testing evenness and oddness using two mutually recursive functions.

Non-tail recursive programs present two examples of general recursive calls and we executed them, altogether with the tail recursive programs, on low input values (not causing `StackOverflow` exceptions in default JVM settings). In addition to that, we executed the tail recursive programs on high input values in which method-based implementations threw `StackOverflow` exceptions in default JVM settings. We show the results in Fig. 5. Its left part shows the result for low input values in IFOs, method implementations in all the other languages and the fastest trampoline implementation (Java); the plot is normalized to the Java method-based implementation's results. The right part shows the result for high input values in IFO- and trampoline-based implementations; the plot is normalized to results of IFO-based implementations. For low input values, we can see that IFO-based implementations run slightly slower than

Low Input Values	fact(20) in *ns*	fib(20) in *ns*	tailfact(20) in *ns*	evenodd(256) in *μs*
IFO	204.84 ± 2.35	35.50 ± 0.47	49.52 ± 0.72	32.95 ± 0.09
Java	147.95 ± 0.65	22.50 ± 0.06	18.18 ± 0.19	30.93 ± 0.12
Java (T)	1280.23 ± 20.99	502.35 ± 9.42	139.39 ± 1.79	474.41 ± 6.29
Scala	130.46 ± 0.40	22.55 ± 0.14	15.94 ± 0.05	32.79 ± 0.09
Clojure	573.95 ± 3.41	314.24 ± 2.25	205.21 ± 0.35	82.61 ± 0.95

High Input Values	evenodd(214748) in *μs*	tailfact(10000) in *μs*
IFO	152.47 ± 0.43	166.64 ± 0.51
Java	1060.35 ± 14.52	644.10 ± 3.89
Scala	1864.34 ± 31.24	1004.13 ± 13.49
Clojure	6533.14 ± 92.65	N/A

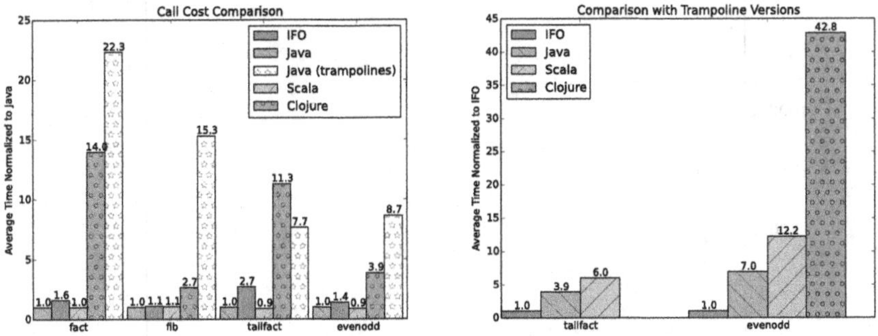

Fig. 5. The isolated call behavior experiments: the reported times are averages of 10 measured runs and corresponding standard deviations. The plots are normalized to Java's (left table and plot) and IFO's (right table and plot) results – the lower, the faster.

method-based ones. However, their overhead is small compared with the fastest trampoline implementations in our evaluation. IFOs ran 0.1 to 1.7-times slower than method-based representations, whereas the fastest trampolines ran 7.7 to 22.3-times slower. In the tail recursive programs, Scala ran slightly faster than standard Java methods due to its compiler optimizations. Clojure has an additional overhead, because its compiler enforces integer overflow checking. For the high input values, the method-based implementations threw a `StackOverflow` exception in default JVM settings, unlike IFOs and trampoline implementations which can continue executing with this input. IFOs ran 3.9 to 12.2-times faster (excluding Clojure) than trampoline implementations. Again, Clojure suffered from its additional overhead and threw an integer overflow exception in the tail recursive factorial. Using BigIntegers would prevent this, but we wanted to isolate the call behavior in this experiment, i.e. avoid any extra overhead from other object allocations.

Time Overhead: DFA Performance. Unlike the first experiment, where the programs isolated costs of plain recursive calls, DFA encoding represents a more realistic behavior with other costs, such as non-recursive method calls and calls to other API methods (e.g. reading input). The setting was the same as in

Input length (time unit)	1000 (μs)	3000 (μs)	10000 (μs)	100000 (μs)
IFO	5.10 ± 0.10	15.98 ± 0.07	77.81 ± 0.83	933.58 ± 13.40
Java (Trampoline-based)	7.03 ± 0.130	26.89 ± 0.10	102.98 ± 2.36	1099.80 ± 15.46
Java (Method-based)	3.80 ± 0.07	11.61 ± 0.10	48.83 ± 0.13	N/A
Java (FAO-based)	6.37 ± 0.01	17.62 ± 0.05	N/A	N/A

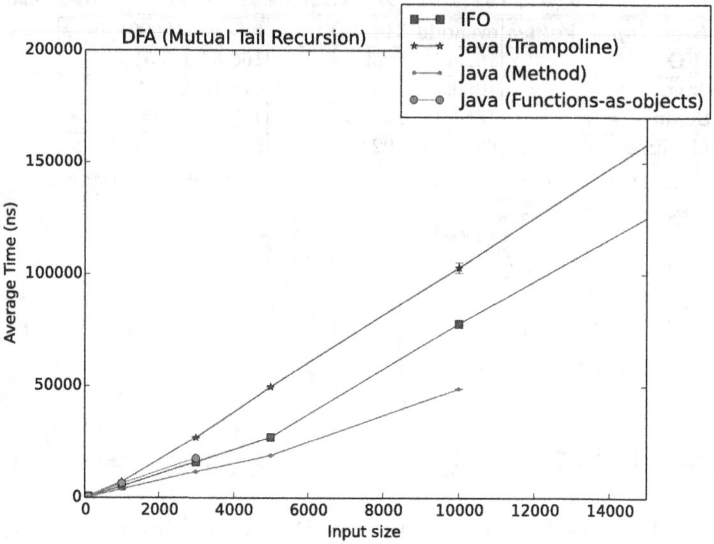

Fig. 6. The DFA encoding: the reported times are averages of 10 measured runs and corresponding standard deviations. Due to space limitations, the x-axes of plots are cropped at 15000 for clarity.

the constant memory experiment and we performed time measurement in the same way as in the isolated call behavior experiment. We show the result of this experiment in Fig. 6. The FAO-based implementation ran slowest out of all implementations and threw `StackOverflow` exception with a smaller input than the method-based implementation. That is because it creates extra objects and performs extra calls due to its representation. As in the isolated calls experiment, the IFO-based implementation ran about 0.5-times slower than method-based implementation. Trampolines, however, ran about 2-times slower. The IFO- and trampoline-based implementations continued executing after method-based one threw a `StackOverflow` exception. The IFO-based implementation was about 0.2-times faster than the trampoline one for larger inputs.

6 Related Work

This section discusses related work: intermediate functional languages on top of the JVM, TCE and function representations, TCE on the JVM, and the JVM modifications.

Intermediate Functional Languages on top of the JVM. A primary objective of our work is to create an efficient intermediate language that targets the JVM. With such intermediate language, compiler writers can easily develop FP compilers in the JVM. System F is an obvious candidate for an intermediate language as it serves as a foundation for ML-style or Haskell-style FP languages. However, there is no efficient implementation of System F in the JVM. The only implementation of System F that we know of (for a JVM-like platform) was done by Kennedy and Syme [12]. They showed that System F can be encoded, in a type-preserving way, into .NET's C#. That encoding could easily be employed in Java or the JVM as well. However, their focus was different from ours. They were not aiming at having an efficient implementation of System F. Instead, their goal was to show that the type system of languages such as C# or Java is expressive enough to faithfully encode System F terms. They used a FAO-based approach and have not exploited the erasure semantics of System F. As a result, the encoding suffers from various performance drawbacks and cannot be realistically used as an intermediate language. MLj [4] compiled a subset of SML'97 (interoperable with Java libraries) to the Monadic Intermediate Language, from which it generated Java bytecode. Various Haskell-to-JVM compiler backends [6,25,27] used different variations of the *graph reduction machine* [26] for their code generation, whereas we translate from System F.

Tail-Call Elimination and Function Representations. A choice of a function representation plays a great role [21] in time and space efficiency as well as in how difficult it is to correctly implement tail calls. Since Steele's pioneering work on tail calls [22], implementors of FP languages often recognize TCE as a necessary feature. Steele's Rabbit Scheme compiler [23] introduced the "UUO handler" that inspired our TCE technique using IFOs. Early on, some Scheme compilers targeted C as an intermediate language and overcame the absence of TCE in the backend compiler by using trampolines. Trampolines incur on performance penalties and different techniques, with "Cheney on the M.T.A."[3] being the most known one, improved upon them. The limitations of the JVM architecture, such as the lack of control over the memory allocation process, prevent a full implementation of Baker's technique.

Tail-Call Elimination on the JVM. Apart from the recent languages, such as Scala [16] or Clojure [10], functional languages have targeted the JVM since its early versions. Several other JVM functional languages support (self) tail recursion optimization, but not full TCE. Examples include MLj [4] or Frege [28]. Later work [15] extended MLj with Selective TCE. This work used an effect system to estimate the number of successive tail calls and introduced trampolines only when necessary. Another approach to TCE in the JVM is to use an explicit stack on the heap (an `Object[]` array) [6]. With such explicit stack for TCE, the approach from Steele's pioneering work [23] can also be encoded in the JVM. Our work avoids the need for an explicit stack by using IFOs, thus allowing for a more direct implementation of this technique. The Funnel compiler for the JVM [19] used standard method calls and shrank the stack only after the execution reached a predefined "tail call limit". This dynamic optimization needs careful tuning of the parameters, but can be possibly used to further improve performance of our approach.

JVM Modifications. Proposals to modify the JVM [14], which would arguably be a better solution for improving support for FP, appeared early on. One reason why the JVM does not support tail calls was due to a claimed incompatibility of a security mechanism based on stack inspection with a global TCE policy. The abstract continuation-marks machine [7] refuted this claim. There exists one modified Java HotSpot™VM [20] with TCE support. The research Maxine VM with its new self-optimizing runtime system [29] allows a more efficient execution of JVM-hosted languages. Despite these and other proposals and JVM implementations, such as IBM J9, we are not aware of any concrete plans for adding TCE support to the next official JVM release. Some other virtual machines designed for imperative languages do not support TCE either. For example, the standard Python interpreter lacks it, even though some enhanced variants can overcome this issue [24]. Hence, ideas from our work can be applied outside of the JVM ecosystem.

7 Conclusion and Future Work

Functional Programming in the JVM is already possible today. However, when efficiency is a concern, programmers and compiler writers still need to be aware of the limitations of the JVM. Some of the problems are the need for two function representations; and the lack of a good solution for TCE. This paper shows that IFOs allow for a uniform representation of functions, while being competitive in terms of time performance and supporting TCE in constant space.

There is much to be done for future work. We would like to prove correctness results for our translation from System F to Java. To achieve this, we will first need a suitable formalization of Java that includes inner classes and imperative features. Furthermore, we will adopt the thread-safe version of our translation – one main difference is that IFOs should be allocated at their call sites rather than at their definition sites. One other aspect is with currying and partial applications, where the uniform function representation is important. FAOs here can have substantial time and memory overheads, especially when defining multi-argument recursive functions, so current languages tend to avoid them and use two representations: JVM methods when possible; and FAOs when necessary. With additional optimizations in **FCore**, such as multi-argument closure optimization and unboxing, IFOs serve as one uniform efficient function representation. We would like to formalize and refine a number of optimizations that we have been experimenting with in **FCore**; and explore what other optimizations are possible with IFOs. Finally, we want to build frontends for realistic functional languages on top of **FCore** and write large functional programs, including a full bootstrapping compiler of **FCore**, in those frontends.

Acknowledgments. We would like to thank T. H. Tse, C.-L. Wang, Vlad Urechte, Rúnar Bjarnason, and **FCore** contributors for help and valuable feedback on previous drafts of this work. We also thank the anonymous reviewers for their helpful suggestions. The work described in this paper was partially supported by a grant from the Research Grants Council of the Hong Kong Special Administrative Region, China (Project No. HKU 27200514).

References

1. Abelson, H., Dybvig, R., Haynes, C., Rozas, G., Adams, N.I.I., Friedman, D., Kohlbecker, E., Steele, G.L., Bartley, D., Halstead, R., Oxley, D., Sussman, G., Brooks, G., Hanson, C., Pitman, K., Wand, M.: Revised^5 report on the algorithmic language scheme. High.-Order Symbolic Comput. **11**(1), 7–105 (1998)
2. Armstrong, J.: Programming Erlang: Software for a Concurrent World, p. 536. Pragmatic Bookshelf, Raleigh (2007)
3. Baker, H.G.: CONS should not CONS its arguments, part II. ACM SIGPLAN Not. **30**(9), 17–20 (1995)
4. Benton, N., Kennedy, A., Russell, G.: Compiling Standard ML to Java Bytecodes. In: Proceedings of the 3rd ACM SIGPLAN International Conference on Functional Programming (1998)
5. Bogdanas, D., Roşu, G.: K-Java: a complete semantics of Java. In: Proceedings of the 42nd Annual ACM SIGPLAN-SIGACT Symposium on Principles of Programming Languages, pp. 445–456. POPL 2015, ACM, New York, NY, USA (2015)
6. Choi, K., Lim, H., Han, T.: Compiling lazy functional programs based on the spineless tagless G-machine for the java virtual machine. In: Kuchen, H., Ueda, K. (eds.) FLOPS 2001. LNCS, vol. 2024, pp. 92–107. Springer, Heidelberg (2001)
7. Clements, J., Felleisen, M.: A tail-recursive machine with stack inspection. ACM Transactions on Programming Languages and Systems **26**(6), 1029–1052 (2004)
8. Friberg, S., Shipilev, A., Astrand, A., Kuksenko, S., Loef, H.: OpenJDK: JMH (2014). openjdk.java.net/projects/code-tools/jmh/
9. Girard, J.Y.: Interprétation fonctionnelle et élimination des coupures de l'arithmétique d'ordre supérieur. Ph.D. thesis, Université Paris VII (1972)
10. Hickey, R.: The Clojure programming language. In: Proceedings of the 2008 Symposium on Dynamic Languages (2008)
11. Hickey, R.: Recur construct, Clojure documentation (2014). clojuredocs.org/clojure.core/recur
12. Kennedy, A., Syme, D.: Transposing F to C#: expressivity of parametric polymorphism in an object-oriented language. Concurrency Comput. Pract. Experience **16**(7), 707–733 (2004)
13. Krishnamurthi, S.: Educational pearl: automata via macros. J. Funct. Program. **16**(3), 253–267 (2006)
14. League, C., Trifonov, V., Shao, Z.: Functional java bytecode. Proceedings 5th World Conference on Systemics, Cybernetics, and Informatics (2001)
15. Minamide, Y.: Selective tail call elimination. In: Proceedings of the 10th International Conference on Static Analysis (2003)
16. Odersky, M.: The scala language specification, Version 2.9. École Polytechnique Fédérale de Lausanne (2014)
17. O'Hair, K.: HPROF: a Heap/CPU profiling tool in J2SE 5.0. Sun Developer Network, Developer Technical Articles & Tips (2004)

18. Reynolds, J.C.: Towards a theory of type structure. In: Symposium on Programming (1974)
19. Schinz, M., Odersky, M.: Tail call elimination on the Java Virtual Machine. Electron. Notes Theor. Comput. Sci. **59**(1), 158–171 (2001)
20. Schwaighofer, A.: Tail Call Optimization in the Java HotSpot™VM, master Thesis, Johannes Kepler Universität Linz (2009)
21. Shao, Z., Appel, A.W.: Space-efficient closure representations. ACM SIGPLAN Lisp Pointers **7**(3), 150–161 (1994)
22. Steele, G.L.: Debunking the "Expensive Procedure Call" myth or, procedure call implementations considered harmful or, LAMDBA: the ultimate GOTO. In: Proceedings of the 1977 Annual Conference (1977)
23. Steele, G.L.: Rabbit: a compiler for scheme. Technical report, Massachusetts Institute of Technology (1978)
24. Tismer, C.: Continuations and stackless Python. In: Proceedings of the 8th International Python Conference, vol. 1 (2000)
25. Tullsen, M.: Compiling Haskell to Java. Technical Report YALEU/DCS/RR-1204, Yale University (1996)
26. Wadsworth, C.: Semantics and Pragmatics of the Lambda-Calculus. Ph.D. thesis, University of Oxford (1971)
27. Wakeling, D.: Compiling lazy functional programs for the Java Virtual Machine. J. Funct. Program. **9**(6), 579–603 (1999)
28. Wechsung, I.: Frege (2014). github.com/Frege/frege
29. Würthinger, T., Wimmer, C., Wöß, A., Stadler, L., Duboscq, G., Humer, C., Richards, G., Simon, D., Wolczko, M.: One VM to rule them all. In: Proceedings of the 2013 ACM International Symposium on New Ideas, New Paradigms, and Reflections on Programming & Software (2013)

A Secure Compiler for ML Modules

Adriaan Larmuseau[1(✉)], Marco Patrignani[2], and Dave Clarke[1,2]

[1] Uppsala University, Uppsala, Sweden
{adriaan.larmuseau,dave.clarke}@it.uu.se
[2] IMinds-Distrinet, K.U. Leuven, Leuven, Belgium
marco.patrignani@cs.kuleuven.be

Abstract. Many functional programming languages compile to low-level languages such as C or assembly. Numerous security properties of those compilers, however, apply only when the compiler compiles whole programs. This paper presents a compilation scheme that securely compiles a *standalone module* of ModuleML, a light-weight version of an ML with modules, into untyped assembly. The compilation scheme is secure in that it reflects the abstractions of a ModuleML module, for every possible piece of assembly code that it interacts with. This is achieved by isolating the compiled module through a low-level memory isolation mechanism and by dynamically type checking its interactions. We evaluate an implementation of the compiler on relevant test scenarios.

1 Introduction

High-level functional programming languages such as ML or Haskell offer programmers numerous security features through abstractions such as type systems, module systems and encapsulation primitives. Motivated by speed, memory efficiency and portability these high-level functional programming languages are often compiled to low-level target languages such as C and assembly [3]. The security features of such low-level target languages, however, rarely coincide with those of high-level source languages. As a result the compiled program might leak confidential information or break integrity when faced with an attacker operating in the low-level target language.

This security risk is rarely considered in existing compilers as it is often assumed that the compiler compiles the whole program, isolating it from malicious attackers. In practice, however, the final executable will consist of more than just the program in the functional language, it will be linked with various, low-level libraries and/or components that may be written with malicious intent or susceptible to code injection attacks. These low-level components have low-level code execution privileges enabling them to inject code into the system and inspect the variables and memory contents of the compiled program.

This paper presents a compilation scheme that compiles ModuleML, a light-weight version of ML featuring references and a module system, into an untyped assembly language running on a machine model enhanced with the Protected Module Architecture (PMA) [19]. PMA is a low-level memory isolation mechanism, that protects a certain memory area by restricting access to that area

X. Feng and S. Park (Eds.): APLAS 2015, LNCS 9458, pp. 29–48, 2015.
DOI: 10.1007/978-3-319-26529-2_3

based on the location of the program counter. Our compilation scheme compiles an input ModuleML module to this protected memory in a way that protects it from low-level attackers while at the same time preserving all of its functionality.

Contributions. The security of a compilation scheme between two programming languages, is often discussed in terms of full abstraction [1]. A fully-abstract compilation scheme preserves and reflects *contextual equivalence* between source and target-level components (Sect. 2). Preservation of contextual equivalence means that the compilation scheme outputs target-level components that behave as their source-level counterparts. Reflection implies that the source-level security properties are not violated by the generated target-level output.

This paper introduces a secure compilation scheme from ModuleML to untyped assembly extended with PMA (Sect. 3), that is proven to reflect contextual equivalence (Sect. 4). As is common in secure compilation works that target a realistic low-level language [16], we assume that preservation holds. Preservation coincides with compiler correctness, it establishes that the secure compiler is a correct ModuleML compiler. While we have tested our implementation intensely (Sect. 5), we consider formally verifying our compiler a separate research subject (Sect. 6). To better explain the secure compilation scheme, this paper also introduces a pattern referred to as the Secure Abstract Data Type pattern (Sect. 2.4). This pattern bundles together some of the techniques applied in previous secure compilation and full abstraction works.

This paper is not the first work to securely compile to untyped assembly extended with PMA. Previous work on secure compilation by Patrignani *et al.* [16] has fully abstractly compiled an object-oriented language to PMAs. The secure compilation scheme introduced in this paper differs from that work in the following three ways. Firstly, the secure compilation scheme of Patrignani *et al.* is limited in its usefulness as a real world compilation scheme in that it does not accept any arguments from the attacker outside of basic values, such as integers and booleans, and shared object identities. In this work we develop a more realistic compiler that accepts attacker defined functions, locations and modules.

Secondly, the abstractions of functional languages are more challenging than those of imperative object-oriented languages. In a functional language such as ModuleML, functions are for example higher-order and thus cannot be compiled into a straight-forward sequence of calls and returns. In this work we address these challenges through the use of an interaction counting masking mechanism.

Lastly, the inclusion of functors, higher-order functions mapping modules to modules, in ModuleML presents a novel secure compilation challenge. The modules created through functors are not analogous to objects, from a secure compilation standpoint. Whereas every object produced by a constructor is of the same type and thus subject to the same type checks and security constraints, functors can produce modules with different types and security constraints. In this work we address all security challenges introduced by functors and develop an efficient method of encoding the required checks.

Limitations. To simplify the compilation scheme, polymorphic types and type kinds have been left out of ModuleML. The effects of certain low-level errors such as stack overflows or out of memory errors are also not considered.

2 Overview

This section introduces the source language ModuleML (Sect. 2.1), the target language A+I (Sect. 2.2), the threat model (Sect. 2.3) and a secure compilation pattern that we reuse throughout this work (Sect. 2.4).

2.1 The Source Language ModuleML

The source language ModuleML is divided into a core language and a module language. The core language is an extension of the simply typed λ-calculus featuring booleans, integers, unit, pairs, references, sequences, recursion and integer and boolean comparison operators. The module system is an adaption of Leroy's variant of the SML module system that features manifest types [11]. It consists of signatures, structures and functors, as illustrated below.

```
signature S = sig
 type T
 val func: T → T
end
```

Signature

```
module M : S =
    struct
 type T = int
 val func x = x +1
end
```

Structure

```
module F = functor(A : S)
struct
 val fd y = (A.func y)
end
module M' = F(M);
```

Functor

A signature is a sequence of signature components that are either value declarations type declarations or module declarations. The signature `S` listed above, for example, defines an abstract type `T` and a value declaration `func` that is a function of type `T` → `T`. A structure is a sequence of structure components that are either value bindings, module bindings or type bindings. The structure `M` listed above, binds the type `T` to **`int`** and binds the value `func` to a simple addition function. A functor can be considered as a parametrized module, a possibly higher-order function mapping modules to modules. The module `F` listed above, is a functor that maps a structure conforming to `S` to a new structure that consists only of a value binding `fd` that applies the value binding `A.func` to the argument `y`. The module `M'`, for example, is the result of applying `F` to `M`.

The typing rules for the ModuleML module system are standard. Note that this work uses SML style generative functors which return *fresh* abstract types with each application [4], as this type of functor provides strong data encapsulation. The interested reader can find a complete formalisation of ModuleML in the accompanying technical report [10].

Contextual Equivalence. The secure compilation scheme aims to reflect ModuleML contextual equivalence in the target language A+I. A ModuleML context

$C : \tau' \rightarrow \tau$ is a well-typed program P of type τ with a single hole $[\cdot]$ that is to be filled with a module M of type τ'. Two ModuleML modules $\mathtt{M}_1$ and $\mathtt{M}_2$ are contextually equivalent if and only if there is no context C that can distinguish them. Contextual equivalence is formalised as follows.

Definition 1 (Contextual Equivalence)

$$M_1 \simeq M_2 \stackrel{def}{=} \forall C : \tau' \rightarrow \tau.\ C[M_1]\Uparrow \iff C[M_2]\Uparrow$$

where $\Uparrow$ indicates divergence.

The following two ModuleML modules $\mathtt{M}_1$ and $\mathtt{M}_2$ are, for example, not contextually equivalent as they are distinguishable by the denoted context C, assuming Ω is a diverging term.

```
module M1 = struct
  val v1 = ref 1
end
```

Module A

```
module M2 = struct
  val v1 = ref 0
end
```

Module B

```
open M
(if (!(M.v1) == 0) Ω
 else true)
```

Context C

Note that the `open M` statement implements the hole of the context C.

2.2 The Low-Level Target Language A+I

To model a realistic compilation scheme, the target language should be close to what is used by modern processors. For this reason this paper adopts A+I (acronym of Assembly plus Isolation), a low-level language that models an idealised von Neumann machine enhanced with a low-level memory protection mechanism referred to as Protected Module Architecture (PMA) [19]. PMA is a fine-grained, program counter-based, memory access control mechanism that divides memory into a protected memory module and unprotected memory. The protected module is further split into two sections: a protected code section accessible only through a fixed collection of designated entry points, and a protected data section that can only be accessed by the code section. As such the unprotected memory is limited to executing the code at entry points. The code section can only be executed from the outside through the entry points and the data section can only be accessed by the code section. An overview of the access control mechanism is given below.

From \To	Protected			Unprotected
	Entry Point	*Code*	*Data*	
Protected	r x	r x	r w	r w x
Unprotected	x			r w x

A variety of PMA implementations exist. While most of them are research prototypes [19], Intel is developing a new instruction set, referred to as SGX, that enables the usage of PMA in commercial processors [15].

Trace Equivalence. Our secure compiler relates contextually equivalent ModuleML modules to contextually equivalent low-level components. Reasoning about contexts is, however, notoriously complex. Reasoning about untyped low-level contexts is especially complex as they lack any inductive structure. In this work we thus adopt the fully abstract *trace semantics* of Patrignani and Clarke for PMA enhanced programs, to reason about trace equivalence instead [17].

The trace semantics transition over a state $\Lambda = (p, r, f, m, s)$, where m represents only the protected memory of PMA and s is a descriptor that details where the protected memory partition starts, as well as the number of entry points and the size of the code and data sections. Additionally, Λ can be $(\textbf{unknown}, m, s)$ a state modelling that A+I code, possibly malicious, is executing in unprotected memory. The trace semantics denote the observations of the A+I contexts that interact with the protected memory through labels L as follows.

$$L ::= \alpha \mid \tau \qquad \alpha ::= \surd \mid \delta! \mid \gamma?$$
$$\gamma ::= call\ p(r; f) \mid ret\ p(r; f) \quad \delta ::= \gamma \mid \omega(a, v).\delta \quad \omega ::= read \mid write$$

A label L can be either an observable action α or a non-observable action τ indicates that an unobservable action occurred in protected memory. Decorations ? and ! indicate the direction of the observable action: from the unprotected memory to the protected memory (?) or vice-versa (!). Observable actions γ are function calls or returns to a certain address p, combined with the registers r and flags f. Registers and flags are in the labels as they convey information on the behaviour of the code executing in the protected memory. Observable actions $\omega(a, v)$ from the protected memory to the unprotected memory detail read and writes to the unprotected memory where a is the memory address and v is the value written to the address. The values will always be data, the compiler does not produce code that writes instructions to the unprotected memory. Additionally, an observable action α can be a tick $\surd$ indicating termination.

Formally the trace semantics of an A+I program L, denoted as $\mathsf{Traces}(L)$, are computed as follows: $\mathsf{Traces}(L) = \{\overline{\alpha} \mid \exists \Lambda. \Lambda_0(L) \stackrel{\overline{\alpha}}{\Longrightarrow} \Lambda\}$. Where Λ_0 is the initial state and the relation $\Lambda \stackrel{\overline{\alpha}}{\Longrightarrow} \Lambda'$ describes the traces generated by transitions between states. An important property of this trace equivalence is that the information they convey is so precise that we can rely on the equality between the traces produced by A+I programs as a replacement for contextual equivalence.

Proposition 1 (Fully Abstract Trace Semantics for A+I *[17]***)**

$$L_1 \simeq_l L_2 \iff \mathsf{Traces}(L_1) = \mathsf{Traces}(L_2)$$

Where $\simeq_l$ denotes contextual equivalence between two A+I programs.

2.3 The Attacker

The attacker considered in this work has kernel-level code injection privileges that can be used to introduce malware into a software system. Kernel-level code injection is a critical vulnerability that bypasses all existing software-based security mechanisms: disclosing confidential data, disrupting applications and so forth. For the sake of simplicity, no differentiation between kernel and user code is defined in A+I. Thus, by modelling the attacker as injecting A+I code, we are modelling kernel-level code injection. Note that PMA is a program counter based mechanism that this attacker model cannot bypass [19].

2.4 The Secure Abstract Data Type Pattern

An A+I context must be able to perform the operations of ModuleML on the compiled ModuleML module. Each of these operations is different, but poses a similar secure compilation challenge: how do we enable the A+I context to perform the relevant operations without exposing the implementation details of the abstraction? In this work we introduce the Secure Abstract Data Type (ADT) pattern as a general approach to addressing this challenge. This pattern bundles together the individual techniques applied in certain secure compilation [16] and full abstraction results [14].

An ADT defines both the values of a data type as well as the functions that apply to it, relying on static typing rules to hide the implementation details of the data type. The Secure ADT pattern, in contrast, protects the implementation details of a source language abstraction τ *without* relying on static typing rules. As illustrated in Fig. 1, it does this by inserting an ADT like interface between the actual implementation of the abstraction and the target language context. Concretely a secure ADT has the following elements: a secured type $\mathsf{Sec}[\tau]$, an interface that defines the operations applicable to the protected type, marshalling rules that handle the transitions between the different representations for τ, and additional run-time checks if required.

Secured Type. The Secure ADT pattern states that values of the type τ, the type of the abstraction that the Secure ADT aims to secure, must be *isolated* and can thus not be shared directly. Instead they can be, for example, shared securely

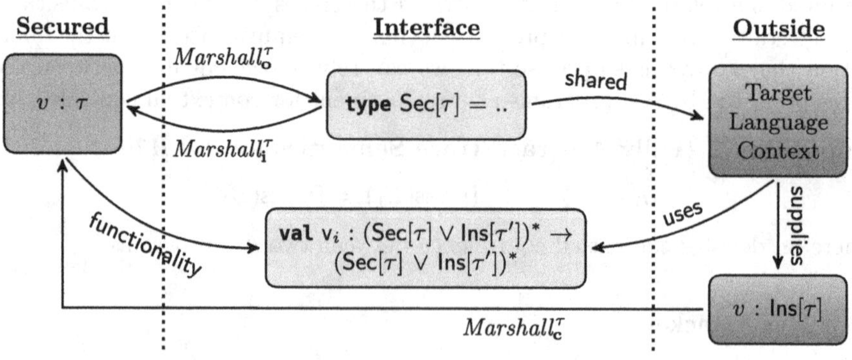

Fig. 1. The Secure ADT pattern isolates an abstraction of type τ through an ADT-like interface that shares secured instances of τ ($\mathsf{Sec}[\tau]$) and accepts outside input ($\mathsf{Ins}[\tau']$).

by encrypting the value or by providing a reference object, an object that refers to the original value. The type of these securely shared instances is denoted as $\mathsf{Sec}[\tau]$. The Secure ADT pattern considers not only the secure sharing of values of type τ, but also input from the target language context. This input is denoted as $\mathsf{Ins}[\tau']$, where τ' denotes the source language type that the input is expected to conform to. We use τ' and not τ as the outside input can be of a different type then the abstraction that the secure ADT pattern secures.

Interface. As illustrated in Fig. 1, the interface defines a series of functions (v_i) that provide the outside context with the functionality of ModuleML. These functions take as arguments some sequence of securely shared values and target language input and return a securely shared or a target language value.

Marshalling. The Secure ADT pattern introduces *type directed* marshalling functions to handle the transitions between the values of type τ, which are the securely compiled values, the values of type $\mathsf{Sec}[\tau]$, which are the securely shared instances, and the values of type $\mathsf{Ins}[\tau]$ which are defined by the outside context. The function $Marshall^{\tau}_{\mathbf{o}} : \tau \rightarrow \mathsf{Sec}[\tau]$ converts values into their secured instances. The function $Marshall^{\tau}_{\mathbf{i}} : \mathsf{Sec}[\tau] \rightarrow \tau$ converts the secured instances back into the original value. Note that this function performs an implicit run-time type check. It fails when given an input that does not correspond to a securely shared value of type τ. Certain secure compilation schemes, such as the one considered in this work, also specify a third type of marshalling function: $Marshall^{\tau}_{\mathbf{c}} : \mathsf{Ins}[\tau] \rightarrow \tau$. Such a marshalling function converts values from the target language context into values of the secured type τ, by converting the input value into the correct representation and by wrapping the result with type checks. Note that if the input is of type $\mathsf{Ins}[\tau']$, where $\tau' \neq \tau$, then the input will only be marshalled in if there exists a marshalling function:$Marshall^{\tau}_{\mathbf{c}} : \mathsf{Ins}[\tau'] \rightarrow \tau'$.

Run-Time Checks. The marshalling rules verify that the input provided by the outside target language context and the output shared to the outside context conform to the typing rules of the source language. This, however, is sometimes not enough to protect the abstractions of the source language. Certain security relevant language properties such as, for example: control-flow integrity, are not always explicitly captured by the typing system. Enforcing these properties must thus be done through *additional* run-time security checks.

3 A Secure Compiler for ModuleML

The secure compilation scheme for ModuleML is a type directed compilation scheme that compiles a standalone ModuleML module and its signature to a protected module (Fig. 2). The secure compilation scheme applies the Secure ADT pattern in a general manner. The entry points of the protected module implement an ADT-like interface to the A+I context. The abstractions of ModuleML are isolated by placing all code and data into the data and code sections of the

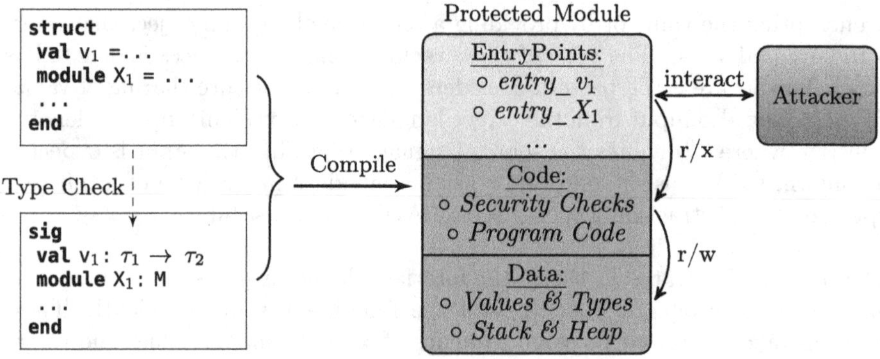

Fig. 2. Our scheme compiles the module and its type into the protected memory.

protected module. The protected data section also includes a heap and stack of a fixed size, that can only be accessed by the securely compiled program. This ensures that the run-time memory of the compiled program is also inaccessible.

The inner workings of how ModuleML is compiled to assembly is of little relevance to this result of this paper. Instead this section focusses on the security relevant aspects of the compilation scheme. This section details how we apply the Secure ADT pattern of Sect. 2.4 to securely compile abstract types (Sect. 3.2), structures and signatures (Sect. 3.3), functions (Sect. 3.4), locations (Sect. 3.5) and functors (Sect. 3.6). Basic types such as integers or pairs are not compiled using the Secure ADT pattern, but must still be marshalled when interacting with the A+I context (Sect. 3.1).

3.1 Booleans, Integers and Pairs

The securely compiled module shares and inputs not only abstractions such as functions, but also basic ModuleML values: booleans, integers and pairs. Booleans and integers are exchanged with the A+I context using their respective A+I representation. The marshalling functions for integers are thus defined as $Marshall_{\mathsf{c}}^{\mathbf{int}} : \mathsf{Ins}[\mathbf{int}] \rightarrow \mathbf{int}$, which converts A+I integers into ModuleML integers, and $Marshall_{\mathsf{o}}^{\mathbf{int}} : \mathbf{int} \rightarrow \mathsf{Ins}[\mathbf{int}]$, which converts ModuleML integers to A+I integers. The marshalling functions for booleans are analogous.

Marshalling pairs is different. When marshalling, for example, a pair $\langle v_1, v_2\rangle$ the marshalling functions for pairs marshall each value with the type appropriate marshalling function as dictated by the Secure ADT pattern. Marshalling *out* the pair $\langle 1, 2\rangle$, for example, will thus produce a value of type $\langle \mathsf{Ins}[\mathbf{int}], \mathsf{Ins}[\mathbf{int}]\rangle$, while marshalling out the pair of lambdas $\langle(\lambda x : \tau.t), (\lambda x : \tau.t')\rangle$ will produce a value of type $\langle \mathsf{Sec}[\tau \rightarrow \tau'], \mathsf{Sec}[\tau \rightarrow \tau'']\rangle$.

3.2 Abstract Types

Abstract types are, as the name indicates, abstract in that associated values are unobservable to an ModuleML context. Consider, for example, the following module A that conforms to the signature S. This signature defines an abstract type T that abstracts the value bindings v_1 and v_2.

```
module A : S = struct
 type T = bool
 val v1 = true
 val v2 = v1
end
```

```
signature S = sig
 type T
 val v1 : T
 val v2 : T
end
```

An A+I context should not be able to observe that $A.v_1$ and $A.v_2$ both return the value true. To achieve this our compilation scheme applies the Secure ADT pattern to compile values of an abstract type. Instead of directly sharing the value of an abstract type T with the A+I context, we share a secured instance of type Sec[T] instead. These secured instances are implemented as indices to a table $\mathcal{A}$. This table $\mathcal{A}$ maps natural numbers to values and their types in a deterministic manner, simply denumerating its entries. Note that this map is *not* a set: it may map different numbers to duplicate elements.

As illustrated in Fig. 3, every time a value of an abstract type is returned the securely compiled module will share a new index i that corresponds to the number of requests that the A+I context has made to abstract types. Note that each member of a pair (Sect. 3.1) counts as a separate request. The marshalling functions $Marshall_{\mathsf{o}}^{\mathsf{T}}$ and $Marshall_{\mathsf{i}}^{\mathsf{T}}$ are thus implemented as extending the table $\mathcal{A}$ and looking up an index in $\mathcal{A}$ respectively, as illustrated in Fig. 3.

We have formally proven in prior work [9], by means of a full abstraction proof, that these request counting indices do not reveal any information to the A+I context other than the number of times the A+I context has requested a value of an abstract type. This is information that the context of any source language with state can reproduce and thus does not harm full abstraction. In the case of ModuleML, a context can count its interactions with the protected module by making use of references (a detail that returns in our proof of Sect. 4).

3.3 Structures and Signatures

Our compiler compiles both structures and signatures into records stored within the data section of the protected memory. As dictated by the Secure ADT pattern

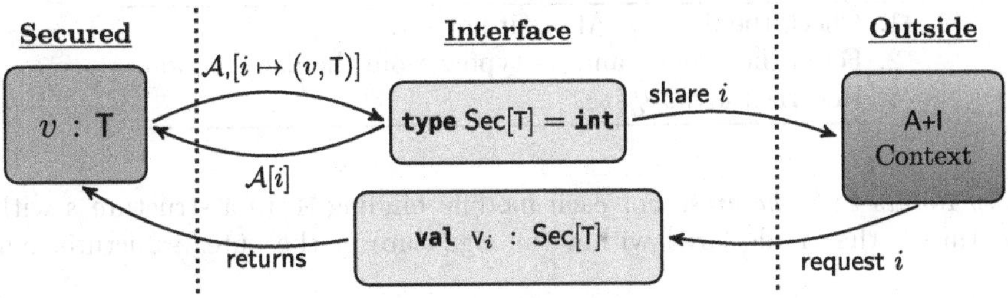

Fig. 3. We use request counting to obscure the value of an abstract type.

these records are not exposed directly to the A+I context. Instead the compilation scheme defines an ADT-like interface of entry points to the protected memory that provide access to the value and structure bindings exposed by the module's signature. Note that, as in previous works [16], these entry points are sorted to obscure their implementation order. The compiler also includes a *load entry point* that evaluates each of the expressions defined within a structure. Our compilation scheme defines marshalling rules that both share secure structures as well as convert in structures created by the A+I context.

Load Entry Point. As is the case in most ML implementations, the value bindings of ModuleML map names to *expressions* not values. These expressions must be reduced to values before the value bindings of a structure can be queried. Our compiler, however, compiles a standalone ModuleML module not a full program, it thus does not have any control over when or if the expressions are evaluated. Instead our compilation scheme provides the A+I context the ability to load the module through a load entry point. This entry point takes no arguments and executes each of the expressions defined throughout the compiled module, storing the result in the appropriate record. Because it is up to the low-level context to invoke this load entry point, a malicious A+I context may attempt to query bindings before the module is loaded or attempt to load the module multiple times. To prevent this, the compiler introduces an additional run-time check in the form of a global flag L_f, that encodes whether or not the module has been loaded. What follows is a pseudo code implementation of the load entry point.

1. Check the flag L_f. Abort if set.
2. For each value binding $\mathtt{v}_i$ with an associated expression e:
   (a) Evaluate e and store the result in the appropriate record.
3. Set L_f.

Value Binding Entry Points. For each value binding $\mathtt{v}_i$ reduced to a value $v : \tau$ declared within the signature of a structure, the compilation scheme creates an entry point of type: $\mathtt{v}_i : \mathsf{Sec}[\tau]$, if τ is an abstraction that must be secured, or $\mathtt{v}_i : \mathsf{Ins}[\tau]$ if τ is a basic type such as **int**. Both are implemented as follows.

1. Check the flag L_f. Abort if not set.
2. Fetch the value v and its type τ from the data section.
3. Return $\mathit{Marshall}_{\mathrm{o}}^{\tau}(v)$

Entry Points to Structures. For each module binding $\mathtt{M}_i$ to a structure s with signature $\mathtt{S}$ that is declared within the signature of the outer structure, our compiler creates an entry point of type: $\mathtt{M}_i$: Sec[S] that takes no arguments and returns a marshalled instance of the structure of secured type Sec[S], as follows.

1. Check the flag L_f. Abort if not set.
2. Return $\mathit{Marshall}^{\mathsf{S}}_{\mathsf{o}}(s)$

$Marshall^{S}_{o}$ and $Marshall^{S}_{i}$. As dictated by the Secure ADT pattern, structures are not shared directly but instead marshalled out using a type directed function $\mathit{Marshall}^{\mathsf{S}}_{\mathsf{o}} : \mathsf{S} \rightarrow \mathsf{Sec}[\mathsf{S}]$. This function converts a structure of signature S into a secured instance Sec[S]: a record that contains an index i to the table $\mathcal{M}$ and references to the entry points of each value/module binding in S. The references to the entry points are included to inform the A+I context of the functionality that the structure provides, simplifying interoperation. Like the table $\mathcal{A}$ of Sect. 3.2, the table $\mathcal{M}$ maps numbers to structures and their signatures. This index i thus enables the marshalling in function $\mathit{Marshall}^{\mathsf{S}}_{\mathsf{i}} : \mathsf{Sec}[\mathsf{S}] \rightarrow \mathsf{S}$ to retrieve the original structure and its signature from $\mathcal{M}$. Note that this marshalling function thus performs an implicit type check as the function fails whenever the retrieved signature is not a *subtype* of S.

$Marshall^{S}_{c}$. Our compilation scheme enables the A+I context to supply its own structures as arguments to the functors of Sect. 3.6. These structures are marshalled in by a function $\mathit{Marshall}^{\mathsf{S}}_{\mathsf{c}} : \mathsf{Ins}[\mathsf{S}] \rightarrow \mathsf{S}$, that iterates through the components of the expected signature S, querying the A+I context's structure for the names of the bindings, marshalling in the results or aborting if a name isn't found. When a value binding is marshalled in it is marshalled in using the type appropriate function. When a module binding is marshalled the marshalling function recurses. Note that this function performs a sub-type check: Ins[S] <: S.

3.4 Higher-Order Functions

To compile the λ-terms of ModuleML the compiler uses closure conversion [18] to eliminate free variables by using an explicit environment that stores bindings between variables and values. As is required by the Secure ADT pattern, these closures are not made available to the A+I context but are instead shared as secured instance of type $\mathsf{Sec}[\tau_1 \rightarrow \tau_2]$: indices to a table $\mathcal{C}$ that maps numbers to closures and their types. As was the case for the indices of Sect. 3.2, these numbers simply denumerate the requests made by the A+I context. The marshalling functions $\mathit{Marshall}^{\tau_1 \rightarrow \tau_2}_{\mathsf{o}}$ and $\mathit{Marshall}^{\tau_1 \rightarrow \tau_2}_{\mathsf{i}}$ are thus implemented as extending the table $\mathcal{C}$ and looking up the closure and its type in $\mathcal{C}$ respectively.

Closure Application Entry Point. As is required by the Secure ADT pattern we enable the A+I context to apply shared closures through an entry point of type: $\mathtt{appl} : \mathsf{Sec}[\tau_1 \rightarrow \tau_2] \rightarrow (\mathsf{Ins}[\tau_1] \vee \mathsf{Sec}[\tau_1]) \rightarrow (\mathsf{Ins}[\tau_2] \vee \mathsf{Sec}[\tau_2])$, where the result is $\mathsf{Ins}[\tau_2]$ if τ_2 is a basic type and $\mathsf{Sec}[\tau_2]$ otherwise. This entry point takes as its arguments an index i to the table $\mathcal{C}$ and as a value v of the appropriate representation for type τ_1. The entry point is implemented as follows.

1. Check the flag L_f. Abort if not set.
2. $c = Marshall_{\mathbf{i}}^{\tau_1 \to \tau_2}(i)$
3. Depending on the representation of v:
   (a) If $\mathsf{Ins}[\tau_1]$: $r = Marshall_{\mathbf{c}}^{\tau_1}(v)$
   (b) If $\mathsf{Sec}[\tau_1]$: $r = Marshall_{\mathbf{i}}^{\tau_1}(v)$
4. Apply c to v, store the result in r'.
5. Return $Marshall_{\mathbf{o}}^{\tau_2}(r')$

Note that the marshalling rules of 3(a) and 3(b) implement the typing rule for function applications, by ensuring that the input value v is of type τ_1.

$Marshall_{\mathbf{c}}^{\tau_1 \to \tau_2}$. Our compilation scheme enables the A+I context to supply its own functions as arguments to the securely compiled entry points that accept an argument of type: $\mathsf{Ins}[\tau_1 \to \tau_2]$. These A+I functions are marshalled by a function $Marshall_{\mathbf{c}}^{\tau_1 \to \tau_2} : \mathsf{Ins}[\tau_1 \to \tau_2] \to (\tau_1 \to \tau_2)$, that takes in a reference to the A+I function f and wraps that function into a new function that performs the following steps, whenever the A+I function f is applied to a ModuleML value v within the securely compiled module.

1. $a = Marshall_{\mathbf{o}}^{\tau_1}(v)$
2. Apply f to a. Store the result in r.
3. Return $Marshall_{\mathbf{c}}^{\tau_2}(r)$

3.5 Locations

As is the case in most commonly used ML variants [13], memory locations do not explicitly appear in the syntax used by programmers. Locations are thus not directly observable to an ModuleML context, leading to many equivalences. Consider, for example, the following two contextually equivalent implementations of the value binding v_1.

```
val v1 = (let x = (ref true) in
 let y = (ref true) in y)
```

```
val v1 = (let x = (ref true) in
 let y = (ref true) in x)
```

No ModuleML context can observe that the left implementation differs from the right implementation in that it returns the second location it created, stored within variable y, and not the first location stored within the variable x.

Again our compilation scheme applies the Secure ADT pattern to protect ModuleML's locations and the operations available on them. Locations are shared with the A+I context in the same manner as higher-order functions (Sect. 3.4) and abstract types (Sect. 3.2): as indices into a table $\mathcal{L}$ that maps numbers to locations and their types. As was the case previously, these numbers simply denumerate the requests made by the A+I context for access to ModuleML locations. The marshalling functions $Marshall_{\mathbf{o}}^{\texttt{ref}\ \tau}$ and $Marshall_{\mathbf{i}}^{\texttt{ref}\ \tau}$ are thus implemented as extending the table $\mathcal{L}$ and looking up an index in $\mathcal{L}$ respectively.

Write and Read Entry Points. To enable the low-level A+I context to write and read to shared locations in the same way that an ModuleML context can, we introduce a *write location* entry point of type: $\texttt{write} : \mathsf{Sec}[\mathbf{ref}\ \tau] \rightarrow (\mathsf{Ins}[\tau] \vee \mathsf{Sec}[\tau]) \rightarrow \mathbf{unit}$, and a *read location* entry point of type $\texttt{read} : \mathsf{Sec}[\mathbf{ref}\ \tau] \rightarrow (\mathsf{Ins}[\tau] \vee \mathsf{Sec}[\tau])$. The write location entry points takes two arguments: an index i to the table $\mathcal{L}$ and a value v of the appropriate representation for type τ. It securely writes v to the appropriate location, as follows.

1. Check the flag L_f. Abort if not set.
2. $l = Marshall_{\mathbf{i}}^{\mathbf{ref}\ \tau}(i)$.
3. Depending on the representation of v:
   (a) If $\mathsf{Ins}[\tau]$: $r = Marshall_{\mathbf{c}}^{\tau}(v)$
   (b) If $\mathsf{Sec}[\tau]$: $r = Marshall_{\mathbf{i}}^{\tau}(v)$
4. Write r to l.

Note again, that the marshalling rules 3(a) and 3(b) implement the assign location typing rule, by ensuring that the input value v is of type τ.

The implementation of the read location entry point is straight-forward: it retrieves the location from $\mathcal{L}$, dereferences it and marshalls the value.

$Marshall_{\mathbf{c}}^{ref\tau}$. A ModuleML context can allocate new locations and share them with the ModuleML module embedded within the context's hole. We thus enable the A+I context to supply its own locations as arguments to entry points that accept an argument of type $\mathsf{Ins}[\mathbf{ref}\ \tau_1]$. As specified by the Secure ADT pattern these locations are marshalled by a function $Marshall_{\mathbf{c}}^{\mathbf{ref}\ \tau} : \mathsf{Ins}[\mathbf{ref}\ \tau] \rightarrow \mathbf{ref}\ \tau$, that takes in a location l_f of the A+I context and wraps it with two functions. The first function enables a ModuleML expression to read the foreign location, the second function enables an ModuleML expression to write to the foreign location. The implementation of the latter is analogous to the implementation of the write entry point. The implementation of the former is simply: $Marshall_{\mathbf{c}}^{\tau}(!l_f)$, where $!l_f$ denotes the dereference of the A+I location l_f.

3.6 Functors

As noted earlier, a ModuleML functor is a higher-order function that maps modules (structures or functors) to modules. Consider the following example.

```
signature Sa =
    sig
 type U
 val v1: int →
     int
 val vs : U
end
```

```
signature Sr = sig
 type T
 val fd: int → int
 val F1:functor(X:Sa)→Sa
 val M1: sig
  val v1: T
 end
end
```

```
module F = functor(A : Sa)
struct
 type T = int
 val fd y = (A.v1 y)
 module F1 = functor(X:Sa)=
    A
 module M1 = A
end : Sr
module M' = F(Mi)
```

```
module F: functor (A : Sa) →
sig
 type T
 val fd: int → int
 module F1: functor(X : S) →(sig
  type U
  val v1: Int
  val vs: U
 end)
 module M1: (sig
  val v1: T end)
end
```

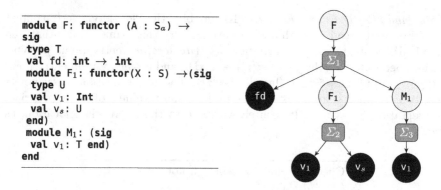

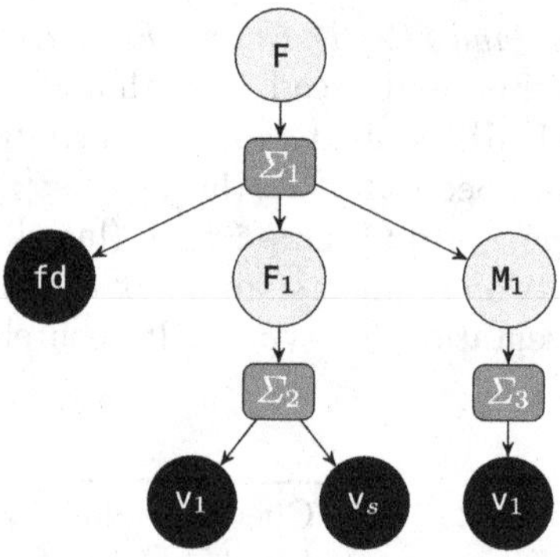

Fig. 4. The secure compiler compiles the signature of F into a tree of unique stamps Σ_i, that enable the functor entry points to identify their arguments.

Module F is a functor that maps a structure that conforms to signature S_a, to a new structure that consists of: a value binding fd, that applies the argument's value binding v_1 to an argument y, and an inner functor F_1 and an inner structure M_1 that copies the argument. This new structure is ascribed with the signature S_r which seals the value binding $M_1.v_1$ with the abstract type T. When compiling functors the compiler operates in two modes. The first mode considers the *static* functor applications within the compiled module, such as, for example, the application of F to an example module M_i in the above listing. Compiling these applications is straightforward, the compiler performs the application and compiles the result in the same way that it compiles any other module.

The second mode considers those functors that are part of the interface to the A+I context. In this case we must securely compile functors into run-time constructs. As is dictated by the Secure ADT pattern we do not share these run-time representations directly with the A+I context, but instead share them (again) as indices into a table $\mathcal{F}$ that maps numbers to functors and their types. As was the case previously, these numbers simply denumerate the requests made by the A+I context for access to ModuleML functors. The marshalling functions $Marshall_{\mathbf{o}}^{\mathbf{functor}(X_i:S)\rightarrow S'}$ and $Marshall_{\mathbf{i}}^{\mathbf{functor}(X_i:S)\rightarrow S'}$, where $\mathbf{functor}(X_i : S) \rightarrow S'$ is the expected type of the functor, are thus implemented by extending the table $\mathcal{F}$ and looking up an index in $\mathcal{F}$ and confirming the type respectively. Our compilation scheme also provides a marshalling rule $Marshall_{\mathbf{c}}^{\mathbf{functor}\ (X_i:S)\rightarrow S'}$ that converts structures of the A+I context.

Compiling Run-Time Functors. Functors are compiled into run-time constructs in a manner similar to the way in which λ-terms are compiled to closures. The functor body is compiled into a function that takes as its arguments a module and an environment of module bindings and returns a new module that conforms to the specification of the functor body. In addition to being compiled into a function, every functor is also compiled into a tree structure of the accessible bindings, assigning a unique stamp Σ_i to each non-leaf node (Fig. 4). These stamps Σ_i are used by the entry points for these bindings to authenticate its arguments.

The module that results from applying a run-time functor is stored as a record that incorporates the resulting module as well as additional run-time data. Additionally the record stores a stamp Σ_i, that identifies the functor that produced it, a module binding environment e, which includes the argument to the functor, and environment of abstract type identifiers e_t. The latter is required to keep track of the abstract types that are created by functors that seal their result, as they generate a new abstract type each time they are applied.

Functor Application Entry Point. To enable the low-level A+I context to apply functors to modules in the same way that a ModuleML context can, we introduce a functor application entry point into the protected memory that has type: $\texttt{fappl} : \mathsf{Sec}[\mathbf{functor}(\texttt{X}_i : \texttt{S}) \rightarrow \texttt{S}'] \rightarrow (\mathsf{Ins}[\texttt{S}] \vee \mathsf{Sec}[S]) \rightarrow \mathsf{Sec}[\texttt{S}']$. The first argument to this entry point is an index to the table $\mathcal{F}$, the second argument m is a shared module or a module defined by the A+I context. The entry point securely applies the appropriate functor f with associated stamp Σ_f to the argument a, as long as a conforms to the signature S, as follows.

1. Check the flag L_f. Abort if not set.
2. $f = \mathit{Marshall}_{\mathbf{i}}^{\mathbf{functor}(\texttt{X}_i:\texttt{S})\rightarrow\texttt{S}'}(i)$.
3. Depending on the representation of m:
   (a) If $\mathsf{Ins}[\texttt{S}]$: $a = \mathit{Marshall}_{\mathbf{c}}^{\texttt{S}}(a)$
   (b) If $\mathsf{Sec}[\texttt{S}]$: $a = \mathit{Marshall}_{\mathbf{i}}^{\texttt{S}}(a)$
4. Apply f to a. Store the result in r.
5. Stamp r with Σ_f.
6. Return $\mathit{Marshall}_{\mathbf{o}}^{S'}(r)$.

Note that as specified in Sect. 3.3, the marshalling rules of 3(a) and 3(b) perform the sub-typing check required by the functor application rule.

Functor Entry Points. The secure compilation scheme outputs entry points that enable the A+I context to gain access to the functor as well as interact with the result of the functor application. The entry points to functor bindings that are not embedded within another functor have a type: $\texttt{M}_i : \mathsf{Sec}[\mathbf{functor}(\texttt{X}_i : \texttt{S}) \rightarrow \texttt{S}']$ and marshall out the associated functor through an index to a table $\mathcal{F}$.

The entry points to the bindings of structures that are defined within the body of a functor, differ from the previously detailed entry points for value, structure and functor bindings in that they take an argument: an index i to the table $\mathcal{M}$. As detailed in the previous paragraph, the functor application entry point marshalls out its result through the marshalling function $\mathit{Marshall}_{\mathbf{o}}^{S}$, which, as explained in Sect. 3.3, stores the result into the structure requests counting table $\mathcal{M}$. The implementations of these entry points extend the previously discussed entry point implementations in that their result is not statically defined but depends on the structure associated with the input index i. The entry points will thus look up index i in $\mathcal{M}$ and check that the retrieved structure is stamped with the correct stamp Σ_i, as follows.

1. $d = Marshall_{\mathbf{i}}^{\mathsf{S}}(i)$.
2. Check that stamp of $d = \Sigma_i$. If not Abort.

To illustrate the necessity of this stamp check, we reconsider the example functor F introduced at the beginning of this section. This functor is assigned the stamp Σ_1 (Fig. 4) and each of its bindings $\mathtt{F.fd}$, $\mathtt{F.F_1}$ and $\mathtt{F.M_1}$, check that the structure associated with input index i is stamped by Σ_1. If they did not do so the A+I context could, for example, violate the typing rules of ModuleML by passing a structure created using F to the bindings of the following functor $\mathtt{F_b}$.

```
signature S_b = sig
 type U
 val v1: int →
      int
 val vs: int
end
```

```
module F_b = functor (A : S_b) struct
 type T = int
 val fd y = (A.v1 y)
 module F1 = functor(X:S_a)struct type U =
      int
  val vs = 0; val v1 = A.vs end
 module M1 = A : S_a
end : S_r
```

While both $\mathtt{F_b}$ and F produce a structure with signature $\mathtt{S_r}$, the argument of $\mathtt{F_b}$ conforms to the signature $\mathtt{S_b}$ not the signature $\mathtt{S_a}$, which seals the binding $\mathtt{v_s}$ whereas $\mathtt{S_b}$ does not. Without the stamp checking mechanism the A+I context could break the abstractions of ModuleML by passing a module produced by applying F to the entry point for $\mathtt{F_b.F_1}$ as the implementation of $\mathtt{F_b.F_1}$ exposes the value binding $\mathtt{A.v_s}$, as highlighted in gray in the listing for $\mathtt{F_b}$.

The entry points for $\mathtt{F.F_1}$ and $\mathtt{F.M_1}$ stamp their result with a stamp Σ_2 and Σ_3 respectively. This further specialization of the stamps within the inner modules is necessary to prevent similar attacks.

$Marshall_{\mathbf{c}}^{\mathsf{functor}(X_i:S)\to S'}$. Our compilation scheme enables the A+I context to supply its own functors as arguments to the functor application entry point. These foreign functors are marshalled into ModuleML functors by a function $Marshall_{\mathbf{c}}^{\mathsf{functor}(X_i:S)\to S'} : \mathsf{Ins}[\mathbf{functor}(\mathsf{X}_i : \mathsf{S}) \to \mathsf{S}'] \to (\mathbf{functor}(\mathsf{X}_i : \mathsf{S}) \to \mathsf{S}')$, that takes in a reference to an A+I function f and wraps that function into a new function that performs the following steps, whenever the foreign functor is applied to a ModuleML module M, within the securely compiled module.

1. $a = Marshall_{\mathbf{o}}^{\mathsf{S}}(\mathtt{M})$
2. Apply f to a. Store the result in r.
3. Return $Marshall_{\mathbf{c}}^{\mathsf{S}'}(r)$

4 Compiler Reflection

Denote the result of compiling the module M down to A+I as $\mathtt{M}^{\downarrow}$. Compiler reflection is formally expressed as.

$$\mathtt{M_1} \simeq \mathtt{M_2} \Rightarrow \mathtt{M_1^{\downarrow}} \simeq \mathtt{M_2^{\downarrow}}$$

It states that the equivalences of the modules M_1 and M_2 are preserved through the secure compilation scheme in the A+I context. To prove this statement we will prove the contra-positive: $M_1^{\downarrow} \not\simeq M_2^{\downarrow} \Rightarrow M_1 \not\simeq M_2$. This contra-positive can be stated as: whenever an A+I context can distinguish between two compiled modules, there exists a ModuleML context that can distinguish between the original modules. As detailed in Sect. 2.2 we do not directly reason about contextual equivalence for A+I programs but instead rely on trace equivalence. As such we can redefine compiler reflection as follows.

Theorem 1 (Module Differentation). *Any two ModuleML modules M_1 and M_2 whose compilation results produce two different low-level traces $\overline{\gamma_1}$ and $\overline{\gamma_2}$ are not contextually equivalent. Formally:* $\mathsf{Traces}(M_1{}^{\downarrow}) \neq \mathsf{Traces}(M_2{}^{\downarrow}) \Rightarrow M_1 \not\simeq M_2$.

To prove the theorem we adopt the established proof technique [8,16] of developing an algorithm that given two ModuleML modules M_1 and M_2 and their differing A+I traces $\overline{\gamma_1}$ and $\overline{\gamma_2}$ can produce a "witness" ModuleML context C that can distinguish between M_1 and M_2.

We have implemented exactly such a witness building algorithm in Ocaml[1]. The algorithm analyses the labels of the low-level traces $\overline{\gamma_1}$ and $\overline{\gamma_2}$ that detail the interactions between an unknown A+I context (it's a black box) and the modules M_1 and M_2. For the algorithm to be correct, it must detect the first two labels γ in the traces that differ. Assuming the first differening labels are at position i, the algorithm produces an ModuleML module that will replicate the first $i - 1$ labels of the traces and at the i-th step will diverge for M_1 and terminate for M_2, distinguishing them as required. The resulting module must thus keep track of the number of interactions it has with the unknown A+I context, which is done through the use of the ModuleML locations. A full explanation of the inner workings of the algorithm is provided in the accompanying technical report [10].

5 Implementation and Experimental Results

We have developped a compiler[2] that compiles ModuleML modules using either the secure compilation scheme detailed in this paper or through a naive and *insecure* compilation scheme that features none of the security checks. The compiler targets the Fides implementation of PMA [19]. Fides implements PMA through use of a hypervisor that runs two virtual machines: one that handles the secure memory module and one handles the outside memory. One consequence of this architecture is that, as the low-level context interacts with the compiled module, the Fides hypervisor will be forced to switch between the two virtual machines for each call and callback between the context and the module.

The security checks described in this paper are only triggered when execution crosses the boundary between protected and unprotected memory. As such we benchmark five scenarios (included with the source code of the compiler) that

[1] https://github.com/sylvarant/moduleml-witness-algorithm.

[2] https://github.com/sylvarant/secure-ml-compiler.

involve boundary crossings. In the first scenario (*Value*) the A+I context retrieves a value binding by calling the appropriate entry point. In the second scenario (*Closure Application*) the A+I context applies a secure closure to another secure closure using the closure application entry point. In the third scenario (*Callback*) the atacker applies a secure closure to a function of the A+I context. In the next scenario (*Functor Application*) the A+I context applies a functor to a module of the A+I context using the functor application entry point. In the final scenario (*Dynamic Value*) the A+I context accesses the value binding of a structure that results from applying a functor at run-time. We have timed the performance of each of these five scenarios, as denoted in Table 1.

The tests were performed on a Dell Latitude with a 2.67 GHz Intel Core i5 and 4GB of DDR3 RAM. The difference between rows "Insecure" and "Insecure + Fides" shows the high overhead of the Fides architecture. It is especially notable in the call back and functor application scenarios which transition between the protected and unprotected memory twice. The security checks of the functor application scenario have by far the biggest performance impact. This is due to the fact that this scenario involves both the dynamic type checking of the structure input by the A+I context as well as the creation of a new module, two computationally intensive operations. The additional performance impact of the security checks in the other scenarios is small, peaking at about 4 % when securing the value binding of a dynamically obtained structure.

Table 1. The average execution time for each test scenario.

	Insecure	**Insecure + Fides**	**Secure + Fides**
Value Binding	0.18 μs	17.59 μs	17.86 μs
Closure Application	0.32 μs	17.68 μs	18.09 μs
Callback	0.31 μs	36.59 μs	36.97 μs
Functor Application	0.57 μs	37.14 μs	106.50 μs
Dynamic Value Binding	0.26 μs	17.73 μs	18.41 μs

6 Related Work

Secure (fully abstract) compilation was first introduced by Abadi [1] as a criticism of the way in which Java was translated into the Java bytecode language. Secure compilation schemes have since been introduced for many different source language and target languages. Closely related to this work is the secure compilation scheme for ML to JavaScript by Fournet *et al.* [5]. Their definition of ML, however, does not feature a module system. Their Javascript attacker model is also more high-level than our untyped assembly contexts with low-level code execution privileges. Another related compilation scheme is the secure compilation scheme for the $\lambda_\mu$hashref-calculus to a machine model with adress space layout randomisation by Jagadeesan *et al.* [7]. Like the ModuleML used in this work the $\lambda_\mu$hashref-calculus features dynamic memory allocation. In contrast to

ModuleML, locations in $\lambda_\mu$hashref are observable through a hash operation. The attacker model differs as well. Whereas the attacker in this work is unable to read the memory of the securely compiled program, due to the PMA mechanism, the attacker considered by Jagadeesan *et al.* can probe the memory.

Verified compilation, is a broad research topic that aims to provide compilers that are proven to be correct [2,12]. The resulting compilers thus come with proofs for the preservation property that we have assumed (Sect. 1). Many established verified compilation results hold only for closed world assumptions, but recently, verified compilers have appeared for partial programs as well. Related to this work is a verified compositional compiler for an ML language, that features references and recursive types, to assembly by Hur and Dreyer [6]. Their compiler preserves the equivalences of ML programs for well-behaved assembly contexts, but does not consider the threats posed by possibly malicious contexts.

Throughout the secure compilation scheme we make use of our previously developed interaction counting masking system [9] to securely share the values of security relevant abstractions. Alternatively, we could have applied the sealing mechanism of Matthews et al. [14], to achieve the same result.

7 Conclusions

This paper presented a secure compiler for ModuleML: a light-weight ML language with higher-order functions, references and a module system. This secure compilation scheme compiles ModuleML to untyped assembly code enhanced with a memory isolation mechanism, known as the Protected Module Architecture, in a way that reflects the equivalences of ModuleML. This security property is proven through the implementation of a witness building algorithm.

References

1. Abadi, M.: Protection in programming-language translations. In: Vitek, J., Jensen, C.D. (eds.) Secure Internet Programming. LNCS, vol. 1603, pp. 19–34. Springer, Heidelberg (1999)
2. Chlipala, A.: A certified type-preserving compiler from lambda calculus to assembly language. In: PLDI 2007, pp. 54–65. ACM, New York, NY, USA (2007)
3. Codognet, P., Diaz, D.: WAMCC: Compiling Prolog to C. In: ICLP, pp. 317–331. MIT PRess (1995)
4. Dreyer, D.: Understanding and evolving the ML module system. PhD thesis, Carnegie Mellon, May 2005
5. Fournet, C., Swamy, N., Chen, J., Dagand, P.-E., Strub, P.-Y., Livshits, B.: Fully abstract compilation to javascript. In: POPL, pp. 371–38 (2013)
6. Hur, C.-K., Dreyer, D.: A Kripke logical relation between ML and assembly. In: POPL 2011, pp. 133–146. ACM (2011)
7. Jagadeesan, R., Pitcher, C., Rathke, J., Riely, J.: Local memory via layout randomization. In: CSF 2011, pp. 161–174. IEEE (2011)
8. Jeffrey, A., Rathke, J.: A fully abstract may testing semantics for concurrent objects. Theor. Comput. Sci. **338**(1–3), 17–63 (2005)

9. Larmuseau, A., Clarke, D.: Formalizing a secure foreign function interface. In: Calinescu, R., Rumpe, B. (eds.) SEFM 2015. LNCS, vol. 9276, pp. 215–230. Springer, Heidelberg (2015)
10. Larmuseau, A., Patrignani, M., Clarke, D.: A secure compiler for ml modules - extended version. Technical Report 2015–028, Uppsala University, September 2015
11. Leroy, X.: Manifest types, modules, and separate compilation. In: POPL 1994, pp. 109–122. ACM, New York, NY, USA (1994)
12. Leroy, X.: Formal verification of a realistic compiler. CACM **52**(7), 107–115 (2009)
13. Leroy, X., Doligez, D., Garrigue, J., Rémy, D., Vôuillon, J.: The Objective Caml system, release 4.02. Technical report, INRIA, August 2014
14. Matthews, J., Ahmed, A.: Parametric polymorphism through run-time sealing or, theorems for low, low prices!. In: Drossopoulou, S. (ed.) ESOP 2008. LNCS, vol. 4960, pp. 16–31. Springer, Heidelberg (2008)
15. McKeen, F., Alexandrovich, I., Berenzon, A., Rozas, C.V., Shafi, H., Shanbhogue, V., Savagaonkar, U.R.: Innovative instructions and software model for isolated execution. In: HASP 2013, ACM (2013)
16. Patrignani, M., Agten, P., Strackx, R., Jacobs, B., Clarke, D., Piessens, F.: Secure compilation to protected module architectures. TOPLAS **37**(2), 6:1–6:50 (2015)
17. Patrignani, M., Clarke, D.: Fully abstract trace semantics of low-level isolation mechanisms. In: SAC 2014, pp. 1562–1569. ACM (2014)
18. Queinnec, C.: Lisp in Small Pieces. Cambridge University Press, Cambridge (2003)
19. Strackx, R., Piessens, F.: Fides: selectively hardening software application components against kernel-level or process-level malware. In: CCS, pp. 2–13 (2012)

Detection of Redundant Expressions: A Complete and Polynomial-Time Algorithm in SSA

Rekha R. Pai(✉)

National Institute of Technology Calicut, Calicut, Kerala, India
rekharamapai@nitc.ac.in

Abstract. Detection of redundant expressions in a program based on values is a well researched problem done with a view to eliminate the redundancies so as to improve the run-time efficiency of the program. The problem entails the detection of equivalent expressions in a program. Here we present an iterative data-flow analysis algorithm to detect equivalent expressions in SSA for the purpose of detection of redundancies. The central challenge in this static analysis is to define a "join" operation to detect all equivalences at a join point such that any later occurrences of redundant expressions are detected in polynomial time. We achieve this by introducing the notion of *value ϕ-function*. We claim the algorithm is complete and takes only polynomial time. We implemented the algorithm in LLVM and demonstrated its performance.

Keywords: Equivalence detection · Global value numbering · Redundancy detection · Value ϕ-function

1 Introduction

Elimination of redundant expressions in a program, based on values, is an important code optimization done with a view to improve run-time efficiency of a program. The fundamental problem here is the detection of equivalent expressions in the program. The detection of all equivalences in a program is undecidable and hence we focus only on the detection of Herbrand equivalences [8], as is done traditionally. Two expressions are *Herbrand equivalent* if they have the same operator and corresponding operands are Herbrand equivalent.

Equivalences are detected by assigning *value numbers* to each expression. The value number v_i is assigned to two expressions if they are detected to be equivalent [3]. Global Value Numbering (GVN) is the problem of assigning value numbers to expressions to detect equivalences in whole programs. Efforts in the literature have been to propose a GVN algorithm which is both complete and efficient. A GVN algorithm is "complete" if it detects all Herbrand equivalences such that all associated total redundancies are detected.

Current GVN algorithms are either complete [5] or take only polynomial time [2–4,6,8–10], but not both, in the context of detection of redundancies. As in a

X. Feng and S. Park (Eds.): APLAS 2015, LNCS 9458, pp. 49–65, 2015.
DOI: 10.1007/978-3-319-26529-2_4

data-flow analysis, the central challenge in GVN is to define a "join" operation to detect equivalences at a *join* point. Though the detection of all equivalences at a join point makes a GVN algorithm complete, it blows up the size of partition of equivalent expressions thus making the algorithm inefficient [5].

In order to make a GVN algorithm polynomial, a solution is to detect only those equivalences at a point p' that may be used later at a point p where an expression, say e, appears. Here, we view the solution from a different perspective. Instead of detecting equivalences that may be used later, we propose that given an expression e at a point p in the program, detect whether e is equivalent to some expression(s) e' that appear in paths to e. For this we use semantics of ϕ-function in Static Single Assignment (SSA) form and introduce the new concept of *value ϕ-function* which is a set of equivalent ϕ-functions. We then propose an iterative data-flow analysis algorithm to detect equivalences in SSA form of programs which is complete and takes only polynomial time. We later prove the soundness and completeness of the algorithm.

We implemented the proposed algorithm and the algorithms by Kildall [5] and Gulwani [4] in LLVM to substantiate our claims on completeness and efficiency. The SPEC2006 programs were analyzed using the three algorithms and experimental results demonstrate that the proposed algorithm is complete as it detects same number of redundancies as the complete algorithm by Kildall. The proposed algorithm is also efficient compared to the widely accepted Gulwani's polynomial time algorithm since it takes less time to analyze the SPEC2006 programs.

The rest of the paper is organized as follows: in Sect. 2 we analyze two classic GVN algorithms to get a clarity on the problems in global value numbering. The terms used in this paper are given in Sect. 3. *Value ϕ-function* and the new algorithm are described in Sect. 4. The algorithm is formally defined in Sect. 5 and an experimental comparison of our algorithm with Kildall's [5] and Gulwani's [4] is made in Sect. 6. In Sect. 7 we review some of the algorithms in the literature. Section 8 concludes the work.

2 Motivation

In this section we analyze the classic works by Kildall [5] and Gulwani [4] to understand the problems in the detection of equivalent expressions. The algorithm by Kildall is complete and the one by Gulwani takes only polynomial time.

2.1 Kildall's Algorithm

The iterative data-flow analysis algorithm by Kildall detects equivalences at each point in the program. The equivalences are represented as a partition of expressions into equivalence classes, known as *expression pool*. The algorithm uses a powerful concept known as "structuring" in its transfer function. When a new equivalence class is created in an expression pool corresponding to an expression e in the program, the algorithm structures the partition by the construction and addition of all expressions (Herbrand) equivalent to e in the new class. This ensures detection of all redundant expressions which means that the algorithm is complete. But this leads to an exponential growth in the size of an equivalence class. The use of value numbers, as given in 'Implementation Notes' section in [5], avoids this problem. Kildall uses *value expression*, a compact representation for a set of equivalent expressions [5,9] to make the size of an equivalence class linear. But the problem of exponential growth in the size of expression pools (expressed in terms of number of equivalence classes) persists due to the definition of join operation as shown by [4]. This is because the join operation applied on n_j input pools may result in an expression pool whose size is exponential in the size of the input pools [4].

2.2 Gulwani's Algorithm

This algorithm works similar to that of Kildall's with equivalence information represented as a directed graph known as *Strong Equivalence DAG* (SED). The SED provides a compact representation of equivalence classes in a partition. The algorithm detects equivalences among all expressions of size at most s, where s is the size of program expression. This reduces the number of equivalence classes in a partition computed by join operation (compared with Kildall's) which makes it take only polynomial time. The join operation as defined in Gulwani (see Sect. 3.5, JOIN algorithm, lines 3–5 in [4]) intersects classes only if they have at least one variable in common. This leads to missing in the detection of some equivalences that will be useful in detecting redundancies [9].

2.3 Our View

The central problem in GVN is to define a *join* operation to detect equivalences at a join point. Detecting all equivalent expressions at a point makes the algorithm exponential. A solution, to overcome this problem, is to detect only those equivalent expressions at a point that are used to detect later occurrences of a redundant expression. To the best of our knowledge, currently there are no methods to precisely predict whether such redundant expressions might appear or not. Here we propose to view the problem from a completely different perspective. Instead of detecting equivalent expressions at a join point j that is used later, we postpone detection of such equivalences till a point where an expression actually occurs.

3 Terminology

Program Representation. The program in SSA is represented as a Control Flow Graph (CFG) [1] that has an empty *entry* and *exit* block. Other blocks contain assignment statements of the form $x = e$, where e is an expression. We assume a block can have at most two predecessors and a block with exactly two predecessors is called *join* block. The input and output points of a block are called *in* and *out* points, respectively, of the block.

Expression. An *expression* can be either a constant, a variable, or of the form $x \oplus y$ where x and y are constants or variables and $\oplus$ is a generic binary operator. An expression can also be of the form $\phi_k(x, y)$ where x and y are variables and k is the join block in which it appears. Such expressions are *ϕ-functions.* We may omit the subscript k when the join block is clear from the context. In the CFGs we draw, ϕ-functions appear in join blocks. But for the sake of clarity, we assume ϕ-functions are transformed to *copy* statements[1] and appended to appropriate predecessors of the join block.

Equivalence. Two expressions e_1 and e_2 are *Herbrand equivalent*, denoted $e_1 \equiv e_2$, if they have the same operator and corresponding operands are Herbrand equivalent. Two expressions e_1 and e_2 in a path $\mathcal{P}$ are said to be *equivalent in the path*, denoted $e_1 \equiv_{\mathcal{P}} e_2$, if they are Herbrand equivalent in that path.

Value Expression. A *value expression* $v_i \oplus v_j$ represents an operation between two equivalent classes where v_i and v_j are the value numbers of the two equivalent classes. $v_i \oplus v_j = \{x \oplus y; x \in C_i$, equivalent class with value number v_i and $y \in C_j$, equivalent class with value number $v_j\}$. A value expression is a representative expression of the set of equivalent expressions. Value expression of an expression $x \oplus y$ is constructed by replacing the operands with their value numbers.

4 Basic Concept

Our goal is to develop a complete and polynomial time algorithm for redundancy detection. The cause of redundancy is the equivalence of expressions in a program and hence detection of redundancies can be stated as a problem of computation of equivalence classes of expressions at each point in the CFG. The problem can be formally stated as: *given an expression e at a point p detect whether there are expressions e' in each path to p such that e' and e are equivalent in that path.* Here the concept of *value ϕ-function* is introduced for the purpose. In this section we first explain value ϕ-function and then propose our method to detect redundancies.

4.1 Value ϕ-function

Consider the code segment in Fig. 1. Depending on the path taken expression $x_3 + 1$ is equivalent to either $x_1 + 1$ or $x_2 + 1$. In other words, depending on the path taken, variable w_3 is equivalent to one of variables y_1 and z_2. That is, w_3 can be viewed as equivalent to the "merge of different variables" – y_1 and z_2 – at the join point, denoted $\phi(y_1, z_2)$. This kind of a "merge of different variables" can be seen as an extended form of the ϕ-function in the literature[2]. We use this extended notion of ϕ-function or "merge of different variables" to

[1] A *copy* statement is an assignment statement of the form $x = y$, where y is a variable.
[2] In the literature, a ϕ-function restricts its operands to different subscripted versions of the same non-SSA variable, say $\phi(x_1, x_2)$.

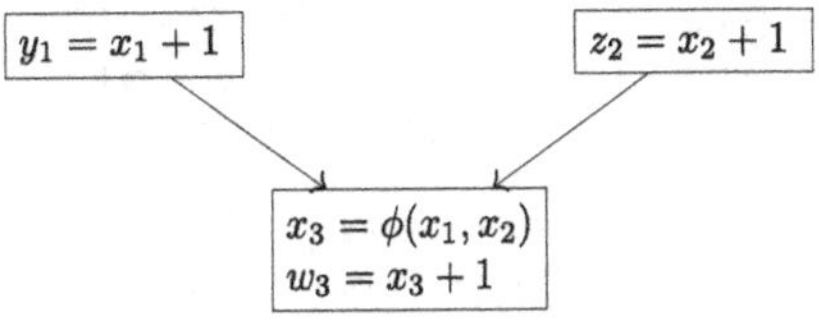

Fig. 1. Program with branches

express equivalences in such cases. Similar to the concept of value expression, we define the concept of *value ϕ-function* as an abstraction of a set of equivalent ϕ-functions.

Partition. A *partition* at a point represents equivalences that hold in the paths to the point. An equivalence class in the partition has a value number and elements like variables, constant, and value expression. It is also annotated with a value ϕ-function when necessary. For example, in a partition $\{\cdots|v_r, x_1, y_1|v_s, z_1, v_r + 1|v_m, x_n : \phi_k(v_i, v_j)|\cdots\}$ at a point p the class with value number v_r represents equivalence among variables x_1 and y_1. The class with value number v_s represents equivalence among expressions represented by value expression $v_r + 1$, that is $x_1 + 1$ and $y_1 + 1$. The expressions are also equivalent to variable z_1. From the class with value number v_m we can infer that variable x_n is equivalent to expressions with value number v_i in the path to point p through left edge to join block k. Also, x_n is equivalent to expressions with value number v_j in the path to p through right edge to the join block. Note that the value ϕ-function $\phi_k(v_i, v_j)$ appears as the last element in the class and is separated from the rest of the elements by ":" symbol to indicate that the value ϕ-function is an annotation of the class.

4.2 Proposed Method

Using the concept of value ϕ-function we propose an iterative data-flow analysis algorithm to compute equivalences at each point in the program. The two main components of this algorithm are *join* operation and *transfer function.*

Join Operation. A *join* operation detects equivalences that are common in all paths to the join point. Since in SSA there is only one definition for a variable, equivalences that hold at a point p, which dominates[3] join point j, hold at the join point. These equivalences are detected at the join point by doing a simple class-wise intersection of partitions. However, the detection of some common equivalences that are generated in branches require extra processing and we illustrate the latter. For clarity we separate the cases of detection of equivalences among variables from those among expressions-with-operators.

[3] Point p in a CFG *dominates* point p' if all paths from *entry* point to p' go through p.

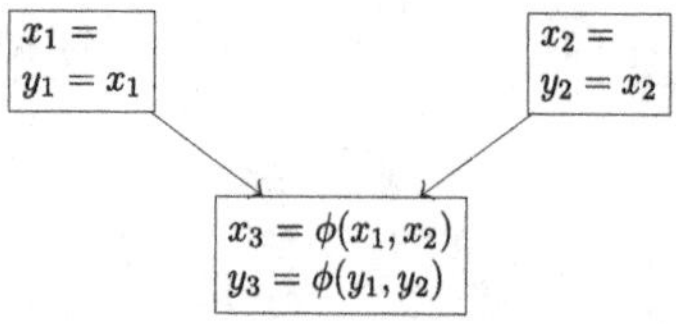

Fig. 2. Detecting equivalence of variables

Equivalence of Variables. Consider the code segment in Fig. 2. In the left path to the join point, variables x_1 and y_1, defined in the left branch, are equivalent. Similarly, x_2 and y_2, defined in the right branch, are equivalent in right path. By the use of ϕ-functions that appears in the join block we can detect that x_1 is equivalent to x_3 in the left path and x_2 is equivalent to x_3 in the right path. Similarly, y_1 is equivalent to y_3 in the left path and y_2 is equivalent to y_3 in the right path. By transitivity of equivalence relation, we conclude that x_3 and y_3 are equivalent at the join point.

In other words, our join operation merge different variables (corresponding to the same non-SSA variable) defined in different branches - x_1 with x_2 and y_1 with y_2 - to obtain x_3 and y_3, respectively, at the join point. We then conclude variables x_3 and y_3 are equivalent at the join point; in addition, they are equivalent to ϕ-functions $\phi(x_1, x_2)$ and $\phi(y_1, y_2)$. The detection of such equivalences are done by the transformation of ϕ-functions to copy statements which are then appended to appropriate predecessors of the join block.

Equivalence of Expressions-with-Operators. Now consider the code segment in Fig. 3. The expressions $x_1 + 1$ and $x_2 + 1$, that appear in different branches are merged[4] to obtain $x_3 + 1$ at the join point. By doing this "merge" we detect the equivalence of $x_1 + 1$ (and $x_2 + 1$) with $x_3 + 1$ if it appears at a point in some path from join point. However, this merge can be avoided if $x_3 + 1$ (or some expression equivalent to it) does not appear.

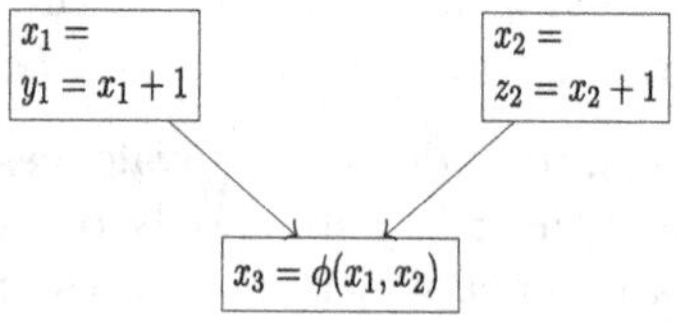

Fig. 3. Detecting equivalence of expressions-with-operators

[4] Merge of expressions can be viewed as an extended notion of merge of variables. "Merge of expressions" $e_{i1} + e_{i2}$ and $e_{j1} + e_{j2}$ is the expression $e_i + e_j$ such that e_i is the merge of e_{i1} and e_{j1}. Similarly, e_j is the merge of e_{i2} and e_{j2}.

As discussed in Sect. 2 the question is whether to merge different expressions at join points to detect equivalences. Here we take a completely different approach and the join operation does not merge the expressions at the join point. Instead merge operation is deferred till the occurrence of x_3+1 (or some expression equivalent to it). This is discussed when the concept of transfer function is explained.

Example. Consider the case of application of join on partitions $P_1 = \{v_1, x_1, x_3|v_2, y_1, y_3, v_1 + 1|v_3, z_1, z_3\}$ and $P_2 = \{v_4, x_2, x_3|v_5, y_2, y_3|v_6, z_2, z_3, v_4 + 1\}$. In the classes with value numbers v_1 in P_1 and v_4 in P_2 there is only one common variable x_3 and it appears in a class in the resulting partition P_3. Since the two classes in P_1 and P_2 have different value numbers v_1 and v_4, respectively, we can infer that x_3 is actually a merge of variables. Hence the resulting class is annotated with value ϕ-function $\phi(v_1, v_4)$. The class is assigned a new value number, say v_7. The resulting class is $|v_7, x_3 : \phi(v_1, v_4)|$.

Now consider the classes with value numbers v_2 in P_1 and v_6 in P_2. There are no obvious common equivalences in the classes; however we can infer from the partitions that the different value expressions $v_1 + 1$ in P_1 and $v_4 + 1$ in P_2 actually represent common equivalences of $x_3 + 1$, which is a merge of different expressions[5] $x_1 + 1$ and $x_2 + 1$. But as stated above the different expressions (or different value expressions to be precise) are not merged now and hence no new class is created in the resulting partition P_3.

Similar strategies are adopted to detect common equivalences in other pairs of classes one each from P_1 and P_2. The resulting partition P_3 is $\{v_7, x_3 : \phi(v_1, v_4)|v_8, y_3 : \phi(v_2, v_5)|v_9, z_3 : \phi(v_3, v_6)\}$.

Transfer Function. Based on the equivalences that hold at *in* point of a statement $s : x = e$, transfer function for the statement defines the equivalences that hold at its *out* point. This involves detection of whether the expression e is equivalent to expression e' in each path to it. Accordingly, the transfer function computes partition at *out* point, denoted $POUT_s$ (from that at *in* point, denoted PIN_s) by updating an existing class or creating a new class. The transfer function we define here is similar to the ones in the literature except that it uses value ϕ-function to detect equivalences in each path to e. The first step is to check partition PIN_s for existence of value expression of e. If not found, the transfer function proceeds to check whether expression e could be expressed as a "merge of different expressions". This is illustrated below using the code segment in Fig. 4.

Consider processing the last statement $w_3 = x_3 + 1$. Since value expression $v_7 + 1$ of expression $x_3 + 1$ does not appear in PIN_3, the transfer function proceeds to check whether $x_3 + 1$ could be expressed as a merge of expressions as follows:

[5] Since x_3 is a merge of variables x_1 and x_2, expression $x_3 + 1$ is a merge of $x_1 + 1$ and $x_2 + 1$.

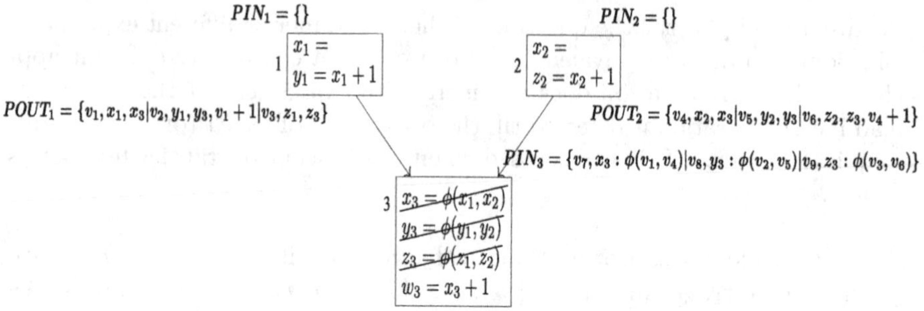

Fig. 4. Concept of transfer function

$x_3 + 1 \equiv v_7 + 1$ // value expression of $x_3 + 1$ computed using PIN_3
$\equiv \phi(v_1, v_4) + 1$ // class with v_7 in PIN_3 is annotated with $\phi(v_1, v_4)$
$\equiv \phi(v_1 + 1, v_4 + 1)$ // using semantics of value ϕ-function
$\equiv \phi(v_2, v_6)$ // $v_1 + 1 \in POUT_1$ having v_2, where block 1 is left predecessor of join block and $v_4 + 1 \in POUT_2$ having v_6, where block 2 is the right predecessor.

Thus using value ϕ-function we detect that $x_3 + 1$ is actually equivalent to expression(s) with value number v_2, when the left path is considered in isolation. Similarly, $x_3 + 1$ is equivalent to expression(s) with value number v_6, when the right path is considered in isolation. That is, $x_3 + 1$ is a "merge of expressions", here $x_1 + 1$ and $x_2 + 1$. In terms of variables, w_3 is merge of different variables, here y_1 and z_2.

Since neither value expression $v_7 + 1$ nor value ϕ-function $\phi(v_2, v_6)$ is present in PIN_3, the transfer function creates a new class in $POUT_3$ with new value number, say v_{10}, and add w_3 and $v_7 + 1$ to it. The class is also annotated with value ϕ-function $\phi(v_2, v_6)$. The classes in PIN_3 are added as such to $POUT_3$. The resulting partition $POUT_3$ is $\{v_7, x_3 : \phi(v_1, v_4)|v_8, y_3 : \phi(v_2, v_5)|v_9, z_3 : \phi(v_3, v_6)|v_{10}, w_3, v_7 + 1 : \phi(v_2, v_6)\}$.

Detection of Redundancies. Expression e in statement $x = e$ is redundant if there exists expression e' equivalent to e in each path to the statement. In terms of variables, this implies x is equivalent to some variable y irrespective of path taken or to the merge of different variables. Given partition $POUT$ at *out* of statement $x = e$, expression e is redundant if there exists a variable in the class of x in $POUT$, other than x, or the class of x in $POUT$ is annotated with value ϕ-function.

In the example code in Fig. 4, redundancy of expression $x_3 + 1$ in the last statement $w_3 = x_3 + 1$ is detected since the class of w_3 in $POUT_3$ (computed in the previous subsection) is annotated with a value ϕ-function.

5 Algorithm

Here we formally present the iterative data-flow analysis algorithm to detect equivalences at each point in the program. The two main components of this algorithm are join operation and transfer function which are defined below. The algorithm to detect redundancies is trivial and is not written here.

5.1 Join

The algorithm JOIN given below defines the join operation. Before the join operation is performed, the ϕ-functions in a join block are transformed to copy statements and appended to appropriate predecessors of the join block. Transfer function is then applied on these copies.

```
JOIN(P1, P2)
    P = {}
    for each pair of classes Ci ∈ P1 and Cj ∈ P2
        Ck = INTERSECT(Ci, Cj)
        P = P ∪ Ck                          // Ignore when Ck is empty
    return P
```

```
INTERSECT(Ci, Cj)
    Ck = Ci ∩ Cj                            // set intersection
    if Ck ≠ {} and Ck does not have value number
        then Ck = Ck ∪ {vk}                 // vk is new value number
             Ck = (Ck − {vpf}) ∪ {φb(vi, vj)}
             // vpf is value φ-function in Ck, vi ∈ Ci, vj ∈ Cj, b is join block
    return Ck
```

Lemma 1. *If $e_1 \equiv e_2$ at a point p and the point p dominates join point j then $e_1 \equiv e_2$ at j iff the* JOIN *algorithm detects their equivalence.*

Lemma 2. *If variable $x \equiv y$ in each path to join point j then $x \equiv y$ at j iff the* JOIN *algorithm detects their equivalence.*

5.2 Transfer Function

Given a partition PIN_s at *in* of a statement s, the transfer function for the statement[6] computes the partition $POUT_s$ at its *out* point and is defined below. The transfer function uses the function VALUEEXPR which accepts an expression e and returns value expression of e, if e is of the form $x \oplus y$, otherwise returns e itself. The function VALUEPHIFUNC accepts value expression and a partition and returns value ϕ-function if the expressions represented by the value expression

[6] Transfer function for a block is the composition of transfer function of each statement in the block [1].

are a merge of expressions. Otherwise it returns NULL. This function assumes partitions at *out* of each block are accessible to it. The concept of this function is given below and the detailed algorithm is in the appendix.

TRANSFERFUNCTION($x = e, PIN_s$)
  $POUT_s = PIN_s$
  if x is in a class C_i in $POUT_s$
    then $C_i = C_i - \{x\}$
  ve = VALUEEXPR(e)
  vpf = VALUEPHIFUNC(ve, PIN_s) // can be NULL
  if ve or vpf is in a class C_i in $POUT_s$ // ignore vpf when NULL
    then $C_i = C_i \cup \{x, ve\}$ // set union
    else $POUT_s = POUT_s \cup \{v_n, x, ve : vpf\}$ // v_n is new value number
  return $POUT_s$

VALUEPHIFUNC(ve, P)
  if ve is of the form $\phi_k(v_{i1}, v_{j1}) \oplus \phi_k(v_{i2}, v_{j2})$
    then v_i = GETVN($POUT_{k_l}, v_{i1} \oplus v_{i2}$)
      if (v_i == NULL)
        then v_i = VALUEPHIFUNC($v_{i1} \oplus v_{i2}, POUT_{k_l}$)
      v_j = GETVN($POUT_{k_r}, v_{j1} \oplus v_{j2}$)
      if (v_j == NULL)
        then v_j = VALUEPHIFUNC($v_{j1} \oplus v_{j2}, POUT_{k_r}$)
  return $\phi_k(v_i, v_j)$ // v_i, v_j are non-NULL

Lemma 3. *Let $x = e$ be a statement at a point p in the program and there exist expressions e_i at points p_i in each path to p such that at least one of the p_i's does not dominate p. Then expression e has a value ϕ-function, as computed by* VALUEPHIFUNC *algorithm, iff expressions e_i and e are equivalent in respective paths.*

Lemma 4. *Let $x = e$ be a statement at a point p in the program and there exist expressions e_i in each path to p. Expressions e_i and e are equivalent in their respective paths iff the* TRANSFERFUNCTION *algorithm detects the equivalences.*

5.3 The Iterative Algorithm

The algorithm DETECTEQUIVALENCES given below analyzes the program (represented as a CFG G) and computes partitions of equivalent expressions at each point in the program. The iterative analysis method is adapted from [1]. The algorithm initializes *out* point of each statement (except first statement) with partition $\top$ (*top*). $\top$ is a special partition with the property JOIN($P, \top$) = P = JOIN($\top, P$). The algorithm iteratively computes partitions at each point till there are no changes in the equivalences detected (from the previous iteration).

```
DETECTEQUIVALENCES(G)
  PIN_1 = {}                            // "1" is the first statement in the program
  POUT_1 = TRANSFERFUNCTION(PIN_1)
  for each statement s other than the first statement in the program
      POUT_s = ⊤
  while changes to any POUT occur     // i.e. changes in equivalences
      for each statement s other than the first statement in the program
          if s appears in block b that has two predecessors
              then PIN_s = JOIN(POUT_s', POUT_s'')^a
              else PIN_s = POUT_s'
          POUT_s = TRANSFERFUNCTION(PIN_s)^b
```

[a] s' and s'' are last statements in respective predecessors.

[b] s' is the statement just before s.

Theorem 1 (Soundness and Completeness). *Let P be a partition at a point p computed by the iterative data-flow analysis algorithm. Two expressions are equivalent at p iff the algorithm detects their equivalence.*

An outline of the correctness proofs of the algorithms are given in appendix.

5.4 Complexity Analysis

Let there be n number of expressions in a program. By definitions of JOIN and TRANSFERFUNCTION a partition can have $O(n)$ classes with each class of $O(v)$ size, where v is the number of variables and constants in the program. The join operation is class-wise intersection of partitions. With efficient data structure that supports lookup, intersection of each class takes $O(v)$ time. With a total of n^2 such intersections, a join takes $O(n^2.v)$ time. If there are j join points, the total time taken by all the join operations in an iteration is $O(n^2.v.j)$. The transfer function involves construction and lookup of value expression or value ϕ-function in the input partition. A value expression is computed and searched for in $O(n)$ time. Computation of value ϕ-function for an expression $x+y$ essentially involves lookup of value expressions, recursively, in partitions at left and right predecessors of a join block. If a lookup table is maintained to map value expressions to value ϕ-functions (or NULL when a value expression does not have a value ϕ-function), then computation of a value ϕ-function can be done in $O(n.j)$ time. Thus transfer function of a statement $x = e$ takes $O(n.j)$ time. In a program with n expressions total time taken by all the transfer functions in an iteration is $O(n^2.j)$. Thus the time taken by all the joins and transfer functions in an iteration is $O(n^2.v.j)$. As shown in [4], in the worst case the iterative analysis takes n iterations and hence the total time taken by the analysis is $O(n^3.v.j)$.

6 Implementation and Results

In this section we compare the new algorithm with the algorithms by Kildall [5] and Gulwani [4]. We chose Kildall's algorithm since it is complete and the widely accepted Gulwani's algorithm was chosen since it takes only polynomial time. The three iterative data-flow analysis algorithms compute equivalence information at each point in the program. We implemented the algorithms in LLVMv3.4 compiler with *clang* as front end. The implementations consider all arithmetic operations, conversion operations, vector operations and aggregate operations, while to simplify the implementations, memory and branch operations were ignored. The implementations uses the *llvm::DenseMap*, *llvm::SmallPtrSet* and *llvm::SmallVector* classes to define the partitions, equivalence classes and value expressions. Instances of partitions are associated with *in* and *out* points of each instruction. The input to the implementations are in SSA form of LLVM-IR. Since Kildall's and Gulwani's algorithm work on non-SSA form of programs, we modified the algorithms to process ϕ-functions. ϕ-functions are transformed to copy statements and appended to predecessors of the join blocks. The implementations were compared using SPEC2006 programs and the results were obtained on 2 GHz Intel Xeon processor with 8 GB RAM running Ubuntu 12.04.

Table 1. Number of redundancies detected by Gulwani, Kildall, and our algorithm

CINT2006	Gulwani	Kildall	Proposed	Improvement(%)
mcf	32	36	36	12.5
astar	130	153	153	17.7
libquantum	210	259	259	23.3
bzip2	580	691	691	19.1
sjeng	1141	1265	1265	10.9
hmmer	3810	4204	4204	10.3
gobmk	8907	10005	10005	12.3
h264ref	8982	10216	10216	13.7
gcc	19837	23300	23300	17.5
CFP2006	Gulwani	Kildall	Proposed	Improvement(%)
milc	775	867	867	11.9
sphinx3	827	919	919	11.1
lbm	1085	1169	1169	07.7
soplex	2685	3022	3022	12.6
povray	3319	3623	3623	09.2

Table 1 shows the number of redundancies detected in SPEC2006 CINT and CFP C/C++ programs using Gulwani, Kildall, and the new algorithm. The table also gives the percentage improvement made by the new algorithm in detecting redundancies over Gulwani. The results show that the proposed algorithm detects same number of redundancies as the complete algorithm by Kildall thus demonstrating completeness. Also both these algorithms detect more redundancies when compared to Gulwani's with an average improvement of 14.2 %.

The figures indicate that there can be statements, say of the form $z = x \oplus y$, in real programs such that variable z is equivalent to different variables in different paths to the statement. Detection of redundancy of $x \oplus y$ is missed by Gulwani while both Kildall and the new algorithm could capture it.

Table 2. Time taken (in seconds) to analyze the input SPEC2006 programs along with their size (when converted to LLVM-IR SSA form)

CINT2006	Size of program		Time for analysis		
	#joins	#instructions	Kildall	Gulwani	Proposed
mcf	171	1815	2.5961	0.8520	0.4917
libquantum	277	5045	7.5244	1.8921	1.1035
astar	450	6586	13.7687	4.1121	2.0936
bzip2	814	13346	66.4680	9.3012	6.3841
sjeng	1874	18658	119.0993	15.7408	9.5835
hmmer	3279	48387	203.3485	34.6138	30.2571
gobmk	9754	105994	361.5141	49.1068	45.5976
h264ref	6804	116253	358.3743	70.6684	67.6074
gcc	45861	605303	750.6864	110.2226	98.3966
CFP2006	#joins	#instructions	Kildall	Gulwani	Proposed
lbm	55	3773	7.6245	3.9202	1.4973
milc	1103	18867	30.4560	8.7964	5.5625
sphinx3	1836	22929	62.6717	22.4852	18.4850
soplex	3206	48513	136.0443	25.3210	21.4148
povray	8349	128305	320.8518	79.0802	74.7350

To show the efficiency of our algorithm, we measured the CPU time taken to perform the analyses during compilation of the SPEC2006 programs. The times were measured using *-ftime-report* option of *clang*. Table 2 gives the time taken (in seconds) by the implementations to analyze the SPEC programs. The table also gives the number of join blocks and instructions considered to indicate the number of join operation and transfer functions being applied on the partitions.

Table 2 shows that the new algorithm takes less time to analyze the SPEC programs than Gulwani's polynomial time algorithm. This we believe is because Gulwani recursively intersects equivalence classes (that has at least one variable in common) to detect equivalent expressions at a join point (see Sect. 3.5, JOIN algorithm, Lines 3–5 in [4]). However, the proposed algorithm does only a simple intersection of equivalence classes. Equivalences in paths to an expression is detected only when needed by computing value ϕ-function. Both these algorithms take considerably less time than Kildall's exponential time algorithm. The join operation in Kildall is similar to that in Gulwani except that, in Kildall's, the join operation recursively intersects equivalence classes even if there are no common variables in the classes which makes it least efficient among the three algorithms.

The results in the tables clearly demonstrate that the proposed algorithm is complete as it detects the same number of redundancies as the complete algorithm by Kildall. Also the algorithm is efficient when compared to the polynomial time algorithm by Gulwani as it takes less time. Since more redundancies can be detected by the proposed algorithm in comparatively less time, the algorithm may be used in redundancy elimination algorithms that aid in the generation of faster code.

7 Related Work

The seminal work on GVN by Kildall [5] detects equivalences at each point in the program using an iterative data-flow analysis algorithm. This algorithm uses "structuring" of partitions of equivalent expressions, which makes it complete. However, structuring of partitions blows up its size and hence affects efficiency of the algorithm. The strive to improve efficiency in the detection of equivalences motivated the algorithm by Alpern and others (referred to as AWZ algorithm) [2] which works on Static Single Assignment (SSA) form of programs and uses the concept of *congruence*. The algorithm though efficient is less precise than Kildall's, one of the reasons being that it does not interpret *ϕ-functions*. Rüthing, Knoop, and Steffen [8] improves on AWZ in terms of the number of equivalences detected by using *normalization rules*. These normalization rules essentially interpret the ϕ-functions. The algorithm is efficient but not complete, as proved by Gulwani [4]. The *Dominator-based value numbering* algorithm by Briggs and others [3] works on SSA form. The algorithm is not complete as it makes pessimistic assumptions about loops in programs. The *SCC-based Value Numbering* algorithm by Simpson [10] considers semantics of operators to improve on AWZ. However the algorithm has similar issues as AWZ since it does not interpret ϕ-functions. The GVN algorithms in SSA by VanDrunen [11] and Odaira [7] detect and eliminate a broader class of partial redundancies and not just total redundancies. The polynomial time algorithm by Gulwani and Necula [4] is claimed to detect all equivalences among expressions of a particular size. However, some of the redundancies could not be detected using this GVN algorithm [9]. Nie proposed an SSA version of Gulwani's algorithm [6]. In general, the algorithms are either complete or take only polynomial time but not both.

8 Conclusion

Detection of equivalent expressions in a program is a static analysis aimed at elimination of redundant expressions. The fundamental problem here is the detection of equivalences at each point in the program such that all redundancies are detected in polynomial time. For this we introduced the novel concept of value ϕ-function. We then presented an iterative data-flow analysis algorithm which uses value ϕ-function to detect equivalences. We showed that the algorithm is complete and takes only polynomial time. Moreover, we implemented our algorithm and compared it with two widely accepted GVN algorithms in the literature. The experimental results demonstrate that the proposed algorithm is complete and efficient.

Acknowledgements. We thank Vineeth Paleri, Muralikrishnan K, Vinith R, and the anonymous reviewers for their insightful comments.

A Appendix

A.1 VALUEPHIFUNC

This recursive function computes value ϕ-function of a given value expression. The function assumes partitions at *out* of each block is available to it. The function uses EQUIVE to replace operands of a given value expression with equivalent value ϕ-functions, whenever possible. Else it returns the value expression as such. The GETVN function used here takes a partition at *out* of either the left or right predecessor of a join block k. It searches for the input value expression in the partition and returns its value number, if present. If the partition was searched for previously then the function returns a new value number. This case can arise with loops in the program.

```
VALUEPHIFUNC(ve, P)
    vi = vj = vpf = NULL
    ve' = EQUIVE(ve, P)
    if ve' is of the form φk(vi1, vj1) + φk(vi2, vj2)
        then vi = GETVN(POUT_kl, vi1 + vi2)
             vj = GETVN(POUT_kr, vj1 + vj2)
             if vi == NULL
                 then vi = VALUEPHIFUNC(vi1 + vi2, POUT_kl)
             if vj == NULL
                 then vj = VALUEPHIFUNC(vj1 + vj2, POUT_kr)
        elseif ve' is of the form φk(vi1, vj1) + vm ^a
             then vi = GETVN(POUT_kl, vi1 + vm)
                  vj = GETVN(POUT_kr, vj1 + vm)
                  if vi == NULL
                      then vi = VALUEPHIFUNC(vi1 + vm, POUT_kl)
                  if vj == NULL
                      then vj = VALUEPHIFUNC(vj1 + vm, POUT_kr)
             elseif ve' is of the form vm + φk(vi2, vj2)
                  then vi = GETVN(POUT_kl, vm + vi2)
                       vj = GETVN(POUT_kr, vm + vj2)
                       if vi == NULL
                           then vi = VALUEPHIFUNC(vm + vi2, POUT_kl)
                       if vj == NULL
                           then vj = VALUEPHIFUNC(vm + vj2, POUT_kr)
    if vi ∧ vj              // both are non-NULL
        then vpf = φk(vi, vj)
    return vpf
```

[a] class with value number v_m does not have value ϕ-function or has $\phi_r(v_s, v_t)$ such that block r *dominates* k.

A.2 Proof

Correctness of JOIN Algorithm

Lemma 1. *If $e_1 \equiv e_2$ at a point p and the point p dominates join point j then $e_1 \equiv e_2$ at j iff the algorithm detects their equivalence.*

Proof. Let expressions e_1 and e_2 be equivalent at a point p such that p dominates join point j. Since a variable is defined only once in SSA the expressions are equivalent in each path to j. Line 1 in the algorithm INTERSECT ensures such common equivalences are detected at the join point. □

Lemma 2. *If variable $x \equiv y$ in each path to join point j then $x \equiv y$ at j iff the algorithm detects their equivalence.*

Proof. Let two variables x and y be equivalent in each path to join point j. Then by suitably transforming the ϕ-functions in the join block j and by line 1 of the INTERSECT algorithm such equivalences could also be detected. □

Let there be expressions e_i in each path to an expression e and $e_i \equiv e$ in respective paths. The equivalences are detected by the TRANSFERFUNCTION algorithm which is proved below.

Correctness of TRANSFERFUNCTION Algorithm

Lemma 3. *Let $x = e$ be a statement at a point p in the program and there exist expressions e_i at points p_i in each path to p such that at least one of the p_i's does not dominate p. Then expression e has a value ϕ-function, as computed by* VALUEPHIFUNC *algorithm, iff expressions e_i and e are equivalent in respective paths.*

Proof. This can be proved by induction on the number of join points in paths with the base case similar to that in Fig. 4. □

Lemma 4. *Let $x = e$ be a statement at a point p in the program and there exists expressions e_i in each path to p. Expressions e_i and e are equivalent in respective paths iff the* TRANSFERFUNCTION *algorithm detects the equivalences.*

Proof. Let the expression(s) e_i appear at point p' such that p' dominate p. Then an equivalence class for e_i with its value expression will appear in the partition at p' (ensured by lines 7 and 8 in the algorithm). Since a variable is defined only once in SSA the partition at *in* point of the statement $x = e$ will have a class with the value expression of e_i. Then line 6 in the algorithm ensures equivalence of e_i and e is detected.

Now consider the case where an expression e_i appear at a point p' such that p' does not dominate p. In this case computation of value ϕ-function in line 5 (Lemma 3) and subsequent check for its existence in line 6 ensures detection of equivalences of e_i and e in respective paths. □

Correctness of Iterative Data-Flow Analysis Algorithm

Theorem 1 (Soundness and Completeness). *Let P be a partition at a point p computed by the iterative data-flow analysis algorithm. Two expressions are equivalent at p iff the algorithm detects their equivalence.*

Proof This follows from Lemmas 1, 2, and 4. □

Correctness of Algorithm for Detection of Redundancies

Theorem 2 (Soundness and Completeness). *Let $s : z = x + y$ be a statement at a point p. The expression $x + y$ is redundant iff the algorithm detects its redundancy.*

Proof This follows from Theorem 1. □

References

1. Aho, A.V., Lam, M.S., Sethi, R., Ullman, J.D.: Compilers: Principles, Techniques, and Tools, 2nd edn. Addison Wesley, Boston (2006)
2. Alpern, B., Wegman, M.N., Zadeck, F.K.: Detecting equality of variables in programs. In: Proceedings of the 15th ACM SIGPLAN-SIGACT Symposium on Principles of Programming Languages, POPL 1988, pp. 1–11. ACM, New York (1988)
3. Briggs, P., Cooper, K., Simpson, L.: Value numbering. Software: Practice and Experience 27(6), 701–724 (1997)
4. Gulwani, S., Necula, G.C.: A polynomial-time algorithm for global value numbering. In: Giacobazzi, R. (ed.) SAS 2004. LNCS, vol. 3148, pp. 212–227. Springer, Heidelberg (2004)
5. Kildall, G.A.: A unified approach to global program optimization. In: Proceedings of the 1st Annual ACM SIGACT-SIGPLAN Symposium on Principles of Programming Languages, POPL 1973, pp. 194–206. ACM, New York (1973)
6. Nie, J.-T., Cheng, X.: An efficient SSA-based algorithm for complete global value numbering. In: Shao, Z. (ed.) APLAS 2007. LNCS, vol. 4807, pp. 319–334. Springer, Heidelberg (2007)
7. Odaira, R., Hiraki, K.: Partial value number redundancy elimination. In: Eigenmann, R., Li, Z., Midkiff, S.P. (eds.) LCPC 2004. LNCS, vol. 3602, pp. 409–423. Springer, Heidelberg (2005)
8. Rüthing, O., Knoop, J., Steffen, B.: Detecting equalities of variables: combining efficiency with precision. In: Cortesi, A., Filé, G. (eds.) SAS 1999. LNCS, vol. 1694, pp. 232–247. Springer, Heidelberg (1999)
9. Saleena, N., Paleri, V.: Global value numbering for redundancy detection: a simple and efficient algorithm. In: Proceedings of the 29th Annual ACM Symposium on Applied Computing, SAC 2014, pp. 1609–1611. ACM, New York (2014)
10. Simpson, L.T.: Value-driven redundancy elimination. Ph.D. thesis, Rice University, Houston, TX, USA (1996)
11. VanDrunen, T., Hosking, A.L.: Value-based partial redundancy elimination. In: Duesterwald, E. (ed.) CC 2004. LNCS, vol. 2985, pp. 167–184. Springer, Heidelberg (2004)

Separation Logic

Separation Logic with Monadic Inductive Definitions and Implicit Existentials

Makoto Tatsuta[1(✉)] and Daisuke Kimura[2]

[1] National Institute of Informatics, Sokendai, Tokyo, Japan
tatsuta@nii.ac.jp
[2] Toho University, Chiba, Japan

Abstract. This paper proves the decidability of entailments in separation logic with monadic inductive definitions and implicit existentials. This system is obtained from the bounded-treewidth separation logic SLRDbtw of Iosif et al. in 2013 by adding implicit existential variables and restricting inductive definitions to monadic ones. The system proposed in this paper is a decidable system where one can use general recursive data structures with pointers as data, such as lists of pointers. The key idea is to reduce the problem to the decidability of SLRDbtw, by assigning local addresses or some distingu ished address to implicit existential variables so that the resulting definition clauses satisfy the establishment condition of SLRDbtw. This paper also proves the undecidability of the entailments when one adds implicit existentials to SLRDbtw. This shows that the implicit existentials are critical for the decidability.

1 Introduction

The theoretical foundations of software verification are important. Among them it is really necessary to obtain a feasible and powerful system for finding memory errors and verifying that software does not have any memory errors. Separation logic made it possible to solve this problem [2,3]. One of the key theoretical properties that supports their framework is the decidability of the truth of entailments of symbolic heaps.

A symbolic-heap system with recursive data structures was first proposed in [2,3]. Their system had a decision procedure of the truth of entailments. However it contained only the inductively defined predicates for list segments and trees. They wanted to extend it to general inductive definitions while keeping its decidability.

The symbolic heap is a conjunction of equalities and disequalities, and a separating conjunction of the empty heap predicate, the points-to predicate, and inductive predicates. In this setting, the expressive power of a system is determined mostly by its inductive predicates.

So far two decidable systems of symbolic heaps with general inductive definitions are known [9,10]. These systems cover complicated recursive data structures such as doubly-linked lists. However, they do not cover the two

X. Feng and S. Park (Eds.): APLAS 2015, LNCS 9458, pp. 69–89, 2015.
DOI: 10.1007/978-3-319-26529-2_5

predicates given in [2,3] for the following reason. In the system of [2,3], they allow field names which can be implicit, for example, $E \mapsto [f_1 : x]$ means $\exists y(E \mapsto [f_1 : x, f_2 : y])$. This implicit field y is formalized by an implicit existential variable. Since the system in [9] do not have implicit existentials, it does not cover the predicates used in [2,3]. Since the list segment predicate used in [2,3] uses disequality, the system in [10] does not cover this predicate.

An *implicit existential* is an existentially quantified variable such that the variable occurs only once in a given formula. So its value is not related to other values. An implicit existential is often denoted by the underscore _ for this reason. Implicit existentials are necessary for keeping data in each node in recursive data structure such as a list of pointers.

It is one of important goals to find the union of these two systems [3,9] where we can use general inductive definitions as well as implicit existentials. In this paper, we first prove that the union becomes undecidable. Namely the truth of entailments in the system obtained from [9] by adding implicit existentials is shown to be undecidable. Hence it is a challenging problem to find certain conditions that allow implicit existentials and show the decidability of the truth of entailments of symbolic heaps with general inductive definitions under the conditions.

We answer this problem by proposing the system Sep obtained from the system SLRD_{btw} in [9] by adding implicit existentials and restricting every inductively defined predicate to essentially unary one. We call this restriction the *monadicity* condition. This restriction disallows some data structures such as doubly-linked lists, but allows several commonly used data structures such as list segments and trees. Then our system Sep contains the system given in [3]. Our system contains a fragment of the system SLRD_{btw} with the restriction that inductive definitions are monadic.

Our main idea is to introduce some distinguished address ∞ and transform the heap into another heap such that implicit existentials point to local addresses or ∞. Then the resulting definition clauses satisfy the establishment condition of SLRD_{btw}. Moreover this transformation does not change the truth of given inductively defined predicates. This solves the difficulty discussed by [9] that implicit existentials may give a heap of arbitrary large treewidth.

Our monadicity condition allows global parameters to weaken the unary-predicate restriction. For example, Sep can inductively define the list segment predicate $\mathrm{ls}(x, y)$ since y is counted as a global parameter and ls is treated as unary for x. It is possible because y is unchanged throughout recursive calls of the predicate, and only the first argument x of the predicate $\mathrm{ls}(x, y)$ can be changed.

Our proof uses two translations. In the first translation, we translate a given inductively defined predicate in Sep into that in the separation logic $\mathrm{Sep}\infty$ with the distinguished address ∞. We transform a given heap into an extended heap which may have the address ∞, but it does not have any dangling, looping, sharing pointers except those to local values or global constants. Then the definition clauses after the translation satisfy the establishment condition. In the second translation, we translate $\mathrm{Sep}\infty$ into the system SLRD_{btw} by [9]. Finally we apply the decidability of the system SLRD_{btw}.

Section 2 defines separation logic Sep with monadic inductive definitions, and explains related work and our main ideas. Section 3 studies our translation from Sep into Sep∞. Section 4 discusses our translation from Sep∞ into a monadic version of SLRD$_{btw}$. Section 5 gives our main theorems of the decidability of Sep. Section 6 proves the undecidability of the system SLRD$_{btw}$ with implicit existentials. Section 7 concludes.

2 Separation Logic with Inductive Definitions

In this section, we first define our separation logic Sep, next we discuss related work, and then we explain our main ideas.

2.1 Symbolic Heaps with Inductive Definitions

This subsection defines the separation logic G with inductive definitions, in order to define our system Sep later. This subsection also gives the definition of the system SLRD$_{btw}$ by Iosif et al. given in [9].

We will use vector notations $\mathbf{x}$ to denote a sequence $x_1, \ldots, x_k$ for simplicity. $|\mathbf{x}|$ denotes the length of the sequence. Sometimes we will also use a notation of a sequence to denote a set for simplicity when it is not ambiguous from a context. We will also write $\mathbf{x} = \mathbf{y}$ to denote $x_i = y_i$ for all i, and $f(\mathbf{x})$ for the sequence $f(x_1), \ldots, f(x_k)$. We write $\equiv$ for the syntactical equivalence. N denotes the set of natural numbers.

Before defining the language of our system Sep, we begin with a general framework G of symbolic heaps with inductive definitions.

The language of G is defined as follows. We have first-order variables Vars $::= x, y, z, w, \ldots$ and inductively defined predicate symbols $P ::= P_1, P_2, \ldots$. Terms t are defined by $t ::= x \mid \text{nil}$. We define the following syntax:

Pure formulas $\Pi ::= t = t \mid t \neq t \mid \Pi \wedge \Pi$,
Spatial formulas $\Sigma ::= \text{Emp} \mid t \mapsto (t_1, \ldots, t_n) \mid P(\mathbf{t}) \mid \Sigma * \Sigma$,
Symbolic Heaps $\phi ::= \Pi \wedge \Sigma$,
Entailments $\phi_1 \vdash \phi_2$.

In G, each cell has n elements. Later a cell will be interpreted by N^n. We write the $(\mathbf{m})_i$ for i-th element m_i of $\mathbf{m}$ in N^n. We assume $*$ is more tightly connected than $\wedge$. We sometimes write $*_k A_k$ for a sequence of separating conjunctions such as $A_1 * A_2 * A_3$.

G has an inductive definition system, which is a finite set of inductive definitions given as follows.

Inductive Definitions $P_i(\mathbf{x}) =_{\text{def}} \bigvee_j R_{ij}(\mathbf{x})$.

Definition Clauses, which are defined as

$$R_{ij}(\mathbf{x}) \equiv \exists \mathbf{z}^{ij} (\Pi_{ij} \wedge *_k w_{ijk} \mapsto (u_1^{ijk}, \ldots, u_n^{ijk}) * *_l P_{f(i,j,l)}(\mathbf{t}^{ijl})),$$

where $f : N^3 \to N$. We write $[t]$ for the equivalence class containing t by the equalities in Π_{ij}.

We want a decidable system for software verification. However, the truth of entailments in the system G is known to be undecidable [1]. So some decidable fragments of this system have been proposed, by imposing some restrictions.

The condition *progress* is that each definition clause has exactly one points-to predicate. For an inductively defined predicate $P(\mathbf{x})$, i is said to be a *cell argument place* of P if every definition clause $R(\mathbf{x})$ of P has $x_i \mapsto (\mathbf{t})$ for some $\mathbf{t}$. The condition *connectivity* is that in every definition clause $R(\mathbf{x})$ and every inductively defined predicate P, if $P(\mathbf{t})$ is in $R(\mathbf{x})$, then P has some cell argument place i, and $R(\mathbf{x})$ has some $w \mapsto (\mathbf{u})$ such that $t_i \in [\mathbf{u}]$.

For an inductively defined predicate P, i is said to be an *allocated argument place* of P if the following holds for each definition clause $R(\mathbf{x})$ of P:

1. it has $x_i \mapsto (\mathbf{t})$ for some $\mathbf{t}$, or
2. it has some $P_l(\mathbf{t})$ such that j is an allocated argument place of P_l and $x_i \in [t_j]$.

For a definition clause $R(\mathbf{x})$ and a variable z existentially quantified in $R(\mathbf{x})$, z is said to be *allocated*, if

1. $R(\mathbf{x})$ has $z \mapsto (\mathbf{t})$ for some $\mathbf{t}$, or
2. $R(\mathbf{x})$ has some $P(\mathbf{t})$ such that i is an allocated argument place of P and $z \in [t_i]$.

The condition *establishment* is that in every definition clause and every existentially quantified variable z in it, z is allocated.

We discuss some known decidable fragments of G with some restrictions.

The first one is the system by Berdine et al. [2,3]. The restriction is to have only the predicate for list segments and that for trees. Namely a general form of inductive definitions is not available in their system. Their list segment predicate ls for the $n = 2$ case is defined as follows

$$\mathrm{ls}(x, y) =_{\mathrm{def}} (x = y \wedge \mathrm{Emp}) \vee (x \neq y \wedge \exists zw(x \mapsto (z, w) * \mathrm{ls}(z, y))). \quad (1)$$

The second one is the system SLRD_{btw} by Iosif et al. in 2013 [9]. Their restrictions are the conditions progress, connectivity, and establishment.

The third one is the system by Iosif et al. in 2014 [10]. We do not discuss details of the definitions of their conditions because of page limitation, but we can say their system allows implicit existentials, which is defined in the next subsection, and does not have disequalities.

2.2 Implicit Existential

This subsection discusses implicit existentials.

For a definition clause $R(\mathbf{x})$ and a variable z existentially quantified in $R(\mathbf{x})$, z is said to be implicit, if $R(\mathbf{x})$ has some $w \mapsto (\mathbf{t})$ such that $z \equiv t_i$ for some i, and z appears only once in $R(\mathbf{x})$.

An example of an implicit existential variable is w in (1). Sometimes one uses the underscore _ for the notation of an implicit existential variable, since it can take an arbitrary value not related to other values. We will sometimes also use this notation. With this notation, (1) can be written as

$$\mathrm{ls}(x, y) =_{\mathrm{def}} (x = y \wedge \mathrm{Emp}) \vee (x \neq y \wedge \exists z(x \mapsto (z, \_) * \mathrm{ls}(z, y))).$$

Implicit existential variables are necessary to keep arbitrary data in each node of recursive data structures such as lists and trees.

Implicit existentials look like small notational difference. Surprisingly, however, it is not the case. Even if the system SLRD_{btw} is decidable, if we allow implicit existentials in their system, the system becomes undecidable. We will prove it in Sect. 6.

So far we do not know any decidable fragment such that a general framework of inductive definitions is available, and it is generalization of the system by Berdine et al. [3]. Hence it is a challenging problem to find certain conditions that allow implicit existentials and show the decidability of the truth of entailments of symbolic heaps with general inductive definitions under the conditions.

2.3 Separation Logic Sep

This subsection defines the separation logic Sep with monadic inductive definitions. This system is obtained from the system SLRD_{btw} by adding implicit existential variables and restricting inductive definitions to monadic inductive definitions.

The language of Sep is the same as that of G except the restriction on the inductive definitions. Namely Sep has the same pure formulas, spatial formulas, symbolic heaps, and entailments. In order to define Sep, we define some conditions for inductive definitions.

The condition *weak establishment* is that in every definition clause and every existentially quantified variable z in it, z is allocated or implicit.

The condition *monadicity* is that for every inductively defined predicate $P(x, \mathbf{y})$ and every definition clause $R(x, \mathbf{y})$ of P, if $P_i(\mathbf{t})$ is in $R(x, \mathbf{y})$, $\mathbf{t}$ is the form $t, \mathbf{y}$.

Monadicity essentially restricts every inductive defined predicate into a unary predicate. Since we want to relax it to some extent, we allow global parameters $\mathbf{y}$. The variables $\mathbf{y}$ are unchanged throughout recursive calls of predicates, and only the first argument x of each predicate can be changed.

The condition *weak progress* is that every definition clause $R(\mathbf{x})$ has either

1. exactly one points-to predicate, or
2. no points-to predicates and we have $\mathbf{x} \in [\mathbf{y}\ \mathrm{nil}]$ where $\mathbf{y}$ are global parameters.

It is the syntax sugar of the progress condition, and we introduce this condition for writing examples in an easier way.

We define Sep as the system obtained from G by imposing the following restrictions:

1. weak progress,
2. connectivity,

3. weak establishment,
4. monadicity.

Since we can simplify the syntax according to the restrictions, we can define the inductive definition system in Sep as follows.

Inductive Definitions $P_i(x, \mathbf{y}) =_{\text{def}} \bigvee_j R_{ij}(x, \mathbf{y})$.

Definition Clauses, which are defined as

$$R_{ij}(x, \mathbf{y}) \equiv \exists \mathbf{z}^{ij}(\Pi_{ij} \wedge \text{Emp}) \text{ and } x \in [\mathbf{y}\,\text{nil}],$$

or

$$R_{ij}(x, \mathbf{y}) \equiv \exists \mathbf{z}^{ij}(\Pi_{ij} \wedge w_{ij} \mapsto (u_1^{ij}, \ldots, u_n^{ij}) * *_l P_{f(i,j,l)}(t_l^{ij}, \mathbf{y})),$$

where $f : N^3 \to N$, $w_{ij} \in [x]$, $t_l^{ij} \in [\mathbf{u}^{ij}]$, and for every z either z is in $[t_l^{ij}]$ for some l or z appears only once in R_{ij}.

We summarize these systems as follows (Table 1).

Table 1. Symbolic-Heap systems

	Berdine et al.	Iosif et al. 2013	Iosif et al. 2014	Iosif et al. 2013 with implicit existentials	Sep
General inductive definitions	No	Yes	Yes	Yes	Yes
Implicit existentials	Yes	No	Yes	Yes	Yes
Disequalities	Yes	Yes	No	Yes	Yes
Without monadicity restriction	Yes	Yes	Yes	Yes	No
Decidable	Yes	Yes	Yes	No	Yes

Example 1. The following ls and ls2 are list segment predicates in Sep. We assume $n = 1$ and 2 for ls and ls2 respectively. ls2 works as the predicate of lists of pointers, since a list specified by ls2 can hold some data at w in each cell.

$$\text{ls}(x, y) =_{\text{def}} (x = y \wedge \text{Emp}) \vee \exists z(x \neq y \wedge x \mapsto (z) * \text{ls}(z, y)),$$
$$\text{ls2}(x, y) =_{\text{def}} (x = y \wedge \text{Emp}) \vee \exists zw(x \neq y \wedge x \mapsto (z, w) * \text{ls2}(z, y)).$$

Note that ls2 is available in [3], but not available in [9] because of implicit existentails, and not available in [10] because of disequalities.

Example 2. The following tree is a ternary tree predicate. We assume $n = 4$. A tree specified by this predicate is a tree with pointers as data, since it can hold some data at u in each cell.

$$\text{tree}(x) =_{\text{def}} (x = \text{nil} \wedge \text{Emp}) \vee \exists yzwu(x \mapsto (y, z, w, u) * \text{tree}(y) * \text{tree}(z) * \text{tree}(w)).$$

Note that the predicate tree is available in [10], but not available in [9] because of implicit existentails, and not available in [3] because their system has only the list predicate and the binary tree predicate.

Example 3. The nested linked list $\mathrm{nll}(x, y)$ is available in Sep. We assume $n = 3$. The following is taken from the competition SL-COMP 2014 (it is modified so that it fits our syntax). According to the monadicity condition, we need a dummy argument y in $\mathrm{ls3}(x, y, z)$. These two predicates have implicit existential variables w.

$$\begin{aligned}
\mathrm{ls3}(x, y, z) =_{\mathrm{def}} & \exists w(x \mapsto (z, w, \mathrm{nil}))\vee \\
& \exists uw(x \neq z \wedge x \mapsto (u, w, \mathrm{nil}) * \mathrm{ls3}(u, y, z)), \\
\mathrm{nll}(x, y, z) =_{\mathrm{def}} & (x = y \wedge \mathrm{Emp})\vee \\
& \exists uvw(x \neq y \wedge x \mapsto (u, v, w) * \mathrm{ls3}(v, y, z) * \mathrm{nll}(u, y, z)).
\end{aligned}$$

Note that the predicate nll is not available in [3] because their system has only the list predicate and the tree predicate. It is not available either in [9] because of implicit existentails. It is not available either in [10] because of disequalities.

Sep can express many useful data structures in the literature. It is because inductive predicates used in the literature are often monadic. For example, Sep can express more than half of benchmarks in the competition SL-COMP 2014. On the other hand, according to the monadicity condition, Sep cannot express some important data structures such as doubly-linked lists and skip lists, whose definition clauses use references to nonlocal addresses.

2.4 Semantics

The semantics $s, h \models_{\mathrm{Sep}} A$ of this logic is defined in a usual way by using the following structure (for example, [15]). An inductively defined predicate is interpreted by the least fixed point in a usual way [9].

$$\begin{aligned}
&\mathrm{Val} = N, \qquad \mathrm{Locs} = \{x \in N \mid x > 0\}, \qquad \mathrm{nil} = 0, \\
&\mathrm{Heaps} = \mathrm{Locs} \to_{fin} \mathrm{Val}^n, \\
&\mathrm{Stores} = \mathrm{Vars} \to \mathrm{Val}.
\end{aligned}$$

We use s and h by assuming $s \in \mathrm{Stores}$ and $h \in \mathrm{Heaps}$. Note that the interpretation $s(t)$ of the term t is defined as 0 for nil. We write $\phi_1 \models_{\mathrm{Sep}} \phi_2$ to denote $\forall sh((s, h \models_{\mathrm{Sep}} \phi_1) \to (s, h \models_{\mathrm{Sep}} \phi_2))$.

2.5 Related Work

Known decision procedures for entailments in separation logic with some general form of inductive definitions are only a system given in [9] and that given in [10], according to our knowledge. In the system SLRD_{btw} in [9], the inductive definitions need to satisfy the conditions of progress, connectivity, and establishment.

Their system covers a wide class of examples in the literature. Its decidability was shown by reducing the entailment problem to the satisfiability problem of MSO on graphs with bounded treewidth. The system given in [10] is obtained from [9] by removing the progress and establishment conditions, disallowing disequalities, and adding some locality condition. Its decidability is shown by reducing the entailment problem to the language inclusion problem of tree automata.

Several semi-decision procedures of separation logic with some general form of inductive definitions have been studied and implemented. For example, a system with lemma mechanism for inductive predicates was proposed and implemented in [11] and a system based on cyclic proofs was proposed and implemented in [4,5].

There are several decision procedures for entailments in separation logic with hard-coded inductive predicates, for example, [2,3,6–8,12–14]. They often have the hard-coded list predicate and tree predicate. Some of them could be generalized to some general form of inductive definitions. The first system among such systems was that given in [2,3], which has implicit existentials, and they showed the decidability by proof-theoretic approach. [6] shows the same decidability with PTIME by graph-theoretic approach. The system in [7,8] also uses graph-theoretic approach to show the decidability for more hard-coded inductive predicates such as cyclic, nesting, and doubly-linked lists.

The system Sep proposed in this paper has a decision procedure for separation logic with some general form of inductive definitions as well as implicit existentials. The system SLRD_{btw} does not have implicit existentials, since they imposed the establishment condition. As we will prove in Theorem 6.2, the truth of the entailments in the system SLRD_{btw} becomes undecidable when we allow implicit existentials. Our system Sep is obtained from the system SLRD_{btw} by allowing implicit existentials and restricting inductively defined predicates into essentially unary predicates. Then our system Sep includes the system in [2,3]. Our system Sep also includes a fragment of SLRD_{btw} with the restriction that inductive definitions are monadic.

2.6 Main Ideas

Our main goal is to find certain conditions that allow implicit existentials and show the decidability of the truth of entailments of symbolic heaps with general inductive definitions under the conditions.

The difficulty comes from implicit existentials that may break the establishment condition, which may lead to unbounded treewidth. For this reason, [9] had to exclude implicit existentials. Since an implicit existential may take an arbitrary value, the corresponding pointer may point to an arbitrary place, so the treewidth of the graph of the heap may become unbounded.

Our observation is that monadicity gives locality. When we assume monadicity, progress, and connectivity in a given definition clause, the formal parameter of an inductively defined predicate has to point to the cell generated in the definition clause. Hence in the definition clause, global information of the other cells is not available. Therefore a pointer to a nonlocal address is only given by an

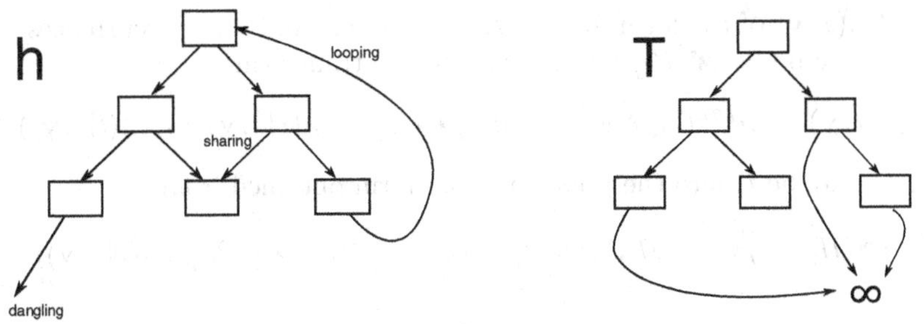

Fig. 1. Heap transformation

implicit existential. Hence the resulting heap also satisfies the definition clause, after we replace a pointer to the nonlocal address by an arbitrary value.

From this observation, our main idea is to transform a given heap h to another heap T by replacing all the pointers to nonlocal addresses to the distinguished address ∞. It is illustrated in the Fig. 1. This transformation keeps the truth and decreases the treewidth of the heap. According to this heap transformation, we will define the translation $P^\infty(x, \mathbf{y})$ of a given inductively defined predicate $P(x, \mathbf{y})$.

We also introduce global parameters. The list segment predicate $\mathrm{ls}(x, y)$ has two arguments, and is not unary. However y is a global parameter which is unchanged in every recursive call of ls, and hence $\mathrm{ls}(x, y)$ is essentially a unary inductive predicate for x. Our system Sep allows such y as global parameters and we treat them in the same way as the constant nil.

The result of the translation is an inductive definition system that satisfies the establishment condition. Hence we can apply the decidability result in [9] to the result of the translation, in order to show the decidability.

3 Translation in Sep∞

We will show our translation of Sep into Sep∞. First we simplify a given inductive definition system in Sep by two steps. Next we define our separation logic Sep∞. Then we translate inductive predicates in Sep into those in Sep∞. Finally we translate symbolic heaps in Sep into those in Sep∞.

3.1 Transformation of Weak Progress into Progress

First we eliminate definition clauses that do not satisfy the progress condition, in order to obtain an inductive definition system that satisfies it. Since the weak progress is the syntax sugar, this elimination is straightforwardly achieved by expanding the definition clauses that do not satisfy the progress condition.

First we expand some inductive predicates by their definition clauses that do not satisfy the progress condition, in a given definition clause R_{pq} that satisfies the progress condition. For an inductively defined predicate P_i, and its definition clauses $R_{ij}(x, \mathbf{y})$ of the form $\exists \mathbf{z}^{ij} \Pi_{ij} \wedge \mathrm{Emp}$, we expand some occurrences of P_i in R_{pq} by the body $\exists \mathbf{z}^{ij} \Pi_{ij} \wedge \mathrm{Emp}$. Namely we transform

$$R_{pq}(x, \mathbf{y}) \equiv \exists \mathbf{z}^{pq}(\Pi_{pq} \wedge w_{pq} \mapsto (\mathbf{u}^{pq}) * *_l P_{f(p,q,l)}(v_l^{pq}, \mathbf{y}) * *_k P_i(t_k^{pq}, \mathbf{y}))$$

($f(p, q, l)$ may be i) into the prenex normal form obtained from

$$\exists \mathbf{z}^{pq}(\Pi_{pq} \wedge \bigwedge_k (\exists \mathbf{z}^{ij} \Pi_{ij})[x := t_k^{pq}] \wedge w_{pq} \mapsto (\mathbf{u}^{pq}) * *_l P_{f(p,q,l)}(v_l^{pq}, \mathbf{y}))$$

by moving $\exists \mathbf{z}^{ij}$ to the head. When the spatial part becomes empty, we put Emp.

We do this expansion of R_{pq} for each P_i, each R_{ij} of this form, and each set of the occurrences of P_i in R_{pq}, and let the results be $R_{pq1}, \ldots, R_{pqr}$. Then for each R_{pq} we replace the original R_{pq} in the original inductive definition system S by $R_{pq1}, \ldots, R_{pqr}$ to obtain the new inductive definition system S'. Then S' is equivalent to S as an inductive definition system, and satisfies the progress condition.

Next we expand some inductive predicates in a given entailment $\phi \vdash \psi$ in a similar way. For ϕ and ψ, we do the same expansion and let the results be $\phi_1, \ldots, \phi_l$ and $\psi_1, \ldots, \psi_m$ respectively. Then the truth of the entailment $\phi \vdash \psi$ under S is equivalent to $\bigwedge_i \bigvee_j (\phi_i \vdash \psi_j)$ under S'. Hence it is sufficient to check the truth of $\phi_i \vdash \psi_j$ under S' for all i, j.

Example. ls2 is transformed into the following ls2:

$$\mathrm{ls2}(x, y) =_{\mathrm{def}} \exists w(x \neq y \wedge x \mapsto (y, w)) \vee \exists zw(x \neq y \wedge x \mapsto (z, w) * \mathrm{ls2}(z, y)).$$

The entailment $x \mapsto y * \mathrm{ls2}(y, z) \vdash \mathrm{ls2}(x, z)$ is transformed into the following entailments: $((y = z \wedge x \mapsto y \vdash x = z \wedge \mathrm{Emp}) \vee (y = z \wedge x \mapsto y \vdash \mathrm{ls2}(x, z))) \wedge ((x \mapsto y * \mathrm{ls2}(y, z) \vdash x = z \wedge \mathrm{Emp}) \vee (x \mapsto y * \mathrm{ls2}(y, z) \vdash \mathrm{ls2}(x, z)))$.

From now on, we assume our inductive definition system in Sep satisfies the progress condition.

3.2 Simplification of Definition Clauses

We simplify definition clauses keeping their expressive power. We need this simplification for defining our main translation.

Suppose the definition clause

$$R(x, \mathbf{y}) \equiv \exists \mathbf{z}(\Pi \wedge w \mapsto (\mathbf{u}) * *_l P_{f(l)}(t_l, \mathbf{y})).$$

For $z_i \not\equiv t$, we eliminate $z_i = t$ in Π by substituting t for z_i, and removing z_i from $\mathbf{z}$. Namely we replace

$$\exists \mathbf{z}(\Pi \wedge w \mapsto (\mathbf{u}) * *_l P_{f(l)}(t_l, \mathbf{y}))$$

by

$$\exists \mathbf{z}'((\Pi \wedge w \mapsto (\mathbf{u}) * *_l P_{f(l)}(t_l, \mathbf{y}))[z_i := t])$$

where $\mathbf{z}' = \mathbf{z} - z_i$.

We remove $t = t$ in Π, since it is redundant.

We split $\mathbf{z}$ into $\mathbf{z}'$ and $\mathbf{z}''$ such that $\mathbf{z}'' = \mathbf{z} \cap \mathbf{t}$ and $\mathbf{z}' = \mathbf{z} - \mathbf{z}''$. We write $\mathbf{z}$ for $\mathbf{z}''$ to save symbols.

Then we have the definition clause

$$\exists \mathbf{z}\mathbf{z}'(\Pi \wedge x \mapsto (\mathbf{u}) * *_l P_{f(l)}(t_l, \mathbf{y}))$$

where

(1) all the equalities in Π do not contain $\mathbf{z}\mathbf{z}'$,
(2) z'_i appears only once, and $\mathbf{z}' = \mathbf{u} - x\mathbf{y}$ nil $\mathbf{t}$,
(3) $\mathbf{z} \subseteq \mathbf{t} \subseteq \mathbf{y}\mathbf{z}$.

From now on, we assume every definition clause has this form.

3.3 Separation Logic Sep∞

We will define our separation logic Sep∞.

Sep∞ is obtained from the separation logic Sep by adding the constant ∞.

Terms $t ::= x|\text{nil}|\infty$.

For defining its semantics, we will use the following structure:

$$N_1 = \{-1\} \cup N, \qquad \text{Val}_1 = N_1, \qquad \infty = -1.$$

We define the interpretation $s(t)$ of the term t as 0 if $t \equiv$ nil, and -1 if $t \equiv \infty$.

Extended heaps are defined by $T : \text{Locs} \to_{fin} \text{Val}_1^n$.

Definition 3.1. We define $s, T \models_{\text{Sep}\infty} \phi$ in the same way as $\models_{\text{Sep}}$ where s is a store $s : \text{Vars} \to \text{Val}$, and T is an extended heap.

3.4 Translation of Inductive Predicates in Sep∞

This subsection gives our translation of inductive predicates in Sep∞ and shows the equivalence of the translation.

For a heap h and an extended heap T, we define $h \in T$ by

(1) $\text{Dom}(h) = \text{Dom}(T)$,
(2) if $(T(x))_i \neq \infty$, we have $(h(x))_i = (T(x))_i$.

For a heap h, an extended heap T, and $a_1, \ldots, a_m \in \text{Val}$, we define $h \rhd_{\mathbf{a}} T$ by

(1) $\text{Dom}(h) = \text{Dom}(T)$,
(2) $(T(x))_i = (h(x))_i$ if $(h(x))_i \in \text{Dom}(T) \cup \{\mathbf{a}, \text{nil}\}$, and
(3) $(T(x))_i = \infty$ if $(h(x))_i \notin \text{Dom}(T) \cup \{\mathbf{a}, \text{nil}\}$.

For a heap h, we define $x \to_i y$ by $x, y \in \mathrm{Dom}(h)$ and $(h(x))_i = y$. We also define $x \to y$ by $x \to_i y$ for some i. We write $\to^*$ for the reflexive transitive closure of $\to$.

Definition 3.2. For $\mathbf{a} \in \mathrm{Val}$, we call an extended heap T *normal* with $\mathbf{a}$ when

(1) there do not exist $x \in \mathrm{Dom}(T)$ and $1 \le i \le n$ such that $(T(x))_i \notin \mathrm{Dom}(T) \cup \{\mathrm{nil}, \infty, \mathbf{a}\}$,
(2) there do not exist $x, y \in \mathrm{Dom}(T)$ such that $x \ne y$, $x \to y$, $y \to^* x$, and $x \notin \mathbf{a}$, and [
(3) there do not exist $x, y \in \mathrm{Dom}(T)$ and $1 \le i, j \le n$ such that $x \ne y$ and $(T(x))_i = (T(y))_j \in \mathrm{Dom}(T) - \{x, y, \mathbf{a}\}$.

We write $\mathrm{Norm}(\mathbf{a}, T)$ when T is normal with $\mathbf{a}$.

$\mathrm{Norm}(\mathbf{a}, T)$ means that T does not have any dangling, looping, or sharing pointers, except for pointers to local addresses and $\mathbf{a}$. Note that we exclude the local looping $x \to x$, the local sharing $x \to_i y$ and $x \to_j y$ for $i \ne j, x \ne y$, and the local sharing $x \to x$ and $y \to x$, since they do not necessarily use implicit existential variables.

Definition 3.3. Suppose an inductive definition system

$$P_i(x, \mathbf{y}) =_{\mathrm{def}} \bigvee_j R_{ij}(x, \mathbf{y}),$$

$$R_{ij}(x, \mathbf{y}) \equiv \exists \mathbf{z}^{\mathbf{ij}} \mathbf{z}'^{\mathbf{ij}} (\Pi_{ij} \wedge x \mapsto (\mathbf{u}^{ij}) * *_l P_{f(i,j,l)}(t_l^{ij}, \mathbf{y})).$$

We define its translation as the following inductive definition system

$$P_i^\infty(x, \mathbf{y}) =_{\mathrm{def}} \bigvee_j R_{ij}^\infty(x, \mathbf{y}),$$

$$R_{ij}^\infty(x, \mathbf{y}) \equiv \bigvee_\alpha \exists \mathbf{z}^{\mathbf{ij}} (\Pi_{ij} \wedge x \mapsto (\alpha(\mathbf{u}^{ij})) * *_l P_{f(i,j,l)}^\infty(t_l^{ij}, \mathbf{y})).$$

where α ranges over $\{\alpha | \alpha : \mathbf{z}'^{\mathbf{ij}} \to \{x, \mathbf{y}, \mathrm{nil}, \mathbf{t}^{ij}, \infty\}\}$, and P_i^∞ is a new inductively defined predicate symbol.

α assigns to $z_k'^{ij}$ some local addresses (that is, x, $\mathbf{t}^{ij}$), or some global values (that is, nil, $\mathbf{y}$), or ∞. Note that $\mathbf{z}'^{\mathbf{ij}}$ do not appear in Π_{ij}.

Example. We transform ls2 in the example in Subsect. 3.1 into the following $\mathrm{ls2}^\infty$:

$$\begin{aligned}
\mathrm{ls2}^\infty(x, y) =_{\mathrm{def}} & (x \ne y \wedge x \mapsto (y, x)) \vee (x \ne y \wedge x \mapsto (y, y)) \vee \\
& (x \ne y \wedge x \mapsto (y, \mathrm{nil})) \vee (x \ne y \wedge x \mapsto (y, \infty)) \vee \\
& \exists z(x \ne y \wedge x \mapsto (z, x) * \mathrm{ls2}^\infty(z, y)) \vee \exists z(x \ne y \wedge x \mapsto (z, y) * \mathrm{ls2}^\infty(z, y)) \vee \\
& \exists z(x \ne y \wedge x \mapsto (z, z) * \mathrm{ls2}^\infty(z, y)) \vee \exists z(x \ne y \wedge x \mapsto (z, \mathrm{nil}) * \mathrm{ls2}^\infty(z, y)) \vee \\
& \exists z(x \ne y \wedge x \mapsto (z, \infty) * \mathrm{ls2}^\infty(z, y)).
\end{aligned}$$

The next lemma shows the equivalence between Sep and its translation for inductive predicates.

Lemma 3.4. *(1)* $s, h \models_{Sep} P(x, \mathbf{y}) \iff \exists T(h \in T \wedge s, T \models_{Sep\infty} P^{\infty}(x, \mathbf{y}))$.
(2) $\exists h \rhd_{s(\mathbf{y})} T(Norm(s(\mathbf{y}), T) \wedge s, h \models_{Sep} P(x, \mathbf{y})) \iff s, T \models_{Sep\infty} P^{\infty}(x, \mathbf{y})$.

It is proved by induction on $|\mathrm{Dom}(h)|$ and $|\mathrm{Dom}(T)|$.

3.5 Translation of Symbolic Heaps in Sep∞

We will translate symbolic heaps in Sep into those in Sep∞.

Definition 3.5. For a symbolic heap

$$\phi(\mathbf{x}) \equiv \Pi \wedge *_k(w_k \mapsto (\mathbf{u}^k)) * *_l P_{f(l)}(t_l, \mathbf{t}^l),$$

we define its translation as the following symbolic heap:

$$\phi^{\infty}(\mathbf{x}) \equiv \Pi \wedge *_k(w_k \mapsto (\mathbf{u}^k)) * *_l P^{\infty}_{f(l)}(t_l, \mathbf{t}^l).$$

The next lemma shows the equivalence between a symbolic heap in Sep and its translation in Sep∞.

Lemma 3.6. *(1)* $s, h \models_{Sep} \phi(\mathbf{x}) \iff \exists T(h \in T \wedge s, T \models_{Sep\infty} \phi^{\infty}(\mathbf{x}))$.
(2) $\exists h \rhd_{s(\mathbf{x})} T(Norm(s(\mathbf{x}), T) \wedge s, h \models_{Sep} \phi(\mathbf{x})) \iff s, T \models_{Sep\infty} \phi^{\infty}(\mathbf{x})$.

It is proved by using Lemma 3.4.

Theorem 3.7. *We have* $\phi_1(\mathbf{x}) \models_{Sep} \phi_2(\mathbf{x}) \iff \phi_1^{\infty}(\mathbf{x}) \models_{Sep\infty} \phi_2^{\infty}(\mathbf{x})$.

It is proved by using Lemma 3.6.

4 Translation in Bounded-Treewidth Separation Logic

In this section, we reduce the entailments in Sep∞ into those in the bounded-treewidth separation logic SLRD_{btw} given in [9]. Since the decidability of the entailments in their system is known, we will obtain the decidability of those in Sep by this reduction.

First we define a monadic version BTW of SLRD_{btw} in terms of this paper. This is essentially the same as their original system except the inductive definitions are restricted to monadic ones, since it is sufficient for our purpose. Our semantics for BTW is an instance of theirs and is obtained from their semantics for SLRD_{btw} in [9] by

1. taking PVar to be $\{\mathrm{nil}, \infty\}$, Loc to be N_1, taking null to be 0,
2. replacing $s : \mathrm{PVar} \to \mathrm{Loc}$ by $s : \mathrm{Vars} \to \mathrm{Locs}$ and defining the interpretation $s(t)$ of the term t by $s(\mathrm{nil}) = 0$ and $s(\infty) \in \mathrm{Loc}$,
3. replacing $h : \mathrm{Loc} - \{0\} \to_{fin} \mathrm{Sel} \to_{fin} \mathrm{Loc}$ by $h : \mathrm{Loc} - \{0\} \to_{fin} \mathrm{Loc}^n$,
4. taking LVar_{sl} to be Vars, and Var_{sl} to be the set of terms,
5. replacing ι by $s : \mathrm{LVar}_{sl} \to \mathrm{Loc}$.

Note that Locs is defined as $\{x \in N | x > 0\}$ in Sect. 2.4.

Definition 4.1 (Bounded-Treewidth System). We define the bounded-treewidth system BTW.

The symbolic heaps ϕ in BTW are the same as those in Sep∞ except the following restrictions for the definition clauses:

- we exclude the definition clause of the first form $R_{ij}(x, \mathbf{y}) \equiv \exists \mathbf{z}^{ij} \Pi_{ij} \wedge \mathrm{Emp}$ (Namely we assume the progress condition),
- we require that for every z, z is in $[t_l^{ij}]$. (Namely we exclude the case where z appears only once in R_{ij}.)

The store s is defined by $s : \mathrm{Vars} \to \mathrm{Val}_1$. The heap h is defined by $h : \mathrm{Locs} \cup \{\infty\} \to_{fin} \mathrm{Val}_1^n$. The interpretation $s(t)$ of the term t is defined by $s(nil) = 0$, $s(\infty) \in \mathrm{Val}_1$. The semantics $s, h \models_{\mathrm{BTW}} \phi$ is defined in a usual way by using the above s, h.

The decidability of the entailments in BTW is known.

Theorem 4.2 (Iosif et al. [9]). *The truth of a given entailment* $\phi_1(\mathbf{x}) \models_{BTW} \phi_2(\mathbf{x})$ *is decidable.*

The semantics of Sep∞ is a special case of that of BTW. Namely the semantics of Sep∞ is obtained from that of BTW by imposing the following restrictions for s, h: $s(\infty) = -1$ and $s : \mathrm{LVar}_{sl} \to \mathrm{Loc} - \{-1\}$, and $-1 \notin \mathrm{Dom}(h)$.

First we state a general lemma that holds for several systems of symbolic heaps. Since the symbolic heaps were invented for characterizing shapes of heaps, the truth is preserved by heap transformation that keeps the shape of heaps. In order to state it, we introduce heap transformation $\eta(s)$ and $\eta(h)$ of s and h respectively.

Definition 4.3. Let $\eta : N_1 - \{0\} \to N_1 - \{0\}$ be a bijection.

For $s : \mathrm{Vars} \to \mathrm{Val}_1$, we define $\eta(s) : \mathrm{Vars} \to \mathrm{Val}_1$ by $\eta(s)(x) = \eta(s(x))$.

For $h : N_1 - \{0\} \to_{fin} \mathrm{Val}_1^n$, we define $\eta(h) : N_1 - \{0\} \to_{fin} \mathrm{Val}_1^n$ by $\eta(h)(x) = \eta(h(\eta^{-1}(x)))$ where we write $\eta((u_1, \ldots, u_n))$ for $(\eta(u_1), \ldots, \eta(u_n))$.

Lemma 4.4. *We have* $s, h \models_{BTW} \phi \iff \eta(s), \eta(h) \models_{BTW} \phi$.

Proof. We first show the claim for the case ϕ is some inductive predicate $P(\mathbf{t})$. This case is proved by induction on $|\mathrm{Dom}(h)|$. Note that η preserves the truth of equalities and the points-to predicate. Next we can prove the claim for ϕ by using it. □

We define the translation of Sep∞ to BTW. The key to this translation is to add both the pure formula nil $\neq \infty$ and the pure formula $w \neq \infty$ for every variable w in a given symbolic heap. Then from nil $\neq \infty$ we can choose $s(\infty) = -1$ by heap transformation. For every variable w occurring in the symbolic heap, from $w \neq \infty$, we have $s(w) \in \mathrm{Val}$, so by replacing the values of the variables not occurring in the symbolic heap by some dummy value such as nil, the range of the resulting store becomes Val.

Definition 4.5 (Translation in BTW). We define the translation $\phi^{\infty\neq}$. First we define the translation $\phi^{\neq}$.

We write $\mathbf{t} \neq \infty$ for $\bigwedge_{t \in \mathbf{t}} t \neq \infty$. Let $\phi(\mathbf{x})$ be a symbolic heap of Sep∞. Note that we assumed the progress condition for Sep and Sep∞.

Suppose an inductive definition system

$$P_i(x, \mathbf{y}) =_{\text{def}} \bigvee_j R_{ij}(x, \mathbf{y}),$$

$$R_{ij}(x, \mathbf{y}) \equiv \exists \mathbf{z^{ij}}(\Pi_{ij} \wedge x \mapsto (\mathbf{u}^{ij}) * *_l P_{f(i,j,l)}(t_l^{ij}, \mathbf{y})).$$

We define its translation as the following inductive definition system:

$$P_i^{\neq}(x, \mathbf{y}) =_{\text{def}} \bigvee_j R_{ij}^{\neq}(x, \mathbf{y}),$$

$$R_{ij}^{\neq}(x, \mathbf{y}) \equiv \exists \mathbf{z^{ij}}(\Pi_{ij} \wedge x\mathbf{yz}\ \text{nil} \neq \infty \wedge x \mapsto (\mathbf{u}^{ij}) * *_l P_{f(i,j,l)}^{\neq}(t_l^{ij}, \mathbf{y})).$$

For a symbolic heap

$$\phi(\mathbf{x}) \equiv \Pi \wedge *_k(w_k \mapsto (\mathbf{u}^k)) * *_l P_{f(l)}(t_l, \mathbf{t}^l),$$

we define its translation by the following symbolic heap:

$$\phi^{\neq}(\mathbf{x}) \equiv \Pi \wedge \mathbf{x}\ \text{nil} \neq \infty \wedge *_k(w_k \mapsto (\mathbf{u}^k)) * *_l P_{f(l)}^{\neq}(t_l, \mathbf{t}^l),$$

We write $\phi^{\infty\neq}$ for $(\phi^{\infty})^{\neq}$ and this completes the definition of the translation.

Example. $(x = y \wedge \text{Emp})^{\infty}$ is $x = y \wedge \text{Emp}$. $(x = y \wedge \text{Emp})^{\infty\neq}$ is $x = y \wedge x \neq \infty \wedge y \neq \infty \wedge \text{nil} \neq \infty \wedge \text{Emp}$.

Since the translation ϕ^{∞} eliminates the implicit existential variables in a given symbolic heap ϕ, ϕ^{∞} becomes a symbolic heap in BTW.

The next lemma tells us the relationship between a symbolic heap ϕ^{∞} and its translation $\phi^{\infty\neq}$.

Definition 4.6. For a store s : Vars $\to$ Val$_1$, we define $\tilde{s}$: Vars $\to$ Val as follows: $\tilde{s}(x) = \text{nil}$ if $s(x) = \infty$, $\tilde{s}(x) = s(x)$ otherwise.

For stores s, s' and $V \subseteq$ Vars, we write $s =_V s'$ when $s(x) = s'(x)$ for all $x \in V$.

Lemma 4.7. *(1)* $s, h \models_{BTW} \phi^{\infty\neq}(\mathbf{x})$ *and* $s(\infty) = -1$ *iff* $s =_{\mathbf{x}} \tilde{s}$ *and* $\tilde{s}, h \models_{Sep\infty} \phi^{\infty}(\mathbf{x})$.

(2) Let η *be the permutation of* $s(\infty)$ *and* -1*. Then we have the following:* $s, h \models_{BTW} \phi^{\infty\neq}(\mathbf{x})$ *iff* $\eta(s) =_{\mathbf{x}} \widetilde{\eta(s)}$ *and* $\widetilde{\eta(s)}, \eta(h) \models_{Sep\infty} \phi^{\infty}(\mathbf{x})$.

Proof. (1) We first show the claim for the case where ϕ is some inductive predicate $P(\mathbf{t})$. This case is proved by induction on $|\text{Dom}(h)|$. Note that for every variable

w in $\mathbf{x}$, we have $s(w) \neq -1$ from $w \neq \infty$, and $s(w) = \tilde{s}(w)$. Next we can prove the claim for ϕ by using the case for inductive predicates.

(2) $\Longrightarrow$: Assume $s, h \models_{\mathrm{BTW}} \phi^{\infty\neq}(\mathbf{x})$. We have $s(\infty) \neq 0$ from $\infty \neq \mathrm{nil}$. Then η is a bijection from $N_1 - \{0\}$ to $N_1 - \{0\}$.

By Lemma 4.4, we have

$$s, h \models_{\mathrm{BTW}} \phi^{\infty\neq}(\mathbf{x}) \Longleftrightarrow (\eta(s), \eta(h) \models_{\mathrm{BTW}} \phi^{\infty\neq}(\mathbf{x})) \wedge \eta(s)(\infty) = -1.$$

By (1), it is equivalent to the righthand side of th claim.

$\Longleftarrow$: Assume that $\eta(s) =_{\mathbf{x}} \widetilde{\eta(s)}$ and $\widetilde{\eta(s)}, \eta(h) \models_{\mathrm{Sep}\infty} \phi^{\infty}(\mathbf{x})$. If $s(\infty) = 0$ were true, then we would have $\eta(s)(\mathrm{nil}) = -1$ by the definition of η, which would contradict $\widetilde{\eta(s)}(\mathrm{nil}) = 0$, which comes from $\widetilde{\eta(s)}, \eta(h) \models_{\mathrm{Sep}\infty} \phi^{\infty}(\mathbf{x})$. Hence $s(\infty) \neq 0$ and η is a bijection from $N_1 - \{0\}$ to $N_1 - \{0\}$.

The rest is the same as the case of $\Longrightarrow$ above. □

The next theorem reduces the entailments in Sep∞ into those in BTW.

Theorem 4.8. *We have* $\phi_1^{\infty}(\mathbf{x}) \models_{Sep\infty} \phi_2^{\infty}(\mathbf{x}) \Longleftrightarrow \phi_1^{\infty\neq}(\mathbf{x}) \models_{BTW} \phi_2^{\infty\neq}(\mathbf{x})$.

Proof. Let η be the permutation of $s(\infty)$ and -1.

$\Longrightarrow$: Assume $\phi_1^{\infty}(\mathbf{x}) \models_{\mathrm{Sep}\infty} \phi_2^{\infty}(\mathbf{x})$ and $s, h \models_{\mathrm{BTW}} \phi_1^{\infty\neq}(\mathbf{x})$.

By Lemma 4.7 (2) $\Longrightarrow$, we have $\widetilde{\eta}(s), \eta(h) \models_{\mathrm{Sep}\infty} \phi_1^{\infty}(\mathbf{x})$. Hence $\widetilde{\eta}(s), \eta(h) \models_{\mathrm{Sep}\infty} \phi_2^{\infty}(\mathbf{x})$. By Lemma 4.7 (2) $\Longleftarrow$, we have $s, h \models_{\mathrm{BTW}} \phi_2^{\infty\neq}(\mathbf{x})$.

$\Longleftarrow$: Assume $\phi_1^{\infty\neq}(\mathbf{x}) \models_{\mathrm{BTW}} \phi_2^{\infty\neq}(\mathbf{x})$ and $s, h \models_{\mathrm{Sep}\infty} \phi_1^{\infty}(\mathbf{x})$.

We have $s(x) \neq s(\infty)$ and $s(\mathrm{nil}) \neq s(\infty)$ from $s, h \models_{\mathrm{Sep}\infty} \phi_1^{\infty}(\mathbf{x})$. Hence $s, h \models_{\mathrm{BTW}} \phi_1^{\infty\neq}(\mathbf{x})$. Then $s, h \models_{\mathrm{BTW}} \phi_2^{\infty\neq}(\mathbf{x})$. Since $s : \mathrm{Vars} \to \mathrm{Val}$, we have $s, h \models_{\mathrm{Sep}\infty} \phi_2^{\infty}(\mathbf{x})$. □

5 Main Theorems

We will give our main theorems for the decidability of the entailments in Sep.

Theorem 5.1. *We have* $\phi_1(\mathbf{x}) \models_{Sep} \phi_2(\mathbf{x}) \Longleftrightarrow \phi_1^{\infty\neq}(\mathbf{x}) \models_{BTW} \phi_2^{\infty\neq}(\mathbf{x})$.

Proof. By Theorems 3.7 and 4.8. □

Theorem 5.2. *The truth of a given entailment* $\phi_1(\mathbf{x}) \models_{Sep} \phi_2(\mathbf{x})$ *is decidable.*

Proof. By Theorems 5.1 and 4.2. □

6 Undecidability of SLRD$_{btw}$ with Implicit Existentials

This section shows that the truth problem of entailments is undecidable in the system SLRD$^{+}_{btw}$ obtained from SLRD$_{btw}$ given in [9] by adding the implicit existentials. (We allow the weak progress condition below, but SLRD$_{btw}$ can express all the definitions below, since the weak progress condition is the syntax sugar of the progress condition.) The system SLRD^{+}_{btw} is the same as the system obtained from our system Sep by dropping the monadicity condition, namely the system where we allow $P(\mathbf{x},\mathbf{y})$ instead of $P(x,\mathbf{y})$.

We will show this undecidability result by reducing it to the undecidability of Post Corresponding Problem (PCP). Our proof is a refinement of the proof given in [1], which shows that the entailment problem of separation logic with general inductive predicates is undecidable. Some predicates used in their proof do not satisfy the weak progress, the connectivity, or the establishment conditions. In order to change their proof to a proof for the undecidability of the system SLRD^{+}_{btw}, we introduce two additional elements in each cell that keep necessary link pointers, by which all the predicates used in the proof satisfy the weak progress, the connectivity, and the establishment conditions.

Assume that K tiles ($K \geq 1$) are given. The i-th tile contains two finite bit sequences v_i and w_i. We will write $v_i(j)$ and $w_i(j)$ for the j-th bit of v_i and w_i respectively.

In the following, we will use the global variables x_0 and x_1 that mean 0 and 1, respectively.

For $1 \leq i \leq K$ and $1 \leq j \leq |v_i| + |w_i|$, the predicate $\mathrm{Tile}_{i,j}(a,b)$ is given by

$$\begin{array}{ll}
\mathrm{Tile}_{i,k}(a,b) & =_{\mathrm{def}} \exists a'(a \mapsto (x_{v_i(k)}, a', _, a') * \mathrm{Tile}_{i,k+1}(a',b)),\\
\mathrm{Tile}_{i,|v_i|}(a,b) & =_{\mathrm{def}} \exists a'(a \mapsto (x_{v_i(|v_i|)}, a', _, b) * \mathrm{Tile}_{i,|v_i|+1}(a',b)),\\
\mathrm{Tile}_{i,|v_i|+l}(a,b) & =_{\mathrm{def}} \exists b'(b \mapsto (x_{w_i(l)}, b', _, b') * \mathrm{Tile}_{i,|v_i|+l+1}(a,b')),\\
\mathrm{Tile}_{i,|v_i|+|w_i|}(a,b) & =_{\mathrm{def}} \exists b'(b \mapsto (x_{w_i(|w_i|)}, b', _, a) * \mathrm{PCP}(a,b'))\\
& \quad\ \vee (a = \mathrm{nil} \wedge b \mapsto (x_{w_i(|w_i|)}, \mathrm{nil}, _, \mathrm{nil})),
\end{array}$$

where $1 \leq k < |v_i|$ and $1 \leq l < |w_i|$. The predicate $\mathrm{PCP}(a,b)$ is defined by

$$\mathrm{PCP}(a,b) =_{\mathrm{def}} \mathrm{Tile}_{1,1}(a,b) \vee \ldots \vee \mathrm{Tile}_{K,1}(a,b).$$

Recall that the symbol _ is an abbreviation of an implicit existential variable. Hence $(x \mapsto (\ldots,\_,\ldots)\ldots)$ should be read as $\exists z(x \mapsto (\ldots,z,\ldots)\ldots)$.

In the above definition, each a points to a cell (x,a',b',c'). The first element x is x_0 or x_1. We sometimes write 'cell q' (q is a bit) to denote a cell whose first element is x_q. We write 'cell list of $q_1,\ldots,q_n$' to mean a list of cells $q_1,\ldots,q_n$. We also write 'cell list of $v_1,\ldots,v_k$' (v_i is a bit sequence) to mean a list of cells $v_1(1),\ldots,v_1(|v_1|),v_2(1),\ldots,v_k(|v_k|)$.

The elements other than the first element of a cell mean pointers for the following three kinds of cell lists. We call the elements of the second (or third, fourth) position of cells the first (or second, third) pointers. The first pointers form a cell list $v_i(1),v_i(2),\ldots,v_k(|v_k|)$ or $w_i(1),w_i(2),\ldots,w_k(|w_k|)$. The second pointers are intended to form a cell list $v_i(1),w_i(1),v_i(2),w_i(2),\ldots$. Note that the above definition of $\mathrm{PCP}(a,b)$ imposes no conditions on the second pointers. Later we will define $\mathrm{NCorList}(a,b)$ in order to force the pointers (at the third position of cells) to satisfy some conditions. The third pointers form a cell list $v_i,w_i,v_j,w_j,\ldots$.

The intuitive meaning of $\mathrm{PCP}(a,b)$ is that a and b point to cell lists of $v_{f(1)},v_{f(2)},v_{f(3)}\ldots$ and $w_{f(1)},w_{f(2)},w_{f(3)}\ldots$ for some function f, respectively.

We define NCorList(a, b) that means some second pointers point to unexpected cells.

$$\begin{aligned}
\text{NCorList}_{1,1}(a,b) &=_{\text{def}} \exists a'(a \mapsto (_, a', b, _) * \text{NCorList}_{1,2}(a', b)),\\
\text{NCorList}_{1,2}(a,b) &=_{\text{def}} \exists b'(b \mapsto (_, b', a, _) * \text{NCorList}(a, b')),\\
\text{NCorList}_{2,1}(a,b) &=_{\text{def}} \exists a'(a \mapsto (_, a', b, _) * \text{NCorList}_{2,2}(a', b)),
\end{aligned}$$

$$\begin{aligned}
\text{NCorList}_{2,2}(a,b) &=_{\text{def}} \exists b'(b \mapsto (_, b', a, _) * \text{NCorList}_{2,3}(a, b') * \text{True1}(b')),\\
\text{NCorList}_{2,3}(a,b) &=_{\text{def}} \exists a', c(c \neq b \wedge a \mapsto (_, a', c, _) * \text{True1}(a')),\\
\text{NCorList}_{3,1}(a,b) &=_{\text{def}} \exists a'(a \mapsto (_, a', b, _) * \text{NCorList}_{3,2}(a', b) * \text{True1}(a')),\\
\text{NCorList}_{3,2}(a,b) &=_{\text{def}} \exists b', c(a \neq c \wedge b \mapsto (_, b', c, _) * \text{True1}(b')),\\
\text{NCorList}_{4}(a,b) &=_{\text{def}} \exists c, d(b \neq c \wedge a \mapsto (_, _, c, d) * \text{True3}(d)),
\end{aligned}$$

where True1(x) and True3(x) are defined by

$$\begin{aligned}
\text{True1}(x) &=_{\text{def}} (x = \text{nil} \wedge \text{Emp}) \vee \exists x'(x \mapsto (_, x', _, _) * \text{True1}(x')),\\
\text{True3}(x) &=_{\text{def}} (x = \text{nil} \wedge \text{Emp}) \vee \exists x'(x \mapsto (_, _, _, x') * \text{True3}(x')).
\end{aligned}$$

Then the predicate NCorList(a, b) is defined as follows:

$$\begin{aligned}
\text{NCorList}(a,b) =_{\text{def}} &\ \text{NCorList}_{1,1}(a,b) \vee \text{NCorList}_{2,1}(a,b)\\
&\vee \text{NCorList}_{3,1}(a,b) \vee \text{NCorList}_{4}(a,b).
\end{aligned}$$

True1(x) means that the cells on the memory make a list whose first cell is pointed by x, and are connected by the first pointers. True3(x) also means a list of cells starting from x, but are connected by the third pointers. NCorList$_{1,1}(a, b)$ means that a and b point to the cells that have correct second pointers, but there will be a cell that has a wrong second pointer after the cells pointed by a and b. The meaning of NCorList$_{2,1}(a, b)$ is that the cells pointed by a and b have correct second pointers, and the cell pointed by a' (the next one pointed by a with respect to the first pointer) has a wrong second pointer. The meaning of NCorList$_{3,1}(a, b)$ is that the cell pointed by a has a correct second pointer, but the cell pointed by b has a wrong second pointer. NCorList$_4(a, b)$ means the cell pointed by a has a wrong second pointer.

Next we define NEqPair(a, b), which means the cell lists connected by the first pointers starting from a and b have different bit sequences.

$$\begin{aligned}
\text{NEqPair}_{1,1}(a,b) &=_{\text{def}} \exists a'(a \mapsto (_, a', b, _) * \text{NEqPair}_{1,2}(a', b)),\\
\text{NEqPair}_{1,2}(a,b) &=_{\text{def}} \exists b'(b \mapsto (_, b', a, _) * \text{NEqPair}(a, b')),\\
\text{NEqPair}_{2,1,i}(a,b) &=_{\text{def}} \exists a'(a \mapsto (x_q, a', b, _) * \text{NEqPair}_{2,2,i}(b) * \text{True1}(a')),\\
\text{NEqPair}_{2,2,i}(a,b) &=_{\text{def}} \exists b'(b \mapsto (x_{\overline{q}}, b', _, _) * \text{True1}(b')),
\end{aligned}$$

where $x_{\overline{0}}$ is x_1 and $x_{\overline{1}}$ is x_0. The predicate NEqPair(a, b) is defined by

$$\text{NEqPair}(a,b) =_{\text{def}} \text{NEqPair}_{1,1}(a,b) \vee \text{NEqPair}_{2,1,0}(a,b) \vee \text{NEqPair}_{2,1,1}(a,b).$$

Intuitively, NEqPair$_{1,1}(a, b)$ means that the sequences starting from a' and b' (the next of a and b with respect to the first pointer) have a different bit at a certain position. The meaning of $\text{NEqPair}_{2,1,i}(a,b)$ is that the bits of the cells pointed by a and b are different.

We define $\text{NEqLen}(a,b)$, which means the lengths of the sequences (that is, lists with respect to the first pointer) pointed by a and b are different.

$$\begin{aligned}
\text{NEqLen}_{1,1,i}(a,b) &=_{\text{def}} \exists a'(a \mapsto (x_i, a', b, _) * \text{NEqLen}_{1,2,i}(a',b)),\\
\text{NEqLen}_{1,2,i}(a,b) &=_{\text{def}} \exists b'(b \mapsto (x_i, b', a, _) * \text{NEqLen}(a,b')),\\
\text{NEqLen}_2(a,b) &=_{\text{def}} \exists a'(b = \text{nil} \wedge a \mapsto (_, a'_, _) * \text{True1}(a')),\\
\text{NEqLen}_{3,1}(a,b) &=_{\text{def}} a \mapsto (_, \text{nil}, b, _) * \text{NEqLen}_{3,2}(b),\\
\text{NEqLen}_{3,2}(b) &=_{\text{def}} \exists b'(b' \neq \text{nil} \wedge b \mapsto (_, b', _, _) * \text{True1}(b')).
\end{aligned}$$

Then the predicate $\text{NEqLen}(a,b)$ is defined by

$$\begin{aligned}
\text{NEqLen}(a,b) =_{\text{def}} & \text{NEqLen}_{1,1,0}(a,b) \vee \text{NEqLen}_{1,1,1}(a,b)\\
& \vee \text{NEqLen}_2(a,b) \vee \text{NEqLen}_{3,1}(a,b).
\end{aligned}$$

Here, $\text{NEqLen}_{1,1}(a,b)$ means that a and b point to the cells which have the same bit, but the sequences starting from a' and b' (the next of a and b with respect to the first pointer) have different lengths. $\text{NEqLen}_2(a,b)$ means that the sequence of b is finished, but the sequence of a has the next cell. The meaning of $\text{NEqLen}_{3,1}(a,b)$ is that a points to the last cell of the sequence, but the cell pointed by b is not the last one.

Finally, the predicate $\overline{\text{PCP}}(a,b)$ is defined by:

$$\overline{\text{PCP}}(a,b) =_{\text{def}} \text{NCorList}(a,b) \vee \text{NEqLen}(a,b) \vee \text{NEqPair}(a,b).$$

The meaning of $\overline{\text{PCP}}(a,b)$ is the cell lists starting from a and b are incorrect, that is, the lists contain a cell that has unexpected second pointer, or the cell lists connected by the first pointer have different bit sequences.

Note that the above definitions satisfy the conditions of weak progress, connectivity, and weak establishment, but do not satisfy the monadicity condition. The following proposition can be shown in a similar way to [1].

Proposition 6.1. *The PCP with tiles* $\mathbf{v}$ *and* $\mathbf{w}$ *is solvable iff* $\exists s,h.(s,h \models x_0 \neq x_1 \wedge \text{PCP}(a,b)$ *and* $s,h \not\models \overline{\text{PCP}}(a,b))$

If we assume decidability of the entailment problem in SLRD^+_{btw}, then we decide the existence of a model (s,h) that satisfies both $s,h \models x_0 \neq x_1 \wedge \text{PCP}(a,b)$ and $s,h \not\models \overline{\text{PCP}}(a,b)$. If the model exists, from the former part, there are two different elements $s(x_0)$ and $s(x_1)$ (say 0 and 1), and $s(a)$ and $s(b)$ point to some sequences of 0 and 1 which are tilings of v_i and w_i. Moreover, these sequences coincide from the latter part. That is, this model gives a solution of PCP. If there is no solution, then there does not exist such a model. This contradicts to the undecidability of PCP. Hence, we have the following undecidability result:

Theorem 6.2. *The entailment problem in the system Sep without the monadicity condition is undecidable.*

7 Conclusion

We have proved the decidability of the truth of entailments of symbolic heaps in separation logic with monadic inductive definitions under the weak progress, connectivity, and weak establishment conditions.

We have also proved the undecidability of the same system when we remove the monadicity condition.

In this paper, we imposed the weak establishment condition and the monadicity condition. We could remove the weak establishment condition by introducing some fixed number of distinguished addresses ∞_k. It could be future work. It could be also future work to relax the monadicity condition by replacing it by some locality condition.

References

1. Antonopoulos, T., Gorogiannis, N., Haase, C., Kanovich, M., Ouaknine, J.: Foundations for decision problems in separation logic with general inductive predicates. In: Muscholl, A. (ed.) FOSSACS 2014 (ETAPS). LNCS, vol. 8412, pp. 411–425. Springer, Heidelberg (2014)
2. Berdine, J., Calcagno, C., O'Hearn, P.W.: A decidable fragment of separation logic. In: Lodaya, K., Mahajan, M. (eds.) FSTTCS 2004. LNCS, vol. 3328, pp. 97–109. Springer, Heidelberg (2004)
3. Berdine, J., Calcagno, C., O'Hearn, P.W.: Symbolic execution with separation logic. In: Yi, K. (ed.) APLAS 2005. LNCS, vol. 3780, pp. 52–68. Springer, Heidelberg (2005)
4. Brotherston, J., Distefano, D., Petersen, R.L.: Automated cyclic entailment proofs in separation logic. In: Bjørner, N., Sofronie-Stokkermans, V. (eds.) CADE 2011. LNCS, vol. 6803, pp. 131–146. Springer, Heidelberg (2011)
5. Brotherston, J., Gorogiannis, N., Petersen, R.L.: A generic cyclic theorem prover. In: Jhala, R., Igarashi, A. (eds.) APLAS 2012. LNCS, vol. 7705, pp. 350–367. Springer, Heidelberg (2012)
6. Cook, B., Haase, C., Ouaknine, J., Parkinson, M., Worrell, J.: Tractable reasoning in a fragment of separation logic. In: Katoen, J.-P., König, B. (eds.) CONCUR 2011. LNCS, vol. 6901, pp. 235–249. Springer, Heidelberg (2011)
7. Enea, C., Saveluc, V., Sighireanu, M.: Compositional invariant checking for overlaid and nested linked lists. In: Felleisen, M., Gardner, P. (eds.) ESOP 2013. LNCS, vol. 7792, pp. 129–148. Springer, Heidelberg (2013)
8. Enea, C., Lengál, O., Sighireanu, M., Vojnar, T.: Compositional entailment checking for a fragment of separation logic. In: Garrigue, J. (ed.) APLAS 2014. LNCS, vol. 8858, pp. 314–333. Springer, Heidelberg (2014)
9. Iosif, R., Rogalewicz, A., Simacek, J.: The tree width of separation logic with recursive definitions. In: Bonacina, M.P. (ed.) CADE 2013. LNCS, vol. 7898, pp. 21–38. Springer, Heidelberg (2013)
10. Iosif, R., Rogalewicz, A., Vojnar, T.: Deciding entailments in inductive separation logic with tree automata. In: Cassez, F., Raskin, J.-F. (eds.) ATVA 2014. LNCS, vol. 8837, pp. 201–218. Springer, Heidelberg (2014)
11. Nguyen, H.H., Chin, W.-N.: Enhancing program verification with lemmas. In: Gupta, A., Malik, S. (eds.) CAV 2008. LNCS, vol. 5123, pp. 355–369. Springer, Heidelberg (2008)

12. Piskac, R., Wies, T., Zufferey, D.: Automating separation logic using SMT. In: Sharygina, N., Veith, H. (eds.) CAV 2013. LNCS, vol. 8044, pp. 773–789. Springer, Heidelberg (2013)
13. Piskac, R., Wies, T., Zufferey, D.: Automating separation logic with trees and data. In: Biere, A., Bloem, R. (eds.) CAV 2014. LNCS, vol. 8559, pp. 711–728. Springer, Heidelberg (2014)
14. Navarro Pérez, J.A., Rybalchenko, A.: Separation logic modulo theories. In: Shan, C. (ed.) APLAS 2013. LNCS, vol. 8301, pp. 90–106. Springer, Heidelberg (2013)
15. Reynolds, J.C.: Separation logic: a logic for shared mutable data structures. In: Proceedings of Seventeenth Annual IEEE Symposium on Logic in Computer Science (LICS2002), pp. 55–74 (2002)

Tree-Like Grammars and Separation Logic

Christoph Matheja(✉), Christina Jansen, and Thomas Noll

Software Modeling and Verification Group, RWTH Aachen University, Aachen, Germany
matheja@cs.rwth-aachen.de
http://moves.rwth-aachen.de/

Abstract. Separation Logic with inductive predicate definitions (SL) and hyperedge replacement grammars (HRG) are established formalisms to describe the abstract shape of data structures maintained by heap-manipulating programs. Fragments of both formalisms are known to coincide, and neither the entailment problem for SL nor its counterpart for HRGs, the inclusion problem, are decidable in general.

We introduce *tree-like grammars* (TLG), a fragment of HRGs with a decidable inclusion problem. By the correspondence between HRGs and SL, we simultaneously obtain an equivalent SL fragment ($\mathtt{SL}_{\mathtt{tl}}$) featuring some remarkable properties including a decidable entailment problem.

Keywords: Heap abstraction · Hyperedge replacement grammars · Separation logic · Entailment checking

1 Introduction

Symbolic execution of heap-manipulating programs builds upon abstractions to obtain finite descriptions of dynamic data structures, like linked lists and trees. Proposed abstraction approaches employ, amongst others, Separation Logic with inductive predicate definitions (SL) [2,13,18] and hyperedge replacement grammars (HRG) [9,12].

While these formalisms are intuitive and expressive, important problems are undecidable. In particular, the *entailment problem* for SL [1], i.e. the question of whether all models of a formula φ are also models of another formula ψ (written $\varphi \models \psi$), as well as its graph-theoretical counterpart, the *inclusion problem* for HRGs [9], are undecidable in general. Unfortunately, as stated by Brotherston, Distefano and Peterson [4], "effective procedures for establishing entailments are at the foundation of automatic verification based on Separation Logic". Consequently, SL-based verification tools, such as SLAYER [3] and PREDATOR [10], often restrict themselves to the analysis of list-like data structures, where the entailment problem is known to be decidable [2]. VERIFAST [14] and CYCLIST [4] allow general user-specified predicates, but are incomplete and/or require additional user interaction. The largest known fragment of SL featuring both inductive predicate definitions and a decidable entailment problem is Separation Logic with bounded tree width ($\mathtt{SL}_{\mathtt{btw}}$) [13].

X. Feng and S. Park (Eds.): APLAS 2015, LNCS 9458, pp. 90–108, 2015.
DOI: 10.1007/978-3-319-26529-2_6

Approaches based on graph grammars suffer from the undecidability of the related inclusion problem: Lee et al. [16] propose the use of graph grammars for shape analysis, but their approach is restricted to trees. The tool JUGGRNAUT [12] allows the user to specify the shape of dynamic data structures by an HRG, but relies on an approximation to check whether newly computed abstractions are subsumed by previously encountered ones. Hence, finding more general fragments of SL and HRGs with good decidability properties is highly desirable.

This paper investigates fragments of HRGs with a decidable inclusion problem. In a nutshell, HRGs are a natural extension of context-free word grammars specifying the replacement of nonterminal-labelled edges by graphs (cf. [11]). Common notions and results for context-free word languages, e.g. decidability of the emptiness problem and existence of derivation trees, can be lifted to HRGs (cf. [19]) which justifies the alternative name "context-free graph grammars".

Most of our results stand on two pillars. The first pillar is an extension of the well-known fact that context-free word languages are closed under intersection with regular word languages, which are, by Büchi's famous theorem [5], exactly the word languages definable in monadic second-order logic (MSO).

Lemma 1 (Courcelle [6]). *For each HRG G and $\mathtt{MSO}_2$ sentence φ, one can construct an HRG G' such that* $L(G') = L(G) \cap L(\varphi) = \{H \in L(G) \mid \underline{H} \models \varphi\}$.

Here, $\mathtt{MSO}_2$ means MSO over graphs with quantification over nodes and edges and $\underline{H}$ denotes the relational structure associated with the hypergraph H. $L(G)$ and $L(\varphi)$ denote the language generated by the grammar G and the set of models of the formula φ, respectively.

The second pillar is the close connection between a fragment of HRGs – called data structure grammars (DSG) – and a fragment of SL studied by Dodds [8] and Jansen et al. [15].

Lemma 2 (Jansen et al. [15]). *Every SL formula can be translated into a language-equivalent data structure grammar and vice versa.*

The overall goal of this paper is to develop fragments of HRGs which can be translated into $\mathtt{MSO}_2$. Then it directly follows from Lemma 1 that the resulting classes of languages have a decidable inclusion problem and are closed under union, intersection and difference as well as under intersection with general context-free graph languages. By Lemma 2, we obtain analogous results for equivalent SL fragments.

The largest fragment we propose are *tree-like grammars* (TLG). Intuitively, every graph H generated by a TLG allows to reconstruct one of its derivation trees by identifying certain nodes, the *anchor* nodes, with positions in a derivation tree. Furthermore, each edge of H is uniquely associated with one of these anchor nodes. These properties allow for each graph H generated by a given TLG G to first encode a derivation tree t in $\mathtt{MSO}_2$ and then to verify that H is in fact the graph derived by G according to t. Our main result is that the two informally stated properties from above guarantee $\mathtt{MSO}_2$-definability.

Theorem 1. *For each TLG G, there exists an* $\mathtt{MSO}_2$ *sentence* φ_G *such that for each hypergraph H, $H \in L(G)$ if and only if* $\underline{H} \models \varphi_G$.

TLGs are introduced in detail in Sect. 4.

Furthermore, we study the fragment of *tree-like Separation Logic* ($\mathtt{SL}_{\mathtt{tl}}$, cf. Sect. 5) which is equivalent to TLGs generating heaps rather than arbitrary graphs.

By Lemma 2, our results on TLGs also hold for $\mathtt{SL}_{\mathtt{tl}}$. Thus, $\mathtt{SL}_{\mathtt{tl}}$ has the following remarkable properties:

1. The satisfiability as well as the *extended* entailment problem, i.e. the question of whether an *arbitrary* SL formula φ entails an $\mathtt{SL}_{\mathtt{tl}}$ formula ψ, are decidable.
2. Although negation and conjunction are restricted to pure formulae, $\mathtt{SL}_{\mathtt{tl}}$ is closed under intersection and difference.

Regarding expressiveness, common data structures like (cyclic) lists, trees, in-trees, $n \times k$-grids for fixed k and combinations thereof are $\mathtt{SL}_{\mathtt{tl}}$-definable. In particular, we show that $\mathtt{SL}_{\mathtt{tl}}$ is strictly more expressive than $\mathtt{SL}_{\mathtt{btw}}$. The same holds for an entirely syntactic fragment of TLGs, called Δ-DSGs, and a corresponding fragment of $\mathtt{SL}_{\mathtt{tl}}$.

The remainder of this paper is structured as follows. Section 2 very briefly recapitulates standard definitions on SL and MSO, while Sect. 3 covers essential concepts of hypergraphs and HRGs. The fragment of TLGs and its MSO-definability result is introduced in Sect. 4. Our results on TLGs are transferred to SL and discussed in Sect. 5. Finally, Sect. 6 concludes.

Some technical details and proofs have been omitted due to lack of space, but are available in a detailed technical report [17].

2 Preliminaries

This section introduces our notation and briefly recapitulates trees, graphs, $\mathtt{MSO}_2$, and SL. On first reading, the well-informed reader might want to skip this part.

Notation. Given a set S, $S^\star$ denotes all finite sequences over S. For $s, s' \in S^\star$, $s.s'$ denotes their concatenation, the i-th element of s is denoted by $s(i)$ and the set of all of its elements is denoted by $\lfloor s \rfloor$. A ranked alphabet is a finite set S with ranking function $rk_S : S \to \mathbb{N}$ and maximal rank $\Re(S)$. We write $\{x_1 \mapsto y_1, \ldots, x_m \mapsto y_m\}$ to denote a finite (partial) function f with domain $\mathrm{dom}(f) = \{x_1, \ldots, x_m\}$ and co-domain $\{y_1, \ldots, y_m\}$ such that $f(x_i) = y_i$ for each $i \in [m] = [1, m] = \{1, 2, \ldots, m\}$. The operators $\uplus$ and $⊎$ denote the disjoint union of two sets and two functions, respectively.

Trees. Given a ranked alphabet S, a *tree* over S is a finite function $t : \mathrm{dom}(t) \to S$ such that $\emptyset \neq \mathrm{dom}(t) \subseteq \mathbb{N}^\star$, $\mathrm{dom}(t)$ is prefix closed and for all $x \in \mathrm{dom}(t)$, $\{i \in \mathbb{N} \mid x.i \in \mathrm{dom}(t)\} = [rk_S(t(x))]$. $x \in \mathrm{dom}(t)$ is a (proper) prefix of $y \in \mathrm{dom}(t)$, written $x \prec y$, if $y = x.i.z$ for some $i \in \mathbb{N}$ and $z \in \mathbb{N}^\star$. The subtree of t with root

$x \in \text{dom}(t)$ is given by $t|_x : \{y \mid x.y \in \text{dom}(t)\} \to S : y \mapsto t(x.y)$. With each tree t, we associate the relational structure $\underline{t} := (\text{dom}(t), (\text{succ}_i)_{i \in [\Re(S)]}, (\text{tlb}_s)_{s \in S})$ where $\text{succ}_i := \{(x, x.i) \in \text{dom}(t) \times \text{dom}(t)\}$ and $\text{tlb}_s := \{x \in \text{dom}(t) \mid t(x) = s\}$.

Graphs. An *edge-labelled graph* over an alphabet S is a tuple $H = (V, E)$ with a finite set of nodes V and edge relation $E \subseteq V \times S \times V$. With each graph H we associate the relational structure $\underline{H} = (V \uplus E, \text{src}, \text{tgt}, (E_s)_{s \in S})$ where src and tgt are the binary source and target relations given by $\text{src} := \{(u, e) \mid e = (u, s, v) \in E\}$, $\text{tgt} := \{(e, v) \mid e = (u, s, v) \in E\}$. For each $s \in S$, there is a unary relation $E_s := \{(u, s, v) \in E \mid u, v \in V\}$ collecting all edges labelled with s.

Monadic Second-Order Logic over Graphs. Given a finite alphabet S, the syntax of $\texttt{MSO}_2$ is given by:

$$\varphi ::= E_s(x) \mid \text{src}(x, y) \mid \text{tgt}(x, y) \mid X(x) \mid \varphi_1 \vee \varphi_2 \mid \neg\varphi \mid \exists x : \varphi \mid \exists X : \varphi \mid x = y$$

where x, y are first-order variables, X is a second-order variable and $s \in S$. For a graph $H = (V, E)$, we write $\underline{H}, \jmath \models \varphi$ iff $\underline{H}$ satisfies φ where $\jmath$ is an interpretation mapping every free first-order variable to an element of $V \uplus E$ and every second-order variable to a subset of either V or E, respectively. The semantics of $\models$ is standard (cf. [7]). Note that the semantics of src, tgt and E_s has been given explicitly in the definition of $\underline{H}$. We allow other operators like conjunction $\wedge$, implication $\to$ and universal quantification $\forall$ that can be obtained from the given ones. To keep formulae readable in the remainder of this paper, we make use of the following shortcuts which are rather straightforward to define in $\texttt{MSO}_2$. If $\mathcal{W}$ is a finite set of variables, $\exists \mathcal{W} : \varphi$ denotes the existential quantification of all variables in $\mathcal{W}$. $\exists! x : \varphi(x) := \exists x : \varphi(x) \wedge \forall y : \varphi(y) \to x = y$ denotes the unique existential quantification of x and $\Pi(X, Y_1, \ldots, Y_m)$ denotes that the sets $Y_1, \ldots, Y_m$ form a partition of X. The formulae $V(x)$ and $E(x)$ state that x is a node or an edge, respectively, and $\text{inc}(x, y)$ is satisfied if and only if x is an edge incident to a node y. If $X_1, \ldots, X_m$ are second order variables and $I \subseteq [m]$, $X_I(x)$ denotes the disjunction $\bigvee_{i \in I} X_i(x)$. Finally, $\text{tree}(X, x)$ means that the nodes in X form the domain of a relational tree structure $\underline{t}$ with root x (cf. [13] for a formal definition).

Heaps. Similarly to the typical RAM model, a heap is understood as a set of locations $Loc := \mathbb{N}$, whose values are interpreted as pointers to other locations. Formally, we define a *heap* as a partial mapping $h : Loc \to Loc \uplus \{\textbf{null}\}$. The set of all heaps is denoted by $\texttt{Hp}$. Let Σ be a finite set of *selectors* equipped with an injective ordering function $\text{cn} : \Sigma \to [0, |\Sigma| - 1]$. We assume a heap to consist of a single kind of objects with a fixed set of fields Σ which are modelled by reserving exactly $|\Sigma|$ successive locations.

Separation Logic with Recursive Definitions. We consider a fragment of Separation Logic, similar to Separation Logic with recursive definitions in [13,15], in which negation $\neg$, **true**, and conjunction $\wedge$ in spatial formulae are disallowed. Let *Pred* be a set of predicate names. The *syntax of* SL is given by:

$$\begin{aligned} E &::= x \mid \textbf{null} \\ P &::= x = y \mid x \neq y \mid P \wedge P && \text{pure formulae} \\ F &::= \textbf{emp} \mid x.s \mapsto E \mid F * F \mid \exists x : F \mid \sigma(x_1, ..., x_n) && \text{spatial formulae} \\ S &::= F \mid S \vee S \mid S \wedge P && \texttt{SL}\text{ formulae} \end{aligned}$$

where $x, y, x_1, ..., x_n \in \mathit{Var}$, $s \in \Sigma$ and $\sigma \in \mathit{Pred}$. We call $x.s \mapsto E$ a *points-to assertion*, $\sigma(x_1, ..., x_n)$ a *predicate call*.

Note that we do not require all selectors of a given variable to be defined by a single points-to assertion. Furthermore, it is straightforward to add program variables to SL, which we omitted for the sake of simplicity. To improve readability, we write $x.(s_1, \ldots, s_k) \mapsto (y_1, \ldots, y_k)$ as a shortcut for $x.s_1 \mapsto y_1 * \ldots * x.s_k \mapsto y_k$.

Predicate calls are specified by means of predicate definitions. A *predicate definition* for $\sigma \in \mathit{Pred}$ is of the form $\sigma(x_1, ..., x_n) := \sigma_1 \vee ... \vee \sigma_m$ where $m, n \in \mathbb{N}$, σ_j is a formula of the form $F \wedge P$, and $x_1, ..., x_n \in \mathit{Var}$ are pairwise distinct and exactly the free variables of σ_j for each $j \in [m]$. The disjunction $\sigma_1 \vee ... \vee \sigma_m$ is called the *body* of the predicate. An *environment* is a set of predicate definitions. *Env* denotes the set of all environments.

The semantics of a predicate call $\sigma(x_1, ..., x_n)$, $\sigma \in \mathit{Pred}$, w.r.t. an environment $\Gamma \in \mathit{Env}$ is given by the predicate interpretation η_Γ. It is defined as the least set of location sequences instantiating the arguments $x_1, \ldots, x_n$ and heaps that fulfil the unrolling of the predicate body. We refer to [15] for a formal definition.

The semantics of the remaining SL constructs is determined by the standard semantics of first-order logic and the following, where $\jmath$ is an interpretation of variables as introduced for $\texttt{MSO}_2$:

$$\begin{aligned} h, \jmath, \eta_\Gamma &\models x.s \mapsto \textbf{null} &&\Leftrightarrow \mathrm{dom}(h) = \{\jmath(x) + \mathit{cn}(s)\}, h(\jmath(x) + \mathit{cn}(s)) = \textbf{null} \\ h, \jmath, \eta_\Gamma &\models x.s \mapsto y &&\Leftrightarrow \mathrm{dom}(h) = \{\jmath(x) + \mathit{cn}(s)\}, h(\jmath(x) + \mathit{cn}(s)) = \jmath(y) \\ h, \jmath, \eta_\Gamma &\models \sigma(x_1, ..., x_n) &&\Leftrightarrow ((\jmath(x_1), ..., \jmath(x_n)), h) \in \eta_\Gamma(\sigma) \\ h, \jmath, \eta_\Gamma &\models \varphi_1 * \varphi_2 &&\Leftrightarrow \exists h_1, h_2 : h = h_1 \uplus h_2, h_1, \jmath, \eta_\Gamma \models \varphi_1,\ h_2, \jmath, \eta_\Gamma \models \varphi_2 \end{aligned}$$

A variable $x \in \mathit{Var}$ is said to be *allocated* in a formula if it (or a variable y with $y = x$) occurs on the left-hand side of a points-to assertion.

From now on, we assume that all existentially quantified variables are eventually allocated. This requirement is similar to the "establishment" condition in [13]. With this assumption, the inequality operator for logical variables $x \neq y$ is redundant with respect to the expressive power of the formalism, because $x.s \mapsto z * y.s \mapsto z'$ already implies that $\jmath(x) \neq \jmath(y)$ in all heaps satisfying the formula. Thus, we assume that two existentially quantified variables refer to different locations if not stated otherwise by a pure formula.

3 Context-Free Graph Grammars

This section introduces HRGs together with some of their properties relevant for the remainder of this paper. For a comprehensive introduction, we refer to [11,19].

Let $\Sigma_N := \Sigma \uplus N$ be a ranked alphabet consisting of terminal symbols Σ and nonterminal symbols N.

Definition 1 (Hypergraph). *A* labelled hypergraph *(HG) over Σ_N is a tuple* $H = (V, E, \text{att}, \text{lab}, \text{ext})$ *where V and E are disjoint sets of nodes and hyperedges,* att : $E \to V^\star$ *maps each hyperedge to a sequence of attached nodes such that* $|\text{att}(e)| = rk_{\Sigma_N}(\text{lab}(e))$, lab : $E \to \Sigma_N$ *is a labelling function, and* ext $\in V^\star$ *a sequence of external nodes. The set of all HGs over Σ_N is denoted by $\mathtt{HG}_{\Sigma_N}$.*

Note that we allow attachments of hyperedges as well as the sequence of external nodes to contain repetitions. Hyperedges with a label from Σ are called *terminal edges*, *nonterminal* otherwise. The set of terminal (nonterminal) hyperedges of an HG H is denoted by E_H^Σ (E_H^N, respectively). In this paper, we assume $rk_{\Sigma_N}(s) = 2$ for each $s \in \Sigma$. Moreover, a hyperedge e with $\text{lab}(e) = s \in \Sigma$ and $\text{att}(e) = u.v$ is interpreted as a directed edge from u to v. The relational structure corresponding to $H \in \mathtt{HG}_\Sigma$ is $\underline{H} := \underline{[H]}$, where the (conventional) graph $[H]$ is defined as $[H] = (V_H, E)$, $E := \{(\text{att}_H(e)(1), \text{lab}_H(e), \text{att}_H(e)(2)) \mid e \in E_H\}$.

Example 1. As an example, consider the HG illustrated in Fig. 1(a) (right). For referencing purpose, we provide a unique index $i \in [|V|]$ inside of each node u_i represented by a circle. External nodes are shaded. For simplicity, we assume them to be ordered according to the provided index. Terminal edges are drawn as directed, labelled edges and nonterminal edges as square boxes with their label inside. The ordinals pictured next to the connections of a nonterminal hyperedge denote the position of the attached nodes in the attachment sequence. For example, if e is the leftmost nonterminal hyperedge in Fig. 1(a), $\text{att}(e) = u_5.u_1.u_3.u_7$.

Two HGs H, H' are *isomorphic*, written $H \cong H'$, if they are identical up to renaming of nodes and edges. In this paper, we will not distinguish between isomorphic HGs. The disjoint union of $H, H' \in \mathtt{HG}_{\Sigma_N}$ is denoted by $H \uplus H'$.

The main concept to specify (infinite) sets of HGs in terms of context-free graph grammars is the replacement of a nonterminal hyperedge by a finite HG. Let K and H be HGs with disjoint sets of nodes and edges. Intuitively, a nonterminal hyperedge e of K is replaced by H by first removing e, adding H to K and identifying the nodes of K originally attached to e with the sequence of external nodes of H. This is formally expressed by a quotient.

Definition 2 (Hypergraph Quotient). *Let* $H \in \mathtt{HG}_{\Sigma_N}$, $R \subseteq V_H \times V_H$ *be an equivalence relation and* $[u]_{/R} = \{v \in V_H \mid (u, v) \in R\}$ *the equivalence class of* $u \in V_H$*, which is canonically extended to sequences of nodes. The R-*quotient graph *of H is* $[H]_{/R} = (V, E, \text{att}, \text{lab}, \text{ext})$, *where* $V = \{[u]_{/R} \mid u \in V_H\}$, $E = E_H$, $\text{att} = \{e \mapsto [\text{att}_H(e)]_{/R} \mid e \in E_H\}$, $\text{lab} = \text{lab}_H$, $\text{ext} = [\text{ext}_H]_{/R}$.

Definition 3 (Hyperedge Replacement). *Let* $H, K \in \mathit{HG}_{\Sigma_N}$ *with disjoint nodes and hyperedges,* $e \in E_H^N$ *with* $rk_{\Sigma_N}(e) = k = |\text{ext}_K|$*. Let* $V = V_H \uplus V_K$*, and* ${}_{H,e}\!\approx_K \subseteq V \times V$ *be the least equivalence relation containing* $\{(\text{att}_H(e)(i), \text{ext}_K(i)) \mid i \in [k]\}$*. Then the* HG obtained from replacing e by K *is* $H[e/K] := [(H \setminus \{e\} \uplus K)]/_{{}_{H,e}\!\approx_K}$ *where* $H \setminus \{e\}$ *is the HG* H *in which* e *has been removed. Moreover, two nodes* $u, v \in V$ *are* merged *by* $H[e/K]$ *if* $u \neq v$ *and* $u \;{}_{H,e}\!\approx_K\; v$*.*

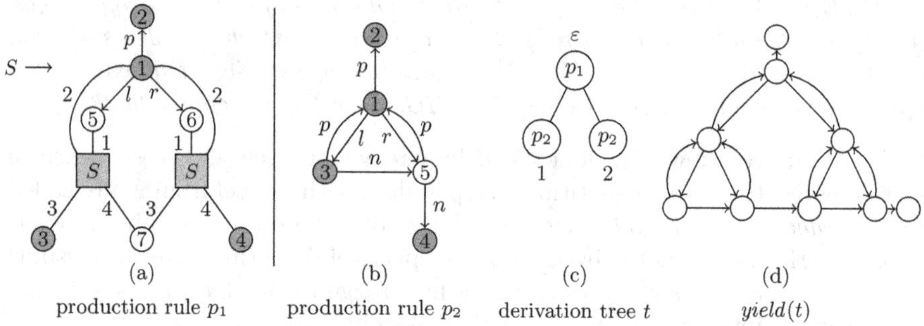

Fig. 1. HRG *TLL* with two production rules p_1 and p_2

We now formally introduce context-free graph grammars based on hyperedge replacement.

Definition 4 (Hyperedge Replacement Grammar). *An* HRG *is a 3-tuple* $G = (\Sigma_N, P, S)$ *where* Σ_N *is a ranked alphabet,* $S \in N$ *is the initial symbol and* $P \subseteq N \times \mathit{HG}_{\Sigma_N}$ *is a finite set of production rules such that* $rk_{\Sigma_N}(X) = |\text{ext}_H| > 0$ *for each* $(X, H) \in P$*. The class of all HRGs is denoted by* **HRG** *and the maximal number of nonterminal hyperedges in any production rule* $p \in P$ *by* $\Bbbk$*.*

Given $p = (X, H) \in P$, we write lhs(p) and rhs(p) to denote X and H, respectively. To improve readability, we write p instead of lhs(p) or rhs(p) whenever the context is clear.

Example 2. The HRG *TLL* depicted in Fig. 1(a) and (b) will serve as a running example. It consists of one nonterminal symbol S, four terminal symbols l, r, p, n and two production rules p_1, p_2. The rule graph of p_2 depicts a fully-branched binary tree of height 1 with additional parent-pointers and two n-connected leaves. Later we will see that the HRG describes arbitrary trees of the aforementioned structure.

A key feature of HRGs is that the order in which nonterminal hyperedges are replaced is irrelevant, i.e. HRGs are confluent (cf. [11,19]). Thus, derivations of HRGs can be described by derivation trees. Towards a formal definition, we assume that the nonterminal hyperedges $E_p^N = \{e_1, ..., e_n\}$ of each production rule $p = (X, H)$ are in some (arbitrary, but fixed) linear order, say $e_1, ..., e_n$. For HRG $G, G[X]$ denotes the HRG (Σ_N, P_G, X).

Definition 5 (Derivation Tree). *Let $G = (\Sigma_N, P, S) \in$ HRG. The set of all* derivation trees *of G is the least set $D(G)$ of trees t over the alphabet P with ranking function $rk_P : P \to \mathbb{N}$ such that $t(\varepsilon) = p$ for some $p \in P$ with* $\text{lhs}(p) = S$. *Moreover, if $E_p^N = \{e_1, \ldots, e_m\}$, then $rk_P(p) = m$ and $t|_i \in D(G[\text{lab}_p(e_i)])$ for each $i \in [m]$. The* yield *of a derivation tree is given by the HG*

$$yield(t) = t(\varepsilon)[e_1/yield(t|_1), \ldots, e_m/yield(t|_m)].$$

We implicitly assume that the nodes and hyperedges of $t(x)$ and $t(y)$ are disjoint if $x \neq y$. The yield of a derivation tree is also called the *derived* HG according to t.

Example 3. Figure 1(c) illustrates a derivation tree t of the HRG *TLL* in which production rule p_1 has been applied once, and production rule p_2 twice. The labels next to the circles provide the position in $\text{dom}(t)$ while the labels inside indicate the applied production rule. The graph on the right (d) illustrates the shape of $yield(t)$. For simplicity, node indices as well as edge labels are omitted.

The language generated by an HRG consists of all HGs without nonterminal edges that can be derived from the initial nonterminal symbol.

Definition 6 (HR Language). *The* language *generated by $G \in$ HRG is the set* $L(G) = \{yield(t) \mid t \in D(G)\}$.

Example 4. The HRG *TLL*, provided in Fig. 1, generates the language of all fully-branched binary trees in which the leaves are connected from left to right and each node has an additional edge to its parent.

Two results for derivation trees are needed in the following. The first result is directly lifted from analogous results for context-free word grammars (cf. [19] below Theorem 3.10).

Lemma 3. *For each $G \in$ HRG, $D(G)$ is a regular tree language. In particular, the emptiness problem for HRGs is decidable in linear time.*

Furthermore, we generalize the notion of merged nodes to multiple successive applications of hyperedge replacement.

Definition 7 (Merged Nodes). *Let $G \in$ HRG, $t \in D(G)$, $x, y \in$* $\text{dom}(t)$ *such that $x \prec y$, i.e. $y = x.i.z$ for some $i \in \mathbb{N}, z \in \mathbb{N}^*$, and let $u \in V_{t(x)}$, $v \in V_{t(y)}$. We say that u and v are* merged *in t, written $u \sim_t v$, if*

- $z = \varepsilon$ *and* $u \;{}_{t(x),e_i}\!\approx_{t(x.i)} v$, *or*
- $z \neq \varepsilon$ *and there exists* $w \in V_{t(x.i)}$ *such that* $u \;{}_{t(x),e_i}\!\approx_{t(x.i)} w$ *and* $w \sim_t v$.

Example 5. Consider the derivation tree t shown in Fig. 1(c) again. In its yield, the node u_7 in $t(\varepsilon)$ is merged with u_4 in $t(1)$ and with u_3 in $t(2)$. In $yield(t)$, this node represents the leftmost leaf of the right subtree.

The relation $\sim_t$ merges exactly the nodes that are identified with each other by *yield*(t).

Lemma 4 (Merge Lemma). *Given $G \in$ HRG and $t \in$ D(G), let $\simeq_t$ denote the least equivalence relation containing $\sim_t$. Then*

$$yield(t) \cong \left[\biguplus_{x \in \mathrm{dom}(t)} \mathrm{rhs}(t(x)) \right]_{/\simeq_t}$$

Proof. By complete induction over the height of derivation trees. □

4 Tree-Like Grammars

This section introduces tree-like grammars (TLG), a fragment of HRGs which can be translated into $\mathtt{MSO}_2$. The main idea of TLGs is that every graph H generated by a TLG G has two properties:

1. A derivation tree t of H is $\mathtt{MSO}_2$-definable in H, i.e. TLGs generate recognisable graph languages in the sense of Courcelle [6].
2. Every edge $e \in E_H$ can be uniquely associated in $\mathtt{MSO}_2$ with some $x \in \mathrm{dom}(t)$ corresponding to the production rule $t(x)$ which added e to H. We call $E^{\Sigma}_{t(x)}$ the *characteristic edges* of x.

Hence, given some $\mathtt{MSO}_2$ formulae encoding t in H and defining $E^{\Sigma}_{t(x)}$ for each $x \in \mathrm{dom}(t)$, one can easily obtain a formula φ ensuring that all edges in every model of φ are edges introduced by the proper application of a production rule. In particular, $K = \biguplus_{x \in \mathrm{dom}(t)} \mathrm{rhs}(t(x))$ is a model of φ for each $t \in \mathtt{D}(\mathrm{G})$. By Lemma 4, it is sufficient to extend φ to an $\mathtt{MSO}_2$ sentence φ' such that only graphs H with $H \cong [K]_{/\simeq_t} \cong yield(t)$, i.e. graphs that resulted from hyperedge replacement steps where exactly the $[K]_{/\simeq_t}$-equivalent nodes were merged, are models of φ'.

Some further notation is needed. Let $H \in \mathtt{HG}_{\Sigma_N}$ with $E^N_H = \{e_1, \ldots, e_m\}$. We call $\mathrm{ext}_H(1)$ the *anchor* node of H and denote it by $\perp_H$. Moreover, the sequence of *context* nodes of H is defined as $\mathrm{ctxt}_H := \mathrm{att}_H(e_1)(1) \ldots \mathrm{att}_H(e_m)(1)$ and the *free* nodes of H are all nodes attached to nonterminal hyperedges only, i.e. $\mathrm{free}(H) := \{u \in V_H \mid \forall e \in E^{\Sigma}_H : u \notin \lfloor \mathrm{att}_H(e) \rfloor\}$.

We will see that TLGs are constructed such that every anchor node u represents an application of a production rule and thus a position in a derivation tree t. The context nodes represent its children as they are merged with anchor nodes after their corresponding nonterminal hyperedges have been replaced. Consequently, by the characteristic edges of an anchor node u we refer to the characteristic edges $E^{\Sigma}_{t(x)}$ of a position $x \in \mathrm{dom}(t)$ represented by u.

We consider a series of simple graph languages to narrow down the class of TLGs step by step. The first example stems from the fact that every context-free word language can be generated by an HRG [11] (if words are canonically encoded by edge-labelled graphs).

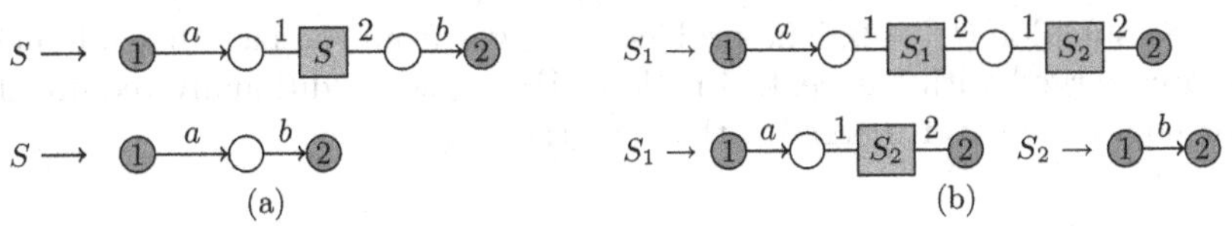

Fig. 2. Two HRGs generating the language $\{a^n.b^n \mid n \geq 1\}$ of string-like graphs.

Example 6. The HRG G shown in Fig. 2(a) generates string-like graphs of the form $a^n.b^n$ for each $n \geq 1$. It is well known that the language $L(\mathrm{G})$ is not $\mathtt{MSO}_2$-definable. We observe that for arbitrary hypergraphs $H \in L(\mathrm{G})$ it is not possible to determine a node that is uniquely associated with all terminal edges in the recursive, upper production rule of Fig. 2(a) (which is in accordance with the idea behind TLGs formulated at the beginning of this section). This is caused by the intermediate nonterminal hyperedge, which can be replaced by an arbitrarily large HG. Thus, to ensure that TLGs generate $\mathtt{MSO}_2$-definable hypergraphs only, we require that every non-free node (and thus every terminal edge) is reachable from the anchor node using terminal edges only.

However, this requirement is insufficient. For instance, Fig. 2(b) depicts an HRG G′ with $L(\mathrm{G}') = L(\mathrm{G})$ which satisfies the condition from above. G′ is obtained by transforming G into the well-known Greibach normal form. In a derivation tree t, a position $x \in \mathrm{dom}(t)$ corresponding to an application of the upper production rule has two children which represent the nonterminal hyperedges labelled with S_1 and S_2, respectively. Since all nodes except for the two leftmost ones are free in this production rule, the parent-child relationship between anchor nodes and context nodes (or any other triple of nodes) cannot be reconstructed in $\mathtt{MSO}_2$. Thus, we additionally require context nodes to be non-free.

In the following we consider *basic* tree-like HGs, which form the building blocks of which a tree-like HG is composed.

Definition 8 (Basic Tree-Like Hypergraphs). *$H \in HG_{\Sigma_N}$ is a* basic *tree-like HG if $\perp_H \in \lfloor \mathrm{att}_H(e) \rfloor$ for each $e \in E_H^{\Sigma}$ and $\lfloor ctxt_H \rfloor \cap free(H) = \emptyset$.*

As a first condition on TLGs, we require right-hand sides of production rules to be (basic) tree-like. In case of string-like graphs, this condition is sufficient to capture exactly the regular word languages (if the direction of edges is ignored), because every such grammar corresponds to a right-linear grammar. If arbitrary graphs are considered, however, there are more subtle cases.

Example 7. Figure 3 (left) depicts an HRG G with three production rules p, q, r. $L(G)$ is the set of "doubly-linked even stars", i.e. a single node u connected by an incoming and an outgoing edge to each of $2n$ nodes for some $n \geq 0$. An HG $H \in L(G)$ is illustrated in Fig. 3 (right). Again, $\mathrm{L}(G)$ is not $\mathtt{MSO}_2$-definable. In particular, no derivation tree can be reconstructed from H by identifying nodes (or edges) in H with positions in a derivation tree, because $|V_H| = 5$ and

$|E_H| = 8$, but $|\text{dom}(t)| = 9$. The problem emerges from the fact that all anchor nodes are merged with the central node u. Hence, we additionally require that anchor nodes are never merged with each other.

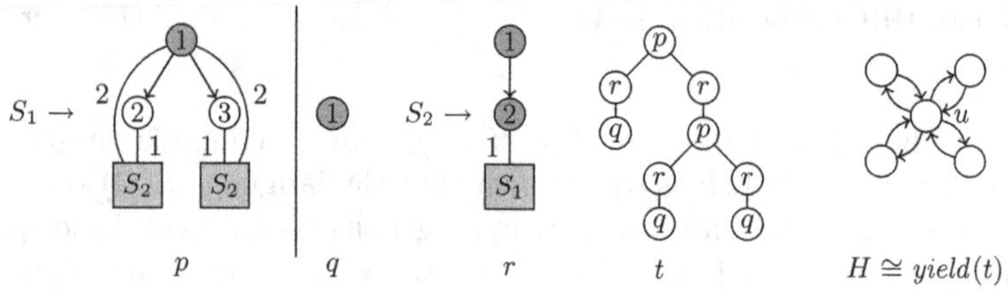

Fig. 3. An HRG G where production rules p, q, r map to tree-like HGs (left) and a generated graph $H \in L(G)$ (right)

Formally, for any $X \in N$, $H \in L(G[X])$ contains merged anchor nodes if for some $t \in \mathtt{D}(G[X])$ with $H \cong \mathit{yield}(t)$, there exist $x, y \in \text{dom}(t)$, $x \neq y$ such that $\downarrow_{t(x)} \simeq_t \downarrow_{t(y)}$. The set of all HGs in $\bigcup_{X \in N} L(G[X])$ containing merged anchor nodes is denoted by $\mathcal{M}(G)$.

Definition 9 (Tree-Like Grammar). *$G = (\Sigma_N, P, S) \in$ HRG is a* TLG *if $\mathcal{M}(G) = \emptyset$ and for each $p \in P$,* rhs(p) *is a basic tree-like HG. The set of all TLGs is denoted by* TLG.

Remark 1. We call an HG H *tree-like* if it can be composed from basic tree-like HGs, i.e. there exists a TLG G with $L(G) = \{H\}$ (where nonterminals of H are considered to be terminal). Although only basic tree-like HGs are considered in all proofs, our results also hold for tree-like HGs. In particular, if all non-free nodes of an HG H are reachable from the anchor node without visiting an external node, a context node or a nonterminal hyperedge, H is tree-like. Intuitively, the anchor nodes of corresponding TLG production rules are determined by a spanning tree with the anchor of H as root. Since this construction is straightforward, but rather tedious, we skip it for space reasons. Analogously, the initial nonterminal S may be mapped to an arbitrary HG provided that it never occurs on the right-hand side of a production rule.

Example 8. According to the previous remark, the recurring example HRG *TLL* illustrated in Fig. 1 is a TLG.

The condition $\mathcal{M}(G) = \emptyset$ is, admittedly, not syntactic. However, it is possible to automatically derive the largest subset of graphs generated by an HRG that satisfies it.

Theorem 2. *For each HRG G, one can construct a TLG G' such that $L(G') = L(G) \setminus \mathcal{M}(G)$.*

Our main result on TLGs is the following.

Theorem 1. *For each TLG G, there exists an MSO_2 sentence φ_G such that for each hypergraph H, $H \in \mathit{HG}$, $H \in L(G)$ if and only if $\underline{H} \models \varphi_G$.*

In order to prove this theorem, we have to encode derivation trees in graphs generated by TLGs. We associate each terminal edge with a unique, characteristic edge of some anchor node and use the constructed derivation tree t to verify that two nodes are identical if and only if they have been merged due to hyperedge replacement, i.e. are equivalent with respect to $\simeq_t$ (see Lemma 4).

Before we present the main steps of the proof, we state two important consequences of Theorem 1 and Lemma 1.

Theorem 3. *The class of languages generated by TLGs is closed under union, intersection and difference.*

Theorem 4. *Given $G \in \mathit{TLG}$ and $G' \in \mathit{HRG}$, it is decidable whether $L(G') \subseteq L(G)$. In particular, the inclusion problem for TLGs is decidable.*

In the following constructions, we use two sets of second-order variables $\mathcal{A}$ and $\mathcal{S}$. Each set variable $A_p \in \mathcal{A} = \{A_p \mid p \in P\}$ collects all anchor nodes corresponding to a position in a derivation tree labelled by $p \in P$. Each set $S_e \in \mathcal{S}$ collects all edges corresponding to the characteristic edge $e \in E_p^{\Sigma}$ of positions labelled by p in a derivation tree. Formally, we introduce an extended set of edge labels $\mathcal{S} := \{S_e \mid e \in E_p^{\Sigma}, p \in P\}$ together with functions $\ell : \mathcal{S} \to \Sigma : S_e \mapsto \mathrm{lab}_p(e)$ and $\rho : \mathcal{S} \to P : S_e \mapsto p$. Let $\mathcal{W} = \mathcal{A} \uplus \mathcal{S}$.

The first auxiliary lemma to prove Theorem 1 states that derivation trees can be encoded in every graph generated by a TLG.

Lemma 5. *For each TLG $G = (\Sigma_N, P, S)$, a set of derivation trees of G is MSO_2-definable with parameters $\mathcal{W}$ in every $H \in \mathit{HG}_{\Sigma}$, i.e. there exists a definition scheme $(\psi, (succ_i)_{i \in [\![k]\!]}, (\mathrm{tlb}_p)_{p \in P})$ such that for each $H \in \mathit{HG}_{\Sigma}$ with $H, \jmath \models \psi(\mathcal{W})$, $\underline{t} := (dom, (\jmath(succ_i))_{i \in [\![k]\!]}, (\jmath(\mathrm{tlb}_p))_{p \in P})$ is a relational tree structure representing a tree $t \in D(G)$, where dom is given by the union of all nodes satisfying exactly one of the formulae tlb_p, $p \in P$.*

In particular, for each $H \in L(\mathrm{G})$, $\mathcal{W}$ can be chosen such that a derivation tree $t \in \mathrm{D(G)}$ with $\mathit{yield}(t) \cong H$ is defined in $\underline{H}$. This is formalised in the following.

Definition 10. *Let $G = (\Sigma_N, P, S)$ be a TLG, $p \in P$ and $E_{p,i} := \{S_e \in \mathcal{S} \mid e \in E_p^{\Sigma}, ctxt_p(i) \in \lfloor \mathrm{att}_p(e) \rfloor\}$ be the set of all extended labels of edges incident to the i-th context node of p.*

A derivation tree $t \in D(G)$ is contained *in $H \in L(G)$ if there exists a set $T \subseteq V_H$ and a bijection $f : T \to \mathrm{dom}(t)$ such that for each $u \in T$ either $f(u) = \varepsilon$ or $f(u) = x.i$, $x \in \mathrm{dom}(t)$, $i \in \mathbb{N}$ and $E_{t(x),i} = \{S_e \in \mathcal{S} \mid f^{-1}(x) \xrightarrow{e} u\}$.*

Lemma 6 *For each TLG $G = (\Sigma_N, P, S)$, $H \in L(G)$ and $t \in D(G)$ with $\mathit{yield}(t) \cong H$, t is contained in H.*

We need one more ingredient before proving Theorem 1: How to use a derivation tree t to check whether two nodes are identical with respect to $\simeq_t$?

Let $t \in \mathtt{D}(G)$. Obviously, each pair of positions $x, y \in \mathrm{dom}(t)$, where $y \prec x$, defines a unique (bottom-up) path $path(x,y) := x_1 \ldots x_m$ in t where $x_1 = x, x_m = y$ and $x_i = x_{i+1}.j_i$ for $j_i \in \mathbb{N}$, $i \in [1, m-1]$. Its corresponding *trace* is given by $\mathrm{trace}(x_1 \ldots x_m) := (j_1, t(x_1)) \ldots (j_{m-1}, t(x_{m-1}))(j, t(x_m))$, where $j = 0$ if $x_m = \varepsilon$. We define a finite (word) automaton running on traces of derivation trees to check whether two given nodes – the i-th external node in $t(x_1)$ and the node $\mathrm{att}(e_j)(k)$ in $t(x_m)$ – are merged. In particular, this merge automaton depends on the HRG G and the indices i, j, k only, but not on a specific derivation tree.

Definition 11 (Merge Automaton). *Let $G = (\Sigma_N, P, S) \in$ HRG, $i, j \in [\Re(G)]$ and $k \in [\![\mathrm{k}]\!]$. The* merge automaton $\mathfrak{A}_{i,j,k} = (Q, \Gamma, 1, \delta, F)$ *running on traces of derivation trees of G is given by the set of states $Q := \{1\} \uplus (\{1,0\} \times [\Re(G)] \times [\![\mathrm{k}]\!])$, input alphabet $\Gamma = [0, \Re(G)] \times P$, initial state q_0, final states $F := \{(0, j, k)\}$ and the partial transition function $\delta : Q \times \Gamma \to Q$, defined by:*

$$
\begin{aligned}
\delta(1, (x, p)) &= (1, i, x) && \textit{if } x > 0, \\
\delta(1, (0, p)) &= (0, i, j) && \textit{if } \mathrm{lhs}(p) = S, E_p^N = \emptyset \textit{ and } i = j, \\
\delta((1, x, y), (z, p)) &= (1, x', z) && \textit{if } \mathrm{att}_p(e_y)(x) = \mathrm{ext}_p(x'), \\
\delta((1, x, y), (z, p)) &= (0, j, k) && \textit{if } u := \mathrm{att}_p(e_y)(x) = \mathrm{att}_p(e_j)(k) \\
& && \textit{and } (z = 0 \textit{ or } u \notin \lfloor \mathrm{ext}_p \rfloor).
\end{aligned}
$$

Intuitively, the automaton records the indices i, j, k in its state space and updates them according to the rules of hyperedge replacement while moving through a derivation tree.

Lemma 7 *Let $G = (\Sigma_N, P, S) \in$ HRG, $t \in D(G)$ and $x, y \in \mathrm{dom}(t)$ such that $y \prec x$. Furthermore, let $u = \mathrm{ext}_{t(x)}(i)$ and $v = \mathrm{att}_{t(y)}(e_j)(k)$. Then, $u \sim_t v$ if and only if $\mathfrak{A}_{i,j,k}$ accepts* $\mathrm{trace}(path(x, y))$.

Proof. By complete induction over the length of $\mathrm{trace}(path(x, y))$. □

We now turn to the proof of Theorem 1, in which the automaton from above is used to verify whether two nodes are merged with each other. To improve readability in the following constructions, we introduce an auxiliary formula which takes three variables x, y, z and is satisfied iff x corresponds to a characteristic edge $e \in E_p^\Sigma$ of anchor node y and is additionally attached to z. Formally, let $e \in E_p^\Sigma$ and $char_e(x, y, z) := E_{\ell(S_e)}(x) \wedge S_e(x) \wedge A_{\rho(e)}(y) \wedge \mathrm{src}(y, x) \wedge \mathrm{tgt}(x, z)$ if $\perp_p = \mathrm{att}_p(e)(1)$ ($\perp_p = \mathrm{att}_p(e)(2)$ with y and z swapped in src and tgt).

Proof (of Theorem 1). Let $G = (\Sigma_N, P, S) \in \mathtt{TLG}$. W.l.o.g., we make two assumptions in order to reduce the technical effort. First, we assume that every production rule is "well-formed", i.e. for each production rule p, all nodes in ext_p and $\mathrm{att}_p(e)$, $e \in E_p^N$, are distinct. It is a classical result that each HRG can be transformed into an equivalent one satisfying this condition (cf. [11], Theorem 4.6).

In particular, this transformation does not change tree-likeness of an HRG. Second, we assume for each $p \in P$ that $\text{rhs}(p)$ does not contain *inner* nodes, i.e. nodes which are neither external nor attached to any nonterminal hyperedge. Otherwise, we introduce a new nonterminal symbol $X \notin \Sigma_N$ with $rk_{\Sigma_N}(X) = 1$ and a single production rule mapping X to a single external node. Then, we attach a new nonterminal hyperedge labelled X to each inner node.

We have to define an $\texttt{MSO}_2$ sentence φ_{G} such that $H \in L(G)$ iff $\underline{H} \models \varphi_{\mathrm{G}}$. In order to construct φ_{G}, a set of derivation trees is encoded in H using the definition scheme $(\psi, (succ_i)_{1 \leq i \leq \Bbbk}, (\text{tlb}_p)_{p \in P})$ from Lemma 5. Recall that this definition scheme depends on a set of parameters $\mathcal{W} = \mathcal{A} \uplus \mathcal{S}$. An evaluation of the parameters $\mathcal{W}$ determines a fixed derivation tree t. Due to Lemma 6, the values of $\mathcal{W}$ can be chosen such that $yield(t) \cong H$ if $H \in L(G)$. Then, φ_{G} is given by

$$\varphi_{\mathrm{G}} := \text{conn} \wedge \exists \mathcal{W} : \psi(\mathcal{W}) \wedge \text{edges}(\mathcal{W}) \wedge \text{anchors}(\mathcal{W}) \wedge \text{mergeNodes}(\mathcal{W}), \quad (1)$$

where all subformulae except for $\psi(\mathcal{W})$ are needed to assert $yield(t) \cong H$. In the following, we explain the components of φ_{G} in more detail.

1. All nodes of H are incident to at least one edge. Together with the conditions on edges provided in (2), this ensures that every model of φ_{G} is a connected graph. Formally, $\text{conn} := \forall x \exists y : \text{inc}(x, y)$.
2. Every edge corresponds to exactly one characteristic edge of an anchor node. In particular, $\mathcal{S}$ forms a partition of all edges E of H.

$$\text{edges}(\mathcal{W}) := \Pi(E, \mathcal{S}) \wedge \bigwedge_{S_e \in \mathcal{S}} \forall x : S_e(x) \rightarrow \exists y, z : char_e(x, y, z) \quad (2)$$

3. Every anchor node $u \in \text{tlb}_p$ has exactly the characteristic edges E_p^{Σ}. Furthermore, if two edges $e, e' \in E_p^{\Sigma}$ are attached to the same nodes in $\text{rhs}(p)$, then the same holds for the corresponding two edges of u:

$$\text{anchors}(\mathcal{W}) := \bigwedge_{p \in P} \forall x : \text{tlb}_p(x, \mathcal{W}) \rightarrow \alpha_p(x, \mathcal{W}) \quad (3)$$

$$\alpha_p(x, \mathcal{W}) := \bigwedge_{u \in V_p \setminus \text{free}(p)} \beta_p^u(x, \mathcal{W}) \wedge \bigwedge_{e \notin E_p^{\Sigma}} \forall y, z : \neg char_e(y, x, z)$$

$$\beta_p^u(x, \mathcal{W}) := \exists y : \bigwedge_{\substack{e \in E_p^{\Sigma} \\ \perp_p \xrightarrow{e} u}} \exists! z : char_e(z, x, y) \wedge \bigwedge_{\substack{e \in E_p^{\Sigma} \\ \neg \perp_p \xrightarrow{e} u}} \forall z : \neg char_e(z, x, y)$$

4. Two nodes $u \in V_{t(x)}, v \in V_{t(y)}$, where $x \neq y$, represent the same node in V_H iff they are merged according to the rules of hyperedge replacement (see Lemma 4). Since G is well-formed and every node is either external or attached to some nonterminal hyperedge, this is the case iff u, v are merged with the same non-external node. In this setting, external nodes of $t(\varepsilon)$ are a corner case and can be considered non-external.

Given an anchor node $x \in \mathrm{dom}(t)$, an inspection of the characteristic edges of x allows us to verify whether a node corresponds to $\mathrm{ext}_{t(x)}(i)$ or $\mathrm{att}_{t(x)}(e_j)(k)$, where $i, j, k \in \mathbb{N}$.

Furthermore, given two anchor nodes x, y, a merge automaton $\mathfrak{A}_{i,j,k}$ running on trace($path(x, y)$) accepts iff the i-th external node of $t(x)$ is merged with the k-th node attached to the j-th nonterminal hyperedge of $t(y)$ (see Lemma 7). Applying Büchi's Theorem [5] yields a corresponding $\mathtt{MSO}_2$ formula for each automaton $\mathfrak{A}_{i,j,k}$. By $\mathfrak{A}_{i,j,k}(x, y, \mathcal{W})$, we denote an $\mathtt{MSO}_2$ formula which is satisfied iff the run of the respective merge automaton on the unique path from x to y in the encoded derivation tree is accepting.

The $\mathtt{MSO}_2$ formula mergeNodes($\mathcal{W}$) then requires for each pair u, v of nodes that $u = v$ iff both represent the same external node of $t(\varepsilon)$ or there exists an anchor node $w \in \mathcal{A}_p, p \in P$, such that $\mathfrak{A}_{i,j,k}(v, w, \mathcal{W})$ as well as $\mathfrak{A}_{i',j,k}(v, w, \mathcal{W})$ holds for some $i, i', k \in \Re(G)$ and $j \in \Bbbk$.

The construction of mergeNodes($\mathcal{W}$) requires several technical auxiliary constructions to identify external and attached nodes. Moreover, some special cases have to be taken into account (the non-external node in question might be free). For lack of space we omit a formal construction. Its correctness is shown by complete induction over the height of encoded derivation trees. □

5 Tree-Like Separation Logic

The close relationship between $\mathtt{SL}$ and HRGs leads to portability of the obtained TLG results to analogous $\mathtt{SL}$ results. As $\mathtt{SL}$ is tailored to reason about heaps, we restrict ourselves to *data structure grammars* (DSG), i.e. HRGs generating heaps only.

Definition 12. *$H \in \mathit{HG}_{\Sigma_N}$ is a* heap configuration *(HC) if $rk_\Sigma(s) = 2$ for all $s \in \Sigma$ and for all $e, e' \in E_H^\Sigma$ with* $\mathrm{lab}(e) = \mathrm{lab}(e')$, $\mathrm{att}(e)(1) \neq \mathrm{att}(e')(1)$. *We denote the set of all HCs over Σ_N by HC_{Σ_N}. $G \in \mathit{HRG}$ is called a DSG if it generates HCs only, i.e. for all $X \in N$, $L(G[X]) \subseteq \mathit{HC}_\Sigma$. The class of all DSGs is denoted by DSG.*

Theorem 5. *For every $G \in \mathit{HRG}$, an HRG G' can be constructed such that $L(G') = L(G) \cap \mathit{HC}_\Sigma$.*

Lemma 2 (Jansen et al. [15]**).** *There exists a translation* $\mathrm{env}[\![.]\!]$: $\mathit{DSG} \to \mathit{SL} \times \mathit{Env}$, *such that G and φ defined over Γ are language-equivalent*[1] *for each $G \in \mathit{DSG}$ with* $\mathrm{env}[\![G]\!] = (\varphi, \Gamma)$. *Conversely, there exists a translation* $\mathrm{hrg}[\![.]\!]$: $\mathit{SL} \times \mathit{Env} \to \mathit{DSG}$ *such that φ and* $\mathrm{hrg}[\![\varphi, \Gamma]\!]$ *are language-equivalent for each $\Gamma \in \mathit{Env}$ and $\varphi \in \mathit{SL}$.*

The largest $\mathtt{SL}$ fragment considered in this paper is $\mathtt{SL}_{\mathtt{tl}}$, which is obtained from applying Lemma 2 to tree-like DSGs.

[1] Intuitively, G and φ are language-equivalent if $L(G)$ equals the set of all graphs corresponding to models of φ.

Definition 13. *An* $\mathtt{SL_{tl}}$ formula *is an SL formula* $\varphi(x_1, ..., x_n)$, $n \geq 1$, *meeting the following conditions:*

- Anchoredness*: All points-to assertions* $y.s \mapsto z$ *occurring in* φ *contain the first parameter* x_1 *of* φ*, either on their left-hand or right-hand side, i.e.* $x_1 = y$ *or* $x_1 = z$*.*
- Connectedness*: The first parameter of every predicate call in* φ *occurs in some points-to assertion of* φ*.*
- Distinctness*:* x_1 *is unequal to the first parameter of every predicate call occurring in* Γ*.*

An SL_{tl} *environment is an SL environment* Γ *where every disjunct of every predicate definition is an* SL_{tl} *formula.*

Theorem 6. *For every* SL_{tl} *formula* φ *defined over an* SL_{tl} *environment* Γ *there exists a language-equivalent tree-like DSG* G *with* $L(G) = L(\text{hrg}[\![\varphi, \Gamma]\!]) \cap HC_\Sigma$ *and vice versa.*

Proof (Sketch). Applying the translation $\text{hrg}[\![\varphi, \Gamma]\!]$ from Lemma 2 to φ and Γ, one observes that every disjunct of every predicate definition is translated into production rules mapping to (basic) tree-like HGs. In particular, the first parameter of every translated predicate definition corresponds to an anchor node in each of these HGs. Thus, by the distinctness condition of $\mathtt{SL_{tl}}$, it is guaranteed that two anchor nodes of the resulting DSG are never merged. Hence, the obtained DSG is tree-like. The converse direction is obtained analogously by applying $\text{env}[\![.]\!]$ to a tree-like DSG. □

As a consequence, our results shown for TLGs presented in Sect. 4 also apply to $\mathtt{SL_{tl}}$. Other fragments of TLGs presented in this paper are transferred to corresponding SL fragments analogously. We omit a formal proof of Theorem 6 for lack of space and provide an example of an $\mathtt{SL_{tl}}$ formula corresponding to the DSG of our running example instead.

Example 9. Consider the $\mathtt{SL_{tl}}$ formula $\varphi := \sigma(x_1, x_2, x_3, x_4)$ defined over an environment Γ consisting of the following predicate definitions.

$$\begin{aligned}\sigma(x_1, x_2, x_3, x_4) := {} & [\exists x_5, x_6, x_7 : x_1.(p, l, r) \mapsto (x_2, x_5, x_6) * \sigma(x_5, x_1, x_3, x_7) \\ & * \sigma(x_6, x_1, x_7, x_4)] \vee [\exists x_5 : x_1.(p, l, r) \mapsto (x_2, x_3, x_5) \\ & * x_3.p \mapsto x_1 * x_5.p \mapsto x_1 * \gamma(x_5, x_3, x_4)] \\ \gamma(x_1, x_2, x_3) := {} & x_2.n \mapsto x_1 * x_1.n \mapsto x_3\end{aligned}$$

Applying the translation $\text{hrg}[\![\varphi, \Gamma]\!]$ yields a tree-like DSG generating the same language as the HRG *TLL* shown in Fig. 1. In particular, the first disjunct of $\sigma(x_1, x_2, x_3, x_4)$ directly corresponds to the production rule in Fig. 1(a), where variable names match with node indices. The other two disjuncts, split across two predicates, translate into basic tree-like HGs and correspond to the second production rule.

We can exploit the additional requirements for DSGs to obtain a simple, yet expressive, *purely syntactical* fragment of TLGs.

Definition 14 (**Δ-DSGs**). *Let $\Delta \subseteq \Sigma$ be a nonempty set of terminal symbols. Then $G = (\Sigma_N, P, S) \in$ DSG is a Δ-DSG if for each $p \in P$, rhs(p) is a tree-like hypergraph and $\perp_p$ has an outgoing edge labelled δ for each $\delta \in \Delta$.*

Example 10. Our example HRG *TLL* shown in Fig. 1 is a $\{p, l, r\}$-DSG.

Lemma 8. *Every Δ-DSG with $\emptyset \neq \Delta \subseteq \Sigma$ is a TLG.*

Proof. If two anchor nodes of a Δ-DSG G are merged, there exists $t \in \mathtt{D}(G)$, $\delta \in \Delta$ and $u \in V_{yield(t)}$ such that u has two outgoing edges labelled with δ, i.e. $G \notin \mathtt{DSG}$. □

A corresponding SL fragment is defined analogously to $\mathtt{SL_{tl}}$ except that the distinctness condition is replaced by a new condition: There exists at least one selector $s \in \Sigma$ such that every disjunct of every predicate definition contains an assertion $x_1.s \mapsto y$, where x_1 is the first paramter of the predicate and y is an arbitrary variable. In terms of expressiveness, we may compare Δ-DSGs to $\mathtt{SL_{btw}}$ [13], which is, to the best of our knowledge, the largest known fragment of SL with a decidable entailment problem.

Theorem 7. *Δ-DSGs are strictly more expressive than $\mathtt{SL_{btw}}$, i.e. for every $\mathtt{SL_{btw}}$ formula there exists a language-equivalent Δ-DSG, but not vice versa.*

Proof (Sketch). Every $\mathtt{SL_{btw}}$ environment over a set of selectors Σ can be normalized such that predicates are connected by their first parameter. Then, applying the translation hrg⟦.⟧ from SL to DSGs (see Lemma 2) yields a language-equivalent Σ-DSG G (see Theorem 5, Lemma 2 and Remark 1).

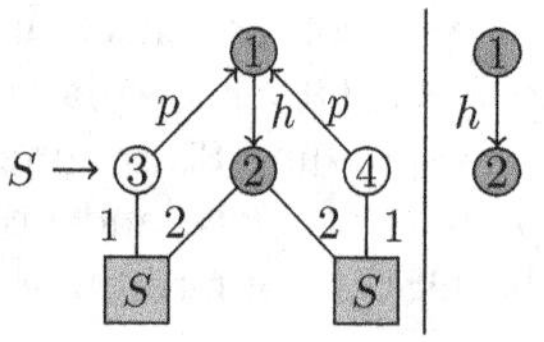

Fig. 4. Tree-like DSG

Conversely, the $\{h\}$-DSG G depicted in Fig. 4 generates reversed binary trees with an additional pointer to the head of another data structure. Obviously, $L(G)$ is $\mathtt{SL_{tl}}$-definable but not $\mathtt{SL_{btw}}$-definable, because the number of allocated locations from which the whole heap is reachable is fixed a priori for every $\mathtt{SL_{btw}}$ formula and a corresponding environment. □

6 Conclusion

SL and DSGs are established formalisms to describe the abstract shape of dynamic data structures. A substantial fragment of SL is known to coincide with the class DSG. However, the entailment problem or, equivalently, the inclusion problem is undecidable.

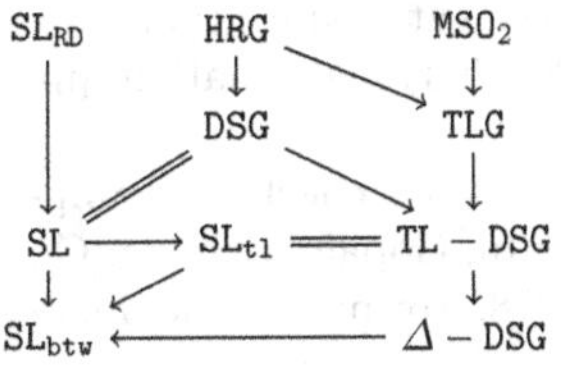

Fig. 5. Fragments of HRG and SL

We introduced the class TLG of tree-like grammars and showed that every TLG is $\mathtt{MSO}_2$-definable. From this, some remarkable properties, like decidability of the inclusion problem and closure under intersection, directly follow from previous work on context-free and recognisable graph languages [7]. Moreover, the close correspondence between HRGs and SL yields several fragments of SL, in particular $\mathtt{SL}_{\mathtt{tl}}$, where an extended entailment problem is decidable. The resulting fragments are more expressive than $\mathtt{SL}_{\mathtt{btw}}$, the largest fragment of SL with a decidable entailment problem known so far.

Figure 5 depicts an overview of the SL and HRG fragments considered in this paper, where an edge from formalism F_1 to formalism F_2 denotes that the class of languages realizable by F_2 is included in the class of languages realizable by F_1. All of these inclusion relations are strict. For completeness, we also added the class $\mathtt{SL}_{\mathtt{RD}}$ of Separation Logic with inductive predicate definitions (cf. [1,13]).

With regard to future research, investigating decision procedures and their tractability for the entailment problem for (fragments of) $\mathtt{SL}_{\mathtt{tl}}$ is of great interest. Although the entailment and inclusion problem is effectively decidable for the fragments presented in this paper, our reliance on Courcelle's theorem does not lead to efficient algorithms. We hope that a combined approach – studying SL as well as HRGs – will lead to further improvements in this area.

References

1. Antonopoulos, T., Gorogiannis, N., Haase, C., Kanovich, M., Ouaknine, J.: Foundations for decision problems in separation logic with general inductive predicates. In: Muscholl, A. (ed.) FOSSACS 2014 (ETAPS). LNCS, vol. 8412, pp. 411–425. Springer, Heidelberg (2014)
2. Berdine, J., Calcagno, C., W.O'Hearn, P.: A decidable fragment of separation logic. In: Lodaya, K., Mahajan, M. (eds.) FSTTCS 2004. LNCS, vol. 3328, pp. 97–109. Springer, Heidelberg (2004)
3. Berdine, J., Cook, B., Ishtiaq, S.: SLAYER: memory safety for systems-level code. In: Gopalakrishnan, G., Qadeer, S. (eds.) CAV 2011. LNCS, vol. 6806, pp. 178–183. Springer, Heidelberg (2011)
4. Brotherston, J., Distefano, D., Petersen, R.L.: Automated cyclic entailment proofs in separation logic. In: Bjørner, N., Sofronie-Stokkermans, V. (eds.) CADE 2011. LNCS, vol. 6803, pp. 131–146. Springer, Heidelberg (2011)
5. Büchi, J.R.: Weak second-order arithmetic and finite automata. Math. Logic Quart. **6**(1–6), 66–92 (1960)
6. Courcelle, B.: The monadic second-order logic of graphs I: Recognizable sets of finite graphs. Inf. Comput. **85**(1), 12–75 (1990)
7. Courcelle, B., Engelfriet, J.: Graph Structure and Monadic Second-Order Logic: A Language-Theoretic Approach, vol. 138. Cambridge University Press, Cambridge (2012)
8. Dodds, M.: From separation logic to hyperedge replacement and back. In: Ehrig, H., Heckel, R., Rozenberg, G., Taentzer, G. (eds.) ICGT 2008. LNCS, vol. 5214. Springer, Heidelberg (2008)

9. Drewes, F., Kreowski, H.J., Habel, A.: Hyperedge replacement graph grammars. In: Handbook of Graph Grammars and Computing by Graph Transformation, pp. 95–162 (1997)
10. Dudka, K., Peringer, P., Vojnar, T.: Predator: a practical tool for checking manipulation of dynamic data structures using separation logic. In: Gopalakrishnan, G., Qadeer, S. (eds.) CAV 2011. LNCS, vol. 6806, pp. 372–378. Springer, Heidelberg (2011)
11. Habel, A.: Hyperedge Replacement: Grammars and Languages. LNCS, vol. 643. Springer, Heidelberg (1992)
12. Heinen, J., Noll, T., Rieger, S.: Juggrnaut: graph grammar abstraction for unbounded heap structures. ENTCS **266**, 93–107 (2010)
13. Iosif, R., Rogalewicz, A., Simacek, J.: The tree width of separation logic with recursive definitions. In: Bonacina, M.P. (ed.) CADE 2013. LNCS, vol. 7898, pp. 21–38. Springer, Heidelberg (2013)
14. Jacobs, B., Smans, J., Philippaerts, P., Vogels, F., Penninckx, W., Piessens, F.: Verifast: a powerful, sound, predictable, fast verifier for C and Java. In: Bobaru, M., Havelund, K., Holzmann, G.J., Joshi, R. (eds.) NFM 2011. LNCS, vol. 6617, pp. 41–55. Springer, Heidelberg (2011)
15. Jansen, C., Göbe, F., Noll, T.: Generating inductive predicates for symbolic execution of pointer-manipulating programs. In: Giese, H., König, B. (eds.) ICGT 2014. LNCS, vol. 8571, pp. 65–80. Springer, Heidelberg (2014)
16. Lee, O., Yang, H., Yi, K.: Automatic verification of pointer programs using grammar-based shape analysis. In: Sagiv, M. (ed.) ESOP 2005. LNCS, vol. 3444, pp. 124–140. Springer, Heidelberg (2005)
17. Matheja, C., Jansen, C., Noll, T.: Tree-like grammars and separation logic. Technical Report 2015–12, RWTH Aachen University (2015)
18. Reynolds, J.C.: Separation logic: A logic for shared mutable data structures. In: LICS, pp. 55–74 (2002)
19. Salomaa, A., Rozenberg, G.: Beyond Words, vol. 3. Springer, Heidelberg (1997)

Static Analysis and Abstract Interpretation

Randomized Resource-Aware Path-Sensitive Static Analysis

Tomasz Dudziak[(✉)]

International Max Planck Research School for Computer Science,
Saarland University, Saarbrücken, Germany
tdudziak@mpi-inf.mpg.de

Abstract. Many interesting properties of programs can only be proved by a path-sensitive analysis. However, path sensitivity may drastically increase analysis time and memory consumption. For existing approaches, the amount of required resources is hard to predict in advance. As a consequence, in a particular analysis run available resources may either be wasted or turn out to be insufficient.

In this paper, we propose a resource-aware approach to path-sensitive analysis that allows to control the maximal amount of required memory. It employs randomly-drawn hash functions to decide which paths to distinguish. Due to randomization, two analysis runs of the same program may yield different results. We show how to use this feature to trade analysis time for space.

Keywords: Static program analysis · Path-sensitive analysis · Abstract interpretation · Software verification · Hashing

1 Introduction

For program analyses formalized in the framework of Abstract Interpretation, it is possible to design generic techniques that augment the precision of any analysis. One such technique is the idea of *path-sensitive* analysis—an analysis that considers program control flow paths in separation. In contrast, classical data-flow analysis usually abstracts from control flow paths and gives invariants about sets of reachable states at each program point.

1.1 Motivating Examples

Figure 1 contains a simple program that computes the sign—either +1 or −1—of an integer variable x whose value is unknown. If analyzed with an interval domain [4, 9.2], the analyzer will discover the following invariants in this function.

- sign $\in [-1, -1]$ after line 4
- sign $\in [1, 1]$ after line 6
- sign $\in [-1, -1] \sqcup [1, 1] = [-1, 1]$ before the assertion in line 8

X. Feng and S. Park (Eds.): APLAS 2015, LNCS 9458, pp. 111–126, 2015.
DOI: 10.1007/978-3-319-26529-2_7

```
int sign;

if (x < 0)
  sign = -1;
else
  sign = 1;

assert(sign != 0);
```

Fig. 1. Program computing the sign of an integer (example from [20])

```
1  int x = 0, y = 0;
2  while(true)
3  {
4    if (x <= 50)
5      y++;
6    else
7      y--;
8    if (y == 0)
9      break;
10   x++;
11 }
12 assert(x == 101);
```

Fig. 2. A complex loop with multiple phases (example from [10])

Due to the precision loss in the join operator ($\sqcup$), the analysis is not able to prove that the assertion always holds. This is also true for more complex abstract domains such as polyhedra [6], octagons [14], or in fact any domain based on convex sets of numbers.

One possible way of dealing with this problem is to abandon the model in which we consider the properties to be associated with program locations and instead express invariants in the context of some control flow history. Such a *path-sensitive* analysis, even when equipped with a convex abstract domain, would be able to prove the assertion in this problem. Path-sensitivity can be considered a generic technique that augments the precision of an analyzer in places where it might be required. Such situations can often be surprising, as demonstrated by the example in Fig. 2.

The loop in this program increments x in every iteration but y can be either incremented or decremented depending on the value of x. For the first 50 loop iterations y will be incremented, then it will be decremented until it drops to zero and the loop exits. Standard numerical analyses are not capable of proving the assertion in line (12) but this particular loop can be handled with techniques dedicated specifically to handling loops with phases, such as lookahead widening [9] or an instance of the guided static analysis framework [10, 4.1].

A static analyzer based on Abstract Interpretation works by discovering properties represented by elements of some *abstract domain*. This approach can only be successful if the loop invariant can be expressed using an element of this domain.

For example, if by a program state we mean the valuation of its variables, the interval analysis will represent program states using intervals. Similarly, polyhedral analysis will use polyhedra.

A good way of getting some insight into what sort of analysis is necessary to solve a particular verification task, is to manually look at the needed properties and invariants. A typical human given the task of formally proving the assertion from Fig. 2 would probably come up with a loop invariant similar to the following.

$$x \geq 0 \wedge y = \begin{cases} x & \text{if} x \leq 50 \\ 102 - x & \text{if} x > 50 \end{cases} \quad (1)$$

Figure 3 shows the set of all (x, y) pairs fulfilling the invariant (1). Any sound analysis will provide a loop invariant including this set of points.

In particular, a polyhedral analysis can do no better than approximate it with a triangle with vertices vertices $(0, 0)$, $(51, 51)$, and $(101, 1)$. Note that, for example, the point $(100, 1)$ is within that triangle but its corresponding state $(x = 100, y = 1)$ is never reached during this program's execution—and if it were reachable, the assertion in line (12) would no longer hold.

Initially, it might not seem like the problem we are facing has anything to do with path sensitivity. To see why this is the case, consider these two separate invariants instead of a single one.

$$I_1 \colon x > 0 \wedge x = y$$
$$I_2 \colon x \geq 0 \wedge y > 0 \wedge x + y = 102$$

I_1 holds if the previous execution of the loop body included statement in line (5). Similarly, I_2 is true if the statement in line (7) was executed.

Both I_1 and I_2 can be represented using common relational domains like octagons [14]. A path-sensitive analyzer that keeps different abstract values depending on the outcome of the `if` condition in line (4) will be able to prove the correctness of this program.

A naive alternative would be to consider each statement in context of the last k control flow points for some fixed parameter k. Given sufficiently large k, this brute-force approach would be able to prove the assertions in both programs from Figs. 1 and 2.

Although such a brute-force technique turned out to perform surprisingly well, it has major drawbacks. With increasing k the number of different traces that an analyzer has to track grows exponentially. Both analysis time and memory consumption become hard to predict and control. Even though we discover occasional path-sensitive properties, we need to pay for that with huge overall slowdown.

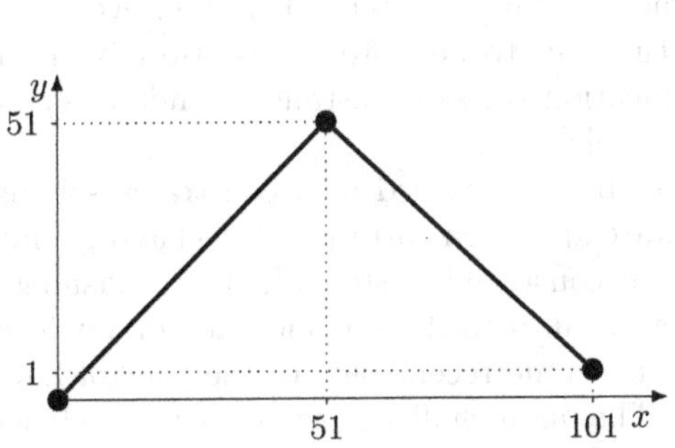

Fig. 3. Set of points representing the loop invariant in the program from Fig. 2

1.2 Trace Hashing

As we have seen in the previous section, the major drawback of the brute-force approach to path sensitivity is its huge and unpredictable memory consumption. The overhead caused by keeping an exponential number of abstract values most of the time is completely in vain, as path-sensitive properties do not occur that frequently. Moreover, the penalty for exceeding the available amount of memory is quite big—it either causes the analyzer to terminate prematurely (and thus all time spent on the analysis is wasted) or causes excessive paging (which increases the analyzer's execution time by several orders of magnitude).

The model checking community encountered similar problems with exponential state explosion. This led to the development of *resource-aware* [23] verification algorithms that take, as an additional input, an integer M. During its execution, the algorithm can keep no more than M states at the same time. An analogous approach for path-sensitive analysis would be to similarly bound the number of simultaneously existing abstract values.

Our approach is based on allocating exactly M buckets, each capable of holding at most one abstract value. A hash function is then used to hash program paths into this space of buckets. The abstract value located in the ith bucket will represent all program states corresponding to a path with hash value i. This can be also viewed as a kind of hash table where conflicts are resolved using the abstract domain's join operator $\sqcup$.

For example, there are exactly 172 paths of length $k = 50$ in the compiled version of the program from Fig. 2. Thus, a naive path-sensitive analysis would need to keep track of 172 abstract values. Our approach would allow a smaller, directly parameterized number of abstract values corresponding to the buckets of the hash table. Thus, the number of abstract values can be decided at runtime depending on available memory. However, we obviously cannot distinguish between all the 172 paths any longer. Depending on how the paths are assigned to hash cells, we may or may not succeed in proving the given assertion.

Our prototype, given an array size of $M = 128$ buckets, will prove the assertion about 30 % of the time. In case of failure, it can be run again—it is expected to succeed within 3-4 trials. It uses less memory than the explicit representation and is, on average, 14 times faster. Therefore, even with multiple retries, this strategy might turn out to be faster. It is also trivially parallelizable with basically no communication between instances (and thus suitable for clustered environments, for example).

Static analysis can be also viewed as a constraint solving problem. In this view, the resource-aware approach corresponds to having a limit M on the number of variables of the constraint system. In trace hashing, the variables are indexed with numbers from 0 to $M - 1$ and each one will in the end describe program states in which some recent part of the control flow history hashes to this variable's index. The main challenge then lies in constructing this system of constraints efficiently—that is, in particular, without enumerating an exponential number of control flow paths.

1.3 Paper Structure and Contributions

The two main contributions of this paper are: the technique of trace partitioning and a hash function that enables an efficient implementation of this technique.

The rest of the paper starts with the formalization of our approach in the abstract interpretation framework (Sect. 2) which provides some insights about the assumptions required for the approach to be sound and efficient. In Sect. 3 we propose a hash function and show how to fulfill all these requirements. Section 4 describes our prototype implementation and some empirical results. We conclude in Sect. 6 by discussing limitations of the technique and future directions.

2 Trace Hashing as Abstract Interpretation

2.1 Basic Definitions and Concrete Semantics

We will work on a graph with a finite set of locations (vertices) Loc and edges Edge $\subseteq$ Loc $\times$ Loc. In an intraprocedural setting, this will be a control flow graph of a procedure. A single entry node entry $\in$ Loc is chosen as the starting point of program execution. We will abstract from the semantics of the underlying language or program representation by assuming some set Env of *program execution environments*. The execution state of the program shall be fully described by a pair from Loc $\times$ Env. Environment is meant to describe the aspects of the state that are not related to the flow of control, such as concrete values of variables or state of the memory store. Each edge $(l, l') \in$ Edge is labeled with a *concrete transfer function* $T_{l,l'}$: Env $\rightarrow$ Env that describes how the environment is transformed when control passes from location l to l'.

Throughout the paper we will use the following sets to describe CFG paths and execution traces.

Definition 1 (paths and traces)

$$\mathrm{Path} = \{l_1 \dots l_i : l_1 = \mathrm{entry} \wedge \forall i \in \{1, \dots, i-1\}.\ (l_i, l_{i+1}) \in \mathrm{Edge}\}$$
$$\mathrm{Trace} = \{(l_1, x_1) \dots (l_i, x_i) \in (\mathrm{Loc} \times \mathrm{Env})^* : (l_1 \dots l_i) \in \mathrm{Path}\}$$

To describe the analysis we will use the framework of Abstract Interpretation [4]. As the concrete domain we will use finite trace semantics [3]. For a program given by Loc and Edge, by its semantics we will understand a set of traces $[\![\mathrm{Loc}, \mathrm{Edge}]\!] \subseteq$ Trace defined to be the least fixed point of the following functional Φ.

Definition 2 (program functional)

$$\begin{aligned}\Phi\colon\ & \mathcal{P}(\mathrm{Trace}) \rightarrow \mathcal{P}(\mathrm{Trace})\\ \Phi(X) = & \ \mathrm{Init}\ \cup \{\omega(l,x)(l',x') \in \mathrm{Trace} :\\ & \qquad\qquad \omega \in \mathrm{Trace} \wedge \omega(l,x) \in X\\ & \qquad\qquad \wedge (l,l') \in \mathrm{Edge} \wedge x' = T_{l,l'}(x)\}\end{aligned}$$

where Init $= \{\mathrm{entry}\} \times$ Env is the set of all possible initial states.

2.2 Assumptions About Underlying Analysis

We will describe our technique as a general-purpose construct that can extend any static analysis expressible in the framework of abstract interpretation. Thus, we assume an arbitrary abstract domain A and an abstraction of environments in the form of a Galois connection $\mathcal{P}(\text{Env}) \underset{\alpha_E}{\overset{\gamma_E}{\leftrightarrows}} A$. Each concrete transfer function $T_{l,l'}$ needs to have a corresponding abstract equivalent $\hat{T}_{l,l'} \colon A \to A$ such that $\hat{T}_{l,l'} \sqsupseteq \alpha_E \circ T_{l,l'} \circ \gamma_E$.

2.3 Path-Sensitive Abstract Domain

Our approach to path sensitivity will employ a hash function $h \colon \text{Path} \to \mathbb{Z}_M$ where $\mathbb{Z}_M = \{0, \ldots, M-1\}$. In this section, we will describe a family of hash functions suitable for use in trace hashing. In the implementation of our technique the function h is drawn at random from this family. Since the main abstract domain is constructed in terms of h, this means that the abstract domain is randomized and the result of the analysis is a random variable.

For the sake of brevity, we will use $[f]$ to denote a function f "lifted" to sets of values.

Definition 3 (lifting functions to sets). *If* $f \colon A \to B$, *then*

$$[f] \colon \mathcal{P}(A) \to \mathcal{P}(B)$$
$$[f](X) = \{f(x) : x \in X\}$$

Figure 4 shows the general setting in terms of Galois connections. Our main abstract domain will be $\mathbb{Z}_M \to A$, connected to the concrete domain with α and γ, as defined below. The environment abstraction α_E is connected to the concrete domain with an implicit abstraction from $\mathcal{P}(\text{Trace})$ to $\mathcal{P}(\text{Env})$ that disregards everything apart from the final environment in each trace. $[h]$, the hash function lifted to sets, is an abstraction of sets of CFG paths obtained from the concrete semantics domain by dropping the environment part of each state.

Definition 4 (abstraction and concretization functions)

$$\alpha(X) = \lambda n.\ \alpha_E(\{x_m : (l_1, x_1)\ldots(l_m, x_m) \in X \wedge h(l_1 \ldots l_m) = n\})$$
$$\gamma(f) = \{(l_1, x_1)\ldots(l_m, x_m) \in \text{Trace} : x_m \in (\gamma_E \circ f \circ h)(l_1 \ldots l_m)\}$$

It is perhaps worth noting that α and γ can be defined as an instance of other, more general, constructions existing in the abstract interpretation literature. The *reduced relative power* [8] of the value abstraction (from $\mathcal{P}(\text{Trace})$ to A) to the control flow abstraction (from $\mathcal{P}(\text{Trace})$ to $\mathcal{P}(\mathbb{Z}_M)$) is isomorphic to our abstract domain $\mathbb{Z}_M \to A$.

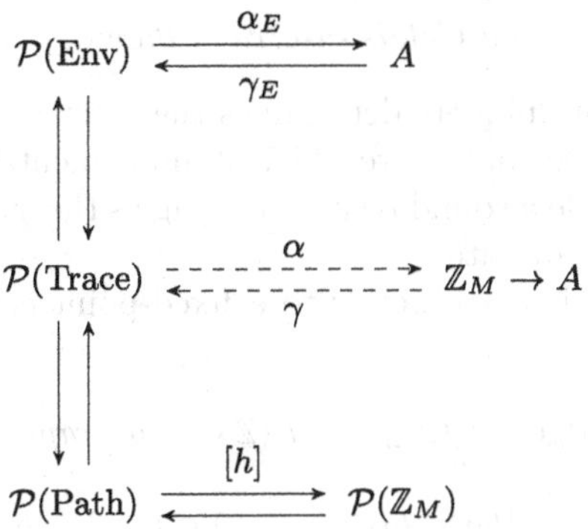

Fig. 4. Abstractions used and defined in the paper

2.4 Hash Update

In contrast to commonly-used hash maps, in our construction the hash function h is not really explicitly evaluated—apart from the initial value $h(\text{entry})$. The hash map will store a value for *every* path from Path, of which there might be an infinite amount. Instead of enumerating this infinite set, we will derive a (finite) system of constraints on values in the buckets of this hash map.

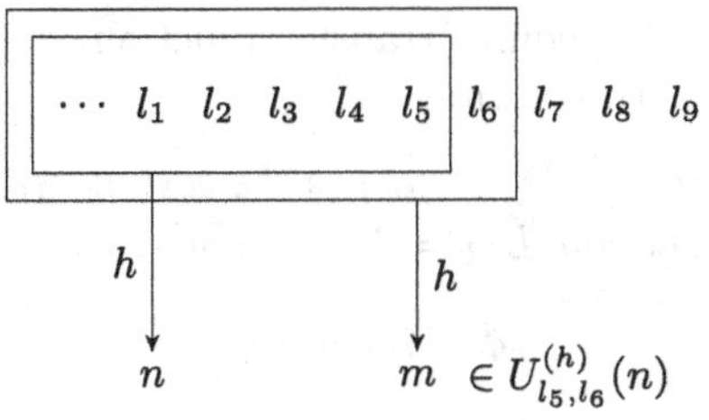

Fig. 5. Concept of a hash function update

Figure 5 shows an example. Knowing the value of $h(\omega l_5) = n$ we would like to compute possible values m of $h(\omega l_5 l_6)$ given $(l_5, l_6) \in \text{Edge}$. We will use $U^{(h)}_{l_5,l_6}(n)$ to describe these possible values.

Definition 5. *For a hash function* $h\colon \text{Path} \to \mathbb{Z}_M$ *by an* ***update function*** *we will understand the following function* U*.*

$$U^{(h)}\colon\ \text{Edge} \to (\mathbb{Z}_M \to \mathcal{P}(\mathbb{Z}_M))$$
$$U^{(h)}_{l,l'}(n) = \{h(l_1 \ldots l_i l l')\colon (l_1 \ldots l_i l l') \in \text{Path} \wedge h(l_1 \ldots l_i l) = n\}$$

Theorem 1. *If* (α_E, γ_E) *is a Galois connection, then* (α, γ) *is a Galois connection.*

Theorem 2. *If (α_E, γ_E) is a Galois insertion, then (α, γ) is a Galois insertion.*

The above definition uniquely determines the most precise update function. However, if a less precise but more efficient implementation is available, the analysis must still provide a sound result—as long as the supplied update returns all results of the precise update.

Formally, our analysis corresponds to a fixed-point computation of the following functional $\hat{\Phi}_{h,\hat{U}}$.

Definition 6. *If $\hat{U}\colon \text{Edge} \to (\mathbb{Z}_M \to \mathcal{P}(\mathbb{Z}_M))$ overapproximates hash update U, i.e.*

$$\forall l_1 \dots l_i l_{i+1} \in \text{Path}.\ h(l_1 \dots l_{i+1}) \in \hat{U}_{l_i,l_{i+1}}(h(l_1 \dots l_i)) \tag{2}$$

then we define

$$\hat{\Phi}_{h,\hat{U}}(f)(n') = \alpha(\text{Init})(n') \sqcup \bigsqcup\{\hat{T}_{l,l'}(f(n)) : n \in \mathbb{Z}_M \wedge (l,l') \in \text{Edge} \wedge n' \in \hat{U}_{l,l'}(n)\}$$

Note that $\alpha(\text{Init})$ is simply

$$\alpha(\text{Init})(n) = \begin{cases} \top & \text{if}\, n = h(\text{entry}) \\ \bot & \text{otherwise} \end{cases} \tag{3}$$

If the abstract transfer and hash update functions are precise enough, then $\hat{\Phi}$ defined here corresponds to the best transformer for our abstract domain. In a more general case, we only require transfer functions to be sound and $\hat{\Phi}$ will overapproximate the best transformer.

Theorem 3. *If $\hat{T}_{l,l'} = (\alpha_E \circ [T_{l,l'}] \circ \gamma_E)$ is the best abstract transformer for our concrete transfer functions and $\hat{U}_{l,l'} = U_{l,l'}$, then*

$$\hat{\Phi} = \alpha \circ \Phi \circ \gamma \tag{4}$$

Theorem 4. *If $\hat{T}_{l,l'} \sqsupseteq (\alpha_E \circ [T_{l,l'}] \circ \gamma_E)$ is a valid transformer for transfer functions and $\hat{U}_{l,l'}(n) \supseteq U_{l,l'}(n)$, then*

$$\hat{\Phi} \sqsupseteq \alpha \circ \Phi \circ \gamma \tag{5}$$

The actual analysis is performed by solving a set of constraints on M variables using a fixpoint iteration algorithm. The abstract transformer from Definition 6 gives rise to the following set of constraints.

$$\begin{aligned} X_{h(\text{entry})} &\sqsupseteq \top \\ X_{n'} &\sqsupseteq \hat{T}_{l,l'}(X_n) \qquad \text{for } (l,l') \in \text{Edge}, n' \in \hat{U}_{l,l'}(n) \end{aligned}$$

The number of constraints, which is directly related to the running time of worklist algorithms [18], depends on the precision of the $\hat{U}_{l,l'}$ operator. The hash function must be chosen carefully such that an efficient and precise implementation of $\hat{U}_{l,l'}$ exists.

3 The Hash Function Family

The update operation that we need to construct the system of constraints can be implemented for a class of hash functions called *recursive hash functions* [2]. The one that we employ here is based on a well-known *polynomial string hash*, originally used in the Karp-Rabin string search algorithm [12]. This function considers a window of the last k locations, based on a parameter k.

Definition 7. *Assuming a prehash function* $g\colon \mathrm{Loc} \to \mathbb{Z}_M$ *the* ***k-sensitive hash function family*** $\mathcal{H}_{k,M}$ *is defined as*

$$\mathcal{H}_{k,M} = \{h_A^{(k)} : A \in \mathbb{Z}_M\} \tag{6}$$

where each individual hash function $h_A^{(k)}\colon \mathrm{Path} \to \mathbb{Z}_M$ *is defined as*

$$h_A^{(k)}(\omega l_1 \ldots l_k) = \left(\sum_{i=1}^{k} g(l_{k-i+1})A^i\right) \bmod M \qquad \text{for any } \omega \in \mathrm{Path}$$

$$h_A^{(k)}(l_1 \ldots l_m) = \left(\sum_{i=1}^{m} g(l_{m-i+1})A^i\right) \bmod M \qquad \text{for } m < k$$

Since we also need to support paths shorter than k, the standard polynomial hash function is applied in reversed order. Conceptually, this is equivalent to having an infinite number of dummy CFG locations before the entry node and assuming a prehash value of 0 on each of these locations.

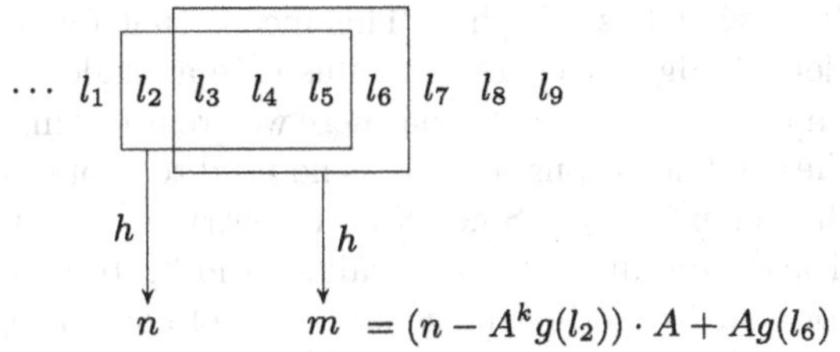

Fig. 6. Updating the k-sensitive hash

Figure 6 demonstrates a useful property of this hash function. The hash value for a path ending in l_6 can be computed from the hash value for the path ending in l_5 as long as $g(l_2)$ is known. This property will be the basis for an update function for this hash and is formalized by Theorems 5 and 6.

Theorem 5. *For any* $(l_1 \ldots l_k l_{k+1}) \in \mathrm{Path}$

$$h_A^{(k)}(l_2 \ldots l_k l_{k+1}) = (h_A^{(k)}(l_1 \ldots l_k) - A^k g(l_1)) \cdot A + A g(l_{k+1}) \tag{7}$$

Theorem 6. *For a path* $(l_1 \dots l_m) \in \text{Path}$ *shorter than* k *elements* $(m < k)$

$$h_A^{(k)}(l_1 \dots l_m l_{m+1}) = A \cdot (h_A^{(k)}(l_1 \dots l_m) + g(l_{m+1})) \tag{8}$$

To compute the precise update $U_{l,l'}$ we need to keep track of k-step reachability information in the control flow graph together with possible hash values for each path connecting its locations. This is done with a precomputed mapping Prev_k defined as follows.

Definition 8. *For fixed parameters* A *and* M *we will consider a function* Prev_k *of type*

$$\text{Prev}_k\colon (\text{Loc} \times \mathbb{Z}_M) \to \mathcal{P}(\text{Loc} \cup \{\_\}) \tag{9}$$

defined by the following rules.

1. $l_s \in \text{Prev}_k(l, n)$ *iff there is a CFG path from* l_s *to* l *of length exactly* k *with hash value* n
2. $\_ \in \text{Prev}_k(l, n)$ *iff there is a path of length smaller than* k *from entry node to* l *with hash value* n

Theorem 7. *Based on* Prev_k, *the update function can be computed as:*

$$U_{l,l'}(n) = \{A \cdot (n + g(l') - A^k g(l_1)) \in \mathbb{Z}_M : n \in \mathbb{Z}_M \wedge l_1 \in \text{Prev}_k(l, n)\} \tag{10}$$

The mapping Prev_k can be constructed iteratively, for increasing k, and without the need to ever enumerate all possible paths of length k. Thus, we can avoid the exponential blowup that is present when trying to represent paths explicitly.

The idea of incremental calculation of Prev_k is depicted in Fig. 7. Since $S \in \text{Prev}_5(B, n)$, we know that there is a path of length 5 from S to B (either $SBCSB$ or $SACSB$) that has a hash n. This means that for paths of length 6 we need to consider all edges from B — in this case a single edge to C — and update n with each new location. Note that here we are updating from hashes on 5 locations to hashes on 6 locations so there is no need to subtract the "starting" location like in Theorems 5 and 6. Since S is the entry node in this control flow graph, Prev_6 will also contain a "blank" value to indicate a path of length 5 from S to B. Algorithm 1 describe the general case of computing Prev_k.

An alternative to explicit calculation of Prev_k would be to employ a *self-annihilating* hash function [2, 2.5] that would no longer require subtracting the term for the location being removed from the hashed path. However, we found that the calculation of Prev_k contributes very little to the overall execution time of the analyzer and existing self-annihilating hash functions have less desirable statistical properties as well as certain limitations (the path length would need to be a power of two, for example).

4 Implementation and Experimental Results

The technique was prototyped as a numerical value analysis on the LLVM intermediate representation [13]. The aim of such analysis is to determine possible

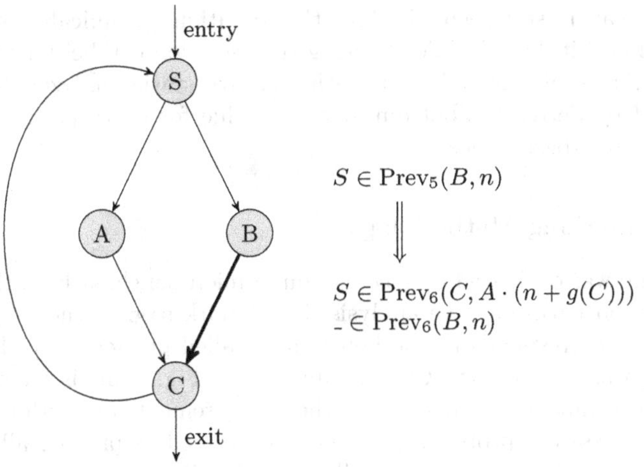

Fig. 7. Idea of incremental computation of Prev_k

Algorithm 1. Constructing Prev_k

```
// initialize Prev as Prev_1
Prev ← fresh empty map (Loc × Z_M) → P(Loc ∪ {_})
for l ∈ Loc do
  Prev[l, A · g(l)] ← {l}
end for

// construct Prev_2, Prev_3, ..., Prev_k
for i = 2, 3, ..., k do
  Prev' ← fresh empty map (Loc × Z_M) → P(Loc ∪ {_})
  for (l, n) ∈ domain(Prev) do
    if l = entry then
      Prev'[l, n] ← Prev'[l, n] ∪ {_}
    end if
    for l' such that (l, l') ∈ Edge do
      n' ← A · (n + g(l'))
      Prev'[l', n'] ← Prev'[l', n'] ∪ Prev[l, n]
    end for
  end for
  Prev ← Prev'
end for
```

values of numerical variables in the program. Multiple abstract domains are supported via the APRON library [11] which includes intervals, polyhedra and octagons.

The analyzer is capable of proving assertions in programs using the standard C `assert` macro, like the ones in Figs. 1 and 2. The C preprocess expands these assertions into an `if` statement checking the condition dynamically and calling a failure function if it doesn't hold. Proving the assertion can be done by proving the unreachability of this call. In a path-sensitive static analyzer, this can be accomplished by deriving a bottom abstract value for every path ending with the corresponding basic block.

4.1 Benchmarking Methodology

The prototype was evaluated on a collection of microbenchmarks gathered from the literature on path-sensitive analysis. Benchmark `sign` is the program from Fig. 1. Figure 2 corresponds to the benchmark called `phased_loop`. Benchmark `loop_noskip` was inspired by a C$^\sharp$ program from [7, Fig. 7] and is shown in Fig. 8.

Since the technique is randomized, the measurement was performed multiple times to assess the probability of success (defined as proving all the assertions contained in the program) as well as the distribution of analysis time and resource usage. The benchmarks were evaluated using the abstract domain of octagons. A standard deterministic path-sensitive analysis that simply considers all paths of length k was used as a baseline for comparison.

The path length parameter k for both the trace hashing approach and baseline was chosen to be 50. For trace hashing, the array size M can be set based on available memory, assuming some fixed heuristic cost per single abstract value. For the benchmarks, its value was $M = 200063$.

4.2 Results

Table 1 shows, for each benchmark, the ratio of runs in which the analyzer have managed to prove the assertion in that benchmark. As we can see, the trace hashing approach succeeds most of the time. The success rate depends on the complexity of the benchmark, with `phased_loop` having the lowest probability of success (71 %).

Table 2 shows observed memory usage and analysis time for trace hashing (TH) and the baseline approach (B) as well as the breakdown of successful and

```
void loop_noskip(int a)
{
  if (a > 0)
  {
    int x = 0;
    for (int i = 0; i < a; i++)
      x = 1;
    assert (x == 1);
  }
}
```

Fig. 8. The `loop_noskip` benchmark

Table 1. Success rates

Benchmark	№ Runs	Success rate
sign	400	100 %
phased_loop	400	71 %
loop_noskip	400	100 %
overall	1200	90 %

Table 2. Analyzer memory consumption and execution time. B=baseline, TH=trace hashing, THS=successful runs of trace hashing, THF=failed runs of trace hashing. Columns p_5, p_{50}, and p_{95} contain, respectively, the 5th, 50th, and 95th percentile.

Benchmark	Variant	№ runs	Memory usage [MiB]			Analysis time [s]		
			p_5	p_{50}	p_{95}	p_5	p_{50}	p_{95}
sign	THS	400	106	106	125	0.10	0.10	0.10
	THF	0	-	-	-	-	-	-
	TH	400	106	106	125	0.10	0.10	0.10
	B	400	178	178	215	0.00	0.00	0.00
phased_loop	THS	284	141	141	160	4.97	4.97	5.29
	THF	116	151	151	1442	5.13	5.13	159.01
	TH	400	142	142	1402	5.01	5.01	147.28
	B	400	292	292	326	13.61	13.61	13.74
loop_noskip	THS	400	97	97	123	0.11	0.11	0.15
	THF	0	-	-	-	-	-	-
	TH	400	97	97	123	0.11	0.11	0.15
	B	400	179	179	216	0.09	0.09	0.09
overall	THS	1084	109	109	151	0.11	0.11	5.16
	THF	116	151	151	1442	5.13	5.13	159.01
	TH	1200	113	113	157	0.11	0.11	5.31
	B	1200	195	195	317	0.09	0.09	13.62

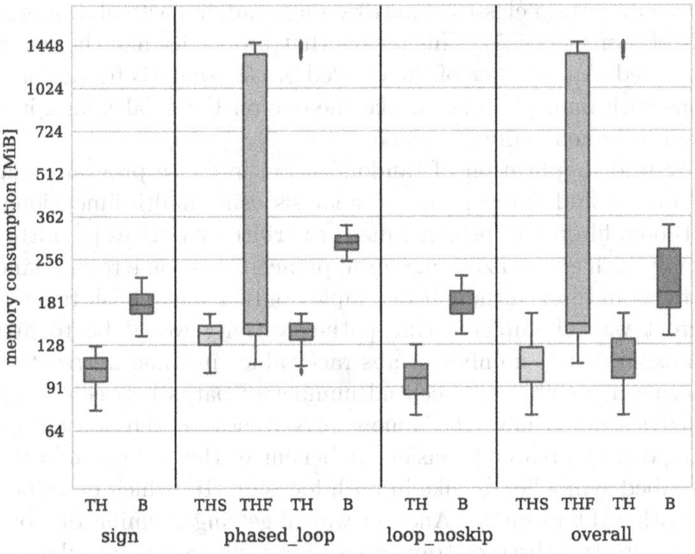

Fig. 9. Distribution of analyzer memory usage

unsuccessful runs of trace hashing. The box-and-whiskers plot in Fig. 9 shows the distribution of memory consumption.

There is a noticeable disparity between successful and unsuccessful runs of trace hashing with successful runs significantly outperforming the baseline approach. In some cases, failure to prove the assertion was combined with very high memory consumption. This is the result of an unfortunate combination of hash collisions which propagate and lead to runaway memory consumption and analysis time.

5 Related Work

Since path-sensitive analysis aims to partially prevent the loss of precision that occurs during joins, one alternative to performing it is to have a distributive domain. *Disjunctive completion* [5, 9.2] of an abstract domain A is the smallest abstract domain containing A that does not lose information in joins. However, even for relatively simple domains like the constant propagation lattice, the disjunctive completion approach becomes essentially equivalent to explicitly representing all possible sets of values.

Trace partitioning [20] provides a very general formalization of path-sensitive abstract domains. The abstraction described in Definition 4 could be also derived as an instance of the trace partitioning framework. The corresponding partitioning $\delta : \mathbb{Z}_M \to \mathcal{P}(\text{Path})$ would be:

$$\delta(n) = \{\boldsymbol{p} \in \text{Path} : h(\boldsymbol{p}) = n\} \tag{11}$$

The practical implementation of the general trace partitioning framework is restricted to only certain classes of partitionings and, in particular, merges traces at the ends of loops [20, 5.1]. This means that properties like the one on Fig. 2 cannot be proved. An instance of the Guided Static Analysis framework [10] can handle loops with multiple phases, like the one on Fig. 2, although it seems to require them to be manually identified.

The only prior application of randomization in static program analysis we have been able to find is the points-to analysis using multi-dimensional Bloom filter [17]. Bloom filters can be generalized to arbitrary lattices [1], although [17] does not apply such generalization. Our approach bears some resemblance to the generalized Bloom filter, although we employ only a single hash function.

A different way of implementing path-sensitivity would be to maintain a small (non-exponential) number of abstract values in some *abstraction points*, while exploring a possibly exponential number of paths between these points. Such an analysis would have the same expressiveness as the non-path-sensitive variant but possibly greater precision. A benefit of this approach is that paths can be described symbolically, like in path focusing [16] which describes control flow paths with SMT formulas. Another way of getting a similar outcome would be to to compute the abstract transformer for a whole acyclic subgraph of the CFG as opposed to individual instructions. There are techniques for automatic derivation of abstract transformers that can be used to that purpose [19,21,22].

6 Extensions and Future Work

Although the work presented in this paper was mostly focused on path-sensitive intraprocedural analysis, there is a potential for applying a similar hashing approach to calling contexts. Context-sensitive interprocedural analysis is often implemented using explicitly-represented call strings of bounded length. In practice, this bound is small—between 1-3—and ideas from this paper can be applied to enable the use of bigger contexts. This can be accomplished by substituting the CFG by a function call graph in the definitions in Sect. 2.

The approach to path-sensitivity presented in this paper is what [20] classifies as a static partitioning—the decision about which parts of the control flow history are distinguished is made prior to the analysis. A dynamic partitioning scheme could be also adapted as a resource-aware algorithm if a hard limit on the number of partitions is imposed. When the number of partitions grows close to the limit, they can be merged according to some heuristic.

The hash function presented in Sect. 3 relies on the parameter k which corresponds to the number of past CFG locations that are taken into account. One could imagine an alternative hash function that does not have this fixed cutoff point but gradually "forgets" history. More formally, for two control flow paths the collision probability of such a hash function would depend on the similarity of these paths—paths sharing a very long common suffix would be mapped into the same hash bucket with high probability. We have briefly experimented with self-designed hash functions having this property but this concept still requires more work.

Acknowledgments. The author would like to thank Jan Reineke and Reinhard Wilhelm of Saarland University for their advice and moral support and all the anonymous reviewers for their constructive comments. This work was partially supported by the Saarbrücken Graduate School of Computer Science which receives funding from the DFG as part of the Excellence Initiative of the German Federal and State Governments.

References

1. Boldi, P., Vigna, S.: Mutable strings in java: design, implementation and lightweight text-search algorithms. Sci. Comput. Program. **54**(1), 3–23 (2005)
2. Cohen, J.D.: Recursive hashing functions for n-grams. ACM Trans. Inf. Syst. **15**(3), 291–320 (1997)
3. Cousot, P.: Constructive design of a hierarchy of semantics of a transition system by abstract interpretation. Theor. Comput. Sci. **277**(1–2), 47–103 (2002)
4. Cousot, P., Cousot, R.: Abstract interpretation: A unified lattice model for static analysis of programs by construction or approximation of fixpoints. In: Proceedings of the 4th ACM SIGACT-SIGPLAN Symposium on Principles of Programming Languages, POPL 1977, pp. 238–252. ACM, New York (1977)
5. Cousot, P., Cousot, R.: Systematic design of program transformation frameworks by abstract interpretation. In: POPL, pp. 178–190 (2002)

6. Cousot, P., Halbwachs, N.: Automatic discovery of linear restraints among variables of a program. In: Conference Record of the Fifth Annual ACM Symposium on Principles of Programming Languages, Tucson, Arizona, USA, pp. 84–96, January 1978. http://doi.acm.org/10.1145/512760.512770
7. Fähndrich, M., Logozzo, F.: Static contract checking with abstract interpretation. In: Beckert, B., Marché, C. (eds.) FoVeOOS 2010. LNCS, vol. 6528, pp. 10–30. Springer, Heidelberg (2011)
8. Giacobazzi, R., Ranzato, F.: The reduced relative power operation on abstract domains. Theor. Comput. Sci. **216**(1–2), 159–211 (1999)
9. Gopan, D., Reps, T.: Lookahead widening. In: Ball, T., Jones, R.B. (eds.) CAV 2006. LNCS, vol. 4144, pp. 452–466. Springer, Heidelberg (2006)
10. Gopan, D., Reps, T.: Guided static analysis. In: Riis Nielson, H., Filé, G. (eds.) SAS 2007. LNCS, vol. 4634, pp. 349–365. Springer, Heidelberg (2007)
11. Jeannet, B., Miné, A.: APRON: a library of numerical abstract domains for static analysis. In: Bouajjani, A., Maler, O. (eds.) CAV 2009. LNCS, vol. 5643, pp. 661–667. Springer, Heidelberg (2009)
12. Karp, R.M., Rabin, M.O.: Efficient randomized pattern-matching algorithms. IBM J. Res. Dev. **31**(2), 249–260 (1987)
13. Lattner, C., Adve, V.: LLVM: A compilation framework for lifelong program analysis & transformation. In: Proceedings of the International Symposium on Code Generation and Optimization: Feedback-directed and Runtime Optimization, CGO 2004, p. 75. IEEE Computer Society, Washington, DC (2004)
14. Miné, A.: The octagon abstract domain. CoRR abs/cs/0703084 (2007). http://arxiv.org/abs/cs/0703084
15. Miné, A., Schmidt, D. (eds.) SAS 2012. LNCS, vol. 7460. Springer, Heidelberg (2012)
16. Monniaux, D., Gonnord, L.: Using bounded model checking to focus fixpoint iterations. In: Yahav, E. (ed.) Static Analysis. LNCS, vol. 6887, pp. 369–385. Springer, Heidelberg (2011)
17. Nasre, R., Rajan, K., Govindarajan, R., Khedker, U.P.: Scalable context-sensitive points-to analysis using multi-dimensional bloom filters. In: Hu, Z. (ed.) APLAS 2009. LNCS, vol. 5904, pp. 47–62. Springer, Heidelberg (2009)
18. Nielson, F., Nielson, H.R., Hankin, C.: Principles of Program Analysis. Springer (2005)
19. Reps, T., Sagiv, M., Yorsh, G.: Symbolic implementation of the best transformer. In: Steffen, B., Levi, G. (eds.) VMCAI 2004. LNCS, vol. 2937, pp. 252–266. Springer, Heidelberg (2004)
20. Rival, X., Mauborgne, L.: The trace partitioning abstract domain. ACM Trans. Program. Lang. Syst. 29(5) (2007). http://doi.acm.org/10.1145/1275497.1275501
21. Thakur, A.V., Elder, M., Reps, T.W.: Bilateral algorithms for symbolic abstraction. In: Miné and Schmidt [15], pp. 111–128
22. Thakur, A.V., Reps, T.W.: A generalization of Stålmarck's method. In: Miné and Schmidt [15], pp. 334–351
23. Tripakis, S.: What is resource-aware verification? (2008). http://www-verimag.imag.fr/~tripakis/papers/what-is.pdf

Quadratic Zonotopes

An Extension of Zonotopes to Quadratic Arithmetics

Assalé Adjé[1,2], Pierre-Loïc Garoche[1,2](✉), and Alexis Werey[1,2]

[1] Onera, the French Aerospace Lab, Toulouse, France
[2] Université de Toulouse, Onera, Toulouse, France
pierre-loic.garoche@onera.fr

Abstract. Affine forms are a common way to represent convex sets of $\mathbb{R}$ using a base of error terms $\epsilon \in [-1, 1]^m$. Quadratic forms are an extension of affine forms enabling the use of quadratic error terms $\epsilon_i \epsilon_j$.

In static analysis, the zonotope domain, a relational abstract domain based on affine forms has been used in a wide range of settings, e.g. set-based simulation for hybrid systems, or floating point analysis, providing relational abstraction of functions with a cost linear in the number of errors terms.

In this paper, we propose a quadratic version of zonotopes. We also present a new algorithm based on semi-definite programming to project a quadratic zonotope, and therefore quadratic forms, to intervals. All presented material has been implemented and applied on representative examples.

Keywords: Affine form · Quadratic form · Affine vectors · Quadratic vectors · Zonotopes · Static analysis

1 Affine Arithmetics and Static Analysis

Context. Affine arithmetics was introduced in the 90 s by Comba and Stolfi [CS93] as an alternative to interval arithmetics, allowing to avoid some pessimistic computation like the cancellation:

$$x - x = [a, b] -_{\mathcal{I}} [a, b] = [a - b, b - a] \neq [0, 0]$$

It relies on a representation of convex subsets of $\mathbb{R}$ keeping dependencies between variables: e.g. $x \in [-1, 1]$ will represented as $0 + 1 * \epsilon_1$ while another variable $y \in [-1, 1]$ will be represented by another ϵ term: $y = 0 + 1 * \epsilon_2$. Therefore $x - x$ will be precisely computed as $\epsilon_1 - \epsilon_1 = 0$ while $x - y$ will result in $\epsilon_1 - \epsilon_2$, i.e. denoting the interval $[-2, 2]$.

In static analysis, affine forms lifted to abstract environments, as vectors of affine forms, are an interesting alternative to costly relational domains. They provide cheap and scalable relational abstractions: their complexity is linear in the

This work has been partially supported by an RTRA/STAE BRIEFCASE project grant, the ANR projects INS-2012-007 CAFEIN, and ASTRID VORACE.

X. Feng and S. Park (Eds.): APLAS 2015, LNCS 9458, pp. 127–145, 2015.
DOI: 10.1007/978-3-319-26529-2_8

number of error terms – the ϵ_i – while most relational abstract domains have a complexity at least cubic. Since their geometric concretization characterizes a zonotope, i.e. a symmetric convex polytope, they are commonly known as zonotopic abstract domains.

However since zonotopes do not have with lattice structure, their use in pure abstract interpretation using a Kleene iteration schema is not common. The definition of an abstract domain based on affine forms requires the definition of an upper bound and lower bound operators since no least upper bound and greatest lower bound exist in general. Choices vary from the computation of a precise minimal upper bound to a coarser upper bound that tries to maintain relationship among variables and error terms. For example, the choices of [GGP09] try to compute such bounds while preserving the error terms of the operands, as much as possible, providing a precise way to approximate a functional.

Related Works. Affine arithmetics and variants of it have been studied in the area of applied mathematics community and global optimization. In global optimization, the objective is to precisely compute the minimum or maximum of a non convex function[1], typically using branch and bound algorithms. In most settings the objective function codomain is $\mathbb{R}$ and interval or affine arithmetics allow to compute such bounds. Bisection, i.e. branch and bound algorithm, improves the precision by considering subcases. The work of [MT06] introduced a quadratic extension of affine forms allowing to express terms in $\epsilon_i\epsilon_j$.

In static analysis, an interval or an affine form is assigned to each variable in an environment. This characterizes the domains of boxes and zonotopes. Zonotopes are mainly used in static analysis to support the formal verification of critical systems performing floating point computation, e.g. aircraft controllers. One can mention a first line of works in which zonotopes are used to precisely over-approximate set of values: 1. hybrid system simulation, for example recent Bouissou *et al.* set-based simulation [BMC12] or earlier Girard work [Gir05]; 2. or floating point error propagation, eg. Goubault *et al.* [Gou13]. In all those cases, a join operator is not necessarily needed nor a partial order check.

A second line of work tries to rely on this representation to perform classic abstract interpretation. Zonotopes are then fitted with a computable partial order and a join, for example in [GGP12,GPV12]. The more complex approach of [GGP09] combines affine abstraction with linear relationship between error terms, and is available in the open-source library APRON [JM09].

As opposed to intervals and their lift to environments as boxes, affine forms and their lift as zonotopes are not well suited for fixed point computation. The absence of a lattice structure imposes the use of an imprecise join which makes the computation of a post fixpoint difficult. In the second line of work mentioned above, either the code analyzed is loop-less or the loops are unrolled a large number of times to improve the precision before computing the join.

[1] When the function or the set of constraints is convex, e.g. conic problems, numerical solvers can be used to efficiently compute a solution. For example, the cases of LP, QP, SOCP, or SDP programming.

Contributions. In the paper, we ambition at using zonotopes based on this quadratic arithmetics. We propose an abstraction based on an extension of zonotopic abstract domains to quadratic arithmetic. Our approach fully handles floating point computations and performs the necessary rounding to obtain a sound result. Furthermore, while keeping the complexity reasonable, i.e. quadratic instead of linear error terms, quadratic forms are best suited to represent non linear computations such as multiplication. Interestingly, the geometric concretization a set of quadratic forms characterizes a non convex, non symmetric subset of $\mathbb{R}^n$, while still being fitted with an algebraic structure.

According to Messine and Touhami, whom defined them in [MT06], quadratic forms were used in reliable computing (global optimization) but never in a comparable setting: $\mathbb{R}^n$ with shared error terms instead of $\mathbb{R}$, set-based interpretation (the concretization) with join and meet operators, and iterative fixpoint computation with the abstract interpretation kleene iteration scheme.

Paper Structure. A first section presents quadratic forms as introduced in [MT06]. Then Sect. 3 presents our extension of zonotopes to quadratic arithmetics. Section 4 motivates our floating point implementation. Section 5 proposes a more precise way to project quadratic zonotopes to intervals using semi-definite programming (SDP) solvers. Finally Sect. 6 addresses our implementation and the evaluation of the approach with respect to existing domains (intervals, affine zonotopes variants).

2 Affine and Quadratic Arithmetics

We formally introduce here some definitions from [MT06] defining quadratic forms. We refer the interested reader to this publication for a wider comparison in a global optimization setting.

Quadratic Forms. A (not so) recent extension of affine arithmetics is quadratic arithmetics [MT06]. It is a comparable representation of values fitted with similar arithmetics operators but quadratic forms also considers products of two errors terms $\epsilon_i \epsilon_j$. A quadratic form is also parametrized by additional error terms used to encode non linear errors: $\epsilon_\pm \in [-1,1], \epsilon_+ \in [0,1]$ and $\epsilon_- \in [-1,0]$. Let us define the set $\mathbf{C}^m \triangleq [-1,1]^m \times [-1,1] \times [0,1] \times [-1,0]$. A quadratic form on m noise symbols is a function q from $\mathbf{C}^m$ to $\mathbb{R}$ defined for all $t = (\epsilon, \epsilon_\pm, \epsilon_+, \epsilon_-) \in \mathbf{C}^m$ by $q(t) = c + b^\intercal \epsilon + \epsilon^\intercal A \epsilon + c_\pm \epsilon_\pm + c_- \epsilon_- + c_+ \epsilon_+$. The A term will generate the quadratic expressions in $\epsilon_i \epsilon_j$. A quadratic form is thus characterized by a 6-tuple $(c, (b)_m, (A)_{m^2}, c_\pm, c_+, c_-) \in \mathbb{R} \times \mathbb{R}^m \times \mathbb{R}^{m \times m} \times \mathbb{R}_+ \times \mathbb{R}_+ \times \mathbb{R}_+$. Without loss of generality, the matrix A can be assumed symmetric. To simplify, we will use the terminology quadratic form for both the function defined on $\mathbf{C}^m$ and the 6-tuple. Let $\mathcal{Q}^m$ denote the set of quadratic forms.

Geometric Interpretation. Let $q \in \mathcal{Q}^m$. Since q is continuous, the image of $\mathbf{C}^m$ by q is a closed bounded interval. In our context, the image of $\mathbf{C}^m$ by q defines its geometric interpretation.

Definition 1 (Concretization of quadratic forms). *The concretization map of a quadratic form $\gamma_{\mathcal{Q}} : \mathcal{Q}^m \to \wp(\mathbb{R})$ is defined by:*

$$\gamma_{\mathcal{Q}}(q) = \{x \in \mathbb{R} \,|\, \exists t \in \mathbf{C}^m \text{ s.t. } x = q(t)\}$$

Remark 1. We can have $\gamma_{\mathcal{Q}}(q) = \gamma_{\mathcal{Q}}(q')$ with $q \neq q'$ e.g. $q = \epsilon_1^2$ and $q' = \epsilon_2^2$. Therefore $\gamma_{\mathcal{Q}}$ could not characterize a antisymmetric relation on $\mathcal{Q}^m$ and therefore not a partial order. We could consider equivalence classes instead to get an order but we would loose the information that q_1 and q_2 are not correlated.

The projection $\mathcal{P}_{\mathcal{Q}} : \mathcal{Q} \to \mathcal{I}$ of q to intervals consists in computing the infimum and the supremum of q over $\mathbf{C}^m$ i.e. the values:

$$\mathbf{b}^q \triangleq \inf\{q(x) \mid x \in \mathbf{C}^m\} \qquad \text{and} \qquad \mathbf{B}^q \triangleq \sup\{q(x) \mid x \in \mathbf{C}^m\} \ . \tag{1}$$

Computing $\mathbf{b}^q$ and $\mathbf{B}^q$ is reduced to solving a non-convex quadratic problem which is NP-hard [Vav90]. The approach described in [MT06] uses simple inequalities to give a safe over-approximation of $\gamma_{\mathcal{Q}}(q)$. The interval provided by this approach is $[\mathbf{b}^q_{MT}, \mathbf{B}^q_{MT}]$ which is defined as follows:

$$\begin{cases} \mathbf{b}^q_{MT} \triangleq c - \sum_{i=1}^{m} |b_i| - \sum_{\substack{i,j=1,\dots,m \\ j\neq i}} |A_{ij}| + \sum_{i=1}^{m} [A_{ii}]^- - c_- - c_\pm \\ \mathbf{B}^q_{MT} \triangleq c + \sum_{i=1}^{m} |b_i| + \sum_{\substack{i,j=1,\dots,m \\ j\neq i}} |A_{ij}| + \sum_{i=1}^{m} [A_{ii}]^+ + c_+ + c_\pm \end{cases} \tag{2}$$

where for all $x \in \mathbb{R}$, $[x]^+ = x$ if $x > 0$ and 0 otherwise and $[x]^- = x$ if $x < 0$ and 0 otherwise.

In practice, we use the interval projection operator $\mathcal{P}^{MT}_{\mathcal{Q}}(q) \triangleq [\mathbf{b}^q_{MT}, \mathbf{B}^q_{MT}]$ instead of $\gamma_{\mathcal{Q}}(q)$, since $\gamma_{\mathcal{Q}}(q) \subseteq \gamma_{\mathcal{I}}\left(\mathcal{P}^{MT}_{\mathcal{Q}}(q)\right)$ where γ_I denotes the concretization of intervals. In Sect. 5, we will present a tighter over-approximation of $\gamma_{\mathcal{Q}}(q)$ using SDP.

We will need a *reverse* map to the concretization map $\gamma_{\mathcal{Q}}$: qn *abstraction map* which associates a quadratic form to an interval. Note that the abstraction map produces a fresh noise symbol.

First, we introduce some notations for intervals. Let $\mathcal{I}$ be the set of closed bounded real intervals i.e. $\{[a,b] \mid a, b \in \mathbb{R}, a \leq b\}$ and $\overline{\mathcal{I}}$ its unbounded extension, i.e. $a \in \mathbb{R} \cup \{-\infty\}, b \in \mathbb{R} \cup \{+\infty\}$. $\forall [a,b] \in \mathcal{I}$, we define two functions $\text{lg}([a,b]) = (b-a)/2$ and $\text{mid}([a,b]) = (b+a)/2$. Let $\sqcup_{\mathcal{I}}$ be the classic join of $\mathcal{I}$ that is $[a,b] \sqcup_{\mathcal{I}} [c,d] \triangleq [\min(a,c), \max(b,d)]$. Let $\sqcap_{\overline{\mathcal{I}}}$ be the classic meet of intervals.

Definition 2 (Abstraction). *The abstraction map $\alpha_{\mathcal{Q}} : \mathcal{I} \to \mathcal{Q}^1$ is defined by:*

$$\alpha_{\mathcal{Q}}([a_1, a_2]) = (c, (b)_1, (0)_1, 0, 0, 0) \textit{ where } c = \text{mid}([a_1, a_2]) \textit{ and } b = \text{lg}([a_1, a_2]).$$

where the vector (b) *of size 1 is associated to a fresh symbol* ϵ. *Ie,* $\alpha_{\mathcal{Q}}([a_1, a_2]) = c + b_1\epsilon$.

Property 1 (Concretization of abstraction). $\gamma_{\mathcal{Q}}(\alpha_{\mathcal{Q}}([a_1, a_2])) \supseteq [a_1, a_2]$.

Arithmetic Operators. Quadratic forms are equipped with arithmetic operators whose complexity is quadratic in the number of error terms. We give here the definitions of the arithmetics operators:

Definition 3 (Arithmetics operator in $\mathcal{Q}$). *Addition, negation, multiplication by scalar are defined by:*

$$
\begin{aligned}
&(c, (b)_m, (A)_{m^2}, c_\pm, c_+, c_-) +_{\mathcal{Q}} (c', (b')_m, (A')_{m^2}, c'_\pm, c'_+, c'_-) = \\
&\qquad (c + c', (b + b')_m, (A + A')_{m^2}, c_\pm + c'_\pm, c_+ + c'_+, c_- + c'_-) \\
&-_{\mathcal{Q}} (c, (b)_m, (A)_{m^2}, c_\pm, c_+, c_-) = (-c, (-b)_m, (-A)_{m^2}, c_\pm, c_-, c_+) \\
&\lambda *_{\mathcal{Q}} (c, (b)_m, (A)_{m^2}, c_\pm, c_+, c_-) = (\lambda c, \lambda(b)_m, \lambda(A)_{m^2}, |\lambda| c_\pm, |\lambda| c_+, |\lambda| c_-)
\end{aligned}
$$

The multiplication is more complex since it introduces additional errors.

$$
\begin{aligned}
&(c, (b)_m, (A)_{m^2}, c_\pm, c_+, c_-) \times_{\mathcal{Q}} (c', (b')_m, (A')_{m^2}, c'_\pm, c'_+, c'_-) = \\
&\begin{cases} (cc', c'(b)_m + c(b')_m, c'(A)_{m^2} + c(A')_{m^2} + (b)_m (b')^\intercal_m, c''_\pm, c''_+, c''_-) \text{ with} \\ c''_x = c''_{x_1} + c''_{x_2} + c''_{x_3} + c''_{x_4}, \forall x \in \{+, -, \pm\} \end{cases}
\end{aligned}
$$

Each c''_{x_i} *accounts for multiplicative errors with more than quadratic degree, obtained in the following four sub terms: (1)* $\epsilon^\intercal A\epsilon \times \epsilon^\intercal A'\epsilon$ *(2)* $b^\intercal\epsilon \times \epsilon^\intercal A'\epsilon$ *and* $b'^\intercal\epsilon \times \epsilon^\intercal A\epsilon$ *(3) multiplication of a matrix element in* A, A' *times an error term in* $\pm, +, -$ *(4) multiplication between error terms or with constant* c, c'. *Their precise definition can be found in [MT06, Sect. 3].*

3 Quadratic Zonotopes: A Zonotopic Extension of Quadratic Forms to Environments

Quadratic vectors are the lift to environments of quadratic forms. They provide a p-dimensional environment in which each dimension/variable is associated to a quadratic form. As for the affine sets used in zonotopic domains [GP09], the different variables share (some) error terms, this characterizes a set of relationships between variables, when varying the values of ϵ within $[-1, 1]^m$. The geometric interpretation of quadratic vectors are non convex non symmetric subsets of $\mathbb{R}^p$. In the current paper, we call them Quadratic Zonotopes to preserve the analogy with affine sets and zonotopes.

Example 1 (quadratic vector). Let us consider the following quadratic vector q:

$$
q = \begin{cases} x = -1 + \epsilon_1 - \epsilon_2 - \epsilon_{1,1} \\ y = 1 + 2\epsilon_2 + \epsilon_{1,2} \end{cases}
$$

Here, ϵ_i denotes the linear dependency with ϵ_i while $\epsilon_{i,j}$ denotes the quadratic one $\epsilon_i \times \epsilon_j$. Note that it corresponds to the following vector of tuples defined over the sequence (ϵ_1, ϵ_2) of error terms:

$$\begin{cases} x = \left(-1, (1,-1)^\intercal, \begin{pmatrix} -1 & 0 \\ 0 & 0 \end{pmatrix}, 0, 0, 0\right) \\ y = \left(1, (0,2)^\intercal, \begin{pmatrix} 0 & 1/2 \\ 1/2 & 0 \end{pmatrix}, 0, 0, 0\right) \end{cases}$$

Figure 1 represents its associated geometric interpretation, a quadratic zonotope.

Let $\mathcal{Z}^p_{\mathcal{Q}^m}$ be the set of quadratic vectors of dimension p: $(q^p) \in \mathcal{Z}^p_{\mathcal{Q}^m} = (c^p, (b)^p_m, (A)^p_{m^2}, c^p_\pm, c^p_+, c^p_-) \in \mathbb{R}^p \times \mathbb{R}^{p\times m} \times \mathbb{R}^{p\times m\times m} \times \mathbb{R}^p_+ \times \mathbb{R}^p_+ \times \mathbb{R}^p_+$.

The Zonotope domain is then a parametric relational abstract domain, parametrized by the vector of m error terms. In practice, its definition mimics a non relational domain based on an abstraction $\mathcal{Z}^p_{\mathcal{Q}^m}$ of $\wp(\mathbb{R}^p)$. Operators are (i) assignment of a variable of the zonotope to a new value defined by an arithmetic expression, using the semantics evaluation of expressions in $\mathcal{Q}$ and the substitution in the quadratic vector; (ii) guard evaluation, i.e. constraint over a zonotope, using the classical combination of forward and backward evaluations of expressions [Min04, Sect. 2.4.4].

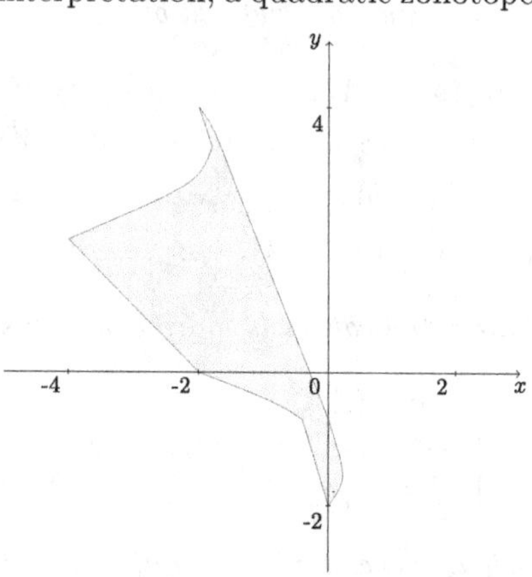

Fig. 1. Zonotopic concretization of the quadratic vector $q \in \mathcal{Z}^p_{\mathcal{Q}^m}$ of Example 1: $\gamma_{\mathcal{Z}_\mathcal{Q}}(q)$

Geometric Interpretation and Box Projection. One can consider the geometric interpretation as the concretization of a quadratic vector to a quadratic zonotope.

From now on, for all $n \in \mathbb{N}$, $[n]$ denotes the set of integers $\{1, \ldots, n\}$.

Definition 4 **(Concretization in $\mathcal{Z}^p_{\mathcal{Q}^m}$).** *The concretization map* $\gamma_{\mathcal{Z}_\mathcal{Q}} : \mathcal{Z}^p_{\mathcal{Q}^m} \mapsto \wp(\mathbb{R}^p)$ *is defined for all* $q = (q_1, \ldots, q_p) \in \mathcal{Z}^p_{\mathcal{Q}^m}$ *by:*

$$\gamma_{\mathcal{Z}_\mathcal{Q}}(q) = \{x \in \mathbb{R}^p \,|\, \exists t \in \mathbf{C}^m \text{ s.t. } \forall k \in [p],\ x_k = q_k(t)\}.$$

Remark 2. Characterizing such subset of $\mathbb{R}^p$ explicitly as a set of constraints is not easy. A classical (affine) zonotope is the image of a polyhedron (hypercube) by an affine map, hence it is a polyhedron and can be represented by a conjunction of affine inequalities. For quadratic vectors a representation in terms of conjunction of quadratic or at most polynomial inequalities is not proven to exist. This makes the concretization of a quadratic set difficult to compute precisely.

To ease the latter interpretation of computed values, we rely on a naive projection to boxes: each quadratic form of the quadratic vector is concretized as an interval using $\mathcal{P}_{\mathcal{Q}} : \mathcal{Q} \to \mathcal{I}$.

Preorder Structure. We equip quadratic vectors with a preorder relying on the geometric inclusion provided by the map $\gamma_{\mathcal{Z}_{\mathcal{Q}}}$.

Definition 5 (Preorder in $\mathcal{Z}^p_{\mathcal{Q}^m}$). *The preorder $\sqsubseteq_{\mathcal{Z}_{\mathcal{Q}}}$ over $\mathcal{Z}^p_{\mathcal{Q}^m}$ is defined by:*

$$x \sqsubseteq_{\mathcal{Z}_{\mathcal{Q}}} y \iff \gamma_{\mathcal{Z}_{\mathcal{Q}}}(x) \subseteq \gamma_{\mathcal{Z}_{\mathcal{Q}}}(y).$$

Remark 3. Since $\gamma_{\mathcal{Z}_{\mathcal{Q}}}$ is not computable, $x \sqsubseteq_{\mathcal{Z}_{\mathcal{Q}}} y$ is not decidable. Note also that, from Remark 1, the binary relation $\sqsubseteq_{\mathcal{Z}_{\mathcal{Q}}}$ cannot be antisymmetric and thus cannot be an order.

Remark 4. The least upper bound of $Z \subseteq \mathcal{Z}^p_{\mathcal{Q}^m}$ i.e. an element z' s.t. $(\forall z \in Z, z \sqsubseteq_{\mathcal{Z}_{\mathcal{Q}}} z' \wedge \forall z'' \in \mathcal{Z}^p_{\mathcal{Q}^m}, \forall z \in Z, z \sqsubseteq_{\mathcal{Z}_{\mathcal{Q}}} z'') \implies z' \sqsubseteq_{\mathcal{Z}_{\mathcal{Q}}} z''$ does not necessarily exists.

Related work [GP09, GGP09, GGP10, GGP12, GPV12] addressed this issue by providing various flavors of join operator computing a safe upper bound or a minimal upper bound. Classical Kleene iteration scheme was adapted[2] to fit this loose framework without (efficient) least upper bound computation. Note that, in general, the aforementioned zonotopic domains do not rely on the geometric interpretation as the concretization to $\wp(\mathbb{R})$.

We now detail a join operator used in our implementation. It is the lifting of the operator proposed in [GP09] to quadratic vectors. The motivation of this operator is to provide an upper bound while minimizing the set of error terms lost in the computation.

First we introduce two functions: a projection function to extract a quadratic form associated to a variable (dimension) in a quadratic vector; and an extension function to introduce new empty error symbols in a quadratic form.

We also need the projection map which selects a specific coordinate of a quadratic vector.

Definition 6 (Projection). *$\forall k \in [p]$, the family of projection maps $\pi_k : \mathcal{Z}^p_{\mathcal{Q}^m} \to \mathcal{Q}^m$ is defined by: $\forall q = (q_1, \ldots, q_p) \in \mathcal{Z}^p_{\mathcal{Q}^m}$, $\pi_k(q) = q_k$.*

When a quadratic form q is defined before a new noise symbol is created, we have to extend q to take into account this fresh noise symbol. We introduce an extension map operator that extend the size of the error term vector considered. Informally, $\text{ext}_{i,j}(q)$ adds i null error terms at the beginning of the error term vector and j at its tail, while keeping the existing symbols in the middle.

[2] Typically this involves a large number of loop unrolling, trying to minimize the number of actual uses of join/meet.

Definition 7 (Extension). *Let $i, j \in \mathbb{N}$. The extension map* $\text{ext}_{i,j} : \mathcal{Q}^m \to \mathcal{Q}^{i+j+m}$ *is defined by:* $\forall q = (c, (b)_m, (A)_{m^2}, c_\pm, c_+, c_-) \in \mathcal{Q}^m, \text{ext}_{i,j}(q) = (c, (b')_{i+j+m}, (A')_{(i+j+m)^2}, c_\pm, c_+, c_-) \in \mathcal{Q}^{i+j+m}$ *where* $b'_k = b_{k-i}$ *if* $i+1 \leq k \leq m+i$ *and 0 otherwise and* $A'_{k,l} = A_{k-i,l-i}$ *if* $i+1 \leq k, l \leq m+i$ *and 0 otherwise.*

Property 2 (Extension properties). Let $i, j \in \mathbb{N}$.

1. Let $(\epsilon, \epsilon_\pm, \epsilon_+, \epsilon_-) \in \mathbf{C}^m$ and $(\epsilon', \epsilon_\pm, \epsilon_+, \epsilon_-) \in \mathbf{C}^{m+i+j}$ s.t. $\forall i+1 \leq k \leq m+i$, $\epsilon'_k = \epsilon_{k-i}$. Then $q(\epsilon', \epsilon_\pm, \epsilon_+, \epsilon_-) = \text{ext}_{i,j}(q)(\epsilon, \epsilon_\pm, \epsilon_+, \epsilon_-)$.
2. For all $q \in \mathcal{Q}^m$, $\mathcal{P}_\mathcal{Q}(q) = \mathcal{P}_\mathcal{Q}(\text{ext}_{i,j}(q))$.

Last, in the following, we rely on the argmin function over reals defined as $\text{argmin}(a, b) = \text{sgn}(a) \min(|a|, |b|)$.

Now, we can give a formal definition of the upper bound of two quadratic vectors.

Definition 8 ($\sqcup_{\mathcal{Z}_\mathcal{Q}}$: Upper bound computation in $\mathcal{Z}^p_{\mathcal{Q}^m}$). *The upper bound* $\sqcup_{\mathcal{Z}_\mathcal{Q}} : \mathcal{Z}^p_{\mathcal{Q}^m} \times \mathcal{Z}^p_{\mathcal{Q}^m} \to \mathcal{Z}^p_{\mathcal{Q}^{m+p}}$ *is defined, for all* $q = (c, b, A, c_\pm, c_+, c_-), q' = (c', b', A', c'_\pm, c'_+, c'_-) \in \mathcal{Z}^p_{\mathcal{Q}^m}$ *by:*

$$q \sqcup_{\mathcal{Z}_\mathcal{Q}} q' = (\text{ext}_{0,p}(q''_k))_{k \in [p]} + q^e \in \mathcal{Z}^p_{\mathcal{Q}^{m+p}}$$

where $q'' = (c'', (b'')^p_m, (A'')^p_{m^2}, c''^p_\pm, c''^p_+, c''^p_-) \in \mathcal{Z}^p_{\mathcal{Q}^m}$ *with, for all* $k \in [p]$*:*

- $(c'')_k = \text{mid}(\mathcal{P}_\mathcal{Q}(\pi_k(q)) \cup_\mathcal{I} \mathcal{P}_\mathcal{Q}(\pi_k(q')))$;
- $\forall t \in \{\pm, +, -\}, c''_{t,k} = \text{argmin}(c_{t,k}, c'_{t,k})$;
- $\forall i \in [m]$, $(b'')_{k,i} = \text{argmin}(b_{k,i}, b'_{k,i})$;
- $\forall i, j \in [m]$, $(A'')_{k,i,j} = \text{argmin}(A_{k,i,j}, A'_{k,i,j})$;

and $\forall k \in [p]$, $q^e_k = \text{ext}_{(m+k-1),(p-k)}(\alpha_\mathcal{Q}(C_k \sqcup_\mathcal{I} C'_k))$ *with* $C_k = \mathcal{P}_\mathcal{Q}(\pi_k(q) - \pi_k(q''))$ *and* $C'_k = \mathcal{P}_\mathcal{Q}(\pi_k(q') - \pi_k(q''))$.

Let us denote the Minkowski sum and the Cartesian product of sets, respectively, by $D_1 \oplus D_2 = \{d_1 + d_2 \mid d_1 \in D_1,\ d_2 \in D_2\}$ and $\prod_i^n D_i = \{(d_1, \ldots, d_n) \mid \forall i \in [n],\ d_i \in D_i\}$. We have the nice characterization of the concretization of the upper bound given by Lemma 1.

Lemma 1. *By construction of q'' and q^e previously defined:*

$$\gamma_{\mathcal{Z}_\mathcal{Q}}\left((\text{ext}_{0,p}(q''_k))_{k \in [p]} + q^e\right) = \gamma_{\mathcal{Z}_\mathcal{Q}}(q'') \oplus \prod_{k=1}^{p} \gamma_{\mathcal{Q}^{m+p}}(q^e_k)$$

Proof. See Appendix.

Now, we state in Theorem 1 that the $\sqcup_{\mathcal{Z}_\mathcal{Q}}$ operator computes an upper bound of its operands with respect to the preorder $\sqsubseteq_{\mathcal{Z}_\mathcal{Q}}$.

Theorem 1 (Soundness of the upper bound operator). *For all* $q, q' \in \mathcal{Z}^p_{\mathcal{Q}^m}$, $q \sqsubseteq_{\mathcal{Z}_\mathcal{Q}} q \sqcup_{\mathcal{Z}_\mathcal{Q}} q'$ *and* $q' \sqsubseteq_{\mathcal{Z}_\mathcal{Q}} q \sqcup_{\mathcal{Z}_\mathcal{Q}} q'$.

Proof. See Appendix.

Example 2. Let Q and Q' be two quadratic vectors:

$$Q = \begin{cases} x = -1 + \epsilon_1 - \epsilon_2 - \epsilon_{1,1} \\ y = 1 + 2\epsilon_2 + \epsilon_{1,2} \end{cases} \quad Q' = \begin{cases} x = -2\epsilon_2 - \epsilon_{1,1} + \epsilon_+ \\ y = 1 + \epsilon_1 + \epsilon_2 + \epsilon_{1,2} \end{cases}$$

The resulted quadratic vector $Q'' = Q \sqcup_{\mathcal{Z}_\mathcal{Q}} Q'$ is

$$Q'' = \begin{cases} x = -\epsilon_2 - \epsilon_{1,1} + 2\epsilon_3 \\ y = 1 + \epsilon_2 + \epsilon_{1,2} + \epsilon_4 \end{cases}$$

Transfer Functions. The two operators **guard** and **assign** over the expressions *RelExpr* and *Expr* are defined like in a non relational abstract domain, as described in [Min04, Sect. 2.4.4]. Each operator relies on the forward semantics of numerical expressions, computed within arithmetics operators in $\mathcal{Q}$: (Fig. 2)

Definition 9 (Semantics of expressions). *Let $\mathcal{V}$ be a finite set of variables. Let $[\![\cdot]\!]_\mathcal{Q}(\mathcal{V} \to \mathcal{Q}) \to \mathcal{Q}$ be the semantics evaluation of an expression in an environment mapping variables to quadratic forms.*

$$\begin{aligned} [\![v]\!]_\mathcal{Q}(Env) &= \pi_k(Env) \text{ where } k \in [p] \text{ is the index of } v \in \mathcal{V} \text{ in } Env \\ [\![e_1 \text{ bop } e_2]\!]_\mathcal{Q}(Env) &= [\![e_1]\!]_\mathcal{Q}(Env) \ \text{bop}_\mathcal{Q}\ [\![e_2]\!]_\mathcal{Q}(Env) \\ [\![\text{uop } e]\!]_\mathcal{Q}(Env) &= \text{uop}_\mathcal{Q}[\![e]\!]_\mathcal{Q}(Env) \end{aligned}$$

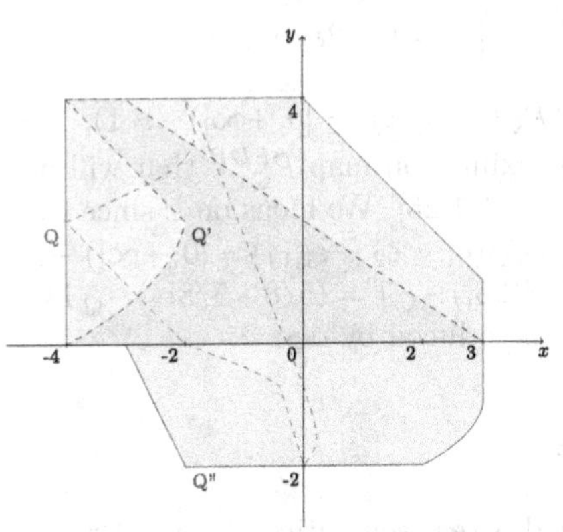

Ex.2: Q (blue), Q' (red), Q" (green)

(a) Upper bound computation

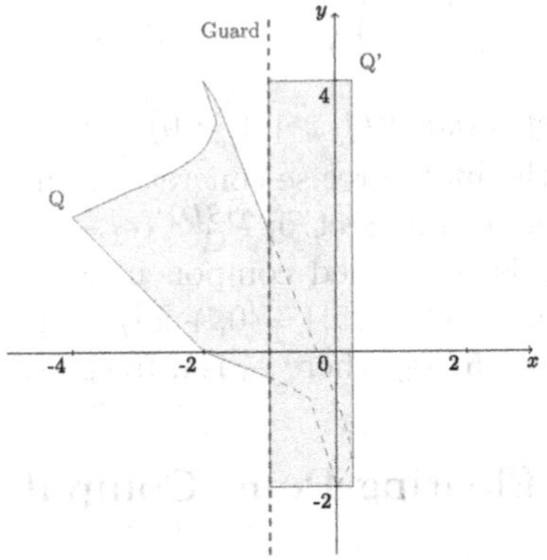

Ex.3: Q (blue), $x + 1 \geqslant 0$ (red), Q' (green)

(b) Guard evaluation

Fig. 2. Zonotopic concretization of operations on Quadratic Zonotopes (Color figure online)

Guards, i.e. tests, are enforced through the classical combination of forward and backward operators. Backward operators are the usual fallback operators, e.g. $[\![x+y]\!]^{\leftarrow} = (x \sqcap_{\mathcal{Q}} ([\![x+y]\!] -_{\mathcal{Q}} y), y \sqcap_{\mathcal{Q}} ([\![x+y]\!] -_{\mathcal{Q}} x))$ where $\sqcap_{\mathcal{Q}}$ denotes the meet of quadratic forms. As for upper bound computation, no best lower bound exists and such meet operator in $\mathcal{Q}$ has to compute a safe but imprecise upper bound of maximal lower bounds.

The meet over $\mathcal{Q}^m$ works as follows: it projects each argument to intervals using $\mathcal{P}_{\mathcal{Q}}$, (i) performs the meet computation and (ii) reinjects the resulting closed bounded interval to $\mathcal{Q}$ using $\alpha_{\mathcal{Q}}$, (iii) introducing it through a fresh noise symbol. For the time being the operator $\mathcal{P}_{\mathcal{Q}}$ used is $\mathcal{P}_{\mathcal{Q}}^{MT}$. It is will later enhanced in Sect. 5.

The meet over $\mathcal{Z}^p_{\mathcal{Q}^m}$ is defined as the lift of $\mathcal{Q}^m$ meet to quadratic vectors. Formally:

Definition 10 ($\sqcap_{\mathcal{Q}}, \sqcap_{\mathcal{Z}_{\mathcal{Q}}}$**: Approximations of maximal lower bounds).** *The meet* $\sqcap_{\mathcal{Q}} : \mathcal{Q}^m \times \mathcal{Q}^m \to \mathcal{Q}^1$ *is defined by:*

$$\forall x, y \in \mathcal{Q}^m, x \sqcap_{\mathcal{Q}} y \triangleq \alpha_{\mathcal{Q}} \left(\mathcal{P}_{\mathcal{Q}}(x) \sqcap_{\mathcal{I}} \mathcal{P}_{\mathcal{Q}}(y) \right).$$

The meet $\sqcap_{\mathcal{Z}_{\mathcal{Q}}} : \mathcal{Z}^p_{\mathcal{Q}^m} \times \mathcal{Z}^p_{\mathcal{Q}^m} \to \mathcal{Z}^p_{\mathcal{Q}^p}$ *is defined, for all* $x, y \in \mathcal{Z}^p_{\mathcal{Q}^m}$ *by* $z = x \sqcap_{\mathcal{Z}_{\mathcal{Q}}} y \in \mathcal{Z}^p_{\mathcal{Q}^p}$ *where:*

$$\forall i \in [p], z_i = \pi_i(x) \sqcap_{\mathcal{Q}} \pi_i(y) \text{ when } \pi_i(x) \neq \pi_i(y), \pi_i(x) \text{ otherwise.}$$

Example 3. Let Q be the following quadratic vector. The meet with the constraint $x + 1 \geq 0$ produces the resulting quadratic vector Q':

$$Q = \begin{cases} x = -1 + \epsilon_1 - \epsilon_2 - \epsilon_{1,1} \\ y = 1 + 2\epsilon_2 + \epsilon_{1,2} \end{cases} \quad Q' = \begin{cases} x = -\frac{3}{8} + \frac{5}{8}\epsilon_3 \\ y = 1 + 2\epsilon_2 + \epsilon_{1,2} \end{cases}$$

Proof. $Guard(Q, x + 1 \geq 0) = Q \sqcap_{\mathcal{Z}_{\mathcal{Q}}} (\alpha_{\mathcal{Q}} (\mathcal{P}_{\mathcal{Q}}(x +_{\mathcal{Q}} 1) \sqcap_{\mathcal{I}} [0, +\infty[) -_{\mathcal{Q}} 1)$. We use the more precise concretization over-approximation map $\mathcal{P}_{\mathcal{Q}}^{SDP}$ that will be introduced in Sect. 5: $\mathcal{P}_{\mathcal{Q}}^{SDP}(\epsilon_1 - \epsilon_2 - \epsilon_{1,1}) = [-3, 1.25]$. We focus on x since the meet is performed component-wise and $\alpha_{\mathcal{Q}} (\mathcal{P}_{\mathcal{Q}}(\epsilon_1 - \epsilon_2 - \epsilon_{1,1}) \sqcap_{\mathcal{I}} [0, +\infty[) -_{\mathcal{Q}} 1 = \alpha_{\mathcal{Q}} ([-3, 1.25] \sqcap_{\mathcal{I}} [0, +\infty[) -_{\mathcal{Q}} 1 = \alpha_{\mathcal{Q}} ([0, 1.25]) -_{\mathcal{Q}} 1 = (5/8 + 5/8\epsilon_3) -_{\mathcal{Q}} 1 = -3/8 + 5/8\epsilon_3$ where ϵ_3 is a fresh error term introduced by $\alpha_{\mathcal{Q}}$.

4 Floating Point Computations

All the operators presentation above assumed a real semantics. As usual when analyzing programs, the domain has to be adapted to deal with floating point arithmetics.

We recall that our use of quadratic zonotopes is to precisely over-approximate reachable reals values. We relied on the approach proposed by Stolfi and De Figueiro [SDF97], creating a new error term for each operation. Other approaches such as generalized intervals [Han75] are typically used in Fluctuat [Gou13].

Their definition in the quadratic setting is given in [MT06]. However, according to [SDF97] the approach with error terms instead of interval arithmetics is more precise but can generate a significative number of error terms.

In the specific case of quadratic forms, the term in $\epsilon_\pm$ is used to accumulate floating point errors: the number of error terms does not increase due to floating point computation. The generalization to zonotopes is straightforward since numerical operations are evaluated at form level.

We illustrate here these principles on the addition and external multiplication operators.

To summarize, all arithmetic operation are provided in Messine and Touhami [MT06]. Our implementation with floating point semantics gathers the additive and multiplicative errors of each operator and accumulate them in $\epsilon_\pm$ terms, following [SDF97] methodology.

Addition. According to Knuth [Knu97, Sect. 4.2.2], the exact computation of $u+v$ with floating point arithmetics is $u+v+e$ where $e = (u - ((u+v) - v)) + (v - ((u+v) - u))$ with all operations performed in floating point arithmetics. Let $e^+(u,v)$ be such additive error e.

We consider the addition of two quadratic forms $x = (x_0, (x_i), (x_{ij}), x_\pm, x_+, x_-)$ and $y = (y_0, (y_i), (y_{ij}), y_\pm, y_+, y_-)$. The addition of x and y is modified to consider these generated errors:

$$(x_0, (x_i), (x_{ij}), x_\pm, x_+, x_-) +_\mathcal{Q} (y_0, (y_i), (y_{ij}), y_\pm, y_+, y_-) =$$
$$(x_0 + y_0, (x_i + y_i), (x_{ij} + y_{ij}), x_\pm + y_\pm + r\_err, x_+ + y_+, x_- + y_-)$$

where

- $r\_err = max(|rup(err)|, |-rup(-err)|)$
- rup denotes the rounding up;
- $err = \sum_{i,j=1}^{n} e^+(x_{ij}, y_{ij}) + \sum_{i=0}^{n} e^+(x_i, y_i) + e^+(x_\pm, y_\pm) + e^+(x_+, y_+) + e^+(x_-, y_-)$.

External Multiplication. Similarly, the algorithm of Dekker and Veltkamp characterizes the multiplicative error obtained when computing $u \times v$. It relies on a constant C depending on the precision used. For single precision floats, $C = 2^{27} + 1$. We denote by $e^\times(u,v)$ such multiplicative error. A more complete presentation is given by Dekker [Dek71].

The operator $*_\mathcal{Q}$ is modified to account such multiplicative errors:

$$\lambda *_\mathcal{Q} (x_0, (x_i), (x_{ij}), x_\pm, x_+, x_-) = (\lambda x_0, \lambda(x_i), \lambda(x_{ij}), |\lambda| x_\pm + r\_err, |\lambda| x_+, |\lambda| x_-)$$

where

- $r\_err = max(|rup(err)|, |-rup(-err)|)$.
- $err = \sum_{i=1}^{n} e^\times(\lambda, x_i) + \sum_{i,j=1}^{n} e^\times(\lambda, x_{ij}) + e^\times(\lambda, x_\pm) + e^\times(\lambda, x_-) + e^\times(\lambda, x_+)$.

All other operators behave similarly: each operation computing an addition or a product generates an additive and a multiplicative error, respectively, accumulated in the $x_\pm$ term.

5 Improving Concretization Using SDP

In this part, we propose a method based on semi-definite programming to compute an over-approximation of the interval concretization of a quadratic form. This method provides tighter bounds than $\mathbf{b}^q_{MT}$ and $\mathbf{B}^q_{MT}$ defined at Eq. (2).

Let us consider a quadratic form $q = (c^q, (b^q)_m, (A^q)_m, c^q_{\pm}, c^q_{+}, c^q_{-}) \in \mathcal{Q}^m$. Recall that $\mathbf{C}^m = [-1,1]^m \times [-1,1] \times [0,1] \times [-1,0] \subseteq \mathbb{R}^{m+3}$, and that the concretization of q is the interval defined $[\mathbf{b}^q, \mathbf{B}^q]$ where $\mathbf{b}^q = \inf\{q(x) \mid x \in \mathbf{C}^m\}$ and $\mathbf{B}^q = \sup\{q(x) \mid x \in \mathbf{C}^m\}$.

In general, a standard quadratic form r from $\mathbb{R}^{m+3}$ to $\mathbb{R}$ is defined by $x \mapsto r(x) = x^\intercal A^r x + b^{r\intercal} x + c^r$ with a $(m+3)\times(m+3)$ symmetric matrix A^r, a vector of $\mathbb{R}^{m+3}$, b^r and a scalar c^r. We can cast q into a standard quadratic form r_q, leading to $r_q(x) = q(x)$ for all $x \in \mathbf{C}^m$. Indeed, it suffices to take the following data:

$$A^{r_q} = \begin{pmatrix} \tilde{A} & 0_{m\times 3} \\ 0_{3\times(m+3)} & \end{pmatrix} \text{ with } \tilde{A} = \frac{A^q + A^{q\intercal}}{2},\ b^{r_q\intercal} = (b^{q\intercal}, c^q_{\pm}, c^q_{+}, c^q_{-}) \text{ and } c^{r_q} = c^q$$

Let tr be the trace function that computes the sum of the elements on the diagonal of a matrix and let $x \in \mathbb{R}^{m+3}$. Then r_q can be rewritten as

$$r_q(x) = \operatorname{tr}(\mathbf{M}^{r_q} X) \text{ where } \mathbf{M}^{r_q} = \begin{pmatrix} A^{r_q} & \frac{1}{2} b^{r_q} \\ \frac{1}{2} b^{r_q\intercal} & c^{r_q} \end{pmatrix} \text{ and } X = \begin{pmatrix} x \\ 1 \end{pmatrix} \begin{pmatrix} x \\ 1 \end{pmatrix}^\intercal.$$

In order to manipulate only matrices, we have to translate the constraints on the vector x into constraints on the matrix X. Let us introduce the set $\mathcal{C}^m$ of $(m+4)\times(m+4)$ symmetric matrices Y such that:

$$\forall i,j \in [m+3],\ i<j,\ Y_{i,j} \in [-1,1] \quad \text{(3a)}$$
$$\forall i \in [m+1],\ Y_{i,(m+4)} \in [-1,1] \quad \text{(3b)}$$
$$\forall i \in [m+3],\ Y_{i,i} \in [0,1] \quad \text{(3c)}$$
$$Y_{(m+2),(m+3)} \in [-1,0] \quad \text{(3d)}$$
$$Y_{(m+2),(m+4)} \in [0,1] \quad \text{(3e)}$$
$$Y_{(m+3),(m+4)} \in [-1,0] \quad \text{(3f)}$$
$$Y_{(m+4),(m+4)} = 1 \quad \text{(3g)}$$

Note by symmetry of Y, for all $i,j \in [m+3]$, $i<j$, $Y_{j,i} \in [-1,1]$; for all $i \in [m+1]$, $Y_{(m+4),i} \in [-1,1]$; $Y_{(m+4),(m+3)} \in [-1,0]$ and $Y_{(m+4),(m+2)} \in [0,1]$. Thus Y can be rewritten as follows:

$$Y = [-1,1] \cap \begin{pmatrix} + & & & & \\ & \ddots & & \top & \\ & & + & - & + \\ & \top & - & + & - \\ & & + & - & \{1\} \end{pmatrix} \begin{matrix} \\ \\ m+2 \\ m+3 \\ m+4 \end{matrix}$$
$$\qquad\qquad\qquad\qquad m+2 \quad m+3 \quad m+4$$

where $\cap$ denotes interval meet: each element of the right handside matrix is intersected with $[-1,1]$.

Let $\mathbb{S}_n^+$ be the set of semi-definite positive matrices of size $n \times n$ i.e. the $n \times n$ symmetric matrices M such that for all $y \in \mathbb{R}^n$, $y^\intercal M y \geq 0$. Recall that the rank of a matrix M is the number of linearly independent rows (or columns), which we denote by $\mathrm{rk}(M)$.

Lemma 2 (Constraint translation). *The following statement holds:*

$$\{X \in \mathbb{S}_{m+4}^+ \mid \mathrm{rk}(X) = 1,\ X \in \mathcal{C}^m\} = \left\{X \in \mathbb{S}_{m+4}^+ \mid \exists x \in \mathbf{C}^m \text{ s.t. } X = \begin{pmatrix} x \\ 1 \end{pmatrix} \begin{pmatrix} x \\ 1 \end{pmatrix}^\intercal \right\}.$$

Proof. See Appendix.

Lemma 2 allows to conclude that optimizing r_q over $\mathbf{C}^m$ and optimizing $X \mapsto \mathrm{tr}(\mathbf{M}^{r_q} X)$ over $\{X \in \mathbb{S}_{m+4}^+ \mid \mathrm{rk}(x) = 1,\ X \in \mathcal{C}^m\}$ is the same. However, the rank one constraint on X leads to a non-convex problem which makes it difficult to solve. A natural and a commonly used relaxation is to remove the rank constraint to get a linear problem over semi-definite positive matrices. This discussion is formulated as Proposition 1.

Proposition 1. *The interval bounds of the concretization of q can be computed from the two following non-convex semi-definite programs:*

$$\mathbf{b}^q = \inf \quad tr(\mathbf{M}^{r_q} X) \quad \text{s.t.} \begin{cases} X \in \mathcal{C}^m \\ X \in \mathbb{S}_{m+4}^+ \\ \mathrm{rk}(X) = 1 \end{cases} \quad \textit{and} \quad \mathbf{B}^q = \sup \quad tr(\mathbf{M}^{r_q} X) \quad \text{s.t.} \begin{cases} X \in \mathcal{C}^m \\ X \in \mathbb{S}_{m+4}^+ \\ \mathrm{rk}(X) = 1 \end{cases}$$

By removing the rank constraint the problem is relaxed into a convex problem. Its resolution becomes feasible with SDP solvers but leads to more conservative bounds.

$$\mathbf{b}_{SDP}^q = \inf \quad tr(\mathbf{M}^{r_q} X) \leq \mathbf{b}^q \quad \text{s.t.} \begin{cases} X \in \mathcal{C}^m \\ X \in \mathbb{S}_{m+4}^+ \end{cases} \quad \textit{and} \quad \mathbf{B}_{SDP}^q = \sup \quad tr(\mathbf{M}^{r_q} X) \geq \mathbf{B}^q \quad \text{s.t.} \begin{cases} X \in \mathcal{C}^m \\ X \in \mathbb{S}_{m+4}^+ \end{cases}$$

Finally, the interval bounds of the concretization are safely approximated by using $\mathbf{b}_{SDP}^q$ and $\mathbf{B}_{SDP}^q$ and we write $\mathcal{P}_{\mathcal{Q}}^{SDP}(q) \triangleq [\mathbf{b}_{SDP}^q, \mathbf{B}_{SDP}^q]$. Moreover, those bounds improve the ones provides by [MT06].

Theorem 2 (Bounds improvements). *Let $q \in \mathcal{Q}^m$. The following inequalities hold:*

$$\gamma_{\mathcal{Q}}(q) \subseteq \gamma_{\mathcal{I}} \circ \mathcal{P}_{\mathcal{Q}}^{SDP}(q) \subseteq \gamma_{\mathcal{I}} \circ \mathcal{P}_{\mathcal{Q}}^{MT}(q)$$

where $\gamma_{\mathcal{I}} : \mathcal{I} \mapsto \wp(\mathbb{R}^n)$ denotes the interval concretization.
i.e. $\quad \mathbf{b}_{MT}^q \leq \mathbf{b}_{SDP}^q \leq \mathbf{b}^q \ \wedge\ \mathbf{B}^q \leq \mathbf{B}_{SDP}^q \leq \mathbf{B}_{MT}^q$

Proof. See Appendix.

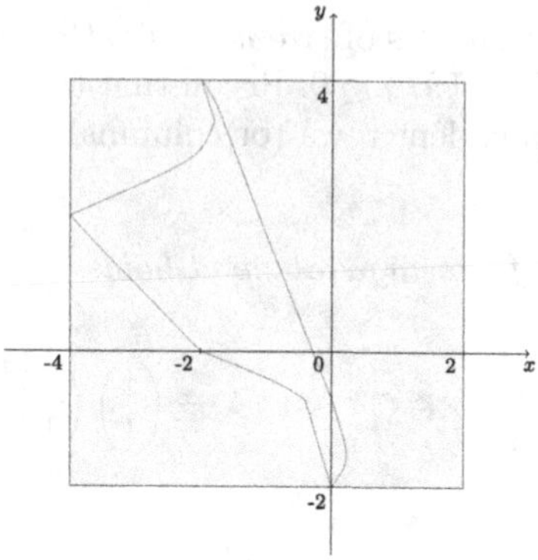

(a) using [MT06]

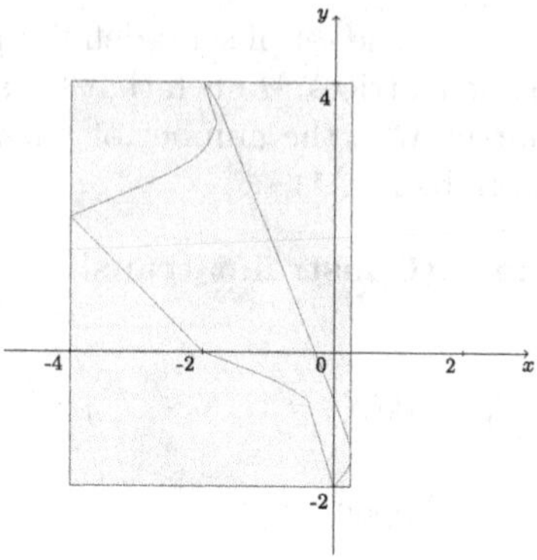

(b) relying on SDP programming

Fig. 3. Projection to intervals

In term of complexity, SDP problems can be solved in polynomial time to an arbitrary prescribed precision by the ellipsoid method [GLS88]. More precisely, let $\alpha > 0$ be a given rational, suppose that the input data of a semi-definite program are rational and suppose that an integer N is known, such that the feasible set lies inside the ball of the radius N around zero. Then a feasible solution – the value of which is at most at a distance α from the optimal value – can be found in a time that is polynomial in the number of bits of the input data and in $-log(\alpha)$. This latter feasible solution can be found in polynomial time by interior point methods [NN94] if a strictly feasible solution is available. The advantage of interior methods is that they are very efficient in practice. We refer the reader to [RP96] for more information.

Corollary 1. *The reals* $\mathbf{b}^q_{SDP}$ *and* $\mathbf{B}^q_{SDP}$ *can be computed in polynomial time.*

The Fig. 3 illustrates such concretization on the quadratic zonotopes defined in Example 1.

In terms of related works, the use of semidefinite programming to compute interval concretisation of nonlinear operation for affine forms already appeared in [Gho11, Proposition 5.1.2]. This approach appears to be the dual version of the semidefinite programs that we presented in this paper.

6 Experimentation

All presented materials has been implemented in an open-source tool written in OCaml[3]. This tool is used for teaching purpose and only consider simple imperative programs without function calls. It implements interval analysis, affine and quadratic zonotopes. The reduced concretization we proposed is integrated through the use of the CSDP or Mosek SDP solvers. Due to the increase cost in

[3] Tool and experiments available at https://cavale.enseeiht.fr/QuadZonotopes/.

terms of computation time, various options enable its use on each call to interval concretization, on some specific calls or disable it.

The quadratic zonotope domain has been evaluated on examples bundled in APRON library, or Fluctuat distribution, as well as simple iterative schemes. We present here the results obtained on an arctan function, the example of [CS93] and the Householder function analyzed in [GGP09].

Let us first consider the arctan function defined in Fig. 4 and the analysis results in Table 1. We can see the dramatic increase in precision obtained with our quadratic extension. This is particularly visible on this example which relies widely on multiplication and division. As a reference the maximal theoretical value for $x \in [-1, 1]$ is $\pi/4$. Intervals or Affine Zonotopes compute a value 144 % bigger while Quadratic Zonotopes obtain a 20 % imprecision.

```
if (x > 1.) {
  y = 1.5708 - 1/x*(1-C1/x^2+C2/x^4+C3/x^6+
        C4/x^8+C5/x^10+C6/x^12+C7/x^14+C8/x^16)
}
if (x < 1.) {
  y = -1.5708 - 1/x*(1-C1/x^2+C2/x^4+C3/x^6+
        C4/x^8+C5/x^10+C6/x^12+C7/x^14+C8/x^16)
}
else {
  y = x*(1-C1*x^2+C2*x^4+C3*x^6+
        C4*x^8+C5*x^10+C6*x^12+C7*x^14+C8*x^16)
}
```

with the constants defined as:

C1	0.0028662257
C2	−0.0161657367
C3	0.0429096138
C4	−0.0752896400
C5	0.1065626393
C6	−0.1420889944
C7	0.1999355085
C8	−0.3333314528

Fig. 4. Arctan program

Table 1. Arctan program analysis results

	$x \in [-1, 1]$	$x \in [-10, 10]$
Domain	Bounds	Bounds
Interval	[-1.919149, 1.919149]	[-1.919149, 1.919149]
Affine Zonotopes	[-1.919149, 1.919149]	[-2.364846, 2.364846]
Quadratic Zonotopes	[-1.002866, 1.002866]	[-1.597501, 1.591769]

In [CS93], Stolfi *et al.* considered the function $\sqrt{(x^2 + x - 1/2)}/\sqrt{(x^2 + 1/2)}$ and the precision obtained using affine arithmetics while evaluating the function on a partition of the input range as sub-intervals. This is the classical bisection or branch-and-bound approach to improve precision. Figure 5a compares the obtained results for subdivision from 1 to 14 partitions. The global error represents the width of the interval obtained and is represented in a log scale. Higher partition divisions (eg. 500) converge in terms of precision and are not shown on the picture. The Table 2 presents the computed values.

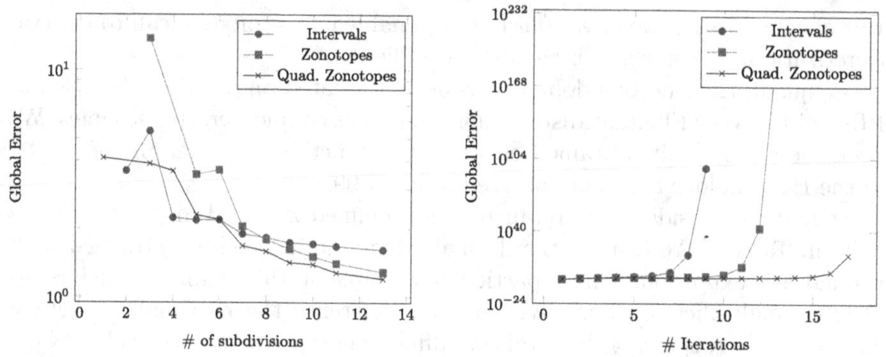

(a) Stolfi [CS93] example evaluated on partitioned input range

(b) Householder precision wrt. number of unrolling.

Fig. 5. Relative precision obtained with different analysis in the experiments (log scale for errors)

Table 2. Stolfi example [CS93] and Householder numerical results

	Intervals		Affine Z.		Quad. Z.	
	val	*ms*	*val*	*ms*	*val*	*ms*
stolfi1	$[0., \infty]$	6	$[-\infty, +\infty]$	0	$[-0.85, 3.25]$	7
stolfi2	$[0., 3.60]$	10	$[-\infty, +\infty]$	7	$[-\infty, +\infty]$	4
stolfi3	$[0., 5.38]$	4	$[-2.98, 10.81]$	5	$[-0.62, 3.24]$	5
stolfi4	$[0., 2.23]$	10	$[-\infty, +\infty]$	6	$[-0.33, 3.26]$	11
stolfi5	$[0., 2.18]$	9	$[-0.42, 3.03]$	3	$[0.08, 2.38]$	11
stolfi6	$[0., 2.18]$	7	$[-0.71, 2.91]$	5	$[0.11, 2.30]$	6
stolfi7	$[0., 1.89]$	7	$[0.19, 2.23]$	3	$[0.29, 1.97]$	10
stolfi30	$[0.35, 1.43]$	15	$[0.48, 1.44]$	20	$[0.48, 1.43]$	18
stolfi40	$[0.40, 1.40]$	15	$[0.49, 1.40]$	20	$[0.50, 1.40]$	18
stolfi50	$[0.43, 1.38]$	19	$[0.50, 1.38]$	34	$[0.50, 1.38]$	21
stolfi55	$[0.44, 1.37]$	24	$[0.51, 1.37]$	33	$[0.51, 1.37]$	35
stolfi100	$[0.48, 1.34]$	29	$[0.52, 1.34]$	80	$[0.52, 1.34]$	66
stolfi200	$[0.51, 1.32]$	48	$[0.53, 1.32]$	337	$[0.53, 1.32]$	269
stolfi300	$[0.52, 1.31]$	73	$[0.53, 1.31]$	916	$[0.53, 1.31]$	554
stolfi400	$[0.52, 1.31]$	91	$[0.53, 1.31]$	1746	$[0.53, 1.31]$	1086
householder #3	$[0.21, 0.24]$	3	$[0.21, 0.24]$	9	$[0.21, 0.24]$	4
householder #4	$[0.17, 0.29]$	0	$[0.22, 0.25]$	7	$[0.22, 0.24]$	8
householder #5	$[0.03, 0.42]$	3	$[0.22, 0.25]$	8	$[0.22, 0.24]$	10
householder #6	$[-0.90, 1.66]$	3	$[0.22, 0.25]$	19	$[0.22, 0.24]$	14
householder #7	$[-1117.82, 1899.48]$	4	$[0.22, 0.25]$	27	$[0.22, 0.24]$	11
householder #8	$[-2.18e^{+18}, 3.70e^{+18}]$	5	$[0.22, 0.25]$	29	$[0.22, 0.24]$	11

Best method is highlighted. Results are shown with two decimal digit precision.

Quadratic zonotopes shows here to be a good alternative to interval or affine zonotopes abstractions. Both in terms of precision and runtime. Interestingly for this example the expected additional cost due to the quadratic error terms is not exhibited. This may be explained by a more direct expression of quadratic terms within our quadratic zonotopes.

Another example analyzed is the Householder function; this dynamical system converges towards $1/\sqrt{A}$:

$$\begin{aligned} x_0 &= 2^{-4} \\ x_{n+1} &= x_n(1 + \tfrac{1}{2}(1 - Ax_n^2) + \tfrac{3}{8}(1 - Ax_n^2)^2) \end{aligned}$$

In our experiments the algorithm was computed with a while loop and a finite bound N on the number of iterations. We analyzed it using loop unrolling with $A \in [16, 20]$ and compared the global errors obtained at the $i - th$ iterate, that is, the difference between the max and min values. Analyzing such system with interval diverges startgin from the 7th iterates while Affine and Quadratic Zonotopes are more stable. The Fig. 5b presents the precision obtained with a variant of the algorithm were $A \in [16, 20]$ is randomly choosen at each loop iteration. While this program is meaningless, its analysis is interesting in terms of precision: intervals diverges from the 7th iteration, affine zonotopes from the 11th and quadratic ones from the 17th. Quadratic zonotopes here provides again better bounds than affine or interval analysis and shows to scale better than all other analyses. The Table 2 presents a selection of iterates computed values.

Most computation are performed within 30 ms. Only the Stolfi example with a large number of partitions shows a much longer time for Affine and Quadratic Zonotopes (about 1 s) than intervals (91 ms).

We do not present here a comparison with existing domains such as the T1P (Taylor 1 plus) abstract domain [GGP09] which is not a pure affine abstract domain. We recall that this domain is not just based on affine arithmetics but also embed linear relationships between error terms in the zonotope. Our motivation here is to show that the quadratic extension of affine zotonopes is feasible and lead to more precise result than the classical case while preserving the computation cost low.

Finally a disappointing result is the cost of the optimized concretization. This algorithm can potentially be used when converting a quadratic form to intervals and impact the computation of meet and join operators. However since meet operators are widely used in backward semantics [Min04], the accumulated overhead of calling an SDP solver impacts widely the overall timing results. Moreover, in most cases the precision is not considerably improved.

7 Conclusion

Zonotopic abstractions are currently the more promising domains when it comes to the formal verification of floating point computations such as the ones found in aircraft controllers. The presented analysis seems to be an interesting alternative to affine zonotopes, increasing precision while keeping the complexity quadratic in the number of error terms. Quadratic zonotopes seems more suited than linear abstractions when analyzing non linear functions such as multiplications. Among the zoo of abstract domains, they belong to the small set of algebraic domains able to synthesize non convex and non symmetric states. This may be later of great impact, e.g. when considering properties involving positivity of products of negative error terms.

Perspectives. On the theoretical side, it would be interesting to compare the abstraction generated by quadratic form with respect to the classical zonotopes, generated by affine forms. While geometrically speaking quadratic zonotopes seem to be strictly included in their affine counterpart, the existence of a Galois connection between the two abstractions is non trivial to exhibit, if ever it exists.

On the application side, our comparison with affine zonotopes in the benchmarks gives overall precision increase with a reasonable cost overhead. In the literature, the work of [GGP09] proposes to combine affine zonotopes with linear constraints to obtain a better precision when computing intersection. A similar extension for our quadratic extension of zonotopes would be interesting in practice.

Finally, both affine and quadratic arithmetics can be seen, respectively, as a first and second order Taylor polynomial abstractions. It would be interesting to evaluate how this approach can be extended and how it combines with other methods aiming at regaining precision such as branch-and-bound algorithms.

References

[BMC12] Bouissou, O., Mimram, S., Chapoutot, A.: Hyson: set-based simulation of hybrid systems. In: RSP, pp. 79–85. IEEE (2012)

[CS93] Comba, J.L.D., Stolfi, J.: Affine arithmetic and its applications to computer graphics (1993)

[Dek71] Dekker, T.J.: A floating-point technique for extending the available precision. Numerische Mathematik **18**(3), 224–242 (1971)

[GGP09] Ghorbal, K., Goubault, E., Putot, S.: The zonotope abstract domain Taylor1+. In: Bouajjani, A., Maler, O. (eds.) CAV 2009. LNCS, vol. 5643, pp. 627–633. Springer, Heidelberg (2009)

[GGP10] Ghorbal, K., Goubault, E., Putot, S.: A logical product approach to zonotope intersection. In: Touili, T., Cook, B., Jackson, P. (eds.) CAV 2010. LNCS, vol. 6174, pp. 212–226. Springer, Heidelberg (2010)

[GGP12] Goubault, E., Le Gall, T., Putot, S.: An accurate join for zonotopes, preserving affine input/output relations. ENTCS **287**, 65–76 (2012)

[Gho11] Ghorbal, K.: Static analysis of numerical programs: constrained affine sets abstract domain. Theses, Ecole Polytechnique X (2011)

[Gir05] Girard, A.: Reachability of uncertain linear systems using zonotopes. In: Morari, M., Thiele, L. (eds.) HSCC 2005. LNCS, vol. 3414, pp. 291–305. Springer, Heidelberg (2005)

[GLS88] Grötschel, M., Lovász, L., Schrijver, A.: Geometric Algorithms and Combinatorial Optimization. Algorithms and Combinatorics. Springer, Heidelberg (1988)

[Gou13] Goubault, E.: Static analysis by abstract interpretation of numerical programs and systems, and FLUCTUAT. In: Logozzo, F., Fähndrich, M. (eds.) Static Analysis. LNCS, vol. 7935, pp. 1–3. Springer, Heidelberg (2013)

[GP09] Goubault, E., Putot, S.: A zonotopic framework for functional abstractions. In: CoRR, abs/0910.1763 (2009)

[GPV12] Goubault, E., Putot, S., Védrine, F.: Modular static analysis with zonotopes. In: Miné, A., Schmidt, D. (eds.) SAS 2012. LNCS, vol. 7460, pp. 24–40. Springer, Heidelberg (2012)

[Han75] Hansen, E.R.: A generalized interval arithmetic. In: Nickel, K. (ed.) Interval Mathematics. LNCS, vol. 29, pp. 7–18. Springer, Heidelberg (1975)

[JM09] Jeannet, B., Miné, A.: APRON: a library of numerical abstract domains for static analysis. In: Bouajjani, A., Maler, O. (eds.) CAV 2009. LNCS, vol. 5643, pp. 661–667. Springer, Heidelberg (2009)

[Knu97] Knuth, D.E.: Art of Computer Programming: Seminumerical Algorithms, vol. 2. Addison-Wesley Professional, New York (1997)

[Min04] Miné, A.: Weakly relational numerical abstract domains. Ph.D. thesis, École Polytechnique, December 2004

[MT06] Messine, F., Touhami, A.: A general reliable quadratic form: an extension of affine arithmetic. Reliable Comput. **12**(3), 171–192 (2006)

[NN94] Nesterov, Y., Nemirovskii, A.: Interior-Point Polynomial Algorithms in Convex Programming, vol. 13. SIAM, Philadelphia (1994)

[RP96] Ramana, M.V., Pardalos, P.M.: Semidefinite programming. In: Terlaky, T. (ed.) Interior Point Methods of Mathematical Programming. Applied Optimization, vol. 5, pp. 369–398. Springer, Heidelberg (1996)

[SDF97] Stolfi, J., De Figueiredo, L.H.: Self-validated numerical methods and applications. In: Brazilian Mathematics Colloquium monograph, IMPA, Rio de Janeiro, Brazil (1997)

[Vav90] Vavasis, S.A.: Quadratic programming is in NP. Inf. Process. Lett. **36**(2), 73–77 (1990)

Abstraction of Optional Numerical Values

Jiangchao Liu(✉) and Xavier Rival

INRIA, ENS, CNRS, PSL*, Paris, France
{jliu,rival}@di.ens.fr

Abstract. We propose a technique to describe properties of numerical stores with optional values, that is, where some variables may have no value. Properties of interest include numerical equalities and inequalities. Our approach lifts common linear inequality based numerical abstract domains into abstract domains describing stores with optional values. This abstraction can be used in order to analyze languages with some form of *option* scalar type. It can also be applied to the construction of abstract domains to describe complex memory properties that introduce symbolic variables, e.g., in order to summarize unbounded sets of program variables, and where these symbolic variables may be undefined, as in some array or shape analyses. We describe the general form of abstract states, and propose sound and automatic static analysis algorithms. We evaluate our construction in the case of an array abstract domain.

1 Introduction

The abstraction of sets of stores is a common problem in static analysis. At a high level, it boils down to identifying a set of predicates over functions that map variables into values. In particular, when the set of variables $\mathbb{X}$ is of fixed and finite size N and the values are scalars (typically, machine integers or floating point numbers), concrete stores are functions of the form $\sigma : \mathbb{X} \rightarrow \mathbb{V}$ (where $\mathbb{V}$ stands for the set of values), and can equivalently be described by finite vectors of scalar values $\sigma \in \mathbb{V}^N$. Then, an abstract state describes a set of finite scalar vectors. Typical sorts of abstract states consist of conjunctions of equality constraints [11] or inequality constraints [3,5,13] over variables.

Optional Values. Many programming languages feature *possibly empty* memory locations. For instance, OCaml and Scala have an `option` type. This type can be defined by `type 'a option = None | Some of 'a`, which means a value of type `int option` may either be an integer, or undefined, represented by `None`. Similarly, spreadsheet environments feature empty cells as well as an `empty` type. When each variable either contains a scalar or no value, then the set of stores is $\mathcal{P}(\mathbb{X} \rightarrow \{\ominus\} \uplus \mathbb{V})$ where $\ominus$ stands for "no value". The conventional abstract domains mentioned above fail to describe such sets, as they require each dimension in the abstract domain to correspond to one concrete memory location, i.e., concrete stores should be of the form $\overrightarrow{\sigma} \in \mathbb{V}^N$. Therefore, they would need to be extended with support for *empty* values in order to deal with optional values.

X. Feng and S. Park (Eds.): APLAS 2015, LNCS 9458, pp. 146–166, 2015.
DOI: 10.1007/978-3-319-26529-2_9

Packing Memory Locations. Another situation where support for optional values would be needed occurs when designing abstract domains for complex data-structures. Indeed, a common technique *packs* sets of memory locations together, so that a single abstract constraint describes the values stored in a group of memory locations. For instance, array analyses often rely on *array partitioning* techniques, that divide an array into groups of cells. Then, the values of the cells of a group are described by a single abstract dimension. Many array analyses do not allow empty groups or treat them in a specific way [4,8,9]. In this case, *summarizing dimensions* [8] can be used in the abstract domain, so as to describe groups of several concrete locations. However, other analyses such as [12] allow empty groups. Then, considering an abstract state, a given abstract dimension may describe an empty set of values, even though the abstract state itself describes a non empty set of stores. A similar situation arises in some shape analyses [18]. Again, the aforementioned numerical domains do not support such an abstraction relation.

Abstraction of Stores in Presence of Possibly Empty Locations. In the previous two paragraphs, we have shown several cases where abstractions for stores with optional numerical values are needed. A first approach relies on disjunctions so as to partition a set of stores S into several sets $S_0, \ldots, S_p$, such that, each S_i corresponds to a fixed set of defined variables. However, when k variables may be empty or not, this would lead to an exponential factor of complexity. Another solution consists in adding a flag $\mathtt{f_x}$ for each variable $\mathtt{x}$, such that $\mathtt{f_x} = 1$ if $\mathtt{x}$ is defined and $\mathtt{f_x} = 0$ otherwise [16]. While this technique nicely describes relations of the form "$\mathtt{x}$ is defined if and only if $\mathtt{y}$ is defined", it is less adapted to infer that a variable is undefined from a set of constraints that show no value can be found for $\mathtt{x}$ thus it is undefined. The latter situation is common in array analyses like [12] and where the emptiness of a group of cells may follow from the numerical constraints over the values of these cells. To alleviate this issue, [6,12] deploy one relational abstract value per possibly empty zone, which is overly costly and limits the relations that can be expressed.

In this paper, we take a radically different approach, where constraints over a variable $\mathtt{x}$ may prove that no value is admissible for $\mathtt{x}$, hence it is undefined. Yet, the concretizations of the existing numerical abstract domains do not cope with one dimension describing the empty set while the others are still defined. Therefore, we let a variable $\mathtt{x}$ that may be undefined be described by a group of *avatars* $\mathtt{x}^0, \ldots, \mathtt{x}^k$, and assume that $\mathtt{x}$ can be defined if and only if all its avatars may be defined to a common value. For instance, constraints $\mathtt{x}^0 < 10 \wedge \mathtt{x}^1 > 20$ cannot be satisfied with a value assignment that maps $\mathtt{x}^0$ and $\mathtt{x}^1$ to the same value, hence this pair of constraints describes states where $\mathtt{x}$ is necessarily undefined. This principle can be applied to any numerical abstract domain where abstract values are finite conjunctions of constraints (the vast majority of numerical abstract domains are of that form). We propose an *abstract domain functor* for linear inequalities abstractions, called the *Maya functor*[1]. We present the following contributions:

[1] Mayas are among the civilizations believed to have independently invented number "zero".

- we define a concrete model for optional values (Sect. 3);
- we set up a general functor lifting a numerical abstract domain without optional dimensions into a domain with optional dimensions (Sect. 4);
- we define sound transfer functions and lattice operators for the automatic analysis of programs with optional variables, with linear inequalities (Sect. 5);
- we handle possibly empty summary dimensions (Sect. 6);
- we evaluate an implementation of the Maya functor (Sect. 7).

2 Overview

In this section, we demonstrate the principle of our abstraction, with a numeric analysis on a program involving optional variables and a basic array analysis applied to an initialization routine.

Abstraction of Optional Variables. We first consider the code fragment shown in Fig. 1. It is written in a C-like language extended with optional variables. An optional variable (as **int option** y in line 1) could be either no value (represented by **None**) or one value (represented by **Some** v_y where v_y is an integer). The statements in line 2 and 3 constrain v_y to be between 20 and the value of x ($20 \leq v_y \leq x$) if optional variable y stores an integer v_y. The test in line 4 constrains variable x to be smaller or equal than 10 ($x \leq 10$). This implies that, if y stores an integer v_y, then v_y is greater or equal than 20 and smaller or equal than 10 ($20 \leq v_y \leq 10$). There exists no such integer, thus, y may only store **None**, and the assertion in line 5 never fails. To prove this assertion by static analysis, we first need to represent all numerical properties using a numerical abstract domain. All the numeric constraints in this example are of the form $\pm x \pm y \leq c$ and can thus be described in the octagons abstract domain [13]. However, an octagon describes either the empty set of stores, or a set containing at least one store, that maps each variable, including y, into a value. Thus, this abstract domain cannot express that y stores **None**, while the other variables hold a value. Siegel et *al.* [16] add a flag variable $\mathtt{f_y}$ to indicate whether y stores one value or no value. However, solving the problem using this approach requires to precisely capture the property that $20 \leq v_y \leq x$ when $\mathtt{f_y} = 1$ and y = **None** when $\mathtt{f_y} = 0$. This property cannot be expressed in a single octagon. Hence, the approach of [16] would require a stronger, more ad hoc abstract domain (most likely, using a disjunction of octagons).

```
1. int option y; int x;
2. if(y == Some v_y)
3.       assume(v_y ≤ x && v_y ≥ 20);
4. if(x ≤ 10)
5.       assert(y == None);
```

Fig. 1. A routine involving optional variables

Abstraction of Possibly Empty Sets of Values. The key idea of our method is to represent a single variable using several instances called *avatars*, carrying different constraints. This way, we ensure both that (1) the abstract domain describes stores which map each variable to one value and (2) we can express either that y must be empty (when it is not possible to find a value all its avatars can be mapped to) or that it may store some value v (when all constraints are satisfied when all the avatars of y are mapped to v). To implement this idea using the octagons abstract domain, we simply distinguish, for a variable y that may have an empty set of values, two sets of constraints: the constraints of the form $\mathtt{y} \pm \mathtt{x} \leq c$ (resp., $-\mathtt{y} \pm \mathtt{x} \leq c$) are carried out by its *upper-bound avatar* $\mathtt{y}^+$ (resp., *lower-bound avatar* $\mathtt{y}^-$). This means, that a (non-bottom) octagon containing constraints $\mathtt{y}^+ \leq 0$ and $1 \leq \mathtt{y}^-$ expresses y is necessarily mapped to no value, as there is no way to satisfy the constraints over its two avatars, while mapping them to a common value. Applying this method to the example in Fig. 1, we associate two avatars $\mathtt{y}^-$ and $\mathtt{y}^+$ to the optional variable y (non-optional variable x is not associated with distinct avatars). Three numeric relations ($20 \leq \mathtt{y}^- \ \wedge\ \mathtt{y}^+ \leq \mathtt{x} \ \wedge\ \mathtt{x} \leq 10$) are observed before the assertion in line 5. According to the constraints, $\mathtt{y}^-$ may take any value greater than 20, whereas $\mathtt{y}^+$ may take any value smaller than 10, so the concretization of this abstract state contains no state that maps both avatars of y to a common value. Thus y stands for no value, which proves the assertion in line 5. Unlike [16], the bi-avatar approach allows constraints $20 \leq \mathtt{y}$ and $\mathtt{y} \leq 10$ to co-exist in a single abstract element, that does not describe the empty set of states. The computation of abstract post-conditions is quite standard, except that it needs to always associate upper and lower constraints to the right avatar.

```
int i = 0; int a[8];
while(i < 8){
  ★ ( 0 ≤ Idx_0 ≤ i − 1 ∧ i ≤ Idx_1 ≤ 7 )
     a[i] = 0;
i = i + 1;
}
```

(a) Array initialization routine and invariant

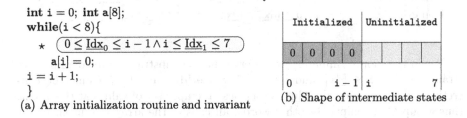

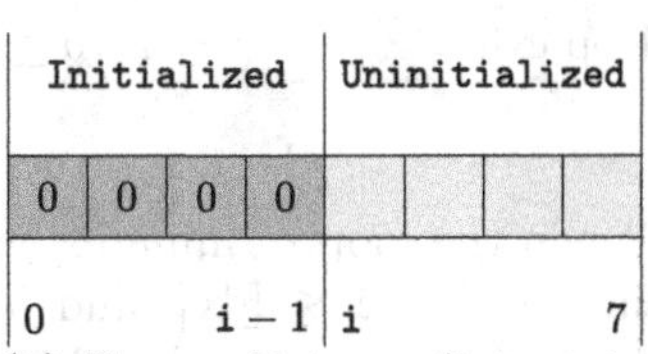

(b) Shape of intermediate states

Fig. 2. An array initialization example

Packing Array Cells. Figure 2(a) shows a C code segment of array initialization. We consider an array analysis inspired by [12], which proceeds by forward abstract interpretation [3] (note that the main emphasis of this section is not the array analysis itself, but the abstraction of optional values). A store observed after 4 iterations is shown in Fig. 2(b). We note the array can be divided into two sets of cells, namely initialized cells and uninitialized cells. As in [12], we consider an abstraction of the array, that partitions it into two groups of cells G_0, G_1 (where all cells in G_0 are initialized to zero and cells in G_1 may hold any value), and we let two summary variables $\underline{\mathtt{Idx}}_0, \underline{\mathtt{Idx}}_1$ over-approximate the sets of indexes corresponding to the cells of each group. Before the loop starts, $\underline{\mathrm{Idx}_0}$ stands for $\emptyset$. In Fig. 2(b), $\underline{\mathrm{Idx}_0}$ stands for set $\{0, 1, 2, 3\}$. Before the loop execution, group G_0 is empty. Actually, [12] will introduce it only during the first iteration of the loop. At this point, the analysis infers that $\underline{\mathrm{Idx}_0} = \{0\}$ (group G_0 has a single element at this point); moreover, it computes that $1 \leq \underline{\mathrm{Idx}_1} \leq 7$. During the loop execution, we observe the following constraints over group indexes form a loop invariant:

$$0 \leq \underline{\mathrm{Idx}_0} \leq \mathtt{i} - 1 \wedge \mathtt{i} \leq \underline{\mathrm{Idx}_1} \leq 7$$

After the loop exit, $8 \leq \mathtt{i}$, therefore the analysis will return $8 \leq \underline{\mathrm{Idx}_1} \leq 7$. Obviously no value satisfies this constraint. This actually means that group G_1 is empty at this stage, thus, the analysis proves the whole array is initialized to 0. The representation of the numerical properties over group indexes suffers from the same issue as for the optional values, in the analysis of the program of Fig. 1: a non bottom octagon element cannot express $8 \leq \underline{\mathrm{Idx}_1} \leq 7$. The solution used in [12] describes each group with a separate octagon. In this layout, an empty group is naturally described by a bottom octagon attached to its $\underline{\mathrm{Idx}_i}$ variable. Yet, this prevents the analysis from inferring constraints across distinct groups.

Using our method, the analysis could describe symbolic variables associated to the groups (that is, in our example, $\underline{\mathrm{Idx}_0}, \underline{\mathrm{Idx}_1}$) by a pair of avatars (while program variables (like i) are not associated to distinct avatars in octagons). It computes the following invariants:

Before the loop	$\mathtt{i} = 0 \wedge 0 \leq \underline{\mathrm{Idx}_1^-} \wedge \underline{\mathrm{Idx}_1^+} \leq 7$
end of the 1st iter	$\mathtt{i} = 1 \wedge 0 \leq \underline{\mathrm{Idx}_0^-} \wedge \underline{\mathrm{Idx}_0^+} \leq 0 \wedge 1 \leq \underline{\mathrm{Idx}_1^-} \wedge \underline{\mathrm{Idx}_1^+} \leq 7$
loop invariant	$0 \leq \mathtt{i} \leq 7 \wedge 0 \leq \underline{\mathrm{Idx}_0^-} \wedge \underline{\mathrm{Idx}_0^+} \leq \mathtt{i} - 1 \wedge \mathtt{i} \leq \underline{\mathrm{Idx}_1^-} \wedge \underline{\mathrm{Idx}_1^+} \leq 7$
loop exit	$8 \leq \mathtt{i} \wedge 0 \leq \underline{\mathrm{Idx}_0^-} \wedge \underline{\mathrm{Idx}_0^+} \leq \mathtt{i} - 1 \wedge \mathtt{i} \leq \underline{\mathrm{Idx}_1^-} \wedge \underline{\mathrm{Idx}_1^+} \leq 7$

When the loop terminates, we observe that the abstract state contains constraints $8 \leq \mathtt{i}$, $\mathtt{i} \leq \underline{\mathrm{Idx}_1^-}$ and $\underline{\mathrm{Idx}_1^+} \leq 7$. Since $\underline{\mathrm{Idx}_1^-}$ and $\underline{\mathrm{Idx}_1^+}$ cannot be concretized to a common value, $\underline{\mathrm{Idx}_1}$ describes an empty set of values at this point, thus group G_1 is empty. In other words, all cells of the array are initialized at this point.

3 A Language with Optional Values and Its Semantics

Before we can formalize the abstraction relation of our domain functor, we need to specify a concrete semantics. To do that, we describe a basic imperative language where some variables have an optional value. It models both languages with an option type as well as the operations shape and array analyses with empty groups require their base domain to provide. The semantics of this language will serve as a basis to state the soundness properties of the transfer functions defined in the functor for the abstraction of optional scalar values.

$$
\begin{array}{lll}
\mathtt{X}: \text{standard (non empty) variables} & (\mathtt{x} \in \mathtt{X}) \\
\mathtt{Y}: \text{optional variables (may be empty)} & (\mathtt{y} \in \mathtt{Y}) \\
\mathtt{V}: \text{values} & (\mathtt{c} \in \mathtt{V})
\end{array}
$$

$$
\begin{array}{rll}
\mathbf{t} ::= \mathbf{x} \mid \mathbf{y} & \oplus ::= + \mid - \mid * \mid \div & \otimes ::= < \mid \leq \mid == \mid != \\
\mathbf{ex} ::= \mathbf{t} \mid \mathbf{c} \mid \mathbf{ex} \oplus \mathbf{ex} & & \text{scalar expressions} \\
\mathbf{cond} ::= \mathtt{TRUE} \mid \mathtt{FALSE} \mid \mathbf{ex} \otimes \mathbf{ex} \mid \mathbf{is\_empty}(\mathtt{y}) & & \text{condition tests} \\
\mathbf{s} ::= \mathbf{skip} \mid \mathbf{t} = \mathbf{ex} \mid \mathbf{assume}(\mathtt{cond}) \mid \mathbf{assert}(\mathtt{cond}) & & \text{basic statements} \\
\mid \ \mathbf{s}; \mathbf{s} \mid \mathbf{if}(\mathtt{cond})\{\mathtt{s}\}\mathbf{else}\{\mathtt{s}\} \mid \mathbf{while}(\mathtt{cond})\{\mathtt{s}\} & & \text{compound statements}
\end{array}
$$

Fig. 3. A language with optional values: syntax

Syntax. The syntax is shown in Fig. 3. We distinguish the variables that may be empty, called the *optional* variables from the *standard* variables, that must store one value. We let $\mathbb{X}$ denote the set of standard variables, and we write $\mathbb{Y}$ for the set of optional variables (we assume $\mathbb{X} \cap \mathbb{Y} = \emptyset$). These two sets are assumed to be fixed throughout the paper. We also let $\mathbb{V}$ stand for the set of values. Values and variables all have scalar type (integer or floating point). Finally, we let $\ominus \notin \mathbb{V}$ denote the absence of value. Conditions include usual arithmetic tests and the emptiness test of an optional variable. Statements include the usual skip statement (that does nothing), assignments, sequences, condition tests and loops.

Memory States. A *concrete memory* (or *store*) σ maps each standard variable into a value and each optional variable to either a scalar value or to the $\ominus$ placeholder, meaning that this variable is not defined. Therefore the set of stores is:

$$\mathbb{S} \stackrel{\text{def.}}{::=} (\mathbb{X} \to \mathbb{V}) \uplus (\mathbb{Y} \to (\mathbb{V} \cup \{\ominus\}))$$

Evaluation of Expressions: $[\![\mathbf{ex}]\!] : \mathtt{S} \to \mathtt{V} \uplus \{\ominus\}$

$$[\![\mathbf{t}]\!](\sigma) = \sigma(\mathbf{t}) \qquad [\![\mathbf{c}]\!](\sigma) = \mathbf{c}$$

$$[\![\mathbf{ex}_0 \oplus \mathbf{ex}_1]\!](\sigma) = \begin{cases} [\![\mathbf{ex}_0]\!](\sigma) \oplus [\![\mathbf{ex}_1]\!](\sigma) & \forall i \in \{0,1\},\ [\![\mathbf{ex}_i]\!](\sigma) \in \mathtt{V} \\ \ominus & \exists i \in \{0,1\},\ [\![\mathbf{ex}_i]\!](\sigma) = \ominus \end{cases}$$

Condition tests: $[\![\mathbf{cond}]\!] : \mathcal{P}(\mathtt{S}) \to \mathcal{P}(\mathtt{S})$

$$[\![\mathtt{TRUE}]\!](\mathtt{S}) = \mathtt{S} \qquad [\![\mathtt{FALSE}]\!](\mathtt{S}) = \emptyset \qquad [\![\mathbf{is\_empty}(\mathtt{y})]\!](\mathtt{S}) = \{\sigma \in \mathtt{S} \mid \sigma(\mathtt{y}) = \ominus\}$$

$$[\![\mathbf{ex}_0 \otimes \mathbf{ex}_1]\!](\mathtt{S}) = \{\sigma \in \mathtt{S} \mid [\![\mathbf{ex}_0]\!](\sigma) \otimes ([\![\mathbf{ex}_1]\!](\sigma) = \mathtt{TRUE}) \vee ([\![\mathbf{ex}_0]\!](\sigma) = \ominus) \vee ([\![\mathbf{ex}_1]\!](\sigma) = \ominus)\}$$

Main statements: $[\![\mathbf{s}]\!] : \mathcal{P}(\mathtt{S}) \to \mathcal{P}(\mathtt{S})$

$$[\![\mathbf{skip}]\!](\mathtt{S}) = \mathtt{S} \qquad [\![\mathtt{s}_0; \mathtt{s}_1]\!](\mathtt{S}) = [\![\mathtt{s}_1]\!] \circ [\![\mathtt{s}_0]\!](\mathtt{S})$$

$$[\![\mathbf{t} = \mathbf{ex}]\!](\mathtt{S}) = \{\sigma[\mathbf{t} \mapsto [\![\mathbf{ex}]\!](\sigma)] \mid \sigma \in \mathtt{S}, [\![\mathbf{ex}]\!](\sigma) \in \mathtt{V} \vee \mathbf{t} \in \mathtt{Y}\}$$

$$[\![\mathbf{if}(\mathtt{cond})\{\mathtt{s}_0\}\mathbf{else}\{\mathtt{s}_1\}]\!](\mathtt{S}) = [\![\mathtt{s}_0]\!] \circ [\![\mathbf{cond}]\!](\mathtt{S}) \cup [\![\mathtt{s}_1]\!] \circ [\![\mathbf{cond} == \mathtt{FALSE}]\!](\mathtt{S})$$

$$[\![\mathbf{while}(\mathtt{cond})\{\mathtt{s}\}]\!](\mathtt{S}) = [\![\mathbf{cond} == \mathtt{FALSE}]\!](\mathbf{lfp}\ \lambda \mathtt{S}' \cdot \mathtt{S} \cup [\![\mathtt{s}]\!]([\![\mathbf{cond}]\!](\mathtt{S}')))$$

Fig. 4. A language with optional values: concrete semantics

Semantics. The concrete semantics is formally defined in Fig. 4 (**assume** and **assert** statements are classical and omitted). While the overall structure of this semantics is standard, a few points should be noticed. The semantics $[\![\mathtt{ex}]\!]$ of expression ex evaluates it in a given store, and produces either a value or the no value $\ominus$ element. It produces $\ominus$ whenever it reads an empty optional variable: all operators are $\ominus$-strict, i.e., they return $\ominus$ whenever one of their arguments is equal to $\ominus$, thus $\ominus$ always propagates. The semantics $[\![\mathtt{cond}]\!]$ of condition cond filters out the stores in which cond does not evaluate to TRUE, thus, it will also include stores where the evaluation encounters $\ominus$.

The semantics $[\![\mathtt{s}]\!]$ of statement s takes a set of input stores and returns the corresponding set of output stores, following an angelic denotational semantics [2] (non terminating behaviors are not represented —this choice simplifies the presentation, while it does not change anything to the core points of the paper). Note that the semantics of an assignment $\mathtt{x} = \mathtt{ex}$ where $\mathtt{x} \in \mathbb{X}$ will produce no output store when ex evaluates to $\ominus$. Intuitively, we consider only executions where the empty value is never assigned to a standard variable.

Example 1. We consider the program below, where $\mathbb{X} = \{\mathtt{x}\}$ and $\mathbb{Y} = \{\mathtt{y}, \mathtt{z}\}$:

```
if(x ≤ y){
    if(y ≤ 6){
        ① z = y + 2;
        ② ...;
```

Assuming that all variables may take any value (including $\ominus$ for optional variables) at the beginning of the execution:

- at point ①, we can observe exactly the stores such that $\sigma(\mathtt{x}) \leq \sigma(\mathtt{y}) \leq 6$, and the stores defined by $\sigma(\mathtt{y}) = \ominus$;
- at point ②, we can observe exactly the stores such that $\sigma(\mathtt{x}) \leq \sigma(\mathtt{y}) \leq 6 \wedge \sigma(\mathtt{z}) = \sigma(\mathtt{y}) + 2$ and the stores where $\sigma(\mathtt{y}) = \ominus$ or $\sigma(\mathtt{z}) = \ominus$.

4 Abstraction in Presence of Optional Numerical Values

In this section, we assume a numerical domain $\mathbb{N}^\sharp$ is fixed, where abstract values correspond to conjunctions of constraints. For instance, linear equalities [11], intervals [3], octagons [13] and polyhedra [5] fit into this category. An abstract value $N^\sharp \in \mathbb{N}^\sharp$ describes constraints over a finite set of "abstract variables" that we refer to as *dimensions* (so as to distinguish them from the "concrete" —standard or optional— variables). Dimensions range over a countable set $\mathbb{D}$, and we write $\mathbf{Dim}(N^\sharp)$ for the dimensions of abstract value $N^\sharp$ ($\mathbf{Dim}(N^\sharp) \subseteq \mathbb{D}$). We let $\gamma_{\mathbb{N}^\sharp} : \mathbb{N}^\sharp \rightarrow \mathcal{P}(\mathbb{D} \rightarrow \mathbb{V})$ denote its concretization function.

Abstract States. An abstract state of the *Maya abstract domain* over $\mathbb{N}^\sharp$ is defined by an abstract value $N^\sharp \in \mathbb{N}^\sharp$ describing constraints over a set of dimensions defined as follows:

- each standard variable x corresponds to exactly one dimension, also noted x;
- each optional variable y corresponds to a finite set of *avatar dimensions* (for clarity, we always mark avatars with superscripts such as: $y^-, y^+, y^0, \ldots$).

Therefore, we attach a function $\mathcal{A} : \mathbb{Y} \to \mathcal{P}(\mathbb{D})$ which describes the mapping of optional variables into their set of avatars to numerical abstract value $N^\sharp$.

Definition 1 (Abstract state). *An abstract state of the* Maya abstract domain *over* $\mathbb{N}^\sharp$ *is a pair* $M^\sharp = (N^\sharp, \mathcal{A})$ *such that:*

$$\mathbf{Dim}(N^\sharp) = \left(\biguplus\{\mathcal{A}(y) \mid y \in \mathbb{Y}\}\right) \uplus \mathbb{X}$$

We let $\mathbb{M}^\sharp$ *denote the set of such states.*

Note that the above definition implicitly asserts that distinct variables are represented by disjoint sets of dimensions.

Example 2. In this example, we assume $\mathbb{N}^\sharp$ is the octagon domain, and that $\mathbb{X} = \{x\}$, $\mathbb{Y} = \{y\}$. Furthermore, as shown in Sect. 2, we let each optional variable be described by two avatars. Thus, $\mathbb{D} = \{x, y^-, y^+\}$. Moreover, an example abstract state is $M^\sharp = (N^\sharp, \mathcal{A})$, with:

$$N^\sharp = \{0 \leq x \wedge x \leq 10 \wedge 5 \leq y^- \wedge y^+ \leq x\} \qquad \mathcal{A} : y \longmapsto \{y^-, y^+\}$$

Concretization. To express the meaning of an abstract state $M^\sharp = (N^\sharp, \mathcal{A})$, we use a valuation ν, that maps all dimensions to a value, as an intermediate step towards the concrete stores. Then, we retain only the concrete stores, that can be obtained by collapsing *all avatars of each optional variable* to a unique value. This second step is described by a pair of *consistency predicates*, which state when a store σ is compatible with ν:

Definition 2 (Concretization). *Given abstract state* $M^\sharp = (N^\sharp, \mathcal{A})$*, we define the following consistency predicates:*

$$\begin{aligned} P_{\mathbb{X}}(\sigma, M^\sharp, \nu) &\overset{def.}{\iff} \forall x \in \mathbb{X},\ \sigma(x) = \nu(x) \\ P_{\mathbb{Y}}(\sigma, M^\sharp, \nu) &\overset{def.}{\iff} \forall y \in \mathbb{Y},\ (\forall d \in \mathcal{A}(y),\ \nu(d) = \sigma(y)) \vee \sigma(y) = \ominus \end{aligned}$$

Then, the concretization of $M^\sharp = (N^\sharp, \mathcal{A})$ *is defined by:*

$$\gamma_{\mathbb{M}^\sharp}(M^\sharp) \overset{def.}{::=} \{\sigma \in \mathsf{S} \mid \exists \nu \in \gamma_{\mathbb{N}^\sharp}(N^\sharp),\ P_{\mathbb{X}}(\sigma, M^\sharp, \nu) \wedge P_{\mathbb{Y}}(\sigma, M^\sharp, \nu)\}$$

Intuitively, consistency predicate $P_{\mathbb{X}}$ asserts that the valuation and the concrete store agree on the mapping of the standard variables, whereas consistency predicate $P_{\mathbb{Y}}$ asserts that the valuation assigns all avatars of each optional variable to the value of that variable in the store.

Example 3. We consider the abstract state shown in Example 2. Its concretization consists of:

– the stores defined by $\sigma(\mathtt{x}) \in [5, 10], \sigma(\mathtt{y}) \in [5, \sigma(\mathtt{x})]$ (the valuation is then fully defined by the store since no variable stores $\ominus$);
– the stores defined by $\sigma(\mathtt{x}) \in [0, 10], \sigma(\mathtt{y}) = \ominus$ (a possible valuation is defined by $\nu(\mathtt{x}) = \sigma(\mathtt{x}), \nu(\mathtt{y}^-) = 15, \nu(\mathtt{y}^+) = \nu(\mathtt{x})$).

This example shows how our domain can distribute the constraints on an optional variable y over several dimensions, so as to express the fact that y must store $\ominus$.

Remark 1. In this example, we also observe that, given $\sigma \in \gamma_{\mathbb{M}^\sharp}(M^\sharp)$, and if σ' is such that, for all standard variable x, $\sigma'(\mathtt{x}) = \sigma(\mathtt{x})$, and for all optional variable y, either $\sigma'(\mathtt{y}) = \sigma(\mathtt{y})$ or $\sigma'(\mathtt{y}) = \ominus$, then $\sigma' \in \gamma_{\mathbb{M}^\sharp}(M^\sharp)$. In other words, our functor cannot express that an optional variable *must not* store $\ominus$. In the context of array analyses such as [12], this is not a limitation: that analysis can already express that a group *cannot* be empty (using size constraints). However, our abstraction also allows to derive emptiness of a group via constraints over multiple avatars of variables denoting its contents or indexes, which [12] does in a rather *ad hoc* manner, at the expense of relations between groups.

Choice of Avatar Dimensions. The definition of abstract elements assumes nothing about the number of avatar dimensions, and about the way the constraints over an optional variable are distributed over its avatars. However, in practice, the way avatar dimensions are managed has a great impact on the efficiency and precision of the analysis. It is the role of the transfer functions and abstract lattice operations to implement an efficient strategy to manage these dimensions. In particular at certain stages, new avatars have to be introduced so as to avoid a loss of precision.

Example 4. We discuss possible abstract invariants for the program shown in Example 1, starting with the set of all stores as a pre-condition, described by abstract state $\top$. After test $\mathtt{x} \leq \mathtt{y}$, the analysis should compute an abstraction of the stores where, either y is mapped only to $\ominus$ or where the numerical constraint is satisfied. Using the octagon abstract domain, and a single avatar $\mathtt{y}^0$ for y, this boils down to abstract state $(\mathtt{x} - \mathtt{y}^0 \leq 0, \mathtt{y} \mapsto \{\mathtt{y}^0\})$. After the second test, we get the set of stores observed at point ①, that is such that, either $\sigma(\mathtt{x}) \leq \sigma(\mathtt{y}) \leq 6$ or $\sigma(\mathtt{y}) = \ominus$. Note that this set of stores cannot be described exactly with octagons using a single avatar. Indeed, this set contains stores such that $\sigma(\mathtt{x}) > 6$ (when $\sigma(\mathtt{y}) = \ominus$). Thus, using a single avatar to describe constraints over y would force the analysis to drop either constraint $\mathtt{y} \leq 6$ or constraint $\mathtt{x} \leq \mathtt{y}$. Keeping both constraints would unsoundly assert $\mathtt{x} \leq 6$. Thus, adding a second avatar for y at this point is necessary in order to maintain maximal precision. In particular, the abstract state below describes exactly the stores that can be observed at point ①:

$$(\mathtt{x} \leq \mathtt{y}^0 \wedge \mathtt{y}^1 \leq 6, \mathtt{y} \mapsto \{\mathtt{y}^0, \mathtt{y}^1\})$$

The above example demonstrates the need to introduce enough avatars so that all constraints on optional variables can be maintained, without "over-constraining" standard variables (which would result in an unsound analysis). Intuitively, each avatar should not carry too much information: the base numerical domain cannot express emptiness of a specific avatar; instead, only the conjunction of all avatars of an optional variable y may express that y is empty. We formalize this as a *sufficient condition*, that we call the *independence* property, and that should be maintained by all abstract operators in the Maya domain. This property states that dropping the constraints over an avatar dimension y^0 associated to variable y should have no impact on the variables other than y. To maintain this property, transfer functions and abstract operators may either pay the cost of adding new avatar dimensions or will have to drop constraints that cannot be represented without adding more avatars. To formalize the independence property, and given abstract value $N^\sharp \in \mathbb{N}^\sharp$ and dimension d, we note $\mathbf{drop}(N^\sharp, d)$ for the abstract value obtained by removing from $N^\sharp$ all the constraints that involve d (this operation is well defined since we assumed elements of abstract domain $\mathbb{N}^\sharp$ correspond to the finite conjunctions of all the constraints of a certain form). Moreover, if ν is a valuation, we write $\nu_{|\neg d}$ for the restriction of ν to $\mathbb{D} \setminus \{d\}$.

Definition 3 (Independence property). *Let $M^\sharp = (N^\sharp, \mathcal{A})$ be an abstract state. We say $M^\sharp$ satisfies the independence property if and only if*

$$\forall y \in \mathbb{Y},\ \forall d \in \mathcal{A}(y),\ \{\nu_{|\neg d} \mid \nu \in \gamma_{\mathbb{N}^\sharp}(N^\sharp)\} = \{\nu_{|\neg d} \mid \nu \in \gamma_{\mathbb{N}^\sharp}(\mathbf{drop}(N^\sharp, d))\}$$

Example 5. The abstract state given at the end of Example 4 satisfies the independence property, using two avatars, that respectively carry the lower and upper bound constraints over y. Section 5 generalizes this approach to lift any domain based on linear inequalities.

Example 6. Intuitively, the independence property is likely to break when an avatar dimension carries several constraints, the conjunction of which may be unsatisfiable. Therefore, an alternate technique to achieve it consists in using one avatar per constraint over each optional variable. As an example, we consider the set of concrete states defined by $\mathbb{X} = \{x\}$ and $\mathbb{Y} = \{y, z\}$ and where the optional variables are either undefined or satisfy the following conditions: $x \leq y \wedge y \leq 2x \wedge y = z + 2$. Then, assuming $\mathbb{N}^\sharp$ is the polyhedra abstract domain, this *multi-avatar* strategy will construct the following abstract state:

$$\begin{aligned} N^\sharp &= \left\{x \leq y^0 \wedge y^1 \leq 2x \wedge y^2 \leq z^0 + 2 \wedge z^1 + 2 \leq y^3\right\} \\ \mathcal{A} &: y \mapsto \{y^0, y^1, y^2, y^3\}, z \mapsto \{z^0, z^1\}, \end{aligned}$$

This strategy is general (it can be applied to, e.g., linear equalities [11]) but costly.

5 Application to Numerical Domains Based on Linear Inequalities

We now propose a strategy to manage avatar dimensions and design abstract operations under the hypothesis that base abstract domain $\mathbb{N}^\sharp$ expresses linear inequality constraints (which includes intervals, octagons, polyhedra, and their variants).

5.1 The Bi-Avatar Strategy

Numerical constraints in the base domain are all of the form $a_0\mathtt{d}_0 + \ldots + a_n\mathtt{d}_n \leq c$ (where $a_0, \ldots, a_n, c$ are constants), thus a constraint involving $\mathtt{d}_i$ (i.e., where $a_i \neq 0$) is either specifying an upper bound for $\mathtt{d}_i$ (if $a_i > 0$) or a lower bound (if $a_i < 0$). The bi-avatar strategy treats those two sets of constraints separately, using two avatar dimensions per optional variable, as shown in Sect. 2:

Definition 4 (The bi-avatar strategy). *Abstract state $M^\sharp = (N^\sharp, \mathcal{A})$ follows the* bi-avatar strategy *if and only if $\mathcal{A}$ maps each optional variable* $\mathtt{y}$ *to a pair of dimensions $\{\mathtt{y}^-, \mathtt{y}^+\}$, and is such that each "upper" avatar $\mathtt{y}^+$ (resp., "lower" avatar $\mathtt{y}^-$) carries only "upper bound constraints" (resp., "lower bound constraints").*

In other words, the bi-avatar strategy fully determines $\mathcal{A}$. In order to implement this strategy, we need to ensure that all abstract operators preserve $\mathcal{A}$, and the property of lower and upper avatars. We define such abstract operations in the next subsections. Interestingly, whenever an abstract state satisfies this strategy, and if we drop all constraints over an (upper or lower) avatar of $\mathtt{y}$, the concretization restricted to the dimensions other than that avatar do not change. This entails:

Theorem 1 (Independence property). *All abstract values following the bi-avatar strategy satisfy the independence property (Definition 3).*

To express the emptiness of an optional variable, we simply need to let its avatars carry a pair of constraints that would be unsatisfiable, if carried by a unique dimension, such as $1 \leq \mathtt{y}^- \wedge \mathtt{y}^+ \leq 0$.

Example 7. Let $\mathbb{X} = \{\mathtt{x}\}, \mathbb{Y} = \{\mathtt{y}\}$, and let $\mathcal{A}$ specify the avatars defined by the bi-avatar strategy. Then, the following numerical abstract values specify the sets of concrete states below:

Abstract numerical state $N^\sharp$	Concretization $\gamma_{\mathbb{M}^\sharp}(N^\sharp, \mathcal{A})$
$1 \leq \mathtt{x} \wedge \mathtt{x} \leq 1 \wedge \mathtt{x} \leq \mathtt{y}^- \wedge \mathtt{y}^+ \leq \mathtt{x}$	$\{\mathtt{x} \mapsto 1, \mathtt{y} \mapsto 1\}, \{\mathtt{x} \mapsto 1, \mathtt{y} \mapsto \ominus\}$
$1 \leq \mathtt{x} \wedge \mathtt{x} \leq 1 \wedge \mathtt{x} \leq \mathtt{y}^- \wedge \mathtt{y}^+ \leq \mathtt{x} - 1$	$\{\mathtt{x} \mapsto 1, \mathtt{y} \mapsto \ominus\}$

Preservation. The abstract operators described in the remainder of this section either discard constraints violating the bi-avatar strategy (such as assignment, in Sect. 5.4), or never apply operations of $\mathbb{N}^\sharp$ that would cause them to bound a $\mathtt{y}^+$ (resp., $\mathtt{y}^-$) avatar below (resp., above). This implies straightforwardly that, in the resulting domain, all abstract elements with a non empty concretization follow the bi-avatar strategy (all $\mathtt{y}^-$ dimensions are not bounded by above and all $\mathtt{y}^+$ dimensions are not bounded by below). The only abstract operation that may input an abstract state with non empty concretization and return an abstract state with empty concretization is the abstract condition test $\mathbf{test}_{\mathbb{N}^\sharp}[.]$ (used in Sect. 5.2) and requires an output check that no constraint violates the bi-avatar strategy.

Expressiveness. Under the bi-avatar strategy, we can compare the expressiveness of Maya domain $\mathbb{M}^\sharp$ with that of its base domain $\mathbb{N}^\sharp$: if a set of stores S with no optional variable containing $\ominus$ can be described exactly by $N^\sharp \in \mathbb{N}^\sharp$, we can still describe S in $\mathbb{M}^\sharp$, up-to the change of any set of optional variable to $\ominus$. Indeed, if we let $\mathbb{S}_{\text{def}} = (\mathbb{X} \uplus \mathbb{Y}) \to \mathbb{V}$, we have:

Theorem 2. *If $\mathcal{A}$ follows the bi-avatar strategy, then:*

$$\forall N_0^\sharp \in \mathbb{N}^\sharp,\ \mathbf{Dim}(N_0^\sharp) = \mathbb{X} \uplus \mathbb{Y} \implies \left(\exists N_1^\sharp \in \mathbb{M}^\sharp,\ \gamma_{\mathbb{N}^\sharp}(N_0^\sharp) = \gamma_{\mathbb{M}^\sharp}(N_1^\sharp, \mathcal{A}) \cap \mathbb{S}_{\text{def}}\right)$$

5.2 Condition Test

The concrete semantics of a condition test `cond` filters out stores for which `cond` does not evaluate to `TRUE`. We assume $\mathbb{N}^\sharp$ provides a sound abstract function $\mathbf{test}_{\mathbb{N}^\sharp}[\texttt{cond}] : \mathbb{N}^\sharp \to \mathbb{N}^\sharp$, and build an abstract operator $\mathbf{test}_{\mathbb{M}^\sharp}[\texttt{cond}] : M^\sharp \to M^\sharp$.

Optional Variable Emptiness Test. To evaluate condition $\mathbf{test}_{\mathbb{M}^\sharp}[\mathbf{is\_empty}(\mathrm{y})]$, and filter out stores that do not map y into $\ominus$, we can simply add two constraints on y^- and y^+ that would be unsatisfiable, if added on a same dimension, such as $1 \leq \mathrm{y}^-$ and $\mathrm{y}^+ \leq 0$. This can be done using $\mathbf{test}_{\mathbb{N}^\sharp}[.]$.

Numerical Tests. We consider only conditions that are linear inequalities, as non-linear conditions are often handled by linearization techniques [14], and a linear equality is equivalent to a pair of inequalities.

Intuitively, $\mathbf{test}_{\mathbb{M}^\sharp}[.]$ should simply add a linear constraint to some abstract state $M^\sharp$ (with some approximation, as this constraint is in general not representable exactly in $\mathbb{N}^\sharp$). Given condition test $a_0\mathrm{x}_0 + \ldots + a_n\mathrm{x}_n + b_0\mathrm{y}_0 + \ldots + b_m\mathrm{y}_m \leq c$ (where $\mathrm{x}_i \in \mathbb{X}$ and $\mathrm{y}_i \in \mathbb{Y}$), we can produce another constraint that involves only standard variables and avatar dimensions by replacing y_i either by y_i^- or by y_i^+ depending on the sign of b_i. This constraint is compatible with the bi-avatar strategy (Sect. 5.1), hence it can be represented precisely in the numerical domain, even if it indirectly entails emptiness of some optional variables (in other words, not using the bi-avatar property would cause a severe precision loss here). Thus, numerical condition test can be applied to this constraint. In turn, the absence of constraints violating the bi-avatar strategy needs to be verified on the output of $\mathbf{test}_{\mathbb{N}^\sharp}[.]$. Moreover, this constraint is equivalent to the initial constraint up-to the $\gamma_{\mathbb{M}^\sharp}$ concretization function. Thus, this principle defines a sound abstract transfer function for condition tests.

Theorem 3 (Soundness of condition test). *The abstract transfer function* $\mathbf{test}_{\mathbb{M}^\sharp}[.]$ *is* sound *in the sense that, for all linear inequality constraint* `cond` *and for all abstract state $M^\sharp$ satisfying the bi-avatar strategy:*

$$[\![\texttt{cond}]\!](\gamma_{\mathbb{M}^\sharp}(M^\sharp)) \subseteq \gamma_{\mathbb{M}^\sharp}(\mathbf{test}_{\mathbb{M}^\sharp}[\texttt{cond}](M^\sharp))$$

Example 8. In this example, we assume that $\mathbb{N}^\sharp$ is the octagon domain, and that $\mathbb{X} = \{\mathtt{x}\}$, and $\mathbb{Y} = \{\mathtt{y}\}$ (thus, $\mathcal{A} : \mathtt{y} \mapsto \{\mathtt{y}^-, \mathtt{y}^+\}$). We consider an abstract pre-condition $M^\sharp = (N_0^\sharp, \mathcal{A})$, where $N_0^\sharp = (5 \leq \mathtt{x} \wedge \mathtt{x} \leq 5)$, and a condition test $\mathtt{y} - \mathtt{x} \leq 3$. Abstract test $\mathbf{test}_{\mathbb{M}^\sharp}[\mathtt{y} - \mathtt{x} \leq 3](M^\sharp)$ first substitutes $\mathtt{y}^+$ for $\mathtt{y}$ in $(\mathtt{y} - \mathtt{x} \leq 3)$, which generates condition $\mathtt{y}^+ - \mathtt{x} \leq 3$. Then, it computes $\mathbf{test}_{\mathbb{N}^\sharp}[\mathtt{y}^+ - \mathtt{x} \leq 3](N_0^\sharp)$. Thus, we obtain the abstract post-condition $(N_1^\sharp, \mathcal{A})$ where $N_1^\sharp = (5 \leq \mathtt{x} \wedge \mathtt{x} \leq 5 \wedge \mathtt{y}^+ - \mathtt{x} \leq 3)$.

5.3 Verifying the Satisfaction of a Constraint

To verify assertions, we need an operator $\mathbf{sat}_{\mathbb{M}^\sharp}[\mathtt{cond}] : \mathbb{M}^\sharp \to \{\mathtt{TRUE}, \mathtt{FALSE}\}$ such that, if $\sigma \in \gamma_{\mathbb{M}^\sharp}(M^\sharp)$ and $\mathbf{sat}_{\mathbb{M}^\sharp}[\mathtt{cond}](M^\sharp) = \mathtt{TRUE}$, then $[\![\mathtt{cond}]\!](\sigma) = \mathtt{TRUE}$. The case of numerical assertions is very similar to the case of numeric tests.

To test whether $\mathtt{y}$ can store only $\ominus$ in any store described by $(N^\sharp, \mathcal{A})$, we simply need to check whether constraint $\mathtt{y}^- = \mathtt{y}^+$ is unsatisfiable. This suggests $\mathbf{sat}_{\mathbb{M}^\sharp}[\mathbf{is\_empty}(\mathtt{y})](N^\sharp, \mathcal{A}) = \mathbf{is\_bot}_{\mathbb{N}^\sharp}(\mathbf{test}_{\mathbb{N}^\sharp}[\mathtt{y}^- = \mathtt{y}^+](N^\sharp))$, where $\mathbf{is\_bot}_{\mathbb{N}^\sharp} : \mathbb{N}^\sharp \to \{\mathtt{TRUE}, \mathtt{FALSE}\}$ is a sound emptiness test (if $\mathbf{is\_bot}_{\mathbb{N}^\sharp}(N^\sharp) = \mathtt{TRUE}$, then $\gamma_{\mathbb{N}^\sharp}(N^\sharp) = \emptyset$).

5.4 Assignment

We now describe a transfer function $\mathbf{assign}_{\mathbb{M}^\sharp}$ that over-approximates the effect of an assignment. We consider assignments with a linear right hand side expression (non linear assignment can be implemented using linearization [14]).

Emptiness Test. If the left-hand side $\mathtt{x}$ is a standard variable and optional variable $\mathtt{y}$ appears in the right hand side, the concrete semantics produces no output state when $\mathtt{y}$ takes no value. Therefore, given abstract pre-condition $M^\sharp$ and optional variable $\mathtt{y}$ appearing in the right hand side, if $\mathbf{sat}_{\mathbb{M}^\sharp}[\mathbf{is\_empty}(\mathtt{y})](M^\sharp)$ (Sect. 5.3), $\mathbf{assign}_{\mathbb{M}^\sharp}$ can safely return $\perp$. The computation of the abstract assignment starts with this check for all optional variables in the right hand side.

Numerical Assignment. We first consider basic assignment $\mathtt{y} = \mathtt{y} + \mathtt{z}$, where $\mathbb{Y} = \{\mathtt{y}, \mathtt{z}\}$, in order to give some intuition. If $M^\sharp = (N^\sharp, \mathcal{A})$ is an abstract pre-condition and $\sigma \in \gamma_{\mathbb{M}^\sharp}(M^\sharp)$ is such that $\sigma(\mathtt{y}) \neq \ominus$ and $\sigma(\mathtt{z}) \neq \ominus$, there exists a valuation $\nu \in \gamma_{\mathbb{N}^\sharp}(N^\sharp)$ such that $\nu(\mathtt{y}^-) = \nu(\mathtt{y}^+) = \sigma(\mathtt{y})$ and the same for $\mathtt{z}$. After the assignment evaluates, we obtain a store σ' such that $\sigma'(\mathtt{y}) = \sigma(\mathtt{y}) + \sigma(\mathtt{z})$ (and is unchanged for all other variables). Therefore, we need to make sure that the abstract post-condition will describe a valuation ν' such that $\nu'(\mathtt{y}^-) = \nu(\mathtt{y}^+) = \sigma(\mathtt{y}) + \sigma(\mathtt{z})$. We can achieve that by performing a pair of assignments to $\mathtt{y}^-, \mathtt{y}^+$ using *any* combination of avatars to represent $\mathtt{y}, \mathtt{z}$ in the right hand side. For instance, the following choices are sound:

$$\begin{cases} \mathtt{y}^- = \mathtt{y}^- + \mathtt{z}^-; \\ \mathtt{y}^+ = \mathtt{y}^+ + \mathtt{z}^+; \end{cases} \qquad \begin{cases} \mathtt{y}^- = \mathtt{y}^- + \mathtt{z}^+; \\ \mathtt{y}^+ = \mathtt{y}^+ + \mathtt{z}^-; \end{cases}$$

Yet, not all choices are of optimal precision. To show this, we assume that the pre-condition bounds both y and z from the above, for example with octagon $N^\sharp = \{\mathtt{y}^+ \leq 0 \wedge \mathtt{z}^+ \leq 0\}$. Then, only the left choice will produce a precise upper bound on $\mathtt{y}^+$. However, this approach may also produce constraints that violate the bi-avatar strategy, such as $\mathtt{y}^+ - \mathtt{z}^+ \leq 0$, where $\mathtt{z}^+$ gets assigned a lower bound. Such a lower bound can be removed by adding a temporary dimension $\mathtt{t}$, assuming that it is positive (using $\mathbf{test}_{\mathbb{M}^\sharp}[\mathtt{t} \geq 0]$), and performing assignment $\mathtt{z}^+ = \mathtt{z}^+ - \mathtt{t}$. To conclude, the analysis of assignment $\mathtt{y} = \sum_{i=0}^{n} a_i \mathtt{x}_i + \sum_{i=0}^{m} b_i \mathtt{y}_i + c$ proceeds as follows:

1. $\mathbf{assign}_{\mathbb{M}^\sharp}$ performs *in parallel* [10] the two assignments $\mathtt{y}^- = \mathtt{ex}^- \,||\, \mathtt{y}^+ = \mathtt{ex}^+$, where $\mathtt{ex}^-, \mathtt{ex}^+$ are obtained from the assignment right hand by substituting $\mathtt{y}_i$ with $\mathtt{y}_i^-$ or $\mathtt{y}_i^+$ depending on the sign of the b_is (see below);
2. then it forces the removal of constraints violating the bi-avatar property, using the aforementioned method.

Expression $\mathtt{ex}^+$ is defined as $\sum_{i=0}^{n} a_i \mathtt{x}_i + \sum_{i=0}^{m} b_i \mathtt{y}_i^{\epsilon_i} + c$ where avatar signs are determined as follows ($\mathtt{ex}^-$ uses the opposite avatar dimensions as $\mathtt{ex}^+$):

- if the assignment is not invertible (y does not appear in the right hand side), then ϵ_i is the sign of b_i;
- if the assignment is invertible and y is $\mathtt{y}_0$, then ϵ_i is the sign of the product $b_0 b_i$.

Finally, an assignment with a standard variable x as a left hand side can be handled in a similar manner (after the emptiness test described earlier): it will boil down to the introduction of a temporary dimension $\mathtt{x}'$, the analysis of two assignments $\mathtt{x} = \mathtt{ex}^+$ and $\mathtt{x}' = \mathtt{ex}^-$ with the above notations, the application of $\mathbf{test}_{\mathbb{M}^\sharp}[\mathtt{x} = \mathtt{x}']$, and finally the removal of $\mathtt{x}'$. By contrast, doing a single assignment would possibly cause relations between x and avatars be discarded.

The resulting abstract operator is sound in the following sense:

Theorem 4 (Soundness). *If* $\mathtt{t} \in \mathbb{X} \uplus \mathbb{Y}$ *and* ex *is a linear expression, then:*

$$\forall M^\sharp \in \mathbb{M}^\sharp,\ [\![\mathtt{t} = \mathtt{ex}]\!](\gamma_{\mathbb{M}^\sharp}(M^\sharp)) \subseteq \gamma_{\mathbb{M}^\sharp}(\mathbf{assign}_{\mathbb{M}^\sharp}(\mathtt{t}, \mathtt{ex}, M^\sharp))$$

Example 9. We assume $\mathbb{X} = \{\mathtt{x}\}$, $\mathbb{Y} = \{\mathtt{y}, \mathtt{z}\}$ and consider the abstract pre-condition defined by octagon $N^\sharp = \{0 \leq \mathtt{y}^- \wedge \mathtt{y}^+ \leq 10 \wedge 0 \leq \mathtt{z}^- \wedge \mathtt{z}^+ \leq 1 + \mathtt{x}\}$.

- non invertible assignment $\mathtt{y} = 1 - \mathtt{z}$ boils down to parallel assignments $\mathtt{y}^+ = 1 - \mathtt{z}^- \,||\, \mathtt{y}^- = 1 - \mathtt{z}^+$ in Octagons [13] and produces numerical post-condition $\{-\mathtt{x} \leq \mathtt{y}^- \wedge \mathtt{y}^+ \leq 1 \wedge 0 \leq \mathtt{z}^- \wedge \mathtt{z}^+ \leq 1 + \mathtt{x}\}$;
- invertible assignment $\mathtt{y} = \mathtt{y} + \mathtt{z}$ boils down to parallel assignments $\mathtt{y}^+ = \mathtt{y}^+ + \mathtt{z}^+ \,||\, \mathtt{y}^- = \mathtt{y}^- + \mathtt{z}^-$, and produces numerical post-condition $\{0 \leq \mathtt{y}^- \wedge \mathtt{y}^+ \leq 11 + \mathtt{x} \wedge 0 \leq \mathtt{z}^- \wedge \mathtt{z}^+ \leq 1 + \mathtt{x}\}$.

5.5 Inclusion Checking, Join and Widening

To analyze condition tests and loops, we also need abstract operations for join, widening and inclusion test. Using the bi-avatar strategy, these operations can be implemented in a straightforward manner, using the operations of the underlying domain, since avatars are the same for all abstract values. We write $\mathcal{A}$ for the set of avatars defined by the bi-avatar strategy in $\mathbb{X} \uplus \mathbb{Y}$. We let $\mathbf{is\_le}_{\mathbb{N}^\sharp}$, $\mathbf{join}_{\mathbb{N}^\sharp}$, $\mathbf{widen}_{\mathbb{N}^\sharp}$ denote the abstract inclusion check, abstract join and abstract widening of abstract domain $\mathbb{N}^\sharp$, satisfying the following soundness conditions:

$$\begin{array}{l}\forall N_0^\sharp, N_1^\sharp \in \mathbb{N}^\sharp,\ \mathbf{is\_le}_{\mathbb{N}^\sharp}(N_0^\sharp, N_1^\sharp) = \mathtt{TRUE} \Longrightarrow \gamma_{\mathbb{N}^\sharp}(N_0^\sharp) \subseteq \gamma_{\mathbb{N}^\sharp}(N_1^\sharp)\\ \forall N_0^\sharp, N_1^\sharp \in \mathbb{N}^\sharp,\ \gamma_{\mathbb{N}^\sharp}(N_0^\sharp) \cup \gamma_{\mathbb{N}^\sharp}(N_1^\sharp) \subseteq \gamma_{\mathbb{N}^\sharp}(\mathbf{join}_{\mathbb{N}^\sharp}(N_0^\sharp, N_1^\sharp))\\ \forall N_0^\sharp, N_1^\sharp \in \mathbb{N}^\sharp,\ \gamma_{\mathbb{N}^\sharp}(N_0^\sharp) \cup \gamma_{\mathbb{N}^\sharp}(N_1^\sharp) \subseteq \gamma_{\mathbb{N}^\sharp}(\mathbf{widen}_{\mathbb{N}^\sharp}(N_0^\sharp, N_1^\sharp))\end{array}$$

Furthermore, we assume that $\mathbf{widen}_{\mathbb{N}^\sharp}$ ensures convergence of any sequence of abstract iterates [3].

Definition 5 (Inclusion checking, join and widening). *We let the operators over* $\mathbb{M}^\sharp$ *be defined by:*

$$\begin{array}{rcl}\mathbf{is\_le}_{\mathbb{M}^\sharp}((N_0^\sharp, \mathcal{A}), (N_1^\sharp, \mathcal{A})) &=& \mathbf{is\_le}_{\mathbb{N}^\sharp}(N_0^\sharp, N_1^\sharp)\\ \mathbf{join}_{\mathbb{M}^\sharp}((N_0^\sharp, \mathcal{A}), (N_1^\sharp, \mathcal{A})) &=& (\mathbf{join}_{\mathbb{N}^\sharp}(N_0^\sharp, N_1^\sharp), \mathcal{A})\\ \mathbf{widen}_{\mathbb{M}^\sharp}((N_0^\sharp, \mathcal{A}), (N_1^\sharp, \mathcal{A})) &=& (\mathbf{widen}_{\mathbb{N}^\sharp}(N_0^\sharp, N_1^\sharp), \mathcal{A})\end{array}$$

These operators trivially inherit the properties of the operators of $\mathbb{N}^\sharp$:

Theorem 5. *Operations* $\mathbf{is\_le}_{\mathbb{M}^\sharp}$, $\mathbf{join}_{\mathbb{M}^\sharp}$ *and* $\mathbf{widen}_{\mathbb{M}^\sharp}$ *satisfy soundness condition of the same form as their underlying counterpart. In particular:*

$$\forall N_0^\sharp, N_1^\sharp \in \mathbb{N}^\sharp,\ \gamma_{\mathbb{N}^\sharp}(N_0^\sharp) \cup \gamma_{\mathbb{N}^\sharp}(N_1^\sharp) \subseteq \gamma_{\mathbb{N}^\sharp}(\mathbf{join}_{\mathbb{N}^\sharp}(N_0^\sharp, N_1^\sharp))$$

Moreover, $\mathbf{widen}_{\mathbb{M}^\sharp}$ *also ensures termination.*

5.6 Analysis

We now propose a static analysis for the language of Sect. 3. We define the abstract semantics of programs in Fig. 5. It uses the abstract operators defined in the previous subsections and an abstract least fixpoint operator $\mathbf{lfp}^\#$, which performs abstract iterations with widening $\mathbf{widen}_{\mathbb{M}^\sharp}$ until convergence can be checked using abstract inclusion test $\mathbf{is\_le}_{\mathbb{M}^\sharp}$ [3]. Operator $\mathbf{lfp}^\#$ ensures that, when $F : \mathcal{P}(\mathbb{S}) \to \mathcal{P}(\mathbb{S})$ is continuous and $F^\# : \mathbb{M}^\sharp \to \mathbb{M}^\sharp$ satisfies $F \circ \gamma_{\mathbb{M}^\sharp} \subseteq \gamma_{\mathbb{M}^\sharp} \circ F^\#$, then $\mathbf{lfp}_{\gamma_{\mathbb{M}^\sharp}(M^\sharp)} \subseteq \gamma_{\mathbb{M}^\sharp}(\mathbf{lfp}^\#_{M^\sharp} F^\#)$. The analysis of statement $\mathbf{assert}(\mathtt{cond})$ (not shown in the figure) simply reports failure to prove the assertion $\mathtt{cond}$ if $\mathbf{sat}_{\mathbb{M}^\sharp}[\mathtt{cond}]$ does not return $\mathtt{TRUE}$.

The abstract semantics $[\![\mathtt{s}]\!]^\# : \mathbb{M}^\sharp \to \mathbb{M}^\sharp$ takes an abstract pre-condition and returns an abstract post-condition. We can prove by induction over the syntax of programs that this abstract semantics is sound:

Theorem 6 (Soundness). *Given a program* $\mathtt{s}$ *and an abstract pre-condition* $M^\sharp$*, the post-condition derived by the analysis is sound:*

$$[\![\mathtt{s}]\!](\gamma_{\mathbb{M}^\sharp}(M^\sharp)) \subseteq \gamma_{\mathbb{M}^\sharp}([\![\mathtt{s}]\!]^\#(M^\sharp))$$

$$\begin{array}{rl}
[\![\mathbf{skip}]\!]^{\#}(M^\sharp) = M^\sharp & [\![\mathtt{z} = \mathtt{ex}]\!]^{\#}(M^\sharp) = \mathbf{assign}_\sharp(M^\sharp, \mathtt{z}, \mathtt{ex}) \\
[\![\mathtt{s_0}; \mathtt{s_1}]\!]^{\#}(M^\sharp) = [\![\mathtt{s_1}]\!]^{\#} \circ [\![\mathtt{s_0}]\!]^{\#}(M^\sharp) & [\![\mathbf{assume}(\mathtt{cond})]\!]^{\#}(M^\sharp) = \mathbf{test}_\sharp[\mathtt{cond}](M^\sharp)
\end{array}$$

$$\begin{array}{rl}
[\![\mathbf{if}(\mathtt{cond})\{\mathtt{s_0}\}\mathbf{else}\{\mathtt{s_1}\}]\!]^{\#}(M^\sharp) = & \mathbf{join}_\sharp([\![\mathtt{s_0}]\!]^{\#} \circ \mathbf{test}_\sharp[\mathtt{cond}](M^\sharp), \\
& [\![\mathtt{s_1}]\!]^{\#} \circ \mathbf{test}_\sharp[\mathtt{cond} == \mathtt{FALSE}](M^\sharp)) \\
[\![\mathbf{while}(\mathtt{cond})\{\mathtt{s}\}]\!]^{\#}(M^\sharp) = & \mathbf{test}_\sharp[\mathtt{cond} == \mathtt{FALSE}](\mathbf{lfp}^{\#}_{M^\sharp} F^{\#}) \\
& \text{where} \quad F^{\#} : M^\sharp \mapsto [\![\mathtt{s}]\!]^{\#}(\mathbf{test}_\sharp[\mathtt{cond}](M^\sharp))
\end{array}$$

Fig. 5. Abstract semantics

6 Possibly Empty Summary Variables

While Sects. 3 to 5 studied the abstraction of stores where optional variables may contain either *one* value or $\ominus$, the array analysis shown in Sect. 2 makes use of *summary dimensions*, which may take no value, one value, or many values. We extend the analysis shown in the previous sections to handle such cases. The construction of Gopan et *al.* [8] handles non empty summary dimensions (the main feature of this abstraction is to perform weak updates when writing into a summary dimension). We apply the same technique to the Maya functor, and call the resulting abstract domain functor Maya+, that lifts an abstraction of numerical vectors into an abstraction of sets of vectors of *sets* of numerical values. As the extension is fairly straightforward, we present only its novel characteristics.

Concrete States and Abstraction. First, we extend the language of Sect. 3. We now let $\mathbb{Y}$ denote summary dimensions, that may take zero, one or several values. The concrete states are now defined by:

$$\sigma_+ \in \mathbb{S}_+ \overset{\text{def.}}{::=} (\mathbb{X} \to \mathbb{V}) \uplus (\mathbb{Y} \to \mathcal{P}(\mathbb{V}))$$

An abstract state $M_+^\sharp$ in the resulting Maya+ domain is a tuple composed of a numeric abstract value $N^\sharp$ and an avatar mapping function $\mathcal{A}$, as in the Maya domain. However, the concretization is different: Maya+ assumes a concretization function γ_+ of a numeric domain with summarized dimensions, which returns sets of valuations ν_+ which map each avatar dimensions into a set of values.

Definition 6 (Concretization). *Given an abstract state $M_+^\sharp = (N^\sharp, \mathcal{A})$, we define the following consistency predicates:*

$$\begin{array}{rl}
P_{\mathbb{X}}(\sigma_+, M_+^\sharp, \nu_+) & \overset{def.}{\Longleftrightarrow} \forall \mathtt{x} \in \mathbb{X},\ \sigma_+(\mathtt{x}) = \nu_+(\mathtt{x}) \\
P_{\mathbb{Y}}(\sigma_+, M_+^\sharp, \nu_+) & \overset{def.}{\Longleftrightarrow} \forall \mathtt{y} \in \mathbb{Y},\ \sigma_+(\mathtt{y}) \subseteq \bigcap_{\mathtt{d} \in \mathcal{A}(\mathtt{y})} \nu_+(\mathtt{d})
\end{array}$$

Then, the concretization of $M_+^\sharp = (N^\sharp, \mathcal{A})$ is defined by:

$$\gamma_{\mathbb{M}_+^\sharp}(M_+^\sharp) \overset{def.}{::=} \left\{ \sigma_+ \in \mathbb{S} \mid \exists \nu_+ \in \gamma_+(N^\sharp),\ P_{\mathbb{X}}(\sigma_+, M_+^\sharp, \nu_+) \wedge P_{\mathbb{Y}}(\sigma_+, M_+^\sharp, \nu_+) \right\}$$

Example 10 (Concretization of Maya+). We assume $\mathbb{X} = \{\mathtt{x}\}$, $\mathbb{Y} = \{\mathtt{y}\}$, and consider the abstract element $(3 \leq \mathtt{x} \wedge \mathtt{x} \leq 4 \wedge 0 \leq \mathtt{y}^- \wedge \mathtt{y}^+ \leq \mathtt{x} - 3, \mathcal{A})$ where $\mathcal{A}$ follows the bi-avatar strategy. These constraints define valid elements of both Maya and Maya+ domains. However, the concretizations of this abstract element in both domains are different as shown below:

$$
\begin{array}{ll}
Maya\colon ① \ \mathtt{x} \mapsto 3 \ \mathtt{y} \mapsto 0 & Maya{+}\colon ① \ \mathtt{x} \mapsto 3 \ \mathtt{y} \mapsto \{0\} \\
② \ \mathtt{x} \mapsto 3 \ \mathtt{y} \mapsto \ominus & ② \ \mathtt{x} \mapsto 3 \ \mathtt{y} \mapsto \emptyset \\
③ \ \mathtt{x} \mapsto 4 \ \mathtt{y} \mapsto 1 & ③ \ \mathtt{x} \mapsto 4 \ \mathtt{y} \mapsto \{1\} \\
④ \ \mathtt{x} \mapsto 4 \ \mathtt{y} \mapsto 0 & ④ \ \mathtt{x} \mapsto 4 \ \mathtt{y} \mapsto \{0\} \\
⑤ \ \mathtt{x} \mapsto 4 \ \mathtt{y} \mapsto \ominus & ⑤ \ \mathtt{x} \mapsto 4 \ \mathtt{y} \mapsto \emptyset \\
 & ⑥ \ \mathtt{x} \mapsto 4 \ \mathtt{y} \mapsto \{0, 1\}
\end{array}
$$

Concrete Semantics. The extension of the concrete semantics is mostly straightforward. We describe its salient aspects below.

– The semantics of arithmetic expressions $[\![\mathbf{ex}]\!] : \mathbb{S}_+ \to \mathcal{P}(\mathbb{V})$ evaluates each expression into a set of values.

$$
[\![\mathtt{c}]\!](\sigma_+) \qquad \forall \mathtt{x} \in \mathbb{X},\ [\![\mathtt{x}]\!](\sigma_+) = \{\sigma_+(\mathtt{x})\} \qquad \forall \mathtt{y} \in \mathbb{Y},\ [\![\mathtt{y}]\!](\sigma_+) = \sigma_+(\mathtt{y})
$$

$$
[\![\mathbf{ex}_0 \oplus \mathbf{ex}_1]\!](\sigma_+) = \begin{cases} \emptyset, \text{ if } \exists i,\ [\![\mathbf{ex}_i]\!](\sigma_+) = \emptyset \\ \{\mathtt{c}_0 \oplus \mathtt{c}_1 \mid \forall i,\ \mathtt{c}_i \in [\![\mathbf{ex}_i]\!](\sigma_+)\}, \text{ otherwise} \end{cases}
$$

– Since the operands of a logical operator are sets of values, the evaluations of logical expressions may also return a set of booleans, thus we can define two semantics for conditions, that filter states where the condition must (resp., may) evaluate to true.

(1) Given $\mathtt{S}_+ \subseteq \mathbb{S}_+$, the strong condition semantics $[\![\mathbf{cond}]\!]_s(\mathtt{S}_+) : \mathcal{P}(\mathbb{S}_+) \to \mathcal{P}(\mathbb{S}_+)$ narrows $\mathtt{S}_+$ to stores that always make $\mathtt{cond}$ evaluate to $\mathtt{TRUE}$:

$$
\begin{aligned}
[\![\mathbf{ex}_0 \otimes \mathbf{ex}_1]\!]_s(\mathtt{S}_+) = \{\sigma_+ \in \mathtt{S}_+ \mid (\forall \mathtt{c}_i \in [\![\mathbf{ex}_i]\!](\sigma_+), i \in \{0,1\}\ \mathtt{c}_0 \otimes \mathtt{c}_1 = \mathtt{TRUE}) \\
\vee [\![\mathbf{ex}_0]\!](\sigma_+) = \emptyset \vee [\![\mathbf{ex}_1]\!](\sigma_+) = \emptyset\}
\end{aligned}
$$

(2) the weak condition semantics $[\![\mathbf{cond}]\!]_w(\mathtt{S}_+)$ narrows $\mathtt{S}_+$ to stores that may make $\mathtt{cond}$ evaluate to $\mathtt{TRUE}$:

$$
\begin{aligned}
[\![\mathbf{ex}_0 \otimes \mathbf{ex}_1]\!]_w(\mathtt{S}_+) = \{\sigma_+ \in \mathtt{S}_+ \mid (\exists \mathtt{c}_i \in [\![\mathbf{ex}_i]\!](\sigma_+), i \in \{0,1\}\ \mathtt{c}_0 \otimes \mathtt{c}_1 = \mathtt{TRUE}) \\
\vee [\![\mathbf{ex}_0]\!](\sigma_+) = \emptyset \vee [\![\mathbf{ex}_1]\!](\sigma_+) = \emptyset\}
\end{aligned}
$$

– In assignment statement $[\![\mathtt{x} = \mathbf{ex}]\!] : \mathcal{P}(\mathbb{S}_+) \to \mathcal{P}(\mathbb{S}_+)$, the evaluation of the right hand side produces a set which may have several elements; in that case, we leave the choice of the new value non-deterministic. Optional variables are now *summaries*. Thus an assignment $\mathtt{y} = \mathbf{ex}$ to an optional variable results in a *weak update*.

$$
\begin{aligned}
&\text{if } \mathtt{x} \in \mathbb{X},\ [\![\mathtt{x} = \mathbf{ex}]\!](\mathtt{S}_+) = \{\sigma_+[\mathtt{x} \mapsto \mathtt{c}] \mid \mathtt{c} \in [\![\mathbf{ex}]\!](\sigma_+)\} \\
&\text{if } \mathtt{y} \in \mathbb{Y},\ [\![\mathtt{y} = \mathbf{ex}]\!](\mathtt{S}_+) = \{\sigma_+[\mathtt{y} \mapsto \sigma_+(\mathtt{y}) \cup [\![\mathbf{ex}]\!](\sigma_+)] \mid \sigma_+ \in \mathtt{S}_+\}
\end{aligned}
$$

- We apply the strong semantics of test in the semantics of **assume** statements and the weak one in semantics of **if** and **while** statements.

$$
\begin{aligned}
[\![\mathbf{assume}((\mathtt{cond})_s)]\!](\mathtt{S}_+) &= [\![\mathtt{cond}]\!]_{\mathrm{s}}(\mathtt{S}_+) \\
[\![\mathbf{if}(\mathtt{cond})\{\mathtt{s}_0\}\mathbf{else}\{\mathtt{s}_1\}]\!](\mathtt{S}_+) &= [\![\mathtt{s}_0]\!] \circ [\![\mathtt{cond}]\!]_{\mathrm{w}}(\mathtt{S}_+) \\
&\quad \cup [\![\mathtt{s}_1]\!] \circ [\![\mathtt{cond} == \mathtt{FALSE}]\!]_{\mathrm{w}}(\mathtt{S}_+) \\
[\![\mathbf{while}(\mathtt{cond})\{\mathtt{s}\}]\!](\mathtt{S}_+) &= [\![\mathtt{cond} == \mathtt{FALSE}]\!]_{\mathrm{w}}(\mathtt{S}''_+) \\
&\quad \text{where } \mathtt{S}''_+ = \mathbf{lfp}\, \lambda \mathtt{S}'_+ \cdot \mathtt{S}_+ \cup [\![\mathtt{s}]\!]([\![\mathtt{cond}]\!]_{\mathrm{w}}(\mathtt{S}'_+))
\end{aligned}
$$

Analysis. The abstract interpretation of this semantics is straightforward, as it simply combines the analysis in Sect. 5 and the classical technique for manipulating summarized dimensions [8]. It is worth noting that, while the abstract condition test described in Sect. 5.2 precisely over-approximates the strong semantics of tests, another abstract transfer function needs to be defined for the weak semantics. When applied to a condition that involves summaries, that function checks whether the condition *cannot* be satisfied (by applying $\mathbf{sat}_{\mathbb{M}^\sharp}[.]$ with the opposite condition), and returns $\bot$ if that is the case; otherwise, it leaves the abstract state unchanged.

Theorem 7 (Soundness). *We let $[\![.]\!]^\#$ represent the abstract semantics. Given a program* s *and an abstract pre-condition $M_+^\sharp$, the post-condition derived by the analysis is sound:*

$$[\![\mathtt{s}]\!](\gamma_{\mathbb{M}_+^\sharp}(M_+^\sharp)) \subseteq \gamma_{\mathbb{M}_+^\sharp}([\![\mathtt{s}]\!]^\#(M_+^\sharp))$$

7 Implementation and Examples

We have implemented abstract domain functors Maya and Maya+ with the bi-avatar strategy (so that they can be applied to numerical abstract domains representing linear inequalities), as well as the analysis of the language of Fig. 3. To assess its precision, we have encoded into this language the computations over array indexes related to possibly empty groups encountered in [12] for a few basic array analyses. This approach allows to assess the optional value analysis, outside of the array analysis. We discuss in details the analysis of the array initialization example shown in Sect. 2. In this analysis $\mathbb{Y} = \{\underline{\mathrm{Idx}}_0, \underline{\mathrm{Idx}}_1\}$, ($\underline{\mathrm{Idx}}_i$ over-approximates the set of indexes of cells in group G_i), and $\mathcal{A}$ is defined according to the bi-avatar strategy ($\mathcal{A}(\underline{\mathrm{Idx}}_i) = \{\underline{\mathrm{Idx}}_i^-, \underline{\mathrm{Idx}}_i^+\}$ —note these are all *summary* dimensions, since a group of cells may span several indexes). The resulting invariants are shown in Fig. 6. At point ⓪, group G_1 contains all the elements of the array (uninitialized elements) and G_0 is empty (initialized elements). The weak update $\underline{\mathrm{Idx}}_0 = \mathtt{i}$ and statement $\mathbf{assume}(\underline{\mathrm{Idx}}_1 != \mathtt{i})$ stem from the assignment $\mathtt{a[i]} = 0$ in the array program (Fig. 2(a)). They are analyzed by $\mathbf{assign}_{\mathbb{M}^\sharp}$ and $\mathbf{test}_{\mathbb{M}^\sharp}[.]$, and effectively extend group G_0 and shrink group G_1 by one cell. The loop exit invariant shown at point ⑤ defines stores where $\underline{\mathrm{Idx}}_1$ is mapped to no value, which indeed means that the group of uninitialized cells is empty.

The analysis was run on a few similar programs encoding the steps that [12] needs to achieve to verify array programs, and the results are shown in Fig. 7. The columns show numbers of lines of codes, standard variables, summary optional variables, runtime, total numbers of assertions and numbers of verified assertions. Test case "array-init" is what we show in Fig. 6. Test cases "array-random-access", "array-traverse" and "array-compare" simulate the array analysis on programs of corresponding algorithm. The analyses are performed with Polyhedra as underlying domain. Runtimes are comparable to those observed in [12] for the numerical domain part. All invariants needed for the verification of array constraints are also verified. Last, the invariants produced express relations between groups, even when those could be empty.

8 Related Works

Numerical abstract domains [1,3,5,7,11,13] describe constraints over sets of vectors, where each dimension is mapped to *one* value. Our work aims at extending such domains so as to abstract vectors of possibly empty sets of scalars.

Abstractions based on summary dimensions [8,17] extend basic numerical domains to abstract vectors of non empty sets, so that one dimension may describe an unbounded family of variables. Summaries are also used in shape analysis [15], with a similar semantics. Empty summaries can be dealt with using disjunctions.

Siegel and Simon [16] abstract dynamic stores, where the set of memory cells is dynamic, and also utilize summary dimensions. In this work, a summary variable may also denote an empty set of values. To abstract precisely which dimension may be empty, a flag is associated to each summary variable, and

int $\mathtt{i} = 0$;

⓪ $0 \leq \mathtt{i} \wedge \mathtt{i} \leq 0 \wedge 1 \leq \underline{\mathrm{Idx}}_0^- \wedge \underline{\mathrm{Idx}}_0^+ \leq 0 \wedge 0 \leq \underline{\mathrm{Idx}}_1^- \wedge \underline{\mathrm{Idx}}_1^+ \leq 7$

while$(\mathtt{i} < 8)\{$

① $0 \leq \mathtt{i} \wedge \mathtt{i} \leq 7 \wedge 0 \leq \underline{\mathrm{Idx}}_0^- \wedge \underline{\mathrm{Idx}}_0^+ \leq \mathtt{i} - 1 \wedge \mathtt{i} \leq \underline{\mathrm{Idx}}_1^- \wedge \underline{\mathrm{Idx}}_1^+ \leq 7$

$\underline{\mathrm{Idx}}_0 = \mathtt{i}$;

② $0 \leq \mathtt{i} \wedge \mathtt{i} \leq 7 \wedge 0 \leq \underline{\mathrm{Idx}}_0^- \wedge \underline{\mathrm{Idx}}_0^+ \leq \mathtt{i} \wedge \mathtt{i} \leq \underline{\mathrm{Idx}}_1^- \wedge \underline{\mathrm{Idx}}_1^+ \leq 7$

assume$(\underline{\mathrm{Idx}}_1 != \mathtt{i})$;

③ $0 \leq \mathtt{i} \wedge \mathtt{i} \leq 7 \wedge 0 \leq \underline{\mathrm{Idx}}_0^- \wedge \underline{\mathrm{Idx}}_0^+ \leq \mathtt{i} \wedge \mathtt{i} + 1 \leq \underline{\mathrm{Idx}}_1^- \wedge \underline{\mathrm{Idx}}_1^+ \leq 7$

$\mathtt{i} = \mathtt{i} + 1$;

④ $0 \leq \mathtt{i} \wedge \mathtt{i} \leq 7 \wedge 0 \leq \underline{\mathrm{Idx}}_0^- \wedge \underline{\mathrm{Idx}}_0^+ \leq \mathtt{i} - 1 \wedge \mathtt{i} \leq \underline{\mathrm{Idx}}_1^- \wedge \underline{\mathrm{Idx}}_1^+ \leq 7$

$\}$

⑤ $8 \leq \mathtt{i} \wedge 0 \leq \underline{\mathrm{Idx}}_0^- \wedge \underline{\mathrm{Idx}}_0^+ \leq \mathtt{i} - 1 \wedge \mathtt{i} \leq \underline{\mathrm{Idx}}_1^- \wedge \underline{\mathrm{Idx}}_1^+ \leq 7$

Fig. 6. Analysis of the array initialization example: invariants over group indexes

Program	LOCs	#Standard	#Optional	Time (ms)	#Assertions	#Verified
array-init	9	1	2	4.7	1	1
array-random-access	30	3	6	36.5	3	3
array-traverse	6	1	1	6.6	1	1
array-compare	10	3	2	14.1	1	1

Fig. 7. Analysis results

it is true if and only if the variable is defined to at least one value. This approach allows to express relations between the emptiness of distinct variables. However, it does not allow to infer that a variable is undefined from conflicting constraints over its value (as needed in, e.g., [12]). This approach is thus orthogonal to ours, and both techniques could actually be combined. Another technique [6,12] uses a conjunction of numerical abstract elements $N_0^\sharp, \ldots, N_p^\sharp$ such that a group of variables that should either all be empty or all be defined are constrained together in a same $N_i^\sharp$. While this approach tracks emptiness precisely and without disjunctions, it is fairly *ad hoc* and expresses no relational constraints across groups.

Last, we note that other works on numerical abstract domains use several dimensions in the abstract domain so as to constrain a single variable. For instance, the implementation of octagons on top of DBMs lets a variable $\mathtt{x}$ be described in a DBM by dimensions $\mathtt{x}^+ = \mathtt{x}$ and $\mathtt{x}^- = -\mathtt{x}$ (so that $\mathtt{x} = \frac{1}{2}(\mathtt{x}^+ - \mathtt{x}^-)$) [13].

9 Conclusion

We have proposed the Maya functor to lift numerical abstract domains into abstractions for sets of stores where some variables may be undefined, and a functor Maya+ that performs the same task in presence of possibly empty summary dimensions. We have fully described the design of abstract operations using a "bi-avatar" strategy, that allows to cope with abstract domains based on linear inequalities. Our construction can be applied either to analyze languages that allow optional values, or as a back-end for static analyses that rely on groups of locations to describe complex memories (such as array and shape analyses). Future work should focus on additional strategies, for instance, based on the multi-avatar strategy (Example 6), to accommodate other kinds of numerical abstract domains. Moreover, it will also be interesting to integrate our functors in array or shape analyses.

References

1. Chen, L., Liu, J., Miné, A., Kapur, D., Wang, J.: An abstract domain to infer octagonal constraints with absolute value. In: Müller-Olm, M., Seidl, H. (eds.) Static Analysis. LNCS, vol. 8723, pp. 101–117. Springer, Heidelberg (2014)

2. Cousot, P.: Constructive design of a hierarchy of semantics of a transition system by abstract interpretation. ENTS **6**, 77–102 (1997)
3. Cousot, P., Cousot, R.: Abstract interpretation: a unified lattice model for static analysis of programs by construction or approximation of fixpoints. In: POPL (1977)
4. Cousot, P., Cousot, R., Logozzo, F.: A parametric segmentation functor for fully automatic and scalable array content analysis. In: POPL (2011)
5. Cousot, P., Halbwachs, N.: Automatic discovery of linear restraints among variables of a program. In: POPL (1978)
6. Cox, A., Chang, B.-Y.E., Sankaranarayanan, S.: QUIC graphs: relational invariant generation for containers. In: VMCAI (2015)
7. Ghorbal, K., Ivančić, F., Balakrishnan, G., Maeda, N., Gupta, A.: Donut domains: efficient non-convex domains for abstract interpretation. In: Kuncak, V., Rybalchenko, A. (eds.) VMCAI 2012. LNCS, vol. 7148, pp. 235–250. Springer, Heidelberg (2012)
8. Gopan, D., DiMaio, F., Dor, N., Reps, T., Sagiv, M.: Numeric domains with summarized dimensions. In: Jensen, K., Podelski, A. (eds.) TACAS 2004. LNCS, vol. 2988, pp. 512–529. Springer, Heidelberg (2004)
9. Halbwachs, N., Péron, M.: Discovering properties about arrays in simple programs. In: PLDI (2008)
10. Jeannet, B., Miné, A.: APRON: a library of numerical abstract domains for static analysis. In: Bouajjani, A., Maler, O. (eds.) CAV 2009. LNCS, vol. 5643, pp. 661–667. Springer, Heidelberg (2009)
11. Karr, M.: Affine relationships among the variables of a program. Acta Informatica **6**(2), 133–151 (1976)
12. Liu, J., Rival, X.: Abstraction of arrays based on non contiguous partitions. In: D'Souza, D., Lal, A., Larsen, K.G. (eds.) VMCAI 2015. LNCS, vol. 8931, pp. 282–299. Springer, Heidelberg (2015)
13. Miné, A.: The octagon abstract domain. HOSC **19**(1), 31–100 (2006)
14. Miné, A.: Relational domains for the detection of floating point run-time errors. In: ESOP (2004)
15. Sagiv, M., Reps, T., Wilhelm, R.: Parametric shape analysis via 3-valued logic. In: POPL (1999)
16. Siegel, H., Mihaila, B., Simon, A.: The undefined domain: precise relational information for entities that do not exist. In: Shan, C. (ed.) APLAS 2013. LNCS, vol. 8301, pp. 74–89. Springer, Heidelberg (2013)
17. Siegel, H., Simon, A.: Summarized dimensions revisited. In: NSAD (2012)
18. Siegel, H., Simon, A.: FESA: fold- and expand-based shape analysis. In: Jhala, R., Bosschere, K. (eds.) Compiler Construction. LNCS, vol. 7791, pp. 82–101. Springer, Heidelberg (2013)

Hoare Logic and Types

Fault-Tolerant Resource Reasoning

Gian Ntzik(✉), Pedro da Rocha Pinto, and Philippa Gardner

Imperial College London, London, UK
{gn408,pmd09,pg}@doc.ic.ac.uk

Abstract. Separation logic has been successful at verifying that programs do not crash due to illegal use of resources. The underlying assumption, however, is that machines do not fail. In practice, machines can fail unpredictably for various reasons, e.g. power loss, corrupting resources. Critical software, e.g. file systems, employ recovery methods to mitigate these effects. We introduce an extension of the Views framework to reason about such methods. We use concurrent separation logic as an instance of the framework to illustrate our reasoning, and explore programs using write-ahead logging, e.g. an ARIES recovery algorithm.

1 Introduction

There are many ways that software can fail: either software itself can be the cause of the failure (e.g. memory overflow or null pointer dereferencing); or the failure can arise independently of the software. These unpredictable failures are either *transient faults*, such as when a bit is flipped by cosmic radiation, or *host failures* (also referred to as crashes). Host failures can be classified into *soft*, such as those arising from power loss which can be fixed by rebooting the host, and *hard*, such as permanent hardware failure.

Consider a simple transfer operation that moves money between bank accounts. Assuming that bank accounts can have overdrafts, the transfer can be regarded as a sequence of two steps: first, subtract the money from one bank account; and then add the money to the other account. In the absence of host failures, the operation should succeed. However, if a host failure occurs in the middle of the transfer, money is lost. Programmers employ various techniques to recover some consistency after a crash, such as write-ahead logging (WAL) and associated recovery code. In this paper, we develop the reasoning to verify programs that can recover from host failures, assuming hard failures do not happen.

Resource reasoning, as introduced by separation logic [15], is a method for verifying that programs do not fail. A triple $\{ P \} \mathbb{C} \{ Q \}$ is given a *fault-avoiding*, partial correctness interpretation. This means that, assuming the precondition P holds then, if program $\mathbb{C}$ terminates, it must be the case that $\mathbb{C}$ does not fail and has all the resource necessary to yield a result which satisfies postcondition Q. Such reasoning guarantees the correct behaviour of the program, ensuring that the software does not crash itself due to bugs, e.g. invalid memory access. However, it assumes that there are no other failures of any form. To reason about

X. Feng and S. Park (Eds.): APLAS 2015, LNCS 9458, pp. 169–188, 2015.
DOI: 10.1007/978-3-319-26529-2_10

programs that can recover from host failures, we must change the underlying assumptions of resource reasoning.

We swap the traditional resource models with one that distinguishes between *volatile* and *durable* resource: the volatile resource (e.g. in RAM) does not survive crashes; whereas the durable resource (e.g. on the hard drive) does. Recovery operations use the durable state to repair any corruptions caused by the host failure. We introduce *fault-tolerant resource reasoning* to reason about programs in the presence of host failures and their associated recovery operations. We introduce a new fault-tolerant Hoare triple judgement of the form:

$$S \vdash \{ P_V \mid P_D \} \mathbb{C} \{ Q_V \mid Q_D \}$$

which has a partial-correctness, *resource fault-avoiding* and *host failing* interpretation. From the standard resource fault avoiding interpretation: assuming the precondition $P_V \mid P_D$ holds, where the volatile state satisfies P_V and the durable P_D, then if $\mathbb{C}$ terminates and there is no host failure, the volatile and durable resource will satisfy Q_V and Q_D respectively. From the host-failing interpretation: when there is a host failure, the volatile state is lost, and after potential recovery operations, the remaining durable state will satisfy the *fault-condition* S.

We extend the Views framework [3], which provides a general account of concurrent resource reasoning, with these fault-tolerant triples to provide a general framework for fault-tolerant resource reasoning. We instantiate our framework to give a fault-tolerant extension of concurrent separation logic [11] as an illustrative example. We use this instantiation to verify the correctness of programs that make use of recovery protocols to guarantee different levels of fault tolerance. In particular, we study a simple bank transaction using write-ahead logging and a simplified ARIES recovery algorithm [8], widely used in database systems.

2 Motivating Examples

We introduce fault-tolerant resource reasoning by showing how a simple bank transfer can be implemented and verified to be robust against host failures.

2.1 Naive Bank Transfer

Consider a simple transfer operation that moves money between bank accounts. Using a separation logic [15] triple, we can specify the transfer operation as:

$$\begin{array}{ll} & \{\mathsf{Account}(\mathtt{from}, v) * \mathsf{Account}(\mathtt{to}, w)\} \\ \vdash & \mathtt{transfer}(\mathtt{from}, \mathtt{to}, \mathtt{amount}) \\ & \{\mathsf{Account}(\mathtt{from}, v - \mathtt{amount}) * \mathsf{Account}(\mathtt{to}, w + \mathtt{amount})\} \end{array}$$

The internal structure of the account is abstracted using the abstract predicate [12], $\mathsf{Account}(x, v)$, which states that there is an account x with balance v. The specification says that, with access to the accounts `from` and `to`, the `transfer` will not fault. It will decrease the balance of account `from` by `amount` and increase the balance of account `to` by the same value. We can implement the transfer operation as follows:

```
function transfer(from, to, amount) {
  widthdraw(from, amount); deposit(to, amount);
}
```

Using separation logic, it is possible to prove that this implementation satisfies the specification, assuming no host failures. This implementation gives no guarantees in the presence of host failures. However, for this example, it is clearly desirable for the implementation to be aware that host failures occur. In addition, the implementation should guarantee that in the event of a host failure the operation is *atomic* : either it happened as a whole, or nothing happened. Note that the word atomic is also used in concurrency literature to describe an operation that takes effect at a single, discrete instant in time. In Sect. 3 we combine concurrency atomicity of concurrent separation logic with host failure atomicity: if an operation is concurrently atomic then it is also host-failure atomic.

2.2 Fault-Tolerant Bank Transfer: Implementation

We want an implementation of `transfer` to be robust against host failures and guarantee atomicity. One way to achieve this is to use write-ahead logging (WAL) combined with a recovery operation. We assume a file-system module which provides standard atomic operations to create and delete files, test their existence, and write to and read from files. Since file systems are critical, their operations have associated internal recovery operations in the event of a host failure.

Given an arbitrary program $\mathbb{C}$, we use $[\mathbb{C}]$ to identify that the program is associated with a recovery. We can now rewrite the `transfer` operation, making use of the file-system operations to implement a stylised WAL protocol as follows:

```
function transfer(from, to, amount) {
  fromAmount := getAmount(from);
  toAmount := getAmount(to);
  [create(log)];
  [write(log, (from, to, fromAmount, toAmount))];
  setAmount(from, fromAmount − amount);
  setAmount(to, toAmount + amount);
  [delete(log)];
}
```

The operation works by first reading the amounts stored in each account. It then creates a log file, `log`, where it stores the amounts for each account. It then updates each account, and finally deletes the log file. If a host failure occurs the log provides enough information to implement a recovery operation. In particular, its absence from the durable state means the transfer either happened or not, while its presence indicates the operation has not completed. In the latter case, we restore the initial balance by reading the log. An example of a recovery operation is the following:

```
function transferRecovery() {
  b := [exists(log)];
  if (b) {
    (from, to, fromAmount, toAmount) := [read(log)];
    if (from ≠ nil && to ≠ nil) {
      setAmount(from, fromAmount); setAmount(to, toAmount);
    }
    [delete(log)];
  }
}
```

The operation tests if the log file exists. If it does not, the recovery completes immediately since the balance is already consistent. Otherwise, the values of the accounts are reset to those stored in the log file which correspond to the initial balance. While the recovery operation is running, a host failure may occur, which means that upon reboot the recovery operation will run again. Eventually the recovery operation completes, at which point the transfer either occurred or did not. This guarantees that `transfer` is atomic with respect to host failures.

2.3 Fault-Tolerant Bank Transfer: Verification

We introduce the following new Hoare triple for specifying programs that run in a machine where host failures can occur:

$$S \vdash \{ P_V \mid P_D \} \mathbb{C} \{ Q_V \mid Q_D \}$$

where P_V, P_D, Q_V, Q_D and S are assertions in the style of separation logic and $\mathbb{C}$ is a program. P_V and Q_V describe the volatile resource, and P_D and Q_D describe the durable resource. The judgement is read as a normal Hoare triple when there are no host failures. The interpretation of the triples is partial *resource fault avoiding* and *host failing*. Given an initial $P_V \mid P_D$, it is safe to execute $\mathbb{C}$ without causing a resource fault. If no host failure occurs, and $\mathbb{C}$ terminates, the resulting state will satisfy $Q_V \mid Q_D$. If a host failure occurs, then the durable state will satisfy the *fault-condition* S.

Given the new judgement we can describe the resulting state after a host failure. Protocols designed to make programs robust against host failures make use of the durable resource to return to a consistent state after reboot. We must be able to describe programs that have a recovery operation running after reboot. We introduce the following triple:

$$R \vdash \{ P_V \mid P_D \} [\mathbb{C}] \{ Q_V \mid Q_D \}$$

The notation $[\mathbb{C}]$ is used to identify a program with an associated recovery. The assertion R describes the durable resource after the recovery takes place.

$$\mathsf{emp} \vee \mathsf{file}(\mathtt{name}, []) \vdash \{\mathsf{emp} \mid \mathsf{emp}\}\ [\mathtt{create}(\mathtt{name})]\ \{\mathsf{emp} \mid \mathsf{file}(\mathtt{name}, [])\}$$

$$\mathsf{emp} \vee \mathsf{file}(\mathtt{name}, xs) \vdash \{\mathsf{emp} \mid \mathsf{file}(\mathtt{name}, xs)\}\ [\mathtt{delete}(\mathtt{name})]\ \{\mathsf{emp} \mid \mathsf{emp}\}$$

$$\mathsf{emp} \vdash \{\mathsf{emp} \mid \mathsf{emp}\}\ [\mathtt{exists}(\mathtt{name})]\ \{\mathsf{ret} = \mathsf{false} \wedge \mathsf{emp} \mid \mathsf{emp}\}$$

$$\mathsf{file}(\mathtt{name}, xs) \vdash \{\mathsf{emp} \mid \mathsf{file}(\mathtt{name}, xs)\}\ [\mathtt{exists}(\mathtt{name})]\ \{\mathsf{ret} = \mathsf{true} \wedge \mathsf{emp} \mid \mathsf{file}(\mathtt{name}, xs)\}$$

$$\mathsf{file}(\mathtt{name}, xs) \vee \mathsf{file}(\mathtt{name}, xs +\!+ [\mathtt{x}]) \vdash \begin{array}{c}\{\mathsf{emp} \mid \mathsf{file}(\mathtt{name}, xs)\} \\ [\mathtt{write}(\mathtt{name}, \mathtt{x})] \\ \{\mathsf{emp} \mid \mathsf{file}(\mathtt{name}, xs +\!+ [\mathtt{x}])\}\end{array}$$

$$\mathsf{file}(\mathtt{name}, []) \vdash \{\mathsf{emp} \mid \mathsf{file}(\mathtt{name}, [])\}\ [\mathtt{read}(\mathtt{name})]\ \{\mathsf{ret} = \mathsf{nil} \wedge \mathsf{emp} \mid \mathsf{file}(\mathtt{name}, [])\}$$

$$\mathsf{file}(\mathtt{name}, [x] +\!+ xs) \vdash \begin{array}{c}\{\mathsf{emp} \mid \mathsf{file}(\mathtt{name}, [x] +\!+ xs)\} \\ [\mathtt{read}(\mathtt{name})] \\ \{\mathsf{ret} = x \wedge \mathsf{emp} \mid \mathsf{file}(\mathtt{name}, [x] +\!+ xs)\}\end{array}$$

Fig. 1. Specification of a simplified journaling file system.

We can now use the new judgements to verify the write-ahead logging `transfer` and its recovery. In their implementation, we use a simplified journaling file system as the durable resource with the operations specified in Fig. 1. We specify the write-ahead logging `transfer` with the following triple:

$$S \vdash \begin{array}{c}\left\{\dfrac{\mathtt{from} = f \wedge \mathtt{to} = t \wedge \mathtt{amount} = a \wedge \mathsf{emp}}{\mathsf{Account}(f, v) * \mathsf{Account}(t, w)}\right\} \\ \mathtt{transfer}(\mathtt{from}, \mathtt{to}, \mathtt{amount}) \\ \left\{\dfrac{\mathtt{from} = f \wedge \mathtt{to} = t \wedge \mathtt{amount} = a \wedge \mathsf{emp}}{\mathsf{Account}(f, v - a) * \mathsf{Account}(t, w + a)}\right\}\end{array}$$

where the fault-condition S describes all the possible durable states if a host failure occurs:

$$\begin{aligned} S = {} & (\mathsf{Account}(f, v) * \mathsf{Account}(t, w)) \\ & \vee (\mathsf{Account}(f, v) * \mathsf{Account}(t, w) * \mathsf{file}(\mathtt{log}, [])) \\ & \vee (\mathsf{Account}(f, v) * \mathsf{Account}(t, w) * \mathsf{file}(\mathtt{log}, [(f, t, v, w)])) \\ & \vee (\mathsf{Account}(f, v - a) * \mathsf{Account}(t, w) * \mathsf{file}(\mathtt{log}, [(f, t, v, w)])) \\ & \vee (\mathsf{Account}(f, v - a) * \mathsf{Account}(t, w + a) * \mathsf{file}(\mathtt{log}, [(f, t, v, w)]) \\ & \vee (\mathsf{Account}(f, v - a) * \mathsf{Account}(t, w + a)) \end{aligned}$$

A proof that the implementation satisfies the specification is shown in Fig. 2. If there is a host failure, the current specification of `transfer` only guarantees that the durable resource satisfies S. This includes the case where money is lost. This is undesirable. What we want is a guarantee that the operation is atomic. In order to add this guarantee, we must combine reasoning about the operation with reasoning about its recovery to establish that undesirable states are fixed after recovery. We formalise the combination of an operation and its recovery in order to provide robustness guarantees against host failures in the *recovery abstraction* rule:

$$
\begin{array}{l}
S \vdash \\
\left\{\frac{\texttt{from} = f \wedge \texttt{to} = t \wedge \texttt{amount} = a \wedge \mathsf{emp}}{\mathsf{Account}(f, v) * \mathsf{Account}(t, w)}\right\} \\
\texttt{fromAmount} := \texttt{getAmount}(\texttt{from}); \\
\texttt{toAmount} := \texttt{getAmount}(\texttt{to}); \\
\left\{\frac{\texttt{from} = f \wedge \texttt{to} = t \wedge \texttt{amount} = a \wedge \texttt{fromAmount} = v \wedge \texttt{toAmount} = w \wedge \mathsf{emp}}{\mathsf{Account}(f, v) * \mathsf{Account}(t, w))}\right\} \\
[\texttt{create}(\texttt{log})]\,; \\
\left\{\frac{\texttt{from} = f \wedge \texttt{to} = t \wedge \texttt{amount} = a \wedge \texttt{fromAmount} = v \wedge \texttt{toAmount} = w \wedge \mathsf{emp}}{\mathsf{Account}(f, v) * \mathsf{Account}(t, w) * \mathsf{file}(\texttt{log}, [])}\right\} \\
[\texttt{write}(\texttt{log}, (\texttt{from}, \texttt{to}, \texttt{fromAmount}, \texttt{toAmount}))]\,; \\
\left\{\frac{\texttt{from} = f \wedge \texttt{to} = t \wedge \texttt{amount} = a \wedge \texttt{fromAmount} = v \wedge \texttt{toAmount} = w \wedge \mathsf{emp}}{\mathsf{Account}(f, v) * \mathsf{Account}(t, w) * \mathsf{file}(\texttt{log}, [(f, t, v, w)])}\right\} \\
\texttt{setAmount}(\texttt{from}, \texttt{fromAmount} - \texttt{amount}); \\
\left\{\frac{\texttt{from} = f \wedge \texttt{to} = t \wedge \texttt{amount} = a \wedge \texttt{fromAmount} = v \wedge \texttt{toAmount} = w \wedge \mathsf{emp}}{\mathsf{Account}(f, v - a) * \mathsf{Account}(t, w) * \mathsf{file}(\texttt{log}, [(f, t, v, w)])}\right\} \\
\texttt{setAmount}(\texttt{to}, \texttt{toAmount} + \texttt{amount}); \\
\left\{\frac{\texttt{from} = f \wedge \texttt{to} = t \wedge \texttt{amount} = a \wedge \texttt{fromAmount} = v \wedge \texttt{toAmount} = w \wedge \mathsf{emp}}{\mathsf{Account}(f, v - a) * \mathsf{Account}(t, w + a) * \mathsf{file}(\texttt{log}, [(f, t, v, w)])}\right\} \\
[\texttt{delete}(\texttt{log})]\,; \\
\left\{\frac{\texttt{from} = f \wedge \texttt{to} = t \wedge \texttt{amount} = a \wedge \mathsf{emp}}{\mathsf{Account}(f, v - a) * \mathsf{Account}(t, w + a)}\right\}
\end{array}
$$

Fig. 2. Proof of transfer operation using write-ahead logging.

$$
\frac{\begin{array}{c} \mathbb{C}_R \textbf{ recovers } \mathbb{C} \\ S \vdash \{P_V \mid P_D\}\,\mathbb{C}\,\{Q_V \mid Q_D\} \\ S \vdash \{\mathsf{emp} \mid S\}\,\mathbb{C}_R\,\{\mathsf{true} \mid R\} \end{array}}{R \vdash \{P_V \mid P_D\}\,[\mathbb{C}]\,\{Q_V \mid Q_D\}}
$$

When implementing a new operation, we use the *recovery abstraction* rule to establish the fault-condition R we wish to expose to the client. In the second premiss we must first derive what the durable resource S will be immediately after a host-failure. In the third premiss, we establish that given S, the associated recovery operation will change the durable resource to the desired R. Note that because the recovery $\mathbb{C}_R$ runs immediately after the host failure, the volatile resource of its precondition is empty. Furthermore, we require the fault-condition of the recovery to be the same as the resource that is being recovered, since the recovery operation itself may fail due to a host-failure; i.e. recovery operations must be able to recover themselves.

We allow recovery abstraction to derive any fault-condition that is established by the recovery operation. If that fault-condition is a disjunction between the durable pre- and postconditions, $P_D \vee Q_D$, then the operation $[\mathbb{C}]$ appears to be atomic with respect to host failures. Either the operation's (durable) resource updates completely, or not at all. No intermediate states are visible to the client.

In order for `transfer` to be atomic, according to the recovery abstraction rule, `transferRecovery` must satisfy the following specification:

$$S \vdash \begin{array}{c} \left\{\dfrac{\mathsf{emp}}{S}\right\} \\ \texttt{transferRecovery}() \\ \left\{\dfrac{\mathsf{true}}{(\mathsf{Account}(f, v) * \mathsf{Account}(t, w)) \vee (\mathsf{Account}(f, v-a) * \mathsf{Account}(t, w+a))}\right\} \end{array}$$

The proof that the implementation satisfies this specification is given in Fig. 3. By applying the abstraction recovery rule we get the following specification for `transfer` which guarantees atomicity in case of a host-failure:

$$R \vdash \begin{array}{c} \left\{\dfrac{\texttt{from} = f \wedge \texttt{to} = t \wedge \texttt{amount} = a \wedge \mathsf{emp}}{\mathsf{Account}(f, v) * \mathsf{Account}(t, w)}\right\} \\ [\texttt{transfer}(\texttt{from}, \texttt{to}, \texttt{amount})] \\ \left\{\dfrac{\texttt{from} = f \wedge \texttt{to} = t \wedge \texttt{amount} = a \wedge \mathsf{emp}}{\mathsf{Account}(f, v-a) * \mathsf{Account}(t, w+a)}\right\} \end{array}$$

where the fault-condition R describes the recovered durable state:

$$R = (\mathsf{Account}(f, v) * \mathsf{Account}(t, w)) \vee (\mathsf{Account}(f, v-a) * \mathsf{Account}(t, w+a))$$

With this example, we have seen how to guarantee atomicity by logging the information required to undo operations. Advanced WAL protocols also store information allowing to redo operations and use concurrency control. We do not go into depth on how to enforce concurrency control in our examples other than the example shown in Sect. 3.1. It follows the common techniques used in concurrent separation logic.[1] However, in Sect. 4 we show ARIES, an advanced algorithm that uses write-ahead logging. A different style of write-ahead logging is used by file systems called journaling [14], which we discuss in the technical report [10].

3 Program Logic

Until now, we have only seen how to reason about sequential programs. For concurrent programs, we use resource invariants, in the style of concurrent separation logic [11], that are updated by primitive atomic operations. Here primitive atomic is used to mean that the operation takes effect at a single, discrete instant in time, and that it is atomic with respect to host failures.

The general judgement that enables us to reason about host failing concurrent programs is:

$$\boxed{J_V \mid J_D}; S \vdash \{P_V \mid P_D\} \ \mathbb{C} \ \{Q_V \mid Q_D\}$$

Here, $P_V \mid P_D$ and $Q_V \mid Q_D$ are pre- and postconditions as usual and describe the volatile and durable resource. S is a durable assertion, which we refer to as the *fault-condition*, describing the durable resource of the program $\mathbb{C}$ after a host failure and possible recovery. The interpretation of these triples is partial

[1] For an introduction to concurrent separation logic see [18].

$$S \vdash$$
$$\left\{\frac{\mathsf{emp}}{S}\right\}$$
$\texttt{b} := [\texttt{exists(log)}]\,;$
$$\left\{\frac{\mathsf{b} = b \wedge \mathsf{emp}}{\begin{array}{c}S \wedge (b \implies \mathsf{file}(\texttt{log}, []) * \mathsf{true} \vee \mathsf{file}(\texttt{log}, [(f, t, v, w)]) * \mathsf{true}) \\ \wedge (\neg b \implies \mathsf{Account}(f, v) * \mathsf{Account}(t, w) \vee \mathsf{Account}(f, v - a) * \mathsf{Account}(t, w + a))\end{array}}\right\}$$
$\texttt{if (b) \{}$
$$\left\{\frac{\mathsf{b} = b \wedge \mathsf{emp}}{S \wedge (\mathsf{file}(\texttt{log}, []) * \mathsf{true} \vee \mathsf{file}(\texttt{log}, [(f, t, v, w)]) * \mathsf{true})}\right\}$$
$(\texttt{from}, \texttt{to}, \texttt{fromAmount}, \texttt{toAmount}) := [\texttt{read(log)}]\,;$
$\texttt{if (from} \neq \texttt{nil \&\& to} \neq \texttt{nil) \{}$
$$\left\{\frac{\mathsf{b} = b \wedge \texttt{from} = f \wedge \texttt{to} = t \wedge \texttt{fromAmount} = v \wedge \texttt{toAmount} = w \wedge \mathsf{emp}}{S \wedge (\mathsf{file}(\texttt{log}, [(f, t, v, w)]) * \mathsf{true})}\right\}$$
$\texttt{setAmount(from, fromAmount); setAmount(to, toAmount);}$
$$\left\{\frac{\mathsf{b} = b \wedge \texttt{from} = f \wedge \texttt{to} = t \wedge \texttt{fromAmount} = v \wedge \texttt{toAmount} = w \wedge \mathsf{emp}}{\begin{array}{c}S \wedge (\mathsf{file}(\texttt{log}, [(f, t, v, w)]) * \mathsf{true}) \wedge \\ (\mathsf{Account}(f, v) * \mathsf{Account}(t, w) * \mathsf{true})\end{array}}\right\}$$
$\}$
$$\left\{\frac{\mathsf{b} = b \wedge \mathsf{emp}}{\begin{array}{c}S \wedge ((\mathsf{file}(\texttt{log}, []) * \mathsf{true}) \vee (\mathsf{file}(\texttt{log}, [(f, t, v, w)]) * \mathsf{true})) \wedge \\ (\mathsf{Account}(f, v) * \mathsf{Account}(t, w) * \mathsf{true})\end{array}}\right\}$$
$[\texttt{delete(log)}]\,;$
$$\left\{\frac{\mathsf{b} = b \wedge \mathsf{emp}}{\mathsf{Account}(f, v) * \mathsf{Account}(t, w)}\right\}$$
$\}$
$$\left\{\frac{\mathsf{b} = b \wedge \mathsf{emp}}{\mathsf{Account}(f, v) * \mathsf{Account}(t, w) \vee \mathsf{Account}(f, v - a) * \mathsf{Account}(t, w + a)}\right\}$$

Fig. 3. Proof that the transfer recovery operation guarantees atomicity.

resource fault avoiding and *host failing*. Starting from an initial state satisfying the precondition $P_V \mid P_D$, it is safe to execute $\mathbb{C}$ without causing a resource fault. If no host failure occurs and $\mathbb{C}$ terminates, the resulting state will satisfy the postcondition $Q_V \mid Q_D$. The shared resource invariant $J_V \mid J_D$ is maintained throughout the execution of $\mathbb{C}$. If a host failure occurs, all volatile resource is lost and the durable state will (after possible recoveries) satisfy $S * J_D$.

We give an overview of the key proof rules of Fault-tolerant Concurrent Separation Logic (FTCSL) in Fig. 4. Here we do not formally define the syntax of our assertions, although we describe the semantics in Sect. 5. In general, volatile and durable assertions can be parameterised by any separation algebra.

The *sequence rule* allows us to combine two programs in sequence as long as they have the same fault-condition and resource invariant. Typically, when the fault-conditions differ, we can weaken them using the *consequence rule*, which adds fault-condition weakening to the standard consequence rule of Hoare logic. The *frame rule*, as in separation logic, allows us to extend the pre- and postconditions with the same unmodified resource $R_V * R_D$. However, here the durable part, R_D, is also added to the fault-condition.

sequence

$$\frac{\boxed{J_V \mid J_D}; S \vdash \{P_V \mid P_D\}\ \mathbb{C}_1\ \{R_V \mid R_D\} \qquad \boxed{J_V \mid J_D}; S \vdash \{R_V \mid R_D\}\ \mathbb{C}_2\ \{Q_V \mid Q_D\}}{\boxed{J_V \mid J_D}; S \vdash \{P_V \mid P_D\}\ \mathbb{C}_1;\mathbb{C}_2\ \{Q_V \mid Q_D\}}$$

consequence

$$\frac{P_V \mid P_D \implies P'_V \mid P'_D \quad Q'_V \mid Q'_D \implies Q_V \mid Q_D \quad S' \implies S \qquad \boxed{J_V \mid J_D}; S' \vdash \{P'_V \mid P'_D\}\ \mathbb{C}\ \{Q'_V \mid Q'_D\}}{\boxed{J_V \mid J_D}; S \vdash \{P_V \mid P_D\}\ \mathbb{C}\ \{Q_V \mid Q_D\}}$$

frame

$$\frac{\boxed{J_V \mid J_D}; S \vdash \{P_V \mid P_D\}\ \mathbb{C}\ \{Q_V \mid Q_D\}}{\boxed{J_V \mid J_D}; S * R_D \vdash \{P_V * R_V \mid P_D * R_D\}\ \mathbb{C}\ \{Q_V * R_V \mid Q_D * R_D\}}$$

atomic

$$\frac{\boxed{\mathsf{emp} \mid \mathsf{emp}}; (P_D * J_D \vee Q_D * J_D) \vdash \{P_V * J_V \mid P_D * J_D\}\ \mathbb{C}\ \{Q_V * J_V \mid Q_D * J_D\}}{\boxed{J_V \mid J_D}; (P_D \vee Q_D) \vdash \{P_V \mid P_D\}\ \langle\mathbb{C}\rangle\ \{Q_V \mid Q_D\}}$$

share

$$\frac{\boxed{J_V * R_V \mid J_D * R_D}; S \vdash \{P_V \mid P_D\}\ \mathbb{C}\ \{Q_V \mid Q_D\}}{\boxed{J_V \mid J_D}; S * R_D \vdash \{P_V * R_V \mid P_D * R_D\}\ \mathbb{C}\ \{Q_V * R_V \mid Q_D * R_D\}}$$

parallel

$$\frac{\boxed{J_V \mid J_D}; S_1 \vdash \{P_{V1} \mid P_{D1}\}\ \mathbb{C}_1\ \{Q_{V1} \mid Q_{D1}\} \qquad \boxed{J_V \mid J_D}; S_2 \vdash \{P_{V2} \mid P_{D2}\}\ \mathbb{C}_2\ \{Q_{V2} \mid Q_{D2}\}}{\boxed{J_V \mid J_D}; (S_1 * S_2) \vee (S_1 * Q_{D2}) \vee (Q_{D1} * S_2) \vdash \begin{array}{c}\{P_{V1} * P_{V2} \mid P_{D1} * P_{D2}\}\\ \mathbb{C}_1 \parallel \mathbb{C}_2 \\ \{Q_{V1} * Q_{V2} \mid Q_{D1} * Q_{D2}\}\end{array}}$$

recovery abstraction

$$\frac{\mathbb{C}_R\ \textbf{recovers}\ \mathbb{C} \qquad \boxed{J_V \mid J_D}; S \vdash \{P_V \mid P_D\}\ \mathbb{C}\ \{Q_V \mid Q_D\} \qquad \boxed{\mathsf{emp} \mid J_D}; S \vdash \{\mathsf{emp} \mid S\}\ \mathbb{C}_R\ \{\mathsf{true} \mid R\}}{\boxed{J_V \mid J_D}; R \vdash \{P_V \mid P_D\}\ [\mathbb{C}]\ \{Q_V \mid Q_D\}}$$

Fig. 4. Selected proof rules of FTCSL

The *atomic rule* allows us to use the resource invariant $J_V \mid J_D$ using a primitive atomic operation. Since the operation executes in a single, discrete, moment in time, we can think of the operation temporarily owning the resources $J_V \mid J_D$. However, they must be reestablished at the end. This guarantees that the every primitive atomic operation maintains the resource invariant. Note that the rule enforces atomicity with respect to host failures. The *share rule* allows us to use local resources to extend the shared resource invariant.

The *parallel rule*, in terms of pre- and postconditions is as in concurrent separation logic. However, the fault-condition describes the possible durable resources that may result from a host failure while running $\mathbb{C}_1$ and $\mathbb{C}_2$ in parallel. In particular, a host-failure may occur while both $\mathbb{C}_1$ and $\mathbb{C}_2$ are running, in which case the fault-condition is $S_1 * S_2$, or when either one of $\mathbb{C}_1$, $\mathbb{C}_2$ has finished, in which case the fault-condition is $S_1 * Q_{D2}$ and $S_2 * Q_{D1}$ respectively.

Finally, the *recovery abstraction rule* allows us to prove that a recovery operation $\mathbb{C}_R$ establishes the fault-condition R we wish to expose to the client. The first premiss requires operation $\mathbb{C}_R$ to be the recovery of $\mathbb{C}$, i.e. it is executed on reboot after a host failure during execution of $\mathbb{C}$. The second premiss guarantees that in such case, the durable resources satisfy S and the shared resource invariant satisfies J_D, while the volatile state is lost after a host failure. The third premiss, takes the resource after the reboot and runs the recovery operation in order to establish R. Note that J_D is an invariant, as there can be potentially parallel recovery operations accessing it using primitive atomic operations. While the recovery operation $\mathbb{C}_R$ is running, there can be any number of host failures, which restart the recovery. This means that the recovery operation must be able to recover from itself. We allow recovery abstraction to derive any fault-condition that is established by the recovery operation. If the fault-condition is a disjunction between the durable pre- and post-conditions, $P_V \vee Q_D$, then the operation $[\mathbb{C}]$ appears to be atomic with respect to host failures.

3.1 Example: Concurrent Bank Transfer

Consider two threads that both perform a transfer operation from account f to account t as shown in Sect. 2. The parallel rule requires that each operation acts on disjoint resources in the precondition. Since both threads update the same accounts, we synchronise their use with the atomic blocks denoted by $\langle \_ \rangle$. A possible specification for the program is the following:

$$\boxed{\mathsf{emp} \mid \mathsf{emp}}; (\exists v, w.\, \mathsf{Account}(f, v) * \mathsf{Account}(t, w)) \vdash$$
$$\left\{\frac{\texttt{from} = f \wedge \texttt{to} = t \wedge \texttt{amount} = a \wedge \texttt{amount2} = b \wedge \mathsf{emp}}{\exists v, w.\, \mathsf{Account}(f, v) * \mathsf{Account}(t, w)}\right\}$$
$$\langle[\texttt{transfer(from, to, amount)}]\rangle;\ \|\ \langle[\texttt{transfer(from, to, amount2)}]\rangle;$$
$$\left\{\frac{\texttt{from} = f \wedge \texttt{to} = t \wedge \texttt{amount} = a \wedge \texttt{amount2} = b \wedge \mathsf{emp}}{\exists v, w.\, \mathsf{Account}(f, v) * \mathsf{Account}(t, w)}\right\}$$

A sketch proof of this specification is given in Fig. 5. We first move the shared resources of the two `transfer` operations to the shared invariant (share rule). We then prove each thread independently by making use of the atomic rule to gain temporary access to the shared invariant within the atomic block, and reuse the specification given in Sect. 2.3. It is possible to get stronger post-conditions, that maintain exact information about the amounts of each bank account, using complementary approaches such as Owicki-Gries or other forms

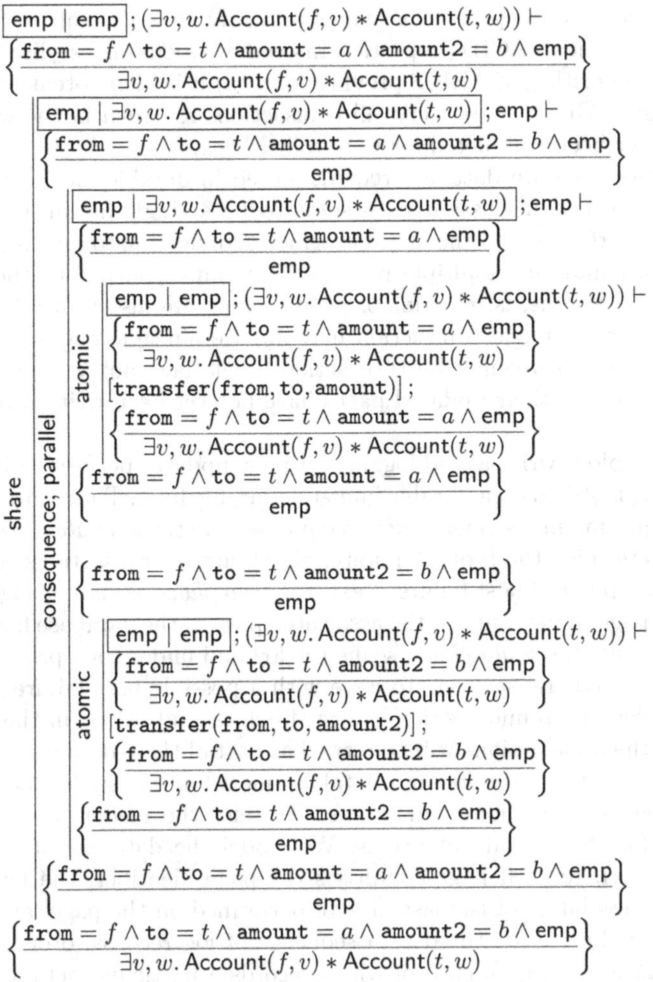

emp | emp ; (∃v, w. Account(f, v) ∗ Account(t, w)) ⊢
from = f ∧ to = t ∧ amount = a ∧ amount2 = b ∧ emp
∃v, w. Account(f, v) ∗ Account(t, w)
emp | ∃v, w. Account(f, v) ∗ Account(t, w) ; emp ⊢
from = f ∧ to = t ∧ amount = a ∧ amount2 = b ∧ emp
emp
emp | ∃v, w. Account(f, v) ∗ Account(t, w) ; emp ⊢
from = f ∧ to = t ∧ amount = a ∧ emp
emp
emp | emp ; (∃v, w. Account(f, v) ∗ Account(t, w)) ⊢
from = f ∧ to = t ∧ amount = a ∧ emp
∃v, w. Account(f, v) ∗ Account(t, w)
[transfer(from, to, amount)] ;
from = f ∧ to = t ∧ amount = a ∧ emp
∃v, w. Account(f, v) ∗ Account(t, w)
from = f ∧ to = t ∧ amount = a ∧ emp
emp
from = f ∧ to = t ∧ amount2 = b ∧ emp
emp
emp | emp ; (∃v, w. Account(f, v) ∗ Account(t, w)) ⊢
from = f ∧ to = t ∧ amount2 = b ∧ emp
∃v, w. Account(f, v) ∗ Account(t, w)
[transfer(from, to, amount2)] ;
from = f ∧ to = t ∧ amount2 = b ∧ emp
∃v, w. Account(f, v) ∗ Account(t, w)
from = f ∧ to = t ∧ amount2 = b ∧ emp
emp
from = f ∧ to = t ∧ amount = a ∧ amount2 = b ∧ emp
emp
from = f ∧ to = t ∧ amount = a ∧ amount2 = b ∧ emp
∃v, w. Account(f, v) ∗ Account(t, w)
share
consequence; parallel
atomic
atomic

Fig. 5. Sketch proof of two concurrent transfers over the same accounts.

of resource ownership [18]. The sequential examples in this paper can be adapted to concurrent applications using these techniques.

4 Case Study: ARIES

In Sect. 2 we saw an example of a very simple transaction and its associated recovery operation employing write-ahead logging. Relational databases support concurrent execution of complex transactions following the established ACID (Atomicity, Consistency, Isolation and Durability) set of properties. ARIES (Algorithms for Recovery and Isolation Exploiting Semantics) [8], is a collection of algorithms involving, concurrent execution, write-ahead-logging and failure recovery of transactions, that is widely-used to establish ACID properties.

It is beyond the scope of this paper to verify that the full set of ARIES algorithms guarantees ACID properties. Instead, we focus on a stylised version of the recovery algorithm of ARIES proving that: (a) it is idempotent with respect to host failures, (b) after recovery, all transactions recorded in the write-ahead log have either been completed, or were rolled-back.

Transactions update database records stored in durable memory, which for the purposes of this discussion we assume to be a single file in a file system. To increase performance, the database file is divided into fixed-size blocks, called pages, containing multiple records. Thus input/output to the database file, instead of records, is in terms of pages, which are also typically cached in volatile memory. A single transaction may update multiple pages. In the event of a host failure, there may be transactions that have not yet completed, or have completed but their updated pages have not yet been written back to the database file.

ARIES employs write-ahead logging for page updates performed by transactions. The log is stored on a durable fault-tolerant medium. The recovery uses the logged information in a sequence of three phases. First, the *analysis phase*, scans the log to determine the (volatile) state, of any active transactions (committed or not), at the point of host failure. Next, the *redo phase*, scans the log and redos each logged page update, unless the associated page in the database file is already updated. Finally, the *undo phase*, scans the log and undos each page update for each uncommitted transaction. To cope with a possible host failure during the ARIES recovery, each undo action is logged beforehand. Thus, in the event of a host failure the undo actions will be retried as part of the redo phase.

In Fig. 6, we define the log and database model and describe the predicates we use in our specifications and proofs. We refer the reader to our technical report [10] for the formal definitions. We model the database state, db, as a set of pages, where each page comprises the page identifier, the log sequence number (defined later) of the last update performed on the page, and the page data. The log, lg, is structured as a sequence of log records, ordered by a *log sequence number*, $lsn \in \mathbb{N}$, each of which records a particular action performed by a transaction. The ordering follows the order in which transaction actions are performed on the database. The logged action, $U[tid, pid, op]$, records that the transaction identifier tid, performs the update $op : \textsc{Data} \rightarrow \textsc{Data}$ on the page identified by pid. We use op^{-1} to denote the operation undoing the update op. $B[tid]$, records the start of a new transaction with identifier tid, and $C[tid]$, records that the transaction with id tid is committed. The information from the above actions is used to construct two auxiliary structures used by the recovery to determine the state of transactions and pages at the point of a host failure. The *transaction table* (TT), records the status of all active transactions (e.g. updating, committed) and the latest log sequence number associated with the transaction. The *dirty page table* (DPT), records which pages are modified but yet unwritten to the database together with the first log sequence number of the action that caused the first modification to each page. To avoid the cost of scanning the entire log, implementations regularly log snapshots of the TT and

Model:

Database state	$db \subseteq \mathbb{N} \times \mathbb{N} \times \text{DATA}$, triples of pid, lsn, d
Logged actions	$act ::= U[tid, pid, op] \mid B[tid] \mid C[tid] \mid CHK[tt, dpt]$
Log state	$lg ::= \varnothing \mid (lsn, act) \mid lg \otimes lg$
Transaction table	$tt \subseteq \mathbb{N} \times \mathbb{N} \times \{C, U\}$, triples of lsn, pid and transaction status
Dirty page table	$dpt \subseteq \mathbb{N} \times \mathbb{N}$, tuples of pid, lsn

Predicates:

$\mathsf{log}\,(lg)$	the state of the log is given by lg (abstract predicate)
$\mathsf{db\_state}\,(db)$	the state of the database is given by db (abstract predicate)
$\mathsf{set}\,(\mathtt{x}, s)$	the set s identified by program variable $\mathtt{x}$ (abstract predicate)
$\mathsf{log\_tt}\,(lg, tt)$	log lg produces the TT entries in tt
$\mathsf{log\_dpt}\,(lg, dpt)$	log lg produces the DPT entries in dpt
$\mathsf{log\_rl}\,(lg, dpt, ops)$	given log lg and DPT dpt the list of redo updates is ops
$\mathsf{ul\_undo}\,(lg, tt, ops)$	given log lg and TT tt the list of undo updates is ops
$\mathsf{log\_undos}\,(ops, lg)$	given list of undos ops the additional log records are lg
$\mathsf{db\_acts}\,(db, ops, db')$	given the list of updates ops, the database db is updated to db'
$\mathsf{recovery\_log}\,(lg, lg')$	given log lg log records added by recovery are lg'
$\mathsf{recovery\_db}\,(db, lg, db)$	given database db and log lg the recovered database state is db'

Axioms:

$$\mathsf{log}\left(lg \otimes lg'\right) \iff \mathsf{log\_bseg}\,(lg) \otimes \mathsf{log\_fseg}\left(lg'\right)$$

Fig. 6. Abstract model of the database and ARIES log, and predicates.

DPT in checkpoints, $CHK[tt, dpt]$. For simplicity, we assume the log contains exactly one checkpoint.

The high level overview of the recovery algorithm in terms of its analysis, redo and undo phases is given in Fig. 7. The analysis phase first finds the checkpoint and restores the TT and DPT. Then, it proceeds to scan the log forwards from the checkpoint, updating the TT and DPT. Any new transaction is added to the TT. For any commit log record we update the TT to record that the transaction is committed. For any update log record, we add an entry for the associated page to the DPT, also recording the log sequence number, unless an entry for the same page is already in it. We give the following specification for the analysis phase:

$$\mathsf{log}\,(lg_i \otimes (lsn, CHK[tt, dpt]) \otimes lg_c\ ) \vdash$$
$$\left\{\frac{\mathsf{emp}}{\mathsf{log}\,(lg_i \otimes (lsn, CHK[tt, dpt]) \otimes lg_c\ )}\right\}$$
$$\mathtt{tt}, \mathtt{dpt} := \mathtt{aries\_analyse}()$$
$$\left\{\frac{\exists tt', dpt'.\, \mathsf{log\_tt}\,(lg_c, tt') \wedge \mathsf{log\_dpt}\,(lg_c, dpt') \wedge \mathsf{set}\,(\mathtt{tt}, tt \oplus tt') * \mathsf{set}\,(\mathtt{dpt}, dpt \uplus dpt')}{\mathsf{log}\,(lg_i \otimes (-, CHK[tt, dpt]) \otimes lg_c\ )}\right\}$$

The specification states that given the database log, the TT and DPT in the log's checkpoint are restored and updated according to the log records following the checkpoint. The analysis does not modify any durable state.

```
function aries_recovery() {
  //ANALYSIS PHASE: restore dirty page table, transaction table
  //and undo list at point of host failure.
  tt, dpt := aries_analyse();
  //REDO PHASE: repeat actions to restore database state at host failure.
  aries_redo(dpt);
  //UNDO PHASE: Undo actions of uncommitted transactions.
  aries_undo(tt);
}
```

Fig. 7. ARIES recovery: high level structure.

The redo phase, follows analysis and repeats the logged updates. Specifically, redo scans the log forward from the record with the lowest sequence number in the DPT. This is the very first update that is logged, but (potentially) not yet written to the database. The updates are redone unless the recorded page associated with that update is not present in the DPT, or a more recent update has modified it. We give the following specification to redo:

$$\begin{gathered}
\exists ops, ops', ops''. \, (ops = ops' \otimes ops'') \wedge \mathsf{db_acts}\,(db, ops', db'') \\
\wedge \, \mathsf{log_fseg}\,((lsn, act) \otimes lg) * \mathsf{db_state}\,(db'') \vdash \\
\left\{ \frac{\mathsf{set}\,(\mathtt{dpt}, dpt) \wedge lsn = min(dpt_{\downarrow 2})}{\mathsf{log_fseg}\,((lsn, act) \otimes lg) * \mathsf{db_state}\,(db)} \right\} \\
\mathtt{aries_redo(dpt)} \\
\left\{ \begin{gathered} \mathsf{set}\,(\mathtt{dpt}, dpt) \wedge lsn = min(dpt_{\downarrow 2}) \\ \hline \mathsf{log_fseg}\,((lsn, act) \otimes lg) * \mathsf{db_state}\,(db') \wedge \mathsf{db_acts}\,(db, ops, db') \\ \wedge \, \mathsf{log_rl}\,((lsn, act) \otimes lg, dpt, ops) \end{gathered} \right\}
\end{gathered}$$

The specification states that the database is updated according to the logged update records following the smallest log sequence number in the DPT. The fault-condition specifies that after a host failure, all, some or none of the redos have happened. Since redo does not log anything, the log is not affected.

The last phase is undo, which reverts the updates of any transaction that is not committed. In particular, undo scans the log backwards from the log record with the largest log sequence number in the TT. This is the log sequence number of the very last update. For each update record scanned, if the transaction exists in the TT and is not marked as committed, the update is reversed. However, each reverting update is logged beforehand. This ensures, that undos will happen even in case of host failure, since they will be re-done in the redo phase of the subsequent recovery run. We give the following specification for the undo phase:

$$\begin{gathered}
\exists lg', lg'', lg''', ops, ops', ops''. \, lg' = lg'' \otimes lg''' \wedge ops = ops' \otimes ops'' \\
\wedge \, \mathsf{db_acts}\,(db, ops', db'') \wedge \mathsf{log_bseg}\,(lg \otimes (lsn, act) \otimes lg'') * \mathsf{db_state}\,(db'') \vdash \\
\left\{ \frac{\mathsf{set}\,(\mathtt{tt}, tt) \wedge lsn = max(tt_{\downarrow 2})}{\mathsf{log_bseg}\,(lg \otimes (lsn, act)) * \mathsf{db_state}\,(db)} \right\} \\
\mathtt{aries_undo(tt)} \\
\left\{ \begin{gathered} \mathsf{set}\,(\mathtt{tt}, tt) \wedge lsn = max(tt_{\downarrow 2}) \wedge \mathsf{ul_undo}\,(tt, lg \otimes (lsn, act), ops) \\ \hline \mathsf{log_bseg}\,(lg \otimes (lsn, act) \otimes lg') \wedge \mathsf{log_undos}\,(ops, lg') \\ * \, \mathsf{db_state}\,(db') \wedge \mathsf{db_acts}\,(db, ops, db') \end{gathered} \right\}
\end{gathered}$$

The specification states that the database is updated with actions reverting previous updates as obtained from the log. These undo actions are themselves logged. In the event of a host failure the fault-condition specifies that all, some, or none of the operations are undone and logged.

Using the specification for each phase and using our logic we can derive the following specification for this ARIES recovery algorithm:

$$
\begin{array}{c}
\exists lg', lg'', db'.\, \mathsf{log}\,(lg \otimes (lsn, CHK[tt, dpt]) \otimes lg') * \mathsf{db\_state}\,(db) \vdash \\
\left\{ \dfrac{\mathsf{emp}}{\mathsf{log}\,(lg \otimes (lsn, CHK[tt, dpt]) \otimes lg') * \mathsf{db\_state}\,(db)} \right\} \\
\texttt{aries\_recovery}() \\
\left\{ \dfrac{\mathsf{true}}{\begin{array}{c}\mathsf{log}\,(lg \otimes (lsn, CHK[tt, dpt]) \otimes lg' \otimes lg'') \\ \wedge\ \mathsf{recovery\_log}\,(lg \otimes (lsn, CHK[tt, dpt]) \otimes lg', lg'') \\ *\ \mathsf{db\_state}\,(db') \wedge \mathsf{recovery\_db}\,(db, lg \otimes (lsn, CHK[tt, dpt]) \otimes lg', db')\end{array}} \right\}
\end{array}
$$

The proof that the high level structure of the ARIES algorithm satisfies this specification is given in Fig. 8. For the implementations of each phase and proofs they meet their specifications we refer the reader to our technical report [10]. The key property of the ARIES recovery specification is that the durable precondition is the same as the fault-condition. This guarantees that the recovery is idempotent with respect to host failures. This is crucial for any recovery operation, as witnessed in the recovery abstraction rule, guaranteeing that the recovery itself is robust against crashes. Furthermore, the specification states that any transaction logged as committed at the time of host failure, is committed after recovery. Otherwise transactions are rolled back.

5 Semantics and Soundness

We give a brief overview of the semantics of our reasoning and the intuitions behind its soundness. A detailed account is given in the technical report [10].

5.1 Fault-Tolerant Views

We define a general fault-tolerant reasoning framework using Hoare triples with fault-conditions in the style of the Views framework [3]. Pre- and postcondition assertions are modelled as pairs of *volatile* and *durable views* (commutative monoids). Fault-condition assertions are modelled as durable views[2]. Volatile and durable views provide partial knowledge reified to concrete volatile and durable program states respectively. Concrete volatile states include the distinguished host-failed state $\lightning$. The semantic interpretation of a primitive operation is given as a state transformer function from concrete states to sets of concrete states.

[2] We use "Views" to refer to the Views framework of Dinsdale-Young et al. [3], and "views" to refer to the monoid structures used within it.

$$\exists lg', lg', db, rl'.\, \mathsf{log}\,(lg \otimes (lsn, CHK[tt, dpt]) \otimes lg') * \mathsf{db\_state}\,(db) \vdash$$
$$\{\mathsf{emp} \mid \mathsf{log}\,(lg \otimes (lsn, CHK[tt, dpt]) \otimes lg') * \mathsf{db\_state}\,(db)\}$$

```
//ANALYSIS PHASE
```

$$\mathsf{log}\,(lg \otimes (lsn, CHK[tt, dpt]) \otimes lg') \vdash$$
$$\{\mathsf{emp} \mid \mathsf{log}\,(lg \otimes (lsn, CHK[tt, dpt]) \otimes lg')\}$$

`tt, dpt := aries_analyse();`

$$\left\{\frac{\exists tt', dpt'.\, \mathsf{log\_tt}\,(lg', tt') \wedge \mathsf{log\_dpt}\,(lg', dpt, dpt') \wedge \mathsf{set}\,(\mathtt{tt}, tt \oplus tt') * \mathsf{set}\,(\mathtt{dpt}, dpt \uplus dpt')}{\mathsf{log}\,(lg \otimes (-, CHK[tt, dpt]) \otimes lg')}\right\}$$

(frame)

$$\left\{\frac{\exists tt', dpt'.\, \mathsf{log\_tt}\,(lg', tt') \wedge \mathsf{log\_dpt}\,(lg', dpt, dpt') \wedge \mathsf{set}\,(\mathtt{tt}, tt \oplus tt') * \mathsf{set}\,(\mathtt{dpt}, dpt \uplus dpt')}{\mathsf{log}\,(lg \otimes (-, CHK[tt, dpt]) \otimes lg') * \mathsf{db\_state}\,(db)}\right\}$$

```
//REDO PHASE: repeat actions to restore database state at host failure.
```

$$\exists lg_i, lg_c, lg, lg', db, db', db'', lsn_{\leq}, act, ops', ops''.\, (ops = ops' \otimes ops'') \wedge$$
$$\mathsf{log\_bseg}\,(lg_i) * \mathsf{log\_fseg}\,((lsn_{\leq}, act) \otimes lg_c) * \mathsf{db\_state}\,(db'') \wedge \mathsf{db\_acts}\,(db, ops', db'') \vdash$$

$$\left\{\frac{\begin{array}{c}\exists tt', dpt'.\, lg \otimes (lsn, CHK[tt, dpt]) \otimes lg' = lg_i \otimes (lsn_{\leq}, act) \otimes lg_c \\ \wedge\, lsn_{\leq} = min((dpt \uplus dpt')_{\downarrow 2}) \wedge \mathsf{log\_tt}\,(lg', tt') \wedge \mathsf{log\_dpt}\,(lg', dpt, dpt') \\ \wedge\, \mathsf{log\_ul}\,(lg', ul) \wedge \mathsf{set}\,(\mathtt{tt}, tt \oplus tt') * \mathsf{set}\,(\mathtt{dpt}, dpt \uplus dpt')\end{array}}{\mathsf{log\_bseg}\,(lg_i) * \mathsf{log\_fseg}\,((lsn_{\leq}, act) \otimes lg_c) * \mathsf{db\_state}\,(db)}\right\}$$

$$\exists db'', ops', ops''.\, (ops = ops' \otimes ops'')$$
$$\wedge\, \mathsf{log\_fseg}\,((lsn_{\leq}, act) \otimes lg) * \mathsf{db\_state}\,(db'') \wedge \mathsf{db\_acts}\,(db, ops', db'') \vdash$$

$$\left\{\frac{\mathsf{set}\,(\mathtt{dpt}, dpt_u) \wedge lsn_{\leq} = min((dpt_u)_{\downarrow 2})}{\mathsf{log\_fseg}\,((lsn_{\leq}, act) \otimes lg_c) * \mathsf{db\_state}\,(db)}\right\}$$

`aries_redo(dpt);`

$$\left\{\frac{\mathsf{set}\,(\mathtt{dpt}, dpt_u) \wedge lsn_{\leq} = min((dpt_u)_{\downarrow 2})}{\begin{array}{c}\mathsf{log\_fseg}\,((lsn_{\leq}, act) \otimes lg_c) * \mathsf{db\_state}\,(db') \\ \wedge\, \mathsf{db\_acts}\,(db, ops, db') \wedge \mathsf{log\_rl}\,((lsn_{\leq}, act) \otimes lg_c, dpt_u, ops)\end{array}}\right\}$$

(frame)

$$\left\{\frac{\begin{array}{c}lg \otimes (lsn, CHK[tt, dpt]) \otimes lg' = lg_i \otimes (lsn_{\leq}, act) \otimes lg_c \\ \wedge\, lsn_{\leq} = min((dpt \uplus dpt')_{\downarrow 2}) \wedge \mathsf{log\_tt}\,(lg', tt') \wedge \mathsf{log\_dpt}\,(lg', dpt, dpt') \\ \wedge\, \mathsf{log\_ul}\,(lg', ul) \wedge \mathsf{set}\,(\mathtt{tt}, tt \oplus tt') * \mathsf{set}\,(\mathtt{dpt}, dpt \uplus dpt') * \mathsf{ulist}\,(\mathtt{ul}, ul)\end{array}}{\begin{array}{c}\mathsf{log\_bseg}\,(lg_i) * \mathsf{log\_fseg}\,((lsn_{\leq}, act) \otimes lg_c) \\ * \,\mathsf{db\_state}\,(db') \wedge \mathsf{log\_rl}\,((lsn_{\leq}, act) \otimes lg_c, dpt_u, ops)\end{array}}\right\}$$

(consequence)

$$\left\{\frac{\begin{array}{c}\exists lg_c, lsn_{\leq}.\, lg' = - \otimes (lsn_{\leq}, act) \otimes lg_c \wedge lsn_{\leq} = min((dpt \uplus dpt')_{\downarrow 2}) \\ \wedge\, \mathsf{log\_tt}\,(lg', tt') \wedge \mathsf{log\_dpt}\,(lg', dpt, dpt') \wedge \mathsf{log\_ul}\,(lg', ul) \\ \wedge\, \mathsf{set}\,(\mathtt{tt}, tt \oplus tt') * \mathsf{set}\,(\mathtt{dpt}, dpt \uplus dpt')\end{array}}{\begin{array}{c}\mathsf{log}\,(lg \otimes (lsn, CHK[tt, dpt]) \otimes lg') * \mathsf{db\_state}\,(db') \\ \wedge\, \mathsf{db\_acts}\,(db, ops, db') \wedge \mathsf{log\_rl}\,((lsn_{\leq}, act) \otimes lg_c, dpt \uplus dpt', rl')\end{array}}\right\}$$

```
//UNDO PHASE: Undo actions of uncommitted transactions.
```

$$\exists lg', lg'', lg''', ops, ops', ops''.\, lg' = lg'' \otimes lg''' \wedge ops = ops' \otimes ops''$$
$$\wedge\, \mathsf{db\_acts}\,(db_r, ops', db_r'') \wedge \mathsf{log\_bseg}\,(lg \otimes (lsn, act) \otimes lg'') * \mathsf{db\_state}\,(db_r'') \vdash$$
$$\{\mathsf{set}\,(\mathtt{tt}, tt) \wedge lsn_{\geq} = max(tt_{\downarrow 2}) \mid \mathsf{log\_bseg}\,(lg \otimes (lsn, act)) * \mathsf{db\_state}\,(db_r)\}$$

`aries_undo(tt, dpt, ul);`

$$\left\{\frac{\mathsf{set}\,(\mathtt{tt}, tt) \wedge lsn = max(tt_{\downarrow 2}) \wedge \mathsf{ul\_undo}\,(tt, lg \otimes (lsn, act), ops)}{\begin{array}{c}\mathsf{log\_bseg}\,(lg \otimes (lsn, act) \otimes lg') \wedge \mathsf{log\_undos}\,(ops, lg') \\ * \,\mathsf{db\_state}\,(db_r') \wedge \mathsf{db\_acts}\,(db_r, ops, db_r')\end{array}}\right\}$$

(consequence, frame; sequence)

$$\left\{\frac{\mathsf{true}}{\begin{array}{c}\mathsf{log}\,(lg \otimes (lsn, CHK[tt, dpt]) \otimes lg' \otimes lg'') \\ \wedge\, \mathsf{recovery\_log}\,(lg \otimes (lsn, CHK[tt, dpt]) \otimes lg', lg'') \\ * \,\mathsf{db\_state}\,(db') \wedge \mathsf{recovery\_db}\,(db, lg \otimes (lsn, CHK[tt, dpt]) \otimes lg', db')\end{array}}\right\}$$

Fig. 8. Proof of the high level structure of ARIES recovery.

To prove soundness, we encode our Fault-tolerant Views (FTV) framework into Views [3]. A judgement[3] $s \vdash \{(p_v, p_d)\}\,\mathbb{C}\,\{(q_v, q_d)\}$, where s, p_d, q_d are durable views and p_v, q_v are volatile views is encoded as the Views judgement: $\{(p_v, q_d)\}\ \mathbb{C}\ \{(q_v, q_d) \vee (\lightning, s)\}$, where volatile views are extended to include $\lightning$ and $\vee$ is disjunction of views. For the general abstraction recovery rule we encode $[\mathbb{C}]$ as a program which can test for host failures, beginning with $\mathbb{C}$ and followed by as many iterations of the recovery $\mathbb{C}_R$ as required in case of a host failure.

We require the following properties for a sound instance of the framework:

Host failure: For each primitive operation, its interpretation function must transform non host-failed states to states including a host-failed state. This guarantees that each operation can be abruptly interrupted by a host failure.

Host failure propagation: For each primitive operation, its interpretation function must leave all host-failed states intact. That is, when the state says there is a host failure, it stays a host failure.

Axiom soundness: The axiom soundness property (property [G] of Views [3]).

The first two are required to justify the general FTV rules, while the final property establishes soundness of the Views encoding itself. When all the parameters are instantiated and the above properties established then the instantiation of the framework is sound.

5.2 Fault-Tolerant Concurrent Separation Logic

We justify the soundness of FTCSL by an encoding into the Fault-tolerant Views framework discussed earlier. The encoding is similar to the concurrent separation logic encoding into Views. We instantiate volatile and durable views as pairs of local views and shared invariants.

The FTCSL judgement $\boxed{(j_v, j_d)}; s \vdash \{(p_v, p_d)\}\ \mathbb{C}\ \{(q_v, q_d)\}$ is encoded as:

$$s \vdash \{((p_v, j_v), (p_d, j_d))\}\,\mathbb{C}\,\{((q_v, j_v), (q_d, j_d))\}$$

The proof rules in Fig. 4 are justified by soundness of the encoding and simple application of FTV proof rules. Soundness of the encoding is established by proving the properties stated in Sect. 5.1.

Theorem 1 (FTCSL Soundness). *If the judgement* $\boxed{J_V \mid J_D}; S \vdash \{P_V \mid P_D\}\ \mathbb{C}\ \{Q_V \mid Q_D\}$ *is derivable in the program logic, then if we run the program* $\mathbb{C}$ *from state satisfying* $P_V * J_V \mid P_D * J_D$*, then* $\mathbb{C}$ *will either not terminate, or terminate in state satisfying* $Q_V * J_V \mid Q_D * J_D$*, or a host failure will occur destroying any volatile state and the remaining durable state (after potential recoveries) will satisfy* $S * J_D$*. The resource invariant* $J_V \mid J_D$ *holds throughout the execution of* $\mathbb{C}$.

[3] Note that judgements, such as those in Fig. 4, using assertions (capital P, Q, S) are equivalent to judgements using views (models of assertions, little p, q, s).

6 Related Work

There has been a significant amount of work in critical systems, such as file systems and databases, to develop defensive methods against the types of failures covered in this paper [1,8,14,19]. The verification of these techniques has mainly been through testing [6,13] and model checking [21]. However, these techniques have been based on building models that are specific to the particular application and recovery strategy, and are difficult to reuse.

Program logics based on separation logic have been successful in reasoning about file systems [5,9] and concurrent indexes [16] on which database and file systems depend. However, as is typical with Hoare logics, their specifications avoid host failures, assuming that if a precondition holds then associated operations will not fail. Faulty Logic [7] by Meola and Walker is an exception. Faulty logic is designed to reason about transient faults, such as random bit flips due to background radiation, which are different in nature from host failure.

Zengin and Vafeiadis propose a purely functional programming language with an operational semantics providing tolerance against processor failures in parallel programs [22]. Computations are check-pointed to durable storage before execution and, upon detection of a failure, the failed computations are restarted. In general, this approach does not work for concurrent imperative programs which mutate the durable store.

In independent work, Chen et al. introduced Crash Hoare Logic (CHL) to reason about host failures and applied it to a substantial sequential journaling file system (FSCQ) written in Coq [2]. CHL extends Hoare triples with fault-conditions and provides highly automated reasoning about host failures. FSCQ performs physical journaling, meaning it uses a write-ahead log for both data and metadata, so that the recovery can guarantee atomicity with respect to host failures. The authors use CHL to prove that this property is indeed true. The resource stored in the disk is treated as durable. Since FSCQ is implemented in the functional language of Coq, which lacks the traditional process heap, the volatile state is stored in immutable variables.

The aim of FSCQ and CHL is to provide a verified implementation of a sequential file system which tolerates host failures. In contrast, our aim is to provide a general methodology for fault-tolerant resource reasoning about concurrent programs. We extend the Views framework [3] to provide a general concurrent framework for reasoning about host failure and recovery. Like CHL, we extend Hoare triples with fault-conditions. We instantiate our framework to concurrent separation logic, and demonstrate that an ARIES recovery algorithm uses the write-ahead log correctly to guarantee the atomicity of transactions. In the technical report [10], we explore the differences in the specifications of fault-tolerance guarantees in physical and logical journaling file systems.

As we are defining a framework, our reasoning of the durable and volatile state (given by arbitrary view monoids) is general. In contrast, CHL reasoning is specific to the durable state on the disk and the volatile state in the immutable variable store. CHL is able to reason modularly about different layers of abstraction of a file-system implementation, using *logical address spaces* which give a systematic pattern of use for standard predicates. We do not explore modular reasoning about layers of abstractions in this paper, since it is orthogonal to reasoning about host failures, and examples have already been studied in instances of the Views framework and other separation logic literature [4,12,17,18,20].

We can certainly benefit from the practical CHL approach to mechanisation and proof automation. We also believe that future work on CHL, especially on extending the reasoning to heap-manipulating concurrent programs, can benefit from our general approach.

7 Conclusions and Future Work

We have developed fault-tolerant resource reasoning, extending the Views framework [3] to reason about programs in the presence of host failures. We have proved a general soundness result. For this paper, we have focused on fault-tolerant concurrent separation logic, a particular instance of the framework. We have demonstrated our reasoning by studying an ARIES recovery algorithm, showing that it is idempotent and that it guarantees atomicity of database transactions in the event of a host failure.

There has been recent work on concurrent program logics with the ability to reason about abstract atomicity [17]. This involves proving that even though the implementation of an operation takes multiple steps, from the client's point of view they can be seen as a single step. Currently, this is enforced by syntactic primitive atomic blocks ($\langle \_ \rangle$) in the programming language. In future, we want to combine abstract atomicity from concurrency with host failure atomicity.

Another direction for future work involves extending existing specifications for file systems [5,9] with our framework. This will allow both the verification of interesting clients programs, such as fault-tolerant software installers or persisted message queues, and the verification of fault-tolerant databases and file systems.

Acknowledgements. We thank Thomas Dinsdale-Young for discussions and useful feedback. This research was supported by EPSRC Programme Grants EP/H008373/1 and EP/K008528/1. Supplementary material and proofs are available in the technical report [10].

References

1. Bonwick, J., Ahrens, M., Henson, V., Maybee, M., Shellenbaum, M.: The zettabyte file system. In: Proceedings of the 2nd Usenix Conference on File and Storage Technologies (2003)
2. Chen, H., Ziegler, D., Chlipala, A., Kaashoek, M.F., Kohler, E., Zeldovich, N.: Using crash hoare logic for certifying the FSCQ file system. In: SOSP (2015)
3. Dinsdale-Young, T., Birkedal, L., Gardner, P., Parkinson, M., Yang, H.: Views: compositional reasoning for concurrent programs. In: POPL, pp. 287–300 (2013)
4. Dinsdale-Young, T., Dodds, M., Gardner, P., Parkinson, M.J., Vafeiadis, V.: Concurrent abstract predicates. In: D'Hondt, T. (ed.) ECOOP 2010. LNCS, vol. 6183, pp. 504–528. Springer, Heidelberg (2010)

5. Gardner, P., Ntzik, G., Wright, A.: Local reasoning for the POSIX file system. In: Shao, Z. (ed.) ESOP 2014 (ETAPS). LNCS, vol. 8410, pp. 169–188. Springer, Heidelberg (2014)
6. Kropp, N., Koopman, P., Siewiorek, D.: Automated robustness testing of off-the-shelf software components. In: 1998 Twenty-Eighth Annual International Symposium on Fault-Tolerant Computing. Digest of Papers, pp. 230–239 (1998)
7. Meola, M.L., Walker, D.: Faulty logic: reasoning about fault tolerant programs. In: Gordon, A.D. (ed.) ESOP 2010. LNCS, vol. 6012, pp. 468–487. Springer, Heidelberg (2010)
8. Mohan, C., Haderle, D., Lindsay, B., Pirahesh, H., Schwarz, P.: ARIES: a transaction recovery method supporting fine-granularity locking and partial rollbacks using write-ahead logging. ACM Trans. Database Syst. **17**, 94–162 (1992)
9. Ntzik, G., Gardner, P.: Reasoning about the POSIX File System: Local Update and Global Pathnames. In: OOPLSA (2015)
10. Ntzik, G., da Rocha Pinto, P., Gardner, P.: Fault-tolerant Resource Reasoning. Technical report, Imperial College London (2015)
11. O'Hearn, P.W.: Resources, concurrency, and local reasoning. Theor. Comput. Sci. **375**(1–3), 271–307 (2007)
12. Parkinson, M., Bierman, G.: Separation logic and abstraction. In: POPL, pp. 247–258 (2005)
13. Prabhakaran, V., Arpaci-Dusseau, A., Arpaci-Dusseau, R.: Model-based failure analysis of journaling file systems. In: 2005 Proceedings of the International Conference on Dependable Systems and Networks. DSN 2005, pp. 802–811, June 2005
14. Prabhakaran, V., Arpaci-Dusseau, A.C., Arpaci-Dusseau, R.H.: Analysis and evolution of journaling file Systems. In: USENIX Annual Technical Conference, General Track (2005)
15. Reynolds, J.: Separation logic: a logic for shared mutable data structures. In: Proceedings. 17th Annual IEEE Symposium on Logic in Computer Science, 2002. pp. 55–74 (2002)
16. da Rocha Pinto, P., Dinsdale-Young, T., Dodds, M., Gardner, P., Wheelhouse, M.: A simple abstraction for complex concurrent indexes. In: OOPSLA, pp. 845–864 (2011)
17. da Rocha Pinto, P., Dinsdale-Young, T., Gardner, P.: TaDA: a logic for time and data abstraction. In: Jones, R. (ed.) ECOOP 2014. LNCS, vol. 8586, pp. 207–231. Springer, Heidelberg (2014)
18. da Rocha Pinto, P., Dinsdale-Young, T., Gardner, P.: Steps in modular specifications for concurrent modules. In: MFPS (2015)
19. Rosenblum, M., Ousterhout, J.K.: The design and implementation of a log-structured file system. ACM Trans. Comput. Syst. **10**, 26–52 (1992)
20. Svendsen, K., Birkedal, L.: Impredicative concurrent abstract predicates. In: Shao, Z. (ed.) ESOP 2014 (ETAPS). LNCS, vol. 8410, pp. 149–168. Springer, Heidelberg (2014)
21. Yang, J., Twohey, P., Engler, D., Musuvathi, M.: Using model checking to find serious file system errors. ACM Trans. Comput. Syst. **24**(4), 393–423 (2006)
22. Zengin, M., Vafeiadis, V.: A Programming Language Approach to Fault Tolerance for Fork-Join Parallelism. In: 2013 International Symposium on Theoretical Aspects of Software Engineering (TASE), pp. 105–112 (July 2013)

Shifting the Blame

A Blame Calculus with Delimited Control

Taro Sekiyama(✉), Soichiro Ueda, and Atsushi Igarashi

Graduate School of Informatics, Kyoto University, Kyoto, Japan
t-sekiym@fos.kuis.kyoto-u.ac.jp

Abstract. We study integration of static and dynamic typing in the presence of delimited-control operators. In a program where typed and untyped parts coexist, the run-time system has to monitor the flow of values between these parts and abort program execution if invalid values are passed. However, control operators, which enable us to implement useful control effects, make such monitoring tricky; in fact, it is known that, with a standard approach, certain communications between typed and untyped parts can be overlooked.

We propose a new cast-based mechanism to monitor all communications between typed and untyped parts for a language with control operators shift and reset. We extend a blame calculus with shift/reset to give its semantics (operational semantics and CPS transformation) and prove two important correctness properties of the proposed mechanism: Blame Theorem and soundness of the CPS transformation.

1 Introduction

Many programming languages support either static or dynamic typing. Static typing makes early error detection and compilation to faster code possible while dynamic typing makes flexible and rapid software development easier. To take the best of both worlds, integration of static and dynamic typing has been investigated. Indeed, several practical programming languages—e.g., C♯, TypeScript, Typed Racket [28], Typed Clojure [4], Reticulated Python [29], Hack (an extension of PHP), etc.—allow typed and untyped parts to coexist in one program and to communicate with each other.

In languages allowing such integration, *casts* [14,22,30] (or *contracts* [13,26,27]) play an important role for monitoring the flow of values between typed and untyped parts. A source program that contains typed and untyped parts is compiled to an intermediate language such that casts are inserted in points where typed and untyped code interacts. Casts are a run-time mechanism to check that a program component satisfies a given type specification. For example, when typed code imports a certain component from untyped code as integer, a cast is inserted to check that it is actually an integer at run time. If it is detected that a component did not follow the specification, an uncatchable exception, called

S. Ueda—Current affiliation: Works Applications Co., Ltd.

X. Feng and S. Park (Eds.): APLAS 2015, LNCS 9458, pp. 189–207, 2015.
DOI: 10.1007/978-3-319-26529-2_11

blame, will be raised to notify that something unexpected has happened. Tobin-Hochstadt and Felleisen [27] originated a *blame calculus* to study integration of static and dynamic typing and Wadler and Findler [30] fined the theory of blame on its variant.

We study integration of static and dynamic typing in the presence of delimited-control operators. As is well known, various control effects—e.g, exception handling [25], backtracking [6], monads [12], generators [25], etc.—can be expressed by using delimited continuations as first-class values. However, control operators make it tricky to monitor the borders between typed and untyped parts; in fact, as is pointed out by Takikawa, Strickland, and Tobin-Hochstadt [26], communications between the two parts via continuations captured by control operators can be overlooked under standard cast semantics.

Our Contributions. In this paper, we propose a blame calculus, based on Wadler and Findler [30], with Danvy and Filinski's delimited-control operators *shift* and *reset* [6] and give a new cast-based mechanism to monitor all communications between typed and untyped parts. The idea of the new cast comes from Danvy and Filinski's type system [5] for shift/reset, where type information about contexts is considered. Using types of contexts, our cast mechanism can monitor all communications.

As a proof of correctness of our idea, we investigate two important properties. One is Blame Theorem [27,30], which states that values that flow from typed code never trigger run-time type errors. The other property is soundness of CPS transformation: it preserves well-typedness and, for any two source terms such that one reduces to the other, their transformation results are equivalent in the target calculus. It turns out that we need a few axioms about casts in addition to usual axioms, such as (call-by-value) β-reduction, for equality in the target calculus.

The Organization of the Paper. In Sect. 2, we review the blame calculus and the control operators shift/reset, explain why the standard cast does not work when they are naively combined, and briefly describe our solution. Section 3 formalizes our calculus with an operational semantics and a type system, and shows type soundness of the calculus. Section 4 shows a Blame Theorem in our calculus and Sect. 5 introduces CPS transformation and shows its soundness. Finally, discussing related work in Sect. 6, we conclude in Sect. 7. We omit proofs from the paper; interested readers are referred to a full version of the paper available at http://www.fos.kuis.kyoto-u.ac.jp/~t-sekiym/papers/decon_blame/APLAS2015_decon_blame_full.pdf.

2 Blame Calculus with Shift and Reset

2.1 Blame Calculus

The blame calculus of Wadler and Findler [30] is a kind of typed lambda calculus for studying integration of static and dynamic typing. It is designed as an intermediate language for gradually typed languages [22], where a program at an early stage is written in an untyped language and parts whose specifications are stable can be gradually rewritten in a typed language, resulting in a program with both typed and untyped parts. In blame calculi, untyped parts are represented as terms of the special, *dynamic type* (denoted by $\star$), where any operation is statically allowed at the risk of causing run-time errors. Blame calculi support smooth interaction between typed and untyped parts—i.e., typed code can use an untyped component and vice versa—via a type-directed mechanism, *casts*.

A cast, taking the form $t : A \Rightarrow^p B$, checks that term t of source type A behaves as target type B at run time; p, called a *blame label*, is used to identify the cast that has failed at run time. For example, using integer type int, cast expression $1 : \mathsf{int} \Rightarrow^p \star$ injects integer 1 to the dynamic type; conversely, $t : \star \Rightarrow^p \mathsf{int}$ coerces untyped term t to int. A cast would fail if the coerced value cannot behave as the target type of the cast. For example, cast expression $(1 : \mathsf{int} \Rightarrow^{p_1} \star) : \star \Rightarrow^{p_2} \mathsf{bool}$, which coërces integer 1 to the dynamic type and then its result to Boolean type bool, causes blame $\mathsf{blame}\, p_2$ at run time since the coerced value 1 cannot behave as bool.

Using casts, in addition to fully typed and fully untyped programs, we can write a program where typed and untyped parts are mixed. For example, suppose that we first write an untyped program as follows:

$$\mathsf{let}\ succ = \lambda x.\, x + 1\ \mathsf{in}\ succ\, 1$$

where we color untyped parts gray.[1] If the successor function is statically typed, we rewrite the program so that it imports the typed successor function:

$$\mathsf{let}\ succ = (\lambda x.\, x + 1) : \mathsf{int} \to \mathsf{int} \Rightarrow^p \star\ \mathsf{in}\ succ\, 1$$

where we color typed parts white. When the source and target types in a cast are not important, as is often the case, we just surround a term by a $\boxed{\text{frame}}$ to indicate the existence of some appropriate cast. So, the program above is presented as below:

$$\mathsf{let}\ succ = \boxed{\lambda x.\, x + 1}\ \mathsf{in}\ succ\, 1$$

Intuitively, a frame in programs in this style means that flows of values between the typed and untyped parts are monitored by casts. Conversely, the absence of a frame between the two parts indicates that the run-time system will overlook their communications.

What happens when a value is coerced to the dynamic type rests on the source type of the cast. If it is a first-order type such as int, the cast simply tags the value with its type. If it is a function type, by contrast, the cast generates a lambda abstraction that wraps the target function and then tags the wrapper. The wrapper, a function over values of the dynamic type, checks, by using a cast, that a given argument has the type expected by the wrapped function and

[1] Precisely speaking, even untyped programs need casts to use values of the dynamic type as functions, integers, etc., but we omit them to avoid the clutter.

coerces the return value of the wrapped function to the dynamic type, similarly to function contracts [13]. For example, cast expression $(\lambda x{:}\mathsf{int}.\, x+1) : \mathsf{int} \rightarrow \mathsf{int} \Rightarrow^{p} \star$ generates lambda abstraction $\lambda y{:}\star.\, (((\lambda x{:}\mathsf{int}.\, x+1)\,(y : \star \Rightarrow^{q} \mathsf{int})) : \mathsf{int} \Rightarrow^{p} \star)$. Here, blame label q is the negation of p, which we will discuss in detail below. Using the notation introduced above, it is easy to understand that all communications between typed and untyped parts are monitored because the program above reduces to:

$$\mathsf{let}\ succ = \lambda y.\ \boxed{(\lambda x.\, x+1)\ \boxed{y}}\ \mathsf{in}\ succ\, 1$$

As advocated by Findler and Felleisen [13], there are two kinds of blame—positive blame and negative blame, which indicate that, when a cast fails, its responsibility lies with the term contained in the cast and the context containing the cast, respectively. Following Wadler and Findler, we introduce an involutive operation $\bar{\cdot}$ of negation on blame labels: for any blame label p, $\bar{p}$ is its negation and $\bar{\bar{p}}$ is the same as p. For a cast with blame label p in a program, $\mathsf{blame}\, p$ and $\mathsf{blame}\, \bar{p}$ denotes positive blame and negative blame, respectively. A key observation, so-called the *Blame Theorem*, in work on blame calculi is that a cast failure is never caused by values from the more precisely typed side in the cast—i.e., if the side of a term contained in a cast with p is more precisely typed, a program including the cast never evaluates to $\mathsf{blame}\, p$, while if the side of a context containing the cast is, the program never evaluates to $\mathsf{blame}\, \bar{p}$.

2.2 Delimited-Control Operators: Shift and Reset

Shift and *reset* are delimited-control operators introduced by Danvy and Filinski [6]. Shift captures the current continuation, like another control operator call/cc, and reset delimits the continuation captured by shift. The captured continuation works as if it is a composable function, namely, unlike call/cc, control is returned to a caller when the call to the captured continuation finishes.

As an example with shift and reset, let us consider the following program:

$$\langle 5 + \mathcal{S}k.\, ((k\,1 + k\,2) = 13)\rangle$$

Here, the shift operator is invoked by the subterm $\mathcal{S}k.\, ((k\,1 + k\,2) = 13)$ and the reset operator $\langle ... \rangle$ encloses the whole term. To evaluate a reset operator, we evaluate its body. Evaluation of the shift operator $\mathcal{S}k.\, ((k\,1 + k\,2) = 13)$ proceeds as follows. First, it captures the continuation up to the closest reset as a function. Since the delimited continuation in this program is $5 + [\,]$ (here, $[\,]$ means a hole of the context), the captured continuation takes the form $\lambda x.\, \langle 5 + x\rangle$ (note that the body of the function is enclosed by reset). Next, variable k is bound to the captured continuation. Finally, the body of the closest reset operator is replaced with the body of the shift operator. Thus, the example program reduces to:

$$\langle (((\lambda x.\, \langle 5 + x\rangle)\, 1) + ((\lambda x.\, \langle 5 + x\rangle)\, 2)) = 13\rangle.$$

Since reset returns the result of its body, it evaluates to true.

Let us consider a more interesting example of function *choice*, a user of which passes a tuple of integers and expects to return one of them. The caller tests the returned integer by some Boolean expression and surrounds it by reset. Then, the whole reset expression evaluates to the index (tagged with Some) to indicate which integer satisfied the test, or None to indicate none of them satisfied. For example, $\langle \texttt{prime?}\,(\mathit{choice}\,(141, 197))\rangle$ will evaluate to Some 2 because the second argument 197 is a prime number. Using shift/reset, such a (two-argument version of) *choice* function can be defined as follows:

$$\mathit{choice} = \lambda(x, y){:}\mathsf{int} \times \mathsf{int}.\, \mathcal{S}k.\, \mathsf{if}\ k\ x\ \mathsf{then\ Some\ 1\ else\ if}\ k\ y\ \mathsf{then\ Some\ 2\ else\ None}$$

It is important to observe k is bound to the predicate (in this case, $\lambda z.\, \langle \texttt{prime?}\ z\rangle$).

Since blame calculi support type-directed casts, it is crucial to consider type discipline in the presence of shift/reset. This work adopts the type system proposed by Danvy and Filinski [5]. Their type system introduces types, called *answer types*, of contexts up to the closest reset to track modification of the body of a reset operator—we have seen above that the body of a reset operator can be modified to the body of a shift operator at run time. In the type system, using metavariables α and β for types, function types take the form $A/\alpha \to B/\beta$, which means that a function of this type is one from A to B and, when applied, it modifies the answer type α to β. For example, using a function of type $(\mathsf{int} \times \mathsf{int})/\mathsf{bool} \to \mathsf{int}/(\mathsf{int\,option})$ ($\mathsf{int\,option}$ means integers tagged with Some and None), its user, when passing a pair of integers, expects to return an integer value and to modify the answer type bool to int option. Conversely, to see how functions are given such a function type, let us consider *choice*, which is typed at $(\mathsf{int} \times \mathsf{int})/\mathsf{bool} \to \mathsf{int}/(\mathsf{int\,option})$. It can be found from the type annotation that it takes pairs of integers. The body captures a continuation and calls it with the first and second components of the argument pair. Since a caller of *choice* obtains a value passed to the continuation k, the return type is int. *choice* demands the answer type of a context be bool because the captured continuation is required to return a Boolean value in conditional expressions; and the shift operator modifies the answer type to int option because the if-expression returns an int option value.

2.3 Blame Calculus with Shift and Reset

We extend the blame calculus with shift/reset so that all value flows between typed and untyped parts are monitored, following the type discipline discussed above. The main question here is how we should give the semantics of casts for function types, which now include answer type information. The standard semantics discussed above does not suffice because it is ignorant of answer types. In fact, it would fail to monitor value flows that occur due to manipulation of delimited contiuations, as we see below. For example, let us consider the situation that untyped code imports typed function *choice* via a cast (represented by a frame):

$$\mathsf{let}\ f = \boxed{\mathit{choice}}\ \mathsf{in}\ 5 + \langle \mathit{succ}\ (f\ (141, 197))\rangle$$

This program contains two errors: first, subterm $succ\,(f\,(141, 197))$ within reset returns an integer, though shift in *choice* expects it to return a Boolean value since the continuation captured by the shift operator is used in conditional expressions; second, as found in subterm $5 + \langle \ldots \rangle$, the computation result of reset is expected to be an integer, though it should be an int option value coming from the body of shift in *choice*. However, if the cast on *choice* behaved as a standard function cast we discussed in Sect. 2.1, these errors would not be detected at run time on borders between typed and untyped parts. To see the reason, let us reduce the program. First, since the choice is coerced to the dynamic type, a wrapper that checks an argument and the return value is generated and then is applied to $(141, 197)$:

$$\mathsf{let}\ f = \boxed{choice}\ \mathsf{in}\ 5 + \langle succ\,(f\,(141, 197))\rangle \longmapsto^* 5 + \langle succ\,(\boxed{choice\,\boxed{(141, 197)}})\rangle$$

The check for $(141, 197)$ succeeds and so *choice* is applied to $(141, 197)$, and then the shift operator in *choice* is invoked.

$$\begin{aligned} \cdots \longmapsto^* & \ 5 + \langle succ\,\boxed{\mathcal{S}k.\ \mathsf{if}\ k\ 141\ \mathsf{then\ Some}\ 1\ \mathsf{else\ if}\ k\ 197\ \mathsf{then\ Some}\ 2\ \mathsf{else\ None}}\rangle \\ \longmapsto^* & \ 5 + \langle \mathsf{if}\ (\lambda x.\ \langle succ\,\boxed{x}\rangle)\ 141\ \mathsf{then\ Some}\ 1\ \mathsf{else\ if}\ \ldots\ \mathsf{then\ Some}\ 2\ \mathsf{else\ None}\rangle \end{aligned}$$

Here, there are one gray area and one white area, both without surrounding frames. The former means that the value flow from the captured continuation $\lambda x.\ \langle succ\,\boxed{x}\rangle$ to typed code will not be monitored, when it should be by the cast from the dynamic type to bool. Similarly, the latter means that the value flow from the result of the (typed) if-expression to untyped code will not be monitored, either, when it should be by the cast from int option to the dynamic type. The problem is that the standard function casts can monitor calls of functions but does not capture and calls of delimited continuations.

Our cast mechanism can monitor such capture and calls of delimited continuations. A wrapper generated by a cast from $A/\alpha \to B/\beta$ to the dynamic type, when applied, ensures that the reset expression enclosing the application returns a value of the dynamic type by inserting injection from β and that the continuation captured during the call to the wrapped function returns a value of α by the cast to α. In the above example of *choice*, our cast mechanism reduces the original program to a term like:

$$5 + \langle \boxed{\mathsf{if}\ (\lambda x.\,\boxed{\langle succ\,\boxed{x}\rangle})\ 141\ \mathsf{then\ Some}\ 1\ \mathsf{else\ if}\ \ldots\ \mathsf{then\ Some}\ 2\ \mathsf{else\ None}}\rangle$$

where two casts are added: one to check that the return value of the continuation has bool and the other to inject the result of the if-expression to the dynamic type.

3 Language

In this section, we formally define a call-by-value blame calculus with delimited-control operators shift and reset and show its type soundness. Our calculus is a variant of the blame calculus by Ahmed et al. [1].

variables	x, y, k	**blame labels**	p, q	**constants**	c	**base types**	ι

$$
\begin{array}{lll}
\textbf{ground types} & G, H & ::= \iota \mid \star/\star \to \star/\star \\
\textbf{types} & A, B, \alpha, \beta, \gamma, \delta & ::= \iota \mid \star \mid A/\alpha \to B/\beta \\
\textbf{values} & v & ::= x \mid c \mid \lambda x.\, t \mid v : G \Rightarrow \star \\
\textbf{terms} & s, t, u & ::= x \mid c \mid op(\overline{t_i}^{\,i}) \mid \lambda x.\, t \mid s\; t \mid \\
& & \quad s : A \Rightarrow^p B \mid s : G \Rightarrow \star \mid \mathsf{blame}\, p \mid \langle s \rangle \mid \mathcal{S}k.\, s
\end{array}
$$

Fig. 1. Syntax.

3.1 Syntax

Figure 1 presents the syntax, which is parameterized over base types, denoted by ι, constants, denoted by c, and primitive operations over constants.

Types consist of base types, the dynamic type, and function types with answer types. Unlike the blame calculus of Wadler and Findler, our calculus does not include refinement types (a.k.a., subset types) for simplicity; we believe that it is not hard to add refinement types if refinements are restricted to be pure [2]. Ground types, denoted by G and H, classify kinds of values. If the ground type is a base type, the values are constants of the base type, and if it is a function type (constituted only of the dynamic type), the values are lambda abstractions.

Values, denoted by v, consist of variables, constants, lambda abstractions, and ground values. A lambda abstraction $\lambda x.\, s$ is standard; variable x is bound in the body s. A ground value $v : G \Rightarrow \star$ is a value of the dynamic type; the kind of v follows ground type G.

Terms, denoted by s and t, extend those in the simply typed blame calculus with two forms, reset expressions and shift expressions. Using the notation $\overline{t_i}^{\,i}$ to denote a sequence $t_1, ..., t_n$ of terms, we allow primitive operators to take tuples of terms. A reset expression is written as $\langle s \rangle$ and a shift expression is as $\mathcal{S}k.\, s$ where k is bound in the body s. The syntax includes blame as a primitive construct despite the fact that exceptions can be implemented by shift and reset because blame is an *uncatchable* exception in a blame calculus. Note that ground values, ground terms ($s : G \Rightarrow \star$), and blame are supposed to be "run-time" citizens that appear only during reduction and not in a source program.

In what follows, as usual, we write $s\,[x := v]$ for capture-avoiding substitution of v for variable x in s. As shorthand, we write $s : G \Rightarrow \star \Rightarrow^p A$ and $s : A \Rightarrow^p G \Rightarrow \star$ for $(s : G \Rightarrow \star) : \star \Rightarrow^p A$ and $(s : A \Rightarrow^p G) : G \Rightarrow \star$, respectively.

3.2 Semantics

The semantics of our calculus is given in a small-step style by using two relations over terms: reduction relation $\longrightarrow$, which represents basic computation such as β-reduction, and evaluation relation $\longmapsto$, in which subterms are reduced.

The reduction rules, shown at the top of Fig. 2, are standard or similar to the previous calculi except (R_Wrap), which is the key of our work. In (R_Op), to

$\boxed{s \longrightarrow t}$ **Reduction rules**

$$
\begin{array}{lll}
op(\overline{v_i}^i) & \longrightarrow \zeta\,(op, \overline{v_i}^i) & \text{R\_OP} \\
(\lambda x.\, s)\, v & \longrightarrow s\,[x := v] & \text{R\_BETA} \\
\langle v \rangle & \longrightarrow v & \text{R\_RESET} \\
\langle F[\mathcal{S}k.\, s] \rangle & \longrightarrow \langle s\,[k := \lambda x.\, \langle F[x] \rangle] \rangle \text{ where } x \notin fv\,(F) & \text{R\_SHIFT} \\
v : \iota \Rightarrow^p \iota & \longrightarrow v & \text{R\_BASE} \\
v : \star \Rightarrow^p \star & \longrightarrow v & \text{R\_DYN} \\
\multicolumn{2}{l}{v : A/\alpha \rightarrow B/\beta \Rightarrow^p A'/\alpha' \rightarrow B'/\beta' \longrightarrow} & \\
\multicolumn{2}{l}{\quad \lambda x.\, \mathcal{S}k.\, (\langle (k\,((v\,(x : A' \Rightarrow^{\bar{p}} A)) : B \Rightarrow^p B')) : \alpha' \Rightarrow^{\bar{p}} \alpha \rangle : \beta \Rightarrow^p \beta')} & \text{R\_WRAP} \\
v : A \Rightarrow^p \star & \longrightarrow v : A \Rightarrow^p G \Rightarrow \star \quad \text{if } A \sim G \text{ and } A \neq \star & \text{R\_GROUND} \\
v : G \Rightarrow \star \Rightarrow^p A & \longrightarrow v : G \Rightarrow^p A \quad \text{if } G \sim A \text{ and } A \neq \star & \text{R\_COLLAPSE} \\
v : G \Rightarrow \star \Rightarrow^p A & \longrightarrow \mathsf{blame}\, p \quad \text{if } G \not\sim A & \text{R\_CONFLICT}
\end{array}
$$

$\boxed{s \longmapsto t}$ **Evaluation rules**

$$
\frac{s \longrightarrow t}{E[s] \longmapsto E[t]}\ \text{E\_STEP} \qquad \frac{E \neq [\,]}{E[\mathsf{blame}\, p] \longmapsto \mathsf{blame}\, p}\ \text{E\_ABORT}
$$

Fig. 2. Reduction and evaluation.

reduce a call to a primitive operator, we assume that there is a function ζ which returns an appropriate value when taking an operator name and arguments to it. The rule (R_SHIFT) presents that the shift operator captures the continuation up to the closest reset operator. In the rule, the captured continuation is represented by pure evaluation contexts, denoted by F, which are evaluation contexts [11] where the hole does not occur in bodies of reset operators. Pure evaluation contexts are defined as follows:

$$F ::= [\,] \mid op(\overline{v_i}^i, F, \overline{t_j}^j) \mid F\, s \mid v\, F \mid F : A \Rightarrow^p B \mid F : G \Rightarrow \star$$

As mentioned earlier, the body of the function representing the captured continuation is enclosed by reset.

There are six reduction rules for cast expressions. The rule (R_BASE) and (R_DYN) means that casts between the same base type and between the dynamic type perform no checks. We find (R_DYN), which does not appear in Ahmed et al. [1], matches well with CPS transformation. The rule (R_GROUND), applied when the target type is the dynamic type but the source type is not, turns a cast expression to a ground term by inserting a cast to the ground type G that represents the kind of the value v. The relation $\sim$, called compatibility, over two types is defined as the least compatible relation closed under $A \sim \star$ and $\star \sim B$. It intuitively means that a cast from A to B (and vice versa) can succeed; in other words, $A \not\sim B$ means that a cast will fail. One interesting fact about compatibility is that, for any nondynamic type A, we can find exactly one ground type that is compatible with A: If A is a base type, then G is equal to A and, if

A is a function type, then G is $\star/\star \rightarrow \star/\star$. As a result, G in (R_GROUND) is uniquely determined. The rules (R_COLLAPSE) and (R_CONFLICT) are applied when a target value is a ground value. When the kind G of the underlying value v is not compatible with the target type of the cast, the cast is blamed with blame label p by (R_CONFLICT). Otherwise, the underlying value is coerced from the ground type of the ground value to the target type of the cast by (R_COLLAPSE).

The reduction rule (R_WRAP), applied to casts between function types, is the most involved. The rule means that the cast expression reduces to a lambda abstraction that wraps the target value v. Since the wrapper function works as a value of type $A'/\alpha' \rightarrow B'/\beta'$, it takes a value of A'. Like function contracts [13], in the wrapper, the argument denoted by x is coerced to argument type A of the source type to apply v to it and the return value of v is coerced to return type B' of the target type. Furthermore, to call the target function in a context of answer type α, the wrapper captures the continuation in which the wrapper is applied by using shift, applies the captured continuation to the result of the target function, and then coerces the result of the captured continuation to α. Since the wrapper is applied in a context of answer type α', the captured continuation returns a value of α'. By enclosing the cast to α with reset, a continuation captured during the call to v returns a value of α. Finally, the wrapper coerces the result of the reset operator from β to β' because the call to the target function modifies the answer type of the context to β, and so the reset expression returns a value of β, and the wrapper is expected to modify the answer type to β'. The rule (R_WRAP) reverses blame labels for casts from A' to A and from α' to α because target values for those casts originate from the context side.

We illustrate how (R_WRAP) makes monitoring of capture and calls of continuations possible, using *choice* in Sect. 2.3. By (R_GROUND), the cast from $(\mathsf{int} \times \mathsf{int})/\mathsf{bool} \rightarrow \mathsf{int}/(\mathsf{int\,option})$ to the dynamic type reduces to that to $\star/\star \rightarrow \star/\star$. By (R_WRAP), the cast generates a wrapper.

$$\mathsf{let}\ f = \boxed{\mathit{choice}}\ \mathsf{in}\ \ldots \longmapsto \mathsf{let}\ f = \lambda x.\, \mathcal{S}k'.\, \boxed{\langle \boxed{k'\ \boxed{(\mathit{choice}\ \boxed{x})}} \rangle}\ \mathsf{in}\ \ldots$$

The check for the argument succeeds, and so the evaluation proceeds as follows:

$$\begin{array}{rl} \cdots \longmapsto^* & 5 + \langle \mathit{succ}\ (\mathcal{S}k'.\, \boxed{\langle \boxed{k'\ \boxed{(\mathcal{S}k.\, \mathsf{if}\ k\ 141\ \mathsf{then\ Some}\ 1\ \mathsf{else}\ \ldots)}} \rangle}) \rangle \\ \longmapsto & 5 + \langle \boxed{\langle \boxed{(\lambda x.\, \langle \mathit{succ}\ x \rangle)\ \boxed{(\mathcal{S}k.\, \mathsf{if}\ k\ 141\ \mathsf{then\ Some}\ 1\ \mathsf{else}\ \ldots)}} \rangle} \rangle \\ \longmapsto & 5 + \langle \boxed{\langle \mathsf{if}\ v\ 141\ \mathsf{then\ Some}\ 1\ \mathsf{else\ if}\ v\ 197\ \mathsf{then\ Some}\ 2\ \mathsf{else\ None} \rangle} \rangle \end{array}$$

where $v = \lambda y.\, \langle \boxed{(\lambda x.\, \langle \mathit{succ}\ x \rangle)\ \boxed{y}} \rangle$. We can observe that all borders in the last term are monitored by casts.

Evaluation rules, presented at the bottom of Fig. 2, are standard: (E_STEP) reduces a subterm that is a redex in a program and (E_ABORT) halts evaluation of a program at blame when cast failure happens. To determine a redex in a program, we use evaluation contexts [11], which are defined as follows.

$$E ::= [\,] \mid op(\overline{v_i}^i, E, \overline{t_j}^j) \mid E\, s \mid v\, E \mid \langle E \rangle \mid E : A \Rightarrow^p B \mid E : G \Rightarrow \star$$

This definition means that terms are evaluated from left to right. Unlike pure evaluation contexts, evaluation contexts include a context where the hole is put in the body of a reset operator.

3.3 Type System

This section presents a type system of our calculus. It is defined as a combination of that of Danvy and Filinski and that of Wadler and Findler. As usual, we use typing contexts, denoted by Γ, to denote a mapping of variables to types:

$$\Gamma ::= \emptyset \mid \Gamma, x{:}A$$

Typing judgments in our type system take the form $\Gamma; \alpha \vdash s : A; \beta$, which means that term s is typed at type A under typing context Γ and it modifies answer type α to β when evaluated. Perhaps, it may be easier to understand what the typing judgment means when its CPS transformation is considered. When we write $[\![\cdot]\!]$ for the CPS transformation, the typing judgment $\Gamma; \alpha \vdash s : A; \beta$ is translated into the form $[\![\Gamma]\!] \vdash [\![s]\!] : ([\![A]\!] \to [\![\alpha]\!]) \to [\![\beta]\!]$ in the simply typed blame calculus (without shift/reset). That is, type A of term s and type α are the argument type and the return type of a continuation, respectively, and type β is the type of the whole computation result when the continuation is passed.

Figure 3 shows typing rules for deriving typing judgments. Typing rules for shift operators, reset operators, and terms from the lambda calculus are the

$\boxed{\Gamma; \alpha \vdash t : A; \beta}$ **Typing rules**

$$\frac{}{\Gamma; \alpha \vdash c : ty(c); \alpha}\ \text{T\_CONST} \qquad \frac{ty(op) = \overline{\iota_i}^i \to \iota \quad \overline{\Gamma; \alpha_i \vdash t_i : \iota_i; \alpha_{i-1}}^i}{\Gamma; \alpha_n \vdash op(\overline{t_i}^i) : \iota; \alpha_0}\ \text{T\_OP}$$

$$\frac{}{\Gamma; \alpha \vdash \mathsf{blame}\, p : A; \beta}\ \text{T\_BLAME} \qquad \frac{\Gamma, x{:}A; \beta \vdash t : B; \gamma}{\Gamma; \alpha \vdash \lambda x.t : A/\beta \to B/\gamma; \alpha}\ \text{T\_ABS}$$

$$\frac{x{:}A \in \Gamma}{\Gamma; \alpha \vdash x : A; \alpha}\ \text{T\_VAR} \qquad \frac{\Gamma; \gamma \vdash t : A/\alpha \to B/\beta; \delta \quad \Gamma; \beta \vdash s : A; \gamma}{\Gamma; \alpha \vdash t\, s : B; \delta}\ \text{T\_APP}$$

$$\frac{\Gamma; \alpha \vdash s : A; \beta \quad A \sim B}{\Gamma; \alpha \vdash (s : A \Rightarrow^p B) : B; \beta}\ \text{T\_CAST} \qquad \frac{\Gamma; \alpha \vdash s : G; \beta}{\Gamma; \alpha \vdash (s : G \Rightarrow \star) : \star; \beta}\ \text{T\_GROUND}$$

$$\frac{\Gamma, k{:}A/\gamma \to \alpha/\gamma; \delta \vdash s : \delta; \beta}{\Gamma; \alpha \vdash \mathcal{S}k.\, s : A; \beta}\ \text{T\_SHIFT} \qquad \frac{\Gamma; \beta \vdash s : \beta; A}{\Gamma; \alpha \vdash \langle s \rangle : A; \alpha}\ \text{T\_RESET}$$

Fig. 3. Typing rules.

same as Danvy and Filinski's type system. In (T_Op), we use function ty from primitive operator names to their (first-order) types. Typing rules for terms from the blame calculus are changed to follow Danvy and Filinski's type system. In (T_Cast), following previous work on the blame calculus, we restrict casts in well typed programs to be ones between compatible types. In other words, (T_Cast) rules out casts that will always fail. The typing rule (T_Blame) seems to allow blame to modify answer types to any type though blame does not invoke shift operator; this causes no problems (and is necessary for type soundness) because blame halts a program.

3.4 Type Soundness

We show type soundness of our calculus in the standard way: Preservation and Progress [31]. In the presence of the dynamic type, we can write a divergent term easily, and blame is a legitimate state of program evaluation. Thus, type soundness in this paper means that any well typed program (a closed term enclosed by reset) evaluates to a well typed value, diverges, or raises blame. In what follows, we write $\longmapsto^*$ for the reflexive and transitive closure of $\longmapsto$.

Theorem 1 (Type Soundness). *If $\emptyset; \alpha \vdash \langle s \rangle : A; \alpha$, then one of the followings holds:*

- *there is an infinite evaluation sequence from $\langle s \rangle$;*
- *$\langle s \rangle \longmapsto^* \mathsf{blame}\, p$ for some p; or*
- *$\langle s \rangle \longmapsto^* v$ for some v such that $\emptyset; \alpha \vdash v : A; \alpha$.*

The outermost reset is assumed to exclude terms stuck at a shift operator without a surrounding reset. The statement of Progress shown after Preservation, however, has to take into account such a possibility for proof by induction to work.

Lemma 1 (Preservation). *If $\emptyset; \alpha \vdash s : A; \beta$ and $s \longmapsto t$, then $\emptyset; \alpha \vdash t : A; \beta$.*

Proof. By induction on the typing derivation with case analysis on the reduction/evaluation rule applied to s. In the case for (R_Shift), we follow the proof in the previous work on shift/reset [3].

Lemma 2 (Progress). *If $\emptyset; \alpha \vdash s : A; \beta$, then one of the followings holds:*

- *$s \longmapsto s'$ for some s';*
- *s is a value;*
- *$s = \mathsf{blame}\, p$ for some p; or*
- *$s = F[\mathcal{S}k.\, t]$ for some F, k and t.*

Proof. Straightforward by induction on the typing derivation.

Proof (Theorem 1). By Progress and Preservation. Note that the evaluation from $\langle s \rangle$ to $F[\mathcal{S}k.\, t]$ as stated in Progress does not happen since s is enclosed by reset and reset does not appear in F.

4 Blame Theorem

Blame Theorem intuitively states that values from the typed code will never be sources of cast failure at run time and, more specifically, clarifies conditions under which some blame never happens. Following the original work [30], we formalize such conditions using a few, different subtyping relations. Our proof is based on that in Ahmed et al.'s work [1], which defined a safety relation for terms and showed Blame Preservation and Blame Progress like preservation and progress for type soundness.

4.1 Subtyping

To state a Blame Theorem, we introduce naive subtyping $<:_n$, which formalizes the notion of being "more precisely typed." Roughly speaking, type A is a naive subtype of B when A is obtained by substituting some types for occurrences of the dynamic type in B. For example, $\mathsf{int} <:_n \star$ and $\mathsf{int}/\mathsf{int} \rightarrow \mathsf{int}/\mathsf{int} <:_n \star/\mathsf{int} \rightarrow \mathsf{int}/\star$. Note that argument types are covariant here. The Blame Theorem states that if type A is a naive subtype of type B, then the side of A is never blamed, that is, a cast $s : A \Rightarrow^p B$ does not cause $\mathsf{blame}\, p$ and $s : B \Rightarrow^p A$ does not $\mathsf{blame}\, \bar{p}$.

To prove the Blame Theorem, we introduce positive and negative subtyping. Intuitively, that type A is a positive (resp. negative) subtype of B expresses that positive (resp. negative) blame never happens for a cast from A to B. It turns out that naive subtyping can be expressed in terms of positive and negative subtyping, from which the Blame Theorem easily follows. In addition, a cast from an ordinary subtype—where argument types of function types are contravariant—to a supertype is shown not to raise blame.

Subtyping relations—ordinary subtyping $<:$, naive subtyping $<:_n$, positive subtyping $<:^+$, and negative subtyping $<:^-$—are reflexive relations satisfying subtyping rules presented in Fig. 4. The idea shared across all subtyping rules for function types is that function type $A/\alpha \rightarrow B/\beta$ is interpreted as if it takes the CPS-transformation form $A \rightarrow (B \rightarrow \alpha) \rightarrow \beta$. In this form, A and α occur at negative positions while B and β occur at positive positions.

We write $A <: B$ to denote that A is a subtype of B. The rule (S_Dyn) means that any (nondynamic) type is a subtype of the dynamic type if it is a subtype of the (unique) ground type compatible to it. The premise is needed for cases that the subtype is higher order. Function types are covariant at positive positions and contravariant at negative positions as usual.

As mentioned before, type A is a naive subtype of B when A is obtained by putting some types in occurrences of the dynamic type in B. The rule (SN_Dyn) means that the dynamic type is least precise. In the rule (SN_Fun), function types for naive subtyping are covariant in both positive and negative positions.

The definitions of positive and negative subtyping are mutually recursive. The rule (S^+_Dyn) means that positive blame never happens when any value is coerced to the dynamic type. Similarly to ordinary subtyping, in (S^+_Fun), function types are covariant at positive positions and contravariant at negative

$\boxed{A <: B}$ **Subtype**

$$\frac{A <: G}{A <: \star}\ \textsc{S\_Dyn} \qquad \frac{A' <: A \quad B <: B' \quad \alpha' <: \alpha \quad \beta <: \beta'}{A/\alpha \to B/\beta <: A'/\alpha' \to B'/\beta'}\ \textsc{S\_Fun}$$

$\boxed{A <:_n B}$ **Naive Subtype**

$$\frac{}{A <:_n \star}\ \textsc{SN\_Dyn} \qquad \frac{A <:_n A' \quad B <:_n B' \quad \alpha <:_n \alpha' \quad \beta <:_n \beta'}{A/\alpha \to B/\beta <:_n A'/\alpha' \to B'/\beta'}\ \textsc{SN\_Fun}$$

$\boxed{A <:^+ B}$ **Positive Subtype**

$$\frac{}{A <:^+ \star}\ \textsc{S}^+\textsc{\_Dyn} \qquad \frac{A' <:^- A \quad B <:^+ B' \quad \alpha' <:^- \alpha \quad \beta <:^+ \beta'}{A/\alpha \to B/\beta <:^+ A'/\alpha' \to B'/\beta'}\ \textsc{S}^+\textsc{\_Fun}$$

$\boxed{A <:^- B}$ **Negative Subtype**

$$\frac{}{\star <:^- A}\ \textsc{S}^-\textsc{\_Dyn} \qquad \frac{A <:^- G}{A <:^- B}\ \textsc{S}^-\textsc{\_Any}$$

$$\frac{A' <:^+ A \quad B <:^- B' \quad \alpha' <:^+ \alpha \quad \beta <:^- \beta'}{A/\alpha \to B/\beta <:^- A'/\alpha' \to B'/\beta'}\ \textsc{S}^-\textsc{\_Fun}$$

Fig. 4. Subtyping rules.

positions. Negative subtyping is a reversed version of positive subtyping except for addition of ($\textsc{S}^-\textsc{\_Any}$), which is a combination of ($\textsc{S}^-\textsc{\_Dyn}$) and the fact that a cast from type A to the dynamic type never gives rise to negative blame when A is a negative subtype of its ground type. The rule ($\textsc{S}^-\textsc{\_Any}$) follows from Ahmed et al.'s work [1] and represents a relaxed form of the system of Wadler and Findler [30]. Notice that polarity of subtyping is reversed at negative positions.

As mentioned above, we show that naive subtyping (and ordinary subtyping) can be expressed in terms of positive and negative subtyping.

Lemma 3. *$A <:_n B$ iff $A <:^+ B$ and $B <:^- A$.*

Lemma 4. *$A <: B$ iff $A <:^+ B$ and $A <:^- B$.*

The proofs of the direction from left to right are straightforward by induction on the derivations of $A <:_n B$ and $A <: B$. The other direction is shown by structural induction on A.

4.2 Blame Theorem

The proof of the Blame Theorem is similar to preservation and progress for type soundness. Instead of a type system, we introduce a safety relation using positive and negative subtyping and show Blame Preservation, which states safety is

$$\frac{s\ \mathsf{sf}\ p \quad A <:^{+} B}{s : A \Rightarrow^{p} B\ \mathsf{sf}\ p} \qquad \frac{s\ \mathsf{sf}\ p \quad A <:^{-} B}{s : A \Rightarrow^{\bar{p}} B\ \mathsf{sf}\ p} \qquad \frac{}{c\ \mathsf{sf}\ p} \qquad \frac{\forall i.\ t_i\ \mathsf{sf}\ p}{op(\overline{t_i}^{\,i})\ \mathsf{sf}\ p} \qquad \frac{}{x\ \mathsf{sf}\ p}$$

$$\frac{s\ \mathsf{sf}\ p}{\lambda x.\, s\ \mathsf{sf}\ p} \qquad \frac{s\ \mathsf{sf}\ p \quad t\ \mathsf{sf}\ p}{s\, t\ \mathsf{sf}\ p} \qquad \frac{q \neq p \quad q \neq \bar{q} \quad s\ \mathsf{sf}\ p}{s : A \Rightarrow^{q} B\ \mathsf{sf}\ p} \qquad \frac{s\ \mathsf{sf}\ p}{s : G \Rightarrow \star\ \mathsf{sf}\ p}$$

$$\frac{q \neq p}{\mathsf{blame}\ q\ \mathsf{sf}\ p} \qquad \frac{s\ \mathsf{sf}\ p}{\mathcal{S}k.\, s\ \mathsf{sf}\ p} \qquad \frac{s\ \mathsf{sf}\ p}{\langle s \rangle\ \mathsf{sf}\ p}$$

Fig. 5. Safety rules.

preserved by evaluation, and Blame Progress, which states that a safe term does not give rise to blame. In this section, we focus only on whether a term gives rise to blame or not and not on whether a term gets stuck or not.

A term s is *safe for blame label* p, written as $s\ \mathsf{sf}\ p$, if every cast with blame label p in s is from a type to its positive supertype and every cast with $\bar{p}$ is from a type to its negative supertype. We present inference rules for the safety relation in Fig. 5. From the definition, it is observed that a term safe for p does not contain blame with p; this does not restrict a source program written by a programmer because it should not contain any blame.

Blame Preservation and Blame Progress show that, if $s\ \mathsf{sf}\ p$, term s never gives rise to blame with label p. We write $s \not\longmapsto t$ and $s \not\longmapsto^{*} t$ to denote that term s does not reduce to term t in a single step and in multiple steps, respectively.

Lemma 5 (Blame Preservation). *If $s\ \mathsf{sf}\ p$ and $s \longmapsto t$, then $t\ \mathsf{sf}\ p$.*

Lemma 6 (Blame Progress). *If $s\ \mathsf{sf}\ p$, then $s \not\longmapsto \mathsf{blame}\ p$.*

Finally, we show the Blame Theorem—values that flow from the more precisely typed side never cause blame—and, furthermore, that casts from one type to its supertype never give rise to blame.

Theorem 2 (Blame Theorem). *Let s be a term with a subterm $t : A \Rightarrow^{p} B$ where cast is labeled by the only occurrence of p in s. Moreover, suppose that $\bar{p}$ does not appear in s.*

1. *If $A <:^{+} B$, then $s \not\longmapsto^{*} \mathsf{blame}\ p$.*
2. *If $A <:^{-} B$, then $s \not\longmapsto^{*} \mathsf{blame}\ \bar{p}$.*
3. *If $A <:_{n} B$, then $s \not\longmapsto^{*} \mathsf{blame}\ p$; if $B <:_{n} A$, then $s \not\longmapsto^{*} \mathsf{blame}\ \bar{p}$.*
4. *If $A <: B$, then $s \not\longmapsto^{*} \mathsf{blame}\ p$ and $s \not\longmapsto^{*} \mathsf{blame}\ \bar{p}$.*

Proof. The first and second cases are shown by Blame Preservation and Blame Progress because $s\ \mathsf{sf}\ p$ in the first case and $s\ \mathsf{sf}\ \bar{p}$ in the second case. The third case (resp. the fourth case) follows from the first and second cases and Lemma 3 (resp. Lemma 4).

5 CPS Transformation

The semantics of programming languages with control operators has often been established by transformation of programs with control operators to continuation passing style (CPS), a programming style where continuations appear in a program as arguments of functions. For example, programs with Reynolds's escape operator [19], call/cc in Scheme, shift/reset [6], and so on can be transformed to CPS form.

As a proof of correctness of our approach, we define a CPS transformation from terms in our calculus to those in the simply typed blame calculus of Ahmed et al. [1] and show that a well typed source term is transformed to a well typed target term and, for any source terms such that one reduces to the other, their CPS-transformation results are equivalent in the target calculus. The equational system is based on call-by-value axioms [20] due to blame, which is effectful.

Our CPS transformation $[\![\cdot]\!]$, shown in Fig. 6, is standard except for the case for ground values $v : G \Rightarrow \star$; if G is the ground function type $\star/\star \to \star/\star$, a ground value is transformed to a value with a cast (the reason is detailed later). To assign a blame label to the cast, we modify the syntax and the reduction rule (R_Ground) of our calculus. Formally, the syntax is changed as follows:

$$v ::= ... \mid v : G \Rightarrow_p \star \qquad s ::= ... \mid s : G \Rightarrow_p \star$$

Blame labels in ground terms and values are given as subscripts for ease of distinction from casts. The reduction rule (R_Ground) takes the following form:

$$v : A \Rightarrow^p \star \longrightarrow (v : A \Rightarrow^p G) : G \Rightarrow_p \star \text{ (if } A \sim G \text{ and } A \neq \star) \quad \text{R\_Ground}$$

Our CPS transformation, which mostly follows Danvy and Filinski [6], is shown in Fig. 6 in three parts: transformation for types, values, and terms. We use variable κ to denote continuations. The CPS transformation for types is standard. A function of type $A/\alpha \to B/\beta$ takes an argument of A, would pass a value of B to a continuation that returns α, and results in a value of β as the computation result. The CPS transformation for values maps values in our calculus to those in the blame calculus without shift/reset. The definition shown in Fig. 6 is easy to understand except for ground values where the ground type is a function type. We might expect that the CPS-transformation result of ground value $v : G \Rightarrow_p \star$ can be defined as $v^* : [\![G]\!] \Rightarrow \star$. However, that form would not be a valid term in the target calculus if the ground type G is a function type, because the ground function type in the target calculus takes only the form $\star \to \star$ but $[\![\star/\star \to \star/\star]\!] = \star \to (\star \to \star) \to \star$. Expecting a value will be translated to a value in the target calculus, we set a ground value $v : \star/\star \to \star/\star \Rightarrow_p \star$ to be mapped to *a value to which* $v^* : [\![G]\!] \Rightarrow^p \star$ *reduces*, instead. (Notice the super-script on $\Rightarrow$. A term $v^* : [\![G]\!] \Rightarrow^p \star$ is a cast and always valid.) In the result, we omit the trivial cast $x : \star \Rightarrow^{\bar{p}} \star$. The CPS transformation for terms is self-explanatory.

It is straightforward to show that well typed source terms are transformed to well typed target terms. For any typing context Γ, we write $[\![\Gamma]\!]$ for the typing context obtained by applying the CPS transformation to types mapped by Γ.

$\boxed{[\![A]\!]}$ **CPS Transformation (Types)**

$$[\![\iota]\!] = \iota \qquad [\![\star]\!] = \star \qquad [\![A/\alpha \to B/\beta]\!] = [\![A]\!] \to ([\![B]\!] \to [\![\alpha]\!]) \to [\![\beta]\!]$$

$\boxed{v^*}$ **CPS Transformation (Values)**

$$x^* = x \qquad c^* = c \qquad (\lambda x.\, s)^* = \lambda x.\, [\![s]\!] \qquad (v : \iota \Rightarrow \star)^* = v^* : \iota \Rightarrow \star$$
$$(v : \star/\star \to \star/\star \Rightarrow_p \star)^* = (\lambda x.\, (v^*\, x) : (\star \to \star) \to \star \Rightarrow^p \star) : \star \to \star \Rightarrow \star$$

$\boxed{[\![s]\!]}$ **CPS Transformation (Terms)**

$$\begin{array}{ll}
[\![v]\!] & = \lambda\kappa.\, \kappa\, v^* \\
[\![op(\overline{t_i}^i)]\!] & = \lambda\kappa.\, [\![t_1]\!]\, (\lambda x_1.\, \ldots\, [\![t_n]\!]\, (\lambda x_n.\, \kappa\, op(\overline{x_i}^i))\, \ldots) \\
[\![s\, t]\!] & = \lambda\kappa.\, [\![s]\!]\, (\lambda x.\, [\![t]\!]\, (\lambda y.\, x\, y\, \kappa)) \\
[\![\langle s \rangle]\!] & = \lambda\kappa.\, \kappa\, ([\![s]\!]\, (\lambda x.\, x)) \\
[\![\mathcal{S}k.\, s]\!] & = \lambda\kappa.\, ([\![s]\!]\, (\lambda x.\, x))\, [k := \lambda x.\, \lambda\kappa'.\, \kappa'\, (\kappa\, x)] \\
[\![s : A \Rightarrow^p B]\!] & = \lambda\kappa.\, [\![s]\!]\, (\lambda x.\, \kappa\, (x : [\![A]\!] \Rightarrow^p [\![B]\!])) \\
[\![s : G \Rightarrow \star]\!] & = \lambda\kappa.\, [\![s]\!]\, (\lambda x.\, \kappa\, (x : G \Rightarrow \star)^*) \\
[\![\mathsf{blame}\, p]\!] & = \lambda\kappa.\, \mathsf{blame}\, p
\end{array}$$

Fig. 6. CPS transformation.

Theorem 3 (Preservation of Type). *If* $\Gamma; \alpha \vdash s : A; \beta$, *then* $[\![\Gamma]\!] \vdash [\![s]\!] : ([\![A]\!] \to [\![\alpha]\!]) \to [\![\beta]\!]$.

Next, we define an equational system in the target calculus. The system consists of axioms about casts as well as usual call-by-value axioms [20]. In what follows, we use metavariables $\mathbb{e}$, $\mathbb{v}$, $\mathbb{E}$, and $\mathbb{A}$ (and $\mathbb{B}$) to denote terms, values, evaluation contexts, and types in the target calculus, respectively, and write $fv\,(\mathbb{v})$ and $fv\,(\mathbb{E})$ for the sets of free variables in $\mathbb{v}$ and $\mathbb{E}$, respectively. In addition, let the relation $\Longrightarrow$ be the evaluation relation in the target calculus.

Definition 1 (Term Equality). *The relation* $\approx$ *is the least congruence that contains the following axioms:*

$$\frac{\mathbb{e}_1 \Longrightarrow \mathbb{e}_2}{\mathbb{e}_1 \approx \mathbb{e}_2} \qquad \frac{x \notin fv\,(\mathbb{v})}{\lambda x.\, \mathbb{v}\, x \approx \mathbb{v}} \qquad \frac{x \notin fv\,(\mathbb{E})}{(\lambda x.\, \mathbb{E}[x])\, \mathbb{e} \approx \mathbb{E}[\mathbb{e}]}$$

$$\mathbb{e} : \star \Rightarrow^p \star \approx \mathbb{e} \qquad \mathbb{e} : \star \Rightarrow^p \star \to \star \Rightarrow^p \mathbb{A} \to \mathbb{B} \approx \mathbb{e} : \star \Rightarrow^p \mathbb{A} \to \mathbb{B}$$

We think that the last two axioms about casts are reasonable. The former, which skips the trivial cast, is found in another blame calculus [24]. This axiom is introduced mainly to ignore redundant casts that often happen in CPS-transformation results. The latter axiom, which collapses two casts into one, is used to show terms reduced by (R_COLLAPSE) are equivalent after CPS transformation.

Now, we show that the relationship between our semantics in direct-style and the CPS transformation.

Theorem 4 (Preservation of Equality). *If* $s \longmapsto t$, *then* $[\![s]\!] \approx [\![t]\!]$.

6 Related Work

Gradual Typing and Blame Theorem. Blame calculi are variants of lambda calculi for gradual typing by Siek and Taha [22], a mechanism to integrate static and dynamic typing. Since the seminal work by Siek and Taha, the notion of gradual typing has spread over various programming constructs—e.g., higher-order functions [22], objects [23], mutable references [16], polymorphism [1], etc. The property that values that flow from typed code never trigger cast failure was studied first in the context of contract checking [27]. Wadler and Findler [30] adopted blame of finer forms (positive and negative blame), following Findler and Felleisen's work [13], and investigated conditions under which blame does not happen. They discovered that the notion of being "more precisely typed" can be formalized as naive subtyping.

Delimited-Control Operators. Roughly speaking, there have been two major families of delimited-control operators: so-called "static" control operators, including shift/reset [5,6], and so-called "dynamic" control operators, including control/prompt [10,15]. In this work, we choose shift/reset because their type system and CPS transformation are well studied. In fact, CPS transformation for shift/reset has served as a guide to designing our cast mechanism. Given recent studies on relationship of control/prompt to their CPS transformation [7,9,21] and a type system for control/prompt [18], we leave an extension of blame calculi to control/prompt for interesting future work.

Gradual Typing with Delimited-Control Operators. Most closely related work is Takikawa et al. [26]; they have also studied integration of static and dynamic typing in the presence of control operators. They proposed a contract system for programs with control operators in Racket [15] and showed that values from typed parts never trigger blame (in the sense of Tobin-Hochstadt and Felleisen [27]) through the complete monitoring property [8]. Aside from an obvious difference in the choice of control operators, our calculus has finer-grained control over how typed and untyped parts can be mixed: e.g., a function of type $\mathsf{int} \to \star$ cannot be expressed in Takikawa et al. because there are only fully typed and fully untyped modules. We also define a CPS transformation for our calculus, and investigate the relationship between our calculus and the CPS transformation. Although shift and reset can be implemented by using control operators in Racket [15], it is not very clear whether their contract system can simulate our casts for function types with answer types naturally.

7 Conclusion

We have proposed a new cast-based mechanism to monitor all communications between typed and untyped code in the presence of shift/reset. It is inspired by Danvy and Filinski's type system. To justify the design of our cast semantics, we have defined a simply typed blame calculus with shift/reset and shown the Blame Theorem and soundness of the CPS transformation. We have found additional axioms for the equational system in the target language in proving the soundness.

There are many directions for future work. First is an extension of our blame calculus with refinement types. Effects in refinements are obviously problematic. One possible solution would be to restrict refinements to be pure. It is interesting to investigate how such purity restriction can be relaxed. Second is to apply succeeding work about blame calculi, such as space-efficiency [16] and parametricity [1], to our calculus. In particular, an extension with parametricity would be challenging because it is not clear how control operators and the ν-operator interact with each other. Finally, we would like to develop a contract system corresponding to our calculus and to inspect more detailed relationship to the contract system of Takikawa et al.

Acknowledgments. We would like to thank Matthias Felleisen, Robby Findler, Philip Wadler, and anonymous reviewers of APLAS 2015 for valuable comments. This work was supported in part by Grant-in-Aid for Scientific Research (B) No. 25280024 from MEXT of Japan. The title is derived from that of a paper by Kameyama, Kiselyov, and Shan [17].

References

1. Ahmed, A., Findler, R.B., Siek, J.G., Wadler, P.: Blame for all. In: Proceedings of ACM POPL, pp. 201–214 (2011)
2. Asai, K., Kameyama, Y.: Polymorphic delimited continuations. In: Shao, Z. (ed.) APLAS 2007. LNCS, vol. 4807, pp. 239–254. Springer, Heidelberg (2007)
3. Asai, K., Kameyama, Y.: Polymorphic delimited continuations. CS-TR-07-10, Department of Computer Science, University of Tsukuba (2007)
4. Bonnaire-Sargeant, A., Davies, R., Tobin-Hochstadt, S.: Practical optional types for Clojure (unpublishded draft)
5. Danvy, O., Filinski, A.: A functional abstraction of typed contexts. 89/12, DIKU, University of Copenhagen (1989)
6. Danvy, O., Filinski, A.: Abstracting control. In: LISP and Functional Programming, pp. 151–160 (1990)
7. Dariusz Biernacki, O.D., Millikin, K.: A dynamic continuation-passing style for dynamic delimited continuations. Research Series RS-06-15, BRICS, DAIMI (2006)
8. Dimoulas, C., Tobin-Hochstadt, S., Felleisen, M.: Complete monitors for behavioral contracts. In: Seidl, H. (ed.) Programming Languages and Systems. LNCS, vol. 7211, pp. 214–233. Springer, Heidelberg (2012)
9. Dybvig, R.K., Jones, S.L.P., Sabry, A.: A monadic framework for delimited continuations. J. Funct. Program. **17**(6), 687–730 (2007)

10. Felleisen, M.: The theory and practice of first-class prompts. In: Proceedings of ACM POPL, pp. 180–190 (1988)
11. Felleisen, M., Hieb, R.: The revised report on the syntactic theories of sequential control and state. Theoret. Comput. Sci. **103**(2), 235–271 (1992)
12. Filinski, A.: Representing monads. In: Proceedings of ACM POPL, pp. 446–457 (1994)
13. Findler, R.B., Felleisen, M.: Contracts for higher-order functions. In: Proceedings of ACM ICFP, pp. 48–59 (2002)
14. Flanagan, C.: Hybrid type checking. In: Proceedings of ACM POPL, pp. 245–256 (2006)
15. Flatt, M., Yu, G., Findler, R.B., Felleisen, M.: Adding delimited and composable control to a production programming environment. In: Proceedings of ACM ICFP, pp. 165–176 (2007)
16. Herman, D., Tomb, A., Flanagan, C.: Space-efficient gradual typing. In: Trends in Functional Programming (2007)
17. Kameyama, Y., Kiselyov, O., Shan, C.: Shifting the stage: staging with delimited control. In: Proceedings of ACM PEPM, pp. 111–120 (2009)
18. Kameyama, Y., Yonezawa, T.: Typed dynamic control operators for delimited continuations. In: Garrigue, J., Hermenegildo, M.V. (eds.) FLOPS 2008. LNCS, vol. 4989, pp. 239–254. Springer, Heidelberg (2008)
19. Reynolds, J.C.: Definitional interpreters for higher-order programming languages. In: Proceedings of ACM Annual Conference, pp. 717–740 (1972)
20. Sabry, A., Felleisen, M.: Reasoning about programs in continuation-passing style. Lisp Symbolic Comput. **6**(3–4), 289–360 (1993)
21. Shan, C.: Shift to control. In: Scheme and Functional Programming Workshop, pp. 99–107 (2004)
22. Siek, J.G., Taha, W.: Gradual typing for functional languages. In: Scheme and Functional Programming Workshop, pp. 81–92 (2006)
23. Siek, J.G., Taha, W.: Gradual typing for objects. In: Ernst, E. (ed.) ECOOP 2007. LNCS, vol. 4609, pp. 2–27. Springer, Heidelberg (2007)
24. Siek, J.G., Wadler, P.: Threesomes, with and without blame. In: Proceedings of ACM POPL, pp. 365–376 (2010)
25. Sitaram, D.: Handling control. In: Proceedings of ACM PLDI, pp. 147–155 (1993)
26. Takikawa, A., Strickland, T.S., Tobin-Hochstadt, S.: Constraining delimited control with contracts. In: Felleisen, M., Gardner, P. (eds.) ESOP 2013. LNCS, vol. 7792, pp. 229–248. Springer, Heidelberg (2013)
27. Tobin-Hochstadt, S., Felleisen, M.: Interlanguage migration: from scripts to programs. In: Dynamic Language Symposium, pp. 964–974 (2006)
28. Tobin-Hochstadt, S., Felleisen, M.: The design and implementation of typed scheme. In: Proceedings of ACM POPL, pp. 395–406 (2008)
29. Vitousek, M.M., Kent, A.M., Siek, J.G., Baker, J.: Design and evaluation of gradual typing for Python. In: Dynamic Language Symposium, pp. 45–56 (2014)
30. Wadler, P., Findler, R.B.: Well-typed programs can't be blamed. In: Castagna, G. (ed.) ESOP 2009. LNCS, vol. 5502, pp. 1–16. Springer, Heidelberg (2009)
31. Wright, A.K., Felleisen, M.: A syntactic approach to type soundness. Inf. Comput. **115**(1), 38–94 (1994)

Aliasing Control in an Imperative Pure Calculus

Marco Servetto[1(✉)] and Elena Zucca[2]

[1] Victoria University of Wellington, Wellington, New Zealand
marco.servetto@ecs.vuw.ac.nz
[2] DIBRIS, Università di Genova, Genoa, Italy
elena.zucca@unige.it

Abstract. We present an imperative object calculus where types are annotated with two modifiers for aliasing control. The `lent` modifier prevents objects to be aliased, whereas the `capsule` modifier characterizes expressions that will reduce to isolated portions of store. There are two key novelties w.r.t. similar proposals. First, the expressivity of the type system is greatly enhanced by *promotion* and *swapping* rules. The former recognizes as `capsule` an expression which only uses external references as `lent`. The latter allows a `lent` reference to be freely aliased, if all the other references are regarded as `lent`. Second, execution is modeled in a *pure* setting, where it is simpler to understand alias control. That is, properties of modifiers can be directly expressed on source terms, rather than as invariants on an auxiliary structure which mimics physical memory. Formally, this is achieved by the block construct, introducing local variable declarations, which play the role of store when evaluated.

1 Introduction

In mainstream languages with state and explicit mutations, unwanted aliasing relations are common bugs. This is exasperated by concurrency mechanisms, since unpredicted aliasing can induce unplanned/unsafe communication points between threads.

For this reasons, in the recent years a massive amount of research has been devoted to make programming with side-effects easier to maintain and understand, notably using type modifiers to control object mutation. Here we focus on two type modifiers: `lent` (preventing objects to be aliased) and `capsule` (characterizing expressions that will reduce to isolated portions of store) which have been previously introduced in the literature. However, original proposals [1,10] were not flexible enough, and later variations [12,19] sacrificed a part of safety allowing programmers to relax the constraints on different object subgraph branches.

The type system proposed in this paper, instead, sticks to full safety: our modifiers constrain the full reachable object graph, allowing simpler reasoning. On the other hand, we avoid the rigidity of original approaches and achieve

This work has been partially supported by MIUR CINA -Compositionality, Interaction, Negotiation, Autonomicity for the future ICT society.

X. Feng and S. Park (Eds.): APLAS 2015, LNCS 9458, pp. 208–228, 2015.
DOI: 10.1007/978-3-319-26529-2_12

expressiveness by *promotion* and *swapping* rules. The former recognizes as `capsule` an expression which only uses external references as `lent`. The latter allows a `lent` reference to be freely aliased, if all the other references are regarded as `lent`. The idea of promotion is similar to the idea of recovery in [9], while the idea of swapping is novel and greatly boosts the expressiveness of promotion/recovery.

Moreover, we differ from former works on type modifiers since they rely on a conventional encoding of a program state as an expression coupled with a flat auxiliary structure called *store* or *memory*. In this model, typing the store is crucial to show the correctness of the approach. However, when modularly typechecking a subterm of an expression, the information about how the whole expression and the store interact is lost. That is, it is hard to know whether a certain memory location is used only locally in the currently typechecked subterm or is aliased somewhere else.

To avoid this problem, we have introduced an innovative model for imperative languages [5,16], which, differently from traditional execution models, is a *pure calculus*. That is, execution is modeled by just rewriting source code terms, in the same way lambda calculus models functional languages.

The main idea is to use local variable declarations, as in the `let` construct, to directly represent memory. For instance, in the following code, where we assume a class `B` with a field of type `B`:

```
B x= new B(y)   B y= new B(x)   y
```

the two declarations can be seen as a store where `x` denotes an object of class `B` whose field is `y`, and conversely. Moreover, store is *hierarchical*, rather than flat as it usually happens in models of imperative languages. This is shown in the example below, where we assume a class `D` with an integer field, and a class `A` with two fields of type `B` and `D`, respectively.

```
D z= new D(0)
A w= ( B x= new B(y)   B y= new B(x)   A u= new A(x,z)   u)
w
```

Here, the store associates to `w` a block introducing local declarations, that is, in turn a store[1]. The advantage of this representation is that it models in a simple and natural way constraints about aliasing among objects, notably:

- the fact that an object is not referenced from outside some enclosing object is directly modeled by the block construct: for instance, the object denoted by `y` can only be reached through `w`
- conversely, the fact that an object does not refer to the outside is modeled by the fact that the corresponding block is closed (that is, has no free variables): for instance, the object denoted by `w` is not closed, since it refers to the external object `z`.

In other words, our calculus smoothly integrates memory representation with shadowing and α-conversion.

[1] In the examples, we omit for readability the brackets of the outermost block.

In this paper, we propose, on top of the calculus, a simple, yet powerful, type system for aliasing control, where types are possibly decorated by the two modifiers mentioned in the beginning.

The `lent` modifier prevents (any subcomponent of) an object to be assigned to external object's fields, and conversely. In other words, no alias to an object can be introduced by using a lent reference, which, however, does not prevent the object from being mutated.[2] The `capsule` modifier characterizes expressions that will reduce to isolated portions of store. In order to preserve this property, a capsule reference can be used only once. That is, uniqueness is guaranteed by linearity, rather than by destructive reads as in [4,9]. The type system achieves expressivity by the *promotion* and *swapping* rules mentioned above. The fact that object graph topologies are directly formalized in syntactic way allows a simple statement and proof of the `capsule` property.

The rest of the paper is organized as follows: we provide syntax and type system in Sect. 2, examples in Sect. 3, reduction rules in Sect. 4, results in Sect. 5, comparison with related work in Sect. 6, and some conclusion and pointer to further work in Sect. 7.

2 Syntax and Type System

Syntax, types, and type contexts are given in Fig. 1. We assume sets of *variables* x, y, z, ..., *class names* C, *field names* f, and *method names* m. We adopt the convention that a metavariable which ends by s is implicitly defined as a (possibly empty) sequence, for example, xs is defined by $xs ::= \epsilon \mid x\ xs$ and xss is defined by $xss ::= \epsilon \mid xs\ xss$, where ϵ denotes the empty string.

$cd ::= \texttt{class}\ C\ \{fds\ mds\}$	class declaration
$fd ::= C\ f$	field declaration
$md ::= T\ m\ \mu\ \texttt{(}T_1\ x_1, \ldots, T_n\ x_n\texttt{)}\ \{\texttt{return}\ e\}$	method declaration
$e ::= x \mid e.f \mid e.m(es) \mid e.f = e' \mid \texttt{new}\ C(es) \mid \texttt{(}ds\ e\texttt{)}$	expression
$d ::= T\ x = e$	variable declaration
$dv ::= T\ x = rv$	evaluated declaration
$rv ::= \texttt{new}\ C(xs) \mid \texttt{(}dvs\ v\texttt{)}$	right value
$v ::= x \mid rv$	value (object)
$T ::= \mu\ C$	type
$\mu ::= \texttt{capsule} \mid \texttt{lent} \mid \epsilon$	optional type modifier
$\Delta ::= \Gamma; xss$	type context
$\Gamma ::= T_1\ x_1 \ldots T_n\ x_n$	type assignment

Fig. 1. Syntax, types, and type contexts

[2] More precisely, `lent` references can be temporarily aliased, e.g., when passed as parameter of a method, but cannot be stored within other objects. That is, aliasing here means *static aliasing* in the sense of [10].

The syntax mostly follows Java and Featherweight Java (FJ) [11]. A *class table cds* is a sequence of class declarations, each one consisting of a class name, a sequence of field declarations and a sequence of method declarations. A field declaration consists of a class name and a field name. A method declaration consists, as in FJ, of a return type, a method name, a list of parameter names with their types, and a body which is an expression. However, there is an additional optional component: the type modifier for `this`, which, if present, is placed before the method name. As in FJ, we assume for each class a canonical constructor whose parameter list exactly corresponds to the class fields. We assume no multiple declarations of classes in a class table, fields and methods in a class declaration.

An expression can be a variable (including the special variable `this` denoting the receiver in a method body), a field access, a method invocation, a field assignment, a constructor invocation and a block consisting of a sequence of variable declarations and a body. A variable declaration consists of a type, a variable and an initialization expression. We assume no multiple declarations for variables in a block, that is, *ds* can be seen as a map from variables into declarations, and we use the notation $\mathsf{dom}(ds)$ and $ds(x)$.

A sequence *dvs* of *evaluated declarations* plays the role of the store in conventional models of imperative languages, that is, each *dv* can be seen as an association of a *right value* to a variable. Right values can be either *object states*, of shape `new` $C(xs)$, or block values, that is, blocks where all declarations have been evaluated, and the body is (recursively) a value. The latter case allows the store to be hierarchical.

A value is the final result of the reduction of an expression[3], and is either a variable (a reference to an object), or an object state, or a block value. A closed expression is expected to reduce to a closed value.

An object state `new` $C(xs)$ represents an elementary allocation unit, and can be considered as a shorter form[4] for a block ($C\ x =$`new` $C(xs)\ x$). Hence, a block value has shape $(dvs_1\ (\ldots\ (dvs_n\ x)\ldots))$, for $n \geq 0$. We call x the *root* of the value, and we assume that in well-formed block values it is bound in some dvs_i.

There are two important *well-formedness constraints* on expressions:

1. In a block $(T_1\ x_1 = e_1 \ldots T_n\ x_n = e_n\ e)$, forward references, that is, occurrences of x_j in e_i for $j \geq i$, are only allowed if the declaration of x_j is evaluated, that is, of shape $T_j\ x_j = rv$. Hence, mutual recursion is only allowed among evaluated declarations, e.g., `(C x= new C(x) x)` is allowed, whereas `(C x= x.f x)`, `(C x= ( x ) x)` and `(C x= x.m() x )` are not. Allowing general recursion would require a sophisticated type system[5], as in [17], but this is not the focus of this paper.
2. Variables of `capsule` types can occur at most once in their scope. Indeed, a capsule variable is a temporary reference, to be used once and for all to

[3] Reduction rules will be given in Sect. 4.
[4] As will be formalized by congruence rule (NEW) in Sect. 4.
[5] To avoid access to objects not initialized yet as in the example.

"move" a capsule object (an isolated portion of store) to another location in the store, as will be formalized in Sect. 4.[6]

A type consists in a class name possibly decorated by a *type modifier* which can be either `capsule` or `lent`. A `capsule` expression is expected to reduce to a capsule object, that is, an object with no references from/to the outside[7], whereas a `lent` expression cannot be used in an assignment, or as constructor argument. A type consisting of a class name with no modifier is called a *standard type*. Note that fields have standard types.[8]

A type context consists of a usual assignment of types to variables Γ, and an additional component $xss = xs_1 \ldots xs_n$ which models aliasing constraints, as will be detailed below. We assume that Γ, xss, and each xs_i are sets (that is, order and repetitions are immaterial), and we use $\emptyset$ for the empty set. Moreover, as usual, Γ is a partial function from variables to types (that is, no variable occurs more than once). Finally, the sets $xs_1 \ldots xs_n$ are disjoint, and their elements are variables of standard type in the domain of Γ, hence they describe a partition of such variables in $n + 1$ sets, called *groups*, one being the set of those not belonging to any xs_i, called the *current group*. To simplify typing rules, type contexts are identified modulo the following equivalence: a type context with a `lent` variable in the domain of Γ is equivalent to one where such variable has the corresponding standard type in Γ and is contained in a singleton set in xss.

The subtyping relation is the reflexive and transitive relation on types induced by

$$\texttt{capsule}\ C \leq C \leq \texttt{lent}\ C$$

However, the (T-CAPSULE) rule can be used to move the type of an expression against the subtype hierarchy, that is, to *promote* an expression of standard type to the corresponding `capsule` type.

Information extracted from the class table is modeled, as usual, by the following functions:

- $\mathsf{fields}(C)$ gives, for each declared class C, the sequence of its fields declarations
- $\mathsf{mbody}(C, m)$ gives, for each method m declared in class C, the pair $\langle x_1 \ldots x_n, e\rangle$ consisting of the sequence of its parameters, and its body[9]
- $\mathsf{mtype}(C, m)$ gives, for each method m declared in class C, the triple $\langle T, \mu, T_1 \ldots T_n\rangle$ consisting of its return type, type modifier for `this`, and parameter types.

[6] See rule (CAPSULE-ELIM). Note that, correspondingly, the association of a right value to a `capsule` variable is not kept in the store, formally there is no such case in the production for dv.

[7] This notion will be formalized in Sect. 4.

[8] It is not straightforward to soundly apply `capsule` and `lent` on fields. We plan to present such extensions in future work, whereas the current paper is focused on promotion and swapping.

[9] This function will be used in Sect. 4.

Of course, we assume a well-typed class table, that is, method bodies are expected to be well-typed w.r.t. the corresponding method type. Formally, if $\mathsf{mtype}(C, m) = \langle T, \mu, T_1 \ldots T_n \rangle$, then it should be

$\mathsf{mbody}(C, m) = \langle x_1 \ldots x_n, e \rangle$, and $\Gamma; \emptyset \vdash e : T$, with
$\Gamma = \mu\, C\, \mathtt{this}\ T_1\, x_1 \ldots T_n\, x_n$.

The typing judgment has shape $\Gamma; xss \vdash e : T$, meaning that expression e has type T under the type assignment Γ, and introduces no alias between (portions of store reachable from) the groups described by xss. More precisely, variables in the current group can be freely used, whereas variables in other groups are *lent-locked*, that is, can only be used as `lent`. A group of lent-locked variables is introduced by applying the *promotion* rule (T-CAPSULE), and can be unlocked, becoming the current group, by applying the *swapping* rule (T-SWAP), as will be explained in detail in the sequel. Typing rules are given in Fig. 2.

$$(\text{T-CAPSULE})\quad \frac{\Gamma; xss\ (xs \backslash xss) \vdash e : C}{\Gamma; xss \vdash e : \mathtt{capsule}\ C}\ \mathsf{dom}^{\mathsf{std}}(\Gamma) = xs$$

$$(\text{T-SWAP})\quad \frac{\Gamma; xss\ (xs' \backslash xss \backslash xs) \vdash e : \mu\, C}{\Gamma; xss\ xs \vdash e : \mu'\, C}\quad \begin{array}{l}\mathsf{dom}^{\mathsf{std}}(\Gamma) = xs' \\ \mu' = \begin{cases} \mathtt{lent} & \text{if } \mu = \epsilon \\ \mu & \text{otherwise}\end{cases}\end{array}$$

$$(\text{T-SUB})\quad \frac{\Delta \vdash e : T}{\Delta \vdash e : T'}\ T \leq T' \qquad (\text{T-VAR})\quad \frac{}{\Gamma; xss \vdash x : \mu'\, C}\quad \begin{array}{l}\Gamma(x) = \mu\, C \\ \mu' = \begin{cases} \mathtt{lent} & \text{if } x \in xss \\ \mu & \text{otherwise}\end{cases}\end{array}$$

$$(\text{T-FIELD-ACCESS})\quad \frac{\Delta \vdash e : \mu\, C}{\Delta \vdash e.f : \mu\, C_i}\ \begin{array}{l}\mathsf{fields}(C) = C_1\, f_1 \ldots C_n\, f_n \\ f = f_i\end{array}$$

$$(\text{T-METH-CALL})\quad \frac{\Delta \vdash e_i : T_i \quad \forall i \in 0..n}{\Delta \vdash e_0.m(e_1, \ldots, e_n) : T}\ \begin{array}{l} T_0 = \mu\, C \\ \mathsf{mtype}(C, m) = \langle T, \mu, T_1 \ldots T_n \rangle\end{array}$$

$$(\text{T-FIELD-ASSIGN})\quad \frac{\Delta \vdash e : C \quad \Delta \vdash e' : C_i}{\Delta \vdash e.f = e' : C_i}\ \begin{array}{l}\mathsf{fields}(C) = C_1\, f_1 \ldots C_n\, f_n \\ f = f_i\end{array}$$

$$(\text{T-NEW})\quad \frac{\Delta \vdash e_i : C_i \quad \forall i \in 1..n}{\Delta \vdash \mathtt{new}\ C(e_1, \ldots, e_n) : C}\ \mathsf{fields}(C) = C_1\, f_1 \ldots C_n\, f_n$$

$$(\text{T-BLOCK})\quad \frac{\Gamma[\Gamma']; xss \vdash e_i : T_i\ \forall i \in 1..n \quad \Gamma[\Gamma']; xss \vdash e : T}{\Gamma; xss \vdash (T_1\ x_1\ \mathtt{=} e_1 \ldots T_n\ x_n\ \mathtt{=} e_n\ e) : T}\ \Gamma' = T_1\, x_1 \ldots T_n\, x_n$$

Fig. 2. Typing rules

Rule (T-CAPSULE) states that an expression can be *promoted* to `capsule` if it can be typed by lent-locking all its free variables (which were not lent-locked yet). Formally, a new group is added to xss. We denote by $\mathsf{dom}^{\mathsf{std}}(\Gamma)$ the set of variables of standard type in Γ, and we write, by abuse of notation, $xs\backslash xss$ for $xs\backslash xs_1 \ldots \backslash xs_n$ if $xss = xs_1 \ldots xs_n$.

By rule (T-SWAP), a group xs of lent-locked variables becomes the current group, by swapping this set with the current group, that is, the standard variables (xs') which are not lent-locked. The type obtained in this way is weakened to `lent`, if it was standard.

Other rules are mostly standard, apart that they model the expected behaviour of type modifiers. Notably, in rule (T-VAR), the type modifier of a variable is weakened to `lent` if the variable belongs to some set in xss. In rule (T-FIELD-ACCESS), the type modifier is propagated to fields. For instance, fields of a `lent` object are `lent` as well. In rule (T-FIELD-ASSIGN), neither the left-hand nor the right-hand side expressions can be `lent`. In rule (T-NEW), analogously, expressions assigned to fields cannot be `lent`.

In rule (T-BLOCK), we write $\Gamma[\Gamma']$ for the concatenation of Γ and Γ' where, for the variables occurring in both domains, Γ' takes precedence.

3 Examples

In this section we illustrate the type system by examples. We first provide some simple examples showing, in particular, how promotion and swapping rules work. Then, we present some more application oriented examples which motivate the usefulness of our modifiers. Finally, we motivate the fact that lent-locked variables are organized in groups.

In the examples, for sake of readability, we feel free to use additional constructs, such as primitive types, static methods and while loops. Moreover, we generally omit the brackets of the outermost block, and abbreviate $(T\ x = e\ e')$ by $e; e'$ when $x \notin \mathsf{FV}(e')$, with $\mathsf{FV}(e)$ the set of the free variables of e.

Consider the following term:

```
D z= new D(0)
capsule C x= ( D y= new D(z.f+1)    new C(y,y) )
x
```

The inner block (right-hand side of the declaration of `x`) can be typed `capsule`, since the free variable `z` is only used in a field access, hence it can be seen as `lent`. Formally, we can apply rule (T-CAPSULE) with $xs =$ `z`. Indeed, the block reduces[10] to `( D y= new D(1) C x = new C(y,y) x )` which is a capsule. As a counterexample, consider the following term:

```
D z= new D(0)
capsule C x= ( D y= z   new C(y,y) )  //ill-typed
x
```

Here the inner block cannot be typed `capsule`, since `z` is internally aliased. Formally, we cannot apply (T-CAPSULE) on the block, since we should typecheck

[10] As will be formalized in Sect. 4.

the block with `z` lent-locked, while (T-BLOCK) requires `D` as type of `z`. Indeed, the block reduces to (`new C(z,z)`) which is not a capsule.

The rule (T-FIELD-ASSIGN) requires *both* e and e' to have standard type. So, how is it possible to modify (the object denoted by) a `lent` reference? Consider the following simple example:

```
lent D z= new D(0)
z.f=z.f+1
```

This is well-typed code, since it is possible to use rule (T-SWAP) to type the expression `z.f=z.f+1`. Indeed, by the assumed equivalence on type contexts, `z: lent D` $,\emptyset$ is just another representation for `z: D`, $\{$`z`$\}$. Hence, we can swap the singleton group `z` of lent-locked variables with the empty set.

Moreover, swapping can be applied to achieve promotion. Consider the following variant of the first example:

```
D z= new D(0)
capsule C x= ( D y= new D(z.f=z.f+1)   new C(y,y) )
x
```

As in the first example, the inner block can be typed `capsule`, by lent-locking free variable `z`. However, now the execution modifies the content of `z`, and rule (T-SWAP) is used to typecheck `z.f=z.f+1`.

The next example shows how a programmer can declare lent references to achieve promotion. The class `Reader` below models reading information about customers out of a text file formatted as shown in the example:

```
Bob
1 500 2 1300
Mark
42 8 99 100
```

That is, in even lines we have customer names and in odd lines we have a shop history, that is, a sequence of product codes.

```
class Reader {
  static capsule Customer readCustomer(lent Scanner s){
    Customer c=new Customer(s.nextLine())
    while( s.hasNextNum() ){
      c.addShopHistory(s.nextNum())
      }
    return c //ok, capsule promotion here
    }
  }
```

The method `readCustomer` takes a `lent Scanner`, assumed to be a class similar to the one in Java, for reading a file and extracting different kinds of data. A `Customer` object is read from the file, and then its shop history is added. Since the scanner is declared `lent`, and there are no other parameters, by promotion the result can be declared `capsule`. Note that `lent` is essential here to express the intention of not mixing the data of the scanner with the result. Previous work offers cumbersome solutions requiring the programmer to manually handle multiple initialization phases like "raw" and "cooked" [20].

Now we show how we can "open" capsules, modify their values and then recover the original `capsule` guarantee. To do so, we show a method `updateCustomer` that takes an old customer (as capsule) and a `lent Scanner` as before.

```
class Reader {...//as before
  static capsule Customer updateCustomer(
                      capsule Customer old,lent Scanner s){
    Customer c=old//here we open the capsule 'old'
    while( s.hasNextNum() ){
      c.addShopHistory(s.nextNum())
      }
    return c //ok, capsule promotion here
    }
  }
```

Every method that does not take mutable parameters can use the pattern illustrated above: one (or many) capsule parameters are opened (that is, assigned to mutable local variables) and, in the end, the result is guaranteed to be again a capsule. This mechanism is not possible in [1,6,8] and relies on destructive reads in [9].

Finally, we show the code of `Scanner` itself, and how swapping can be used to update the fields of a `lent` scanner in a safe way.

```
class Scanner{
  InputStream stream;
  String nextLine(){...}
  bool hasNextNum(){...}
  int nextNum(){...}
  }

lent Scanner s=...
InputStream stream1=...
capsule InputStream stream2 = ...
//s.stream=stream1 //(a) wrong
s.stream=new InputStream("www. ...") //(b) ok, swapping
s.stream=stream2 //(c) ok, swapping
```

In our type system, a `lent` reference can be regarded as standard, if all the standard references are regarded as `lent`, as formally modeled by rule (T-SWAP). This mechanism is similar to *viewpoint adaptation* as in [8].

This can be trivially applied to the line (b), where `s` is the only free variable, and to the line (c), where the other free variable is declared `capsule`. In the line (a), instead, swapping would assign a `lent` type to `stream1`.

We conclude the section by an example showing that promotions can be nested, hence lent-locked variables must be organized in groups. Consider the following code, where implementation of `A` is omitted to emphasize that only type information provided by modifiers is significant.[11]

```
class A{...
  A mix(A a2){...}
  //a1.mix(a2) inserts a2 in the reachable object graph
  // of a1 and returns a1
  capsule A clone lent(){...}
  //a.clone() returns a capsule clone of a
  static A parse(){...} //A.parse() reads an A from input
}

A a1= A.parse() //outside of promotions
capsule A outerA=(//outer promotion here
  A a2= A.parse()//inside outer promotion
  capsule A nestedA=(//nested promotion here
    A a3= A.parse()//inside nested promotion
    A res= ???
    res.mix(a3)//this is promoted and assigned to nestedA
  )
  nestedA.mix(a2)//this is promoted and assigned to outerA
)
...//program continues here, using outerA as capsule
```

The question is, what can we write instead of ???, and why. Clearly, (1) `a3` is allowed, while (2) `a1` and `a2` are not. However, (3) `a1.clone()` and `a2.clone()` are allowed.

In the same way, (4) `a2.mix(a2).clone()` is allowed, as well as `a1.mix(a1).clone()`.

However, when we start mixing different variables, things become trickier. For example, (5) `a2.mix(a1).clone())` is not well-typed in our type system. Indeed, even though, thanks to cloning, mixing `a2` and `a1` does not compromise the capsule well-formedness of `nestedA` (that is, nested promotion can be safely applied), the fact that `a2` and `a1` are mixed could compromise the capsule well-formedness of `outerA` when `outerA` is computed (that is, outer promotion would be unsafe).

In summary, mixing as lent-locked for different promotions must be avoided. Rule (T-SWAP) swaps one set with another, thus keeping them distinct.

This last example illustrates many of the differences w.r.t. the type system proposed in [9], whose notion of *recovery* is similar to our promotion, but less expressive. Their system allows (1), and rejects (2) and (5), as ours. However, they conservatively rejects (3) and (4), since the flow is not tracked at a fine enough granularity. Depending on the concrete application, programmers may need to work around the limitations of [9] by reordering local variables, introducing stricter type modifiers or, in general, re-factoring their code. However, there may be cases where there is no possible reordering.

---

[11] Recall that, in the declaration of `clone`, `lent` is the modifier of the receiver, that is, the method takes the receiver as `lent`.

4 Calculus

Evaluation contexts, expressing standard left-to-right evaluation, are defined in Fig. 3, where we report values as well for reader's convenience. We write $\mathsf{FV}(e)$ and $\mathsf{FV}(ds)$ for the free variables of an expression and a sequence of declarations, respectively (the standard formal definition is omitted).

dv	$::= C\ x\ \texttt{=}rv$	evaluated declaration
rv	$::= \texttt{new}\ C(xs) \mid \texttt{(}dvs\ v\texttt{)}$	right value
v	$::= x \mid rv$	value (object)
$\mathcal{E}$	$::= [\,] \mid \mathcal{E}.f \mid \mathcal{E}.m(es) \mid x.m(xs, \mathcal{E}, es) \mid \mathcal{E}.f = e' \mid x.f = \mathcal{E}$	evaluation context
	$\mid \texttt{new}\ C(xs, \mathcal{E}, es) \mid \texttt{(}dvs\ T\ x\ \texttt{=}\mathcal{E}\ ds\ e\texttt{)} \mid \texttt{(}dvs\ \mathcal{E}\texttt{)}$	

Fig. 3. Values and evaluation contexts

Semantics is defined by a *congruence* relation, which captures structural equivalence, and a *reduction* relation, which models actual computation, similarly to what happens, e.g., in π-calculus [13].

The congruence relation, denoted by $\cong$, is defined as the smallest congruence satisfying the axioms given in Fig. 4. Rule (ALPHA) is the usual α-conversion. The condition $x, y \notin \mathsf{dom}(ds\ ds')$ is implicit by well-formedness of blocks.

By the following two rules we can manipulate the declarations in a block. Rule (REORDER) states that we can move evaluated declarations first, in an arbitrary order. Informally, this is safe since they have no longer side effects. Rule (GARBAGE) states that we can remove (or, conversely, add) a useless sequence of evaluated declarations from a block. Note that it is only possible to safely remove/add declarations which are evaluated, since, otherwise, their evaluation could have side effects.

By the following two rules we can eliminate and introduce blocks. Rule (ELIM) states the obvious fact that a block with no declarations is equivalent to its body. In rule (NEW), a constructor invocation can be seen as an elementary block where a new object is allocated. Note that, differently from what happens in traditional models with memory, x is an arbitrary variable, not required to be fresh. However, if x is moved outside of the block by applying other congruence rules, α-conversion is needed to avoid conflicts. Note also that the fields refer to external objects, hence the new object is not a capsule, differently from approaches providing shallow uniqueness, where freshly created objects have a unique/fresh type [3]. In our approach, instead, `capsule` prevents aliasing of the whole reachable object graph, and capsules are only obtained using promotions.

By the remaining rules we can move a sequence of declarations from a block to the directly enclosing block, or conversely, as it happens with rules for *scope extension* in the π-calculus [13].

In the first two rules, (BODY) and (RHS), the inner block is the body, or the right-hand side of a declaration, respectively, of the enclosing block. The side

(ALPHA) $\dfrac{}{\texttt{(}ds\ T\ x\ \texttt{=}e\ ds'\ e'\texttt{)} \cong \texttt{(}ds\ T\ y\ \texttt{=}e\ ds'\ e'\texttt{)}[y/x]}$

(REORDER) $\dfrac{}{\texttt{(}ds\ T\ x\ \texttt{=}rv\ ds'\ e\texttt{)} \cong \texttt{(}T\ x\ \texttt{=}rv\ ds\ ds'\ \ e\texttt{)}}$

(GARBAGE) $\dfrac{}{\texttt{(}dvs\ ds\ e\texttt{)} \cong \texttt{(}ds\ e\texttt{)}}\ \mathsf{FV}(\texttt{(}ds\ e\texttt{)}) \cap \mathsf{dom}(dvs) = \emptyset$

(ELIM) $\dfrac{}{\texttt{(}\ e\texttt{)} \cong e}$ (NEW) $\dfrac{}{\texttt{new}\ C(es) \cong \texttt{(}C\ x\ \texttt{=new}\ C(es)\ x\texttt{)}}$

(BODY) $\dfrac{}{\texttt{(}ds\ \texttt{(}ds_1\ ds_2\ e\texttt{))} \cong \texttt{(}ds\ ds_1\ \texttt{(}ds_2\ e\texttt{))}}\ \begin{array}{l}\mathsf{FV}(ds_1) \cap \mathsf{dom}(ds_2) = \emptyset\\ \mathsf{FV}(ds) \cap \mathsf{dom}(ds_1) = \emptyset\end{array}$

(RHS) $\dfrac{}{\texttt{(}ds\ T x\texttt{=(}ds_1\ ds_2\ e\texttt{)}\ ds'\ e'\texttt{)} \cong \texttt{(}ds\ ds_1\ T x\texttt{=(}ds_2\ e\texttt{)}\ ds'\ e'\texttt{)}}\ \begin{array}{l}\mathsf{FV}(ds_1) \cap \mathsf{dom}(ds_2) = \emptyset\\ \mathsf{FV}(ds\ ds') \cap \mathsf{dom}(ds_1) = \emptyset\end{array}$

(FIELD-ACCESS-RCV) $\dfrac{}{\texttt{(}ds\ e\texttt{)}.f \cong \texttt{(}ds\ e.f\texttt{)}}$

(INVK-RCV) $\dfrac{}{\texttt{(}ds\ e\texttt{)}.m(es) \cong \texttt{(}ds\ e.m(es)\texttt{)}}\ \mathsf{FV}(es) \cap \mathsf{dom}(ds) = \emptyset$

(INVK-ARG) $\dfrac{}{e.m(es, \texttt{(}dvs\ e'\texttt{)}, es') \cong \texttt{(}dvs\ e.m(es, e', es')\texttt{)}}\ \mathsf{FV}(e, es, es') \cap \mathsf{dom}(dvs) = \emptyset$

(FIELD-ASSIGN-LEFT) $\dfrac{}{\texttt{(}ds\ e\texttt{)}.f\texttt{=}\ e' \cong \texttt{(}ds\ e.f\texttt{=}\ e'\texttt{)}}\ \mathsf{FV}(e') \cap \mathsf{dom}(ds) = \emptyset$

(FIELD-ASSIGN-RIGHT) $\dfrac{}{e.f\texttt{=}\ \texttt{(}dvs\ e'\texttt{)} \cong \texttt{(}dvs\ e.f\texttt{=}\ e'\texttt{)}}\ \mathsf{FV}(e) \cap \mathsf{dom}(dvs) = \emptyset$

(NEW-ARG) $\dfrac{}{\texttt{new}\ C(es, \texttt{(}dvs\ e\texttt{)}, es') \cong \texttt{(}dvs\ \texttt{new}\ C(es, e, es')\texttt{)}}\ \mathsf{FV}(es, es') \cap \mathsf{dom}(dvs) = \emptyset$

Fig. 4. Congruence rules

conditions ensure that the declarations can be safely moved. More precisely: the former prevents from moving outside a declaration which depends on local variables of the inner block. Conversely, the latter prevents from moving inside a declaration which is used by other declarations of the enclosing block. Note that both these conditions *cannot* be obtained by α-conversion. Moreover, note that the conditions $\mathsf{dom}(ds_1) \cap \mathsf{dom}(ds_2) = \emptyset$ and $\mathsf{dom}(ds_1) \cap \mathsf{dom}(ds) = \emptyset$ ($\mathsf{dom}(ds_1) \cap \mathsf{dom}(ds\ ds') = \emptyset$ in the second rule) are implicit from well-formedness of blocks.

The other rules handle the cases when the inner block is a direct subterm of a field access, method invocation, field assignment or constructor invocation. In all such cases, the action to be executed is propagated to the body of the block, within the scope of the declarations. Hence, we must avoid capture of free variables, as specified by the side conditions of the rules, which can be always obtained by α-renaming. Moreover, as in rules (REORDER) and

$$\text{(CTX)}\ \frac{e \longrightarrow e'}{\mathcal{E}[e] \longrightarrow \mathcal{E}[e']} \qquad \text{(CONGR)}\ \frac{e_1 \longrightarrow e}{e_2 \longrightarrow e}\ \begin{array}{l} e_1 \cong e_2 \\ \vdash e_1 : T \\ \vdash e_2 : T \end{array}$$

$$\text{(FIELD-ACCESS)}\ \frac{}{(dvs\ \mathcal{E}[x.f]) \longrightarrow (dvs\ \mathcal{E}[y])}\ \begin{array}{l} dvs(x) = \mu\ C\ x = rv \\ x \notin \mathsf{HB}(\mathcal{E}), y \notin \mathsf{HB}(\mathcal{E}) \\ \mathsf{fields}(C) = C_1\ f_1 \ldots C_n\ f_n \text{ and } f = f_i \\ \mathsf{get}(rv, i) = y \text{ and } y \in \mathsf{FV}(rv) \end{array}$$

$$\text{(INVK)}\ \frac{}{(dvs\ \mathcal{E}[x.m(xs)]) \longrightarrow (dvs\ \mathcal{E}[e[x/\mathtt{this}][xs/ys]])}\ \begin{array}{l} dvs(x) = \mu\ C\ x = rv \\ x \notin \mathsf{HB}(\mathcal{E}), xs \cap \mathsf{HB}(\mathcal{E}) = \emptyset \\ \mathsf{mbody}(C, m) = \langle ys, e \rangle \end{array}$$

$$\text{(FIELD-ASSIGN)}\ \frac{}{(dvs\ \mathcal{E}[x.f = y]) \longrightarrow (dvs[x = rv']\ \mathcal{E}[y])}\ \begin{array}{l} dvs(x) = \mu\ C\ x = rv \\ x \notin \mathsf{HB}(\mathcal{E}), y \notin \mathsf{HB}(\mathcal{E}) \\ \mathsf{fields}(C) = C_1\ f_1 \ldots C_n\ f_n \text{ and } f = f_i \\ \mathsf{set}(rv, i, y) = rv' \end{array}$$

$$\text{(DEC)}\ \frac{(dvs\ e) \longrightarrow (dvs'\ e')}{(dvs\ \mu\ C\ x = e\ ds\ e'') \longrightarrow (dvs'\ \mu\ C\ x = e'\ ds\ e'')}$$

$$\text{(ALIAS-ELIM)}\ \frac{}{(dvs\ \mu\ C\ x = y\ ds\ e) \longrightarrow (dvs\ ds\ e)[y/x]}$$

$$\text{(CAPSULE-ELIM)}\ \frac{}{(dvs\ \mathtt{capsule}\ C\ x = rv\ ds\ e) \longrightarrow (dvs\ ds\ e)[rv/x]}$$

Fig. 5. Reduction rules

(GARBAGE) above, we must preserve the evaluation order, hence in some cases declarations are required to be evaluated, that is, to have no longer side effects.

Reduction rules are given in Fig. 5. We write $e[e'/x]$ for the expression obtained by replacing all (free) occurrences of x in e by e', and $\mathsf{HB}(\mathcal{E})$ for the *hole binders* of $\mathcal{E}$, that is, the variables declared in blocks enclosing the context hole. The standard formal definition is omitted.

The most interesting reduction rules are those for reading/assigning a field, so we first illustrate these rules in detail, also providing examples, then explain the others.

In rule (FIELD-ACCESS), given a field access of shape $x.f$, the first enclosing declaration for x is found (side condition $x \notin \mathsf{HB}(\mathcal{E})$ ensures that it is the first), and fields of the class C of x are retrieved from the class table. If f is actually the name of a field of C, say, the i-th field, then the field access is reduced to the reference y stored in this field. The function get returning the i-th field of a right value is defined below (The auxiliary function auxGet also returns the root of a value.)

- $\mathsf{get}(\mathtt{new}\ C(x_1, \ldots, x_n), i) = x_i$
- $\mathsf{get}((dvs\ v), i) = y$ if $\mathsf{auxGet}((dvs\ v), i) = \langle x, y \rangle$

- $\mathsf{auxGet}(x, i) = \langle x, \bot \rangle$
- $\mathsf{auxGet}((dvs\ v), i) = \begin{cases} \langle x, y \rangle & \text{if } \mathsf{auxGet}(v, i) = \langle x, \bot \rangle, \mathsf{get}(dvs(x), i) = y \\ \mathsf{auxGet}(v, i) & \text{otherwise} \end{cases}$

The side condition $y \notin \mathsf{HB}(\mathcal{E})$ ensures that there are no inner declarations for y (otherwise y would be erroneously bound), and can be always obtained by α-renaming. For instance, assuming a class table where class `A` has an `int f` field, and class `B` has an `A f` field, the term

```
A a= new A(0) B b= new B(a) ( A a= new A(1) b.f )
```

is reduced to

```
A a= new A(0) B b= new B(a) ( A a1= new A(1) a )
```

Note that before the reduction the outer declaration of `a` is hidden in the inner scope. Using α-conversion, we get two differently named local variables `a` and `a1` coexisting in the same scope. The same technique allows correct execution of recursive methods with local variables.

The side condition $y \in \mathsf{FV}(rv)$, requiring that the reference y is not locally declared in rv, prevents scope extrusion, and can always be guaranteed by congruence, that is, by applying rule (CONGR). For instance, without this side condition, the term

```
B x= ( A y= new A(0) B z= new B(y) z)  x.f
```

would reduce to

```
B x= ( A y= new A(0) B z= new B(y) z)  y
```

Instead, we can take the equivalent term

```
A y= new A(0) B x= ( B z=new B(y) z)  x.f
```

which correctly reduces to

```
A y= new A(0) B x= ( B z=new B(y) z)  y
```

In rule (FIELD-ASSIGN), given a field assignment of shape $x.f = y$, the first enclosing declaration for x is found (side condition $x \notin \mathsf{HB}(\mathcal{E})$ ensures that it is the first), and fields of the class C of x are retrieved from the class table. If f is actually the name of a field of C, say, the i-th, then the i-th field of the right value of x is updated to y. We write $dvs[x{=}rv']$ for the sequence of evaluated declarations obtained from dvs by replacing the right-hand side of the declaration of x by rv' (the obvious formal definition is omitted).

The function set returning a right value where a field has been updated is defined below (the auxiliary function auxSet also returns the root of a value).

- $\mathsf{set}(\mathtt{new}\ C(x_1, \ldots, x_n), i, y) = \mathtt{new}\ C(x_1, \ldots, x_{i-1}, y, x_{i+1}, \ldots, x_n)$
- $\mathsf{set}((dvs\ v), i, y) = rv$ if $\mathsf{auxSet}((dvs\ v), i, y) = \langle x, rv \rangle$
- $\mathsf{auxSet}(x, i, y) = \langle x, \bot \rangle$
- $\mathsf{auxSet}((dvs\ v), i, y) = \begin{cases} \langle x, (dvs[x{=}\mathsf{set}(rv, i, y)]\ v) \rangle & \text{if } \mathsf{auxSet}(v, i, y) = \langle x, \bot \rangle, dvs(x) = rv \\ \mathsf{auxSet}(v, i, y) & \text{otherwise} \end{cases}$

The side condition $y \notin \mathsf{HB}(\mathcal{E})$, requiring that there are no inner declarations for the reference y, prevents scope extrusion, and can be always guaranteed by congruence, that is, by applying rule (CONGR). For instance, without this side condition, the term

```
B x=new B(...)  (A y=new C(0)  x.f=y)
```

would reduce to

```
B x=new B(y)  (A y=new C(0)  y)
```

Rule (CTX) is the usual contextual closure. Rule (CONGR) states that congruence is preserved by reduction, and can be used, as shown above, to reduce a term which otherwise would be stuck, as it happens for α-rule in lambda calculus. The side condition, where $\vdash e : T$ abbreviates $\emptyset; \emptyset \vdash e : T$, restricts congruence to preserve types. Otherwise, for instance, (GARBAGE) could be used to insert some ill-typed *dvs*, and (BODY) or (RHS) could be used to move some ds_1 of a block of `capsule` type at an outer level.

In rule (INVK), given a method invocation of shape $x.m(xs)$, the first enclosing declaration for x is found (side condition $x \notin \mathsf{HB}(\mathcal{E})$ ensures that it is the first), and method m of the class C of x is retrieved from the class table, if actually provided. In this case, the call is reduced to the method body where `this` has been replaced by (the reference to) the receiver object, and parameters have been replaced by arguments. The side condition $xs \cap \mathsf{HB}(\mathcal{E}) = \emptyset$ ensures that there are no inner declarations for some argument (which, otherwise, would be erroneously bound), and can be always obtained by α-renaming.

Rule (DEC) avoids the need of duplicating the above rules for field access, method invocation and field assignment, to handle the case where they occur in the right-hand side of a declaration, rather than in the body, of the block containing that of the receiver object.

In rule (ALIAS-ELIM), a reference x which is initialized as an alias of another reference y is eliminated by replacing all its occurrences. In rule (CAPSULE-ELIM), a `capsule` reference is eliminated by replacing its (unique by assumption) occurrence by its right value.

5 Results

We use the abbreviations $e \longrightarrow$ for $e \longrightarrow e'$ for some e', $\vdash e : T$ for $\emptyset; \emptyset \vdash e : T$, and $\vdash e$ for $\vdash e : T$ for some T.

The soundness theorem states that reduction of well-typed expressions with no free variables does not get stuck.

Theorem 1 (Soundness). *If $\vdash e$, and $e \longrightarrow^\star e'$, then either e' is a value, or $e' \longrightarrow$.*

Soundness is obtained, as usual, as a consequence of progress and subject reduction theorems. Note that, since our operational model is a pure calculus, in the proofs we do not need invariants on auxiliary structures such as memory.

Theorem 2 (Progress). *If $\vdash e$, then either e is a value, or $e \longrightarrow$.*

The progress theorem is obtained as an immediate corollary of extended progress.

Theorem 3 (Extended Progress). *If $\Gamma; xss \vdash e : T$, then one of the following cases holds:*

1. *e is a value, with* $\mathsf{FV}(e) \subseteq \mathsf{dom}(\Gamma)$
2. $e \longrightarrow$
3. $e = \mathcal{E}[x.f]$, $x \notin \mathsf{HB}(\mathcal{E})$, *and* $x \in \mathsf{dom}(\Gamma)$
4. $e = \mathcal{E}[x.m(xs)]$, $x \notin \mathsf{HB}(\mathcal{E})$, *and* $x \in \mathsf{dom}(\Gamma)$
5. $e = \mathcal{E}[x.f = y]$, $x \notin \mathsf{HB}(\mathcal{E})$, *and* $x \in \mathsf{dom}(\Gamma)$.

Theorem 4 (Subject reduction). *If $\Delta \vdash e : T$, and $e \longrightarrow e'$, then $\Delta \vdash e : T$.*

In addition to soundness, we state that the `capsule` modifier actually ensures the expected behaviour. A nice consequence of our non standard operational model is that this can be easily formally expressed and proved, as shown below, since a capsule is simply a closed value.

Let $\mathsf{typectx}(\mathcal{E})$ be the type context extracted from a context $\mathcal{E}$, whose trivial definition is omitted. Moreover, to trace the reduction of an expression inside a context, let us assume that in the result $\mathcal{E}[e]$ of filling the hole of a context, we can still recover the subterm e (for instance, we can replace the hole by $[e]$, with square brackets immaterial for reduction rules).

Lemma 1. *If $\vdash \mathcal{E}[e]$, $\mathsf{typectx}(\mathcal{E}); \emptyset \vdash e : T$, and $\mathcal{E}[e] \longrightarrow \mathcal{E}'[e']$, then $\vdash \mathcal{E}'[e']$ and $\mathsf{typectx}(\mathcal{E}'); \emptyset \vdash e' : T$.*

Theorem 5 *(Capsule).* *If $\vdash \mathcal{E}[e]$, $\mathsf{typectx}(\mathcal{E}); \emptyset \vdash e :$ `capsule` C, and $\mathcal{E}[e] \longrightarrow^\star \mathcal{E}'[v]$, then either v is a variable having a `capsule` type in $\mathsf{typectx}(\mathcal{E}')$, or v is closed.*

Proof. We know that $\mathsf{typectx}(\mathcal{E}'); \emptyset \vdash v :$ `capsule` C by Lemma 1. Set $\Gamma' = \mathsf{typectx}(\mathcal{E}')$. By structural induction on v.

- ***x*** We can assign a `capsule` type to x only by rule (T-CAPSULE) or (T-VAR). However, to apply rule (T-CAPSULE) we should assign a standard type to x in a type context where all standard variables are lent-locked, and this is not possible. Hence, we have applied rule (T-VAR), and we have $\Gamma'(x) =$ `capsule` C.
- **`new`** ***C(xs)*** We can assign a `capsule` type to `new` $C(xs)$ only by rule (T-CAPSULE). However, we should assign a standard type to `new` $C(xs)$ in a type context where all standard variables are lent-locked, whereas variables in xs are required to have standard type. Hence `new` $C(xs)$ has no free variables, that is, $xs = \epsilon$.
- **(*dvs v*)** We can assign a `capsule` type to a block only by rule (T-CAPSULE) or (T-BLOCK). If we have applied rule (T-CAPSULE), then all free variables are required to be lent-locked. Free variables in block values only occur as values of fields (the root variable is necessarily bound), which cannot be `lent`,

hence the block has no free variables. If we have applied rule (T-BLOCK), then v has a `capsule` type as well, hence by inductive hypothesis v is either a variable x having a `capsule` type, or v is closed. In the former case, x is necessarily bound in *dvs* by well-formedness of blocks, hence cannot have a `capsule` type. Hence, the latter case holds, and (*dvs* v) is equivalent to v by congruence rules (GARBAGE) and (ELIM). □

6 Related Work

Our type system combines in a novel and powerful way different features existing in previous work. Notably, the `capsule` notion has many variants in the literature (*external uniqueness* [6], *balloon* [1,18], *island* [8]). Our meaning is essentially that introduced in [9], that is, a capsule is a reachable object subgraph where all non immutable nodes cannot be reached from the outside. The fact that aliasing can be controlled by using *lent* (*borrowed*) references is well-known [14]. Our promotion is inspired to *recovery* [9]. However, our promotion is much more expressive, as illustrated by the last example in Sect. 3, since external references are not forbidden once and for all, but only restricted, by means of the `lent` notion. Moreover, uniqueness is guaranteed by linearity, that is, by allowing at most one use of a `capsule` reference, rather than by destructive reads as in [4,9].[12] In our approach, the `capsule` modifier cannot be applied to fields. Indeed, the "only once" use of capsule local variables, ensured by linear types, makes no sense on fields. Other approaches support field properties similar to our `capsule` using destructive reads, as for example *isolated* in [9]. This leads to the style of programming outlined below:

```
a.f=c.doStuff(a.f) //style suggested by other authors
//during execution of doStuff, 'a.f' is null
```

The object referenced by `a` has an *isolated* field `f` containing an object `b`. This object `b` is passed to a client `c`, which can use (potentially modifying) it. A typical pattern is that the result of such computation is a reference to `b`, which `a` can then recover. This approach allows *isolated* fields, as shown above, but has also a serious drawback: an *isolated* field can become unexpectedly not available (in the example, during execution of `doStuff`), hence any object contract involving such field can be broken. Instead, we introduce the `lent` modifier, that removes the need of destructive reads: mutable objects can be passed to clients as `lent`, in order to control aliasing behaviour. Thus, previous code can be rewritten as follows:

```
c.doStuff(a.f()) //our suggested style
//doStuff takes a lent parameter
//during execution of doStuff, 'a.f()' is still there
```

This simple usage pattern of `lent`, if combined with `capsule`, allows one to control the ownership of a subgraph. Assume for example a graph with a list

[12] See [3] for another alternative to destructive reads, in a work aiming to ensure shallow uniqueness.

of nodes, and a constructor taking in input such list. In Java, in order to be sure to control/own the list of nodes, the graph object must clone the parameter object, since it comes from an external client environment. This solution, called *defensive cloning* [2], is very popular in the Java community, but inefficient, since it requires to duplicate the reachable object graph of the parameter, until immutable nodes are reached. Indeed, many programmers prefer to write unsafe code instead of using defensive cloning for efficiency reasons.

The following code establishes the ownership invariant using `capsule`, and ensures that it cannot be violated using `lent`. Here we assume private and static members as in Java.

```
class Graph{
  private final ListNode nodes;
  private Graph(ListNode nodes){this.nodes=nodes;}
  public static Graph factory(capsule ListNode nodes){
    return new Graph(nodes);}
  public lent ListNode getNodes(){return nodes;}
}
```

This approach is the specular opposite of that offered by many ownership approaches (see an overview in [8]), where to guarantee that the ownership invariant holds when an object is created the programmer is required to internally create the representation, that is, to use defensive cloning. This leads to an unnatural initialization strategy: first the composite objects are created, then the leaves are initialized during the initialization process of the composite object. The `capsule` modifier allows the programmer to create composite objects in the natural way: first the leaves are created and then the composite objects are recursively initialized by simply initializing their fields.

The choice to allow dynamic aliases [10] for `lent` references, but to prevent storage within other objects (static aliasing), allows `Graph` instances to release the mutation control of their nodes without permanently loosing the alias control.[13]

7 Conclusion

We have presented an imperative object calculus where types are annotated with `lent` and `capsule` modifiers. The type system includes a promotion rule to type an expression as `capsule`, if it can be typed by lent-locking all its variables currently available of standard type. By multiple applications of this rule, typechecking takes place in a context where there exist many sets of lent-locked variables, and a set of variables with standard type. The swapping rule allows one to swap the latter set with one of the sets of lent-locked variables.

The operational model of the language is given as a pure calculus, where aliasing properties can be directly expressed at the syntax level. To illustrate this advantage, let us consider typing rule (T-CAPSULE) in Fig. 2. Here we want

[13] In an hypothetical extension, we would need to prevent storage also within closures or threads.

to express that an expression e, subterm of a program, can be typed `capsule` if it can modify only its local objects. Objects which are reachable from other parts of the program, instead, can only be used as `lent`. In our model, objects reachable from other parts of the program are simply those denoted by free variables in e, whereas local objects are those denoted by local variables declared in e. In other terms, the portion of memory only reachable from e is encoded in e itself. In a conventional model with global memory, to express the same property, we should, first of all, type the memory locations as well, and add invariants on the memory to prove subject reduction. Then, we should require to use only as `lent` the locations which are reachable from other parts of the program. However, this information is lost in the global memory. To be concrete, consider the following example:

```
A a= new A(...)  B b=( C c=new C()   c.foo() )
```

In the conventional model, this program is reduced by first adding to the memory two new locations, say ι_a and ι_c, which are then used to replace variables a and c, respectively. We then get to execute ι_c`.foo()`. To type this expression, we would use the following judgement: $\emptyset; \iota_a{:}A, \iota_c{:}C \vdash \iota_c$`.foo()`$:B$. Here, there is no information about how ι_c is used inside the rest of the program. For example ι_c could be reachable from ι_a. In our approach `C c=new C()` is kept in place, and we use the following judgment: $a{:}A \vdash$ `( C c=new C() c.foo() )`$:B$.

This work is part of a larger project: the development of L42, a novel programming language designed to support massive use of libraries. Description and prototype for the full language (in progress) can be found at `L42.is`. The current L42 prototype is important as proof-of-evidence that the type system presented in this paper can be smoothly integrated with other features of a realistic language.

On a more foundational side, we believe that the novel pure setting presented in this paper has a great potential of really achieving a better understanding of aliasing. Notably, in future work, we plan to extend the type system to express and formally verify other properties of object graphs, e.g., immutability, and others among those proposed in the wide literature about ownership, see, e.g., [7]. As a long term goal, we also plan to investigate (a form of) Hoare logic on top of our model. We believe that the hierarchical structure of our memory representation should help local reasoning, allowing specifications and proofs to mention only the relevant portion, analogously to what is achieved by separation logic [15].

We also plan to formally state and prove behavioural equivalence of the calculus with conventional imperative models. A corollary of such theorem would be that our calculus is confluent, since conventional imperative models are deterministic.

Finally, it should be possible to use our approach to enforce safe parallelism, on the lines of [9,18].

Acknowledgement. We thank the anonymous referees for their helpful comments, and Matthew Parkinson (author of [9]) for his help in the comparison with our work.

References

1. Almeida, P.S.: Balloon types: controlling sharing of state in data types. In: Akşit, M., Matsuoka, S. (eds.) ECOOP 1997. LNCS, vol. 1241, pp. 32–59. Springer, Heidelberg (1997)
2. Bloch, J.: Effective Java (2Nd Edition) (The Java Series), 2nd edn. Prentice Hall PTR, Upper Saddle River (2008)
3. Boyland, J.: Alias burying: Unique variables without destructive reads. Softw. Pract. Exper. **31**(6), 533–553 (2001)
4. Boyland, J.: Semantics of fractional permissions with nesting. ACM Trans. Program. Lang. Syst. **32**(6), 1–33 (2010)
5. Capriccioli, A., Servetto, M., Zucca, E.: An imperative pure calculus. In: ICTCS 2015 - Italian Conference on Theoretical Computer Science (2015)
6. Clarke, D., Wrigstad, T.: External uniqueness is unique enough. In: Cardelli, L. (ed.) ECOOP 2003. LNCS, vol. 2743, pp. 176–200. Springer, Heidelberg (2003)
7. Clarke, D.G., Potter, J., Noble, J.: Ownership types for flexible alias protection. In: ACM Symposium on Object-Oriented Programming: Systems, Languages and Applications 1998, pp. 48–64 (1998)
8. Dietl, W., Drossopoulou, S., Müller, P.: Generic universe types. In: Ernst, E. (ed.) ECOOP 2007. LNCS, vol. 4609, pp. 28–53. Springer, Heidelberg (2007)
9. Gordon, C.S., Parkinson, M.J., Parsons, J., Bromfield, A., Duffy, J.: Uniqueness and reference immutability for safe parallelism. In: ACM SIGPLAN Conference on Object-Oriented Programming, Systems, Languages and Applications (OOPSLA 2012), pp. 21–40. ACM Press (2012)
10. Hogg, J.: Islands: aliasing protection in object-oriented languages. In: ACM Symposium on Object-Oriented Programming: Systems, Languages and Applications 1991, pp. 271–285. ACM Press (1991)
11. Igarashi, A., Pierce, B.C., Wadler, P.: Featherweight Java: a minimal core calculus for Java and GJ. ACM Trans. Program. Lang. Syst. **23**(3), 396–450 (2001)
12. Li, P., Cameron, N., Noble, J.: Cloning in ownership. In: Proceedings of the ACM International Conference Companion on Object Oriented Programming Systems Languages and Applications Companion, OOPSLA 2011, pp. 63–66. ACM, New York (2011)
13. Milner, R.: Communicating and Mobile Systems - The Pi-Calculus. Cambridge University Press, Cambridge (1999)
14. Naden, K., Bocchino, R., Aldrich, J., Bierhoff, K.: A type system for borrowing permissions. In: ACM Symposium on Principles of Programming Languages 2012, pp. 557–570. ACM Press (2012)
15. Reynolds, J.C.: Separation logic: a logic for shared mutable data structures. In: Proceedings of the IEEE Symposium on Logic in Computer Science 2002, pp. 5–74. IEEE Computer Society (2002)
16. Servetto, M., Groves, L.: True small-step reduction for imperative object-oriented languages. IN: FTfJP 2013- Formal Techniques for Java-like Programs (2013)
17. Servetto, M., Mackay, J., Potanin, A., Noble, J.: The billion-dollar fix: safe modular circular initialisation with placeholders and placeholder types. In: Castagna, G. (ed.) ECOOP 2013. LNCS, vol. 7920, pp. 205–229. Springer, Heidelberg (2013)
18. Servetto, M., Pearce, D.J., Groves, L., Potanin, A.: Balloon types for safe parallelisation over arbitrary object graphs. In: WODET 2014 - Workshop on Determinism and Correctness in Parallel Programming (2013)

19. Tschantz, M.S., Ernst, M.D.: Javari: adding reference immutabilityto Java. In: Object-Oriented Programming Systems, Languages, and Applications (OOPSLA 2005), San Diego, CA, USA, October 18–20, pp. 211–230 (2005)
20. Zibin, Y., Potanin, A., Li, P., Ali, M., Ernst, M.D.: Ownership and immutability in generic Java. In: ACM SIGPLAN Conference on Object-Oriented Programming, Systems, Languages and Applications (OOPSLA 2010), pp. 598–617 (2010)

Functional Programming and Semantics

A Strong Distillery

Beniamino Accattoli[1], Pablo Barenbaum[2], and Damiano Mazza[3(✉)]

[1] LIX, Inria-École Polytechnique, Palaiseau, France
beniamino.accattoli@inria.fr
[2] CONICET, University of Buenos Aires, Buenos Aires, Argentina
pbarenbaum@dc.uba.ar
[3] LIPN, CNRS-Université Paris 13, Sorbonne Paris Cité,Villetaneuse, France
Damiano.Mazza@lipn.univ-paris13.fr

Abstract. Abstract machines for the strong evaluation of λ-terms (that is, under abstractions) are a mostly neglected topic, despite their use in the implementation of proof assistants and higher-order logic programming languages. This paper introduces a machine for the simplest form of strong evaluation, leftmost-outermost (call-by-name) evaluation to normal form, proving it correct, complete, and bounding its overhead. Such a machine, deemed *Strong Milner Abstract Machine*, is a variant of the KAM computing normal forms and using just one global environment. Its properties are studied via a special form of decoding, called a *distillation*, into the Linear Substitution Calculus, neatly reformulating the machine as a standard micro-step strategy for explicit substitutions, namely *linear leftmost-outermost reduction*, *i.e.* the extension to normal form of linear head reduction. Additionally, the overhead of the machine is shown to be linear both in the number of steps and in the size of the initial term, validating its design. The study highlights two distinguished features of strong machines, namely backtracking phases and their interactions with abstractions and environments.

1 Introduction

The computational model behind functional programming is the weak λ-calculus, where *weakness* is the fact that evaluation stops as soon as an abstraction is obtained. Evaluation is usually defined in a small-step way, specifying a strategy for the selection of weak β-redexes. Both the advantage and the drawback of λ-calculus is the lack of a machine in the definition of the model. Unsurprisingly implementations of functional languages have been explored for decades.

Implementation schemes are called *abstract machines*, and usually account for two tasks. First, they switch from small-step to *micro-step* evaluation, delaying the costly meta-level substitution used in small-step operational semantics and replacing it with substitutions of one occurrence at a time, when required. Second, they also *search the next redex* to reduce, walking through the program according to some evaluation strategy. Abstract machines are *machines* because they are deterministic and the complexity of their steps can easily be measured,

X. Feng and S. Park (Eds.): APLAS 2015, LNCS 9458, pp. 231–250, 2015.
DOI: 10.1007/978-3-319-26529-2_13

and are *abstract* because they omit many details of a real implementation, like the actual representation of terms and data-structures or the garbage collector.

Historically, the theory of λ-calculus and the implementation of functional languages have followed orthogonal approaches. The former rather dealt with *strong* evaluation, and it is only since the seminal work of Abramsky and Ong [1] that the theory took weak evaluation seriously. Dually, practical studies mostly ignored *strong* evaluation, with the notable exception of Crégut [13,14] (1990) and, more recently, the semi-strong approach of Grégoire and Leroy [23] (2002)—see also the *related work* paragraph below. Strong evaluation is nonetheless essential in the implementation of proof assistants or higher-order logic programming, typically for type-checking in frameworks with dependent types as the Edinburgh Logical Framework or the Calculus of Constructions, as well as for unification modulo $\beta\eta$ in simply typed frameworks like λ-prolog.

The aim of this paper is to move the first steps towards a systematic and theoretical exploration of the implementation of strong evaluation. Here we deal with the simplest possible case, call-by-name evaluation to strong normal form, implemented by a variant of the Krivine Abstract Machine. The study is carried out according to the *distillation methodology*, a new approach recently introduced by the authors and previously applied only to weak evaluation [3].

Distilling Abstract Machines. Many abstract machines can be rephrased as strategies in λ*-calculi with explicit substitutions* (ES for short), see at least [9,10,14,15,24,25]. The Linear Substitution Calculus (LSC)—a variation over a λ-calculus with ES by Robin Milner [27] developed by Accattoli and Kesner [2,5]—provides more than a simple reformulation: it disentangles the two tasks carried out by abstract machines, retaining the *micro-step operational semantics* and omitting the *search for the next redex*. Such a neat disentangling, that we prefer to call a *distillation*, is a decoding based on the following key points:

1. *Partitioning*: the machine transitions are split in two classes. *Principal transitions* are mapped to the rewriting rules of the calculus, while *commutative transitions*—responsible for the search for the redex—are mapped on a notion of structural equivalence, specific to the LSC.
2. *Rewriting*: structural equivalence accounts both for the search for the redex and garbage collection, and commutes with evaluation. It can thus be postponed, isolating the micro-step strategy in the rewriting of the LSC.
3. *Logic*: the LSC itself has only two rules, corresponding to cut-elimination in linear logic proof nets. A distillation then provides a logical reading of an abstract machine (see [3] for more details).
4. *Complexity*: by design, a principal transition has to take linear time in the input, while a commutative transition has to be constant.

A *distillery* is then given by a machine, a strategy, a structural equivalence, and a decoding function satisfying the above points. In bilinear distilleries, the number of commutative transitions is linear in both the *number of principal transitions* and the *size of the initial term*. Bilinearity guarantees that distilling away the commutative part by switching to the LSC preserves the asymptotical behavior, *i.e.* it does not forget too much. At the same time, the bound on the commutative overhead justifies the design of the abstract machine, providing a provably bounded implementation scheme.

A Strong Distillery. Our machine is a strong version of the Milner Abstract Machine (MAM), a variant with just one *global environment* of the Krivine Abstract Machine (KAM), introduced in [3].

The first result of the paper is the design of a distillery relating the Strong MAM to *linear leftmost-outermost reduction* in the LSC [5,6]—that is at the same time a refinement of leftmost-outermost (LO) β-reduction and an extension of linear head reduction [2,16,26] to normal form—together with the proof of correctness and completeness of the implementation. Moreover, the linear LO strategy is *standard* and *normalizing* [5], and thus we provide an instance of Plotkin's approach of mapping abstract machines to such strategies [28].

The second result is the complexity analysis showing that the distillery is bilinear, *i.e.* that the cost of the additional search for the next redex specific to the machine is negligible. The analysis is simple, and yet subtle and robust. It is subtle because it requires a global analysis of executions, and it is robust because the overhead is bilinear for *any* evaluation sequence, not necessarily to normal form, and even for diverging ones.

For the design of the Strong MAM we make various choices:

1. *Global Environment*: we employ a *global* environment, which is in opposition to having closures (pairing subterms with *local* environments), and it models a store-based implementation scheme. The choice is motivated by future extensions to more efficient strategies as call-by-need, where the global environment allows to integrate sharing with a form of memoization [3,18].
2. *Sequential Exploration and Backtracking*: we fix a sequential exploration of the term (according to the leftmost-outermost order), in opposition to the parallel evaluation of the arguments (once a head normal form has been reached). This choice internalizes the handling of the recursive iterations, that would be otherwise left to the meta-level, providing a finer study of the data-structures needed by a strong machine. On the other hand, it forces to have backtracking transitions, activated when the current subterm has been checked to be normal and evaluation needs to retrieve the next subterm on the stack. Call-by-value machines usually have a similar but simpler backtracking mechanism, realized via an additional component, the *dump*.
3. *(Almost) No Garbage Collection*: we focus on time complexity, and thus ignore space issues, that is, our machine does not account for garbage collection. In particular, we keep the global environment completely unstructured, similarly to the (weak) MAM. Strong evaluation however is subtler, as to establish a precise relationship between the machine and the calculus with ES, garbage collection cannot be completely ignored. Our approach is to isolate it within the meta-level: we use a system of parenthesized markers, to delimit subenvironments created under abstractions that could be garbage collected once the machine backtracks outside those abstraction. These labels are not inspected

by the transitions, and play a role only for the proof of the distillation theorem. Garbage collection then is somewhat accounted for by the analysis, but there are no dedicated transitions nor rewriting rules, it is rather encapsulated in the decoding and in the structural equivalence.

Efficiency? It is known that LO evaluation is not efficient. Improvements are possible along three axis: refining the strategy (by turning to strong call-by-value/need, partially done in [8,14,23]), speeding up the substitution process (by forbidding the substitution of variables, see [7,8]), and avoiding useless substitutions (by adding *useful sharing*, see [6,8]). These improvements however require sophisticated machines, left to future work.

LO evaluation is nonetheless a good first case study, as it allows to isolate the analysis of backtracking phases and their subtle interactions with abstractions and environments. We expect that the mentioned optimizations can be added in a quite modular way, as they have all been addressed in the complementary study in [8], based on the same technology (*i.e.* LSC and distilleries).

(Scarce) Related Work. Beyond Crégut's [13,14], we are aware of only two other similar works on strong abstract machines, García-Pérez, Nogueira and Moreno-Navarro's [22] (2013), and Smith's [30] (unpublished, 2014). Two further studies, de Carvalho's [12] and Ehrhard and Regnier's [20], introduce strong versions of the KAM but for theoretical purposes; in particular, their design choices are not tuned towards implementations (*e.g.* rely on a naïve parallel exploration of the term). Semi-strong machines for call-by-value (*i.e.* dealing with weak evaluation but on open terms) are studied by Grégoire and Leroy [23] and in a recent work by Accattoli and Sacerdoti Coen [8] (see [8] for a comparison with [23]). More recent work by Dénès [19] and Boutiller [11] appeared in the context of term evaluation in Coq. These works, which do offer the nice perspective of concretely dealing with proof assistants, are focused on quite specific Coq-related tasks (such as term simplification) and the difference in reduction strategy and underlying motivations makes a comparison difficult.

Of all the above, the closest to ours is Crégut's work, because it defines an implementation-oriented strong KAM, thus also addressing leftmost-outermost reduction. His machine uses local environments, sequential exploration and backtracking, scope markers akin to ours, and a calculus with ES to establish the correctness of the implementation. His calculus, however, has no less than 13 rewriting rules, while ours just 2, and so our approach is simpler by an order of magnitude. Moreover, we want to stress that our contribution does not lie in the machine *per se*, or the chosen reduction strategy (as long as it is strong), but in the combined presence of a robust and simple abstraction of the machine, provided by the LSC, and the complexity analysis showing that such an abstraction does not miss too much. In this respect, none of the above works comes with an analysis of the overhead of the machine nor with the logical and rewriting perspective we provide. In fact, our approach offers general guidelines for the design of (strong) abstract machines. The choice of leftmost-outermost reduction showcases the idea while keeping technicalities to a minimum, but it is by no means a limitation. The development of strong distilleries for call-by-value or lazy strategies, which may be more attractive from a programming languages perspective, are certainly possible and will be the object of future work (again, an intermediary step has already been taken in [8]).

Global environments are explored by Fernández and Siafakas in [21], and used in a minority of works, *e.g.* [18,29]. We introduced the distillation technique in [3] to revisit the relationship between the KAM and weak linear head reduction pointed out by Danos and Regnier [16]. Distilleries have also been used in [8]. The idea to distinguish between *operational content* and *search for the redex* in an abstract machine is not new, as it underlies in particular the *refocusing semantics* of Danvy and Nielsen [17]. The LSC, with its roots in linear logic proof nets, allows to see this distinction as an avatar of the principal/commutative divide in cut-elimination, because machine transitions may be seen as cut-elimination steps [3,9]. Hence, it is fair to say that distilleries bring an original refinement where logic, rewriting, and complexity enlighten the picture, leading to formal bounds on machine overheads.

Omitted proofs may be found in [4].

2 Linear Leftmost-Outermost Reduction

The language of the *linear substitution calculus* (LSC for short) is given by the following term grammar:

$$\text{LSC Terms}\quad t,u,w,r ::= x \mid \lambda x.t \mid tu \mid t[x{\leftarrow}u].$$

The constructor $t[x{\leftarrow}u]$ is called an *explicit substitution, shortened ES* (of u for x in t). Both $\lambda x.t$ and $t[x{\leftarrow}u]$ bind x in t, and we silently work modulo α-equivalence of these bound variables, *e.g.* $(xy)[y{\leftarrow}t]\{x{\leftarrow}y\} = (yz)[z{\leftarrow}t]$.

The operational semantics of the LSC is parametric in a notion of (one-hole) context. General *contexts*, that simply extend the contexts for λ-terms with the two cases for ES, and the special case of *substitution contexts* are defined by:

$$\begin{array}{rl} \text{Contexts} & C, C' ::= \langle\cdot\rangle \mid \lambda x.C \mid Ct \mid tC \mid C[x{\leftarrow}t] \mid t[x{\leftarrow}C]; \\ \text{Substitution Contexts} & L, L' ::= \langle\cdot\rangle \mid L[x{\leftarrow}t]. \end{array}$$

The *plugging* $C\langle t\rangle$ of a term t into a context C is defined as $\langle\cdot\rangle\langle t\rangle := t$, $(\lambda x.C)\langle t\rangle := \lambda x.(C\langle t\rangle)$, and so on. As usual, plugging in a context can capture variables, *e.g.* $((\langle\cdot\rangle y)[y{\leftarrow}t])\langle y\rangle = (yy)[y{\leftarrow}t]$. The plugging $C\langle C'\rangle$ of a context C' into a context C is defined analogously.

We write $C \prec_p t$ if there is a term u s.t. $C\langle u\rangle = t$, call it the *prefix relation.*

The rewriting relation is $\rightarrow := \rightarrow_{\mathtt{m}} \cup \rightarrow_{\mathtt{e}}$ where $\rightarrow_{\mathtt{m}}$ and $\rightarrow_{\mathtt{e}}$ are the *multiplicative* and *exponential* rules, defined by

	Rule at Top Level	Contextual closure
Multiplicative	$L\langle \lambda x.t\rangle u \mapsto_{\mathtt{m}} L\langle t[x{\leftarrow}u]\rangle$	$C\langle t\rangle \rightarrow_{\mathtt{m}} C\langle u\rangle$ if $t \mapsto_{\mathtt{m}} u$
Exponential	$C\langle x\rangle[x{\leftarrow}u] \mapsto_{\mathtt{e}} C\langle u\rangle[x{\leftarrow}u]$	$C\langle t\rangle \rightarrow_{\mathtt{e}} C\langle u\rangle$ if $t \mapsto_{\mathtt{e}} u$

The rewriting rules are assumed to use *on-the-fly* α-equivalence to avoid variable capture. For instance, $(\lambda x.t)[y{\leftarrow}u]y \to_{\mathtt{m}} t\{y{\leftarrow}z\}[x{\leftarrow}y][z{\leftarrow}u]$ for $z \notin \mathtt{fv}(t)$, and $(\lambda y.(xy))[x{\leftarrow}y] \to_{\mathtt{e}} (\lambda z.(yz))[x{\leftarrow}y]$. Moreover, in $\to_{\mathtt{e}}$ the context C is assumed to not capture x, in order to have $(\lambda x.x)[x{\leftarrow}y] \not\to_{\mathtt{e}} (\lambda x.y)[x{\leftarrow}y]$.

The above operational semantics ignores garbage collection. In the LSC, this may be realized by an additional rule which may always be postponed, see [2].

Taking the external context into account, an exponential step has the form $C'\langle C\langle x\rangle[x{\leftarrow}u]\rangle \to_{\mathtt{e}} C'\langle C\langle u\rangle[x{\leftarrow}u]\rangle$. We shall often use a *compact* form:

Exponential Rule in Compact Form

$$C''\langle x\rangle \to_{\mathtt{e}} C''\langle u\rangle \qquad \text{if } C'' = C'\langle C[x{\leftarrow}u]\rangle$$

Definition 1 (Redex Position). *Given a $\to_{\mathtt{m}}$-step $C\langle t\rangle \to_{\mathtt{m}} C\langle u\rangle$ with $t \mapsto_{\mathtt{m}} u$ or a compact $\to_{\mathtt{e}}$-step $C\langle x\rangle \to_{\mathtt{e}} C\langle t\rangle$, the* position *of the redex is the context C.*

We identify a redex with its position, thus using C, C', C'' for redexes, and use $d : t \to^k u$ for derivations, *i.e.* for possibly empty sequences of rewriting steps. We write $|t|_{[\cdot]}$ for the number of substitutions in t, and use $|d|$, $|d|_{\mathtt{m}}$, and $|d|_{\mathtt{e}}$ for the number of steps, m-steps, and e-steps in d, respectively.

Linear Leftmost-Outermost Reduction, Two Definitions. We give two definitions of linear LO reduction $\to_{\mathtt{LO}}$, a traditional one based on ordering redexes and a new contextual one not mentioning the order, apt to work with LSC and relate it to abstract machines. We start by defining the LO order on contexts.

Definition 2 (LO Order). *The* outside-in order *$C \prec_O C'$ is defined by*

1. Root*: $\langle\cdot\rangle \prec_O C$ for every context $C \neq \langle\cdot\rangle$;*
2. Contextual closure*: if $C \prec_O C'$ then $C''\langle C\rangle \prec_O C''\langle C'\rangle$ for any context C''.*

Note that $\prec_O$ can be seen as the prefix relation $\prec_p$ on contexts. The left-to-right order *$C \prec_L C'$ is defined by*

1. Application*: if $C \prec_p t$ and $C' \prec_p u$ then $Cu \prec_L tC'$;*
2. Substitution*: if $C \prec_p t$ and $C' \prec_p u$ then $C[x{\leftarrow}u] \prec_L t[x{\leftarrow}C']$;*
3. Contextual closure*: if $C \prec_L C'$ then $C''\langle C\rangle \prec_L C''\langle C'\rangle$ for any context C''.*

Last, the left-to-right outside-in order *is defined by $C \prec_{LO} C'$ if $C \prec_O C'$ or $C \prec_L C'$.*

Two examples of the outside-in order are $(\lambda x.\langle\cdot\rangle)t \prec_O (\lambda x.(\langle\cdot\rangle[y{\leftarrow}u]))t$ and $t[x{\leftarrow}\langle\cdot\rangle] \prec_O t[x{\leftarrow}uC]$, and an example of the left-to-right order is $t[x{\leftarrow}C]u \prec_L t[x{\leftarrow}w]\langle\cdot\rangle$. The next immediate lemma guarantees that we defined a total order.

Lemma 1 (Totality of $\prec_{LO}$). *If $C \prec_p t$ and $C' \prec_p t$ then either $C \prec_{LO} C'$ or $C' \prec_{LO} C$ or $C = C'$.*

Remember that we identify redexes with their position context and write $C \prec_{LO} C'$. We can now define linear LO reduction, first considered in [5], where it is proved that it is standard and normalizing, and then in [6], extending linear head reduction [2,16,26] to normal form.

Definition 3 (Linear LO Reduction $\rightarrow_{\mathtt{LO}}$). *Let t be a term. C is the* leftmost-outermost *(LO for short) redex of t if $C \prec_{LO} C'$ for every other redex C' of t. We write $t \rightarrow_{\mathtt{LO}} u$ if a step reduces the LO redex.*

We now define LO contexts and prove that the position of a linear LO step is always a LO context. We need two notions.

Definition 4 (Neutral Term). *A term is* neutral *if it is $\rightarrow$-normal and it is not of the form $L\langle \lambda x.t \rangle$.*

Neutral terms are such that their plugging in a context cannot create a multiplicative redex. We also need the notion of left free variable of a context, *i.e.* of a variable occurring free at the left of the hole.

Definition 5 (Left Free Variables). *The set $\mathtt{lfv}(C)$ of* left free variables *of C is defined by:*

$$\begin{array}{rlrl} \mathtt{lfv}(\langle\cdot\rangle) &:= \emptyset & \mathtt{lfv}(tC) &:= \mathtt{fv}(t) \cup \mathtt{lfv}(C) \\ \mathtt{lfv}(\lambda x.C) &:= \mathtt{lfv}(C) \setminus \{x\} & \mathtt{lfv}(C[x{\leftarrow}t]) &:= \mathtt{lfv}(C) \setminus \{x\} \\ \mathtt{lfv}(Ct) &:= \mathtt{lfv}(C) & \mathtt{lfv}(t[x{\leftarrow}C]) &:= (\mathtt{fv}(t) \setminus \{x\}) \cup \mathtt{lfv}(C) \end{array}$$

Definition 6 (LO Contexts). *A context C is* LO *if*

1. Right Application*: whenever $C = C'\langle tC''\rangle$ then t is neutral, and*
2. Left Application*: whenever $C = C'\langle C''t\rangle$ then $C'' \neq L\langle \lambda x.C'''\rangle$.*
3. Substitution*: whenever $C = C'\langle C''[x{\leftarrow}u]\rangle$ then $x \notin \mathtt{lfv}(C'')$.*

Lemma 2 (LO Reduction and LO Contexts). *Let $t \rightarrow u$ by reducing a redex C. Then C is a $\rightarrow_{\mathtt{LO}}$ step iff C is LO.*

Structural Equivalence. A peculiar trait of the LSC is that the rewriting rules do not propagate ES. Therefore, evaluation is usually stable by structural equivalences moving ES around. In this paper we use the following equivalence, including garbage collection ($\equiv_{\mathtt{gc}}$), that we prove to be a strong bisimulation.

Definition 7 (Structural equivalence). *The* structural equivalence $\equiv$ *is the symmetric, reflexive, transitive, and contextual closure of the following axioms:*

$$\begin{array}{rcll} (\lambda x.t)[y{\leftarrow}u] &\equiv_{\lambda}& \lambda x.t[y{\leftarrow}u] & \text{if } x \notin \mathtt{fv}(u) \\ (t\,u)[x{\leftarrow}w] &\equiv_{@1}& t[x{\leftarrow}w]\,u & \text{if } x \notin \mathtt{fv}(u) \\ (t\,u)[x{\leftarrow}w] &\equiv_{@r}& t\,u[x{\leftarrow}w] & \text{if } x \notin \mathtt{fv}(t) \\ t[x{\leftarrow}u][y{\leftarrow}w] &\equiv_{\mathtt{com}}& t[y{\leftarrow}w][x{\leftarrow}u] & \text{if } y \notin \mathtt{fv}(u) \text{ and } x \notin \mathtt{fv}(w) \\ t[x{\leftarrow}u][y{\leftarrow}w] &\equiv_{[\cdot]}& t[x{\leftarrow}u[y{\leftarrow}w]] & \text{if } y \notin \mathtt{fv}(t) \\ t[x{\leftarrow}u] &\equiv_{\mathtt{gc}}& t & \text{if } x \notin \mathtt{fv}(t) \\ t[x{\leftarrow}u] &\equiv_{\mathtt{dup}}& t_{[y]_x}[x{\leftarrow}u][y{\leftarrow}u] & \end{array}$$

In $\equiv_{\mathtt{dup}}$, $t_{[y]_x}$ *denotes a term obtained from* t *by renaming some (possibly none) occurrences of* x *as* y*, with* y *a fresh variable.*

Proposition 1 (Structural Equivalence $\equiv$ is a Strong Bisimulation). *If* $t \equiv u \rightarrow_{\mathtt{LO}} w$ *then exists* r *s.t.* $t \rightarrow_{\mathtt{LO}} r \equiv w$ *and the steps are either both multiplicative or both exponential.*

3 Distilleries

An abstract machine $\mathtt{M}$ is meant to implement a strategy $\multimap$ via a *distillation*, *i.e.* a decoding function $\underline{\cdot}$. A machine has a state s, given by a *code* $\overline{t}$, *i.e.* a λ-term t without ES and not considered up to α-equivalence, and some data-structures like stacks, dumps, environments, and heaps. The data-structures are used to implement the search for the next $\multimap$-redex and some form of substitution, and they decode to evaluation contexts for $\multimap$. Every state s decodes to a term $\underline{s}$, having the shape $C_s\langle\overline{t}\rangle$, where $\overline{t}$ is the code currently under evaluation and C_s is the evaluation context given by the data-structures.

A machine computes using transitions, whose union is denoted by $\rightsquigarrow$, of two types. The *principal* one, denoted by $\rightsquigarrow_{\mathtt{p}}$, corresponds to the firing of a rule defining $\multimap$, up to structural equivalence $\equiv$. The *commutative* transitions, denoted by $\rightsquigarrow_{\mathtt{c}}$, only rearrange the data structures, and on the calculus are either invisible or mapped to $\equiv$. The terminology reflects a proof-theoretic view, as machine transitions can be seen as cut-elimination steps [3,9]. The transformation of evaluation contexts is formalized in the LSC as a structural equivalence $\equiv$, which is required to commute with evaluation $\multimap$, *i.e.* to satisfy

$$\begin{array}{ccc} t & \multimap & r \\ \equiv & & \\ u & & \end{array} \quad \Rightarrow \exists q \text{ s.t.} \quad \begin{array}{ccc} t & \multimap & r \\ \equiv & & \equiv \\ u & \dashrightarrow\!\circ & q \end{array}$$

for each of the rules of $\multimap$, preserving the kind of rule. In fact, this means that $\equiv$ is a *strong* bisimulation (*i.e. one* step to *one* step) with respect to $\multimap$, that is what we proved in Proposition 1 for the equivalence at work in this paper. Strong bisimulations formalize transformations which are transparent with respect to the behavior, even at the level of complexity, because they can be delayed without affecting the length of evaluation:

Lemma 3 (Postponement of $\equiv$). *If* $\equiv$ *is a strong bisimulation,* $t\ (\multimap \cup \equiv)^*\ u$ *implies* $t \multimap^* \equiv u$ *and the number and kind of steps of* $\multimap$ *in the two reduction sequences is exactly the same.*

We can finally introduce distilleries, *i.e.* systems where a strategy $\multimap$ simulates a machine $\mathtt{M}$ up to structural equivalence $\equiv$ via the decoding $\underline{\cdot}$.

Definition 8. *A* distillery $\mathtt{D} = (\mathtt{M}, \multimap, \equiv, \underline{\cdot})$ *is given by:*

1. *An* abstract machine $\mathtt{M}$, *given by*
   (a) *a deterministic labeled transition system (lts)* $\rightsquigarrow$ *over states* s, *with labels in* $\{\mathtt{m}, \mathtt{e}, \mathtt{c}\}$; *the transitions labelled by* $\mathtt{m}, \mathtt{e}$ *are called* principal, *the others* commutative;
   (b) *a distinguished class of states deemed* initial, *in bijection with closed* λ*-terms; from these, the* reachable *states are obtained by applying* $\rightsquigarrow^*$;
2. *a deterministic* strategy $\multimap$, *i.e., a deterministic lts over the terms of the LSC induced by some strategy on its reduction rules, with labels in* $\{\mathtt{m}, \mathtt{e}\}$.
3. *a* structural equivalence $\equiv$ *on terms which is a strong bisimulation with respect to* $\multimap$;
4. *a* decoding function $\underline{\cdot}$ *from states to terms whose graph, when restricted to reachable states, is a weak simulation up to* $\equiv$ *(the commutative transitions are considered as* τ *actions). More explicitly, for all reachable states:*
   - projection of principal transitions: $s \rightsquigarrow_{\mathtt{p}} s'$ *implies* $\underline{s} \multimap_{\mathtt{p}} \equiv \underline{s'}$ *for all* $\mathtt{p} \in \{\mathtt{m}, \mathtt{e}\}$;
   - distillation of commutative transitions: $s \rightsquigarrow_{\mathtt{c}} s'$ *implies* $\underline{s} \equiv \underline{s'}$.

The simulation property is a minimum requirement, but a stronger form of relationship is usually desirable. Additional hypotheses are required in order to obtain the converse simulation and provide complexity bounds.

Terminology: an *execution* ρ is a sequence of transitions from an initial state. With $|\rho|$, $|\rho|_p$ and $|\rho|_c$ we denote respectively the length, the number of principal and commutative transitions of ρ, whereas $|t|$ denotes the size of a term t.

Definition 9 (Distillation Qualities). *A distillery is*

- Reflective *when on reachable states:*
  - Termination: $\rightsquigarrow_{\mathtt{c}}$ *terminates;*
  - Progress: *if* s *is final then* $\underline{s}$ *is a* $\multimap$*-normal form.*
- Bilinear *when, given an execution* ρ *from an initial term* t:
  - Execution Length: *the number of commutative steps* $|\rho|_c$ *is linear in both* $|t|$ *and* $|\rho|_p$, *i.e.* $|\rho|_c \leq c\cdot(1+|\rho|_p)\cdot|t|$ *for some non-zero constant* c *(when* $|\rho|_p = 0$, $O(|t|)$ *time is still needed to recognize that* t *is normal).*
  - Commutative: *each commutative transition is implementable in* $O(1)$ *time on a RAM;*
  - Principal: *each principal transition is implementable in* $O(|t|)$ *time on a RAM.*

A reflective distillery is enough to obtain a weak *bi*simulation between the strategy $\multimap$ and the machine $\mathtt{M}$, up to structural equivalence $\equiv$ (again, the weakness is with respect to commutative transitions). With $|\rho|_{\mathtt{m}}$ and $|\rho|_{\mathtt{e}}$ we denote respectively the number of multiplicative and exponential transitions of ρ.

Theorem 1 (Correctness and Completeness). *Let* $\mathtt{D}$ *be a reflective distillery and* s *an initial state.*

1. Simulation up to $\equiv$: *for every execution* $\rho : s \rightsquigarrow^* s'$ *there is a derivation* $d : \underline{s} \multimap^* \equiv \underline{s'}$ *s.t.* $|\rho|_{\mathtt{m}} = |d|_{\mathtt{m}}$ *and* $|\rho|_{\mathtt{e}} = |d|_{\mathtt{e}}$.

2. Reverse Simulation up to $\equiv$: *for every derivation* $d : \underline{s} \multimap^* t$ *there is an execution* $\rho : s \rightsquigarrow^* s'$ *s.t.* $t \equiv \underline{s'}$ *and* $|\rho|_{\mathtt{m}} = |d|_{\mathtt{m}}$ *and* $|\rho|_{\mathtt{e}} = |d|_{\mathtt{e}}$.

Bilinearity, instead, is crucial for the low-level theorem.

Theorem 2 (Low-Level Implementation Theorem). *Let* $\multimap$ *be a strategy on terms with ES s.t. there exists a bilinear reflective distillery* $\mathtt{D} = (\mathtt{M}, \multimap, \equiv, \underline{\cdot})$. *Then a derivation* $d : t \multimap^* u$ *is implementable on RAM machines in* $O((1 + |d|) \cdot |t|)$ *steps, i.e. bilinear in the size* $|t|$ *of the initial term and the length* $|d|$ *of the derivation.*

Proof. Given $d : t \multimap^n u$ by Theorem 1.2 there is an execution $\rho : s \rightsquigarrow^* s'$ s.t. $u \equiv \underline{s'}$ and $|\rho|_p = |d|$. The cost of implementing ρ is the sum of the costs of implementing the commutative and the principal transitions. By bilinearity, $|\rho|_c = O((1 + |\rho|_p) \cdot |t|)$ and so all the commutative transitions in ρ require $O((1 + |\rho|_p) \cdot |t|)$ steps, because a single one takes a constant number of steps. Again by bilinearity, each principal one takes $O(|t|)$, and so all the principal transitions together require $O(|\rho|_p \cdot |t|)$ steps. □

4 Strengthening the MAM

The machine we are about to introduce implements leftmost-outermost reduction and may therefore be seen as a strong version of the Krivine abstract machine (KAM). However, it differs from the KAM in the fundamental point of using global, as opposed to local, environments. It is therefore more appropriate to say that it is a strong version of the machine we introduced in [3], which we called MAM (Milner abstract machine). Let us briefly recall its definition:

Code	Stack	Env		Code	Stack	Env	
$\overline{t}\overline{u}$	π	E	$\rightsquigarrow_{\mathtt{c}_1}$	$\overline{t}$	$\overline{u} : \pi$	E	
$\lambda x.\overline{t}$	$\overline{u} : \pi$	E	$\rightsquigarrow_{\mathtt{m}}$	$\overline{t}$	π	$[x{\leftarrow}\overline{u}] : E$	
x	π	E	$\rightsquigarrow_{\mathtt{e}}$	$\overline{t}^{\alpha}$	π	E	if $E(x) = \overline{t}$

Note that the stack and the environment of the MAM contain *codes*, not *closures* as in the KAM. A global environment indeed circumvents the complex mutually recursive notions of *local environment* and *closure*, at the price of the explicit α-renaming $\overline{t}^{\alpha}$ which is applied *on the fly* in $\rightsquigarrow_{\mathtt{e}}$. The price however is negligible, at least theoretically, as the asymptotic complexity of the machine is not affected, see [3] (the same can be said of variable names vs de Bruijn indexes/levels).

We know that the MAM performs *weak* head reduction, whose reduction contexts are (informally) of the form $\langle\cdot\rangle\pi$. This justifies the presence of the stack. It is immediate to extend the MAM so that it performs full head reduction, *i.e.*, so that the head redex is reduced even if it is under an abstraction. Since head contexts are of the form $\Lambda.\langle\cdot\rangle\pi$ (with Λ a list of abstractions), we simply add a stack of abstractions Λ and augment the machine with the following transition:

Abs	Code	Stack	Env		Abs	Code	Stack	Env
Λ	$\lambda x.\overline{t}$	ϵ	E	$\rightsquigarrow_{\mathtt{c}_2}$	$x : \Lambda$	$\overline{t}$	ϵ	E

The other transitions do not touch the Λ stack.

LO reduction is nothing but iterated head reduction. LO reduction contexts, which we formally introduced in Definition 6, when restricted to the pure λ-calculus (without ES) are of the form $\Lambda.rC\pi$, where: Λ and π are as above; r, if present, is a neutral term; and C is either $\langle\cdot\rangle$ or, inductively, a LO context. Then LO contexts may be represented by stacks of triples of the form (Λ, r, π), where r is a neutral term. These stacks of triples will be called *dumps*.

The states of the machine for full LO reduction are as above but augmented with a dump and a *phase* φ, indicating whether we are executing head reduction ($\blacktriangledown$) or whether we are backtracking to find the starting point of the next iteration ($\blacktriangle$). To the above transitions (which do not touch the dump and are always in the $\blacktriangledown$ phase), we add the following:

Abs	Code	Stack	Env	Dump	Ph		Abs	Code	Stack	Env	Dump	Ph
Λ	x	π	E	D	$\blacktriangledown$	$\leadsto_{c_3}$	Λ	x	π	E	D if $E(x) = \bot$	$\blacktriangle$
$x : \Lambda$	$\overline{t}$	ϵ	E	D	$\blacktriangle$	$\leadsto_{c_5}$	Λ	$\lambda x.\overline{t}$	ϵ	E	D	$\blacktriangle$
ϵ	$\overline{u}$	ϵ	E	$(\Lambda, \overline{t}, \pi) : D$	$\blacktriangle$	$\leadsto_{c_7}$	Λ	$\overline{t}\overline{u}$	π	E	D	$\blacktriangle$
Λ	$\overline{t}$	$\overline{u} : \pi$	E	D	$\blacktriangle$	$\leadsto_{c_6}$	ϵ	$\overline{u}$	ϵ	E	$(\Lambda, \overline{t}, \pi) : D$	$\blacktriangledown$

where $E(x) = \bot$ means that the variable x is undefined in the environment E.

In the machine we actually use we join the dump and the Λ stack into the *frame* F, to reduce the number of machine components (the analysis will however somewhat reintroduce the distinction). In the sequel, the reader should bear in mind that a state of the Strong MAM introduced below corresponds to a state of the machine just discussed according to the following correspondence:[1]

Discussed Machine:

Abs	Code	Stack	Env	Dump	Ph
Λ_0	$\overline{t}$	π	E	$(\Lambda_1, \overline{t}_1, \pi_1) : \cdots : (\Lambda_n, \overline{t}_n, \pi_n)$	φ

$\updownarrow$

Strong MAM :

Frame	Code	Stack	Env	Ph
$\Lambda_0 : (\overline{t}_1, \pi_1) : \Lambda_1 : \cdots : (\overline{t}_n, \pi_n) : \Lambda_n$	$\overline{t}$	π	E	φ

5 The Strong Milner Abstract Machine

The components and the transitions of the Strong MAM are given by the first two boxes in Fig. 1. As above, we use $\overline{t}, \overline{u}, \ldots$ to denote *codes*, *i.e.*, terms not containing ES and *well-named*, by which mean that distinct binders bind distinct variables and that the sets of free and bound variables are disjoint (codes are not considered up to α-equivalence). The Strong MAM has two phases: *evaluation* ($\blacktriangledown$) and *backtracking* ($\blacktriangle$).

[1] Modulo the presence of markers of the form $\blacktriangle x$ and $\blacktriangledown x$ in the environment, which are needed for bookkeeping purposes and were omitted here.

Frames	$F ::= \epsilon \mid (\overline{t}, \pi) : F \mid x : F$	Stacks	$\pi ::= \epsilon \mid \overline{t} : \pi$
Environments	$E ::= \epsilon \mid [x{\leftarrow}\overline{t}] : E \mid \blacktriangledown x : E \mid \blacktriangle x : E$	Phases	$\varphi ::= \blacktriangledown \mid \blacktriangle$

Frame	Code	Stack	Env	Ph		Frame	Code	Stack	Env	Ph
F	$\overline{t}\overline{u}$	π	E	$\blacktriangledown$	$\rightsquigarrow_{\blacktriangledown c_1}$	F	$\overline{t}$	$\overline{u} : \pi$	E	$\blacktriangledown$
F	$\lambda x.\overline{t}$	$\overline{u} : \pi$	E	$\blacktriangledown$	$\rightsquigarrow_{\mathtt{m}}$	F	$\overline{t}$	π	$[x{\leftarrow}\overline{u}] : E$	$\blacktriangledown$
F	$\lambda x.\overline{t}$	ϵ	E	$\blacktriangledown$	$\rightsquigarrow_{\blacktriangledown c_2}$	$x : F$	$\overline{t}$	ϵ	$\blacktriangledown x : E$	$\blacktriangledown$
F	x	π	E	$\blacktriangledown$	$\rightsquigarrow_{\mathtt{e}}$	F	$\overline{t}^{\alpha}$	π	E	$\blacktriangledown$
									if $E(x) = \overline{t}$	
F	x	π	E	$\blacktriangledown$	$\rightsquigarrow_{\blacktriangledown c_3}$	F	x	π	E	$\blacktriangle$
									if $E(x) = \blacktriangledown$	
$x : F$	$\overline{t}$	ϵ	E	$\blacktriangle$	$\rightsquigarrow_{\blacktriangle c_4}$	F	$\lambda x.\overline{t}$	ϵ	$\blacktriangle x : E$	$\blacktriangle$
$(\overline{t}, \pi) : F$	$\overline{u}$	ϵ	E	$\blacktriangle$	$\rightsquigarrow_{\blacktriangle c_5}$	F	$\overline{t}\overline{u}$	π	E	$\blacktriangle$
F	$\overline{t}$	$\overline{u} : \pi$	E	$\blacktriangle$	$\rightsquigarrow_{\blacktriangle c_6}$	$(\overline{t}, \pi) : F$	$\overline{u}$	ϵ	E	$\blacktriangledown$

Frames (Ordinary, Weak, Trunk)	Environments (Well-Formed, Weak, Trunk)
$F ::= F_{\mathrm{w}} \mid F_{\mathrm{t}} \mid F_{\mathrm{w}} : F_{\mathrm{t}}$	$E ::= E_{\mathrm{w}} \mid E_{\mathrm{t}} \mid E_{\mathrm{w}} : E_{\mathrm{t}}$
$F_{\mathrm{w}} ::= \epsilon \mid (\overline{t}, \pi) : F$	$E_{\mathrm{w}} ::= \epsilon \mid [x{\leftarrow}\overline{t}] : E_{\mathrm{w}} \mid \blacktriangle x : E_{\mathrm{w}} : \blacktriangledown x : E'_{\mathrm{w}}$
$F_{\mathrm{t}} ::= \epsilon \mid x : F$	$E_{\mathrm{t}} ::= \epsilon \mid \blacktriangledown x : E$

Fig. 1. The strong MAM.

Initial States. The *initial states* of the Strong MAM are of the form $\epsilon \mid \overline{t} \mid \epsilon \mid \epsilon \mid \blacktriangledown$, where $\overline{t}$ is a closed code called the *initial term*. In the sequel, we abusively say that a state is reachable from a term meaning that it is reachable from the corresponding initial state.

Scope Markers. The two transitions to evaluate and backtrack on abstractions, $\rightsquigarrow_{\blacktriangledown c_2}$ and $\rightsquigarrow_{\blacktriangle c_4}$, add markers to delimit subenvironments associated to scopes. The marker $\blacktriangledown x$ is introduced when the machine starts evaluating under an abstraction λx, while $\blacktriangle x$ marks the end of such a subenvironment.

Slight Notation Abuse. The data structures we are going to use are defined as lists, using ϵ for the empty list and ":" for *both* the cons and append operation. The overloading of : means that in the case of, *e.g.*, an environment E we have $E : \epsilon = E = \epsilon : E$, and in particular $\epsilon : \epsilon = \epsilon$. Such an abuse will be used thoughout the whole paper.

Weak and Trunk Frames. A frame F may be uniquely decomposed into $F = F_{\mathrm{w}} : F_{\mathrm{t}}$, where $F_{\mathrm{w}} = (\overline{t}_1, \pi_1) : \cdots : (\overline{t}_n, \pi_n)$ (with n possibly null) is a *weak frame*, *i.e.* where no abstracted variable appear, and F_{t} is a *trunk frame*, *i.e.* not of the form $(\overline{t}, \pi) : F'$ (it either starts a variable entry or it is empty). More precisely, we rely on the alternative grammar in the third box of Fig. 1. We denote by $\Lambda(F)$ the set of variables in F, *i.e.* the set of x s.t. $F = F' : x : F''$.

Weak, Trunk, and Well-Formed Environments. Similarly to the frame, the environment of a reachable state has a weak/trunk structure. In contrast to frames, however, not every environment can be seen this way, but only the well-formed ones (reachable environments will be shown to be well-formed). A weak environment E_{w} does not contain any open scope, *i.e.* whenever in E_{w} there is a scope opener marker ($\blacktriangledown x$) then one can also find the scope closer marker ($\blacktriangle x$), and (globally) the closed scopes of E_{w} are well-parenthesized. A trunk environment E_{t} may instead also contain open scopes that have no closing marker in E_{t} (but not unmatched closing markers $\blacktriangle x$). Formally, weak E_{w}, trunk E_{t}, and well-formed environments E (all the environments that we will consider will be well-formed, that is why we note them E) are defined in the third box in Fig. 1.

Closed Scopes and Meta-level Garbage Collection. Fragments of the form $\blacktriangle x : E_{\mathrm{w}} : \blacktriangledown x$ within an environment will essentially be ignored; this is how a simple form of garbage collection is encapsulated at the meta-level in the decoding. In particular, for a well-formed environment E we define $E(x)$ as:

$$\begin{array}{rclrcl} \epsilon(x) & := & \bot & (\blacktriangle y : E_{\mathrm{w}} : \blacktriangledown y : E)(x) & := & E(x) \\ ([x{\leftarrow}\overline{t}] : E)(x) & := & \overline{t} & (\blacktriangledown x : E)(x) & := & \blacktriangledown \\ ([y{\leftarrow}\overline{t}] : E)(x) & := & E(x) & (\blacktriangledown y : E)(x) & := & E(x) \end{array}$$

Note that the only potential source of non-determinism for the Strong MAM is the choice among $\rightsquigarrow_{\mathsf{e}}$ and $\rightsquigarrow_{\blacktriangle c_4}$ in the variable case. The operation $E(x)$, however, is a function, and so the machine is deterministic.

We write $\Lambda(E)$ to denote the set of variables bound to $\blacktriangledown$ by an environment E, *i.e.* those variables whose scope is not closed with $\blacktriangle$.

Lemma 4 (Weak Environments Contain only Closed Scopes). *If E_{w} is a weak environment then $\Lambda(E_{\mathrm{w}}) = \emptyset$.*

Compatibility. In the Strong MAM , both the frame and the environment record information about the abstractions in which evaluation is currently taking place. Clearly, such information has to be coherent, otherwise the decoding of a state becomes impossible. The following compatibility predicate captures the correlation between the structure of the frame and that of the environment.

Definition 10 (Compatibility $F \propto E$). *Compatibility $F \propto E$ between frames and environments is defined by*

1. Base*: $\epsilon \propto \epsilon$;*
2. Weak Extension*: $(F_{\mathrm{w}} : F_{\mathrm{t}}) \propto (E_{\mathrm{w}} : E_{\mathrm{t}})$ if $F_{\mathrm{t}} \propto E_{\mathrm{t}}$;*
3. Abstraction*: $(x : F) \propto (\blacktriangledown x : E)$ if $F \propto E$;*

Lemma 5 (Properties of Compatibility).

1. Well-Formed Environments*: if F and E are compatible then E is well-formed.*
2. Factorization*: every compatible pair $F \propto E$ can be written as $(F_{\mathrm{w}} : F_{\mathrm{t}}) \propto (E_{\mathrm{w}} : E_{\mathrm{t}})$ with $F_{\mathrm{t}} = x : F'$ iff $E_{\mathrm{t}} = \blacktriangledown x : E'$;*
3. Open Scopes Match*: $\Lambda(F) = \Lambda(E)$.*
4. Compatibility and Weak Structures Commute*: for all F_{w} and E_{w}, $F \propto E$ iff $(F_{\mathrm{w}} : F) \propto (E_{\mathrm{w}} : E)$.*

Invariants. The properties of the machine that are needed to prove its correctness and completeness are given by the following invariants.

Lemma 6 (Strong MAM Invariants). *Let* $s = F \mid \overline{u} \mid \pi \mid E \mid \varphi$ *be a state reachable from an initial term* $\overline{t}_0$*. Then:*

1. Compatibility: *F and E are compatible, i.e.* $F \propto E$.
2. Normal Form:
   (1) Backtracking Code: *if* $\varphi = \blacktriangle$, *then* $\overline{u}$ *is normal, and if* π *is non-empty, then* $\overline{u}$ *is neutral;*
   (2) Frame: *if* $F = F' : (\overline{w}, \pi') : F''$, *then* $\overline{w}$ *is neutral.*
3. Backtracking Free Variables:
   (1) Backtracking Code: *if* $\varphi = \blacktriangle$ *then* $\mathtt{fv}(\overline{u}) \subseteq \Lambda(F)$*;*
   (2) Pairs in the Frame: *if* $F = F' : (\overline{w}, \pi') : F''$ *then* $\mathtt{fv}(\overline{w}) \subseteq \Lambda(F'')$.
4. Name:
   (1) Substitutions: *if* $E = E' : [x{\leftarrow}\overline{t}] : E''$ *then x is fresh wrt* $\overline{t}$ *and* E''*;*
   (2) Markers: *if* $E = E' : \blacktriangledown x : E''$ *and* $F = F' : x : F''$ *then x is fresh wrt* E'' *and* F''*, and* $E'(y) = \bot$ *for any free variable y in* F''*;*
   (3) Abstractions: *if* $\lambda x.\overline{t}$ *is a subterm of* F, $\overline{u}$, π, *or* E *then x may occur only in* $\overline{t}$ *and in the closed subenvironment* $\blacktriangle x : E_{\mathtt{w}} : \blacktriangledown x$ *of* E*, if it exists.*
5. Closure:
   (1) Environment: *if* $E = E' : [x{\leftarrow}\overline{t}] : E''$ *then* $E''(y) \neq \bot$ *for all* $y \in \mathtt{fv}(\overline{t})$*;*
   (2) Code, Stack, and Frame: $E(x) \neq \bot$ *for any free variable in* $\overline{u}$ *and in any code of* π *and* F.

Since the statement of the invariants is rather technical, let us summarize the dependencies (or lack thereof) of the various points and their use in the distillation proof of the next section.

- The compatibility, normal form and backtracking free variables invariants are independent of each other and of the subsequent invariants.
- The name invariant relies on the compatibility invariant only.
- The closure invariant relies on the compatibility, name and backtracking free variable invariants only. It is crucial for the progress property (because in the variable case at least one among $\rightsquigarrow_{\mathtt{e}}$ and $\rightsquigarrow_{\blacktriangle \mathtt{c}_4}$ applies).

The proof of every invariant is by induction on the number of transitions leading to the reachable state. In this respect, the various points of the statement of each invariant (*e.g.* points 5.1 and 5.2) are entangled, in the sense that each point needs to use the induction hypothesis of one of the other points, and thus they cannot be proved separately.

Implementing Environments. Note that substitutions in closed scopes are never used by the machine, because the operation $E(x)$ is defined by ignoring them. Moreover, the name invariant guarantees that if $E(x) = \blacktriangledown x$ then E does not contain a substitution on x. These two facts imply that the scope markers $\blacktriangle x$ and $\blacktriangledown x$ are not really needed in an actual implementation: the test $E(x) = \blacktriangledown x$ in $\rightsquigarrow_{\blacktriangledown \mathtt{c}_3}$ can indeed be replaced—in the variant without markers (also redifining

$E(x)$ as simple look-up in E)—by a test of undefinedness. The markers are in fact needed only for the analysis, as they structure the frame and the environment of a reachable state into *weak* and *trunk* parts, allowing a simple decoding towards terms with ES.

Moreover, variables are meant to be implemented as memory locations, so that the environment is simply a store, and the list structure of environments is not necessary either. Such an assumption allows to access the environment in constant time on RAM, and will be essential for the proof of the bilinearity of the distillery (to be defined).

Therefore, the structure of environments—given by the scope markers and the list structure—is an artifice used to define the decoding and develop the analysis, but it is not meant to be part of the actual implementation.

6 Distilling the Strong MAM

The definition of the decoding relies on the notion of compatible pair.

Definition 11 (Decoding). *Let $s = (F, \overline{t}, \pi, E, \varphi)$ be a state s.t. $F \propto E$ is a compatible pair. Then s decodes to a state context C_s and a term $\underline{s}$ as follows:*

Weak Environments:

$$\begin{aligned} \underline{\epsilon} &:= \langle\cdot\rangle \\ \underline{[x{\leftarrow}\overline{u}] : E_{\mathrm{w}}} &:= \underline{E_{\mathrm{w}}}\langle\langle\cdot\rangle[x{\leftarrow}\overline{u}]\rangle \\ \underline{\blacktriangle x : E_{\mathrm{w}} : \blacktriangledown x : E'_{\mathrm{w}}} &:= \underline{E'_{\mathrm{w}}} \end{aligned}$$

Compatible Pairs:

$$\begin{aligned} \underline{\epsilon \propto \epsilon} &:= \langle\cdot\rangle \\ \underline{(F_{\mathrm{w}} : F_{\mathrm{t}}) \propto (E_{\mathrm{w}} : E_{\mathrm{t}})} &:= \underline{F_{\mathrm{t}} \propto E_{\mathrm{t}}}\langle\underline{E_{\mathrm{w}}}\langle\underline{F_{\mathrm{w}}}\rangle\rangle \\ \underline{(x : F) \propto (\blacktriangledown x : E)} &:= \underline{F \propto E}\langle\lambda x.\langle\cdot\rangle\rangle \end{aligned}$$

Weak Frames:

$$\begin{aligned} \underline{\epsilon} &:= \langle\cdot\rangle \\ \underline{(\overline{u}, \pi) : F_{\mathrm{w}}} &:= \underline{F_{\mathrm{w}}}\langle\underline{\pi}\langle\overline{u}\langle\cdot\rangle\rangle\rangle \end{aligned}$$

Stacks:

$$\begin{aligned} \underline{\epsilon} &:= \langle\cdot\rangle \\ \underline{\overline{u} : \pi} &:= \underline{\pi}\langle\langle\cdot\rangle\overline{u}\rangle \end{aligned}$$

States:

$$\begin{aligned} C_s &:= \underline{F \propto E}\langle\underline{\pi}\rangle \\ \underline{s} &:= C_s\langle\overline{t}\rangle \end{aligned}$$

The following lemmas sum up the properties of the decoding.

Lemma 7 (Closed Scopes Disappear). *Let $F \propto E$ be a compatible pair. Then $\underline{F \propto (\blacktriangle x : E_{\mathrm{w}} : \blacktriangledown x : E)} = \underline{F \propto E}$.*

Lemma 8 (LO Decoding Invariant). *Let $s = F \mid \overline{u} \mid \pi \mid E \mid \varphi$ be a reachable state. Then $\underline{F \propto E}$ and C_s are LO contexts.*

Lemma 9 (Decoding and Structural Equivalence $\equiv$)

1. Stacks and Substitutions Commute*: if x does not occur free in π then $\underline{\pi}\langle t[x{\leftarrow}u]\rangle \equiv \underline{\pi}\langle t\rangle[x{\leftarrow}u]$;*
2. Compatible Pairs Absorb Substitutions*: if x does not occur free in F then $\underline{F \propto E}\langle t[x{\leftarrow}u]\rangle \equiv \underline{F \propto ([x{\leftarrow}u] : E)}\langle t\rangle$.*

The next theorem is our first main result. By the abstract approach presented in Sect. 3 (Theorem 1), it implies that the Strong MAM is a correct and complete implementation of linear LO evaluation to normal form.

Theorem 3 (Distillation). *(Strong MAM* $, \to_{\mathtt{LO}}, \equiv, \underline{\cdot})$ *is an explicit and reflective distillery. In particular:*

1. Projection of Principal Transitions*:*
   (a) Multiplicative*: if* $s \rightsquigarrow_{\mathtt{m}} s'$ *then* $\underline{s} \to_{\mathtt{m}} \equiv \underline{s'}$*;*
   (b) Exponential*: if* $s \rightsquigarrow_{\mathtt{e}} s'$ *then* $\underline{s} \to_{\mathtt{e}} \underline{s'}$*, duplicating the same subterm.*
2. Distillation of Commutative Transitions*:*
   (a) Garbage Collection of Weak Environments*: if* $s \rightsquigarrow_{\mathtt{c}_4} s'$ *then* $\underline{s} \equiv_{\mathtt{gc}} \underline{s'}$*;*
   (b) Equality Cases*: if* $s \rightsquigarrow_{\mathtt{c}_{1,2,3,5,6}} s'$ *then* $\underline{s} = \underline{s'}$*.*

Proof. Recall, the decoding is defined as $\underline{(F, \overline{t}, \pi, E, \varphi)} := \underline{F} \propto \underline{E}\langle\underline{\pi}\langle\overline{t}\rangle\rangle$. Determinism of the machine follows by the deterministic definition of $E(x)$, and that of the strategy follows from the totality of the LO order (Lemma 1). Transitions:

- **Case** $s = (F, \lambda x.\overline{t}, \overline{u} : \pi, E, \blacktriangledown) \rightsquigarrow_{\mathtt{m}} (F, \overline{t}, \pi, [x{\leftarrow}\overline{u}] : E, \blacktriangledown) = s'$. Note that $C_{s'} = \underline{F} \propto \underline{E}\langle\underline{\pi}\rangle$ is LO by the LO decoding invariant (Lemma 8). Moreover by the closure invariant (Lemma 6.5) x does not occur in F nor π, justifying the use of Lemma 9 in:

$$\begin{array}{rl} \underline{(F, \lambda x.\overline{t}, \overline{u} : \pi, E, \blacktriangledown)} = & \underline{F} \propto \underline{E}\langle\underline{\overline{u} : \pi}\langle\lambda x.\overline{t}\rangle\rangle \\ = & \underline{F} \propto \underline{E}\langle\underline{\pi}\langle(\lambda x.\overline{t})\overline{u}\rangle\rangle \\ \to_{\mathtt{m}} & \underline{F} \propto \underline{E}\langle\underline{\pi}\langle\overline{t}[x{\leftarrow}\overline{u}]\rangle\rangle \\ \equiv_{L.9.1} & \underline{F} \propto \underline{E}\langle\underline{\pi}\langle\overline{t}\rangle[x{\leftarrow}\overline{u}]\rangle \\ \equiv_{L.9.2} & \underline{F} \propto \underline{([x{\leftarrow}\overline{u}] : E)}\langle\underline{\pi}\langle\overline{t}\rangle\rangle = \underline{(F, \overline{t}, \pi, [x{\leftarrow}\overline{u}] : E, \blacktriangledown)} \end{array}$$

- **Case** $s = (F, x, \pi, E, \blacktriangledown) \rightsquigarrow_{\mathtt{e}} (F, \overline{t}^{\alpha}, \pi, E, \blacktriangledown) = s'$ with $E(x) = \overline{t}$ As before, C_s is LO by Lemma 8. Moreover, $E(x) = \overline{t}$ guarantees that E, and thus C_s, have a substitution binding x to $\overline{t}$. Finally, $C_s = C_{s'}$. Then

$$\underline{s} = C_s\langle x\rangle \to_{\mathtt{e}} C_s\langle\overline{t}^{\alpha}\rangle = \underline{s'}$$

- **Case** $s = (x : F, \overline{t}, \epsilon, E, \blacktriangle) \rightsquigarrow_{\blacktriangle\mathtt{c}_4} (F, \lambda x.\overline{t}, \epsilon, \blacktriangle x : E, \blacktriangle) = s'$ By Lemma 6.1 $x : F \propto E$, and by Lemma 5.2 $E = E_{\mathtt{W}} : \blacktriangledown x : E'$. Then

$$\underline{(x : F) \propto E} = \underline{(x : F) \propto (E_{\mathtt{W}} : \blacktriangledown x : E')} = \underline{(x : F) \propto (\blacktriangledown x : E')}\langle\underline{E_{\mathtt{W}}}\rangle$$

Since we are in a backtracking phase ($\blacktriangle$), the backtracking free variables invariant (Lemma 6.3.1) and the open scopes matching property (Lemma 5.3) give $\mathtt{fv}(\overline{t}) \subseteq_{L.6.3.1} \Lambda(F) =_{L.5.3} \Lambda(E_{\mathtt{W}} : \blacktriangledown x : E') =_{L}.4 \Lambda(\blacktriangledown x : E')$, *i.e.* $\underline{E_{\mathtt{W}}}$ does not bind any variable in $\mathtt{fv}(\overline{t})$. Then $\underline{E_{\mathtt{W}}}\langle\overline{t}\rangle \equiv_{\mathtt{gc}}^{*} \overline{t}$, and

$$\begin{array}{rl} \underline{(x : F, \overline{t}, \epsilon, E, \blacktriangle)} = & \underline{(x : F) \propto E}\langle\overline{t}\rangle \\ = & \underline{(x : F) \propto (E_{\mathtt{W}} : \blacktriangledown x : E')}\langle\overline{t}\rangle \\ = & \underline{(x : F) \propto (\blacktriangledown x : E')}\langle\underline{E_{\mathtt{W}}}\langle\overline{t}\rangle\rangle \\ \equiv_{\mathtt{gc}}^{*} & \underline{(x : F) \propto (\blacktriangledown x : E')}\langle\overline{t}\rangle \\ = & \underline{F \propto E'}\langle\lambda x.\overline{t}\rangle \\ =_{L.7} & \underline{F \propto (\blacktriangle x : E_{\mathtt{W}} : \blacktriangledown x : E')}\langle\lambda x.\overline{t}\rangle \\ = & \underline{F \propto (\blacktriangle x : E)}\langle\lambda x.\overline{t}\rangle \qquad = \underline{(F, \lambda x.\overline{t}, \epsilon, \blacktriangle x : E, \blacktriangle)} \end{array}$$

- **Case** $(F, \overline{t}\overline{u}, \pi, E, \blacktriangledown) \rightsquigarrow_{\blacktriangledown c_1} (F, \overline{t}, \overline{u} : \pi, E, \blacktriangledown)$.

$$\underline{(F, \overline{t}\overline{u}, \pi, E, \blacktriangledown)} = \underline{F} \propto \underline{E}\langle \underline{\pi}\langle \overline{t}\overline{u} \rangle \rangle = \underline{F} \propto \underline{E}\langle \underline{\overline{u} : \pi}\langle \overline{t} \rangle \rangle = \underline{(F, \overline{t}, \overline{u} : \pi, E, \blacktriangledown)}$$

- **Case** $(F, \lambda x.\overline{t}, \epsilon, E, \blacktriangledown) \rightsquigarrow_{\blacktriangledown c_2} (x : F, \overline{t}, \epsilon, \blacktriangledown x : E, \blacktriangledown)$.

$$\begin{aligned} \underline{(F, \lambda x.\overline{t}, \epsilon, E, \blacktriangledown)} &= \underline{F} \propto \underline{E}\langle \lambda x.\overline{t} \rangle \\ &= \underline{(x : F)} \propto \underline{(\blacktriangledown x : E)}\langle \overline{t} \rangle = \underline{(x : F, \overline{t}, \epsilon, \blacktriangledown x : E, \blacktriangledown)} \end{aligned}$$

- **Case** $(F, x, \pi, E, \blacktriangledown) \rightsquigarrow_{\blacktriangledown c_3} (F, x, \pi, E, \blacktriangle)$.

$$\underline{(F, x, \pi, E, \blacktriangledown)} = \underline{F} \propto \underline{E}\langle \underline{\pi}\langle x \rangle \rangle = \underline{(F, x, \pi, E, \blacktriangle)}$$

- **Case** $((\overline{t}, \pi) : F, \overline{u}, \epsilon, E, \blacktriangle) \rightsquigarrow_{\blacktriangle c_5} (F, \overline{t}\overline{u}, \pi, E, \blacktriangle)$.

$$\underline{((\overline{t}, \pi) : F, \overline{u}, \epsilon, E, \blacktriangle)} = \underline{(\overline{t}, \pi) : F} \propto \underline{E}\langle \overline{u} \rangle = \underline{F} \propto \underline{E}\langle \underline{\pi}\langle \overline{t}\,\overline{u} \rangle \rangle = \underline{(F, \overline{t}\overline{u}, \pi, E, \blacktriangle)}$$

- **Case** $(F, \overline{t}, \overline{u} : \pi, E, \blacktriangle) \rightsquigarrow_{\blacktriangle c_6} ((\overline{t}, \pi) : F, \overline{u}, \epsilon, E, \blacktriangledown)$.

$$\begin{aligned} \underline{(F, \overline{t}, \overline{u} : \pi, E, \blacktriangle)} &= \underline{F} \propto \underline{E}\langle \underline{\overline{u} : \pi}\langle \overline{t} \rangle \rangle \\ &= \underline{F} \propto \underline{E}\langle \underline{\pi}\langle \overline{t}\,\overline{u} \rangle \rangle \\ &= \underline{((\overline{t}, \pi) : F)} \propto \underline{E}\langle \overline{u} \rangle = \underline{((\overline{t}, \pi) : F, \overline{u}, \epsilon, E, \blacktriangledown)} \end{aligned}$$

For what concerns reflectiveness, *termination* of commutative transitions is subsumed by bilinearity (Theorem 4 below). For *progress*, note that

1. *the machine cannot get stuck during the evaluation phase*: for applications and abstractions it is evident and for variables one among $\rightsquigarrow_{e}$ and $\rightsquigarrow_{\blacktriangledown c_3}$ always applies, because of the closure invariant (Lemma 6.5).
2. *final states have the form* $(\epsilon, t, \epsilon, E, \blacktriangle)$, because
   (a) by the previous consideration they are in a backtracking phase,
   (b) if the stack is non-empty then $\rightsquigarrow_{\blacktriangle c_6}$ applies,
   (c) otherwise if the frame is not empty then either $\rightsquigarrow_{\blacktriangle c_4}$ or $\rightsquigarrow_{\blacktriangle c_5}$ applies.
3. *final states decode to normal terms*: a final state $s = (\epsilon, t, \epsilon, E, \blacktriangle)$ decodes to $\underline{s} = \underline{E}\langle t \rangle$ which is normal and closed by the normal form (Lemma 6.2.1) and backtracking free variables (Lemma 6.3.1) invariants □

7 Complexity Analysis

The complexity analysis requires a further invariant, bounding the size of the duplicated subterms. For us, $\overline{u}$ is a subterm of $\overline{t}$ if it does so up to variable names, both free and bound. More precisely: define t^- as t in which all variables (including those appearing in binders) are replaced by a fixed symbol $*$. Then, we will consider u to be a subterm of t whenever u^- is a subterm of t^- in the usual sense. The key property ensured by this definition is that the size $|\overline{u}|$ of $\overline{u}$ is bounded by $|\overline{t}|$.

Lemma 10 (Subterm Invariant). *Let ρ be an execution from an initial code $\overline{t}$. Every code duplicated along ρ using $\leadsto_{\mathtt{e}}$ is a subterm of $\overline{t}$.*

Via the distillation theorem (Theorem 3), the invariant provides a new proof of the subterm property of linear LO reduction (first proved in [6]).

Lemma 11 (Subterm Property for $\to_{\mathtt{LO}}$). *Let d be a $\to_{\mathtt{LO}}$-derivation from an initial term t. Every term duplicated along d using $\to_{\mathtt{e}}$ is a subterm of t.*

The next theorem is our second main result, from which the low-level implementation theorem (Theorem 2) follows. Let us stress that, despite the simplicity of the reasoning, the analysis is subtle as the length of backtracking phases (Point 2) can be bound only *globally*, by the whole previous evaluation work.

Theorem 4 (Bilinearity). *The Strong MAM is bilinear, i.e. given an execution $\rho : s \leadsto^* s'$ from an initial state of code t then:*

1. Commutative Evaluation Steps are Bilinear*:* $|\rho|_{\blacktriangledown\mathtt{c}} \leq (1 + |\rho|_{\mathtt{e}}) \cdot |t|$.
2. Commutative Evaluation Bounds Backtracking*:* $|\rho|_{\blacktriangle\mathtt{c}} \leq 2 \cdot |\rho|_{\blacktriangledown\mathtt{c}}$.
3. Commutative Steps are Bilinear*:* $|\rho|_{c} \leq 3 \cdot (1 + |\rho|_{\mathtt{e}}) \cdot |t|$.

Proof. 1. We prove a slightly stronger statement, namely $|\rho|_{\blacktriangledown\mathtt{c}} + |\rho|_{\mathtt{m}} \leq (1 + |\rho|_{\mathtt{e}}) \cdot |t|$, by means of the following notion of size for stacks/frames/states:

$$
\begin{array}{rclrcl}
|\epsilon| &:=& 0 & |x : F| &:=& |F| \\
|\overline{t} : \pi| &:=& |\overline{t}| + |\pi| & |(\overline{t}, \pi) : F| &:=& |\pi| + |F| \\
|(F, \overline{t}, \pi, E, \blacktriangledown)| &:=& |F| + |\pi| + |\overline{t}| & |(F, \overline{t}, \pi, E, \blacktriangle)| &:=& |F| + |\pi|
\end{array}
$$

By direct inspection of the rules of the machine it can be checked that:

- *Exponentials Increase the Size*: if $s \leadsto_{\mathtt{e}} s'$ is an exponential transition, then $|s'| \leq |s| + |t|$ where $|t|$ is the size of the initial term; this is a consequence of the fact that exponential steps retrieve a piece of code from the environment, which is a subterm of the initial term by Lemma 10;
- *Non-Exponential Evaluation Transitions Decrease the Size*: if $s \leadsto_a s'$ with $a \in \{\mathtt{m}, \blacktriangledown\mathtt{c}_1, \blacktriangledown\mathtt{c}_2, \blacktriangledown\mathtt{c}_3\}$ then $|s'| < |s|$;
- *Backtracking Transitions do not Change the Size*: if $s \leadsto_a s'$ with $a \in \{\blacktriangle\mathtt{c}_4, \blacktriangle\mathtt{c}_5, \blacktriangle\mathtt{c}_6\}$ then $|s'| = |s|$.

Then a straightforward induction on $|\rho|$ shows that

$$|s'| \leq |s| + |\rho|_{\mathtt{e}} \cdot |t| - |\rho|_{\blacktriangledown\mathtt{c}} - |\rho|_{\mathtt{m}}$$

i.e. that $|\rho|_{\blacktriangledown\mathtt{c}} + |\rho|_{\mathtt{m}} \leq |s| + |\rho|_{\mathtt{e}} \cdot |t| - |s'|$.

Now note that $|\cdot|$ is always non-negative and that since s is initial we have $|s| = |t|$. We can then conclude with

$$
\begin{array}{rll}
|\rho|_{\blacktriangledown\mathtt{c}} + |\rho|_{\mathtt{m}} & \leq |s| + |\rho|_{\mathtt{e}} \cdot |t| - |s'| & \\
& \leq |s| + |\rho|_{\mathtt{e}} \cdot |t| & = |t| + |\rho|_{\mathtt{e}} \cdot |t| = (1 + |\rho|_{\mathtt{e}}) \cdot |t|
\end{array}
$$

2. We have to estimate $|\rho|_{\blacktriangle c} = |\rho|_{\blacktriangle c_4} + |\rho|_{\blacktriangle c_5} + |\rho|_{\blacktriangle c_6}$. Note that
   (a) $|\rho|_{\blacktriangle c_4} \leq |\rho|_{\blacktriangledown c_2}$, as $\leadsto_{\blacktriangle c_4}$ pops variables from F, pushed only by $\leadsto_{\blacktriangledown c_2}$;
   (b) $|\rho|_{\blacktriangle c_5} \leq |\rho|_{\blacktriangle c_6}$, as $\leadsto_{\blacktriangle c_5}$ pops pairs $(\bar{t}, \pi)$ from F, pushed only by $\leadsto_{\blacktriangle c_6}$;
   (c) $|\rho|_{\blacktriangle c_6} \leq |\rho|_{\blacktriangledown c_3}$, as $\leadsto_{\blacktriangle c_6}$ ends backtracking phases, started only by $\leadsto_{\blacktriangledown c_3}$.
   Then $|\rho|_{\blacktriangle c} \leq |\rho|_{\blacktriangledown c_2} + 2|\rho|_{\blacktriangledown c_3} \leq 2|\rho|_{\blacktriangledown c}$.
3. We have $|\rho|_c = |\rho|_{\blacktriangledown c} + |\rho|_{\blacktriangle c} \leq_{P.2} |\rho|_{\blacktriangledown c} + 2|\rho|_{\blacktriangledown c} =_{P.1} 3 \cdot (1 + |\rho|_{e}) \cdot |t|$.

Last, every transition but $\leadsto_{e}$ takes a constant time on a RAM. The renaming in a $\leadsto_{e}$ step is instead linear in $|\bar{t}|$, by the subterm invariant (Lemma 10). □

Acknowledgments. This work was partially supported by projects LOGOI ANR-2010-BLAN-0213-02, COQUAS ANR-12-JS02-006-01, ELICA ANR-14-CE25-0005, the Saint-Exupéry program funded by the French embassy and the Ministry of Education in Argentina, and the French–Argentinian laboratory in Computer Science INFINIS.

References

1. Abramsky, S., Ong, C.L.: Full abstraction in the lazy lambda calculus. Inf. Comput. **105**(2), 159–267 (1993)
2. Accattoli, B.: An abstract factorization theorem for explicit substitutions. In: RTA, pp. 6–21 (2012)
3. Accattoli, B., Barenbaum, P., Mazza, D.: Distilling abstract machines. In: ICFP, pp. 363–376 (2014)
4. Accattoli, B., Barenbaum, P., Mazza, D.: A strong distillery. CoRR abs/1509.00996 (2015). http://arxiv.org/abs/1509.00996
5. Accattoli, B., Bonelli, E., Kesner, D., Lombardi, C.: A nonstandard standardization theorem. In: POPL, pp. 659–670 (2014)
6. Accattoli, B., Dal Lago, U.: Beta Reduction is Invariant, Indeed. In: CSL-LICS, p. 8 (2014)
7. Accattoli, B., Sacerdoti Coen, C.: On the value of variables. In: Kohlenbach, U., Barceló, P., de Queiroz, R. (eds.) WoLLIC. LNCS, vol. 8652, pp. 36–50. Springer, Heidelberg (2014)
8. Accattoli, B., Sacerdoti Coen, C.: On the relative usefulness of fireballs. In: LICS, pp. 141–155 (2015)
9. Ariola, Z.M., Bohannon, A., Sabry, A.: Sequent calculi and abstract machines. ACM Trans. Program. Lang. Syst. **31**(4) (2009). Article No. 13
10. Biernacka, M., Danvy, O.: A concrete framework for environment machines. ACM Trans. Comput. Log. 9(1) (2007). Article No. 6
11. Boutiller, P.: De nouveaus outils pour manipuler les inductif en Coq. Ph.D. thesis, Université Paris Diderot - Paris 7 (2014)
12. de Carvalho, D.: Execution time of lambda-terms via denotational semantics and intersection types. CoRR abs/0905.4251 (2009)
13. Crégut, P.: An abstract machine for lambda-terms normalization. In: LISP and Functional Programming, pp. 333–340 (1990)
14. Crégut, P.: Strongly reducing variants of the Krivine abstract machine. High.-Order Symbolic Comput. **20**(3), 209–230 (2007)
15. Curien, P.: An abstract framework for environment machines. Theor. Comput. Sci. **82**(2), 389–402 (1991)
16. Danos, V., Regnier, L.: Head linear reduction (2004). (unpublished)

17. Danvy, O., Nielsen, L.R.: Refocusing in reduction semantics. Technical Report RS-04-26, BRICS (2004)
18. Danvy, O., Zerny, I.: A synthetic operational account of call-by-need evaluation. In: PPDP, pp. 97–108 (2013)
19. Dénès, M.: Étude formelle d'algorithmes efficaces en algèbre linéaire. Ph.D. thesis, Université de Nice - Sophia Antipolis (2013)
20. Ehrhard, T., Regnier, L.: Böhm trees, Krivine's machine and the taylor expansion of lambda-terms. In: Beckmann, A., Berger, U., Löwe, B., Tucker, J.V. (eds.) CiE 2006. LNCS, vol. 3988, pp. 186–197. Springer, Heidelberg (2006)
21. Fernández, M., Siafakas, N.: New developments in environment machines. Electr. Notes Theor. Comput. Sci. **237**, 57–73 (2009)
22. García-Pérez, Á., Nogueira, P., Moreno-Navarro, J.J.: Deriving the full-reducing krivine machine from the small-step operational semantics of normal order. In: PPDP, pp. 85–96 (2013)
23. Grégoire, B., Leroy, X.: A compiled implementation of strong reduction. In: ICFP, pp. 235–246 (2002)
24. Hardin, T., Maranget, L.: Functional runtime systems within the lambda-sigma calculus. J. Funct. Program. **8**(2), 131–176 (1998)
25. Lang, F.: Explaining the lazy Krivine machine using explicit substitution and addresses. High.-Order Symbolic Comput. **20**(3), 257–270 (2007)
26. Mascari, G., Pedicini, M.: Head linear reduction and pure proof net extraction. Theor. Comput. Sci. **135**(1), 111–137 (1994)
27. Milner, R.: Local bigraphs and confluence: two conjectures. Electr. Notes Theor. Comput. Sci. **175**(3), 65–73 (2007)
28. Plotkin, G.D.: Call-by-name, call-by-value and the lambda-calculus. Theor. Comput. Sci. **1**(2), 125–159 (1975)
29. Sands, D., Gustavsson, J., Moran, A.: Lambda calculi and linear speedups. In: Mogensen, T.Æ., Schmidt, D.A., Sudborough, I.H. (eds.) The Essence of Computation. LNCS, vol. 2566, pp. 60–82. Springer, Heidelberg (2002)
30. Smith, C.: Abstract machines for higher-order term sharing, Presented at IFL 2014

From Call-by-Value to Interaction by Typed Closure Conversion

Ulrich Schöpp(✉)

LMU Munich, Munich, Germany
Ulrich.Schoepp@ifi.lmu.de

Abstract. We study the efficient implementation of call-by-value using the structure of interactive computation models. This structure has been useful in applications to resource-bounded compilation, but much of the existing work in this area has focused on call-by-name programming languages. This paper works towards the goal of a simple, efficient treatment of call-by-value languages. In previous work we have studied CPS-translation as an approach to implementing call-by-value and have observed that it needs to be refined in order to achieve efficient space usage. In this paper we give an alternative presentation of the refined translation, which is close to existing methods of typed closure conversion. We show that a simple correctness proof following Benton and Hur is possible for this formulation. Moreover, we extend previous work to cover full recursion in the source language.

1 Introduction

Recent advances in compiler verification, resource-bounded compilation, and resource usage certification underline the value of a good understanding of the properties of low-level computation. Certifying correctness and resource usage of compiled low-level programs makes it important to have a good understanding of their structure. While individually low-level programs have little structure, interesting structure appears when one considers them collectively and studies how they can be constructed and composed. For example for separate compilation and low-level program linking, perhaps of programs written in different programming languages, one is interested in the possible ways of composing of low-level programs. For resource-bounded compilation, one is interested in the resource usage of compiled programs, e.g. with respect to memory usage or execution time. Resource usage is a property of low-level programs and it is desirable to obtain a compositional understanding of such resource usage properties.

One line of investigation to identify useful mathematical structure of low-level computation consists of applying ideas from interaction semantics to low-level computation. Ideas from interaction semantics have been applied independently in a number of contexts, mainly for applications where particular control of low-level aspects is required. Examples include the interactive implementation of functional programs [12], abstract machines [4], hardware synthesis from functional programs [7], functional programming with logarithmic space [3], distributed programming [6], quantum programming languages [8], to mention just a

X. Feng and S. Park (Eds.): APLAS 2015, LNCS 9458, pp. 251–270, 2015.
DOI: 10.1007/978-3-319-26529-2_14

few. While much of the work in this area was concerned with call-by-name programming languages, the success of the approach motivates an increasing interest in applying these ideas to call-by-value computation. In addition to early approaches [5], call-by-value has received more attention recently [10,11,17].

In this paper we study a decomposition of call-by-value into the structure found in interactive models. This continues the work reported in [17,18] which investigates an approach of factoring the translation from a call-by-value source language to a first-order low-level language through a higher-order low-level calculus INT. This calculus is based on the structure of interactive computation models and captures structure of low-level computation in terms of a higher-order λ-calculus. Higher-order functions capture concepts of low-level code modules, their interfaces and their composition, see [18] for details. Factoring the translation from call-by-value to a first-order low-level language through this higher-order calculus allows one to use standard high-level proof techniques from semantics to show correctness of the translation from call-by-value to the first-order low-level language [17].

Here we develop the work reported in [17] on a decomposition of call-by-value computation that is suitable for targeting a calculus of interactive computation, such as INT. The aim of this paper is first to simplify the translation from [17], to formulate it in a direct style, close to other approaches to typed closure conversion [1,13], and second to generalise the correctness argument to include recursion in the source language.

The first contribution of this paper is to simplify the translation from [17], which is defined as a CPS-translation. It is observed in [17] that while it is possible to use a standard call-by-value CPS-translation to translate a call-by-value source language to INT, this would lead to an implementation of call-by-value with inefficient space usage. To address this, we propose in [17] a refined CPS-translation that makes the environment of all values explicit, so that unneeded values may be discarded explicitly when they are not needed anymore. The idea is to use a continuation "monad" of the form

$$(\forall \alpha.\ X(\alpha) \multimap \bot^{\alpha}) \multimap \bot^{\beta}, \tag{1}$$

where $\multimap$ can be thought of as a function type that formalises module abstraction and composition (similar to functors in ML) and where $\bot^{\alpha}$ denotes a standard strict function space $\alpha \to \bot$. Terms of the above type represent source programs as follows. The type β should be thought of as a first-order type of the environments of the source program, e.g. the tuples of the values of its free variables, and the type α is a first-order type whose values can encode the possible values of the source term. To compute the source program, one throws its environment into $\bot^{\beta}$. This forces the computation of the program value, whose code will be returned to us by being thrown into $\bot^{\alpha}$. That α is universally quantified means that we must accept any possible encoding of the source value. In order to nevertheless make use of such an encoding, we are also provided with an argument of type $X(\alpha)$. This gives us an interface for making use of the value of type α we were give as the code for a source value. In the case of functions, $X(\alpha)$ will provide a way to apply any function given to us in the form of a code in α.

In this paper we simplify the translation by formulating it in a direct way. Instead of the above type we use a type of the form

$$\exists \alpha.\, X(\alpha) \otimes (\beta \to \alpha), \tag{2}$$

where $\otimes$ can be understood as a pairing operation on modules. This translation can be explained just as above; it represents the above way of computing source values more directly. The simplification makes it easier to define and hopefully also to understand the translation. The result is a translation that is quite close to existing methods of typed closure conversion [1,13], which allows us to connect such techniques to work on the applications of interaction semantics [7,10].

We note that, when we use INT as a target for the translation, then the reformulation has no effect on the resulting first-order low-level programs. In INT (suitably extended with existential types) the types $(\forall\alpha.\, X(\alpha) \multimap \bot^{\alpha}) \multimap \bot^{\beta}$ and $\exists\alpha.X(\alpha) \times (\beta \to \alpha)$ lead to first-order low-level programs with the same interface. The translations are such that the programs turn out to be the same too. This establishes a formal connection between a CPS-translation and a typed closure conversion. In this paper, we use the term closure conversion to mean a conversion that makes the representation and manipulation of function closures fully explicit.

The second main contribution of this paper is to extend the correctness proof of the translation to cover recursion in the source language. To do so we follow the approach of Benton and Hur [2]. The resulting correctness proof uses a form of $^{\top\top}$-lifting and turns out to be pleasingly simple.

While the translation of call-by-value presented in this paper is intended to target languages such as INT, it is not necessary to explain the particular details of INT. We present the translation more generally as a translation from a call-by-value source language to a variant of Idealized Algol [14]. Indeed, INT can be seen as variant of Idealized Algol with type annotations that make low-level computation details explicit. The point of this paper is to present the translation and its soundness proof. While the low-level details of the implementation of the target Algol-like language are interesting for understanding the overall implementation of call-by-value, here we focus just on the step to such an Algol-like language.

As a result we obtain a simple typed translation of call-by-value to the structure found in interaction semantics. The translation is quite similar to existing typed closure conversion approaches, which makes the results from this work available in the interactive context. While the translation presented in this paper is close to existing methods of closure conversion, it is not exactly the same, and it is not immediate to re-target the existing ones directly to Algol-like target languages with a call-by-name semantics.

By targeting Algol-like languages, we hope to be able to apply the results on call-by-value to resource-bounded situations. In particular, the Geometry of Synthesis [7] and the LOGSPACE-fragment of INT [3] are instances of Algol-like languages that are based on interaction semantics and that are interesting to study in further work.

An important feature of the translation in this paper is its compositionality. Open terms of the source language are translated to target programs with a well-specified interface. By composing the translation with an interpretation in INT, one obtains a well-defined interface of the low-level code arising from open source terms. This may be used to define a low-level calling convention for call-by-value.

The interfaces are formulated so that the choice of closure representation remains abstract. It is possible to translate parts of the same source terms using different closure representations and combine the translated programs to obtain a correct whole program. We believe that this is useful for studying separate compilation and linking of programs that are written in different languages.

2 Source Language

Our source language is a variant of call-by-value PCF. In this section we begin by fixing the details of this language. Its types and terms are defined as follows.

$$
\begin{aligned}
X, Y &::= \mathbb{N} \mid X \to Y \\
s, t &::= x \mid \mathtt{fn}\ x \Rightarrow t \mid \mathtt{fun}\ f\ x \Rightarrow t \mid s\ t \\
&\quad\mid \mathtt{zero} \mid \mathtt{succ}(s) \mid \mathtt{if0}\ s\ \mathtt{then}\ t_1\ \mathtt{else}\ t_2
\end{aligned}
$$

The term $\mathtt{fun}\ f\ x \Rightarrow t$ represents a recursive function definition with the intended operational semantics $(\mathtt{fun}\ f\ x \Rightarrow t)\ v \longrightarrow t[(\mathtt{fun}\ f\ x \Rightarrow t)/f, v/x]$. We omit type annotations on abstractions, as we will work with typing derivations, so that such annotations are not important for our purposes.

The typing rules for the source language appear in Fig. 1. We make the structural rules explicit, as this makes it clear where variable duplication is needed later in the translation. The typing rule for `if-then-else` is restricted to base types. This simplifies the technical development and allows us to focus on the issues pertaining to recursion. We believe that the results in this paper can be extended to an unrestricted instance of this rule. For the time being, one may reduce case-distinction on function types to base-type case-distinction in the source language, e.g. replacing $\mathtt{if0}\ x\ \mathtt{then}\ (\mathtt{fn}\ y \Rightarrow t_1)\ \mathtt{else}\ (\mathtt{fn}\ y \Rightarrow t_2)$ with $\mathtt{fn}\ y \Rightarrow \mathtt{if0}\ x\ \mathtt{then}\ t_1\ \mathtt{else}\ t_2$.

The aim in this paper is to give a correct implementation of this source language. The proof of correctness proceeds by an argument close to that of Benton and Hur [2]. It shows that the implementation correctly implements the standard denotational semantics of the source language [19]. The semantics of types is given by $[\![\mathbb{N}]\!] = \mathbb{N}$ and $[\![X \to Y]\!] = [\![X]\!] \Rightarrow [\![Y]\!]_\bot$, where $\mathbb{N}$ is the discrete cpo of the natural numbers, where $(-)_\bot$ denotes the lifting operation, and where $D \Rightarrow E$ is the cpo of continuous functions from cpo D to cpo E. We write $\lfloor - \rfloor \colon D \to D_\bot$ for the injection of a cpo D into its lifting. The interpretation of types is extended to contexts in the standard way, i.e. if Γ is $x_1{:}X_1, \dots, x_n{:}X_n$, then $[\![\Gamma]\!]$ is $[\![X_1]\!] \times \dots \times [\![X_n]\!]$.

For each derivation Π of $\Gamma \vdash t \colon X$ in the source language, one defines an interpretation $[\![\Pi]\!] \in [\![\Gamma]\!] \Rightarrow [\![X]\!]_\bot$ in the usual way [19].

$$\text{VAR}\ \frac{}{x{:}X \vdash x\colon X} \qquad \text{WEAK}\ \frac{\Gamma \vdash t\colon Y}{\Gamma, \Delta \vdash t\colon Y} \qquad \text{EXCH}\ \frac{\Gamma,\ y{:}Y,\ x{:}X,\ \Delta \vdash t\colon Z}{\Gamma,\ x{:}X,\ y{:}Y,\ \Delta \vdash t\colon Z}$$

$$\text{CONTR}\ \frac{\Gamma,\ x{:}X,\ y{:}X,\ \Delta \vdash t\colon Y}{\Gamma,\ z{:}X,\ \Delta \vdash t[z/x, z/y]\colon Y} \qquad \text{ZERO}\ \frac{}{\Gamma \vdash \mathtt{zero}\colon \mathbb{N}} \qquad \text{SUCC}\ \frac{\Gamma \vdash t\colon \mathbb{N}}{\Gamma \vdash \mathtt{succ}(t)\colon \mathbb{N}}$$

$$\text{ABS}\ \frac{\Gamma,\ x{:}X \vdash t\colon Y}{\Gamma \vdash \mathtt{fn}\, x \Rightarrow t\colon X \to Y} \qquad \text{APP}\ \frac{\Gamma \vdash s\colon X \to Y \qquad \Delta \vdash t\colon X}{\Gamma, \Delta \vdash s\, t\colon Y}$$

$$\text{IF}\ \frac{\Gamma \vdash s\colon \mathbb{N} \qquad \Delta_1 \vdash t_1\colon \mathbb{N} \qquad \Delta_2 \vdash t_2\colon \mathbb{N}}{\Gamma, \Delta_1, \Delta_2 \vdash \mathtt{if0}\ s\ \mathtt{then}\ t_1\ \mathtt{else}\ t_2\colon \mathbb{N}} \qquad \text{REC}\ \frac{\Gamma,\ f{:}X \to Y,\ x{:}X \vdash t\colon Y}{\Gamma \vdash \mathtt{fun}\, f\, x \Rightarrow t\colon X \to Y}$$

Fig. 1. Source typing rules

3 Target Language

We translate the source language to a target language that is close in spirit to Idealized Algol [14]. As outlined in the Introduction, this choice is motivated by the development of the calculus INT [16,18], which can be seen as an Algol-like language with a type system that allows for the control of low-level aspects of computation. By translating the source language to INT, one obtains a fully specified translation to a simple first-order low-level language. Here, we concentrate on the translation from the source language to Algol-like languages, as definition of the translation and its correctness does not depend on the particular details of INT. This allows us to concentrate on the essential issues of the translation.

The core of the target language has the following types.

$$\begin{aligned} \text{Value Types } A, B &::= \alpha \mid \mathtt{void} \mid \mathtt{unit} \mid \mathtt{nat} \mid A \times B \\ \text{Types } X, Y &::= \mathtt{exp}(A, B) \mid X \to Y \mid X \times Y \mid \forall \alpha.\, X \mid \exists \alpha.\, X \end{aligned}$$

The type $\mathtt{exp}(A, B)$ is meant to contain (strict) functions that map values of type A to values of type B. This is a slight generalisation of Idealized Algol, which only has a type $\mathtt{exp}(A)$ corresponding to $\mathtt{exp}(\mathtt{unit}, A)$.

At first it may appear that this target language is of similar expressiveness as the source language. However, note first that in the type $\mathtt{exp}(A, B)$, both A and B are restricted to be value types. This means that call-by-value functions are not available directly in this language. Of course, it is possible to represent call-by-value computation by means of a call-by-value CPS-translation, for example. However, we have observed in [17] that such a CPS-translation would generally not result in a space-efficient implementation of the source language.

In the target language, the terms of type $\mathtt{exp}(A, B)$ are our basic notion of computation. We use the higher-order structure only to compose such computations and to organise them, much like in [18]. The reader should think of a term of type $\mathtt{exp}(A, B) \to \mathtt{exp}(C, D)$ less as a function and more as a program that expects to be connected with a module that contains a function from A to B and that then provides a function from C to D. In OCaml notation this would roughly amount to functor of the following type:

```
functor (X: sig val t: A -> B end) -> sig val t: C -> D end
```

Indeed, one could use a language with ML-style modules as a target language in this paper. Notice, in particular, that the universal and existential quantification in the target language are restricted to range over value types only. However, it seems that a lambda-calculus is more convenient as a language for defining and composing modules [15,18].

The terms of the target language are standard for all but the type $\mathtt{exp}(A, B)$. For this type it is also possible to follow the standard approach for Idealized Algol and define the terms of this type using suitable constants. In Idealized Algol one finds constants like $\mathtt{succ}\colon \mathtt{exp(nat)} \to \mathtt{exp(nat)}$ and a similar approach can be taken for $\mathtt{exp}(A, B)$. A possible choice of constants for this type could include constants such as the following:

$$\begin{aligned} \mathtt{proj}\colon & \mathtt{exp}(A \times B, B) \\ \mathtt{pair}\colon & \mathtt{exp}(C, A) \times \mathtt{exp}(C, B) \to \mathtt{exp}(C, A \times B) \\ \mathtt{seq}\colon & \mathtt{exp}(C, A) \times \mathtt{exp}(C \times A, B) \to \mathtt{exp}(C, B) \end{aligned}$$

However, working with such constants is somewhat awkward syntactically.

We therefore define a slightly extended target calculus that allows a simpler, more direct, definition of terms of type $\mathtt{exp}(A, B)$ as in [18]. It also contains the type $\mathtt{exp}(A)$, which is familiar from Idealized Algol and corresponds to $\mathtt{exp}(\mathtt{unit}, A)$.

$$\begin{aligned} \text{Value Types } A, B &::= \alpha \mid \mathtt{void} \mid \mathtt{unit} \mid \mathtt{nat} \mid A \times B \\ \text{Types } X, Y &::= \mathtt{exp}(A) \mid \mathtt{exp}(A, B) \mid X \to Y \mid X \times Y \mid \forall \alpha.\, X \mid \exists \alpha.\, X \end{aligned}$$

We use the abbreviations $I := \mathtt{exp}(\mathtt{void}, \mathtt{void})$ for a vacuous type with a single inhabitant $\star := (\mathtt{fn}\ v{:}\mathtt{void} \Rightarrow \mathtt{return}\ v)$. (Note that I is not isomorphic to $\mathtt{exp}(\mathtt{unit}, \mathtt{unit})$, which has two inhabitants, the function returning $\langle\rangle$ and the non-terminating function.)

The terms are given by the grammar below, in which n ranges over natural numbers.

$$\begin{aligned} \text{Values } v, w &::= x \mid \langle\rangle \mid \langle v, w\rangle \mid n \\ \text{Terms } s, t &::= x \mid \mathtt{return}\ v \mid \mathtt{let}\ x = s\ \mathtt{in}\ t \mid \mathtt{if0}\ v\ s\ t \mid \mathtt{fn}\ x{:}A \Rightarrow t \mid t(v) \\ &\mid \lambda x{:}X.t \mid s\ t \mid \langle s, t\rangle \mid \mathtt{let}\ \langle x, y\rangle = s\ \mathtt{in}\ t \\ &\mid \Lambda\alpha.t \mid t\ A \mid \mathtt{pack}_X(A, t) \mid \mathtt{let}\ \mathtt{pack}(\alpha, x) = s\ \mathtt{in}\ t \\ &\mid \mathtt{fix}_X^n \mid \mathtt{fix}_X \end{aligned}$$

We write $\langle t_1, t_2, \ldots, t_k\rangle$ as an abbreviation for $\langle \ldots \langle t_1, t_2\rangle \ldots, t_k\rangle$, i.e. pairs associate to the left. We will often omit type annotations, such as the X in $\mathtt{pack}_X(A, t)$, for readability.

The terms include constructs that allow one to view the elements of type $\mathtt{exp}(A, B)$ as functions. Terms of this type can be defined using an abstraction $\mathtt{fn}\ x{:}A \Rightarrow t$. In this term the body t must have type $\mathtt{exp}(B)$, which is why we have included types of the form $\mathtt{exp}(B)$ in the language. Elements of type

$$\frac{}{\Gamma,\, x{:}A \vdash x\colon A} \qquad \frac{}{\Gamma \vdash \langle\rangle\colon \mathtt{unit}} \qquad \frac{}{\Gamma \vdash n\colon \mathbb{N}}$$

$$\frac{\Gamma \vdash v\colon A \qquad \Gamma \vdash w\colon B}{\Gamma \vdash \langle v, w\rangle\colon A \times B} \qquad \frac{\Gamma \vdash v\colon A \times B \qquad \Gamma,\, x{:}A,\, y{:}B \vdash w\colon C}{\Gamma \vdash \mathtt{let}\ \langle x, y\rangle = v\ \mathtt{in}\ w\colon C}$$

Fig. 2. Target language: Terms of value types

$$\frac{}{\Gamma \mid \Delta,\, x{:}X \vdash x\colon X}$$

$$\frac{\Gamma \vdash v\colon A}{\Gamma \mid \Delta \vdash \mathtt{return}\ v\colon \mathtt{exp}(A)} \qquad \frac{\Gamma \mid \Delta \vdash s\colon \mathtt{exp}(A) \qquad \Gamma,\, x{:}A \mid \Delta \vdash t\colon \mathtt{exp}(B)}{\Gamma \mid \Delta \vdash \mathtt{let}\ x = s\ \mathtt{in}\ t\colon \mathtt{exp}(B)}$$

$$\frac{\Gamma \vdash v\colon \mathbb{N} \qquad \Gamma \mid \Delta \vdash s\colon \mathtt{exp}(A) \qquad \Gamma \mid \Delta \vdash t\colon \mathtt{exp}(A)}{\Gamma \mid \Delta \vdash \mathtt{if0}\ v\ \mathtt{then}\ s\ \mathtt{else}\ t\colon \mathtt{exp}(A)}$$

$$\frac{\Gamma,\, x{:}A \mid \Delta \vdash t\colon \mathtt{exp}(B)}{\Gamma \mid \Delta \vdash \mathtt{fn}\ x{:}A \Rightarrow t\colon \mathtt{exp}(A, B)} \qquad \frac{\Gamma \mid \Delta \vdash t\colon \mathtt{exp}(A, B) \qquad \Gamma \vdash v\colon A}{\Gamma \mid \Delta \vdash t(v)\colon \mathtt{exp}(B)}$$

$$\frac{\Gamma \mid \Delta,\, x{:}X \vdash t\colon Y}{\Gamma \mid \Delta \vdash \lambda x{:}X.\, t\colon X \to Y} \qquad \frac{\Gamma \mid \Delta \vdash s\colon X \to Y \qquad \Gamma \mid \Delta \vdash t\colon X}{\Gamma \mid \Delta \vdash s\, t\colon Y}$$

$$\frac{\Gamma \mid \Delta \vdash s\colon X \qquad \Gamma \mid \Delta \vdash t\colon Y}{\Gamma \mid \Delta \vdash \langle s, t\rangle\colon X \times Y} \qquad \frac{\Gamma \mid \Delta \vdash s\colon X \times Y \qquad \Gamma \mid \Delta,\, x{:}X,\, y{:}Y \vdash t\colon Z}{\Gamma \mid \Delta \vdash \mathtt{let}\ \langle x, y\rangle = s\ \mathtt{in}\ t\colon Z}$$

$$\frac{\Gamma \mid \Delta \vdash t\colon X}{\Gamma \mid \Delta \vdash \Lambda\alpha.\, t\colon \forall\alpha.\, X}\ (*) \qquad \frac{\Gamma \mid \Delta \vdash t\colon \forall\alpha.\, X}{\Gamma \mid \Delta \vdash t\, A\colon X[A/\alpha]}$$

$$\frac{\Gamma \mid \Delta \vdash t\colon X[A/\alpha]}{\Gamma \mid \Delta \vdash \mathtt{pack}_{\exists\alpha.\, X}(A, t)\colon \exists\alpha.\, X} \qquad \frac{\Gamma \mid \Delta \vdash s\colon \exists\alpha.\, X \qquad \Gamma \mid \Delta,\, x{:}X \vdash t\colon Z}{\Gamma \mid \Delta \vdash \mathtt{let}\ \mathtt{pack}(\alpha, x) = s\ \mathtt{in}\ t\colon Z}\ (*)$$

$$\frac{}{\Gamma \mid \Delta \vdash \mathtt{fix}_X\colon (X \to X) \to X} \qquad \frac{}{\Gamma \mid \Delta \vdash \mathtt{fix}^i_X\colon (X \to X) \to X}$$

$(*)$ — α not free in Γ, Δ

Fig. 3. Target language: Terms

$\mathtt{exp}(B)$ can be defined using $\mathtt{return}\ v$, and the term $\mathtt{let}\ x = t_1\ \mathtt{in}\ t_2$ can be used to sequence computations $t_1 \colon \mathtt{exp}(B_1)$ and $t_2 \colon \mathtt{exp}(B_2)$. For a term t of type $\mathtt{exp}(A, B)$, there is an application $t(v)$. It is restricted to values as arguments, which corresponds to the view of $\mathtt{exp}(A, B)$ as strict functions from values of type A to values of type B.

The typing rules for the target calculus are given in Figs. 2 and 3. The typing judgements have the form $\Gamma \vdash t \colon A$ for value types A and $\Gamma \mid \Delta \vdash t \colon X$ for types X, where Γ is a value context of the form $x_1{:}A_1, \dots, x_n{:}A_n$ (the A_i range over value types) and Δ is a context $y_1{:}Y_1, \dots, y_n{:}Y_n$ (the Y_i range over types). We identify these contexts up to reordering of variable declarations.

The value context is there to allow the formulation of the term constructs for the types $\mathtt{exp}(A)$ and $\mathtt{exp}(A, B)$. If one were to prefer a formulation of the calculus with constants for $\mathtt{exp}(A, B)$, as mentioned above, then the value context Γ could be replaced with a context of the form $x_1{:}\mathtt{exp}(A_1), \dots, x_n{:}\mathtt{exp}(A_n)$. We prefer the version with two contexts, as it clarifies which terms can be assumed to denote values.

3.1 Equational Theory

We assume a standard equational theory for the target language. Equations are given in context, i.e. they are given by a judgement of the form $\Gamma \mid \Delta \vdash s = t \colon X$. For brevity, we state equations without typing contexts, but with the understanding that the equations are subject to suitable typing constraints.

$$
\begin{aligned}
\mathtt{let}\ \langle x, y\rangle = \langle s, t\rangle\ \mathtt{in}\ u &= u[s/x, t/y] && (\times\beta)\\
\mathtt{let}\ \langle x, y\rangle = s\ \mathtt{in}\ t[\langle x, y\rangle/z] &= t[s/z] \quad \text{if } x, y \text{ not free in } t && (\times\eta)\\
(\lambda x{:}X.\, s)\ t &= s[t/x] && (\to\beta)\\
\lambda x{:}X.\, (t\ x) &= t \quad \text{if } x \text{ not free in } t && (\to\eta)\\
(\Lambda\alpha.\, t)\ A &= t[A/\alpha] && (\forall\beta)\\
\Lambda\alpha.\, t\ \alpha &= t \quad \text{if } \alpha \text{ not free in } t && (\forall\eta)\\
\mathtt{let}\ \mathtt{pack}(\alpha, x) = \mathtt{pack}(A, s)\ \mathtt{in}\ t &= t[A/\alpha, s/x] && (\exists\beta)\\
\mathtt{let}\ \mathtt{pack}(\alpha, x) = s\ \mathtt{in}\ t[\mathtt{pack}(\alpha, x)/y] &= t[s/y] \quad \text{if } \alpha, x \text{ not free in } t && (\exists\eta)\\
\mathtt{fix}_X\ t &= t\ (\mathtt{fix}_X\ t) && (\mathtt{fix}\beta)\\
\mathtt{fix}_X^{i+1}\ t &= t\ (\mathtt{fix}_X^{i}\ t) && (\mathtt{fix}^i\beta)
\end{aligned}
$$

Equation $(\times\eta)$ is formulated with $t[\langle x, y\rangle/z]$ instead of just $\langle x, y\rangle$, in order to make commuting conversions derivable.

For the terms for the types $\mathtt{exp}(A)$ and $\mathtt{exp}(A, B)$ and for value types, we assume the following equations.

$$
\begin{aligned}
(\mathtt{fn}\ x{:}A \Rightarrow t)(v) &= t[v/x] && (\mathtt{exp}\beta)\\
\mathtt{fn}\ x{:}A \Rightarrow (t(x)) &= t \quad \text{if } x \text{ not free in } t && (\mathtt{exp}\eta)\\
\mathtt{let}\ x = \mathtt{return}\ v\ \mathtt{in}\ t &= t[v/x] && (\mathtt{let1})
\end{aligned}
$$

$$\texttt{let } x = (\texttt{let } y = s \texttt{ in } t) \texttt{ in } u = \texttt{let } y = s \texttt{ in let } x = t \texttt{ in } u \qquad (\texttt{let2})$$

$$\texttt{succ}(n) = n + 1 \qquad (\texttt{succ})$$

$$\texttt{if0 } 0 \texttt{ then } v \texttt{ else } w = v \qquad (\texttt{if1})$$

$$\texttt{if0 } n \texttt{ then } v \texttt{ else } w = w \quad \text{if } n > 0 \qquad (\texttt{if2})$$

(The equations for $\times$ also hold for terms of value types; we do not repeat them here.) Finally, there are rules for reflexivity, symmetry, transitivity and there are congruence rules that allow one to apply these equations in any context.

4 Translation

We are now ready to define the translation from source to target language. It is compositional and identifies an interface in the target language for the translation of each subterm of a source term.

For each source type X, we define a family $\mathcal{C}[\![X]\!]_A$ of value types and a family $\mathcal{I}[\![X]\!]_A$ of types, both families being indexed by a value type A.

$$\mathcal{C}[\![\mathbb{N}]\!]_A := \texttt{nat} \qquad \mathcal{C}[\![X \to Y]\!]_A := A$$

$$\mathcal{I}[\![\mathbb{N}]\!]_A := I \qquad \mathcal{I}[\![X \to Y]\!]_A := \forall \beta. \mathcal{I}[\![X]\!]_\beta \to \mathcal{M}[\![Y]\!]_{A \times \mathcal{C}[\![X]\!]_\beta}$$

where

$$\mathcal{M}[\![X]\!]_A := \exists \beta. \mathcal{I}[\![X]\!]_\beta \times \texttt{exp}(A, \mathcal{C}[\![X]\!]_\beta)$$

The intention is that a source language value of type X is represented by a target language value $c\colon \mathcal{C}[\![X]\!]_A$ and a term $a\colon \mathcal{I}[\![X]\!]_A$, where A may be any value type. The type $\mathcal{M}[\![X]\!]_A$ corresponds to (2) in the Introduction.

For the type of natural numbers, the choice of $\mathcal{C}[\![\mathbb{N}]\!]_A$ is such that we can simply choose c to be the represented number. The term a is not important for natural numbers, as all relevant information is already in c. Therefore, we choose the type $\mathcal{I}[\![\mathbb{N}]\!]_A$ to be vacuous.

Values of function type $X \to Y$, are represented by a value $c\colon A$ and a term a of type $\forall \beta. \mathcal{I}[\![X]\!]_\beta \to \mathcal{M}[\![Y]\!]_{A \times \mathcal{C}[\![X]\!]_\beta}$, where A may be an arbitrary value type. The idea is that c is a code value for the function, which may be encoded in any way using an arbitrary value type A. Of course, if we allow an arbitrary encoding, then we must explain how the code c can be used to apply the function. This is what the term a does. Suppose $c_x\colon \mathcal{C}[\![X]\!]_{A_X}$ and $a_x\colon \mathcal{I}[\![X]\!]_{A_X}$ represent a value of type X. Then a allows us to obtain a code for the result of the application of the function encoded by c and a to the argument encoded by c_x and a_x. Applying a to A_x and a_x amounts to connecting the module a_x to a. We obtain a term $a\ A_x\ a_x$ of type $\exists \alpha. \mathcal{I}[\![Y]\!]_\alpha \times \texttt{exp}(A \times \mathcal{C}[\![X]\!]_{A_x}, \mathcal{C}[\![Y]\!]_\alpha)$. The function in the second component takes a pair of type $A \times \mathcal{C}[\![X]\!]_{A_x}$ consisting of the code for the function and the code for the argument. It returns a code for the result of the function application. Since the type α is existentially quantified, the type that is used to represent the result of the function application is abstract. The first component $\mathcal{I}[\![Y]\!]_\alpha$ allows us to make use of values encoded using α.

This application procedure is captured by the following application term.

$$\begin{aligned}\texttt{app}((A,a,c),(A_x,a_x,c_x))&\colon \exists\alpha.\,\mathcal{I}[\![Y]\!]_\alpha\times\texttt{exp}(\texttt{unit},\mathcal{C}[\![Y]\!]_\alpha)\\ \texttt{app}((A,a,c),(A_x,a_x,c_x)) &:= \texttt{let pack}(\alpha_y,\langle a_y,e_y\rangle)=a\ A_x\ a_x\ \texttt{in}\\ &\qquad \texttt{pack}(\alpha_y,\langle a_y,\texttt{fn}\ \langle\rangle\Rightarrow e_y(\langle c,c_x\rangle)\rangle)\end{aligned}$$

Here, and in the rest of the paper, we allow ourselves some syntactic sugar for pattern matching in fn-function and to avoid nested let-terms.

The translation from source to target language is defined by induction on the typing derivation. To define it, we extend the definition of $\mathcal{C}[\![-]\!]$ to source contexts by:

$$\mathcal{C}[\![\text{empty}]\!] := \texttt{unit} \qquad\qquad \mathcal{C}[\![\Gamma,\ x{:}X]\!]_{\vec{B},A} := \mathcal{C}[\![\Gamma]\!]_{\vec{B}}\times\mathcal{C}[\![X]\!]_A$$

A derivation Π of a source sequent $\Gamma\vdash t\colon Y$, where Γ is $x_1{:}X_1,\dots,x_k{:}X_k$, is then translated to a closed target term $(|\Pi|)$ of type

$$\forall\alpha_1\dots\alpha_k.\ \mathcal{I}[\![X_1]\!]_{\alpha_1}\to\cdots\to\mathcal{I}[\![X_k]\!]_{\alpha_k}\to\mathcal{M}[\![Y]\!]_{\mathcal{C}[\![\Gamma]\!]_{\vec{\alpha}}}.$$

The definition of $(|\Pi|)$ is given by induction on the derivation Π of $\Gamma\vdash t\colon X$.

- Case: Π is

$$\text{VAR}\frac{}{x{:}X\vdash x\colon X}$$

$$(|\Pi|) := \Lambda\alpha.\,\lambda a\colon\mathcal{I}[\![X]\!]_\alpha.\,\texttt{pack}(\alpha,\langle a,\texttt{fn}\ \langle\langle\rangle,x\rangle\Rightarrow\texttt{return}\ x\rangle)$$

- Case: Π ends with rule (WEAK), whose premise is derived by Π_t.

$$\text{WEAK}\frac{\Gamma\vdash t\colon Y}{\Gamma,\Delta\vdash t\colon Y}$$

$$\begin{aligned}(|\Pi|) &:= \Lambda\vec{\alpha}\vec{\beta}.\,\lambda\vec{a}\vec{b}.\ \texttt{let pack}(A_t,\langle a_t,e_t\rangle)=(|\Pi_t|)\ \vec{\alpha}\ \vec{a}\ \texttt{in}\\ &\qquad\texttt{pack}(A_t,\langle a_t,\texttt{fn}\ (\vec{x},\vec{y})\Rightarrow e_t(\vec{x})\rangle)\end{aligned}$$

  Here we use an informal pattern matching notation $(\vec{x},\vec{y})$ that matches $\vec{x}$ against the code values for Γ and $\vec{y}$ against the values for Δ.

  We omit the similar cases for the other structural rules.

- Case: Π ends with rule (ABS), whose premise is derived by Π_t.

$$\text{ABS}\frac{\Gamma,\ x{:}X\vdash t\colon Y}{\Gamma\vdash\texttt{fn}\ x\Rightarrow t\colon X\to Y}$$

$$(|\Pi|) := \Lambda\vec{\alpha}.\,\lambda\vec{x}.\,\texttt{pack}(\mathcal{C}[\![\Gamma]\!]_{\vec{\alpha}},\langle(\Lambda\beta.\,\lambda x{:}\mathcal{I}[\![X]\!]_\beta.\,(|\Pi_t|)\ \vec{\alpha}\ \beta\ \vec{x}\ x),\texttt{fn}\ c\Rightarrow\texttt{return}\ c\rangle)$$

In this definition we choose the type $\mathcal{C}[\![\Gamma]\!]_{\vec{\alpha}}$ for the code type to represent the function defined by the abstraction. The function $\mathtt{fn}\ c \Rightarrow \mathtt{return}\ c$ gets as argument the tuple of the values of the variables in Γ and returns the code unchanged as the code for the function.

Notice that the term $(|\Pi_t|)\ \vec{\alpha}\ \beta\ \vec{x}\ x$ has type $\mathcal{M}[\![Y]\!]_{\mathcal{C}[\![\Gamma,\, x:X]\!]_{\vec{\alpha},\beta}}$, which is the same as $\mathcal{M}[\![Y]\!]_{\mathcal{C}[\![\Gamma]\!]_{\vec{\alpha}} \times \mathcal{C}[\![X]\!]_{\beta}}$. By our choice of $\mathcal{C}[\![\Gamma]\!]_{\vec{\alpha}}$ as the code type, the pair $\mathcal{C}[\![\Gamma]\!]_{\vec{\alpha}} \times \mathcal{C}[\![X]\!]_{\beta}$ can be understood as the pair of the function code and its argument, as is required for the translation of functions.

While we have chosen the tuple of the free variables for function codes here, other choices are possible, and can be made differently on a case-by-case basis.

- Case: Π ends with rule (APP), whose premises are derived by Π_s and Π_t.

$$\text{APP}\frac{\Gamma \vdash s\colon X \to Y \qquad \Delta \vdash t\colon X}{\Gamma,\, \Delta \vdash s\ t\colon Y}$$

$$\begin{aligned}(|\Pi|) \ :=\ \Lambda\vec{\alpha}\vec{\beta}.\,\lambda\vec{x}.\,\lambda\vec{y}.\ & \mathtt{let\ pack}(\varphi, \langle f, e_f\rangle) = (|\Pi_s|)\ \vec{\alpha}\ \vec{x}\ \mathtt{in} \\ & \mathtt{let\ pack}(\xi, \langle x, e_x\rangle) = (|\Pi_t|)\ \vec{\beta}\ \vec{y}\ \mathtt{in} \\ & \mathtt{let\ pack}(\rho, \langle y, a\rangle) = f\ \xi\ x\ \mathtt{in} \\ & \mathtt{pack}(\rho, \langle y, e\rangle)\end{aligned}$$

where e is $\mathtt{fn}\ (\vec{x}, \vec{y}) \Rightarrow \mathtt{let}\ v_f = e_f(\vec{x})\ \mathtt{in\ let}\ v_x = e_x(\vec{y})\ \mathtt{in}\ a(\langle v_f, v_x\rangle)$.

- Case: Π ends with rule (ZERO).

$$\text{ZERO}\frac{}{\Gamma \vdash \mathtt{zero}\colon \mathbb{N}}$$

$$(|\Pi|) \ :=\ \Lambda\vec{\alpha}.\,\lambda\vec{x}.\,\mathtt{pack}(\mathtt{unit}, \langle \star, \mathtt{fn}\ g \Rightarrow \mathtt{return}\ 0\rangle)$$

- Case: Π ends with rule (SUCC), whose premise is derived by Π_t.

$$\text{SUCC}\frac{\Gamma \vdash t\colon \mathbb{N}}{\Gamma \vdash \mathtt{succ}(t)\colon \mathbb{N}}$$

$$\begin{aligned}(|\Pi|) \ :=\ \Lambda\vec{\alpha}.\,\lambda\vec{x}.\ & \mathtt{let\ pack}(\alpha_t, \langle a_t, e_t\rangle) = (|\Pi_t|)\ \vec{\alpha}\ \vec{x}\ \mathtt{in} \\ & \mathtt{pack}(\alpha_t, \langle a_t, \mathtt{fn}\ g \Rightarrow \mathtt{let}\ y = e_t(g)\ \mathtt{in\ return\ succ}(y)\rangle)\end{aligned}$$

- Case: Π ends with rule (IF) whose premises are derived by Π_s, Π_{t_1} and Π_{t_2}.

$$\text{IF}\frac{\Gamma \vdash s\colon \mathbb{N} \qquad \Delta_1 \vdash t_1\colon \mathbb{N} \qquad \Delta_2 \vdash t_2\colon \mathbb{N}}{\Gamma, \Delta_1, \Delta_2 \vdash \mathtt{if0}\ s\ \mathtt{then}\ t_1\ \mathtt{else}\ t_2\colon \mathbb{N}}$$

$$\begin{aligned}(|\Pi|) \ :=\ \Lambda\vec{\alpha}\vec{\beta}\vec{\gamma}.\,\lambda\vec{x}\vec{y}\vec{z}.\ & \mathtt{let\ pack}(\alpha_s, \langle a_s, e_s\rangle) = (|\Pi_s|)\ \vec{\alpha}\ \vec{x}\ \mathtt{in} \\ & \mathtt{let\ pack}(\alpha_1, \langle a_1, e_1\rangle) = (|\Pi_{t_1}|)\ \vec{\beta}\ \vec{y}\ \mathtt{in} \\ & \mathtt{let\ pack}(\alpha_2, \langle a_2, e_2\rangle) = (|\Pi_{t_2}|)\ \vec{\gamma}\ \vec{z}\ \mathtt{in} \\ & \mathtt{pack}(\mathtt{unit}, \langle \star, e\rangle)\end{aligned}$$

where e is $(\mathtt{fn}\ (\vec{x}, \vec{y}, \vec{z}) \Rightarrow \mathtt{let}\ v = e_s\ \vec{x}\ \mathtt{in\ if0}\ v\ \mathtt{then}\ e_1(\vec{y})\ \mathtt{else}\ e_2(\vec{z}))$.

– Case: Π ends with rule (REC), whose premise is derived by Π_t.

$$\text{REC}\ \frac{\Gamma,\ f{:}X \to Y,\ x{:}X \vdash t\colon Y}{\Gamma \vdash \mathtt{fun}\ f\ x \Rightarrow t\colon X \to Y}$$

$$\Lambda\vec{\alpha}.\,\lambda\vec{x}.\,\mathtt{pack}(\mathcal{C}[\![\Gamma]\!], \langle \mathtt{fix}\ \mathit{step}, \mathtt{fn}\ g \Rightarrow \mathtt{return}\ g\rangle)$$

where

$$\begin{aligned}\mathit{step}\ :=\ &\lambda f.\,\Lambda\beta.\,\lambda x.\ \mathtt{let}\ \mathtt{pack}(\rho, \langle a, e\rangle) = (|\Pi_t|)\ \vec{\alpha}\ \mathcal{C}[\![\Gamma]\!]_{\vec{\alpha}}\ \beta\ \vec{x}\ f\ x\ \mathtt{in}\\ &\qquad\qquad \mathtt{pack}(\rho, \langle a, \mathtt{fn}\ \langle c, x\rangle \Rightarrow e(\langle\langle c, c\rangle, x\rangle)\rangle).\end{aligned}$$

Here, c is the tuple of the values in the context Γ. This tuple is used as the code for the recursive function f.

4.1 Examples

Let us spell out the translation of the following simple source term.

$$\vdash (\mathtt{fn}\ s \Rightarrow s\ \mathtt{zero})\ (\mathtt{fn}\ x \Rightarrow \mathtt{succ}(x))\colon \mathbb{N}$$

We spell out the non-trivial subterms:

– $(|s{:}\mathbb{N} \to \mathbb{N} \vdash s\ \mathtt{zero}\colon \mathbb{N}|)$ is defined to be

$$\begin{aligned}\Lambda\alpha.\,\lambda s\colon \mathcal{I}[\![\mathbb{N} \to \mathbb{N}]\!]_\alpha.\ &\mathtt{let}\ \mathtt{pack}(\varphi, \langle f, e_f\rangle) = (|s{:}\mathbb{N} \to \mathbb{N} \vdash s\colon \mathbb{N} \to \mathbb{N}|)\ \alpha\ s\ \mathtt{in}\\ &\mathtt{let}\ \mathtt{pack}(\xi, \langle x, e_x\rangle) = (|\ \vdash 0\colon \mathbb{N}|)\ \mathtt{in}\\ &\mathtt{let}\ \mathtt{pack}(\rho, \langle y, a\rangle) = f\ \xi\ x\ \mathtt{in}\\ &\mathtt{pack}(\rho, \langle y, e\rangle)\end{aligned}$$

where e is $\mathtt{fn}\ \langle\langle\rangle, c_s\rangle \Rightarrow \mathtt{let}\ c_f = e_f(\langle\langle\rangle, c_s\rangle)\ \mathtt{in}\ \mathtt{let}\ c_x = e_x(\langle\rangle)\ \mathtt{in}\ a(\langle c_f, c_x\rangle)$. Using the equational theory, this term may be simplified as follows:

$$\begin{aligned}&(|s{:}\mathbb{N} \to \mathbb{N} \vdash s\ \mathtt{zero}\colon \mathbb{N}|)\\ &= \Lambda\alpha.\,\lambda s\colon \mathcal{I}[\![\mathbb{N} \to \mathbb{N}]\!]_\alpha.\ \mathtt{let}\ \mathtt{pack}(\rho, \langle y, a\rangle) = s\ \mathtt{unit}\ \star\ \mathtt{in}\\ &\qquad\qquad\qquad\qquad\qquad \mathtt{pack}(\rho, \langle y, \mathtt{fn}\ \langle\langle\rangle, c_s\rangle \Rightarrow a(c_s, 0)\rangle)\end{aligned}$$

– $(|\ \vdash \mathtt{fn}\ s \Rightarrow s\ \mathtt{zero}\colon \mathbb{N}|)$ is then given by:

$$\mathtt{pack}(\mathtt{unit}, \langle (|s{:}\mathbb{N} \to \mathbb{N} \vdash s\ \mathtt{zero}\colon \mathbb{N}|), \mathtt{fn}\ g \Rightarrow \mathtt{return}\ g\rangle)$$

– For the function argument, we get:

$$\begin{aligned}&(|\ \vdash \mathtt{fn}\ x{:}\mathbb{N} \Rightarrow \mathtt{succ}(x)\colon \mathbb{N} \to \mathbb{N}|)\\ &= \mathtt{pack}(\mathtt{unit}, \langle \Lambda\alpha.\,\lambda x\colon I.\,\mathtt{pack}(\alpha, \langle x, \mathtt{fn}\ \langle\langle\rangle, c_x\rangle \Rightarrow \mathtt{return}\ \mathtt{succ}(c_x)\rangle),\\ &\qquad\qquad \mathtt{fn}\ c \Rightarrow \mathtt{return}\ c\rangle)\end{aligned}$$

- Putting these terms together the translation of the whole term we can be calculated and simplified as follows.

$$
\begin{aligned}
&(\!| \vdash (\texttt{fn}\ s \Rightarrow s\ \texttt{zero})\ (\texttt{fn}\ x \Rightarrow \texttt{succ}(x)\colon \mathbb{N}|\!)\\
&= \texttt{let pack}(\varphi, \langle f, e_f\rangle) = (\!|\ \vdash \texttt{fn}\ s \Rightarrow s\ \texttt{zero}|\!)\ \texttt{in}\\
&\quad \texttt{let pack}(\xi, \langle x, e_x\rangle) = (\!|\ \vdash \texttt{fn}\ x \Rightarrow \texttt{succ}(x)|\!)\ \texttt{in}\\
&\quad \texttt{let pack}(\rho, \langle y, a\rangle) = f\ \xi\ x\ \texttt{in}\\
&\quad \texttt{pack}(\rho, \langle y, \texttt{fn}\ \langle\rangle \Rightarrow \texttt{let}\ c_f = e_f(\langle\rangle)\ \texttt{in let}\ c_x = e_x(\langle\rangle)\ \texttt{in}\ a(\langle c_f, c_x\rangle)\rangle)\\
&= \texttt{let pack}(\xi, \langle x, e_x\rangle) = (\!|\ \vdash \texttt{fn}\ x \Rightarrow \texttt{succ}(x)|\!)\ \texttt{in}\\
&\quad \texttt{let pack}(\rho, \langle y, a\rangle) = (\!|s\ \texttt{zero}|\!)\ \xi\ x\ \texttt{in}\\
&\quad \texttt{pack}(\rho, \langle y, \texttt{fn}\ \langle\rangle \Rightarrow \texttt{let}\ c_x = e_x(\langle\rangle)\ \texttt{in}\ a(\langle\langle\rangle, c_x\rangle)\rangle)\\
&= \texttt{let pack}(\rho, \langle y, a\rangle) = (\!|s\ \texttt{zero}|\!)\ \texttt{unit}\ (\Lambda\alpha.\, \lambda x\colon I.\, \texttt{pack}(\alpha, \langle x, e\rangle))\ \texttt{in}\\
&\quad \texttt{pack}(\rho, \langle y, \texttt{fn}\ \langle\rangle \Rightarrow a(\langle\langle\rangle, \langle\rangle\rangle)\rangle)\ \text{where } e \text{ is } \texttt{fn}\ \langle\langle\rangle, c_x\rangle \Rightarrow \texttt{return succ}(c_x)\\
&= \texttt{let pack}(\rho, \langle y, a\rangle) = \texttt{pack}(\texttt{unit}, \langle\star, \texttt{fn}\ \langle\langle\rangle, c_f\rangle \Rightarrow 1\rangle)\ \texttt{in}\\
&\quad \texttt{pack}(\rho, \langle y, \texttt{fn}\ \langle\rangle \Rightarrow a(\langle\langle\rangle, \langle\rangle\rangle)\rangle)\\
&= \texttt{pack}(\texttt{unit}, \langle\star, \texttt{fn}\ \langle\rangle \Rightarrow 1\rangle)
\end{aligned}
$$

While we have used the equational theory here to illustrate that the translation produces the right result, we emphasise that computation is not intended to be implemented by rewriting on target terms, but by a compilation of target programs to low-level programs. Rewriting may be used for optimisation, of course.

To illustrate that the translation correctly implements the call-by-value evaluation strategy, consider a function that takes a function as an argument and applies it more than once:

$$\texttt{fn}\ s \Rightarrow \texttt{if0}\ (s\ \texttt{zero})\ \texttt{then}\ (s\ \texttt{zero})\ \texttt{else zero}$$

The translation of the body of this function can be calculated as

$$
\begin{aligned}
&(\!|s{:}\mathbb{N} \to \mathbb{N} \vdash \texttt{if0}\ (s\ \texttt{zero})\ \texttt{then}\ (s\ \texttt{zero})\ \texttt{else zero}\colon \mathbb{N}|\!)\\
&= \Lambda\alpha.\, \lambda s\colon \mathcal{I}[\![\mathbb{N} \to \mathbb{N}]\!]_\alpha.\ \texttt{let pack}(\rho, \langle y, a\rangle) = s\ \texttt{unit}\ \star\ \texttt{in}\\
&\qquad \texttt{pack}(\texttt{unit}, \langle\star, \texttt{fn}\ \langle\langle\rangle, c_s\rangle\rangle \Rightarrow e\rangle),
\end{aligned}
$$

where e is $\texttt{let}\ x = a(c_s, \texttt{zero})\ \texttt{in if0}\ x\ \texttt{then}\ a(c_s, \texttt{zero})\ \texttt{else return}\ 0$. Thus, the function value c_s is computed only once, but the function itself is invoked twice, as would be expected from an implementation of call-by-value.

5 Correctness

In this section we show the correctness of the translation. The main result is that a closed source term of base type $\mathbb{N}$ evaluates to a value n if and only if the translated term for this term returns the code value n.

The basic idea for the correctness proof is to formalise the intuition when a target term of type $\mathcal{M}[\![X]\!]_{\mathtt{unit}}$ represents a source term of type X, as outlined in Sect. 4 above. This naturally leads one to considering a realisability argument using logical relations. In the simply-typed case, soundness can be shown using a straightforward argument. With recursion, however, we must account for the effect of non-termination. This naturally leads to an argument using $^{\top\top}$-lifting. It turns out that an argument very similar to that of Benton and Hur [2] suffices to treat our translation.

5.1 Lower Bound

First we show that translated terms do not return wrong results.

In Sect. 4 we have outlined how $c\colon \mathcal{C}[\![X]\!]_A$ and $a\colon \mathcal{I}[\![X]\!]_A$ represent a source value of type X. Here we make precise in which sense triples (A, a, e) represent source values (or rather their domain-theoretic denotation). We extend this definition to computations by means of a form of $^{\top\top}$-lifting. To define it, we need some notation.

Define a type of continuations for type X as follows.

$$\mathcal{K}[\![X]\!] \ := \ \forall\alpha.\, \mathcal{I}[\![X]\!]_\alpha \to \mathtt{exp}(\mathcal{C}[\![X]\!]_\alpha, \mathtt{unit})$$

A continuation $k\colon \mathcal{K}[\![X]\!]$ can be composed with any term of type $p\colon \mathcal{M}[\![X]\!]_{\mathtt{unit}}$ to give us a term $p \bullet k\colon \mathtt{exp}(\mathtt{unit})$.

$$p \bullet k \ := \ \mathtt{let}\ \mathtt{pack}(A, \langle a, e\rangle) = p\ \mathtt{in}\ \mathtt{let}\ c = e(\langle\rangle)\ \mathtt{in}\ (k\ A\ a)(c)$$

We say that a closed term $t\colon \mathtt{exp}(\mathtt{unit})$ *terminates* if the equation $t = \mathtt{return}\ \langle\rangle$ is derivable and that it *diverges* otherwise.

$$\begin{aligned} \downarrow^X V \ &:= \ \{k\colon \mathcal{K}[\![X]\!] \mid \forall (A, a, c) \in V.\ k\ A\ a\ c \text{ diverges}\} \\ \Uparrow^X K \ &:= \ \{p\colon \mathcal{M}[\![X]\!]_{\mathtt{unit}} \mid \forall k \in K.\ p \bullet k \text{ diverges }\} \end{aligned}$$

The reader should think of $\Uparrow^X \downarrow^X V$ as the set of all terms that produce only values – encoded as a triple (A, a, c) – that are indistinguishable from one in V. It would be possible to make an intensional definition to this effect, but the extensional definition using $\Uparrow^X$ and $\downarrow^X$ appears to be more natural and general.

For any source type X, we define a relation

$$(A, a, c) \preceq^X d$$

where A is a base type and $\vdash a\colon \mathcal{I}[\![X]\!]_A$ and $\vdash c\colon \mathcal{C}[\![X]\!]_A$ and $d \in [\![X]\!]$ (recall that $[\![X]\!]$ is the denotational interpretation of X). This relation expresses that the triple (A, a, c) implements only behaviour that is also found in d. It is defined by induction on the type X:

- Base type: $v \leq^{\mathbb{N}} n$ if and only if v is of the form $(A, \star, n)$ for some A.
- Function type: $v \leq^{X \to Y} f$ if and only if:

$$\forall w, x.\ \ w \leq^X x \implies \mathtt{app}(v, w) \in \Uparrow^Y \downarrow^Y \{r \mid \exists d.\ f(x) = \lfloor d \rfloor \wedge r \leq^Y d\}.$$

This approximation relation $\leq^X$ is extended to the interpretation of typing sequents. For any source context $\Gamma = x_1{:}X_1, \ldots, x_n{:}X_n$, the relation $p \leq^{\Gamma,X} d$ relates a term

$$p\colon \forall \alpha_1 \ldots \alpha_k.\ \mathcal{I}[\![X_1]\!]_{\alpha_1} \to \cdots \to \mathcal{I}[\![X_k]\!]_{\alpha_k} \to \mathcal{M}[\![Y]\!]_{\mathtt{unit} \times \mathcal{C}[\![X_1]\!]_{\alpha_1} \times \cdots \times \mathcal{C}[\![X_k]\!]_{\alpha_k}}$$

to a domain element $d \in [\![X_1]\!] \times \cdots \times [\![X_n]\!] \Rightarrow [\![X]\!]_\perp$. It is defined such that $p \leq^{\Gamma,Y} f$ holds if and only if: Whenever $v_i \leq^{X_i} x_i$ for $i = 1, \ldots, n$, then

$$\mathtt{inst}(p, v_1, \ldots, v_n) \in \Uparrow^Y \downarrow^Y \{v \mid \exists d.\ f(x_1, \ldots, x_n) = \lfloor d \rfloor \wedge v \leq^Y d\}.$$

Here, inst is defined by:

$$\begin{aligned} &\mathtt{inst}(p, (A_1, a_1, c_1), \ldots, (A_n, a_n, c_n)) \\ &\quad := \mathtt{let\ pack}(\alpha_y, \langle a_y, e_y \rangle) = p\ A_1 \ldots A_n\ a_1 \ldots a_n\ \mathtt{in} \\ &\qquad \mathtt{pack}(\alpha_y, a_y, \mathtt{fn}\ \langle\rangle \Rightarrow e_y\ \langle\langle\rangle, c_1, \ldots, c_n\rangle) \end{aligned}$$

Lemma 1. *If $v \leq^X d$ and $d \sqsubseteq e$, then $v \leq^X e$.*

The proof is a straightforward induction on the type X.

Lemma 2. *For any derivation Π of $\Gamma \vdash t\colon X$, we have $(\!|\Pi|\!) \leq^{\Gamma,X} [\![\Pi]\!]$.*

Proof. The proof goes by induction on the derivation Π. We continue by case distinction on the last rule in Π and show just the cases for application and recursion.

- Case (App): Denote the derivations of the two premises by Π_s and Π_t.
  Suppose Γ is $x_1{:}X_1, \ldots, x_n{:}X_n$ and Δ is $y_1{:}Y_1, \ldots, y_m{:}Y_m$. Assume $v_i \leq^{X_i} x_i$ and $w_j \leq^{Y_j} y_j$ for $i = 1, \ldots, n$ and $j = 1, \ldots, m$. We have to show the relation $\mathtt{app}((\!|\Pi|\!), \vec{v}, \vec{w}) \leq^Y [\![s]\!](\vec{x}, [\![t]\!](\vec{y}))$.
  By induction hypothesis, we get $\mathtt{app}((\!|\Pi_s|\!), \vec{v}) \in \Uparrow^{X \to Y} \downarrow^{X \to Y} \{u \mid u \leq^{X \to Y} [\![s]\!](\vec{x})\}$ and $\mathtt{app}((\!|\Pi_t|\!), \vec{w}) \in \Uparrow^X \downarrow^X \{r \mid v \leq^X [\![t]\!](\vec{y})\}$. To show $\mathtt{app}((\!|\Pi_s|\!), \vec{v}) \bullet k$ diverges, it therefore suffices to show that $k\ A_u\ a_u\ c_u$ diverges for all A_u, a_u and c_u with $(A_u, a_u, c_u) \leq^{X \to Y} [\![s]\!](\vec{x})$, and likewise for Π_t.
  This means that to show that

$$\begin{aligned} &\mathtt{let\ pack}(A_u, \langle a_u, e_u \rangle) = \mathtt{inst}((\!|\Pi_s|\!), \vec{v})\ \mathtt{in} \\ &\mathtt{let}\ c_u = e_u()\ \mathtt{in} \\ &\mathtt{let\ pack}(A_r, \langle a_r, e_r \rangle) = \mathtt{inst}((\!|\Pi_t|\!), \vec{w})\ \mathtt{in} \\ &\mathtt{let}\ c_r = e_r()\ \mathtt{in} \\ &\mathtt{app}((A_u, a_u, c_u), (A_r, a_r, c_r)) \bullet k \end{aligned}$$

diverges, it suffices to show that $\mathsf{app}((A_u, a_u, c_u), (A_r, a_r, c_r)) \bullet k$ diverges for any $(A_u, a_u, c_u) \leq^{X \to Y} [\![s]\!](\vec{x})$ and any $(A_r, a_r, c_r) \leq^X [\![t]\!](\vec{y})$. The definition of $\leq^{X \to Y}$ gives us that this is true when k is in $\downarrow^Y \{y \mid y \leq^Y [\![s]\!](\vec{x}, [\![t]\!](\vec{y}))\}$.

But this means that to show $\mathsf{app}((|\Pi|), \vec{v}, \vec{w}) \in \Uparrow^Y \downarrow^Y \{y \mid y \leq^Y [\![s]\!](\vec{x}, [\![t]\!](\vec{y}))\}$, it suffices to show that $\mathsf{app}((|\Pi|), \vec{v}, \vec{w})$ is equal to the above program. But this follows by unfolding the definitions and direct equational reasoning.

- Case (Rec): Write Π_t for the derivation of the premise of this rule. Suppose Γ is $x_1{:}X_1, \ldots, x_n{:}X_n$. Assume $(A_i, a_i, c_i) \leq^{X_i} x_i$ for $i = 1, \ldots, n$.

  Let $f_0 := \bot$ and $f_i := [\![\Pi_t]\!](\vec{x}, f_{i-1})$ and $f := \bigsqcup_i f_i$.

  We have to show that

$$\begin{aligned}&\mathtt{let\ pack}(A, \langle a, e\rangle) = (|\Pi|)\ A_1\ \ldots\ A_n\ a_1\ \ldots\ a_n\ \mathtt{in}\\ &\mathtt{pack}(A, a, \mathtt{fn}\ \langle\rangle \Rightarrow e(\langle\langle\rangle, c_1, \ldots, c_n\rangle))\end{aligned}$$

is in $\Uparrow^{X \to Y} \downarrow^{X \to Y} \{v \mid v \leq^{X \to Y} f\}$.

By definition of $(|\Pi|)$, the above program equals

$$\mathtt{pack}(\mathcal{C}[\![\Gamma]\!], a_\Pi, \mathtt{fn}\ \langle\rangle \Rightarrow (\langle\langle\rangle, c_1, \ldots, c_n\rangle)).$$

It therefore suffices to show $(\mathcal{C}[\![\Gamma]\!], a_\Pi, \langle\langle\rangle, c_1, \ldots, c_n\rangle) \leq^{X \to Y} f$. By definition, a_Π has the form $\mathtt{fix}(step)$. Let $b_i := \mathtt{fix}^i(step)$.

First we show $\forall i.\ (\mathcal{C}[\![\Gamma]\!], b_i, \langle\langle\rangle, c_1, \ldots, c_n\rangle) \leq^{X \to Y} f_i$ by a straightforward induction on i. This implies $\forall i.\ (\mathcal{C}[\![\Gamma]\!], b_i, \langle\langle\rangle, c_1, \ldots, c_n\rangle) \leq^{X \to Y} f$ by monotonicity.

From this we can conclude $(\mathcal{C}[\![\Gamma]\!], a_\Pi, \mathtt{fn}\ \langle\rangle \Rightarrow \langle\langle\rangle, c_1, \ldots, c_n\rangle) \leq^{X \to Y} f$ as follows. Suppose $(A_x, a_x, c_x) \leq^X x$. We have to show that

$$\begin{aligned}&\mathtt{let\ pack}(A_y, \langle a_y, e_y\rangle) = a_\Pi\ A_x\ a_x\ \mathtt{in}\\ &\mathtt{pack}(A_y, a_y, \mathtt{fn}\ \langle\rangle \Rightarrow e_y(\langle\langle\rangle, c_1, \ldots, c_n, c_x\rangle))\end{aligned}$$

is in $\Uparrow^Y \downarrow^Y \{v \mid \exists d.\ f(x) = [d] \wedge v \leq^Y d\}$. For this, we have to show that

$$\begin{aligned}&\mathtt{let\ pack}(A_y, \langle a_y, e_y\rangle) = a_\Pi\ A_x\ a_x\ \mathtt{in}\\ &\mathtt{let}\ c_y = e_y(\langle\langle\rangle, c_1, \ldots, c_n, c_x\rangle)\ \mathtt{in}\\ &k\ A_y\ a_y\ c_y\end{aligned}$$

diverges, given that k diverges for all inputs v with $\exists d.\ f(x) = [d] \wedge v \leq^Y d$. But we know that, for any i, the program with b_i in place of a_Π diverges. Thus, if the program were to terminate, then it would already terminate with an approximation of $\mathtt{fix}$. But this would also mean that, for some i, the program with b_i in place of a_Π were to terminate, leading to a contradiction.

5.2 Upper Bound

It now remains to show that the translation produces target terms that compute at least the information specified by the domain interpretation. To this end we define a relation $(A, a, c) \geq^X d$ expressing that the triple (A, a, c) implements at least the behaviour specified by d. The proof that the translation of each source program is $\geq$-related to the domain-theoretic interpretation of the program also follows [2].

As in [2], some care needs to be taken with recursion, in order to make the definition of $\geq$ closed under taking the least upper bound in its second argument. We therefore first define a relation $\geq_0$ and then define $\geq$ from it by closing under limits.

$$\underline{\downarrow}^X V = \{k\colon \mathcal{K}[\![X]\!] \mid \forall (A, a, c) \in V.\, k\ A\ a\ c \text{ terminates}\}$$
$$\overline{\Uparrow}^X K = \{p\colon \mathcal{M}[\![X]\!]_{\texttt{unit}} \mid \forall k \in K.\, \texttt{let}\ (A, \langle a, c\rangle) = p\ \texttt{in}\ k\ A\ a\ c \text{ terminates}\}$$

Define $\geq_0^X$ between triples (A, a, c) with $a\colon \mathcal{I}[\![X]\!]_A$ and $c\colon \mathcal{C}[\![X]\!]_A$, and elements of $[\![X]\!]$ to be the least relation with the following properties:

- Base type: $(A, \star, n) \geq_0^{\mathbb{N}} n$
- Function type: $v \geq_0^{X \to Y} f$ if and only if:

$$\forall w, x, d.\ \ w \geq_0^X x \wedge f(x) = \lfloor d \rfloor \implies \mathsf{app}(v, w) \in \overline{\Uparrow}^Y \underline{\downarrow}^Y \{v \mid v \geq_0^Y d\}$$

For a source context $\Gamma = x_1{:}X_1, \ldots, x_n{:}X_n$, we define $p \geq_0^{\Gamma,Y} f$ to mean: Whenever $w_i \geq_0^{X_i} x_i$ for $i = 1, \ldots, n$ and $f(x_1, \ldots, x_n) = \lfloor d \rfloor$, then also $\texttt{inst}(p, w_1, \ldots, w_n) \in \overline{\Uparrow}^Y \underline{\downarrow}^Y \{v \mid v \geq_0^Y d\}$.

This definition is then closed under least upper bounds, as in [2]:

$$v \geq^X x \iff \text{for some } \omega\text{-chain } (x_i)_{i \geq 0}\colon\ x \sqsubseteq \bigsqcup_i x_i \ \wedge\ \forall i.\, v \geq_0^X x_i$$

$$v \geq^{\Gamma,X} x \iff \text{for some } \omega\text{-chain } (x_i)_{i \geq 0}\colon\ x \sqsubseteq \bigsqcup_i x_i \ \wedge\ \forall i.\, v \geq_0^{\Gamma,X} x_i$$

Lemma 3. *For any derivation Π of $\Gamma \vdash t\colon X$, we have $(\!|\Pi|\!) \geq^{\Gamma,X} [\![\Pi]\!]$.*

Proof. With the explicit closure under limits, the case for recursion is straightforward this time, but we have to check that all operations are compatible with closing under limits. For example, in the case of application we use continuity of function application, i.e. $\bigsqcup_i f_i(\bigsqcup_i x_i) = \bigsqcup_i f_i(x_i)$. Using this equality it suffices to show that $v \geq_0^{X \to Y} f_i$ and $w \geq_0^X x_i$ implies $\mathsf{app}(v, w) \geq_0^Y f_i(x_i)$ for all i, which follows using the same kind of reasoning as for the lower bound. □

Theorem 1. *Suppose Π derives $\vdash t\colon \mathbb{N}$. Define the target term $p\colon \mathit{exp}(\mathit{nat})$ to be $\mathtt{let}\ \mathit{pack}(\alpha, \langle a, e\rangle) = (\!|\Pi|\!)\ \mathit{in}\ e(\langle\rangle)$. Then the following are true.*

1. *If $[\![\Pi]\!] = \bot$, then p diverges.*
2. *If $[\![\Pi]\!] = \lfloor n \rfloor$, then $\vdash p = \mathit{return}\ n\colon \mathbb{N}$.*

Proof. If $[\![\Pi]\!] = \bot$, then $(|\Pi|) \in \Uparrow^{\mathbb{N}}\downarrow^{\mathbb{N}}\emptyset$ by $(|\Pi|) \leq^{\texttt{empty},\mathbb{N}} [\![\Pi]\!]$. This means that $(|\Pi|) \bullet k$ must diverge for any k, in particular also $\Lambda\alpha.\,\lambda x.\,\texttt{fn}\ m \Rightarrow \texttt{return}\ \langle\rangle$. Hence, $(|\Pi|)$ cannot be equal to $\texttt{return}\ m$ for any m.

By $(|\Pi|) \geq^{\texttt{empty},\mathbb{N}} [\![\Pi]\!]$ and the fact that $\mathbb{N}_\bot$ is a flat cpo, we obtain that $(|\Pi|)$ is in $\overline{\Uparrow^{\mathbb{N}}\downarrow^{\mathbb{N}}}\{v \mid v \geq_0^{\mathbb{N}} n\}$. This means that $(|\Pi|) \bullet k$ must terminate for the continuation defined by the pseudo-code $\Lambda\alpha.\,\lambda x.\,\texttt{fn}\ m \Rightarrow \texttt{if}\ m = n\ \texttt{then}\ \texttt{return}\ \langle\rangle\ \texttt{else}$ diverge. But this can only be the case if $(|\Pi|)$ returns n. □

6 Conclusion and Further Work

We have defined a simple typed closure conversion from a call-by-value source language to an Algol-like target language. The target language is modelled on the structure of interactive models of computation. Overall, we have there arrived at a simple implementation of call-by-value in models of interactive computation, simplifying earlier work in this direction, in particular [17]. Moreover, the translation in this paper also covers recursion. The formulation should be general enough to account for effects other than non-termination as well.

While the translation in this paper is similar to other typed closure conversion methods [1,13], it does not appear to be exactly the same. In addition to corresponding to the CPS-translation from [17], we believe that the translation here is also canonical in the sense that it is an implementation of call-by-value game semantics [9]. This was observed in discussions with Nikos Tzevelekos.

Let us consider the definition of arenas in call-by-value games [9]. Arenas are forests of labelled trees (with additional information) that explain which sequences of moves are allowed as plays. For a source type X, define the labelled forest $\mathcal{M}(X)$ as shown below, where $\mathcal{C}(\mathbb{N})$ is the set of natural numbers and $\mathcal{C}(X \to Y) = \{*\}$.

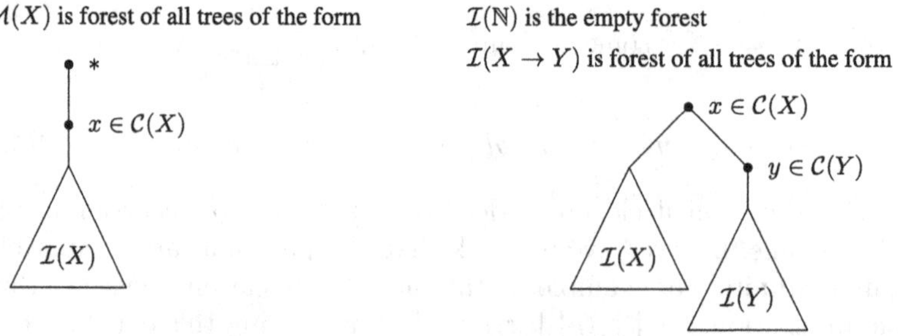

In call-by-value games, the semantics of a closed PCF term of type X is explained in terms of plays on $\mathcal{M}(X)$. Such a play is a sequences of nodes $m_1, \ldots, m_n$ with the property (among others) that, for all $i > 1$ there exists $j < i$ such that m_j is the parent node of m_i in the forest $\mathcal{M}(X)$.

Now, consider an implementation of the target language in this paper which records the trace of values that terms of type $\texttt{exp}(A, B)$ receive as arguments and that they return. The types $\mathcal{I}[\![X]\!]_A$ and $\mathcal{M}[\![X]\!]_A$ specify an ordering on the traces that can appear at these types. Consider $\mathcal{I}[\![(\mathbb{N} \to \mathbb{N}) \to \mathbb{N}]\!]_A$, i.e.

$\forall\beta_1.\,(\forall\beta_2.\,I \times \mathtt{exp}(\beta_1 \times \mathtt{nat}, \mathtt{nat})) \to \exists\gamma.\,I \times \mathtt{exp}(A \times \beta_1, \mathtt{nat})$. A trace of a term of this type must start with a value of type $A \times \beta_1$ (invoking the function). This can be followed by a message of type $\beta_1 \times \mathtt{nat}$ (invoking the argument function) and then the corresponding return value of type $\mathtt{nat}$. Such a call to the argument function can be repeated until the final value of type $\mathtt{nat}$ is returned. If we spell out the constraints on the traces in terms of forests as above, then we get the following forests, in which type variables range over arbitrary types.

$\mathcal{M}(X)_{\mathtt{unit}}$ **is forest of all trees of the form**

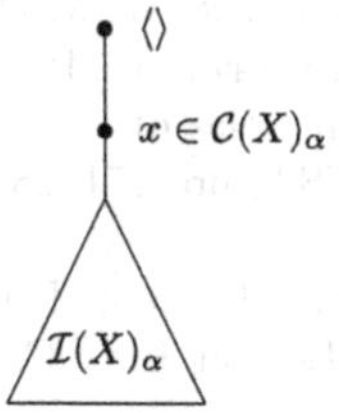

$\mathcal{I}(\mathbb{N})_\alpha$ **is the empty forest**

$\mathcal{I}(X \to Y)_\alpha$ **is forest of all trees of the form**

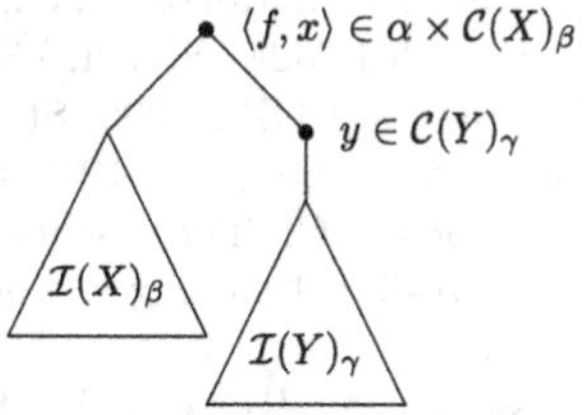

The trees from the game semantic arenas are obtained from these trees by removing all values whose type is a type variable. In game semantic plays, this removed information is not needed, as it can be recovered from the history. This makes it reasonable to expect that the translation in this paper can be seen as an efficient, *history-free* implementation of call-by-value game semantics. We intend to make the relation precise in further work.

References

1. Ahmed, A., Blume, M.: Typed closure conversion preserves observational equivalence. In: International Conference on Functional Programming, ICFP 2008, pp. 157–168 (2008)
2. Benton, N., Hur, C.: Biorthogonality, step-indexing and compiler correctness. In: International Conference on Functional program ming, ICFP 2009, pp. 97–108 (2009)
3. Dal Lago, U., Schöpp, U.: Functional programming in sublinear space. In: Gordon, A.D. (ed.) ESOP 2010. LNCS, vol. 6012, pp. 205–225. Springer, Heidelberg (2010)
4. Danos, V., Herbelin, H., Regnier, L.: Game semantics and abstract machines. In: Logic in Computer Science, LICS 1996, pp. 394–405. IEEE (1996)
5. Fernández, M., Mackie, I.: Call-by-value lambda-graph rewriting without rewriting. in: International Conference on Graph Transformation, ICGT 2002, pp. 75–89 (2002)
6. Fredriksson, O., Ghica, D.R.: Seamless distributed computing from the geometry of interaction. In: Palamidessi, C., Ryan, M.D. (eds.) TGC 2012. LNCS, vol. 8191, pp. 34–48. Springer, Heidelberg (2013)
7. Ghica, D.R.: Geometry of synthesis: a structured approach to VLSI design. In: Hofmann, M., Felleisen, M. (eds.) Principles of Programming Languages, POPL 2007, pp. 363–375. ACM (2007)
8. Hasuo, I., Hoshino, N.: Semantics of higher-order quantum computation via geometry of interaction. In: Logic in Computer Science, LICS 2011, pp. 237–246. IEEE (2011)

9. Honda, K., Yoshida, N.: Game-theoretic analysis of call-by-value computation. Theor. Comput. Sci. **221**(1–2), 393–456 (1999)
10. Hoshino, N., Muroya, K., Hasuo, I.: Memoryful geometry of interaction: from coalgebraic components to algebraic effects. In: Computer Science Logic - Logic in Computer Science, CSL-LICS 2014. ACM (2014)
11. Lago, U.D., Faggian, C., Hasuo, I., Yoshimizu, A.: The geometry of synchronization. In: Computer Science Logic - Logic in Computer Science, CSL-LICS 2014, pp. 35:1–35:10 (2014)
12. Mackie, I.: The geometry of interaction machine. In: Cytron, R.K., Lee, P. (eds.) Principles of Programming Languages, POPL 1995, pp. 198–208. ACM (1995)
13. Minamide, Y., Morrisett, G., Harper, R.: Typed closure conversion. In: Proceedings of the 23rd ACM SIGPLAN-SIGACT Symposium on Principles of Programming Languages, POPL 1996, St. Petersburg Beach, Florida, USA, pp. 271–283. ACM, New York (1996). doi:10.1145/237721.237791
14. Reynolds, J.C.: The essence of ALGOL. In: O'Hearn, P.W., Tennent, R.D. (eds.) ALGOL-like Languages, vol. 1, pp. 67–88. Birkhauser Boston Inc., Cambridge (1997)
15. Rossberg, A., Russo, C.V., Dreyer, D.: F-ing modules. J. Funct. Program. **24**(5), 529–607 (2014)
16. Schöpp, U.: Computation-by-Interaction for Structuring Low-Level Computation. Habilitation thesis, Ludwig-Maximilians-Universität München (2015)
17. Schöpp, U.: Call-by-value in a basic logic for interaction. In: Garrigue, J. (ed.) APLAS 2014. LNCS, vol. 8858, pp. 428–448. Springer, Heidelberg (2014)
18. Schöpp, U.: Organising low-level programs using higher types. In: Principles and Practice of Declarative Programming, PPDP 2014. ACM, New York, to appear 2014
19. Winskel, G.: The Formal Semantics of Programming Languages - An Introduction. MIT Press, Cambridge (1993). ISBN: 0-262-23169-7

Kripke Open Bisimulation

A Marriage of Game Semantics and Operational Techniques

Guilhem Jaber[1](✉) and Nicolas Tabareau[2]

[1] Queen Mary University, London, UK
[2] Inria, Nantes, France
g.jaber@qmul.ac.uk

Abstract. Proving that two programs are contextually equivalent is notoriously hard, particularly for functional languages with references (i.e., local states). Many operational techniques have been designed to prove such equivalences, and fully abstract denotational model, using game semantics, have been built for such languages. In this work, we marry ideas coming from trace semantics, an operational variant of game semantics, and from Kripke logical relations, notably the notion of worlds as transition systems of invariants, to define a new operational technique: Kripke open bisimulations. It is the first framework whose completeness does not rely on any closure by contexts.

1 Introduction

Many operational methods have been designed to reason about contextual equivalence of stateful programs. This profusion comes mainly from the difficulty to know exactly what kind of equivalence can be proven or not by a particular method. Even if completeness have been stated for some of those methods, the proof of completeness always relies on a notion of closure by contexts, which prevents to conclude that all the proofs of equivalence can be performed. For instance, Kripke logical relations (KLR), one of the most popular (and complete) method, were in their first version insufficient to prove the equivalence of two simple programs, dubbed at the time the "awkward example". This is because the notion of worlds as invariants introduced in the seminal paper of Pitts and Stark [12] is too restricted. KLR have later been refined by Ahmed, Dreyer et al. [1,2], where a *transition system* between such invariant is used to overcome this restriction. A sibling relational method to reason about contextual equivalence is given by bisimulations. Environmental [13,16] and Normal Form (a.k.a. Open) Bisimulations [7,8,15] are (set of) relations on terms defined coinductively w.r.t. the operational reduction. Their underlying idea is that contextual equivalence can be seen as the greatest adequate bisimulation which is also a congruence. The issue with this approach is that building a bisimulation is a complex task, especially when contexts do not have control operators and thus are not powerful enough to discriminate terms. Recently, Relation Transition Systems [3] (RTS)

X. Feng and S. Park (Eds.): APLAS 2015, LNCS 9458, pp. 271–291, 2015.
DOI: 10.1007/978-3-319-26529-2_15

have been introduced to take the best of the two approaches. While in the work on bisimulation, a class of bisimulation is defined and then shown to be a congruence, RTS provide a single bisimulation, whose definition is parametrized by a transition system—as it is done for KLR—plus a notion of *global knowledge*. This means that when proving equivalence of two terms, only the transition system of heap invariants and the global knowledge need to be constructed. Then it just remains to show that the two terms are in the corresponding bisimulation. But RTS are not known to be complete (the first version do not cover, e.g., η-equivalence).

On another line of work, fully-abstract denotational model of higher-order references have been designed, in terms of trace semantics [6] or game semantics [9]. In theory, it is thus possible to prove equivalence of programs by computing their denotation in such models, then prove that the denotations are equal. This is however in general a really complex task. *Algorithmic game semantics* [10] has been designed to perform automatically this task, using an automaton representation of the denotation of a term. However, this can be done only for fragments of the language where the type of terms is restricted. Thus this methods cannot be applied to unrestricted terms.

Overall, transition systems constitute a central object in this area. One can wonder whether they have been used for the same purpose. In trace semantics [6], the *interactive reduction* which generates traces can be seen as a bipartite *Labeled Transition System* (LTS) between player (i.e., the term) and opponent (i.e., contexts) configurations. Such LTSs carry a lot of information: the control flow between the term and any context, on each transition the actions performed, and on each state the configuration that the interactive reduction has reached. In the work on KLR and RTS, the transition system is rather an abstraction of the control flow, which is shared between two terms, and states only provide invariants on heaps. But among these works, those that are complete all use a notion of closure by context at one point in their definition. The only exception is the work of Stovring and Lassen [15], but for an *untyped* λ-calculus with a control operator (contexts having access to such operators, they can discriminate more terms). It is interesting to notice that in [7], the completeness of their bisimulation, once references are added to their language, was conjectured (albeit for a continuation passing style calculus, where reasoning on divergence is easier).

In this paper, we propose *Kripke Open Bisimulations* (KOBs), which are derived from bisimulations on configurations of the LTS generating traces, but are rather defined directly on terms with the usual operational semantics. The motto of KOBs could be:

"*to prove equivalence of programs, only a transition system of invariants is needed*"

Indeed, its definitions can be carried on in a simple logic that does not make use of quantification over λ-terms nor of a notion of closure. So once the transition system of invariants on heaps has been provided, it is straightforward to conduct the proof of equivalence, by simply reducing the terms operationally and checking that we get synchronized behavior. Via the link to trace semantics, we prove full abstraction of KOBs, without relying on any kind of closure, which suggests that all the reasoning principles necessary to reason about equivalence of stateful programs are present in KOBs.

Reasoning Principles behind Kripke Open Bisimulations. When reasoning on contextual equivalence, the key notion is to determine what can be observed by a context. This, of course, depends on the programming language in which contexts are written. For example, when contexts have access to a mutable memory, they can store how many times a function (or callback) provided to a term is called. This means that two terms are equivalent only when they perform the same callbacks, e.g., $\lambda f.f();f()$ is not equivalent in that case to $\lambda f.f()$. Moreover, with such a memory, contexts can also keep track of the order in which arguments are applied to callbacks. Thus, $\lambda f.(f\ 1) + (f\ 2)$ is not equivalent to $\lambda f.(f\ 2) + (f\ 1)$ in this setting. To sum-up, when reasoning on a language with a mutable memory, two terms are contextually equivalent only if the control flow between the term and contexts are equal, such control flow taking into account the functional values provided by a term to the context via callbacks. This idea shows up in game semantics, where the intensional model is fully abstract for a language with store, without considering a quotient of the model.

But in this setting, contexts can also observe memory cells created or modified by a term. This is however only the case for languages with unrestricted memory management like C or assembly code, where pointer arithmetic is allowed. This is not the case for languages like ML, where memory is implemented with *references*, represented using locations, on which the typing system forbids any kind of arithmetic. Locations can yet be passed as arguments to functions. This means that a disclosure process of locations can happen between a term and the context. So part of the references created by a term can become observable by the context, as soon as the corresponding locations are disclosed. For example, $\texttt{let x} = \text{ref}\,0\ \texttt{in}\ \lambda\texttt{y} : (\text{ref Int}).\texttt{x} == \texttt{y}$ and $\lambda\texttt{y} : (\text{ref Int}).\textbf{false}$ are equivalent. Indeed, the location stored in x has not been disclosed and remains private to the term, so that contexts have no access to it and cannot pass it as an argument to the λ-abstraction. This means that we need to keep track of such disclosure process of locations to reason about equivalence of programs for languages like ML. But, we must also keep track of the way references that remain private to a term evolve. Indeed, when a term recovers the control, after performing a callback or returning a higher-order value, its execution also depends on its private part of the heap, and not only on the values provided by the context (either directly as arguments or via the disclosed part of the heap).

Transition systems representing the control flow between a term and a context, together with labels on transitions representing the invariants on heaps and the disclosure of locations, are thus important pieces of information to reason about equivalence of programs in the presence of a mutable memory. Following the work on KLR [2], some states of transition systems are tagged as *inconsistent* to deal with the so-called deferred divergence examples. This technique corresponds to the restriction to *complete plays* in game semantics, and would not be necessary if the language we consider featured some simple notion of control flow operator to abort the reduction.

The goal of this paper is to marry the notion of worlds as evolving invariants of KLR to the direct style reasoning provided by open bisimulations to provide a framework in which the transition system is the only external information needed to decide the equivalence of two programs. The price to pay for this unified framework is a complex proof of soundness and completeness as it can no longer rely on a biorthogonality argument (because of direct-style reasoning) nor on a generic notion of bisimulation (because bisimulations are restricted to particular ones, specified by a *relational* transition system). The proof is performed using ideas coming from nominal game semantics [9] and its connection to trace semantics, an operational variant initiated by Laird [6].

All the detailed proofs appear in the technical Appendix [5].

2 RefML

The programming language considered in this paper is RefML, a typed call-by-value functional language with *nominal higher-order references*, which is a fragment of ML.

2.1 Syntax of RefML

The syntax of types τ, values u, terms M, contexts C and evaluation contexts K of RefML is defined in Fig. 1. As usual, `let` x `=` N `in` M is defined as $(\lambda x.M)N$ and $M;N$ is defined as $(\lambda x.N)M$ with x fresh in M. Evaluation contexts K are particular kinds of contexts, the ones that start by reducing terms that fill their hole $\bullet$. For each type τ, we use a special term $\bot_\tau$ that always diverges.

Heaps h are defined as finite partial maps Loc $\rightharpoonup$ Val. The empty heap is written ε. Adding a new element to a partial map h is written $h \cdot [l \hookrightarrow v]$, and is defined only if $l \notin \mathrm{dom}(h)$. We also define $h[l \hookrightarrow v]$, for $l \in \mathrm{dom}(h)$, as the partial function h' which satisfies $h'(l') = h(l')$ when $l' \neq l$, and $h'(l) = u$. The restriction of a heap h to a set of locations L is written $h_{|L}$. A heap is said to be *closed* when, for all $l \in \mathrm{dom}(h)$, if $h(l)$ is itself a location then $h(l) \in \mathrm{dom}(h)$. Taking a set L of locations and a heap h, we define the image of L by h, written $h^*(L)$ as $h^*(L) \stackrel{def}{=} \cup_{j \geq 0} h^j(L)$ where $h^0(L) = L$ and $h^{j+1}(L) = h(h^j(L)) \cap \mathrm{Loc}$.

$$
\begin{array}{ll}
\tau,\sigma & \stackrel{def}{=} \mathrm{Unit} \mid \mathrm{Bool} \mid \mathrm{Int} \mid \mathrm{ref}\,\tau \mid \mid \tau \times \sigma \mid \tau \to \sigma \\
u,u' & \stackrel{def}{=} () \mid \mathbf{true} \mid \mathbf{false} \mid \hat{n} \mid x \mid l \mid \langle u,u' \rangle \mid \lambda x.M \quad (\text{where } n \in \mathbb{Z}, x \in \mathrm{Var}, l \in \mathrm{Loc}) \\
M,M' & \stackrel{def}{=} u \mid MM' \mid M + M' \mid \mathtt{if}\ M\ \mathtt{then}\ M'\ \mathtt{else}\ M'' \mid M == M' \mid \\
 & \quad \mathrm{ref}\,M \mid !M \mid M := M' \mid \mid \langle M,M' \rangle \mid \pi_1(M) \mid \pi_2(M) \mid \bot_\tau \\
C & \stackrel{def}{=} \bullet \mid \lambda x.C \mid CM \mid MC \mid \mathrm{ref}\,C \mid C := M \mid M := C \mid !C \mid C == M \mid \ldots \\
K & \stackrel{def}{=} \bullet \mid KM \mid uK \mid \mathrm{ref}\,K \mid K := M \mid u := K \mid !K \mid K == M \mid u == K \mid \ldots
\end{array}
$$

Fig. 1. Definition of RefML

Typing Rules. Typing judgments are of the form $\Sigma; \Gamma \vdash M : \tau$, where Σ and Γ are respectively typing contexts for locations and variables. Such typing contexts are partial maps between locations or variables to types. The typing rules of RefML are standard, and given in Appendix A. We write $\Sigma; \Gamma \vdash C : \tau \rightsquigarrow \sigma$ when $\Sigma; \Gamma, x : \tau \vdash C[x] : \sigma$, with $x \notin \Gamma$. Then, we write $\Gamma \vdash h : \Sigma$ if $\mathrm{dom}(h) = \mathrm{dom}(\Sigma)$ and $\Sigma; \Gamma \vdash h(l) : \Sigma(l)$.

2.2 Operational Semantics

The small-step operational semantics of RefML, written $(M, h) \mapsto (M', h')$, is defined in Fig. 2[1]. We write $M\{v/x\}$ to represent the (capture-free) substitution of x by v in M. This reduction is deterministic, and in particular we suppose that the reduction $(K[\mathrm{ref}\ v], h) \mapsto (K[l], h \cdot [l \hookrightarrow v])$ chooses a location $l \notin \mathrm{dom}(h)$. Using higher-order references, usual fixpoints $\mathtt{fix\ f(x).M}$ of type $\tau \to \sigma$ can be defined using the *Landin's Knot*: $\mathtt{let\ y} = \mathtt{ref}\ (\lambda \mathtt{x}.\bot_\sigma)\ \mathtt{in\ y} := (\lambda \mathtt{x.let\ f} = !\mathtt{y\ in\ M}); !\mathtt{y}$.

In the following, we say that a pair (M, h) is irreducible, written $\mathbf{irred}(M, h)$, if it cannot be reduced anymore. Taking an irreducible pair formed by a well-typed term M and a closed well-typed heap, where all the free variables are of functional types, we get that M is either equal to a value or to a *callback*, i.e., a term of the form $K[f\ v]$ with f a free variable and v a value.

Contextual (a.k.a. observational) equivalence is defined as:

Definition 1. *Taking two terms M_1, M_2 of the same type τ in a context Σ, Γ, we say that M_1 and M_2 are* contextually equivalent, *written $\Sigma; \Gamma \vdash M_1 \simeq_{ctx} M_2 : \tau$, when $\forall \Sigma' \supseteq \Sigma. \forall h : \Sigma'$ closed. $\forall C$ s.t. $\Sigma'; \Gamma \vdash C : \tau \rightsquigarrow$ Unit. $(C[M_1], h) \Downarrow$ iff $(C[M_2], h) \Downarrow$, where $(C[M_1], h) \Downarrow$ means $(C[M_1], h) \mapsto^* ((), h')$.*

Using closed heaps containing Σ ensures that the reduction of $(C[M_i], h)$ cannot get stuck, i.e., either reduces to () or diverges.

$$
\begin{array}{llllll}
(K[(\lambda x.M)u], h) & \mapsto (K[M\{u/x\}], h) & (K[\hat{n} + \hat{m}], h) & \mapsto (K[\widehat{n+m}], h) & \\
(K[\hat{n} == \hat{n}], h) & \mapsto (K[\mathbf{true}], h) & (K[\hat{n} == \hat{m}], h) & \mapsto (K[\mathbf{false}], h) & (n \neq m) \\
(K[l == l], h) & \mapsto (K[\mathbf{true}], h) & (K[l == l'], h) & \mapsto (K[\mathbf{false}], h) & (l \neq l') \\
(K[\bot_\tau], h) & \mapsto (K[\bot_\tau], h) & (K[!l], h) & \mapsto (K[h(l)], h) & \\
(K[\mathrm{ref}\ u], h) & \mapsto (K[l], h \cdot [l \hookrightarrow u]) & (K[l := u], h) & \mapsto (K[()], h[l \hookrightarrow u]) & \\
\multicolumn{3}{l}{(K[\pi_i \langle M_1, M_2 \rangle], h)} & \mapsto (K[M_i], h) & \\
\multicolumn{3}{l}{(K[\mathtt{if}\ \ b\ \mathtt{then}\ \ M_{\mathbf{true}}\ \mathtt{else}\ \ M_{\mathbf{false}}], h)} & \mapsto (K[M_b], h) &
\end{array}
$$

Fig. 2. Operational Semantics of RefML

[1] We also consider the non-deterministic reduction $\mapsto_{nd}$, defined in the same way but for the rule of allocation, which is defined as $(K[\mathrm{ref}\ v], h) \mapsto_{nd} (K[l], h \cdot [l \hookrightarrow v])$ for any $l \notin \mathrm{dom}(h)$.

2.3 Abstract Values and Nominal Reasoning

In the following, we represent functional values (i.e., λ-abstractions) using *functional names* belonging to a set FN. Abstract values[2] v are then defined as:

$$v, v' \stackrel{def}{=} () \mid \mathbf{true} \mid \mathbf{false} \mid \widehat{n} \mid f \mid l \mid \langle v, v' \rangle \quad \text{with } n \in \mathbb{Z}, l \in \text{Loc and } f \in \text{FN}.$$

To each type τ, we associate a set $[\![\tau]\!]$ formed by pairs (v, ϕ) of abstract values and typing function for functional names.

$$[\![\text{Unit}]\!] \stackrel{def}{=} \{((), \varepsilon)\} \qquad [\![\sigma \to \tau]\!] \stackrel{def}{=} \{(f, [f \mapsto (\sigma \to \tau)]) \mid f \in \text{FN}\}$$
$$[\![\text{Int}]\!] \stackrel{def}{=} \{(\widehat{n}, \varepsilon) \mid n \in \mathbb{Z}\} \qquad [\![\theta_1 \times \theta_2]\!] \stackrel{def}{=} \{(\langle v_1, v_2 \rangle, \phi_1 \cdot \phi_2) \mid (v_i, \phi_i) \in [\![\theta_i]\!]\}$$
$$[\![\text{Bool}]\!] \stackrel{def}{=} \{(\mathbf{true}, \varepsilon), (\mathbf{false}, \varepsilon)\} \qquad [\![\text{ref}\, \tau]\!] \stackrel{def}{=} \{(l, \varepsilon) \mid l \in \text{Loc}\}$$

Taking a typing context Γ, we define $[\![\Gamma]\!]$ as the set of pairs of substitution functions and typing function of functional names defined as

$$\{(\rho, \phi) \mid \text{dom}(\rho) = \text{dom}(\Gamma), \forall (x, \tau) \in \Gamma, \exists \phi_x.(\rho(x), \phi_x) \in [\![\tau]\!], \phi = \biguplus_{x \in \text{dom}(\Gamma)} \phi_x\}.$$

Then, we need to reason up-to permutations of both functional names and locations. To do so, we use *nominal sets*, as introduced by Pitts [11]. Fixing a set of names $\mathbb{A}$, we consider the group of finite permutations $\text{Perm}(\mathbb{A})$ of $\mathbb{A}$, i.e., the bijections π of $\mathbb{A}$ s.t. the set $\{a \in \mathbb{A} \mid \pi(a) \neq a\}$ is finite. Then an $\mathbb{A}$-*nominal set* is a set X equipped with a group action (noted $*$) on $\text{Perm}(\mathbb{A})$. We omit to indicate $\mathbb{A}$ when it is clear from the context. A subset S of $\mathbb{A}$ is said to *support* an element t of a nominal set X when

$$\forall \pi \in \text{Perm}(\mathbb{A}).\ (\forall a \in S.\ \pi(a) = a) \Rightarrow \pi * t = t.$$

The smallest subset of $\mathbb{A}$ which supports t is called the *support* of t, written $\nu_{\mathbb{A}}(t)$. Terms and heaps of RefML can be seen as a nominal set over both Loc and FN. Then, the support of a term is (i) its set of locations if it is seen as nominal over Loc, or (ii) its set of free functional names if it is seen as nominal over FN.

Two elements t, u of a nominal set X are said to be *nominally-equivalent*, written $t \sim_{\mathbb{A}} u$ if there exists π in $\text{Perm}(\mathbb{A})$ s.t. $t = \pi * u$ holds. We sometimes need to be explicit in the permutation when working with two nominally equivalent elements t, u of a nominal set X. However, when this is the case, it is more convenient to work with (typed) *spans* rather than permutations because spans are easier to extend than permutations. Spans, which are equivalent to permutations, have already been used by Stark to reason about locations, when defining logical relations for the ν-calculus [14].

Definition 2. *A* span $\mathcal{S} : (\mathbb{A} \times \text{Types}) \rightleftharpoons (\mathbb{A} \times \text{Types})$ *is a pair of partial finite injections* $(\mathbb{A} \times \text{Types}) \hookleftarrow \mathcal{S} \hookrightarrow (\mathbb{A} \times \text{Types})$ *preserving types. We write* $\text{Span}_{\mathbb{A}}$ *for the set of spans over* $\mathbb{A}$.

---

[2] By seeing functional names as variables, the operational semantics of RefML can be extended straightforwardly to abstract values.

We write ε for the empty span. The image of a span $\mathcal{S}$ by the left (resp. right) injection is written $\mathcal{S}_1$ (resp. $\mathcal{S}_2$). Such images can be seen as typing contexts. Reciprocally, from a typing context Γ, we define the span $\widehat{\Gamma}$ as $\{(x, x, \tau) \mid (x, \tau) \in \Gamma\}$. The extension of a span $\mathcal{S}$ at type τ with $(a_1, a_2) \in \mathbb{A}$ is written $\mathcal{S}\cdot(a_1, a_2, \tau)$, when $a_1 \notin \mathcal{S}_1$ and $a_2 \notin \mathcal{S}_2$. We say that $\mathcal{S}'$ extends $\mathcal{S}$, written $\mathcal{S}' \sqsupseteq \mathcal{S}$, when $\mathcal{S}'$ is a span which includes $\mathcal{S}$ as a set. Two spans are disjoints, written $\mathcal{S}\#\mathcal{S}'$, when both $\mathcal{S}_i, \mathcal{S}'_i$ are disjoint sets. A span $\mathcal{S}$ induces a finite permutation $\pi_{\mathcal{S}} : \mathbb{A} \to \mathbb{A}$, using the so-called "Homogeneity Lemma" of [11] (Lemma 1.14). Then, we define a restriction of the nominal equivalence $\sim_{\mathbb{A}}$ with respect to a span $\mathcal{S}$, written $X \sim_{\mathcal{S}} Y$, if $X = \pi_{\mathcal{S}} * Y$. We usually write Φ and $\mathcal{D}$ for spans respectively over functional names and locations, and write $x \sim_{\Phi}^{\mathcal{D}} y$ for the nominal equivalence induced by those spans on a nominal set over both FN and Loc.

3 Trace Semantics

This section presents a fully abstract model of RefML, based on a trace representation of game semantics which will be used to prove soundness and completeness of Kripke open bisimulations and at the same time to shed light on the intuitions coming from game semantics that have been used to define Kripke open bisimulations. Rather than working with the fully abstract game model of RefML defined by Murawski and Tzevelekos [9], it appears to be more convenient to work with a typed variant [4] of the trace model introduced by Laird [6]. This is because trace semantics, which provides as well a fully-abstract model of RefML, has a strong operational flavor, since it is generated via an *interactive reduction*, representing exactly all the possible interactions between terms and contexts.

3.1 Interactive Reduction

The denotation of terms is defined as set of traces, whose basic blocks are *actions* a, of four kinds (following game semantics terminology, actions of terms and contexts are respectively called Player and Opponent actions):

- a question of Player (resp. Opponent) via a functional name f with argument an abstract value v, represented by the action $\bar{f}\langle v\rangle$ (resp. $f\langle v\rangle$);
- an answer by Player (resp. Opponent) with the abstract value v, represented by the action $\langle\bar{v}\rangle$ (resp. $\langle v\rangle$).

A *trace* is then defined as a sequence of actions-with-heap (a, h), where a is an action and h is a closed abstract heap. An important point is that h represents the disclosed part of the heap, common to the term and the context.

Traces are generated using an *interactive reduction*. This reduction is defined on "*evaluation stacks*" $\mathcal{S}$, which are either

- *passive*, $(K^n[\bullet_{\sigma_n}], \tau_n) :: \ldots :: (K^1[\bullet_{\sigma_1}], \tau_1)$, formed by typed evaluations contexts, for *Opponent configurations*,
- or active, $(M, \theta) :: \mathcal{S}'$ formed by a term M of type θ and a passive stack $\mathcal{S}'$, for *Player configurations*.

The empty stack is simply written $\Diamond$. When Player provides a higher-order value to Opponent, either via a callback (i.e., a question) or directly when reducing to a λ-abstraction (i.e., an answer), it is stored in an environment γ, which is a partial maps from FN to Val. Then Opponent can recover what is stored in γ, by asking a question. We associate a type to every functional names using a typing function $\phi : \text{FN} \rightharpoonup \text{Types}$, such that $\text{dom}(\gamma) \subseteq \text{dom}(\phi)$. Functional names in $\text{dom}(\phi)\backslash\text{dom}(\gamma)$ are the one provided by Opponent, which can then be used by Player. To represent disclosure of locations, we use a typing function $D : \text{Loc} \rightharpoonup \text{Types}$, that we often see as a relation, which grows as the term or the context discloses new locations.

Definition 3. *The disclosed locations coming from a value v and a heap h and already disclosed locations in D is computed using the fonction* $\text{discl}(v, h, D)$, *defined as a typing function D' such that $(l, \tau) \in D'$ iff $l \in h^*(\nu_{\text{Loc}}(v, D))$ and $D'; \phi \vdash h(l) : \tau$.*

The interactive reduction is defined in Fig. 3 as a bipartite LTS between Player and Opponent configurations $\langle \mathcal{S}, \gamma, \phi, h, D \rangle$, where labels are actions-with-heap. The basic idea is that if a term reduces:

- to a callback $K[f\ u]$, the corresponding Player configuration performs a question $\bar{f}\ \langle v \rangle$, reducing to an Opponent configuration with K on top of the evaluation stack,
- to a value u, the corresponding Player configuration performs an answers $\langle \bar{v} \rangle$, reducing to an Opponent configuration where the head of the evaluation stack has been popped,

where v is an abstract values which, together with an environment γ' mapping its functional names to values, represents u. This γ' is added to the player environment. An opponent configuration can perform a question $f\ \langle v \rangle$ by interrogating

Intern $\langle (M, \tau) :: \mathcal{S}, \gamma, \phi, h, D \rangle \longrightarrow \langle (M', \tau) :: \mathcal{S}, \gamma, \phi, h', D \rangle$
(when $(M, h) \mapsto_{nd} (M', h')$)

P-Ans $\langle (u, \tau) :: \mathcal{S}, \gamma, \phi, h, D \rangle \xrightarrow{\langle \bar{v} \rangle, h'_{|D'}} \langle \mathcal{S}, \gamma', \phi', h[h'], D' \rangle$

P-Quest $\langle (K[f\ u], \sigma) :: \mathcal{S}, \gamma, \phi, h, D \rangle \xrightarrow{\bar{f}\langle v \rangle, h'_{|D'}} \langle (K[\bullet_{\tau'}], \sigma) :: \mathcal{S}, \gamma', \phi', h[h'], D' \rangle$
(with $\phi(f) = \tau \to \tau'$)

in all P-rules: $(v, \gamma_v, \phi_v) \in \mathbf{AVal}_u(\tau)$, $D' = \text{discl}(u, h, D)$,
$(h', \gamma_h, \phi_h) \in \mathbf{AHeap}_{D'}(h')$, $\gamma' = \gamma \cdot \gamma_v \cdot \gamma_h$, $\phi' = \phi \cdot \phi_v \cdot \phi_h$

O-Ans $\langle (K[\bullet_\tau], \sigma) :: \mathcal{S}, \gamma, \phi, h, D \rangle \xrightarrow{\langle v \rangle, h'_{|D'}} \langle (K[v], \sigma) :: \mathcal{S}, \gamma, \phi', h[h'], D' \rangle$

O-Quest $\langle \mathcal{S}, \gamma, \phi, h, D \rangle \xrightarrow{f\langle v \rangle, h'_{|D'}} \langle (u\, v, \sigma) :: \mathcal{S}, \gamma, \phi', h[h'], D' \rangle$
(with $\gamma(f) = u$)

in all O-Rules: $(v, \phi_v) \in [\![\tau]\!]$, $(h', \phi_h) \in [\![D']\!]$, $\phi' = \phi \cdot \phi_v \cdot \phi_h$, $D' = \text{discl}(v, h, D)$

Fig. 3. Definition of the interaction reduction

a functional name f in γ, or, if its evaluation stack is non-empty, it can perform an answer $\langle v \rangle$, filling the hole of the first context of the stack.

The representation of a value u of type τ as a triple (v, ϕ, γ) formed by an abstract value, and two functions mapping its fresh functional names to values and types, is defined via the following set $\mathbf{AVal}_u(\tau)$:

$$\begin{array}{lll}
\mathbf{AVal}_v(\iota) & \stackrel{def}{=} & \{(v, \varepsilon, \varepsilon)\} \text{ for } \iota = \text{Unit}, \text{Bool}, \text{Int}, \text{ref}\,\tau \\
\mathbf{AVal}_{\langle u_1, u_2 \rangle}(\tau_1 \times \tau_2) & \stackrel{def}{=} & \{(\langle v_1, v_2 \rangle, \gamma_1 \cdot \gamma_2, \phi_1 \cdot \phi_2) \mid (v_i, \gamma_i, \phi_i) \in \mathbf{AVal}_{u_i}(\tau_i)\} \\
\mathbf{AVal}_u(\tau \to \sigma) & \stackrel{def}{=} & \{(f, [f \mapsto u], [f \mapsto (\tau \to \sigma)]) \mid f \in \text{FN}\}
\end{array}$$

We also define a function $\mathbf{AHeap}_D(h)$ to transform a heap h into a triple (h', γ, ϕ) formed by an abstract heap, and two functions mapping its fresh functional names to values and types, defined, using the typing information on locations contains in D, as:

$$\begin{array}{lll}
\mathbf{AHeap}_D(\varepsilon) & \stackrel{def}{=} & \{(\varepsilon, \varepsilon, \varepsilon)\} \\
\mathbf{AHeap}_D(h \cdot [l \mapsto u]) & \stackrel{def}{=} & \{(h' \cdot [l \mapsto v], \gamma \cdot \gamma', \phi \cdot \phi') \mid (h', \gamma', \phi') \in \mathbf{AHeap}_D(h), \\
& & \quad (v, \gamma, \phi) \in \mathbf{AVal}_u(\tau) \text{ with } (l, \tau) \in D\}
\end{array}$$

We write $C \stackrel{a}{\Rightarrow} C'$ when, if C is a Player configuration then there exists a Player configuration C'' such that $C \to C'' \stackrel{a}{\to} C'$, otherwise if C is an Opponent configuration then $C \stackrel{a}{\to} C'$. A trace T is *generated* by a configuration C when it can be written as a sequence $a_1 \cdots a_n$ of actions-with-heap s.t. $C \stackrel{a_1}{\Rightarrow} C_1 \stackrel{a_2}{\Rightarrow} \ldots \stackrel{a_n}{\Rightarrow} C_n$, in which case we write $C \stackrel{T}{\Rightarrow} C_n$. The set of traces generated by C is written $\text{Tr}(C)$. A trace $T \in \text{Tr}(C)$ is said to be *complete* if the number of answers occurring in the trace is greater than its number of questions plus the length of the evaluation stack of C. They can also be seen as the traces for which C reduces to a *final* Opponent configuration, that is one with an empty stack. The set of complete traces of a configuration C is written $\mathbf{comp}(\text{Tr}(C))$. To define the denotation associated to an *open* term M, an extra action $?\langle v \rangle$, the *initial Opponent question*, is added to fix the choice of abstract values for the free variables of M.

Definition 4. *The set of complete traces generated by M, written $[\![\Sigma; \Gamma \vdash M : \tau]\!]$, is*

$$\bigcup \mathbf{comp}(\{?\langle \text{codom}(\rho) \rangle \cdot \text{Tr}(\langle (\rho(M), \tau), \varepsilon, \phi_\Gamma \cdot \phi_\Sigma, h, \Sigma' \rangle \mid (\rho, \phi_\Gamma) \in [\![\Gamma]\!],$$
$$\Sigma' \supseteq \Sigma, (h, \phi_\Sigma) \in [\![\Sigma']\!], \nu_{\text{Loc}}(\rho) \subseteq \text{dom}(\Sigma')\}).$$

As proven by Laird in [6] for closed, and more generally for open terms in [4], we get a full abstraction result:

Theorem 1. $\Sigma; \Gamma \vdash M_1 \simeq_{ctx} M_2 : \tau \Leftrightarrow [\![\Sigma; \Gamma \vdash M_1 : \tau]\!] = [\![\Sigma; \Gamma \vdash M_2 : \tau]\!]$.

3.2 Nominal Equivalence of Traces

In the following, we decompose traces forming the denotation of terms, thus loosing the initial Opponent question which fixes the choice of names. To overtake this problem, we reason up to nominal equivalence of traces, with permutations which fix these names via two spans Φ and $\mathcal{D}$ on Loc and FN. We write $T \simeq_{\Phi}^{\mathcal{D}} T'$ if $T = a_1 \cdot \ldots \cdot a_n, T' = a'_1 \cdot \ldots \cdot a'_n$ and there exist two spans $\Phi' \sqsupseteq \Phi$ and $\mathcal{D}' \sqsupseteq \mathcal{D}$ such that for all $i, a_i \sim_{\Phi'}^{\mathcal{D}'} a'_i$. We then apply such nominal reasoning on *compatible configurations*

Definition 5. *Two configurations* C_1, C_2 *are* compatible *for* $\Phi, \mathcal{D}$ *when, writing* C_i *as* $\langle \mathcal{S}_i, \gamma_i, \phi_i, h_i, D_i \rangle$, *we have* $\Phi_i = \phi_i$, $\mathcal{D}_i = D_i$, *there exists a subspan* $\Phi_P \sqsubseteq \Phi$ *such that* $\mathrm{dom}(\gamma_i) = \Phi_i$, *and writing* n_i *for the evaluation stack* $\mathcal{S}_i$, *for all* $j \in \{1, \ldots, \mathbf{min}(n_1, n_2)\}$, *the* j*-th elements of* $\mathcal{S}_1$ *and* $\mathcal{S}_2$ *are of the same type, and* $n_1 = 0$ *iff* $n_2 = 0$ *(i.e.,* C_1 *is a final configuration iff* C_2 *is).*

Taking two compatible configurations C_1, C_2 for $\Phi, \mathcal{D}$, we write $C_1 \simeq_{\Phi}^{\mathcal{D}} C_2$ when for all $T_1 \in \mathbf{comp}(\mathrm{Tr}(C_1))$, there exists $T_2 \in \mathbf{comp}(\mathrm{Tr}(C_2))$ such that $T_1 \simeq_{\Phi}^{\mathcal{D}} T_2$, and for all $T_2 \in \mathbf{comp}(\mathrm{Tr}(C_2))$, there exists $T_1 \in \mathbf{comp}(\mathrm{Tr}(C_1))$ such that $T_1 \simeq_{\Phi}^{\mathcal{D}} T_2$.

Theorem 2. *Suppose that* $\Sigma; \Gamma \vdash M_1, M_2 : \tau$, *then* $\Sigma; \Gamma \vdash M_1 \simeq_{ctx} M_2 : \tau$ *if and only if for all* $(\rho, \phi_\Gamma) \in [\![\Gamma]\!], \Sigma' \supset \Sigma$ *and* $(h, \phi_\Sigma) \in [\![\Sigma']\!]$ *closed s.t.* $\nu_{\mathrm{Loc}}(\rho) \subseteq \mathrm{dom}(\Sigma')$, *we have* $C_1 \simeq_{\hat{\phi}}^{\widehat{\Sigma'}} C_2$, *where* $C_i = \langle (\rho(M_i), \tau), \varepsilon, \phi, h, \Sigma' \rangle$ *with* $\phi = \phi_\Gamma \cdot \phi_\Sigma$.

3.3 A Simple Bisimulation on Traces

One can see the LTS that generates traces as a (possibly infinite) automaton, where the final states correspond to opponent configurations with an empty evaluation stack. Then, bisimulations on this automaton can be defined in a standard way in order to capture the equality of the two languages recognized from two states (i.e. two configurations).

Using the fact that the LTS is bipartite, deterministic, and that a Player configuration can generate at most one action (up to nominal equivalence), we introduce a notion of bisimilation on traces as a family of pairs of relations $(\mathcal{P}_{\Phi,\mathcal{D}}, \mathcal{O}_{\Phi,\mathcal{D}})$ on *compatible* Player and Opponent configurations for Φ and $\mathcal{D}$ two spans respectively on functional names and locations, whose mutual coinductive definitions is given in Fig. 4. Its definition is somehow complicated by the fact that the LTS is not complete, since for any configuration there exists some action a such that C does not produce a. This is particularly the case of diverging Player configurations, which simply do not produce any actions. We cannot complete the LTS by adding a unique "garbage state", since this state would not be compatible with the other diverging states. So for an Opponent (non-final) configuration C and two spans $\Phi, \mathcal{D}$, we consider the associated diverging compatible state $C_{\Phi,\mathcal{D}}^{\not{\downarrow} i}$ defined as $\langle \mathcal{S}^{\not{\downarrow} i}, \gamma^{\not{\downarrow} i}, \Phi_i, h, \mathcal{D}_i \rangle$, where we write $\mathcal{S}^{\not{\downarrow} i}$ for the evaluation stack $(\lambda\_.\bot_\tau)\bullet_\sigma, \tau)$ such that the top element of the evaluation

$$
\begin{aligned}
\mathcal{O}_{\Phi,\mathcal{D}} &\stackrel{def}{=} \Big\{(C_1, C_2) \mid \forall \Phi' \sqsupseteq \Phi, \forall \mathcal{D}' \sqsupseteq \mathcal{D} \forall a_1 \sim_{\Phi'}^{\mathcal{D}'} a_2 . \exists (C_1', C_2') \in \mathcal{P}_{\Phi',\mathcal{D}'} . \\
&\qquad ((C_1 \stackrel{a_1}{\Rightarrow} C_1') \Leftrightarrow (C_2 \stackrel{a_1}{\Rightarrow} C_2'))\Big\} \\
\mathcal{P}_{\Phi,\mathcal{D}} &\stackrel{def}{=} \{(C_1, C_2) \mid (\forall i \in \{1,2\}. C_i \in \mathcal{P}^{\lightning i}) \vee (\exists \Phi' \sqsupseteq \Phi . \exists \mathcal{D}' \sqsupseteq \mathcal{D} . \\
&\qquad \exists (C_1', C_2') \in \mathcal{O}_{\Phi',\mathcal{D}'} . \exists a_1 \sim_{\Phi'}^{\mathcal{D}'} a_2 . (\forall i \in \{1,2\}. C_i \stackrel{a_i}{\Rightarrow} C_i')\} \\
\mathcal{P}^{\lightning i} &\stackrel{def}{=} \{C \mid C \Uparrow \vee \exists C' \in \mathcal{O}^{\lightning i} . \exists a . C \stackrel{a}{\Rightarrow} C'\} \\
\mathcal{O}^{\lightning 1} &\stackrel{def}{=} \{C \mid \exists \Phi, \mathcal{D} . \Phi_1 = C.\phi \wedge \mathcal{D}_1 = C.D \wedge (C, C^{\lightning 1}_{\Phi,\mathcal{D}}) \in \mathcal{O}_{\Phi,\mathcal{D}}\} \\
\mathcal{O}^{\lightning 2} &\stackrel{def}{=} \{C \mid \exists \Phi, \mathcal{D} . \Phi_2 = C.\phi \wedge \mathcal{D}_2 = C.D \wedge (C^{\lightning 2}_{\Phi,\mathcal{D}}, C) \in \mathcal{O}_{\Phi,\mathcal{D}}\}
\end{aligned}
$$

Fig. 4. Bisimulations on traces

stack of C is of type $\sigma \rightsquigarrow \tau$ and $\gamma^{\lightning 1}$ is defined as $\{(f, \lambda\_ : \sigma.\bot_{\sigma'}) \mid \exists f' \in \mathrm{dom}(C.\gamma).(f', f, \sigma \to \sigma') \in \Phi\}$ (the symmetric definitions applies for $i = 2$).

This notion of bisimulation captures equality of complete traces in the following sense (the proof can be found in Appendix B).

Theorem 3. *Taking C_1, C_2 be two configurations of polarity $X \in \{O, P\}$, we have $C_1 \simeq_{\Phi}^{\mathcal{D}} C_2$ iff $(C_1, C_2) \in X_{\Phi,\mathcal{D}}$.*

4 Kripke Open Bisimulations

Bisimulations on traces can be somehow difficult to use as the LTS they are defined on is in most cases infinite. Indeed, Opponent has always the possibility to question a function f in γ as many times as he wants. The interaction generated by this question depends on both the value and the heap provided by Opponent. It is possible to characterizes them by knowing what are the disclosed locations (living in D) and the private part of the heap ($h_{\overline{D}}$), at any point after the introduction of f. To do so, we use a notion of world w, formed by such invariants on private heaps and a span on disclosed locations, and a transition system $\mathcal{A}$ describing how these worlds evolve. One can check the equivalence of two functional values disclosed by Player by checking their equivalence for any "future" world. This is the basic reasoning principle of Kripke Open Bisimulations, which is in fact taken from Kripke Logical Relations.

4.1 Transition Systems and Worlds

As in the work on RTS, we choose to work with "small" worlds, which only states *local* invariants relevant to the terms we reason on, but nothing about the invariants of the global contexts. But compared to the worlds used in RTS, we choose to do not incorporate the transition system inside the definition of worlds, but to use instead an external definition of transition system which dictates the evolution of worlds. Doing so, we can see transitions as pairs of pre- and post-conditions on heaps. We call them *World Transition Systems*

(WTS, defined in Fig. 5), since they are simply transition functions between worlds. Worlds w are tuples formed by a state s from an abstract set State, two heaps (describing the private part of the heap) h_1, h_2, a typed span on locations $\mathcal{D}$ and a boolean indicating if the world is inconsistent or not. We suppose that for $i \in \{1,2\}, \text{dom}(h_i) \cap \mathcal{D}_i = \varnothing$. In practice, State can simply be taken as natural numbers. For a world $w = (s, h_1, h_2, \mathcal{D}, b)$ we define the predicates $\mathbf{cons}(w)$ and $\mathbf{incons}(w)$ respectively as $b = \mathbf{false}$ and $b = \mathbf{true}$. WTS are formed by a pair $(\delta, \delta_{\mathbf{pub}})$ respectively for private and public transitions, which are simply relations between worlds. Since worlds do not fully specify the disclosed part of heaps, there can be some branching on the values stored inside, which explains the non-deterministic representation of transitions, rather than just using a partial function. Private transitions represent transitions that only terms can take, while public ones can be taken by both terms and contexts. This explains the condition $\delta_{\mathbf{pub}} \subseteq \delta^*_{\mathbf{priv}}$. Moreover, private transitions cannot transform an inconsistent world into a consistent one.

Worlds specify heaps precisely, since there is no freedom on the private part of the heap, while on the public part, the span is used to induce a nominal equivalence. But depending on whether the disclosed part is an abstract heap or a usual heap, we use two different predicates, defined in Fig. 5:

- $\mathbf{P}_\Phi(w)$, which characterizes tuples $(h_1, h_2, \mathcal{D}, \Phi')$ of heaps together with a span on disclosed locations and a span on functional names Φ' that extends Φ, and which is used to collect the functional names used as abstract values on the $h_{i|\mathcal{D}_i}$
- $\mathbf{Q}_\Phi(w)$, which characterizes tuples $(h_1, h_2, \mathcal{D})$, where the $h_{i|\mathcal{D}_i}$ can contain λ-abstraction on which $\mathcal{V}_\mathcal{A}\,[\![\tau]\!]_\Phi w$, introduced in the next section, is used to reason about (via a mutual definition).

Transitions of a WTS $\mathcal{A}$ are used to define private and public notions of future worlds.

Definition 6. *Let $\mathcal{A}$ be a WTS and w_1, w_2 two worlds. We say that w_2 is a future (w.r.t. $\mathcal{A}$) of w_1, written $w_2 \sqsupseteq w_1$ if either $w_1 = w_2$ or $\delta_{\mathbf{priv}}(w_1, w_2)$. Note that strictly speaking, $\sqsupseteq$ depends on $\mathcal{A}$ but it is not explicit in the notation as $\mathcal{A}$ is always clear from context. Public futures (noted with $\sqsupseteq_{\mathbf{pub}}$) are defined similarly using $\delta_{\mathbf{pub}}$.*

Because contexts may create fresh disclosed locations during execution, we also introduce a notion of *freshened* extension $\mathcal{F}(w)$ of a world w which forces the existence of a state creating an arbitrary number of fresh disclosed locations. $\mathcal{F}(w)$ is defined as $\{(s, h_1, h_2, \mathcal{D}) \mid s = w.s, h_1 = w.h_1, h_2 = w.h_2, \exists \mathcal{D}'.\mathcal{D} = \mathcal{D}' \uplus w.\mathcal{D}\}$. We then write $w' \sqsupseteq^{\mathcal{F}} w$ (resp. $w' \sqsupseteq^{\mathcal{F}}_{\mathbf{pub}} w$) when there exists w'' such that $w'' \sqsupseteq w$ (resp. $w'' \sqsupseteq_{\mathbf{pub}} w$) and $w' \in \mathcal{F}(w'')$. We write $\sqsupseteq^{\mathcal{F}*}$ and $\sqsupseteq^{\mathcal{F}*}_{\mathbf{pub}}$ respectively for the transitive closure of $\sqsupseteq^{\mathcal{F}}$ and $\sqsupseteq^{\mathcal{F}}_{\mathbf{pub}}$.

$$\mathrm{World} \stackrel{def}{=} \mathrm{State} \times \mathrm{Heap}^2 \times \mathrm{Span}_{\mathrm{Loc}} \times \mathrm{Bool}$$

$$\begin{aligned}\mathrm{WTS} \stackrel{def}{=} \{(\delta_{\mathbf{priv}}, \delta_{\mathbf{pub}}) \mid \delta_{priv}, \delta_{pub} \subseteq \mathcal{P}(\mathrm{World} \times \mathrm{World}), \delta_{\mathbf{pub}} \subseteq \delta^*_{\mathbf{priv}}, \\ \forall (w, w') \in \delta_{\mathbf{priv}}.\mathbf{cons}(w') \Rightarrow \mathbf{cons}(w)\}\end{aligned}$$

$$\begin{aligned}\mathbf{P}_\Phi(w) \stackrel{def}{=} \{(h_1, h_2, \mathcal{D}, \Phi') \mid \exists \Phi''. \exists h_1^d, h_2^d. \Phi' = \Phi \cdot \Phi'' \wedge h_1^d \sim^{\mathcal{D}}_{\Phi''} h_2^d \wedge \mathcal{D} = w.\mathcal{D} \\ \wedge \forall i \in \{1,2\}. h_i = w.h_i \cdot h_i^d \wedge h_i^d \in [\![\mathcal{D}_i]\!]\}\end{aligned}$$

$$\begin{aligned}\mathbf{Q}_\Phi(w) \stackrel{def}{=} \{(h_1, h_2, \mathcal{D}) \mid \forall (l_1, l_2, \tau) \in \mathcal{D}.(h_1(l_1), h_2(l_2)) \in \mathcal{V}_\mathcal{A} [\![\tau]\!]_\Phi \, w \\ \wedge \mathcal{D} = w.\mathcal{D} \wedge \forall i \in \{1,2\}. h_i = w.h_i \cdot h_i^d \wedge \mathrm{dom}(h_i^d) = \mathcal{D}_i\}\end{aligned}$$

$$\mathcal{V}_\mathcal{A} [\![\iota]\!]_\Phi \, w \stackrel{def}{=} \{(v_1, v_2) \mid v_1, v_2 \in [\![\iota]\!], v_1 \sim_{w.D} v_2\}$$

$$\mathcal{V}_\mathcal{A} [\![\tau_1 \times \tau_2]\!]_\Phi \, w \stackrel{def}{=} \{(\langle v_1, v_2\rangle, \langle v_1', v_2'\rangle) \mid \forall i \in \{1,2\}.(v_i, v_i') \in \mathcal{V}_\mathcal{A} [\![\tau_i]\!]_\Phi \, w\}$$

$$\begin{aligned}\mathcal{V}_\mathcal{A} [\![\tau \to \sigma]\!]_\Phi \, w \stackrel{def}{=} \{((u_1, u_2) \mid \forall w' \sqsupseteq^{\mathcal{F}*} w. \forall \Phi' \# \Phi. \forall (v_1, \Phi_1'), (v_2, \Phi_2') \in [\![\tau]\!]. \\ v_1 \sim_{\Phi', w'.\mathcal{D}} v_2 \Rightarrow (u_1 \, v_1, u_2 \, v_2) \in \mathcal{E}_\mathcal{A} [\![\sigma]\!]_{\Phi.\Phi'} (w', w')\}\end{aligned}$$

$$\mathcal{G}_\mathcal{A} [\![\Phi_P]\!]_\Phi \, w \stackrel{def}{=} \{(\gamma_1, \gamma_2) \mid \forall (f_1, f_2, \tau) \in \Phi_P.(\gamma_1(f_1), \gamma_2(f_2)) \in \mathcal{V}_\mathcal{A} [\![\tau]\!]_\Phi \, w\}$$

$$\begin{aligned}\mathcal{K}_\mathcal{A} [\![\tau, \sigma]\!]_\Phi (w, w_0) \stackrel{def}{=} \{(K_1, K_2) \mid \forall w' \sqsupseteq^{\mathcal{F}*}_{\mathbf{pub}} w. \forall \Phi' \# \Phi. \forall (v_1, \Phi_1'), (v_2, \Phi_2') \in [\![\tau]\!]. \\ v_1 \sim_{\Phi', w'.\mathcal{D}} v_2 \Rightarrow (K_1[v_1], K_2[v_2]) \in \mathcal{E}_\mathcal{A} [\![\sigma]\!]_{\Phi.\Phi'} (w', w_0)\}\end{aligned}$$

$$\begin{aligned}&\mathcal{E}_\mathcal{A} [\![\tau]\!]_\Phi (w, w_0) \stackrel{def}{=} \Big\{(M_1, M_2) \mid \forall (h_1, h_2, \mathcal{D}, \Phi') \in \mathbf{P}_\Phi(w). \\ &\Big(\exists M_1', M_2'. \exists w' \sqsupseteq w. \exists (h_1', h_2', \mathcal{D}') \in \mathbf{Q}_{\Phi'}(w'). \\ &\quad \forall i \in \{1,2\}.((M_i, h_i) \mapsto^* (M_i', h_i') \wedge \mathbf{irred}(M_i', h_i')) \\ &\quad \wedge \Big(\big(\exists (u_1, u_2) \in \mathcal{V}_\mathcal{A} [\![\tau]\!]_{\Phi'} \, w' \wedge w' \sqsupseteq^*_{\mathbf{pub}} w_0 \wedge \forall i \in \{1,2\}. M_i' = u_i \wedge \mathrm{discl}(u_i, h_i', \mathcal{D}_i) \subseteq \mathcal{D}_i'\big) \\ &\quad\quad \vee \big(\exists (f_1, f_2, \sigma \to \sigma') \in \Phi'. \exists (u_1, u_2) \in \mathcal{V}_\mathcal{A} [\![\sigma]\!]_{\Phi'} \, w'. \exists (K_1, K_2) \in \mathcal{K}_\mathcal{A} [\![\sigma', \tau]\!]_{\Phi'} (w', w_0) \\ &\quad\quad\quad \forall i \in \{1,2\}. M_i' = K_i[f_i \, u_i] \mathrm{discl}(u_i, h_i', \mathcal{D}_i) \subseteq \mathcal{D}_i'\big)\Big)\Big) \\ &\vee \big(\forall i \in \{1,2\}.(M_i, h_i, \mathcal{D}_i) \in \mathcal{E}^i_\mathcal{A} [\![\tau]\!]_{\Phi_i'} (w, w_0)\big)\Big\}\end{aligned}$$

$$\begin{aligned}&\mathcal{E}^i_\mathcal{A} [\![\tau]\!]_\phi (w, w_0) \stackrel{def}{=} \Big\{(M, h, D) \mid (M, h) \Uparrow \vee \Big(\exists M'. \exists w' \sqsupseteq w. \exists (h', D') \in \mathbf{Q}^i_\phi(w'). \\ &\quad (M, h) \mapsto^* (M', h') \wedge \mathbf{irred}(M', h') \wedge \mathbf{incons}(w') \wedge \\ &\quad \Big(\big(\exists u \in \mathcal{V}^i_\mathcal{A} [\![\tau]\!]_\phi \, w'. M' = u \wedge \mathrm{discl}(u, h', D) \subseteq D' \wedge w' \sqsupseteq^*_{\mathbf{pub}} w_0\big) \vee \big(\exists (f, \sigma \to \sigma') \in \phi. \\ &\quad\quad \exists u \in \mathcal{V}^i_\mathcal{A} [\![\sigma]\!]_\phi \, w'. \exists K \in \mathcal{K}^i_\mathcal{A} [\![\sigma', \tau]\!]_\phi (w', w_0). M' = K[f \, u]\big) \wedge \mathrm{discl}(u, h', D') \subseteq D'\Big)\Big)\Big\}\end{aligned}$$

$$\begin{aligned}\Sigma; \Gamma \vdash M_1 \simeq_{kob} M_2 : \tau \stackrel{def}{=} \exists \mathcal{A} \in \mathrm{WTS}. \exists s \in \mathrm{State}. \forall (\rho, \phi) \in [\![\Gamma]\!]. \forall \Sigma' \supseteq \Sigma. \\ \nu_{\mathrm{Loc}}(\rho) \subseteq \mathrm{dom}(\Sigma') \Rightarrow (\rho(M_1), \rho(M_2)) \in \mathcal{E}_\mathcal{A} [\![\tau]\!]_{\widehat{\phi}} (w_0, w_0)\end{aligned}$$

where $w_0 = (s, \varepsilon, \varepsilon, \widehat{\Sigma'}, \mathbf{false})$. and for all $w \sqsupseteq^*_{\mathbf{pub}} w_0.\mathbf{cons}(w)$

Fig. 5. Definition of Kripke Open Bisimulations for RefML.

4.2 Definition of KOBs

This section introduces Kripke open bisimulations. For space limitation, we have illustrated in Appendix F, on well-known examples of the literature, how to use direct-style reasoning, spans of names, WTSs and reasoning about divergence—which constitute the main concepts of KOBs.

Kripke open bisimulations, defined via a mutual coinduction in Fig. 5, are a family of relations on values ($\mathcal{V}_{\mathcal{A}}\llbracket\tau\rrbracket_{\Phi}w$), evaluation contexts[3] ($\mathcal{K}_{\mathcal{A}}\llbracket\tau,\sigma\rrbracket_{\Phi}w$) and terms ($\mathcal{E}_{\mathcal{A}}\llbracket\tau\rrbracket_{\Phi}w$), that represents a particular kind of bisimulation, indexed by a world w of the WTS $\mathcal{A}$ and by a span on functional names Φ.

Compared to the bisimulations on traces, here we do not reason anymore on configurations, but simply on terms. The bisimulation on Player configurations corresponds to $\mathcal{E}_{\mathcal{A}}\llbracket\tau\rrbracket$, while the bisimulation on Opponent configurations corresponds to $\mathcal{V}_{\mathcal{A}}\llbracket\tau\rrbracket w$ for the questions, and $\mathcal{K}_{\mathcal{A}}\llbracket\sigma,\tau\rrbracket$ for the answers.

Forgetting a moment about the necessary predicative reasoning principle for diverging terms, Kripke open bisimulations mainly guarantee that, once reducing two terms with heaps satisfying the invariants of the current world w, they either diverge, or there exists a future world w' of w such that the heaps produced by the reduction satisfy its invariants, and if the resulting terms are values, they are related, otherwise the resulting terms are callbacks which are synchronized, with the evaluation contexts surrounding them being related. The span on functional names Φ is used to keep track of functional names given by the context to the terms. Indeed, compared to logical relations, when τ is of functional type, the definition of $\mathcal{V}_{\mathcal{A}}\llbracket\tau\to\sigma\rrbracket_{\Phi}w$ does not quantify over related values v_1, v_2 of type τ, but uses instead fresh functional names f_1, f_2, remembering in Φ that they are related.

The definition of $\mathcal{E}_{\mathcal{A}}\llbracket\tau\rrbracket_{\Phi}(w, w_0)$ is indexed by an extra world w_0, corresponding to the initial world where the reduction of the two terms has been considered, and which is thus freshened in the definition of $\mathcal{V}_{\mathcal{A}}\llbracket\tau\to\sigma\rrbracket_{\Phi}w$. We enforce the existence of a *public* transition between a future world w' of w, and w_0 when terms have been reduced to values (but not callbacks). This corresponds to a well-bracketed behavior, where the question, which happens in the world w_0, is answered in the world w'.

Finally, the "full" KOB $\Sigma;\Gamma_f,\Gamma_g \vdash M_1 \simeq_{kob} M_2 : \tau$ is defined for terms with open ground variables, that must be substituted by ground values. All the futures worlds of the initial world w_0 used in its definition must be consistent. The main difference with Kripke logical relations is that there is an existential quantification over the WTS $\mathcal{A}$ which fixes the possible futures instead of a universal over all possible world extensions.

Predicative Reasoning. When considering diverging terms, synchronization of callbacks is no longer valid, since the two terms can diverge at different time during the execution. This is taken into account by a predicative reasoning involving:

- $\mathbf{Q}^i_{\phi}(w)$ defined as $\{(h,D) \mid h = (w.h_i)\cdot h^d \wedge D = (w.\mathcal{D})_i \wedge \mathrm{dom}(h^d) = D \wedge \forall (l,\tau)\in D, h(l) \in \mathcal{V}^i_{\mathcal{A}}\llbracket\tau\rrbracket_{\phi}w\}$
- $\mathcal{V}^1_{\mathcal{A}}\llbracket\iota\rrbracket_{\Phi}w$, defined as the set of closed values of type ι, for ι a ground type,
- $\mathcal{V}^1_{\mathcal{A}}\llbracket\tau\to\sigma\rrbracket_{\Phi}w$, defined as the set of values $\{v \mid \exists\Phi\in\mathrm{Span}_{\mathrm{FN}}.\Phi_1 = \phi \wedge (v, \lambda x.\bot_{\sigma}) \in \mathcal{V}_{\mathcal{A}}\llbracket\tau\to\sigma\rrbracket_{\Phi}w\}$,

[3] Even if we use a relation $\mathcal{K}_{\mathcal{A}}\llbracket\sigma,\tau\rrbracket$ on evaluation contexts, our definition does not make any use of biorthogonality.

- $\mathcal{K}^1_{\mathcal{A}}[\![\tau, \sigma]\!]_\phi(w, w_0)$, defined as the set of contexts $\{K \mid \exists \Phi \in \mathrm{Span}_{\mathrm{FN}}.\Phi_1 = \phi \wedge (K, (\lambda\_.\bot_\sigma)\bullet) \in \mathcal{K}_{\mathcal{A}}[\![\tau, \sigma]\!]_\Phi(w, w_0)\}$

and $\mathcal{V}^2_{\mathcal{A}}[\![\tau]\!]_\Phi w$, $\mathcal{K}^2_{\mathcal{A}}[\![\tau, \sigma]\!]_\Phi(w, w_0)$ defined in a symmetric way. Then, we use inconsistent states to allow predicative reasoning, however this is not allowed in a public future of the initial world used in the definition $\Sigma; \Gamma_f, \Gamma_g \vdash M_1 \simeq_{kob} M_2 : \tau$, to avoid having unrelated "final" answers. This condition is also present in the definition of KLR [2].

4.3 An Example: Well-Bracketed State Change

We now see how KOBs work, using the WTS in Fig. 6. on the "well-bracketed state change" example:

$$M_1 = \texttt{let x} = \mathrm{ref}\,0\ \texttt{in}\ \lambda\texttt{f.x} := 0; \texttt{f}(); \texttt{x} := 1; \texttt{f}();\ !x$$
$$M_2 = \lambda\texttt{f.f}(); \texttt{f}();\ 1$$

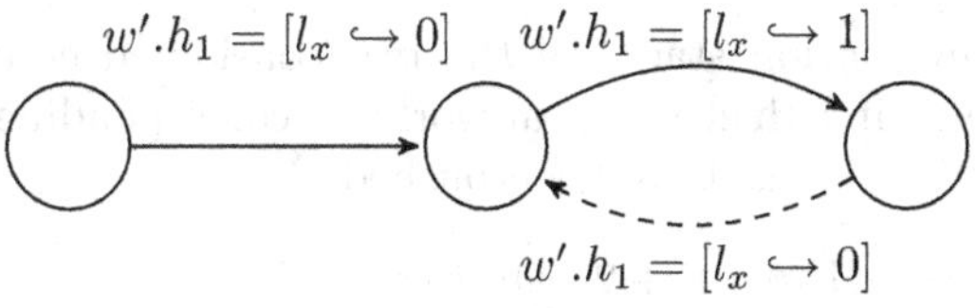

Fig. 6. WTS for the well-bracketed state change example.

The transitions from the left to the middle state and from the middle to the right state are public, so that both the term and contexts can take it. The other one is only private to the term. Then, to prove the equivalence, we begin in the left state, and we reduce (M_1, ε) to $(v_1, h_1) = (\lambda\texttt{f.l}_\texttt{x} := 0; \texttt{f}(); \texttt{l}_\texttt{x} := 1; \texttt{f}();\ !l_x, [\texttt{l}_\texttt{x} \mapsto 0])$. Then, to prove the equivalence of v_1 and M_2, we must reason about all the future state of the middle one. This correspond to the fact that such λ-abstractions can be called at any point of the execution by the context, via nested calls.

Suppose we are in the right state. Then we know that $l_x \hookrightarrow 1$ and to prove that the two λ-abstractions are equivalent in this state, we directly reason on the corresponding open terms where the bindings of f have been removed. We reduce them, and since l_x is set to 0, we go back to the middle state, which is (privately) accessible. They both perform the same callback with the same value (), so far they are related. Then, we must prove that the two contexts $\bullet; \texttt{l}_\texttt{x} := 1; \texttt{f}();\ !l_x$ and $\bullet; \texttt{f}(); 1$ are related. To do so, we can go to any state *publicly* accessible from the current one. That is, we can be in the middle or right state as both are publicly accessible. Moreover, the contexts we consider have a hole of type Unit, so we just have to prove that the two terms $(); \texttt{l}_\texttt{x} := 1; \texttt{f}();\ !l_x$ and $(); \texttt{f}(); 1$ are related. Reducing them, the callbacks are again related, and we must find a state where the post-condition $l_x \mapsto 1$ is valid, i.e., we move to the right state. Finally, we travel to any public future state from this one, so we stay in the same place, to prove that the contexts $\bullet; !l_x$ and $\bullet; 1$ are equivalent, which is straightforward since we know that l_x points to 1. The reasoning for the state where $l_x \hookrightarrow 0$ is similar. We see that the proof is done via a simple reasoning on the transition system, reducing the terms step by step. We have not simplified it in any way.

5 Soundness

We now prove a correspondence between bisimulations on traces and KOBs (the complete proofs are given in Appendix D). To do so, since KOBs are defined using the usual operational semantics, we need a lemma to validate the transformation of values into abstract values and functional environments defined via $\mathbf{AVal}_u(\tau)$

Lemma 1. *Let us consider* $(u_1, u_2) \in \mathcal{V}_\mathcal{A} [\![\tau]\!]_{\Phi_O} w$. *Taking* $(v_1, \phi_1, \gamma_1) \in \mathbf{AVal}_{u_1}(\tau)$ *and* $(v_2, \phi_2, \gamma_2) \in \mathbf{AVal}_{u_2}(\tau)$ *such that* $\mathrm{dom}(\phi_i) \cap \mathrm{dom}(\Phi_{O,i}) = \varnothing$, *there exists a span* Φ_P *satisfying* $\Phi_{P,i} = \phi_i$ *such that* $v_1 \sim^{w.\mathcal{D}}_{\Phi_P} v_2$ *and* $(\gamma_1, \gamma_2) \in \mathcal{G}_\mathcal{A} [\![\Phi_P]\!]_{\Phi_O} w$.

To relate the evaluation stacks of the two considered configurations, it is necessary to relate their j-th elements at world w_j corresponding to the invariant when these evaluation stacks have been pushed.

Theorem 4. *Let* $n \in \mathbb{N}$ *and* $n+2$ *world* $w_{n+1} \sqsupseteq^{\mathcal{F}*} w_n \sqsupseteq^{\mathcal{F}*} \dots \sqsupseteq^{\mathcal{F}*} w_0$ *such that*

- $\forall w' \sqsupseteq^*_{\mathbf{pub}} w_0.\mathbf{cons}(w')$,
- $(M_1, M_2) \in \mathcal{E}_\mathcal{A} [\![\tau]\!]_{\Phi_O}(w_{n+1}, w_n)$,
- *for all* $j \in \{1, \dots, n\}$, $(K_1^j, K_2^j) \in \mathcal{K}_\mathcal{A} [\![\sigma_j, \tau_j]\!]_{\Phi_O}(w_{n+1}, w_{j-1})$,
- $(\gamma_1, \gamma_2) \in \mathcal{G}_\mathcal{A} [\![\Phi_P]\!]_{\Phi_O} w_{n+1}$.

Then for all $(h_1, h_2, \mathcal{D}, \Phi') \in \mathbf{P}_{\Phi_P \cdot \Phi_O}(w_{n+1})$, *writing* $\mathcal{S}_i$ *for* $(K_i^n[\bullet_{\sigma_n}], \tau_n) :: \dots :: (K_i^1[\bullet_{\sigma_1}], \tau_1)$, $(\langle (M_1, \tau) :: \mathcal{S}_1, \gamma_1, \Phi'_1, h_1, \mathcal{D}_1 \rangle, \langle (M_2, \tau) :: \mathcal{S}_2, \gamma_2, \Phi'_2, h_2, \mathcal{D}_2 \rangle) \in \mathcal{P}_{\Phi', \mathcal{D}}$.

From Theorems 2, 3 and 4, we get the wanted result.

Corollary 1. *Suppose that* $\Sigma; \Gamma \vdash M_1 \simeq_{kob} M_2 : \tau$, *then* $\Sigma; \Gamma \vdash M_1 \simeq_{ctx} M_2 : \tau$.

6 Completeness

As opposed to KLR, completeness of KOBs can no longer be proven "for free" using biorthogonality. The proof needs to be more constructive and relies crucially on the connection to the fully-abstract trace semantics introduced in Sect. 3. However, it is not possible to use directly bisimulations on traces as they do not enforce the existence of a WTS $\mathcal{A}$ and a world w validating the equivalence. We introduce instead a variant notion of bisimulation on traces—*faithful Kripke bisimulation on traces*—whose definition is indexed by a WTS $\mathcal{A}$

$$\overline{\mathcal{O}}_{\mathcal{A}}(\Phi, L) \stackrel{def}{=} \Big\{(\langle \mathcal{S}_1, \gamma_1\rangle, \langle \mathcal{S}_2, \gamma_2\rangle) \mid \forall (h_1, h_2, \mathcal{D}, \Phi') \in \mathbf{P}_{\Phi}(w), \forall \Phi'' \sqsupseteq \Phi,$$
$$\forall w' \in \mathcal{F}(w), \forall a_1, a_2. a_1 \sim_{\Phi''}^{w';\mathcal{D}} a_2 \Rightarrow \exists \mathcal{S}_1', \mathcal{S}_2'.(\langle \mathcal{S}_1', \gamma_1\rangle, \langle \mathcal{S}_2', \gamma_2\rangle) \in \mathcal{P}_{\mathcal{A}}(\Phi', L')$$
$$\wedge\big((C_1 \stackrel{a_1}{\Longrightarrow} \langle \mathcal{S}_1', \gamma_1, \Phi_1'', h_1', \mathcal{D}_1'\rangle) \Leftrightarrow (C_2 \stackrel{a_2}{\Longrightarrow} \langle \mathcal{S}_2', \gamma_2, \Phi_2'', h_2', \mathcal{D}_2'\rangle)\big)$$
$$\wedge(\langle \mathcal{S}_1, \gamma_1\rangle, \langle \mathcal{S}_2, \gamma_2\rangle) \in (\mathbf{Faitful}_{\Phi}(L) \cap \mathbf{Faitful}_{\mathbf{pub},\Phi}(L))\Big\}$$

$$\overline{\mathcal{P}}_{\mathcal{A}}(\Phi, L) \stackrel{def}{=} \Big\{(\langle \mathcal{S}_1, \gamma_1\rangle, \langle \mathcal{S}_2, \gamma_2\rangle) \mid \forall (h_1, h_2, \mathcal{D}, \Phi') \in \mathbf{P}_{\Phi}(w).(\forall i \in \{1,2\}. C_i \in \overline{\mathcal{P}}_{\mathcal{A}}^{\lightning i}(\Phi_i', L)$$
$$\vee\big(\exists w' \sqsupseteq w.\ \ \exists (h_1', h_2', \mathcal{D}', \Phi'') \in \mathbf{P}_{\Phi''}(w').\exists (\langle \mathcal{S}_1', \gamma_1'\rangle, \langle \mathcal{S}_2', \gamma_2'\rangle) \in \overline{\mathcal{O}}_{\mathcal{A}}(\Phi'', L').$$
$$\exists (a_1 \sim_{\Phi''}^{\mathcal{D}'} a_2). \forall i \in \{1,2\}.\big(C_i \stackrel{a_i}{\Longrightarrow} \langle \mathcal{S}_i', \gamma_i', \phi_i'', h_i', D_i'\rangle\big) \wedge (a_1, a_2 \text{ answer} \Rightarrow w' \sqsupseteq_{\mathbf{pub}} w)\big)\Big\}$$

where (in both definitions) $C_i = \langle \mathcal{S}_i, \gamma_i, \Phi_i', h_i, \mathcal{D}_i\rangle$, $L = w :: L''$

$L' = w' :: L$ if both a_i are questions, otherwise $L' = w' :: L''$

$$\overline{\mathcal{P}}_{\mathcal{A}}^{\lightning i}(\phi, L)) \stackrel{def}{=} \{C \mid C \uparrow \vee \exists w' \sqsupseteq w. \exists (h', D', \phi') \in \mathbf{P}_{\phi}^{i}(w'). \exists \langle \mathcal{S}', \gamma'\rangle \in \overline{\mathcal{O}}_{\mathcal{A}}^{\lightning i}(\phi', L').$$
$$\exists a.(C \stackrel{a}{\Rightarrow} \langle \mathcal{S}', \gamma', \phi', h', D'\rangle) \wedge \mathbf{incons}(w') \wedge (a \text{ answer} \Rightarrow w' \sqsupseteq_{\mathbf{pub}} w)\}$$

where $L = w :: L''$ and $L' = w' :: L$ if both a_i are questions, otherwise $L' = w' :: L''$

$$\overline{\mathcal{O}}_{\mathcal{A}}^{\lightning 1}(\phi, L) \stackrel{def}{=} \{\langle \mathcal{S}, \gamma\rangle \mid \exists \Phi. \Phi_1 = \phi \wedge (\langle \mathcal{S}, \gamma\rangle, \langle \mathcal{S}^{\lightning i}, \gamma^{\lightning i}\rangle) \in \overline{\mathcal{O}}_{\mathcal{A}}(\Phi, L)\}$$

$$\mathbf{Faitful}_{\Phi}(w :: L) \stackrel{def}{=} \{(\langle \mathcal{S}_1, \gamma_1\rangle, \langle \mathcal{S}_2, \gamma_2\rangle) \mid \forall w' \sqsupseteq^{\mathcal{F}*} w. \forall (h_1', h_2', \mathcal{D}', \Phi'') \in \mathbf{P}_{\Phi}(w'),$$
$$\exists (h_1, h_2, \mathcal{D}, \Phi') \in \mathbf{P}_{\Phi}(w), \exists T_1, T_2. \exists (\langle \mathcal{S}_1', \gamma_1'\rangle, \langle \mathcal{S}_2', \gamma_2'\rangle) \in \overline{\mathcal{O}}_{\mathcal{A}}(\Phi'', (w' :: L')).$$
$$\langle \mathcal{S}_i, \gamma_i, \Phi_i', h_i, \mathcal{D}_i\rangle \stackrel{T_i}{\Longrightarrow} \langle \mathcal{S}_i', \gamma_i', \Phi_i'', h_i', \mathcal{D}_i'\rangle\}$$

$$\mathbf{Faitful}_{\mathbf{pub},\Phi}(w :: L) \stackrel{def}{=} \{(\langle \mathcal{S}_1, \gamma_1\rangle, \langle \mathcal{S}_2, \gamma_2\rangle) \mid \forall w' \sqsupseteq_{\mathbf{pub}}^{\mathcal{F}*} w. \forall (h_1', h_2', \mathcal{D}', \Phi'') \in \mathbf{P}_{\Phi}(w'),$$
$$\exists (h_1, h_2, \mathcal{D}, \Phi') \in \mathbf{P}_{\Phi}(w), \exists T_1, T_2. \exists \gamma_1', \gamma_2'.(\langle \mathcal{S}_1, \gamma_1'\rangle, \langle \mathcal{S}_2, \gamma_2'\rangle) \in \overline{\mathcal{O}}_{\mathcal{A}}(\Phi'', (w' :: L)) \wedge$$
$$\langle \mathcal{S}_i, \gamma_i, \Phi_i', h_i, \mathcal{D}_i\rangle \stackrel{T_i}{\Longrightarrow} \langle \mathcal{S}_i, \gamma_i', \Phi_i'', h_i', \mathcal{D}_i'\rangle\}$$

Fig. 7. Faithful Kripke bisimulations

and a list of world L, and which satisfies the property that being related for these new bisimulations implies being related for KOBs. We conclude by constructing an *exhaustive WTS* associated to a pair of configurations in the bisimulation on traces, which shows that two equivalent programs produce traces that are related by a faithful Kripke bisimulation (the complete proofs are given in Appendix E).

6.1 Faithful Kripke Bisimulations on Traces

To prove completeness of KOBs, we introduce an intermediate notion—between bisimulations on traces and KOBs: *faithful Kripke bisimulations on traces*, defined in Fig. 7. They are pairs of relations $(\overline{\mathcal{P}}_{\mathcal{A}}(\Phi, L), \overline{\mathcal{O}}_{\mathcal{A}}(\Phi, L))$ on *partial configurations*, that is pairs formed by an evaluation stack and a functional environment, whose definitions is indexed by a span Φ on functional names and by stack of worlds, of size those of the evaluation stacks plus two, $L = w_n :: \ldots :: w_1$ such that $w_n \sqsupseteq^{\mathcal{F}*} \ldots \sqsupseteq^{\mathcal{F}*} w_1$. Restriction to *partial configurations* is harmless since we can always complete them using the span Φ and the top element of L. Faithful Kripke bisimulations on traces are used to enforce two main properties on a WTS $\mathcal{A}$: (i) the existence of accessible worlds validating the possible heaps obtained from reachable configurations, (ii) from $(C_1, C_2) \in \mathcal{O}_{\Phi,w}$ and $w' \sqsupseteq^* w$, the existence of equivalent execution of C_1, C_2 to configurations which satisfies the invariants of w'. Their definition can be seen as a mix between the bisimulations on traces introduced in Sect. 3.3, since they are defined on (partial) configurations and use interactive reduction, and the KOBs, since they use worlds and WTS to deduce and enforce invariants on heaps. However, there is a crucial distinction in the use of the WTS, that is the enforcement of *faithfulness* via the two predicates $\mathbf{Faitful}_{\Phi}(L), \mathbf{Faitful}_{\mathbf{pub},\Phi}(L)$ respectively on private and public transitions. Indeed, these predicates enforce that all the transition of the WTS can be taken by some reduction of the LTS generating the traces (notice that $\mathbf{Faitful}_{\mathbf{pub},\Phi}(L)$ enforces a stronger condition that this reduction should not change the stack of the configurations). These properties are not enforce by the KOBs, and it is indeed possible to use them with some WTS where they are not true. Thanks to those properties, faithful Kripke bisimulations on traces implies KOBs in the following sense.

Theorem 5. *Let M_1, M_2 two terms, w and w_0 two worlds, $\Phi = \Phi_P \cdot \Phi_O$ a span on functional names such that $(w.\mathcal{D})_i; \Phi_{O,i} \vdash M_i : \tau$, and γ_1, γ_2 two functional environments with* $\mathrm{dom}(\gamma_i) = \Phi_{P,i}$. *If* $(\langle M_1, \gamma_1\rangle, \langle M_2, \gamma_2\rangle) \in \overline{\mathcal{P}}_{\mathcal{A}}(\Phi(w, w_0))$, *then* $(M_1, M_2) \in \mathcal{E}_{\mathcal{A}} [\![\tau]\!]_{\Phi_O}(w, w_0)$.

6.2 Exhaustive WTS

It remains to construct the exhaustive relational WTS, which can be seen as the merge of two WTS coming from trace semantics. Its construction is obfuscated by nominal reasoning and diverging terms and requires some basic operations on WTSs:

- Add a private transition r: $\mathcal{A} \overset{\mathbf{priv}}{\oplus} r \overset{def}{=} (\delta_{\mathbf{priv}} \cup \{r\}, \delta_{\mathbf{pub}})$
- Add a public transition r: $\mathcal{A} \overset{\mathbf{pub}}{\oplus} r \overset{def}{=} (\delta_{\mathbf{priv}}, \delta_{\mathbf{pub}} \cup \{r\})$
- Union of two transition systems: $\mathcal{A}_1 \sqcup \mathcal{A}_2 \overset{def}{=} (\delta_{1,\mathbf{priv}} \cdot \delta_{2,\mathbf{priv}}, \delta_{1,\mathbf{pub}} \cdot \delta_{2,\mathbf{pub}})$.

$$\mathbf{SE}^{w::L}_{\Phi}(\langle \mathcal{S}_1, \gamma_1\rangle, \langle \mathcal{S}_2, \gamma_2\rangle) \overset{def}{=} \bigsqcup_{(h_1,h_2,\mathcal{D},\Phi')\in \mathbf{P}_{\Phi}(w)} \Big(\bigsqcup_{a_1 \sim^{\mathcal{D}'}_{\Phi''} a_2} \mathbf{SK}^{L'}_{\Phi'}(\langle \mathcal{S}'_1, \gamma'_1\rangle, \langle \mathcal{S}'_2, \gamma'_2\rangle) \overset{\mathbf{priv}}{\oplus} (w, w') \underbrace{\overset{\mathbf{pub}}{\oplus} (w_0, w')}_{\text{only if } a_i\text{'s are Player answers}} \Big) \bigsqcup \Big(\bigsqcup_i \mathbf{SE}^{\not{z}\, i, w::L}(C_i)\Big)$$

$$\mathbf{SE}^{\not{z}\, i, w::L}(\langle \mathcal{S}, \gamma, \phi, h, D\rangle) \overset{def}{=} \bigsqcup_a \mathbf{SK}^{\not{z}\, i, L}_{\phi'}(\langle \mathcal{S}', \gamma'\rangle) \overset{\mathbf{priv}}{\oplus} (w, w') \underbrace{\overset{\mathbf{pub}}{\oplus} (w_0, w')}_{\text{only if } a \text{ is a Player answer}})$$

$$\mathbf{SK}^{w::L}_{\Phi}(\langle \mathcal{S}_1, \gamma_1\rangle, \langle \mathcal{S}_2, \gamma_2\rangle) \overset{def}{=} \bigsqcup_{a_1 \sim^{\mathcal{D}'}_{\Phi'} a_2} \Big(\mathbf{SE}^{L'}_{\Phi'}(\langle \mathcal{S}'_1, \gamma_1\rangle, \langle \mathcal{S}'_2, \gamma_2\rangle) \Big)$$

$$\mathbf{SK}^{\not{z}\, 1, L}_{\phi}(\langle \mathcal{S}, \gamma\rangle) \overset{def}{=} \mathbf{SK}^{L}_{\Phi}(\langle \mathcal{S}, \gamma\rangle, \langle \mathcal{S}^{\not{z}}, \gamma^{\not{z}}\rangle)$$

Fig. 8. The exhaustive relational WTS

The exhaustive WTS (for terms) $\mathbf{SE}_{\Phi}^{L}$ is defined by mutual coinduction with its corresponding WTS (for contexts) $\mathbf{SK}_{\Phi}^{L}$, where L is a list of worlds whose head corresponds to the current one, while its tail corresponds to the public transitions that must be added once a value is reached in the interactive reduction. The definition is given in Fig. 8.

The definition of $\mathbf{SE}_{\Phi}^{w::L}$ is done on Player evaluation stacks $\mathcal{S}_1, \mathcal{S}_2$. In the definition, writing C_i for $\langle \mathcal{S}_i, \gamma_i, \Phi_i', h_i, \mathcal{D}_i \rangle$, we have $C_i \overset{a_i}{\Rrightarrow} \langle \mathcal{S}_i', \gamma_i', \Phi_i'', h_i', \mathcal{D}_i' \rangle$ and w' is equal to $(s, h'_{1|\overline{\mathcal{D}_1'}}, h'_{2|\overline{\mathcal{D}_1'}}, \mathcal{D}'', w.b)$ with s a fresh state. $L' = w'::L''$ where, if the a_i are Player questions, then $L'' = L$, otherwise, $w_0::L'' = L$. To deal with divergence, we use the auxilliary definition $\mathbf{SE}^{\not\downarrow i, w::L}$ to consider actions a such that $C \overset{a}{\Rrightarrow} \langle \mathcal{S}', \gamma', \phi_1', h_1', D_1' \rangle$, In these case, $w' = (s, h'_{1|\overline{D_1'}}, w.h_2, \mathcal{D}', \mathbf{true})$ with $\mathcal{D}'$ any span s.t. $\mathcal{D}_i' = D_i'$. $L' = w' :: L''$ such that, if a is a Player questions, then $L = L''$, otherwise, $L = w_0 :: L'$. The definition of $\mathbf{SK}_{\Phi}^{L}$ is done on two Opponent evaluation stacks, with $\Phi' \sqsupseteq \Phi$, $w' \in \mathcal{F}(w)$ and both $\langle \mathcal{S}_i, \gamma_i, \Phi_i', h_i, (w.\mathcal{D})_i \rangle \overset{a_i}{\Rrightarrow} \langle \mathcal{S}_i', \gamma_i', \Phi_i'', h_i', (w'.\mathcal{D})_i \rangle$. $L' = w' :: L''$ and, if the a_i are Opponent questions, $L'' = w :: L$, otherwise, $L'' = L$.

Using the tree structure of the exhaustive WTS, we can prove the following theorem, which, combined with Theorems 2, 3 and 5, allows to conclude on completeness of KOBs.

Theorem 6. *Let $\langle \mathcal{S}_1, \gamma_1 \rangle, \langle \mathcal{S}_2, \gamma_2 \rangle$ be two Player reduced configuration such that both $\mathcal{S}_1, \mathcal{S}_2$ have the same size n, Φ a spans on functional names, L a list of n worlds whose top element is w, and $(h_1, h_2, \mathcal{D}, \Phi) \in \mathbf{P}_{\Phi}(w)$. Writing C_i for $\langle \mathcal{S}_i, \gamma_i, \Phi_i, h_i, \mathcal{D}_i \rangle$, if $(C_1, C_2) \in \mathcal{P}_{\Phi,\mathcal{D}}$ then $(\langle \mathcal{S}_1, \gamma_1 \rangle \langle \mathcal{S}_2, \gamma_2 \rangle) \in \overline{\mathcal{P}}_{\mathbf{SE}_{\Phi}^{L}(\langle \mathcal{S}_1, \gamma_1 \rangle \langle \mathcal{S}_2, \gamma_2 \rangle)}(\Phi L)$.*

7 Future Work

Toward Automation of Proofs of Equivalence. The ultimate goal of this work is to reason automatically on contextual equivalence. That is, given two terms M_1, M_2 and supposing that a WTS $\mathcal{A}$ is provided, we would like to prove automatically that $(M_1, M_2) \in \mathcal{E}_{\mathcal{A}} [\![\tau]\!]_e w_0$. This is why we have removed quantification over "complex" objects in the definition of KOBs. By introducing a symbolic execution for fragments of the language (without higher-order references), one can automatically check whether two terms of these fragmets are in $\mathcal{E}_{\mathcal{A}} [\![\tau]\!]_e w_0$. This can be seen as *model-checking* equivalence of programs w.r.t. a WTS. Going further, we want to study fragments of the language where some WTS $\mathcal{A}$, being of course a lot more compact than the exhaustive one, can be built automatically. Doing so, we should be able to *decide* equivalence of programs. We have begun to implement these ideas, using an SMT-solver. It gives promising results, being able to decide automatically the (in)-equivalence of many examples from the literature. It would then be interesting to compare such results from the one from *algorithmic game semantics* [10].

Semantic Cube. One of the most impressive result of game semantics is the characterization of various imperative features via constraint on strategies (e.g., first-order references = visibility condition), coined the "semantic cube" by Abramsky. Following this idea, Dreyer et al. [2] give a characterization of such imperative features via constraints on the shape of worlds and on the way we can reason about them. The restriction to first-order references corresponds to the possibility to backtrack in the world. In our framework, it should be possible to modify the definition of $\mathcal{E}_{\mathcal{A}} [\![\tau]\!]_e(w, w_0)$ so that future worlds of successive callbacks would be branching over w_0 instead of being linearly related—branching corresponds to backtracking. Finally, adding a control operator corresponds to removing the distinction between private and public transitions (and inconsistent states), since the restriction to complete traces is not necessary, which would lead to an interesting comparison with the work of Støvring and Lassen [15].

Compositionality. Because we use "small worlds", so that the *frame rule* is not baked in the definitions of KOBs, we cannot get compositionality results for free. It should however be possible to prove it, by defining a product $\mathcal{A}_1 \otimes \mathcal{A}_2$ of two LTSs, with an associated weakening lemma on LTS stating that if $(M_1, M_2) \in \mathcal{E}_{\mathcal{A}_1} [\![\tau]\!]_{\Phi} w_1$, then $(M_1, M_2) \in \mathcal{E}_{(\mathcal{A}_1 \otimes \mathcal{A}_2)} [\![\tau]\!]_{\Phi}(w_1 \otimes w_2)$. The crucial point is that we should only require $\text{discl}(u_i, h'_i, \mathcal{D}_i) \subseteq \mathcal{D}'_i$ in the definition of $\mathcal{E}_{\mathcal{A}} [\![\tau]\!]_{\Phi} w$, instead of equality. This should allow to prove the composition theorem: if $(M_1, M_2) \in \mathcal{E}_{\mathcal{A}_1} [\![\tau \to \sigma]\!]_{\Phi} w_1$ and $(N_1, N_2) \in \mathcal{E}_{\mathcal{A}_2} [\![\tau]\!]_{\Phi} w_2$ then $(M_1\ N_1, M_2\ N_2) \in \mathcal{E}_{(\mathcal{A}_1 \otimes \mathcal{A}_2)} [\![\tau]\!]_{\Phi}(w_1 \otimes w_2)$. Its proof should follows quite closely the proof of compositionality for RTS [3].

References

1. Ahmed, A., Dreyer, D., Rossberg, A.: State-dependent representation independence. In: Proceedings of POPL (2009)
2. Dreyer, D., Neis, G., Birkedal, L.: The impact of higher-order state and control effects on local relational reasoning. J. Funct. Program. **22**(9), 477–528 (2012)
3. Hur, C.-K., Dreyer, D., Neis, G., Vafeiadis, V.: The marriage of bisimulations and Kripke logical relations. Proc. of POPL **47**, 59–72 (2012)
4. Jaber, G.: Operational nominal game semantics. In: Pitts, A. (ed.) FOSSACS 2015. LNCS, vol. 9034, pp. 264–278. Springer, Heidelberg (2015)
5. Jaber, G., Tabareau, N.: Kripke open bisimulation, a marriage of game semantics and operational techniques (2015). Technical Appendix http://guilhem.jaber.fr/aplas2015-full.pdf
6. Laird, J.: A fully abstract trace semantics for general references. In: Arge, L., Cachin, C., Jurdziński, T., Tarlecki, A. (eds.) ICALP 2007. LNCS, vol. 4596, pp. 667–679. Springer, Heidelberg (2007)
7. Lassen, S.B., Levy, P.B.: Typed normal form bisimulation. In: Duparc, J., Henzinger, T.A. (eds.) CSL 2007. LNCS, vol. 4646, pp. 283–297. Springer, Heidelberg (2007)
8. Lassen, S., Levy, P.: Typed normal form bisimulation for parametric polymorphism. In: Proceedings of LICS, pp. 341–352. IEEE (2008)
9. Murawski, A., Tzevelekos, N.: Game semantics for good general references. In: Proceedings of LICS, pp. 75–84. IEEE (2011)
10. Murawski, A.S., Tzevelekos, N.: Algorithmic games for full ground references. In: Czumaj, A., Mehlhorn, K., Pitts, A., Wattenhofer, R. (eds.) ICALP 2012, Part II. LNCS, vol. 7392, pp. 312–324. Springer, Heidelberg (2012)

11. Pitts, A.: Nominal logic, a first order theory of names and binding. Inf. Comput. **186**(2), 165–193 (2003)
12. Pitts, A., Stark, I.: Operational reasoning for functions with local state. Higher Order Operational Techniques in Semantics, pp. 227–273. CUP (1998)
13. Sangiorgi, D., Kobayashi, N., Sumii, E.: Environmental bisimulations for higher-order languages. ACM Trans. Program. Lang. Syst. (TOPLAS), **33** (2011)
14. Stark, I.: Names, equations, relations: practical ways to reason about new. Fundamenta Informaticae **33**(4), 369–396 (1998)
15. Støvring, K., Lassen, S.: A complete, co-inductive syntactic theory of sequential control and state. In: Proceedings of POPL, pp. 161–172. ACM (2007)
16. Sumii, E.: A complete characterization of observational equivalence in polymorphic λ-calculus with general references. In: Grädel, E., Kahle, R. (eds.) CSL 2009. LNCS, vol. 5771, pp. 455–469. Springer, Heidelberg (2009)

Model Checking

Automata-Based Abstraction for Automated Verification of Higher-Order Tree-Processing Programs

Yuma Matsumoto[1], Naoki Kobayashi[1](✉), and Hiroshi Unno[2]

[1] The University of Tokyo, Tokyo, Japan
koba@is.s.u-tokyo.ac.jp
[2] University of Tsukuba, Tsukuba, Japan

Abstract. Higher-order model checking has been recently applied to automated verification of higher-order functional programs, but there have been difficulties in dealing with algebraic data types such as lists and trees. To remedy the problem, we propose an automata-based abstraction of tree data, and a counterexample-guided refinement of the abstraction. By combining them with higher-order model checking, we can construct a fully-automated verification tool for higher-order, tree-processing functional programs. We formalize the verification method, prove its correctness, and report experimental results.

1 Introduction

Higher-order model checking [9,15], or the model checking of higher-order recursion schemes (HORS), has been recently applied to automated verification of functional programs [9,11,16,18,19]. Since a HORS is essentially a simply-typed higher-order functional program with recursion and finite base types (such as Booleans, not integers), the control structure of a (higher-order) functional program can be precisely modeled and verified. Thus, with a suitable abstraction of data, we can verify functional programs fully automatically by using higher-order model checking. For example, Kobayashi et al. [11] used predicate abstraction and CEGAR (counterexample-guided abstraction refinement) for abstracting integers to Booleans, and constructed a fully automated verification tool MoCHi for simply-typed higher-order functional programs with recursion and integers.

There have, however, been limitations in the treatment of algebraic data types such as trees and lists. Sato et al. [18] extended MoCHi to deal with algebraic data types by encoding algebraic data into functions; for example, a list may be encoded as a function that maps an index to the corresponding element. That approach has not been so successful, because the encoding makes both programs and specifications complex. In another line of work, Kobayashi et al. [12] proposed a verification method for HMTT, a kind of higher-order tree transducers. The HMTT model is however much more restricted than the usual functional programs: there is a distinction between input and output trees, and input trees are read-only, and output trees are write-only. Unno et al. [19] later extended

X. Feng and S. Park (Eds.): APLAS 2015, LNCS 9458, pp. 295–312, 2015.
DOI: 10.1007/978-3-319-26529-2_16

HMTT to allow conversion between input and output trees so that the model is as expressive as an ordinary functional language, but annotations are required for the conversion. Ong and Ramsay [16] introduced a verification method for an extension of HORS called pattern-matching recursion schemes (PMRS). PMRS supports pattern matching on tree-structured data, but the verification method, however, uses pattern-based abstraction, which is not powerful enough.

To remedy the situation above, we propose a new approach to using higher-order model checking for automated verification of higher-order tree-processing programs. As in [11], we apply abstraction to approximate a source program by a higher-order functional program over finite base types, so that the latter can be verified by higher-order model checking. Instead of using predicates on integers, however, we use an automaton for abstracting tree data: each tree is abstracted to a state of the automaton that accepts the tree. Using the automata-based abstraction, we can transform a higher-order tree-processing program to a higher-order functional program with finite data domains, so that the latter overapproximates the behavior of the source program. Thus, verification problems for the former can be reduced to those for the latter, which can further be reduced to higher-order model checking.

As an example, consider the following program.

```
double x = twice (add x) Z.     twice f x = f(f x).
add x y = match x with Z => y | S x' => add x' (S y).
```

Here, Z and S are tree constructors. The program consists of two functions *double* and *add*. The main function *double* takes a natural number x (in the unary tree representation) and returns $x + x$. Suppose that we wish to verify that the output of *double* is always even, i.e., a unary tree of the form $(\mathtt{S})^{2n}\mathtt{Z}$. We can use a tree automaton that distinguishes $(\mathtt{S})^{2n}\mathtt{Z}$ and $(\mathtt{S})^{2n+1}\mathtt{Z}$, consisting of two states q_0, from which trees of the form $(\mathtt{S})^{2n}\mathtt{Z}$ is accepted, and q_1, from which trees of the form $(\mathtt{S})^{2n+1}\mathtt{Z}$ is accepted. Using the automaton, the program above is abstracted to:

```
main() = (double q0)□(double q1).     double x = twice (add x) Z.
twice f x = f(f x).    s x = match x with q0 => q1 | q1 => q0
add x y = match x with q0 => y□(add q1 (s y)) | q1 => add q0 (s y).
```

Here, □ represents a non-deterministic choice, and s is now a function on states. The new main function main non-deterministically invokes double q_0 or double q_1; here, the argument of double is now a state of the automaton, instead of a tree. The call double q_0 (double q_1, resp.) simulates the case where the input is an even (odd, resp.) number. The case analysis on tree x in function add has now been replaced by a case analysis on states. The case $x = q_0$ models the case where x is of the form $(\mathtt{S})^{2n}$ z in the source program; since both of the branches are possible in the source program, the abstract program non-deterministically evaluates (the abstract version of) them. On the other hand, the case $x = q_1$ models the case where x is of the form $(\mathtt{S})^{2n+1}$ Z; since only the second branch of the source program is possible, the abstract program evaluates add q_0 (s y) deterministically. To check that the return value of the source program is always

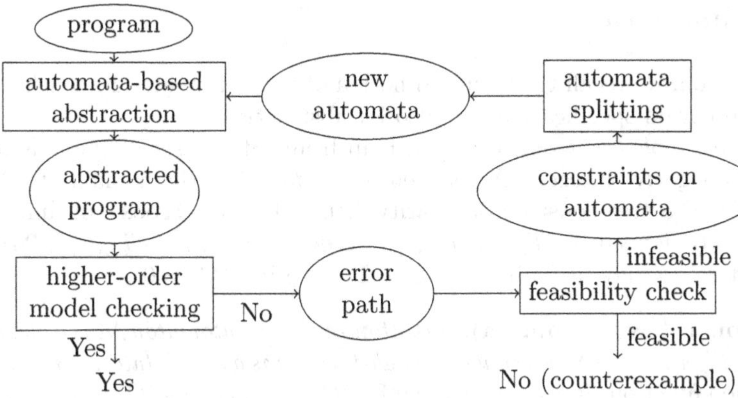

Fig. 1. Our method

even (given $(\mathtt{S})^n\mathtt{Z}$) as an input), it suffices to check that the return value of the abstract program is always q_0.

Figure 1 illustrates our overall method. As mentioned above, we apply an automata-based abstraction to reduce a given verification problem to that on a functional program with *finite* data domains. The latter problem can be decided by a reduction to higher-order model checking [9]. If the abstract program has no error path then we can conclude that the answer to the original verification problem is "yes". Otherwise, we inspect an error path returned by a higher-order model checker. If a source program has a corresponding error path, we can conclude that the answer to the original verification problem is "no". Otherwise, the abstraction was not precise enough, so the automaton used for abstraction is refined, and the cycle is repeated until the answer is found. (Since the verification problem is undecidable, the cycle may be repeated forever.)

A challenge arises on how to refine the automaton used for abstraction when a spurious error path is found. Unlike the case for predicate abstraction for integer values [11], we cannot use an interpolant-based method for predicate discovery. Given an initial automaton for abstraction, we split each state of the automaton to obtain a new automaton with an unknown transition function. From spurious error paths, we accumulate constraints on the transition function, which represent necessary conditions for eliminating spurious error paths. Then by using an SMT solver, we obtain a transition function that satisfies the constraints.This refinement procedure is relatively complete, in the sense that if there exists an automaton with which the abstract program can be proved to be safe, the procedure can eventually find such an automaton and the verification succeeds. The rest of this paper is organized as follows. Section 2 reviews the definitions of tree automata. Section 3 introduces our verification problem. Section 4 formalizes the automata-based abstraction. Section 5 describes an abstraction refinement method. Section 6 reports experimental results. Section 7 discusses related work, and Sect. 8 concludes this paper.

2 Preliminaries

In this section, we recall the standard notion of tree automata [4], which will be used for program specification and also for abstraction.

A *ranked alphabet*, written Σ, is a map from a finite set of symbols to the set of non-negative integers. An element C of $dom(\Sigma)$ (the domain of Σ) may be considered a tree constructor of arity $\Sigma(C)$. The set $\mathbf{Trees}_\Sigma$ of finite trees is inductively defined by: $T_1, \ldots, T_{\Sigma(C)} \in \mathbf{Trees}_\Sigma \Rightarrow C\,T_1 \cdots T_{\Sigma(C)} \in \mathbf{Trees}_\Sigma$. Note that $\Sigma(C)$ may be 0 above, so $C \in \mathbf{Trees}_\Sigma$ if $\Sigma(C) = 0$.

Definition 1 (tree automata). *A (bottom-up) tree automaton $\mathcal{M}$ is a quadruple (Σ, Q, Δ, F) where (i) Σ is a ranked alphabet. (ii) Q is a set of states. (iii) Δ, called a* transition function, *is a subset of $dom(\Sigma) \times Q^* \times Q$ such that $(C, q_1 \cdots q_n, q) \in \Delta$ implies $n = \Sigma(C)$. (iv) F is a subset of Q. Elements of F are called* final states. *We define the transition relation $T \longrightarrow_\mathcal{M} T'$ on $\mathbf{Trees}_{\Sigma \cup \{q \mapsto 0 \mid q \in Q\}}$ by:*

$$C\,q_1 \cdots q_n \longrightarrow_\mathcal{M} q \qquad \textit{if } (C, q_1 \cdots q_n, q) \in \Delta.$$

A tree $T \in \mathbf{Trees}_\Sigma$ is accepted *by $\mathcal{M}$ if $T \longrightarrow^*_\mathcal{M} q \in F$ for some q. The language accepted by $\mathcal{M}$, written $\mathcal{L}(\mathcal{M})$, is the set of trees accepted by $\mathcal{M}$. We often write $\Sigma_\mathcal{M}, Q_\mathcal{M}, \Delta_\mathcal{M}, F_\mathcal{M}$ for the four components of $\mathcal{M}$. We write $\mathcal{L}(\mathcal{M}, q)$ and $\mathcal{L}(\mathcal{M}, Q)$ for $\mathcal{L}((\Sigma_\mathcal{M}, Q_\mathcal{M}, \Delta_\mathcal{M}, \{q\}))$ and $\mathcal{L}((\Sigma_\mathcal{M}, Q_\mathcal{M}, \Delta_\mathcal{M}, Q))$ respectively. An automaton (Σ, Q, Δ, F) is deterministic if for every $C \in dom(\Sigma)$ and $q_1 \cdots q_{\Sigma(C)} \in Q^*$, there exists at most one q such that $(C, q_1 \cdots q_{\Sigma(C)}, q) \in \Delta$. An automaton (Σ, Q, Δ, F) is total if for every $C \in dom(\Sigma)$ and $q_1 \cdots q_{\Sigma(C)} \in Q^*$, there exists at least one q such that $(C, q_1 \cdots q_{\Sigma(C)}, q) \in \Delta$. When an automaton $\mathcal{M}$ is deterministic and total, we write $\Delta_\mathcal{M}(C, q_1 \cdots q_{\Sigma_\mathcal{M}(C)})$ for the state q such that $(C, q_1 \cdots q_{\Sigma_\mathcal{M}(C)}, q) \in \Delta_\mathcal{M}$.*

Example 1. Consider an automaton $\mathcal{M} = (\Sigma, \{q_1, q_2, q_3\}, \Delta, \{q_1, q_2\})$ where $\Sigma = \{\mathtt{E} \mapsto 0, \mathtt{A} \mapsto 1, \mathtt{B} \mapsto 1\}$ and

$$\Delta = \{(\mathtt{E}, \epsilon, q_1), (\mathtt{A}, q_1, q_2), (\mathtt{A}, q_2, q_2), (\mathtt{A}, q_3, q_3), (\mathtt{B}, q_1, q_1), (\mathtt{B}, q_2, q_3), (\mathtt{B}, q_3, q_3)\}$$

The automaton $\mathcal{M}$ is total and deterministic, and $\mathcal{L}(\mathcal{M}) = \mathtt{A}^*\mathtt{B}^*\mathtt{E}$. Here, we have identified unary trees with words, and used a regular expression for a set of unary trees. The regular expression $\mathtt{A}^*\mathtt{B}^*\mathtt{E}$ denotes

$$\{\underbrace{\mathtt{A}(\cdots(\mathtt{A}}_{m}\underbrace{(\mathtt{B}(\cdots(\mathtt{B}}_{n}\,\mathtt{E})))))\mid m \geq 0, n \geq 0\}.$$

We often use this kind of notation for a set of unary trees.

Henceforth, we consider only deterministic and total automata; this does not lose generality, as we are considering bottom-up automata.

3 The Verification Problem

This section introduces the language of tree processing programs, which is used as the target of our verification, and defines the verification problem. The target of verification is a higher-order, tree-processing functional program. We fix a ranked alphabet Σ. We sometimes write $\{e_i\}_{i=1}^n$ for $\{e_1, \ldots, e_n\}$, and also write $\{f(x)\}_{x \in S}$ for $\{f(x) \mid x \in S\}$.

Definition 2. *The set of* expressions, *ranged over by e, is given by:*

$$e ::= C \mid x \mid \mathbf{fail} \mid e_1\ e_2 \mid\ \mathbf{case}\, e\, \mathbf{of} \{C_i\ \widetilde{y_i} \Rightarrow e_i\}_{i=1}^n.$$

Here, C ranges over $dom(\Sigma)$, and x ranges over the set of variables and function symbols. A program *$\mathcal{P}$ is a set of function definitions $\{f_1\ \widetilde{x_1} = e_1, \ldots f_m\ \widetilde{x_m} = e_m\}$ where f_i is a function symbol, and $\widetilde{x_i}$ is a sequence of variables. The set of function symbols $\{f_1, \ldots, f_m\}$ must contain the main function symbol "main". We write arity (f_i) for the length of the sequence $\widetilde{x_i}$.*

The expression **fail** aborts the execution. The expression $\mathbf{case}\, e\, \mathbf{of} \{C_i\ \widetilde{y_i} \Rightarrow e_i\}_{i=1}^n$ evaluates e to a tree, and then evaluates $[\widetilde{T}/\widetilde{y_i}]e_i$ if the tree matches $C_i\ \widetilde{T}$. We assume that the patterns of every case expression are exhaustive; if not, we can insert a clause $C_i\ \widetilde{y_i} \Rightarrow \mathbf{fail}$. We consider only programs that are well-typed in the standard simple type system. The set of (simple) types, ranged over by κ, is given by: $\kappa ::= \mathsf{o} \mid \kappa_1 \to \kappa_2$. Here, o is the type of trees, and $\kappa_1 \to \kappa_2$ is the type of functions from κ_1 to κ_2. A type judgment is of the form $\mathcal{K} \vdash e : \kappa$, where $\mathcal{K}$ is a map from a finite set of variables (which may include function symbols) to the set of types. It is defined by the following rules.

$$\frac{}{\mathcal{K} \vdash C : \underbrace{\mathsf{o} \to \cdots \to \mathsf{o}}_{\Sigma(C)} \to \mathsf{o}} \qquad \frac{}{\mathcal{K}, x : \kappa \vdash x : \kappa} \qquad \frac{\mathcal{K} \vdash e_1 : \kappa_1 \to \kappa_2 \qquad \mathcal{K} \vdash e_2 : \kappa_1}{\mathcal{K} \vdash e_1\ e_2 : \kappa_2}$$

$$\frac{}{\mathcal{K} \vdash \mathbf{fail} : \kappa} \qquad \frac{\mathcal{K} \vdash e : \mathsf{o} \qquad \mathcal{K}, \widetilde{y_i} : \widetilde{\mathsf{o}} \vdash e_i : \kappa (\text{for each } i \in \{1, \ldots, n\})}{\mathcal{K} \vdash \mathbf{case}\, e\, \mathbf{of} \{C_i\ \widetilde{y_i} \Rightarrow e_i\}_{i=1}^n : \kappa}$$

We write $\vdash \mathcal{P} : \mathcal{K}$ if: (i) $\mathcal{P} = \{f_i\, x_{i,1} \cdots x_{i,k_i} = e_i\}_{i=1}^n$; (ii) $dom(\mathcal{K}) = \{f_1, \ldots, f_n\}$; (iii) $\mathcal{K}(f_i) = \kappa_{i,1} \to \cdots \to \kappa_{i,k_i} \to \mathsf{o}$ and $\mathcal{K}, x_{i,1} : \kappa_{i,1}, \ldots, x_{i,k_i} : \kappa_{i,k_i} \vdash e_i : \mathsf{o}$ for every $i \in \{1, \ldots, n\}$; and (iv) $\mathcal{K}(main) = \mathsf{o} \to \mathsf{o}$. A program $\mathcal{P}$ is *well-typed* if $\vdash \mathcal{P} : \mathcal{K}$ for some $\mathcal{K}$. Henceforth, we consider only well-typed programs.

The sets of *evaluation contexts* and *values* are defined respectively by:

$$E \text{ (evaluation contexts)} ::= [\,] \mid E\ v \mid e\ E \mid\ \mathbf{case}\ E\ \mathbf{of}\ \{C_i\ \widetilde{y_i} \Rightarrow e_i\}_{i=1}^n$$
$$v \text{ (values)} ::= f\ v_1 \cdots v_n\ (n < arity(f)) \mid C\ v_1 \cdots v_n\ (n \leq \Sigma(C))$$

The reduction relation $e \longrightarrow_{\mathcal{P}} e'$ is defined by: (i) $E[\mathbf{fail}] \longrightarrow_{\mathcal{P}} \mathbf{fail}$; (ii) $E[f\ v_1 \cdots v_n] \longrightarrow_{\mathcal{P}} E[[v_1 \cdots v_n/x_1 \cdots x_n]e]$ if $f\ x_1 \cdots x_n = e \in \mathcal{P}$; and (iii) $E[\mathbf{case}\, a_k\ \widetilde{v}\, \mathbf{of}\ \{C_i\ \widetilde{y_i} \Rightarrow e_i\}_{i=1}^n] \longrightarrow_{\mathcal{P}} E[[\widetilde{v}/\widetilde{y_k}]e_k]$. We often omit the subscript $\mathcal{P}$.

Example 2. The program in Sect. 1 is expressed as:

$$\mathcal{P}_1 = \{main\ x = twice\,(add\ x)\,\mathtt{Z},\ twice\ f\ x = f\,(f\,x),\\ add\ x\ y = \mathbf{case}\ x\ \mathbf{of}\ \mathtt{Z} \Rightarrow y \mid \mathtt{S}\ x' \Rightarrow add\ x'\ (\mathtt{S}\ y)\}$$

The expression $main\,(\mathtt{S}(\mathtt{Z}))$ is evaluated as follows.

$$main\,(\mathtt{S}(\mathtt{Z})) \longrightarrow twice\,(add\ (\mathtt{S}(\mathtt{Z})))\,\mathtt{Z} \longrightarrow add\ (\mathtt{S}(\mathtt{Z}))(add\ (\mathtt{S}(\mathtt{Z}))\,\mathtt{Z}) \longrightarrow^* \mathtt{S}(\mathtt{S}(\mathtt{Z})).$$

Definition 3 (verification problem). *Let $\mathcal{M}_I$ and $\mathcal{M}_O$ be tree automata. We write $\models (\mathcal{P}, \mathcal{M}_I, \mathcal{M}_O)$ if, for every $T \in \mathcal{L}(\mathcal{M}_I)$, $main\ T \not\longrightarrow^*_{\mathcal{P}}$ **fail** and $main\ T \longrightarrow^*_{\mathcal{P}} t' \in$ **Trees**$_\Sigma$ implies $t' \in \mathcal{L}(\mathcal{M}_O)$. The verification problem $(\mathcal{P}, \mathcal{M}_I, \mathcal{M}_O)$ is the problem of deciding whether $\models (\mathcal{P}, \mathcal{M}_I, \mathcal{M}_O)$ holds.*

Intuitively, $\models (\mathcal{P}, \mathcal{M}_I, \mathcal{M}_O)$ means that given a tree accepted by $\mathcal{M}_I$ as an input, P does not fail, and if it returns a (finite) tree, it is accepted by $\mathcal{M}_O$.

Example 3. Consider the verification problem $(\mathcal{P}_1, \mathcal{M}_1, \mathcal{M}_2)$ where $\mathcal{P}_1$ is the program given in Example 2, and

$$\mathcal{M}_1 = (\Sigma, \{q_1\}, \Delta_1, \{q_1\}) \quad \Delta_1 = \{(\mathtt{Z}, \epsilon, q_1), (\mathtt{S}, q_1, q_1)\}\\ \mathcal{M}_2 = (\Sigma, \{q_2, q_3\}, \Delta_2, \{q_2\})\ \Delta_2 = \{(\mathtt{Z}, \epsilon, q_2), (\mathtt{S}, q_2, q_3), (\mathtt{S}, q_3, q_2)\}$$

The languages accepted by $\mathcal{M}_1$ and $\mathcal{M}_2$ are $(\mathtt{S})^*\mathtt{Z}$ and $(\mathtt{S}\ \mathtt{S})^*\mathtt{Z}$ respectively. The answer to the verification problem $(\mathcal{P}_1, \mathcal{M}_1, \mathcal{M}_2)$ is "yes".

4 Automata-Based Abstraction

This section formalizes our automata-based abstraction method.

4.1 Abstract Programs

The target language of the automata-based abstraction has a finite enumeration type as the base type, instead of tree types. The enumeration type consists of the states of automata used for abstraction.

Definition 4 (abstract programs). *The set of* (abstract) expressions, *ranged over by t, is given by: $t ::= q \mid x \mid t_1\ t_2 \mid$ **case** t **of** $\{q_i \Rightarrow t_i\}_{i=1}^m \mid t_1 \Box t_2 \mid$ **fail**. Here, q ranges over the set $\{q_1, \ldots, q_m\}$ of values of the finite enumeration type and x ranges over a set of variables (including defined function symbols f_i's). An* abstract program $\mathcal{D}$ *is a set of function definitions $\{f_1\ \widetilde{x_1} = t_1, \ldots, f_n\ \widetilde{x_n} = t_n\}$, where $main \in \{f_1, \ldots, f_n\}$.*

The expression **case** t **of** $\{q_i \Rightarrow t_i\}_{i=1}^m$ is a case analysis on the finite enumeration type; it first evaluates t, and evaluates t_i if the value is q_i. The expression $t_1 \Box t_2$ evaluates t_1 or t_2 in a non-deterministic manner. As for source programs, we require that abstract programs are simply-typed. The set of types is given by: $\tau ::= \mathtt{d} \mid \tau_1 \rightarrow \tau_2$. Here, $\mathtt{d}$ is the finite enumeration type, consisting of values

$q_1, \ldots, q_m$. We show only the typing rules for q and case-expressions; the other typing rules for expressions are essentially the same as those for source programs.

$$\frac{}{\Theta \vdash q : \mathtt{d}} \qquad \frac{\Theta \vdash t : \mathtt{d} \qquad \Theta \vdash t_i : \tau}{\Theta \vdash \mathbf{case}\, t\, \mathbf{of} \{q_i \Rightarrow t_i\}_{i=1}^m : \tau}$$

We write $\vdash \mathcal{D} : \Theta$ if: (i) $\mathcal{D} = \{f_i\, x_{i,1} \cdots x_{i,k_i} = t_i\}_{i=1}^n$; (ii) $dom(\Theta) = \{f_1, \ldots, f_n\}$; (iii) $\Theta(f_i) = \tau_{i,1} \to \cdots \to \tau_{i,k_i} \to \mathtt{d}$ and $\Theta, x_{i,1}{:}\tau_{i,1}, \ldots, x_{i,k_i}{:}\tau_{i,k_i} \vdash t_i : \mathtt{d}$ for every $i \in \{1, \ldots, n\}$; and (iv) $\Theta(main) = \mathtt{d} \to \mathtt{d}$.

We define the call-by-value, small-step reduction relation below. The sets of evaluation contexts and values, ranged over by E and v, are defined by:

$$E ::= [\,] \mid E\ v \mid t\ E \mid \mathbf{case}\, E\, \mathbf{of}\ \{q_i \Rightarrow t_i\}_{i=1}^m \qquad v ::= f\ v_1 \cdots v_n\ (n < arity(f)) \mid q$$

The relation $t_1 \longrightarrow_{\mathcal{D}} t_2$ is defined by: (i) $E[f\ v_1 \cdots v_n] \longrightarrow_{\mathcal{D}} E[[v_1 \cdots v_n/x_1 \cdots x_n]t]$ if $f\ x_1 \cdots x_n = t \in \mathcal{D}$; (ii) $E[\mathbf{case}\, q_k\, \mathbf{of}\ \{q_i \Rightarrow t_i\}_{i=1}^m] \longrightarrow_{\mathcal{D}} E[t_k]$; (iii) $E[\mathbf{fail}] \longrightarrow_{\mathcal{D}} \mathbf{fail}$; and (iv) $E[t_1 \Box t_2] \longrightarrow_{\mathcal{D}} E[t_i]$ for $i \in \{1, 2\}$.

Definition 5 (safety problem). *Let $\mathcal{D}$ be an abstracted program and F_I and F_O be finite subsets of $\{q_1, \ldots, q_m\}$. We write $\models (\mathcal{D}, F_I, F_O)$ if, for every $q \in F_I$, (i) main $q \not\longrightarrow_{\mathcal{D}}^* \mathbf{fail}$; and (ii) main $q \longrightarrow_{\mathcal{D}}^* q'$ implies $q' \in F_O$. The safety problem $(\mathcal{D}, F_I, F_O)$ is the problem of deciding whether $\models (\mathcal{D}, F_I, F_O)$ holds.*

The safety problem above is decidable by a reduction to higher-order model checking [9]. Furthermore, if $\models (\mathcal{D}, F_I, F_O)$ does not hold, we can obtain an error reduction sequence $main\ q \longrightarrow_{\mathcal{D}}^* \mathbf{fail}$ or $main\ q \longrightarrow_{\mathcal{D}}^* q' \notin F_O$ by using a higher-order model checker [3,8]. The knowledge of higher-order model checking and the reduction method is not required for understanding the rest of this paper; an interested reader may wish to consult [9].

4.2 Abstraction Method

We now formalize the automata-based abstraction. In order to allow a different automaton to be used for abstracting each expression of tree type, we use *abstraction types*, which specify how each expression should be abstracted.

The set of abstraction types is defined by: $\sigma ::= \mathtt{o}_{\mathcal{M}} \mid \sigma_1 \to \sigma_2$. Here, $\mathcal{M}$ is a (total, deterministic) automaton. Intuitively, $\mathtt{o}_{\mathcal{M}}$ describes trees that should be abstracted by using the automaton $\mathcal{M}$. The type $\sigma_1 \to \sigma_2$ describes functions whose argument should be abstracted according to σ_1, and return value should be abstracted according to σ_2. For example, consider the automata $\mathcal{M}_1$ and $\mathcal{M}_2$ in Example 3. The type $\mathtt{o}_{\mathcal{M}_1} \to \mathtt{o}_{\mathcal{M}_2}$ describes a function whose input tree should be abstracted using the automaton $\mathcal{M}_1$, and output tree should be abstracted using the automaton $\mathcal{M}_2$. Using this type, the identity function $\lambda x.x$ would be abstracted to $\lambda x.\, \mathbf{case}\, x\, \mathbf{of}\ q_1 \Rightarrow (q_2 \Box q_3)$; the argument is abstracted to q_1, and since there is no information about whether the original value of x is even or not, the function returns q_2 (which is an abstraction of trees of the form $\mathtt{s}^{2n}\mathtt{z}$) or q_3 (which is an abstraction of trees of the form $\mathtt{s}^{2n+1}\mathtt{z}$) non-deterministically. If the abstraction type was $\mathtt{o}_{\mathcal{M}_2} \to \mathtt{o}_{\mathcal{M}_2}$, then $\lambda x.x$ would be abstracted to $\lambda x.x$.

The abstraction is formalized as a type-based program transformation relation $\Gamma \vdash e{:}\sigma \rightsquigarrow t$, where Γ, called an *abstraction type environment*, is a map from a finite set of variables to the set of abstraction types. Intuitively, $\Gamma \vdash e : \sigma \rightsquigarrow t$ means that assuming that each variable x has been abstracted according to $\Gamma(x)$, the expression e should be abstracted to t according to the abstraction type σ. How to obtain an appropriate abstraction type environment is discussed in [13] The transformation relation is defined by the following rules.

$$\frac{}{\Gamma, x : \sigma \vdash x : \sigma \rightsquigarrow x} \qquad \frac{}{\Gamma \vdash a : \underbrace{\mathsf{o}_{\mathcal{M}} \rightarrow \cdots \rightarrow \mathsf{o}_{\mathcal{M}}}_{\Sigma(a)} \rightarrow \mathsf{o}_{\mathcal{M}} \rightsquigarrow f_{a,\mathcal{M}}}$$

$$\frac{\Gamma \vdash e : \mathsf{o}_{\mathcal{M}} \rightsquigarrow t \qquad \Gamma, \widetilde{y_i} : \widetilde{\mathsf{o}_{\mathcal{M}}} \vdash e_i : \sigma \rightsquigarrow t_i \text{ (for each } i \in \{1, \ldots, n\})}{\Gamma \vdash \mathbf{case}\, e\, \mathbf{of} \{C_i\ \widetilde{y_i} \Rightarrow e_i\}_{i=1}^n : \sigma \rightsquigarrow \mathbf{case}\, t\, \mathbf{of} \{q \Rightarrow \Box\ \{[\widetilde{q}/\widetilde{y_\ell}]t_\ell\}_{(C_\ell, \widetilde{q}, q) \in \Delta_{\mathcal{M}}}\}_{q \in Q_{\mathcal{M}}}}$$

$$\frac{\Gamma \vdash e_1 : \sigma_1 \rightarrow \sigma_2 \rightsquigarrow t_1 \qquad \Gamma \vdash e_2 : \sigma_1 \rightsquigarrow t_2}{\Gamma \vdash e_1\ e_2 : \sigma_2 \rightsquigarrow t_1\ t_2} \qquad \frac{}{\Gamma \vdash \mathbf{fail} : \sigma \rightsquigarrow \mathbf{fail}}$$

Here, $\Box\ \{t_1, \ldots, t_n\}$ is an abbreviation of $t_1 \Box (t_2 \Box \cdots \Box (t_{n-1} \Box t_n))$. In the rule for case-expressions, $\widetilde{y_i} : \widetilde{\mathsf{o}_{\mathcal{M}}}$ abbreviates $y_{i,1} : \mathsf{o}_{\mathcal{M}}, \ldots, y_{i,k} : \mathsf{o}_{\mathcal{M}}$; note that the type of $y_{i,k}$ is the same as that of e.

A variable is abstracted to itself. A tree constructor is transformed to a function $f_{a,\mathcal{M}}$ defined below. A case expression is transformed to a case expression on the states of $\mathcal{M}$. If the value of t matches q, then the value T of the original expression e is accepted by $\mathcal{M}$ from state q. So, T must be of the form $a\,T_1 \cdots T_k$ such that $(a, q_1 \cdots q_k, q) \in \Delta_M$ with $T_i \in \mathcal{L}(\mathcal{M}, q_i)$. Thus, the body of the clause for q is a non-deterministic branch on such cases. For example, consider the expression: $\mathbf{case}\, x\, \mathbf{of} \{\mathtt{Z} \Rightarrow e_1, \mathtt{S}\, y \Rightarrow e_2\}$, with the abstraction type $x : \mathsf{o}_{\mathcal{M}_2}$ (where $\mathcal{M}_2$ is that of Example 3). It is transformed to: $\mathbf{case}\, x\, \mathbf{of} \{q_2 \Rightarrow (t_1 \Box [q_3/y]t_2),\quad q_3 \Rightarrow [q_2/y]t_2\}$, where $x : \mathsf{o}_{\mathcal{M}_2} \vdash e_1 : \sigma \rightsquigarrow t_1$ and $x{:}\mathsf{o}_{\mathcal{M}_2}, y{:}\mathsf{o}_{\mathcal{M}_2} \vdash e_2 : \sigma \rightsquigarrow t_2$. The rule for applications transforms e_1 and e_2 in a compositional manner, but it ensures that the argument abstraction type of e_1 is equal to the abstraction type of e_2, so that the abstraction is consistent.

A program is transformed by the following rule.

$$\frac{\begin{array}{c}\mathcal{P} = \{f_i\,\widetilde{x}_i = e_i\}_{i=1}^n \qquad \mathcal{D} = \{f_i\,\widetilde{x}_i = t_i\}_{i=1}^n \cup \mathcal{D}' \\ \Gamma = \{f_i : \widetilde{\sigma}_i \rightarrow \mathsf{o}_{\mathcal{M}_i}\}_{i=1}^n \qquad \Gamma, \widetilde{x}_i : \widetilde{\sigma}_i \vdash e_i : \mathsf{o}_{\mathcal{M}_i} \rightsquigarrow t_i \text{ (for each } i) \\ \mathcal{D}' = \{f_{C,\mathcal{M}}\, x_1 \cdots x_{\Sigma(C)} = t_{C,\mathcal{M}}\}_{C \in dom(\Sigma), \mathcal{M} \in Automata(\Gamma)}\end{array}}{\vdash \mathcal{P} : \Gamma \rightsquigarrow \mathcal{D}} \quad \text{(A-PROG)}$$

Here, *Automata*(Γ) is the set of automata occurring in Γ, and $t_{C,\mathcal{M}}$ is:

$$\mathbf{case}\ (x_1, \ldots, x_{\Sigma(C)})\, \mathbf{of} \{(q_1, \ldots, q_{\Sigma(C)}) \Rightarrow q\}_{(C, q_1 \cdots q_{\Sigma(C)}, q) \in \Delta}.$$

We have used a case expression on tuples for clarity; it can be easily flattened to case expressions on each of $x_1, \ldots, x_{\Sigma(C)}$. In the rule A-PROG , $\widetilde{\sigma} \rightarrow \mathsf{o}_{\mathcal{M}}$ and $\widetilde{x} : \widetilde{\sigma}$ abbreviate $\sigma_1 \rightarrow \cdots \rightarrow \sigma_k \rightarrow \mathsf{o}_{\mathcal{M}}$ and $x_1 : \sigma_1, \ldots, x_k : \sigma_k$ respectively.

The soundness of the abstraction is stated as follows; see [13] for a proof.

Theorem 1 (soundness). *Let* $(\mathcal{P}, \mathcal{M}_I, \mathcal{M}_O)$ *be a verification problem. If* $\vdash \mathcal{P} : \Gamma \rightsquigarrow \mathcal{D}$ *and* $\Gamma(main) = \mathsf{o}_{\mathcal{M}'_I} \to \mathsf{o}_{\mathcal{M}'_O}$ *with* $\mathcal{L}(\mathcal{M}'_I, F_I) = \mathcal{L}(\mathcal{M}_I)$ *and* $\mathcal{L}(\mathcal{M}'_O, F_O) = \mathcal{L}(\mathcal{M}_O)$*, then* $\models (\mathcal{D}, F_I, F_O)$ *implies* $\models (\mathcal{P}, \mathcal{M}_I, \mathcal{M}_O)$.

Example 4. Consider the verification problem $(\mathcal{P}_1, \mathcal{M}_1, \mathcal{M}_2)$ where $\mathcal{P}_1$ is defined in Example 2 and the automata $\mathcal{M}_1$ and $\mathcal{M}_2$ are given in Example 3. Let Γ_1 be:

$$\{main : \mathsf{o}_{\mathcal{M}_1} \to \mathsf{o}_{\mathcal{M}_2},\ add : \mathsf{o}_{\mathcal{M}_1} \to \mathsf{o}_{\mathcal{M}_2} \to \mathsf{o}_{\mathcal{M}_2},$$
$$twice : (\mathsf{o}_{\mathcal{M}_2} \to \mathsf{o}_{\mathcal{M}_2}) \to \mathsf{o}_{\mathcal{M}_2} \to \mathsf{o}_{\mathcal{M}_2}\}.$$

Then, $\vdash \mathcal{P}_1 : \Gamma_1 \rightsquigarrow \mathcal{D}_1$, where $\mathcal{D}_1$ consists of:

$$main\ x = twice\ (add\ x)\ q_2 \qquad f_{\mathrm{S},\mathcal{M}_2}\ x = \textbf{case}\, x\, \textbf{of}\ q_2 \Rightarrow q_3 \mid q_3 \Rightarrow q_2$$
$$twice\ f\ x = f\ (f\ x) \qquad add\ x\ y = \textbf{case}\, x\, \textbf{of}\ q_1 \Rightarrow y \,\Box\, (add\ q_1\ (f_{\mathrm{S},\mathcal{M}_2}\ y)).$$

The verification problem has been reduced to the safety problem $(\mathcal{D}_1, \{q_1\}, \{q_2\})$. ($\models (\mathcal{D}_1, \{q_1\}, \{q_2\})$ does not hold, however, as shown in Sect. 5.1; we need to refine the abstraction using the method described in Sect. 5.2.) □

5 Abstraction Refinement

This section discusses how to refine the automata used for abstraction when they are not precise enough. The pseudo code of our verification method is shown in Fig. 2. Our method first infers the initial abstraction type environment, and performs some initialization (line 2). The verification problem is reduced to a safety problem as explained in Sect. 4.2 (line 4). The safety problem is solved by an existing higher-order model checker (line 5). If the answer to the problem is "no" (line 7), we inspect whether the abstract error path returned by the model checker is feasible, i.e., the source program has a corresponding error path (lines 8–9). If the error path is feasible, the answer to the verification problem is "no" (line 10). Otherwise, our method refines the abstraction by splitting each state of the automaton for abstraction so that the spurious error path is eliminated from the future abstraction (lines 12–17).

We explain below the feasibility checking (lines 8–9) and the abstraction refinement (lines 12–17) in Sects. 5.1 and 5.2 respectively. The inference of the initial abstraction type environment (line 2) is explained in the full version [13].

5.1 Feasibility Check

If the answer to a safety problem is "no", a higher-order model checker [3,8] outputs an error path of the abstract program. To check whether the source program has a corresponding error execution path, we evaluate the source program symbolically along the error path, and generate constraints on variables (line 8). We then check the satisfiability of constraints (line 9).

function VERIFY$(\mathcal{P}, \mathcal{M}_I, \mathcal{M}_O)$
  $\Gamma_0 :=$ INFER_ABST_TENV$(\mathcal{P}, \mathcal{M}_I, \mathcal{M}_O)$; $Split := 1$; $CnstSet := \emptyset$; $\Gamma := \Gamma_0$;
  loop
    let $(\mathcal{D}, F_I, F_O) =$ ABSTRACT$((\mathcal{P}, \mathcal{M}_I, \mathcal{M}_O), \Gamma)$
    case CHECK_REACHABILITY$(\mathcal{D}, F_I, F_O)$ **of**
    | $Yes \rightarrow$ **return** Yes;
    | $No(ep) \rightarrow$
      let $Cnst =$GEN_CNST$(ep, (\mathcal{P}, \mathcal{M}_I, \mathcal{M}_O))$
      case SOLVE_CNST$(Cnst)$ **of**
      | $Satisfiable(\theta) \rightarrow$ **return** No;
      | $Unsatisfiable \rightarrow$
        $CnstSet := CnstSet \cup \{Cnst\}$;
        loop
          let $cond =$GENSMT$(CnstSet, \Gamma_0, Split)$
          case SMT_SOLVER$(cond)$ **of**
          | $Satisfiable(sol) \rightarrow \Gamma :=$ REFINE$(\Gamma_0, Split, sol)$; **break**;
          | $Unsatisfiable \rightarrow Split := Split + 1;\}\}$

Fig. 2. Pseudo code of our method

For example, recall the safety problem $(\mathcal{D}_1, \{q_1\}, \{q_2\})$ in Example 4. The answer to this safety problem is "no", and one of the error paths output by a model checker is as follows.

$$\begin{aligned} &main\ q_1 \longrightarrow_{\mathcal{D}_1} twice\ (add\ q_1)\ q_2 \longrightarrow_{\mathcal{D}_1} add\ q_1\ (add\ q_1\ q_2) \\ &\longrightarrow^*_{\mathcal{D}_1} add\ q_1\ (q_2 \,\Box\, (add\ q_1\ (f_{\mathtt{S},\mathcal{M}_2}\ q_2))) \longrightarrow_{\mathcal{D}_1} add\ q_1\ q_2 \\ &\longrightarrow^*_{\mathcal{D}_1} q_2 \,\Box\, (add\ q_1\ (f_{\mathtt{S},\mathcal{M}_2}\ q_2)) \longrightarrow_{\mathcal{D}_1} add\ q_1\ (f_{\mathtt{S},\mathcal{M}_2}\ q_2) \\ &\longrightarrow^*_{\mathcal{D}_1} add\ q_1\ q_3 \longrightarrow^*_{\mathcal{D}_1} q_3 \,\Box\, (add\ q_1\ (f_{\mathtt{S},\mathcal{M}_2}\ q_3)) \longrightarrow_{\mathcal{D}_1} q_3 \end{aligned}$$

We first prepare a concise version of the error path (of the abstract program), which is just a sequence TR of the transition rules used for abstracting the values inspected by each case expression. Here, we ignore the case-expressions in the definition of $f_{C,\mathcal{M}}$, which have no corresponding case-expressions in the source program. For the example above, $TR = (\mathtt{Z}, \epsilon, q_1)(\mathtt{S}, q_1, q_1)(\mathtt{Z}, \epsilon, q_1)$. The i-th element ($i \in \{1, 2, 3\}$) corresponds to the evaluation of the i-th case expression evaluated in the error path above. For example, the first element corresponds to the first case expression; since the expression being evaluated to q_1 means that the corresponding value of the source program has been considered Z, and it was abstracted to q_1 by using the transition rule $(\mathtt{Z}, \epsilon, q_1)$.

Given a concise error sequence TR, we replace TR with a corresponding concise transition sequence TR_0 for the initial abstraction, which is obtained by replacing each transition rule $(C, \widetilde{q}, q)$ with the corresponding transition rule $(C, \widetilde{q}', q')$ of the automata occurring in the *initial* abstraction type environment Γ_0. This is always possible by the construction of the refinement procedure described in Sect. 5.2; each state of an automaton in the current abstraction type environment is of the form $q^{(i)}$, and we just need to replace $q^{(i)}$ with q.

The symbolic evaluation of the original program is formalized as the relation $(e, Cnst, TR) \longrightarrow_{\mathcal{P}} (e', Cnst', TR')$, where e is an expression of the original program, $Cnst$ is the set of constraints being accumulated, and TR is a concise error sequence. The relation is defined by the following rules:

$$\frac{f\ x_1 \cdots x_n = e \in \mathcal{P}}{(E[f\ v_1 \cdots v_n], Cnst, TR) \longrightarrow_{\mathcal{P}} (E[[v_1 \cdots v_n/x_1 \cdots x_n]e], Cnst, TR)}$$

$$\frac{TR = (C_k, \widetilde{q}, q) \cdot TR' \qquad Cnst' = \{(v = C_k\ \widetilde{x}), v : q, (\widetilde{x} : \widetilde{q})\} \cup Cnst \quad (\widetilde{x} \text{ fresh})}{(E[\mathbf{case}\, v\, \mathbf{of}\, \{C_i\ \widetilde{y_i} \Rightarrow e_k\}_{i=1}^m], Cnst, TR) \longrightarrow_{\mathcal{P}} (E[[\widetilde{x}/\widetilde{y_k}]e_k], Cnst', TR')}$$

The first rule is for a function call, which is a deterministic evaluation that does not require information about the error path. The second rule is for case-expressions, where the first element of TR is looked up (and consumed) to decide which branch should be taken. The premise $TR = (C_k, \widetilde{q}, q).\ TR'$ means that v has been abstracted to q using the transition rule $(C_k, \widetilde{q}, q)$. So, the constraints $v = C_k\ \widetilde{x}$, $v : q$, and $\widetilde{x} : \widetilde{q}$ are added. Here, v is a tree expression consisting of variables and tree constructors; the latter constraint $\widetilde{x} : \widetilde{q}$ is an abbreviation of $x_1 : q_1, \ldots, x_k : q_k$, which means that the value of x_i should belong to $\mathcal{L}(\mathcal{M}, q_i)$. (Here, the states of automata in $Automata(\Gamma)$ are disjoint from each other; so $\mathcal{M}$ is uniquely identified by q_i.) By applying the rules above, we obtain a symbolic execution sequence: $(main\, x, \emptyset, TR_0) \longrightarrow_{\mathcal{P}}^{*} (e, Cnst, \epsilon)$. We let $Cnst$ be the output of GEN_CONST on line 8 of Fig. 2. By the rules, it should be clear that if we instantiate each variable in the symbolic evaluation sequence so that $Cnst$ is satisfied, then we get an actual error path of the source program. Therefore, $Cnst$ is satisfiable if and only if the source program has an error path corresponding to the abstract error path TR_0. The satisfiability of $Cnst$ can be easily checked by first solving equality constraints using a standard unification algorithm, and then checking the remaining condition $v : q$ based on the transition rules of the automaton.

Example 5. Recall the verification problem $(\mathcal{D}_1, \{q_1\}, \{q_2\})$ and the (concise) abstract error path $TR = (\mathtt{Z}, \epsilon, q_1)(\mathtt{S}, q_1, q_1)(\mathtt{Z}, \epsilon, q_1)$ considered above. We have the following symbolic execution sequence.

$$
\begin{aligned}
&(main\ x_1, \emptyset, (\mathtt{Z}, \epsilon, q_1)(\mathtt{S}, q_1, q_1)(\mathtt{Z}, \epsilon, q_1)) \\
\longrightarrow^{*}&(add\, x_1\, (\mathbf{case}\, x_1\, \mathbf{of}\, \mathtt{Z} \Rightarrow \mathtt{Z} \mid \mathtt{S}\, x' \Rightarrow add\, x' (\mathtt{S}\, \mathtt{Z})), \emptyset, (\mathtt{Z}, \epsilon, q_1)(\mathtt{S}, q_1, q_1)(\mathtt{Z}, \epsilon, q_1)) \\
\longrightarrow\ &(add\ x_1\ \mathtt{Z}, \{x_1 : q_1, x_1 = \mathtt{Z}\}, (\mathtt{S}, q_1, q_1)(\mathtt{Z}, \epsilon, q_1)) \\
\longrightarrow\ &(\mathbf{case}\, x_1\, \mathbf{of}\, \mathtt{Z} \Rightarrow \mathtt{Z} \mid \mathtt{S}\, x' \Rightarrow add\, x'\ (\mathtt{S}\, \mathtt{Z})), \{x_1 : q_1, x_1 = \mathtt{Z}\}, (\mathtt{S}, q_1, q_1)(\mathtt{Z}, \epsilon, q_1)) \\
\longrightarrow\ &(add\ x_2\ (\mathtt{S}\ \mathtt{Z}), \{x_1 : q_1, x_1 = \mathtt{Z}, x_1 = \mathtt{S}\ x_2, x_2 : q_1\}, (\mathtt{Z}, \epsilon, q_1)) \\
\longrightarrow\ &(\mathbf{case}\, x_2\, \mathbf{of}\, \mathtt{Z} \Rightarrow \mathtt{S}\ \mathtt{Z} \mid \mathtt{S}\ x' \Rightarrow add\ x'\ (\mathtt{S}\ (\mathtt{S}\ \mathtt{Z})), \\
&\qquad \{x_1 : q_1, x_1 = \mathtt{Z}, x_1 = \mathtt{S}\ x_2, x_2 : q_1\}, (\mathtt{Z}, \epsilon, q_1)) \\
\longrightarrow\ &(\mathtt{S}\ \mathtt{Z}, \{x_1 : q_1, x_1 = \mathtt{Z}, x_1 = \mathtt{S}\ x_2, x_2 : q_1, x_2 = \mathtt{Z}\}, \epsilon)
\end{aligned}
$$

We therefore get constraints $\{x_1 : q_1, x_1 = \mathtt{Z}, x_1 = \mathtt{S}\ x_2, x_2 : q_1, x_2 = \mathtt{Z}\}$. Because the constraints are unsatisfiable (there are conflicting equalities $x_1 = \mathtt{Z}$ and $x_1 = \mathtt{S}\ x_2$), the error path is infeasible. Note that the infeasible error path has been obtained because the variable x_1 has been copied as *add* x_1 (*add* x_1 Z) and instantiated differently (the first occurrence as S Z and the second as Z) due to the imprecise abstraction, which abstracts both Z and S Z to the same state q_1. The procedure described in the next subsection refines the abstraction by splitting the state q_1 in order to avoid this confusion between Z and S Z.

5.2 Abstraction Refinement

As mentioned above, when the error path of the abstracted program is infeasible, our method refines the abstraction by splitting each automaton state q to $q^{(1)}, \ldots, q^{(n)}$, where n, called the *split number*, is kept in variable *Split* in Fig. 2. It is set to 1 initially (line 2), and gradually increased.

We refine each automaton $\mathcal{M} \in \mathit{Automata}(\Gamma_0)$ to $\mathcal{M}'$, so that: (i) $\forall q \in Q_{\mathcal{M}}.\mathcal{L}(\mathcal{M}, q) = \mathcal{L}(\mathcal{M}', \{q^{(1)}, \ldots, q^{(n)}\})$; and (ii) the same error path (TR_0 in Sect. 5.1) never occurs again.

To guarantee the first condition, it suffices to guarantee that for each rule $(C, q_1 \cdots q_k, q) \in \Delta_{\mathcal{M}}$,

$$\forall i_1, \ldots, i_k \in \{1, \ldots, n\}.\exists i \in \{1, \ldots, n\}.(C, q_1^{(i_1)} \cdots q_k^{(i_k)}, q^{(i)}) \in \Delta_{\mathcal{M}'}$$

holds. Thus, $\mathcal{M}'$ is determined by a function $g_{(C,q_1\cdots q_k,q)} \in \{1, \ldots, \mathit{Split}\}^k \rightarrow \{1, \ldots, \mathit{Split}\}$ for each $(C, q_1 \cdots q_k, q) \in \Delta_{\mathcal{M}}$. We prepare an uninterpreted function symbol $g_{(C,q_1\cdots q_k,q)}$ for representing the unknown function, and generate the constraints on $g_{(C,q_1\cdots q_k,q)}$'s so that the second condition is guaranteed.

To guarantee the second condition, for each constraint *Cnst* in *CnstSet* (which accumulates the set of constraints generated from spurious error paths found so far), we generate the following SMT formula F_{Cnst}.

$$\forall x_1, \ldots, x_\ell \in \{1, \ldots, \mathit{Split}\}. \bigvee_{v_1 = v_2 \in \mathit{Cnst}} (\mathit{state}(v_1) \neq \mathit{state}(v_2)).$$

Here, $\mathit{state}(v)$ is defined by: (i) $\mathit{state}(x) = x$; and (ii) $\mathit{state}(C\, v_1 \cdots v_k) = g_{(C,q_1\cdots q_k,q)}(\mathit{state}(v_1), \ldots, \mathit{state}(v_k))$ if $\Delta'(v_1) = q_1, \ldots, \Delta'(v_k) = q_k$, and $\Delta'(C\, v_1, \ldots v_k) = q$, where $\Delta'(v)$ is defined by:

$$\Delta'(v) = \begin{cases} q & (\text{if } v = x \wedge (x : q) \in \mathit{Cnst}) \\ \Delta(C, \Delta'(v_1) \cdots \Delta'(v_{\Sigma(C)})) & (\text{if } v = C\, v_1 \cdots v_{\Sigma(C)}) \end{cases}$$

with $\Delta = \bigcup\{\Delta_{\mathcal{M}} \mid \mathcal{M} \in \mathit{Automata}(\Gamma_0)\}$ for the initial abstraction type environment Γ_0. Then, GENSMT outputs the conjunction of the above formula $\bigwedge_{\mathit{Cnst} \in \mathit{CnstSet}} F_{\mathit{Cnst}}$. If it is satisfiable, then we obtain a refined abstraction type environment Γ. Otherwise, we increase *Split* until the SMT constraint becomes satisfiable.

Example 6. Recall the verification problem in Example 5 and suppose $\mathit{Split} = 2$. The generated SMT formula is:

$$\forall x_1, x_2 \in \{1, 2\}.x_1 \neq g_{(\mathtt{Z},\epsilon,q_1)}() \vee x_1 \neq g_{(\mathtt{S},q_1,q_1)}(x_2) \vee x_2 \neq g_{(\mathtt{Z},\epsilon,q_1)}()$$

One of the solutions is $g_{(\mathtt{Z},\epsilon,q_1)} = 1, g_{(\mathtt{S},q_1,q_1)}(1) = 2, g_{(\mathtt{S},q_1,q_1)}(2) = 1$. The transition function of the refined automaton is: $\{(\mathtt{Z},\epsilon,q_1^{(1)}),(\mathtt{S},q_1^{(1)},q_1^{(2)}),(\mathtt{S},q_1^{(2)},q_1^{(1)})\}$. Using this automaton, the verification succeeds.

The following theorem ensures that if there is an appropriate abstraction type environment with which the verification succeeds, then the algorithm eventually find such an abstraction type environment. See [13] for a proof.

Theorem 2 (relative completeness). *Let $(\mathcal{P},\mathcal{M}_I,\mathcal{M}_O)$ be a verification problem. Suppose there exists Γ such that $\vdash \mathcal{P} : \Gamma \leadsto \mathcal{D}$, $\models (\mathcal{D},F_I,F_O)$, and $\Gamma(main) = \mathsf{o}_{\mathcal{M}'_I} \to \mathsf{o}_{\mathcal{M}'_O}$ with $\mathcal{L}(\mathcal{M}_I) = \mathcal{L}(\mathcal{M}'_I,F_I)$ and $\mathcal{L}(\mathcal{M}_O) = \mathcal{L}(\mathcal{M}'_O,F_O)$. Then the algorithm eventually terminates and outputs "Yes".*

We say that CHECK_REACHABILITY in Fig. 2 is *fair* if every concise error path is eventually generated; it is guaranteed if CHECK_REACHABILITY always returns a shortest concise error path, for example. We can also guarantee:

Theorem 3 (completeness of refutation). *Let $(\mathcal{P},\mathcal{M}_I,\mathcal{M}_O)$ be a verification problem such that $\not\models (\mathcal{P},\mathcal{M}_I,\mathcal{M}_O)$. If* CHECK_REACHABILITY *is fair, then the algorithm eventually terminates and outputs "No".*

6 Implementation and Experiments

We have implemented a verification tool based on our method, and evaluated it through experiments. The experiments were conducted on a machine with Intel(R) Xeon(R) CPU E5620 2.40 GHz and 3.73 GB memory. We used HORSAT [3] as the higher-order model checker (except for the program "homrep-rev" for which we used [8] due to a problem of HORSAT) and Z3 [5] as the SMT solver.

Table 1 shows the result of the experiments. The column "S" represents the size of the programs. The size of a program is the number of occurrences of constants and variables on the right side of the rules in the program. The column "O" represents the order of the programs. The order of a program is the largest order of the types of functions. Here, the order $order(\kappa)$ of the type κ is defined by: $order(\mathsf{o}) = 0$, $order(\kappa_1 \to \kappa_2) = \max\{order(\kappa_1)+1, order(\kappa_2)\}$. The column "R" represents the number of refinements in the verification. The column "T" shows the running time (measured in seconds). We ran each program 3 times and show the average running time. "TO" in the column "T" means a time-out, where we set the time-out to 1000 seconds. For comparison, we have also run the verification tools for HMTT [12] and EHMTT [19] and show their running times in the columns "$\mathrm{T_H}$" and "$\mathrm{T_E}$" respectively. The "N/A" means that the tool is inapplicable; that is the case for the HMTT verification tool, when trees are repeatedly constructed and deconstructed inside the program. The EHMTT verification tool is inapplicable when there is no appropriate annotation; see the discussion below. We have also tried to compare our tool with the PMRS verification tool [16], but unfortunately we could not obtain its source code.

The benchmark programs consist of three categories (separated by lines in the table). The first category (the programs from "reverse" to "mincaml-k") has been taken from the benchmark set for the EHMTT verification tool [19]. The original programs contain annotations required for EHMTT, and they have been removed for the experiments on our new tool. The second category has been taken from the benchmark set for the PMRS verification tool [16], available at http://mjolnir.cs.ox.ac.uk/cgi-bin/horsc/recheck-horsc/input. The third category contains a new benchmark set. The program "double" is the verification problem given in Example 3. The program "isort2" sorts a given list consisting of "A" and "B" by the insertion sort algorithm. The specification asserts that the result is a sorted list. The program "issorted" sorts a given list consisting of "A" and "B" by the insertion sort, and then (inside the program) checks that the result is a sorted list; if not, the program fails. The specification is that the program does not fail. The program "mergesort2" is the same as "insertionsort" except that the merge sort algorithm is used. The program "mapswsort" sorts a given list and maps a function that swaps "A" and "B" on the list. In the programs above, lists are encoded as trees constructed from `cons`, `nil`, `A`, and `B`. The program "remove0" takes a list of integers (in the unary representation) and removes 0 from the list.

Our tool could verify the benchmark programs, except "xmarkq1" and "gapid". For the program "xmarkq1", the tool failed to construct the initial abstraction. This is because the automata given as the specification of the program is large, and the current tool naively applies a product construction to make the automaton used for abstraction. For the program "gapid", the abstraction refinement loop did not terminate within the given time limit. This is because the automaton required for abstracting intermediate trees is quite different from the automata given as the input/output specification.

As for the comparison with the HMTT/EHMTT verification tools, the HMTT tool is applicable to only a few of the benchmark programs. That is because HMTT [12] classifies trees into input trees and output trees, and pattern matching can be applied only to input trees, and tree constructors can be applied only to output trees. Most of the programs in the benchmark set repeatedly construct and deconstruct trees.

The EHMTT tool works for the first benchmark set, but it relies on user annotations. Like HMTT, EHMTT also distinguishes between input and output trees, but allows an explicit coercion of output trees to input trees. Each coercion must be annotated with an invariant on the shape of trees that are coerced, and that invariant is used for abstraction. Thus, since an appropriate abstraction is given by hand, EHMTT is faster than our tool when it is applicable. For the second and third categories, we have also added annotations for EHMTT, when applicable. For many of the benchmark programs in the second and third categories, however, there are no appropriate annotations that make the EHMTT verification succeed. There are two main reasons for this. One reason, which is somehow specific to the current implementation, is that the EHMTT tool allows only deterministic top-down automata as output specifications. Since the class of deterministic top-down tree automata is a strict subclass of deterministic bottom-up tree automata, some of the specifications cannot be handled by the

EHMTT tool. The other reason is more fundamental. Consider the following function "*iszero*".

$$iszero\ x\ t\ f = \mathbf{case}\, x\, \mathbf{of}\, \mathtt{Z} \Rightarrow t \mid \mathtt{S}\, y \Rightarrow f.$$

If the first argument of the function "*iszero*" is an output tree, the argument requires an annotation as follows.

$$iszero\ (\mathtt{coerce}^{\mathcal{L}} e)\ e_t\ e_f$$

Here, $\mathtt{coerce}^{\mathcal{L}} e$ converts an output tree constructed by e to an input tree, so that pattern matching can be applied again. The annotation $\mathcal{L}$ is an invariant on the value of e; in this case, $\mathcal{L}$ would be typically `S*Z` (unless the value of e can be statically determined). Given the annotation, the EHMTT converts the body of *iszero* to a non-deterministic choice between t and f, ignoring the actual value. Thus, if the property to be verified requires a case analysis on whether x is `Z` or not, the EHMTT verification fails.

To summarize, compared with the HMTT/EHMTT verification tools, our new tool works for a larger set of programs, requiring no special annotations, although it may be slower when the previous tools are applicable. For the programs such as `xmarkq1` and `gapid`, a compromise would be to allow users to provide abstraction types as annotations. Such annotations do not suffer from the problem of EHMTT annotations discussed above.

Table 1. Experimental results

Program	S	O	R	T	T_H	T_E	Program	S	O	R	T	T_H	T_E
reverse	46	1	16	4.215	N/A	0.032	mkground	46	1	4	0.892	N/A	0.043
isort	29	1	0	0.103	N/A	0.022	filter-nz	31	2	1	0.472	N/A	N/A
mergesort	173	2	0	1.711	N/A	0.303	safe-tail	100	2	9	11.48	N/A	N/A
homrep-rev	97	4	14	2.338	N/A	0.043	maphead	53	2	5	2.489	N/A	N/A
split2	108	2	53	589.3	N/A	0.089	risers	78	1	3	2.006	N/A	0.079
bib2html	103	2	1	3.568	N/A	0.376	safe-init	113	2	13	22.76	N/A	N/A
xmarkq1	89	2	-	TO	N/A	0.767	checknz	8	1	0	0.018	0.011	0.009
xmarkq2	157	1	0	100.8	N/A	1.531	checkpairs	35	1	0	0.082	N/A	N/A
gapid	393	3	14	TO	N/A	0.148	double	12	1	0	0.041	0.040	N/A
jwig-cal	96	1	0	143.5	N/A	0.570	isort2	40	1	1	1.058	N/A	N/A
jwig-guess	99	2	6	65.8	N/A	1.411	issorted	127	1	6	12.45	N/A	N/A
mincaml-k	683	2	0	532.3	N/A	1.830	mapswsort	61	2	20	22.63	N/A	N/A
last	20	1	1	0.129	N/A	0.027	mergesort2	96	1	0	3.178	N/A	N/A
safe-head	67	2	1	0.888	N/A	N/A	remove0	32	1	1	0.409	0.015	0.012

7 Related Work

As mentioned in Sect. 1, several approaches have been proposed for automated verification of functional programs based on higher-order model checking. Kobayashi et al. [11] proposed predicate abstraction and CEGAR (counterexample-guided abstraction refinement) for higher-order model checking, but they used only predicates on integers for abstraction. They later supported some algebraic data structures by encoding them into functions on integers. That encoding approach, however, complicates both programs and specifications. For example, since a list is encoded into a pair consisting of its length and a function that maps an index to the corresponding element, the property of a list: "1 occurs in the list" would be converted to a refinement type specification:

$$n : \mathtt{int} \times \{f : \mathtt{int} \to \mathtt{int} \mid \exists x.(0 \le x < n \wedge f(x) = 1)\},$$

which would be simply represented by $\_^*1\_^*$ with a regular language (or automaton) specification. The above specification involves function variables and existential quantifiers, which cannot be handled even by the recent extension of `MoCHi` [1]. Even if the encoding works, the resulting program and specification tends to become too complex and large, making automated verification difficult; in fact, the current implementation of `MoCHi` does not work for the benchmark programs in Sect. 6. That said, a limitation of our new approach is that we cannot verify some co-relation between arguments and return values, like "Function f takes a list of length n, and returns a list of length $2 \times n$." This is because we use automata for abstracting information about each tree, which loses the relationship between multiple trees. A possible remedy to this problem would be to use tree automatic relations [2] for abstraction. Another approach would be to integrate our new approach with that of `MoCHi`.

We have already discussed HMTT [12] and EHMTT [19] in Sect. 6. Although HMTT also abstracts trees by using an automaton, the automaton used for the abstraction is fixed to the one specified as the input automaton. EHMTT decompose the verification problem to multiple HMTT verification problems, by using annotations. Again, the abstraction relies on the automata given as specifications or annotations. There was no abstraction refinement loop mechanism in the above work on HMTT/EHMTT verification. We have recently extended the HMTT verification with abstraction refinement loops [14], but it was restricted to HMTT (where there is a distinction between input/output trees), and the relative completeness (cf. Theorem 2) was not guaranteed. In short, our new method requires no annotations unlike EHMTT verification, and works (at least in theory) for a strictly larger set of verification problems than our previous work on HMTT/EHMTT verification.

Ong and Ramsay [16] introduced a verification method for tree-processing programs called PMRS. Their method abstracts trees based on finite patterns, so it cannot deal with general regular properties like "a tree contains an even number of `S`". For example, for the program $\mathcal{P}_1$ in Example 2: they abstract the argument x of *add* based on the information about whether x matches `Z` or `S` x'.

If the verification fails, they expand patterns by unfolding functions; in the case of the above example, the new set of patterns would be $\{\mathtt{Z}, \mathtt{S}\,\mathtt{Z}, \mathtt{S}\,(\mathtt{S}\,x)\}$. Thus, their abstraction never captures properties like "x is an even number" (i.e., x is of the form $\mathtt{S}^{2n}\mathtt{Z}$). For the benchmark programs used in our experiments, PMRS works for the second category (because it has been taken from the benchmark of the PMRS tool), but it would not work for most of the benchmarks in the first and third categories.

Automata-based abstraction has also been recently used for μHORS model checking [10]. The μHORS model checking is an extension of higher-order model checking, where HORS has been extended with recursive types. They abstract the whole program configuration (which can be represented as applicative terms) by using a tree automaton, and gradually refines the abstraction using a similar technique utilizing an SMT solver. Since μHORS is Turing complete, their approach can in theory be applied to the verification problems considered in the present paper, but our approach would scale much better for tree-processing programs. They abstract both control and data structures using automata in a monolithic way, whereas we abstract only tree data using automata, and precisely analyze control structures thanks to the decidability of higher-order model checking.

Besides approaches based on higher-order model checking, there have been a few other approaches to (semi-)automated verification of higher-order functional programs that support algebraic data types. Liquid types [7,17,20] is a notable approach based on refinement types, but it requires a user's hints on the predicates used in refinement types. Genet [6] applies a tree automata completion technique for term rewriting systems to static analysis of functional programs. His approach uses tree automata for modeling the whole program state (like in the μHORS model checking mentioned above), while our approach uses tree automata only for abstracting tree data. His method does not guarantee the relative completeness in the sense of ours.

8 Conclusion

In this paper, we have introduced a new method for fully automated verification of tree-processing, higher-order functional programs. We have introduced automata-based abstraction, and combined it with higher-order model checking. The automata-based abstraction is formalized as a type-based program transformation, and the abstraction is gradually refined based on counterexamples. Compared with the previous methods based on higher-order model checking, the new method is more automated (requires no annotations), and can deal with a larger class of programs. Future work includes improvement of the scalability of the verification method, and an integration of the proposed technique with the predicate abstraction approach of `MoCHi` [1,11,18].

Acknowledgments. We thank anonymous reviewers for useful comments. This work was partially supported by JSPS Kakenhi 15H05706, 23220001, and 25730035.

References

1. Asada, K., Sato, R., Kobayashi, N.: Verifying relational properties of functional programs by first-order refinement. In: Proceedings of PEPM 2015, pp. 61–72 (2015)
2. Blumensath, A., Grädel, E.: Automatic structures. In: Proceedings of LICS 2000, pp. 51–62 (2000)
3. Broadbent, C.H., Kobayashi, N.: Saturation-based model checking of higher-order recursion schemes. In: Proceedings of CSL 2013. LIPIcs, vol. 23, pp. 129–148 (2013)
4. Comon, H., et al.: Tree automata techniques and applications (2007). http://www.grappa.univ-lille3.fr/tata
5. de Moura, L., Bjørner, N.S.: Z3: An efficient SMT solver. In: Ramakrishnan, C.R., Rehof, J. (eds.) TACAS 2008. LNCS, vol. 4963, pp. 337–340. Springer, Heidelberg (2008)
6. Genet, T.: Towards static analysis of functional programs using tree automata completion. In: Escobar, S. (ed.) WRLA 2014. LNCS, vol. 8663, pp. 147–161. Springer, Heidelberg (2014)
7. Kawaguchi, M., Rondon, P., Jhala, R.: Type-based data structure verification. In: Proceedings of PLDI 2009, pp. 304–315. ACM (2009)
8. Kobayashi, N.: Model-checking higher-order functions. In: Proceedings of PPDP 2009. pp. 25–36 (2009)
9. Kobayashi, N.: Model checking higher-order programs. J. ACM **60**(3), 20:1–20:62 (2013)
10. Kobayashi, N., Li, X.: Automata-based abstraction refinement for μHORS model checking. In: Proceedings of LICS 2015 (2015)
11. Kobayashi, N., Sato, R., Unno, H.: Predicate abstraction and cegar for higher-order model checking. In: Proceedings of PLDI 2011, pp. 222–233 (2011)
12. Kobayashi, N., Tabuchi, N., Unno, H.: Higher-order multi-parameter tree transducers and recursion schemes for program verification. In: Proceedings of POPL 2010, pp. 495–508. ACM (2010)
13. Matsumoto, Y., Kobayashi, N., Unno, H.: Automata-based abstraction for automated verification of higher-order tree-processing programs (2015). an extended version, available from the second author's web page
14. Matsumoto, Y., Kobayashi, N., Unno, H.: Counterexample finding and abstraction refinement for automated verification of higher-order transducers. Comput. Softw. **31**(1), 161–178 (2015). (in Japanese)
15. Ong, C.-H.L.: On model-checking trees generated by higher-order recursion schemes. In: Proceedings of LICS 2006, pp. 81–90. IEEE Computer Society (2006)
16. Ong, C.-H.L., Ramsay, S.J.: Verifying higher-order functional programs with pattern-matching algebraic data types. In: Proceedings of POPL 2011, pp. 587–598. ACM (2011)
17. Rondon, P.M., Kawaguchi, M., Jhala, R.: Liquid types. In: PLDI 2008, pp. 159–169 (2008)
18. Sato, R., Unno, H., Kobayashi, N.: Towards a scalable software model checker for higher-order programs. In: Proceedings of PEPM 2013, pp. 53–62. ACM (2013)
19. Unno, H., Tabuchi, N., Kobayashi, N.: Verification of tree-processing programs via higher-order model checking. In: Ueda, K. (ed.) APLAS 2010. LNCS, vol. 6461, pp. 312–327. Springer, Heidelberg (2010)
20. Vazou, N., Rondon, P.M., Jhala, R.: Abstract refinement types. In: Felleisen, M., Gardner, P. (eds.) ESOP 2013. LNCS, vol. 7792, pp. 209–228. Springer, Heidelberg (2013)

Decision Algorithms for Checking Definability of Order-2 Finitary PCF

Sadaaki Kawata([✉]), Kazuyuki Asada, and Naoki Kobayashi

The University of Tokyo, Tokyo, Japan
Kawata@kb.is.s.u-tokyo.ac.jp

Abstract. We consider a definability problem for finitary PCF, which asks whether, given a function (as an element of a cpo), there exists a term of finitary PCF whose interpretation is the function. The definability problem for finitary PCF is known to be decidable for types of order at most 2. However, its complexity and practical algorithms have not been well studied. In this paper, we give two algorithms for checking definability: one based on Sieber's sequentiality relation, which runs in quadruply exponential time for the size of the type of the given function, and the other based on a saturation method, which runs in triply exponential time for the size. With the recent advance of higher-order model checking, our result may be useful for implementing a tool for deciding observational equivalence between finitary PCF terms of types of order at most 3.

1 Introduction

Finitary PCF [11] (FPCF for short) is a simply typed λ-calculus with a single ground type o of booleans and recursion. Any FPCF term can be interpreted as a continuous function between finite cpos. However, some continuous functions such as "parallel-or" cannot be represented by any FPCF term. The FPCF definability is the problem of deciding whether a continuous function can be represented by an FPCF term or not.

Loader [11] proved that definability is undecidable if the order of an input function is greater than 2. He also mentioned that definability is decidable for functions of order at most 2, which is an immediate consequence of Sieber's result [23]. Nevertheless, practical algorithms and the complexity of the definability problem have not been studied well. To our knowledge, the only exception is Stoughton's work [24], which gave an algorithm for the definability problem of order at most 2 and its implementation.[1] However, she did not discuss the complexity of her algorithm.

In this paper, we give two algorithms for deciding the definability problem for order-2 FPCF. We first introduce an algorithm for checking definability based on Sieber's result [23] and prove that the algorithm runs in $\mathcal{O}(2^{2^{2^{2^{\mathrm{poly}(m)}}}})$ time where

[1] We thank an anonymous reviewer for providing us the information of Stoughton's work.

X. Feng and S. Park (Eds.): APLAS 2015, LNCS 9458, pp. 313–331, 2015.
DOI: 10.1007/978-3-319-26529-2_17

the type of an input function is $(\overbrace{\mathsf{o} \to \cdots \to \mathsf{o}}^{m_1} \to \mathsf{o}) \to \cdots \to (\overbrace{\mathsf{o} \to \cdots \to \mathsf{o}}^{m_n} \to \mathsf{o}) \to \mathsf{o}$, $m = \max(n, m_1, \ldots, m_n)$ and $\text{poly}(m)$ is a polynomial of m. Then, we give another algorithm based on a saturation method, which runs in $\mathcal{O}(2^{2^{2^{\text{poly}(m)}}})$ time. Unlike the algorithm based on Sieber's result, this saturation-based algorithm can output a witness term M defining d, if d is indeed definable.

Decision algorithms for definability of order at most 2 can be used to decide the observational equivalence between FPCF terms of types of order at most 3. Since the interpretation $[\![\tau]\!]$ of a type τ has only finitely many elements, and since we can check definability of all the elements in $[\![\tau]\!]$, we can enumerate all the definable elements of $[\![\tau]\!]$. Then, we can decide the observational equivalence between closed terms M_1 and M_2 of type $\tau \to \mathsf{o}$, by checking whether $[\![M_1]\!]d = [\![M_2]\!]d$ for every definable element d in $[\![\tau]\!]$. For computing $[\![M]\!]d$, we can use higher-order model checking [9,17]. Given a closed FPCF term N of type o and a value $V \in \{\mathbf{T}, \mathbf{F}\}$, higher-order model checking can be used for deciding whether N evaluates to V or not. Thus, given M and d, we can compute $[\![M]\!]d$ by first preparing a term N such that $[\![N]\!] = d$, and then invoking a higher-order model checker (e.g. [4,9,21]) to compute the value of $M\,N$.

The rest of this paper is structured as follows. In Sect. 2, we recall finitary PCF and define the definability problem and data representation for discussing the complexities. In Sect. 3, we show the algorithm using Sieber's result and calculate its complexity. Section 4 describes the more efficient saturation-based algorithm for checking definability. Section 5 discusses an application to equivalence checking. Section 6 discusses related work, and Sect. 7 concludes this paper.

2 Preliminaries

2.1 Finitary PCF

FPCF is a call-by-name simply typed λ-calculus with a single ground type o as defined below.

The set of *types* of FPCF (ranged over by $\tau, \sigma, \ldots$) is defined by

$$\tau ::= \mathsf{o} \mid \tau_1 \to \tau_2.$$

The *order* of types is defined by

$$\begin{aligned} \mathbf{order}(\mathsf{o}) &:= 0 \\ \mathbf{order}(\tau_1 \to \tau_2) &:= \max(\mathbf{order}(\tau_1) + 1, \mathbf{order}(\tau_2)). \end{aligned}$$

The set of *terms* of FPCF (ranged over by $M, N, \ldots$) is defined as follows:

$$M ::= x \mid c \mid M_1\ M_2 \mid \lambda x\!:\!\tau.\, M.$$

We sometimes omit the type annotation "$:\tau$" of $\lambda x\!:\!\tau.\, M$ for simplicity. The metavariable c is used to denote constants and the set of *constants* (ranged over by c) is given by:

$$c ::= \mathbf{T} \mid \mathbf{F} \mid \mathbf{if} \mid \mathbf{Y}_\tau.$$

T and **F** are ground type constants, **if** has type $o \to o \to o \to o$, and $\mathbf{Y}_\tau$ is a fixed-point operator of type $(\tau \to \tau) \to \tau$. We often write **if** M_1 **then** M_2 **else** M_3 for **if** $M_1\ M_2\ M_3$, and write $\boldsymbol{\Omega}_\tau$ for the non-terminating term $\mathbf{Y}_\tau\ (\lambda x : \tau. x)$.

We write $\Gamma \vdash M : \tau$ when M has type τ under context Γ. Typing rules for FPCF terms are given in the usual way for the simply-typed λ-calculus.

We give an operational semantics of FPCF by defining the binary relation $\Downarrow$ between closed FPCF terms and values. Note that a term is *closed* if the term does not contain free variables. The set of *values* (ranged over by V) is given by

$$V ::= \mathbf{T} \mid \mathbf{F} \mid \lambda x : \tau. M$$

where $\lambda x : \tau. M$ must be closed. The relation $\Downarrow$ is defined inductively by the following rules:

$$\frac{}{V \Downarrow V} \qquad \frac{M \Downarrow \lambda x : \tau. M' \qquad M'[N/x] \Downarrow V}{M\ N \Downarrow V} \qquad \frac{M\ (\mathbf{Y}_\tau\ M) \Downarrow V}{\mathbf{Y}_\tau\ M \Downarrow V}$$

$$\frac{M_1 \Downarrow \mathbf{T} \qquad M_2 \Downarrow V}{\mathbf{if}\ M_1\ \mathbf{then}\ M_2\ \mathbf{else}\ M_3 \Downarrow V} \qquad \frac{M_1 \Downarrow \mathbf{F} \qquad M_3 \Downarrow V}{\mathbf{if}\ M_1\ \mathbf{then}\ M_2\ \mathbf{else}\ M_3 \Downarrow V}$$

Next, let us recall the standard cpo semantics (e.g. [25]) for FPCF. A type τ is interpreted as a pointed cpo D_τ, i.e., an ordered set with the least upper bound (denoted by lub A) of any directed subset A and the least element (denoted by $\bot$). The cpos D_τ are defined inductively by:

$$D_o = (\{\underline{\mathbf{T}}, \underline{\mathbf{F}}, \bot\}, \leq_o)$$
$$D_{\tau_1 \to \tau_2} = ([D_{\tau_1} \to D_{\tau_2}], \leq_{\tau_1 \to \tau_2}).$$

Here, $[D \to D']$ is the set of continuous[2] functions from D to D', and

$$x \leq_o y \overset{\text{def}}{\iff} (x = y) \vee (x = \bot)$$
$$x \leq_{\tau_1 \to \tau_2} y \overset{\text{def}}{\iff} \forall z \in D_{\tau_1}.\ x(z) \leq_{\tau_2} y(z).$$

We often identify a cpo $D = (S, \leq)$ with a set S. The least element $\bot_\tau$ for each cpo D_τ is given inductively by:

$$\bot_o = \bot$$
$$\bot_{\tau_1 \to \tau_2} = \lambda x : \tau_1. \bot_{\tau_2}$$

The interpretation function $[\![-]\!]$ maps a term $x_1 : \tau_1, \ldots, x_n : \tau_n \vdash M : \tau$ to a function in $D_{\tau_1} \times \cdots \times D_{\tau_n} \to D_\tau$.[3] The definition of $[\![x_1 : \tau_1, \ldots, x_n : \tau_n \vdash M : \tau]\!]$ is given inductively by:

---

2 A function f between pointed cpos is *continuous* if f is monotonic and preserves the least upper bound of any directed subset. Note that, if f is a function between finite cpos, f is continuous if and only if f is monotonic.

3 A cartesian product of two cpos $D_1 = (S_1, \leq_1)$ and $D_2 = (S_2, \leq_2)$ is a cpo $(S_1 \times S_2, \leq_{D_1 \times D_2})$ where $(d_1, d_2) \leq_{D_1 \times D_2} (d_1', d_2') \overset{\text{def}}{\iff} d_1 \leq_1 d_1' \wedge d_2 \leq_2 d_2'$.

$$[\![x_1:\tau_1,\ldots,x_n:\tau_n \vdash x_i:\tau_i]\!](d_1,\ldots,d_n) := d_i$$
$$[\![\Gamma \vdash (M\,N):\tau]\!](\vec{d}) := [\![\Gamma \vdash M:\sigma \to \tau]\!](\vec{d})([\![\Gamma \vdash N:\sigma]\!](\vec{d}))$$
$$[\![\Gamma \vdash (\lambda x:\tau.\,M):\tau \to \sigma]\!](\vec{d})(d) := [\![\Gamma, x:\tau \vdash M:\sigma]\!](\vec{d}, d)$$
$$[\![\Gamma \vdash \mathbf{Y}_\tau :(\tau \to \tau) \to \tau]\!](\vec{d})(f) := \mathrm{lub}\{f^n(\bot) \mid n \in \mathbb{N}\}$$
$$[\![\Gamma \vdash \mathbf{T}:\mathsf{o}]\!](\vec{d}) := \underline{\mathbf{T}}$$
$$[\![\Gamma \vdash \mathbf{F}:\mathsf{o}]\!](\vec{d}) := \underline{\mathbf{F}}$$
$$[\![\Gamma \vdash \mathbf{if}:\mathsf{o} \to \mathsf{o} \to \mathsf{o} \to \mathsf{o}]\!](\vec{d})(v)(v')(v'') := \begin{cases} v' & (\text{if } v = \underline{\mathbf{T}}) \\ v'' & (\text{if } v = \underline{\mathbf{F}}) \\ \bot & (\text{if } v = \bot). \end{cases}$$

Here, $f^0(\bot) := \bot$, $f^{n+1}(\bot) := f(f^n(\bot))$, and $\vec{d}$ denotes a sequence $d_1,\ldots,d_n$. Note that the interpretation of $\mathbf{Y}_\tau$ is well-defined since $\bot \le f(\bot) \le f^2(\bot) \le \ldots$ always holds by the monotonicity of f. Also note that in the interpretation of $M\,N$, the type σ is uniquely determined by the typing judgment $\Gamma \vdash (M\,N) : \tau$. If M is closed, $[\![\vdash M:\tau]\!]$ is a function in $\{*\} \to D_\tau$, and we often abbreviate $[\![\vdash M:\tau]\!](*)$ to $[\![M]\!]$.

Definition 1. *An element $d \in D_\tau$ is* definable *if there exists a closed FPCF term M such that $[\![M]\!] = d$.*

Note that not all the elements are definable. For example, an element $\underline{\mathbf{por}}$ (parallel-or) such that

$$\underline{\mathbf{por}}\,\underline{\mathbf{T}}\,\bot = \underline{\mathbf{T}} \qquad \underline{\mathbf{por}}\,\bot\,\underline{\mathbf{T}} = \underline{\mathbf{T}} \qquad \underline{\mathbf{por}}\,\underline{\mathbf{F}}\,\underline{\mathbf{F}} = \underline{\mathbf{F}}$$

is not definable [18], as explained in Sect. 3.1.

2.2 FPCF Definability Problem

Let τ be a type of order at most 2. We define the *FPCF definability problem* for type τ as follows: given an input $d \in D_\tau$, output whether d is definable or not.

Here, we represent $d \in D_\tau$ as follows: Suppose that τ is of the form $\tau_1 \to \cdots \to \tau_n \to \mathsf{o}$ where τ_i is a type of the form $\overbrace{\mathsf{o} \to \cdots \to \mathsf{o}}^{m_i} \to \mathsf{o}$. Since a function $e \in D_{\tau_i}$ can be seen as a family $(e\,v_1\,\ldots\,v_{m_i})_{(v_1,\ldots v_{m_i}) \in D_\mathsf{o}^{m_i}}$ of elements in D_o, we represent e as an array of the form:

$$(e\,\underline{\mathbf{T}}\,\ldots\,\underline{\mathbf{T}}\,\underline{\mathbf{T}},\;\; e\,\underline{\mathbf{T}}\,\ldots\,\underline{\mathbf{T}}\,\underline{\mathbf{F}},\;\; e\,\underline{\mathbf{T}}\,\ldots\,\underline{\mathbf{T}}\,\bot,\;\; \ldots,\;\; e\,\bot\,\ldots\,\bot).$$

Here, the length of the array for $e \in D_{\tau_i}$ is $|D_\mathsf{o}|^{m_i}$, and an index $(v_1,\ldots,v_{m_i})$ of the family is represented by the ternary representation of an index of the array. For example, the parallel-or $\underline{\mathbf{por}}$ is represented by

$$(\underline{\mathbf{por}}\,\underline{\mathbf{T}}\,\underline{\mathbf{T}},\; \underline{\mathbf{por}}\,\underline{\mathbf{T}}\,\underline{\mathbf{F}},\; \underline{\mathbf{por}}\,\underline{\mathbf{T}}\,\bot,$$
$$\underline{\mathbf{por}}\,\underline{\mathbf{F}}\,\underline{\mathbf{T}},\; \underline{\mathbf{por}}\,\underline{\mathbf{F}}\,\underline{\mathbf{F}},\; \underline{\mathbf{por}}\,\underline{\mathbf{F}}\,\bot,$$
$$\underline{\mathbf{por}}\,\bot\,\underline{\mathbf{T}},\; \underline{\mathbf{por}}\,\bot\,\underline{\mathbf{F}},\; \underline{\mathbf{por}}\,\bot\,\bot),$$

i.e.,

$$(\underline{\mathbf{T}}, \underline{\mathbf{T}}, \underline{\mathbf{T}}, \underline{\mathbf{T}}, \underline{\mathbf{F}}, \bot, \underline{\mathbf{T}}, \bot, \bot).$$

Next, we represent a function $d \in D_\tau (\subseteq D_{\tau_1} \times \cdots \times D_{\tau_n} \to D_\circ)$ as its graph, i.e. as a list $[s_1, \ldots, s_l]$ of elements, where each s_j in $(D_{\tau_1} \times \cdots \times D_{\tau_n}) \times D_\circ$ is of the form:

$$((e_1, \ldots, e_n), d\, e_1 \ldots e_n)$$

and $e_i \in D_{\tau_i}$ is represented by an array as explained above. Here, we only list $(e_1, \ldots, e_n)$ such that each e_i $(i \in \{1, \ldots, n\})$ is continuous. The length of the list d is therefore $|D_{\tau_1} \times \cdots \times D_{\tau_n}|$. We further assume that the list $[s_1, \ldots, s_l]$ is sorted according to a certain linear order on $D_{\tau_1} \times \cdots \times D_{\tau_n}$. (Thus, the part $(e_1, \ldots, e_n)$ is actually redundant, but it does not matter for the order of the input size.) We also assume that the input d represents a continuous function. Note that the continuity, i.e., the monotonicity of d can be checked in time polynomial in the length of d i.e., in time $\mathcal{O}(3^{3^{\mathrm{poly}(m)}})$ $(=\mathcal{O}(2^{2^{\mathrm{poly}(m)}}))$ where $m = \max(n, m_1, \ldots, m_n)$. We often identify an element d in a cpo D with the above representation of d.

3 Algorithm Using Sieber's Relation

In this section, we give an algorithm for the FPCF definability using Sieber's sequentiality relations, and discuss its complexity.

3.1 Logical Relation

We first explain logical relations [19], which can be used to check definability.

Definition 2. *For $n \in \mathbb{N}$, an n-ary* logical relation *R is a type-indexed family $(R_\tau)_{\tau \in \mathbf{Types}}$ of relations $R_\tau \subseteq (D_\tau)^n$ such that for all types τ_1, τ_2 and $f_1, \ldots, f_n \in D_{\tau_1 \to \tau_2}$,*

$$R_{\tau_1 \to \tau_2}\, f_1 \,\ldots\, f_n \iff \forall d_1, \ldots, d_n \in D_{\tau_1}.\ (R_{\tau_1}\, d_1 \,\ldots\, d_n \Rightarrow R_{\tau_2} (f_1\, d_1) \,\ldots\, (f_n\, d_n)).$$

Note that R is uniquely determined by $R_\circ$.

Definition 3. *Let R be a logical relation. An element $d \in D_\tau$ is* invariant under *R if $R_\tau\, d \ldots d$. Also, a closed term M of type τ is* invariant under *R if so is $[\![M]\!]$.*

Theorem 1 (Basic Lemma [20]). *Let R be a logical relation. If every constant c is invariant under R, then every closed FPCF term M is invariant under R.*

This theorem can be used to prove the non-definability of some elements. To prove the non-definability of d, it is sufficient to construct a logical relation R such that all the PCF constants are invariant under R but d is not invariant under R. A classical example for showing the non-definability of $\underline{\mathbf{por}}$ is the logical relation R defined by:

$$R_o\ x_1\ x_2\ x_3 \overset{\text{def}}{\Longleftrightarrow} (x_1 = \bot) \lor (x_2 = \bot) \lor (x_1 = x_2 = x_3). \tag{1}$$

All the constants of FPCF are invariant under R; however, $\underline{\mathbf{por}}$ is not invariant under R, because $R_o\ \bot\ \underline{\mathbf{T}}\ \underline{\mathbf{F}}$ and $R_o\ \underline{\mathbf{T}}\ \bot\ \underline{\mathbf{F}}$ hold but

$$R_o\ (\underline{\mathbf{por}}\ \bot\ \underline{\mathbf{T}})\ (\underline{\mathbf{por}}\ \underline{\mathbf{T}}\ \bot)\ (\underline{\mathbf{por}}\ \underline{\mathbf{F}}\ \underline{\mathbf{F}}), \quad \text{i.e.,} \quad R_o\ \underline{\mathbf{T}}\ \underline{\mathbf{T}}\ \underline{\mathbf{F}}$$

does not hold.

3.2 Characterization of Definability

Sieber [23] gave a characterization of the logical relations under which all the FPCF constants are invariant. The algorithm for the definability problem given in Sect. 3.3 uses this characterization.

Definition 4. *For $n \geq 0$ and $A \subseteq B \subseteq \{1, \ldots, n\}$, let $S^n_{A,B} \subseteq (D_o)^n$ be a relation defined by*

$$S^n_{A,B}\ v_1\ \ldots\ v_n \overset{\text{def}}{\Longleftrightarrow} (\exists i \in A.\ v_i = \bot) \lor (\forall i, j \in B.\ v_i = v_j).$$

A logical relation R is a sequentiality relation *R if R_o is an intersection of relations of the form $S^n_{A,B}$.*

Sieber proved that the sequentiality characterizes the logical relations under which all the PCF constants are invariant [23]. The following is the FPCF version of Sieber's theorem, due to [3].

Theorem 2 ([3, Theorem 4.5.17]). *A logical relation R is a sequentiality relation if and only if all the FPCF constants are invariant under R.*

The theorem below, again due to Sieber [23], is a key theorem for deriving a decision algorithm for definability. We have slightly strengthened the original statement, so that f is required to be invariant for sequentiality relations of a fixed arity; in the original one, d was required to be invariant under all sequentiality relations.

Theorem 3 ([23, Theorem 4.1]). *Let $\tau = \tau_1 \to \cdots \to \tau_n \to o$ be a type of order at most 2, and let $(e_{i1}, \ldots, e_{in}) \in D_{\tau_1} \times \cdots \times D_{\tau_n}$ for every $i \in \{1, \ldots, m\}$. If $f \in D_\tau$ is invariant under all the sequentiality relations of arity m, then there exists a closed PCF term M of type τ such that*

$$\forall i \in \{1, \ldots, m\}.\, d\, e_{i1} \cdots e_{in} = [\![M]\!]\, e_{i1} \cdots e_{in}.$$

Note that the theorem above is for PCF, and that terms and cpo's are different from those for FPCF given in Sect. 2.1. However, the same theorem also holds for FPCF, as stated below. We omit the proof, since it is essentially the same proof as that of [23, Theorem 4.1].

Theorem 4. *Let* $\tau = \tau_1 \to \cdots \to \tau_n \to \mathsf{o}$ *be a type of order at most 2, and* $(e_{i1}, \ldots, e_{in}) \in D_{\tau_1} \times \cdots \times D_{\tau_n}$ *for every* $i \in \{1, \ldots, m\}$*. If* $d \in D_\tau$ *is invariant under all the sequentiality relations of arity* m*, there exists a closed FPCF term* M *of type* τ *such that*

$$\forall i \in \{1, \ldots, m\}. d\, e_{i1} \cdots e_{in} = [\![M]\!]\, e_{i1} \cdots e_{in}.$$

As a corollary of the above theorems, we obtain a decidable characterization of definability for FPCF.

Corollary 1. *Let* $\tau = \tau_1 \to \cdots \to \tau_n \to \mathsf{o}$ *be a type of order at most 2 and* $K = \prod_i |D_{\tau_i}|$*. Then* $d \in D_\tau$ *is definable if and only if* d *is invariant under all the sequentiality relations of arity* K*.*

Proof. **"only if"**: Suppose that d is definable and that R is a sequentiality relation of arity K. Then by Theorem 2, all the FPCF constants are invariant under R. Therefore, by Theorem 1, d must be invariant under R.

"if": Let $t_1 = (e_{11}, \ldots, e_{1n}), \ldots, t_K = (e_{K1}, \ldots, e_{Kn})$ be all the elements in $\prod_i D_{\tau_i}$. By Theorem 4, there exists M such that

$$\forall i \in \{1, \ldots, K\}. d\, e_{i1} \ldots e_{in} = [\![M]\!]\, e_{i1} \ldots e_{in}$$

This means that $d = [\![M]\!]$. Hence d is definable. □

3.3 Algorithm

Using Corollary 1, we can solve the FPCF definability problem for a type $\tau = \tau_1 \to \cdots \to \tau_n \to \mathsf{o}$ of order at most 2 by the following algorithm: Let d be a given element in D_τ, and τ_i be of the form $\overbrace{\mathsf{o} \to \cdots \to \mathsf{o}}^{m_i} \to \mathsf{o}$.

1. Enumerate all the pairs (A, C) such that $A, C \subseteq \{1, \ldots, K\}$ and $A \cap C = \emptyset$; each pair (A, C) is intended to be the representation of the $S^K_{A, A \cup C}$ in Definition 4.
2. Enumerate all the subsets of the pairs created in Step 1; each set $\{(A_1, C_1), \ldots, (A_l, C_l)\}$ is intended to be the representation of $R_\mathsf{o} = S^K_{A_1, A_1 \cup C_1} \cap \cdots \cap S^K_{A_l, A_l \cup C_l}$, hence also the representation of the corresponding sequential relation R.
3. For each (representation of) sequentiality relation R enumerated in Step 2, check whether d is invariant under R, as follows.
   (a) Enumerate all the elements $v = (v_1, \ldots, v_K) \in R_\mathsf{o}$ by first enumerating all the elements of D_o and then checking whether $R_\mathsf{o}\, v_1 \ldots v_K$ holds. In order to check this, first enumerate all the pair in $L = \{(A_1, C_1), \ldots (A_l, C_l)\}$, where L is a representation of R, and then check that for all $(A, C) \in L$, $S^K_{A, A \cup C}\, v_1, \ldots, v_K$ holds by checking there exists $i \in A$ such that $v_i = \bot$ or $v_i = v_j$ holds for all $i, j \in A \cup C$.

(b) For each $i \in \{1,\ldots,n\}$, enumerate all the elements $e = (e_1,\ldots,e_K) \in R_{\tau_i} (\subseteq D_{\tau_i}^K)$ by first enumerating all the elements of $D_{\tau_i}^K$, and then checking whether

$$R_\circ\ (e_1\, v_1^1 \ldots v_1^{m_i}) \ldots (e_K\, v_K^1 \ldots v_K^{m_i})$$

holds for all $(v^1,\ldots,v^{m_i}) \in R_\circ^{m_i} (= \overbrace{R_\circ \times \cdots \times R_\circ}^{m_i})$ where $v^j = (v_1^j,\ldots,v_K^j)$.

(c) Check whether d is invariant under R by checking whether

$$R_\circ\ (d\, e_1^1 \ldots e_1^n) \ldots (d\, e_K^1 \ldots e_K^n)$$

holds for all $(e^1,\ldots,e^n) \in \prod_i R_{\tau_i}$ where $e^i = (e_1^i,\ldots,e_K^i)$.

4. If d is invariant under all the sequentiality relations of arity K, output "Yes" (i.e., "definable") and "No" otherwise.

3.4 Complexity

We show that the algorithm above runs in $\mathcal{O}(2^{2^{2^{2^{\mathrm{poly}(m)}}}})$ time where $m = \max(n, m_1,\ldots,m_n)$.

Before discussing the complexity of the algorithm, we first fix data representations and describe the complexity of some basic operations. Since the representation of $e \in D_{\tau_i}$ is the array $(e\,\underline{\mathbf{T}}\ldots\underline{\mathbf{T}}, e\,\underline{\mathbf{T}}\ldots\underline{\mathbf{F}}, \ldots)$ of size 3^{m_i} as described in Sect. 2.2, for $v_1,\ldots,v_{m_i} \in D_\circ$, we can compute the value of $e\,v_1 \ldots v_{m_i}$ in $\mathcal{O}(\mathrm{poly}(m_i))$ time by computing an appropriate index for $e\,v_1 \ldots v_{m_i}$ in the array. Similarly, since the representation of $d \in D$ is the sorted list $[(\overrightarrow{e_1}, d\,\overrightarrow{e_1}), (\overrightarrow{e_2}, d\,\overrightarrow{e_2}), \ldots]$ of size $\mathcal{O}(3^{3^m})$ for $\overrightarrow{e} \in \prod_{i=1}^n D_{\tau_i}$, we can compute the value of $d\,\overrightarrow{e}$ in $\mathcal{O}(\log(3^{3^{\mathrm{poly}(m)}})) = \mathcal{O}(3^{\mathrm{poly}(m)})$ time by finding $\overrightarrow{e}$ in the list using a binary search. We can equip $D_\circ^K$ with some total order; therefore, we can represent $R_\circ \subseteq D_\circ^K$ as a self-balancing binary search tree consisting of elements in $D_\circ^K$. Note that $K = \prod_{i=1}^n |D_{\tau_i}| = \mathcal{O}(2^{2^{\mathrm{poly}(m)}})$ since $2^{(2^{m_i})} \leq |D_{\tau_i}| \leq 3^{(3^{m_i})}$ holds for each $i \in \{1,\ldots,n\}$.

Now, we examine the complexity of the algorithm given in Sect. 3.3. The cost of each step is estimated as follows:

1. Since there are 3^K pairs (A,C) such that $A, C \subseteq \{1,\ldots,K\}$ and $A \cap C = \emptyset$, this step takes $\mathcal{O}(3^{\mathrm{poly}(K)})$ time.
2. Since there are $2^{(3^K)}$ subsets of the set of all the pairs created in Step 1, this step costs $\mathcal{O}(2^{3^{\mathrm{poly}(K)}})$ time.
3. (a) For each $v \in D_\circ^K$, we can check whether $v \in R_\circ$ holds in $3^K\mathrm{poly}(K) = \mathcal{O}(3^{\mathrm{poly}(K)})$ time, since $\mathrm{poly}(K)$ time is needed to check whether $v \in S_{A,A\cup C}^K$ holds for each pair (A,C), and since a representation for R contains at most 3^K pairs. If $v \in R_\circ$, v is added to a self-balancing binary search tree representing $R_\circ$. This addition takes $\mathcal{O}(\log(|R_\circ|))$ time for each $v \in R_\circ$. Hence this step costs

$$|D_\circ^K| \times \mathcal{O}(3^{\mathrm{poly}(K)}) + |R_\circ| \times \mathcal{O}(\log(|R_\circ|)) = \mathcal{O}(3^{\mathrm{poly}(K)})$$

time.

(b) Since we created $R_\circ$ as a self-balancing binary search tree, the membership $v \in R_\circ$ can be checked in $\mathcal{O}(\log(|R_\circ|))$ time. Therefore, for each $e = (e_1, \ldots, e_K) \in D^K_{\tau_i}$ and $(v^1, \ldots, v^{m_i}) \in R^{m_i}_\circ$ where $v^j = (v^j_1, \ldots, v^j_K)$, the time cost to check whether $R_\circ\ (e_1\, v^1_1 \ldots v^{m_i}_1) \ldots (e_K\, v^1_K \ldots v^{m_i}_K)$ holds is

$$K \times \mathcal{O}(\mathrm{poly}(m_i)) + \mathcal{O}(\log(|R_\circ|)) = \mathrm{poly}(K),$$

where $\mathcal{O}(\mathrm{poly}(m_i))$ is the time cost to compute the value of $e_k\, v^1_k\ \ldots\ v^{m_i}_k$ for each $k \in \{1, \ldots, K\}$. We represent $R_{\tau_i} (\subseteq D^K_{\tau_i})$ simply as a list; thus the insertion takes $\mathcal{O}(1)$ time. Hence this step takes

$$\sum_{i=1}^{n} (|D^K_{\tau_i}| \times (|R^{m_i}_\circ| \times \mathrm{poly}(K) + \mathcal{O}(1))) = \mathcal{O}(3^{\mathrm{poly}(K)})$$

time.

(c) For each $(e^1, \ldots, e^n) \in \prod_{i=1}^n R_{\tau_i}$ where $e^i = (e^i_1, \ldots, e^i_K)$, the time cost to check whether $R_\circ(d\, e^1_1\ \ldots\ e^n_1) \ldots (d\, e^1_K\ \ldots\ e^n_K)$ holds is

$$K \times \mathcal{O}(3^{\mathrm{poly}(m)}) + \mathcal{O}(\log(|R_\circ|)) = \mathrm{poly}(K),$$

where $\mathcal{O}(3^{\mathrm{poly}(m)})$ is the time cost to compute the value of $d\, e^1_k\ \ldots\ v^n_k$ for each $k \in \{1, \ldots, K\}$. Hence this step costs

$$\left(\prod_{i=1}^{n} |R_{\tau_i}|\right) \times \mathrm{poly}(K) = \mathcal{O}(3^{\mathrm{poly}(K)})$$

time.

Thus, for each sequentiality relation R, the time cost to check whether $d \in R$ is $\mathcal{O}(3^{\mathrm{poly}(K)})$. Hence, Step 3 needs $\mathcal{O}(2^{(3^K)} 3^{\mathrm{poly}(K)})$ time.

Therefore, the time cost of the whole algorithm is

$$\mathcal{O}(3^{\mathrm{poly}(K)} + 2^{(3^{\mathrm{poly}(K)})} + 2^{(3^K)} 3^{\mathrm{poly}(K)}),$$

which is doubly exponential in K; hence this algorithm runs in $\mathcal{O}(2^{2^{2^{2^{\mathrm{poly}(m)}}}})$ time.

4 Saturation-Based Algorithm Using Finite Canonical Forms

In this section, we introduce a more efficient algorithm for deciding definability, which is saturation-based and runs in $\mathcal{O}(2^{2^{2^{\mathrm{poly}(m)}}})$ time.

We first give an overview of our algorithm. In this algorithm, the set of all the definable elements is computed; thus, the definability problem is reduced to checking whether an input is in the set. To compute the set, we use finite canonical forms of FPCF which we will describe in Sect. 4.1. Any FPCF term has an equivalent finite canonical form, and the set of finite canonical forms of an FPCF type of order at most 2 can be defined inductively. By the inductive definition, we have an increasing chain $(F^i(T_0))_{i\in\mathbb{N}}$ of sets of finite canonical forms, repeating the induction step F from the base case T_0. In the algorithm, we compute the image of this chain in the cpo model: $(\{[\![M]\!] \mid M \in F^i(T_0)\})_{i\in\mathbb{N}}$. Since the interpretation of an FPCF type is a finite set, the latter increasing chain is saturated with all the definable elements at some step $i \in \mathbb{N}$.

We give the detail of the above algorithm in Sect. 4.2 and discuss the complexity of the algorithm in Sect. 4.3.

4.1 Finite Canonical Forms of FPCF

Hyland and Ong [8] and Abramsky et.al. [1] showed that the compact elements in their (intensional) game models of PCF bijectively correspond to the *finite canonical forms.* FPCF also has similar canonical forms:

Definition 5. *The set* $\mathrm{FCF}[f_1 : \tau_1, \ldots, f_n : \tau_n]$ *of* finite canonical forms *with free variables* $f_1, \ldots, f_n$ *is defined as the least set that satisfies the following conditions:*

1. $\mathbf{\Omega}_\mathrm{o}, \mathbf{T}, \mathbf{F} \in \mathrm{FCF}[f_1 : \tau_1, \ldots, f_n : \tau_n]$
2. *Let* $i \in \{1, \ldots, n\}$, $\tau_i = \sigma_1 \to \cdots \to \sigma_m \to \mathrm{o}$ *and* $\sigma_j = \sigma_{j1} \to \cdots \to \sigma_{jp_j} \to \mathrm{o}$ *for each* $j \in \{1, \ldots, m\}$.

$$\mathbf{if}\ f_i\ (\lambda g_1 \ldots g_{p_1}. N_1)\ \ldots\ (\lambda g_1 \ldots g_{p_m}. N_m)\ \mathbf{then}\ M_1\ \mathbf{else}\ M_2 \in \mathrm{FCF}[f_1 : \tau_1, \ldots, f_n : \tau_n]$$

if

$$N_j \in \mathrm{FCF}[f_1 : \tau_1, \ldots, f_n : \tau_n, g_1 : \sigma_{j1}, \ldots, g_{p_j} : \sigma_{jp_j}] \text{ for each } j \in \{1, \ldots, m\} \text{ and } M_1, M_2 \in \mathrm{FCF}[f_1 : \tau_1, \ldots, f_n : \tau_n].$$

If the order of $\tau_1 \to \cdots \to \tau_n \to \mathrm{o}$ is at most 2, the second item above can be specialized to:

2'. *Let* $i \in \{1, \ldots, n\}$ *and* $\tau_i = \overbrace{\mathrm{o} \to \cdots \to \mathrm{o}}^{m} \to \mathrm{o}$.

$$\mathbf{if}\ f_i\ N_1 \ldots N_m\ \mathbf{then}\ M_1\ \mathbf{else}\ M_2 \in \mathrm{FCF}[f_1 : \tau_1, \ldots, f_n : \tau_n]$$

if

$$N_1, \ldots, N_m, M_1, M_2 \in \mathrm{FCF}[f_1 : \tau_1, \ldots, f_n : \tau_n].$$

Note that the general definition for arbitrary order of types is a potentially *infinite* simultaneous induction, since the definition of $\mathrm{FCF}[f_1 : \tau_1, \ldots, f_n : \tau_n]$ refers to $\mathrm{FCF}[f_1 : \tau_1, \ldots, f_n : \tau_n, g_1 : \sigma_{j1}, \ldots, g_{p_j} : \sigma_{jp_j}]$ where the number of the contexts such as $(f_1 : \tau_1, \ldots, f_n : \tau_n, g_1 : \sigma_{j1}, \ldots, g_{p_j} : \sigma_{jp_j})$ is unbounded, while in the case of order at most 2, the definition with *2'* is a single inductive definition only on $\mathrm{FCF}[f_1, \ldots, f_n]$. This finiteness is the key of the algorithm given in Sect. 4.2.

The following theorem states that any closed FPCF term has an equivalent canonical form. Here, we consider the equality in the cpo semantics, instead of the observational equivalence. Note that the equality in the cpo semantics implies the observational equivalence, so that it suffices for our purpose of enumerating all the elements up to the observational equivalence (possibly with duplications).

Theorem 5. *Let M be a closed FPCF term of type $\tau = \tau_1 \to \cdots \to \tau_n \to \mathrm{o}$. There exists a finite canonical form $N \in \mathrm{FCF}[f_1 : \tau_1, \ldots, f_n : \tau_n]$ such that*

$$[\![M]\!] = [\![\lambda f_1 : \tau_1. \ldots \lambda f_n : \tau_n. N]\!].$$

Proof sketch. We give an overview of the proof. We call a term **Y**-*free* if it contains no **Y** but $\boldsymbol{\Omega}$ $(= \mathbf{Y}(\lambda x.x))$.

First, we can obtain a **Y**-free term M' such that $[\![M]\!] = [\![M']\!]$ as follows. For some term C that does not contain **Y**, $M =_\beta C\mathbf{Y}$. Then,

$$\begin{aligned}[\![M]\!] = [\![C]\!][\![\mathbf{Y}]\!] &= [\![C]\!](\mathrm{lub}_n[\![\lambda f.f^n(\boldsymbol{\Omega})]\!]) \\ &= \mathrm{lub}_n[\![C]\!][\![\lambda f.f^n(\boldsymbol{\Omega})]\!] = \mathrm{lub}_n[\![C\lambda f.f^n(\boldsymbol{\Omega})]\!].\end{aligned}$$

Since D_τ is a finite set, the ascending chain $[\![C\lambda f.f^n(\boldsymbol{\Omega})]\!]$ must be saturated in D_τ, i.e., there exists some n such that $[\![M]\!] = [\![C\lambda f.f^n(\boldsymbol{\Omega})]\!]$. Thus, we have obtained $M' := C\lambda f.f^n(\boldsymbol{\Omega})$.

Next, a finite canonical form is a kind of $\beta\eta$-long normal form, and we can normalize any **Y**-free term M' to some $\lambda f_1 : \tau_1. \ldots \lambda f_n : \tau_n. N$ where $N \in \mathrm{FCF}[f_1 : \tau_1, \ldots, f_n : \tau_n]$. Here, note that, in FPCF, variable f of type $\tau = \sigma_1 \to \cdots \to \sigma_m \to \mathrm{o}$ in M' (e.g., f in $M' = \lambda f.f$) can be normalized by η-expansion of function types and that of the boolean type ($M \longrightarrow$ **if** M **then T else F**) to a curried finite canonical form, $P_{f,\tau}$, which is defined by induction on τ as follows:

$$P_{f,\tau} \;:=\; \lambda x_1 : \sigma_1. \ldots \lambda x_m : \sigma_m. \ \mathbf{if}\ f P_{x_1,\sigma_1} \cdots P_{x_m,\sigma_m}\ \mathbf{then\ T\ else\ F}.$$

(On the other hand, in PCF we cannot normalize variables of infinite-domain types to *finite* canonical forms.) The normalization consists of η-expansions, β-reductions, commuting conversions, and Ω-reductions (**if** $\boldsymbol{\Omega}$ **then** M_1 **else** $M_2 \longrightarrow \boldsymbol{\Omega}$). Clearly, all these reductions are sound for the cpo semantics; hence,

$$[\![M']\!] = [\![\lambda f_1 : \tau_1. \ldots \lambda f_n : \tau_n. N]\!]. \qquad \square$$

4.2 Algorithm

Let τ be a type of order at most 2 and d be an element of D_τ. Suppose that $\tau = \tau_1 \to \cdots \to \tau_n \to \mathsf{o}$, where $\tau_i = \overbrace{\mathsf{o} \to \cdots \to \mathsf{o}}^{m_i} \to \mathsf{o}$.

The definability of d can be decided by the following algorithm.

1. Let $P_0 = \{[\![\lambda f_1 \dots f_n.\mathbf{T}]\!], [\![\lambda f_1 \dots f_n.\mathbf{F}]\!], [\![\boldsymbol{\Omega}_\tau]\!]\} \subseteq D_\tau$
2. For $P \subseteq D_\tau$, we define

$$F(P) := P \cup \{\, h_i(d_1, \dots, d_{m_i+2}) \in D_\tau \mid i \in \{1, \dots, n\},\, d_1, \dots, d_{m_i+2} \in P \,\}$$
$$h_i(d_1, \dots, d_{m_i+2})(\overrightarrow{e}) := [\![\mathbf{if}]\!]\big(e_i(d_1 \overrightarrow{e}) \dots (d_{m_i} \overrightarrow{e})\big)\big(d_{m_i+1} \overrightarrow{e}\big)\big(d_{m_i+2} \overrightarrow{e}\big)$$

   where $\overrightarrow{e} \in \prod_{i=1}^{n} D_{\tau_i}$. Compute $P_{j+1} := F(P_j) \subseteq D_\tau$ for $j = 0, 1, \dots,$ until $P_{j+1} = P_j$ holds. Let k be the least j such that $P_{j+1} = P_j$.
3. Output "Yes" (i.e., "definable") if $d \in P_k$, and "No" otherwise.

For example, for $\tau = ((\mathsf{o} \to \mathsf{o}) \to \mathsf{o}) \to \mathsf{o}$,

$$\begin{aligned}
P_1 = P_0 \cup \{&[\![\lambda f.\, \mathbf{if}\ (f\, v_1)\ \mathbf{then}\ v_2\ \mathbf{else}\ v_3]\!] \mid v_1, v_2, v_3 \in \{\mathbf{T}, \mathbf{F}, \boldsymbol{\Omega}\}\},\\
P_2 = P_1 \cup \{&[\![\lambda f.\, (\mathbf{if}\ (f\ (\mathbf{if}\ (f\, v_1)\ \mathbf{then}\ v_2\ \mathbf{else}\ v_3))\\
&\qquad \mathbf{then}\, v_4\ \mathbf{else}\, v_5)]\!] \mid v_1, \dots, v_5 \in \{\mathbf{T}, \mathbf{F}, \boldsymbol{\Omega}\}\}\\
\cup \{&[\![\lambda f.\, (\mathbf{if}\ (f\, v_1)\\
&\qquad \mathbf{then}\, (\mathbf{if}\ (f\, v_2)\ \mathbf{then}\ v_3\ \mathbf{else}\ v_4)\\
&\qquad \mathbf{else}\, v_5)]\!] \mid v_1, \dots, v_5 \in \{\mathbf{T}, \mathbf{F}, \boldsymbol{\Omega}\}\}\\
\cup \{&[\![\lambda f.\, (\mathbf{if}\ (f\, v_1)\\
&\qquad \mathbf{then}\, v_2\\
&\qquad \mathbf{else}\, (\mathbf{if}\ (f\, v_3)\ \mathbf{then}\ v_4\ \mathbf{else}\ v_5))]\!] \mid v_1, \dots, v_5 \in \{\mathbf{T}, \mathbf{F}, \boldsymbol{\Omega}\}\}\\
\cup \{&[\![\lambda f.\, (\mathbf{if}\ (f\, v_1)\\
&\qquad \mathbf{then}\, (\mathbf{if}\ (f\, v_2)\ \mathbf{then}\ v_3\ \mathbf{else}\ v_4)\\
&\qquad \mathbf{else}\, (\mathbf{if}\ (f\, v_5)\ \mathbf{then}\ v_6\ \mathbf{else}\ v_7))]\!] \mid v_1, \dots, v_7 \in \{\mathbf{T}, \mathbf{F}, \boldsymbol{\Omega}\}\}\\
\cup \{&[\![\lambda f.\, (\mathbf{if}\ (f\ (\mathbf{if}\ (f\, v_1)\ \mathbf{then}\ v_2\ \mathbf{else}\ v_3))\\
&\qquad \mathbf{then}\, v_4\\
&\qquad \mathbf{else}\, (\mathbf{if}\ (f\, v_5)\ \mathbf{then}\ v_6\ \mathbf{else}\ v_7))]\!] \mid v_1, \dots, v_7 \in \{\mathbf{T}, \mathbf{F}, \boldsymbol{\Omega}\}\}\\
\cup \{&[\![\lambda f.\, (\mathbf{if}\ (f\ (\mathbf{if}\ (f\, v_1)\ \mathbf{then}\ v_2\ \mathbf{else}\ v_3))\\
&\qquad \mathbf{then}\, (\mathbf{if}\ (f\, v_4)\ \mathbf{then}\ v_5\ \mathbf{else}\ v_6)\\
&\qquad \mathbf{else}\, v_7)]\!] \mid v_1, \dots, v_7 \in \{\mathbf{T}, \mathbf{F}, \boldsymbol{\Omega}\}\}\\
\cup \{&[\![\lambda f.\, (\mathbf{if}\ (f\ (\mathbf{if}\ (f\, v_1)\ \mathbf{then}\ v_2\ \mathbf{else}\ v_3))\\
&\qquad \mathbf{then}\, (\mathbf{if}\ (f\, v_4)\ \mathbf{then}\ v_5\ \mathbf{else}\ v_6)\\
&\qquad \mathbf{else}\, (\mathbf{if}\ (f\, v_7)\ \mathbf{then}\ v_8\ \mathbf{else}\ v_9))]\!] \mid v_1, \dots, v_9 \in \{\mathbf{T}, \mathbf{F}, \boldsymbol{\Omega}\}\}.
\end{aligned}$$

Note that the above algorithm terminates since $P_0, P_1, P_2, \dots$ is an increasing chain over the finite set 2^{D_τ}.

We show that this algorithm is correct.

Theorem 6. *In the above algorithm, d is definable iff $d \in P_k$.*

Proof. In this proof, we often abbreviate $\mathrm{FCF}[f_1 : \tau_1, \ldots, f_n : \tau_n]$ as $\mathrm{FCF}[\overrightarrow{f_i : \tau_i}]$.

Let us define $T_j \subseteq \mathrm{FCF}[\overrightarrow{f_i : \tau_i}]$ $(j = 0, 1, \ldots)$ as

$$T_0 := \{\mathbf{T}, \mathbf{F}, \boldsymbol{\Omega}_\circ\}$$
$$T_{j+1} := F'(T_j)$$

where for $T \subseteq \mathrm{FCF}[\overrightarrow{f_i : \tau_i}]$,

$$F'(T) = T \cup \{\textbf{if } f_i\ M_1\ \ldots\ M_{m_i} \textbf{ then } M_{m_i+1} \textbf{ else } M_{m_i+2} \mid i \in \{1, \ldots, n\}, M_1, \ldots, M_{m_i+2} \in T\}.$$

Then, $\mathrm{FCF}[\overrightarrow{f_i : \tau_i}] = \bigcup_j T_j$. Define $[\![-]\!]'$ as follows:

$$[\![M]\!]' = [\![\lambda f_1 : \tau_1 . \ldots \lambda f_n : \tau_n . M]\!] \qquad (M \in \mathrm{FCF}[\overrightarrow{f_i : \tau_i}])$$
$$[\![T]\!]' = \{[\![M]\!]' | M \in T\} \qquad (T \subseteq \mathrm{FCF}[\overrightarrow{f_i : \tau_i}])$$

We can easily show that $[\![T_0]\!]' = P_0$ and that $[\![T]\!]' = P$ implies $[\![F'(T)]\!]' = F(P)$; hence we get $[\![T_j]\!]' = P_j$ for all j.

If $d \in P_k$, since $P_k = [\![T_k]\!]'$, there exists $M \in \mathrm{FCF}[\overrightarrow{f_i : \tau_i}]$ such that $d = [\![\lambda f_1 : \tau_1 \ldots \lambda f_n : \tau_n . M]\!]$. Hence d is definable.

If $d \notin P_k$, there is no $M \in \mathrm{FCF}[\overrightarrow{f_i : \tau_i}]$ such that $d = [\![M]\!]'$, because $P_k = \cup_j P_j = [\![\cup_j T_j]\!]' = [\![\mathrm{FCF}[\overrightarrow{f_i : \tau_i}]]\!]'$. By Theorem 5, this implies that there is no closed FPCF term M of type τ such that $d = [\![M]\!]$. That is, d is not definable. □

It is clear that the above algorithm can also find concrete terms that define definable elements: For that purpose, we just need to modify the algorithm slightly, so that each element d in P_j is associated with a representative element M of $[\![P_j]\!]'$ such that $d = [\![M]\!]$.

4.3 Complexity

We show that the algorithm above runs in $\mathcal{O}(2^{2^{2^{\mathrm{poly}(m)}}})$ time where $m = \max(n, m_1, \ldots, m_n)$.

We first fix the data representations and estimate the cost of basic operations. In Sect. 2.2, we have represented each $d \in D_\tau$ as a list of the form $[(\vec{e}_1, d\,\vec{e}_1), (\vec{e}_2, d\,\vec{e}_2), \ldots]$. In the algorithm, we actually represent it as a pair of lists $([\vec{e}_1, \vec{e}_2, \ldots], [d\,\vec{e}_1, d\,\vec{e}_2, \ldots])$. Since the part $[\vec{e}_1, \vec{e}_2, \ldots]$ is common among all the elements of D_τ, we actually need to keep only the second element for each d. It can be viewed as a ternary number consisting of $\mathcal{O}(2^{2^{\mathrm{poly}(m)}})$ ternary digits; we write $n(d)$ for it. Each set P_j is then represented as a bit vector having $n(d)$ as an index. The membership $d \in P_j$ can then be checked in time $\mathcal{O}(2^{2^{\mathrm{poly}(m)}})$. For $d \in D_\tau$ and $\vec{e} \in D_{\tau_1} \times \cdots \times D_{\tau_n}$, computing $d\vec{e}$ amounts to finding the corresponding element in the list $[d\vec{e}_1, d\vec{e}_2, \ldots]$, which can be performed (e.g., using binary search) in time $\mathcal{O}(2^{\mathrm{poly}(m)})$.

Now we estimate the cost for each step. First, we discuss the time cost needed for Step 2. Since $h_i(d_1, \ldots, d_{m_i+2})(\vec{e})$ can be computed in time $\mathcal{O}(2^{\mathrm{poly}(m)})$, the time cost to compute $h_i(d_1, \ldots, d_{m_i+2})$ is:

$$|\prod_{i=1}^{n} D_{\tau_i}| \times \mathcal{O}(2^{\mathrm{poly}(m)}) = \mathcal{O}(2^{2^{\mathrm{poly}(m)}}).$$

We can then add $h_i(d_1, \ldots, d_{m_i+2})$ to P_{j+1} in time $\mathcal{O}(2^{2^{\mathrm{poly}(m)}})$, as discussed above. Since the number of tuples $(d_1, \ldots, d_{m_i+2})$ is $\mathcal{O}(2^{2^{2^{\mathrm{poly}(m)}}})$, the total cost needed for computing P_{j+1} is also $\mathcal{O}(2^{2^{2^{\mathrm{poly}(m)}}}) \times (\mathcal{O}(2^{\mathrm{poly}(m)}) + \mathcal{O}(2^{2^{\mathrm{poly}(m)}})) = \mathcal{O}(2^{2^{2^{\mathrm{poly}(m)}}})$. Finally, since k is at most $|D_\tau| = \mathcal{O}(2^{2^{2^{\mathrm{poly}(m)}}})$, the overall time cost for Step 2 is $\mathcal{O}(2^{2^{2^{\mathrm{poly}(m)}}})$.

Checking whether $d \in P_k$ in Step 3 costs $\mathcal{O}(2^{2^{\mathrm{poly}(m)}})$ time. Therefore, the whole algorithm runs in $\mathcal{O}(2^{2^{2^{\mathrm{poly}(m)}}})$ time.

5 Application to Program Equivalence Checking

As an application of the algorithms for the definability problem, we discuss an automated method for deciding the observational equivalence of order-3 FPCF terms.

5.1 Observational Equivalence Problem

First, we define the notions of context and observational equivalence.

Definition 6. *An FPCF term with one hole* $[\,]$ *is called a* context *(ranged over by* $C, \ldots$*). We write* $C[M]$ *for a term obtained by replacing* $[\,]$ *in a context* C *with a term* M*. If* $C[M]$ *has type* τ' *for any term* M *of type* τ*,* C *is called a* τ*-*τ' context.

In general, a context C may capture free variable in M when replacing a hole $[\,]$ in a context C with a term M, but we do not consider such context in this paper.

Definition 7. *Two closed FPCF terms* M_1 *and* M_2 *of a type* τ *are called* observationally equivalent *(denoted by* $M_1 \equiv M_2$*) if for any* $\tau - \mathsf{o}$ *context* C *and value* $V \in \{\mathbf{T}, \mathbf{F}\}$*,* $C[M_1] \Downarrow V \Longleftrightarrow C[M_2] \Downarrow V$*.*

If M_1 and M_2 are observational equivalent, we can replace a subterm M_1 of a program with M_2 without changing the output of the whole program.

We define the *equivalence problem for FPCF* as follows: given a type τ and closed terms M_1, M_2 of type τ, output whether M_1 and M_2 are observationally equivalent or not.

To prove the observational equivalence, we do not need to consider all contexts:

Theorem 7 (Context Lemma [12]). *For closed FPCF terms M_1 and M_2 of type $\tau = \tau_1 \to \cdots \to \tau_n \to \mathsf{o}$, $M_1 \equiv M_2$ if and only if for all closed FPCF terms $N_1, \ldots, N_n$ (of types $\tau_1, \ldots, \tau_n$, respectively) and $V \in \{\mathbf{T}, \mathbf{F}\}$,*

$$M_1\ N_1\ \ldots\ N_n \Downarrow V \iff M_2\ N_1\ \ldots\ N_n \Downarrow V.$$

The observational equivalence of order-3 FPCF terms is non-trivial. Let us define ETest_V ($V = \mathbf{T}, \mathbf{F}$) as follows.

$$\begin{aligned}&\mathrm{ETest}_V := \lambda e{:}(\mathsf{o} \to \mathsf{o}) \to \mathsf{o}.\,\mathbf{if}\ E\ \mathbf{then}\ V\ \mathbf{else}\ \mathbf{\Omega}\\ &E := e(\lambda x.\mathbf{if}\ x\ \mathbf{then}\ \mathbf{T}\ \mathbf{else}\ \mathbf{\Omega}) \wedge e(\lambda x.\mathbf{if}\ x\ \mathbf{then}\ \mathbf{\Omega}\ \mathbf{else}\ \mathbf{T}) \wedge \neg(e(\lambda x.\mathbf{F}))\,.\end{aligned}$$

This example is obtained by a simple modification to the well-known "**por**-test" terms, which distinguish **por** from (F)PCF terms; we changed **por** to (a finitary version of) Plotkin's *continuous existential quantifier* [18], whose interpretation $\exists \in D_{(\mathsf{o} \to \mathsf{o}) \to \mathsf{o}}$ is defined by

$$\begin{aligned}\exists(f) &:= \underline{\mathbf{T}} \ \text{ if } \ f\,\underline{\mathbf{T}} = \underline{\mathbf{T}} \text{ or } f\,\underline{\mathbf{F}} = \underline{\mathbf{T}}\,,\\ \exists(f) &:= \underline{\mathbf{F}} \ \text{ if } \ f\,\bot = \underline{\mathbf{F}}\,,\\ \exists(f) &:= \bot \ \text{ otherwise.}\end{aligned}$$

Terms $\mathrm{ETest}_{\mathbf{T}}$ and $\mathrm{ETest}_{\mathbf{F}}$ are observationally equivalent but not equal in the cpo model as explained below. First, since $[\![E]\!](\exists) = \underline{\mathbf{T}}$ and $[\![\mathrm{ETest}_V]\!](\exists) = [\![V]\!]$, we have $[\![\mathrm{ETest}_{\mathbf{T}}]\!] \neq [\![\mathrm{ETest}_{\mathbf{F}}]\!]$. Next, we show the observational equivalence. For the logical relation R defined by (1) and for $d \in D_{(\mathsf{o} \to \mathsf{o}) \to \mathsf{o}}$ such that $[\![E]\!]\,d = \underline{\mathbf{T}}$, we have

$$\begin{aligned}&R_{\mathsf{o} \to \mathsf{o}}\,[\![\lambda x.\mathbf{if}\ x\ \mathbf{then}\ \mathbf{T}\ \mathbf{else}\ \mathbf{\Omega}]\!]\ [\![\lambda x.\mathbf{if}\ x\ \mathbf{then}\ \mathbf{\Omega}\ \mathbf{else}\ \mathbf{T}]\!]\ [\![\lambda x.\mathbf{F}]\!],\\ &d[\![\lambda x.\mathbf{if}\ x\ \mathbf{then}\ \mathbf{T}\ \mathbf{else}\ \mathbf{\Omega}]\!] = \underline{\mathbf{T}},\\ &d[\![\lambda x.\mathbf{if}\ x\ \mathbf{then}\ \mathbf{\Omega}\ \mathbf{else}\ \mathbf{T}]\!] = \underline{\mathbf{T}},\\ &d[\![\lambda x.\mathbf{F}]\!] = \underline{\mathbf{F}},\end{aligned}$$

but not $R_{\mathsf{o}}\,\underline{\mathbf{T}}\,\underline{\mathbf{T}}\,\underline{\mathbf{F}}$; hence, d is not invariant under R and not definable. Therefore, for any FPCF term M, $\mathrm{ETest}_V M$ diverges, and so, by the context lemma above, $\mathrm{ETest}_{\mathbf{T}}$ and $\mathrm{ETest}_{\mathbf{F}}$ are observationally equivalent.

5.2 Algorithm for the Equivalence Problem

As a trivial consequence of Theorem 7, we obtain the following algorithm for deciding the equivalence of terms of an order-3 type. Let M_1, M_2 be given terms of a type $\tau = \tau_1 \to \cdots \to \tau_l \to \mathsf{o}$. Here, note that the order restriction applies to only the interface; M_1, M_2 may internally use terms of order higher than 3.

1. For every $i \in \{1, \ldots, l\}$, compute the set Q_{τ_i} of all the definable elements in D_{τ_i}, using one of the algorithms discussed in the previous sections.
2. Output "Yes" (i.e., "observationally equivalent") if $[\![M_1]\!]\overrightarrow{d} = [\![M_2]\!]\overrightarrow{d}$ for all $\overrightarrow{d} \in \prod_i Q_{\tau_i}$, and "No" otherwise.

The correctness of this algorithm follows from Theorem 7 and the adequacy [25] of the cpo semantics. (The adequacy says that, for all ground closed term M and $V \in \{\mathbf{T}, \mathbf{F}\}$, $[\![M]\!] = [\![V]\!]$ iff $M \Downarrow V$.)

For example, we can check that $\mathrm{ETest}_{\mathbf{T}}$ and $\mathrm{ETest}_{\mathbf{F}}$ of type $((\mathsf{o} \to \mathsf{o}) \to \mathsf{o}) \to \mathsf{o}$ are observationally equivalent by this algorithm. Continuous existential quantifier $\exists$ is excluded from the set $Q_{(\mathsf{o} \to \mathsf{o}) \to \mathsf{o}}$ of all the definable elements.

When input terms M_1 and M_2 are not equivalent, the above algorithm can output a witness $\overrightarrow{d} \in \prod_i Q_{\tau_i}$ such that $[\![M_1]\!]\overrightarrow{d} \neq [\![M_2]\!]\overrightarrow{d}$. Further, if we use the saturation-based algorithm, which can output a defining term N of a definable element d, we obtain terms N_i of type τ_i such that $[\![M_1 N_1 \ldots N_l]\!] \neq [\![M_2 N_1 \ldots N_l]\!]$.

For example, so-called Kierstead terms $K_1 = \lambda f : \tau_1 .\, f(\lambda x : \mathsf{o}.\, f(\lambda y : \mathsf{o}.\, x))$ and $K_2 = \lambda f : \tau_1 .\, f(\lambda x : \mathsf{o}.\, f(\lambda y : \mathsf{o}.\, y))$ where $\tau_1 = (\mathsf{o} \to \mathsf{o}) \to \mathsf{o}$ are not observational equivalent, and the above algorithm based on the saturation-based algorithm can find N such that $[\![K_1 N]\!] \neq [\![K_2 N]\!]$. The following term may, for example, be output as N:

$$\lambda g.\, \mathbf{if}\ (g\, \mathbf{T})\ \mathbf{then}\ (\mathbf{if}\ (g\, \mathbf{F})\ \mathbf{then}\ \mathbf{F}\ \mathbf{else}\ \mathbf{T})\ \mathbf{else}\ \mathbf{T}.$$

To compute $[\![M_i]\!]\overrightarrow{d}$ in the second step of the algorithm, we can use higher-order model checking [9,17]. Higher-order model checking can decide a property on the tree generated by a tree grammar called a higher-order recursion scheme. Using the technique of [9,17], given a closed FPCF term K of type o, one can construct a higher-order recursion scheme G_K such that $[\![K]\!] = v$ if and only if the tree generated by G_K is a singleton tree consisting of v. Thus, to compute $[\![M_i]\!]\overrightarrow{d}$, we just need to pick terms $\overrightarrow{N} = N_1, \ldots, N_l$ such that $[\![\overrightarrow{N}]\!] = \overrightarrow{d}$ (e.g., using the saturation-based algorithm in the previous section), apply the above translation for $K = M_i\overrightarrow{N}$, and invoke a higher-order model checker (e.g. [4,9,21]) to check whether $G_{M_i\overrightarrow{N}}$ generates $\perp$, $\mathbf{T}$, or $\mathbf{F}$. This is expected to run much faster than semantically computing $[\![M_i]\!]\overrightarrow{d}$ in a naive manner.

6 Related Work

As already mentioned, Loader proved that the definability problem for FPCF is undecidable for order-3 types [10] and the equivalence problem for FPCF is undecidable for order-4 types [11]. Loader [11] also mentioned that the definability problem for FPCF types of order at most 2 is decidable from Sieber's result [23]. We remark that the definability problem is trivial if FPCF is extended with **por**: any element in D_τ is definable for FPCF+**por** [18]. As a consequence, the equivalence problem for FPCF+**por** is also decidable for any order.

Stoughton [24] gave an explicit algorithm for the definability problem and its implementation. Her algorithm is built on Sieber's result [23], but does not use Sieber's sequentiality relation, unlike the algorithm discussed in Sect. 3. Her algorithm is actually similar to the saturation-based algorithm introduced in Sect. 4; all the β-η-long normal forms are enumerated (up to equivalence), until the set of interpretations of terms is saturated with the set of all the definable elements. We expect that our algorithm is more efficient than her algorithm, because we enumerate only finite canonical forms instead of all the β-η-long normal forms. Whilst she did not discuss the complexity of her algorithm, we have analyzed the complexity of our saturation-based algorithm, and shown that the saturation-based algorithm is exponentially faster than the naive algorithm using Sieber's sequentiality relation.

There are several pieces of work on the equivalence problem for functional languages, but they are mainly for those with references. There is a series of work [7,13,15,16] on Idealized Algol (IA for short) [22], the call-by-name simply typed λ-calculus extended with block-allocated references of ground types. The observational equivalence is decidable for order-3 finitary IA with iteration (while-loop) terms of order at most 3 is decidable, but it is undecidable for order-2 finitary IA with recursion [16] or order-4 finitary IA without iteration or recursion [13]. There is another series of work [5,6,14] on RML [2], a call-by-value simply typed λ-calculus extended with dynamically allocated references of ground types. The observational equivalence is decidable for terms of a certain class of types [14]. Please note that for the decidability results on IA and RML mentioned above, the restriction on types applies to all the subterms. In contrast, in our method for equivalence checking of FPCF terms, the order restriction applies to only the type of the terms being compared; arbitrary recursion at any order is allowed inside the terms.

7 Conclusion

We have given two algorithms for deciding definability for FPCF; one is based on Sieber's result, and the other is a saturation-based algorithm using the finite canonical forms of FPCF. The latter is exponentially faster than the former. As discussed in Sect. 5, those algorithms for the definability problem can be used for implementing a tool for deciding the equivalence between order-3 FPCF terms.

Acknowledgments. We thank anonymous reviewers for useful comments. This work was partially supported by JSPS Kakenhi 15H05706, and 23220001.

References

1. Abramsky, S., Jagadeesan, R., Malacaria, P.: Full abstraction for PCF. Inf. Comput. **163**(2), 409–470 (2000)
2. Abramsky, S., McCusker, G.: Call-by-value games. In: Nielsen, M. (ed.) CSL 1997. LNCS, vol. 1414, pp. 1–17. Springer, Heidelberg (1998)
3. Amadio, R.M., Curien, P.L.: Domains and Lambda-Calculi. Cambridge University Press, Cambridge (1998)
4. Broadbent, C.H., Kobayashi, N.: Saturation-based model checking of higher-order recursion schemes. In: Proceedings of CSL 2013. LIPIcs, vol. 23, pp. 129–148 (2013)
5. Hopkins, D., Murawski, A.S., Ong, C.-H.L.: HECTOR: an equivalence checker for a higher-order fragment of ML. In: Madhusudan, P., Seshia, S.A. (eds.) CAV 2012. LNCS, vol. 7358, pp. 774–780. Springer, Heidelberg (2012)
6. Hopkins, D., Murawski, A.S., Ong, C.-H.L.: A fragment of ML decidable by visibly pushdown automata. In: Aceto, L., Henzinger, M., Sgall, J. (eds.) ICALP 2011, Part II. LNCS, vol. 6756, pp. 149–161. Springer, Heidelberg (2011)
7. Hopkins, D., Ong, C.-H.L.: HOMER: a higher-order observational equivalence model checkER. In: Bouajjani, A., Maler, O. (eds.) CAV 2009. LNCS, vol. 5643, pp. 654–660. Springer, Heidelberg (2009)
8. Hyland, J.M.E., Ong, C.-H.L.: On full abstraction for PCF: I, II, and III. Inf. Comput. **163**(2), 285–408 (2000)
9. Kobayashi, N.: Model checking higher-order programs. J. ACM **60**(3), 1–62 (2013)
10. Loader, R.: The undecidability of lambda-definability. In: The Church Festschrift. CSLI/University of Chicago Press (1994)
11. Loader, R.: Finitary PCF is not decidable. Theor. Comput. Sci. **266**(1), 341–364 (2001)
12. Milner, R.: Fully abstract models of typed λ-calculi. Theor. Comput. Sci. **4**(1), 1–22 (1977)
13. Murawski, A.S.: On program equivalence in languages with ground-type references. In: Proceedings of LICS 2003, pp. 108–108. IEEE (2003)
14. Murawski, A.S.: Functions with local state: regularity and undecidability. Theor. Comput. Sci. **338**(1–3), 315–349 (2005)
15. Murawski, A.S., Walukiewicz, I.: Third-order Idealized Algol with iteration is decidable. Theor. Comput. Sci. **390**(2–3), 214–229 (2008)
16. Ong, C.-H.L.: Observational equivalence of 3rd-order Idealized Algol is decidable. In: Proceedings of LICS 2002, pp. 245–256. IEEE (2002)
17. Ong, C.-H.L.: On model-checking trees generated by higher-order recursion schemes. In: Proceedings of LICS 2006, pp. 81–90. IEEE (2006)
18. Plotkin, G.D.: LCF considered as a programming language. Theor. Comput. Sci. **5**(3), 223–255 (1977)
19. Plotkin, G.D.: Lambda-definability and logical relations. Technical report, SAI-RM-4, School of Artificial Intelligence, University of Edinburgh (1973)
20. Plotkin, G.D.: Lambda-definability in the full type hierarchy. To HB Curry: Essays on Combinatory Logic, Lambda Calculus and Formalism, pp. 363–373 (1980)
21. Ramsay, S.J., Neatherway, R., Ong, C.-H.L.: An abstraction refinement approach to higher-order model checking. In: Proceedings of POPL 2014, pp. 61–72. ACM (2014)
22. Reynolds, J.C.: The essence of ALGOL. In: O'Hearn, P.W., Tennent, R.D. (eds.) ALGOL-like Languages. Progress in Theoretical Computer Science, pp. 67–88. Springer, Heidelberg (1997)

23. Sieber, K.: Reasoning about sequential functions via logical relations. In: Applications of Categories in Computer Science. London Mathematical Society Lecture Note Series, vol. 177, pp. 258–269. Cambridge University Press (1992)
24. Stoughton, A.: Mechanizing logical relations. In: Main, M.G., Melton, A.C., Mislove, M.W., Schmidt, D., Brookes, S.D. (eds.) MFPS 1993. LNCS, vol. 802, pp. 359–377. Springer, Heidelberg (1994)
25. Winskel, G.: Formal Semantics of Programming Languages. The MIT Press, Cambridge (1993)

Program Analysis - I

Uncovering JavaScript Performance Code Smells Relevant to Type Mutations

Xiao Xiao[1](✉), Shi Han[2], Charles Zhang[1], and Dongmei Zhang[2]

[1] The Hong Kong University of Science and Technology, Hong Kong, Hong Kong
{richardxx,charlesz}@cse.ust.hk
[2] Microsoft Research, Beijing, China
{shihan,dongmeiz}@microsoft.com

Abstract. In dynamic typing languages such as JavaScript, object types can be mutated easily such as by adding a field to an object. However, compiler optimizations rely on a fixed set of types, unintentional type mutations can invalidate the speculative code generated by the type-feedback JIT and deteriorate the quality of compiler optimizations. Since type mutations are invisible, finding and understanding the performance issues relevant to type mutations can be an overwhelming task to programmers. We develop a tool JSweeter to detect performance bugs incurred by type mutations based on the type evolution graphs extracted from program execution. We apply JSweeter to the Octane benchmark suite and identify 46 performance issues, where 19 issues are successfully fixed with the refactoring hints generated by JSweeter and the average performance gain is 5.3 % (up to 23 %). The result is persuasive because those issues are hidden in such well developed benchmark programs.

1 Introduction

JavaScript has become a pivotal building block for web and mobile applications. As a dynamically typed language, considerable academic and industrial effort is invested to optimize its performance. One of the important techniques that contributed to the dramatic improvement of the speed of JavaScript is the type-feedback Just-in-time (JIT) compilation adopted by almost all modern JavaScript engines. The type-feedback JIT is a speculative technique that leverages the runtime information to generate fast code and use it in future executions if types remain unchanged [15]. Therefore, unlike statically typed languages, programmers of dynamic languages such as JavaScript can significantly influence the success rate of the speculations.

If the code conforms to some coding idioms such as asm.js [1] to restrict the type generation and variation, the type-feedback speculations, along with all dynamic optimization techniques, can be very effective. The underlying reason is that JavaScript engines such as V8 employ two contradictory designs in dealing with types: The *fat* type design and the type *equality* testing for validating speculations. The spirit of fat type design is binding certain instance specific information such as pointer to the prototype to the type. Thus, the JIT optimizers can perform aggressive optimizations to generate type-specific and more

X. Feng and S. Park (Eds.): APLAS 2015, LNCS 9458, pp. 335–355, 2015.
DOI: 10.1007/978-3-319-26529-2_18

efficient code. However, a fat type is also *fragile* that programmers can easily mutate it unconsciously, such as changing the prototype of a function. Therefore, the failure rate of type equality testing, which is the key component to validate speculative assumptions for JITed code, can be high.

(a)
```
1 function Foobar() {
2   this.abc = 1;
3   this.test = function (n) {
4     this.abc = n;
5   };
6 }
7 Foobar.prototype.runTest =
8 function (N) {
9   for (var i=0; i<N; ++i) {
10    this.test(i);
11  }
12 };
13 var N = 10000000;
14 (new Foobar()).runTest(N);
15 (new Foobar()).runTest(N);
```

(b)
```
1 Foobar.prototype.test =
2 function (n) {
3   this.abc = n;
4 };
```

Fig. 1. The "Foobar" Objects created at Line 14 and Line 15 have different types due to the method binding optimization for *test* field.

Figure 1(a) extracted from V8's user group[1] illustrates a case where the two "Foobar" objects created at Line 14 and Line 15 have different types on Google's V8 JavaScript engine, even their allocation sites are literally the same. The reason is that the field assigned to a closure instance such as *test* (Line 3) is stored in the type descriptor rather than in the object instance. This is called *method binding*, because V8 recognizes that a field referring to a closure rarely changes [4]. When calling `Foobar` again at Line 15, *test* is assigned to a different closure instance and V8 cancels method binding for *test*. Therefore, the type of the first "Foobar" object is unequal to the type of the second "Foobar" object. As a side effect, the `runTest` function optimized against the first "Foobar" object will be invalidated when it operates on the second "Foobar" object. A quick solution is moving the field *test* to the prototype of `FooBar` as shown in Fig. 1(b). This simple change gains 10× speedup.

In this paper, we present a technique that can automatically recognize the performance code smells relevant to unintentional type mutations and generate a sketched execution path for programmers to understand the smell. Moreover, refactoring hints for programmers to eliminate the type mutations are also generated. For our goal, conventional profiling techniques offer insufficient help. One could use timing functions to find the expensive code fragments. However, this gives programmers a very coarse view of performance symptoms, which cannot be used to distinguish the performance issues incurred by type mutations from other causes. Since type is implicitly represented by the JavaScript engine, programmers need to link the clues from the engine logs of internal events, the JITed code, and the source code, to understand how types are generated and evolved. This bug hunting process is overwhelming for application programmers. Moreover, the engine logs vary from one engine to another. These factors make application programmers inhibitive to understand how type mutations impact performance.

[1] https://groups.google.com/forum/#!topic/v8-users/Ofc_SmwDCUM.

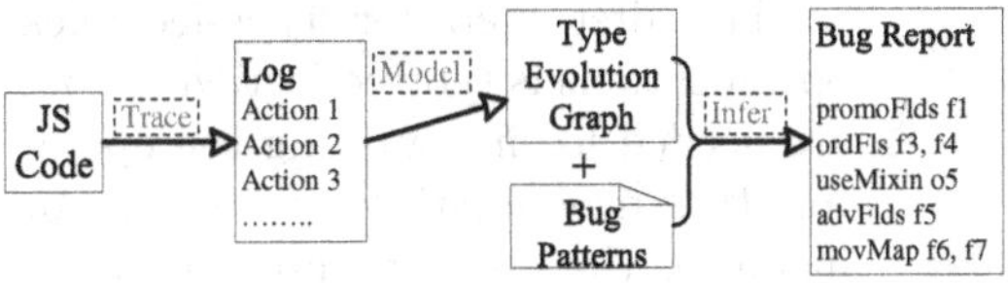

Fig. 2. Workflow of our algorithm.

We employ program execution information other than timing results to diagnose performance issues. The workflow of our technique is summarized in Fig. 2. First, we trace the operations that could change the types of objects. Tracing is performed at the engine side, where changes are not required for the traced code. In the second step, we build the *type evolution graphs* (TEG), one for all the objects that are created by the same constructor. In this way, precise type evolution track for each object may be lost, but we gain the knowledge of how the objects that could have the same usage evolve to different types. Third, for each type equality testing failure, we study the path on TEG between the type expected by the testing and the type being tested, and match it to one of our predefined code patterns drawn from empirical study. If the pattern matching succeeded, we generate a refactoring suggestion.

We implement our algorithm in a tool JSweeter and apply it to the Octane benchmark suite. Our tool reports 46 performance issues relevant to type mutations. By successfully fixing 19 issues, we improve the benchmark score by up to 23 %. Since the programs in Octane are all well tuned, finding performance bugs for these programs is challenging and our results are worth mentioning. In summary, our contributions are:

1. We carefully examine V8 and Firefox bug repositories and identify five common ways to cause performance issues by type mutations. Meanwhile, we identify six types of code smells that often mutate types unintentionally and conclude seven refactoring approaches to eliminate these code smells.
2. We develop an algorithm to detect the performance issues incurred by type mutations based on type evolution graph. Our approach also generates actionable refactoring suggestions by matching execution patterns to six performance issues.
3. We implement a tool JSweeter and apply it to the benchmark suite Octane. We find 46 performance bugs and 19 of the 46 issues are successfully fixed. The average speedup is 5.3 % and one has significant 23 % speedup.

2 Types in Type-Feedback JavaScript Engine

2.1 Type Collection

Due to lack of types, JavaScript programs cannot be compiled to fully optimized binary code ahead of time. *Type-feedback* is a profiling technique that dynamically collects type information for variables [16]. The type information is fed to the JIT compiler for generating efficient speculative code. Type-feedback JITs are pervasively used by all modern browsers such as Firefox and Chrome.

(a)
```
1 function test(a, b)
2 {
3   c = a + b;
4   return c;
5 }
6 test("foo", "bar");
7 test(1, 2);
```

(b)
```
1 function test(a, b)
2 {
3   if (is_str(a) && is_str(b))
4     c = strcat(a, b);
5   else
6     c = runtime_plus(a, b);
7   return c;
8 }
```

Fig. 3. Inline cache example. **is_str(s)** tests if s is a string. **strcat** concatenates two strings. **runtime_plus** is a runtime function to interpret the "+" operator.

The first step for type-feedback optimizations is type collection. Types are needed for interpreting the operators that have multiple semantics. For instance, the "+" operator could be applied to both numbers and strings. *Inline cache* (IC) is an effective way to collect the types and speedup the execution of the operators whose semantics depend on the types of their arguments. IC dynamically weaves the fast paths for observed types into the binary code [14]. An example is in Fig. 3(a), after the first call to `test` is executed (Line 6), a fast path for processing string is embedded into the code. We show a proof-of-concept implementation of IC in Fig. 3(b), where the *if* statement is called *type guard.* When we call `test` again with string arguments, the fast path will be taken. If "a" or "b" are integers next time, such as in Line 7 of 3(a), the *else* branch is taken and the slower runtime function **runtime_plus** is called. After processing the integer arguments, a fast path for the integer type is also built, resulting in a *polymorphic IC* (PIC). Types are collected in the way of continuously patching the ICs and a JavaScript engine often provides sufficient warm-up time for type collection.

2.2 Type Mutations

Inside JavaScript engine, every piece of memory, such as an object, array, string, and closure, is associated to a *type descriptor* (TD), which is also known as *hidden class* in V8, *shape* in IonMonkey, and *structure* in JavaScript-Core. A type descriptor records certain information for correctly inferring the code behaviors such as field access. For example, a type for an object usually contains fields descriptors that describe the value type (*e.g.* integer or double) of each field and fields layout that records the offset of each field.

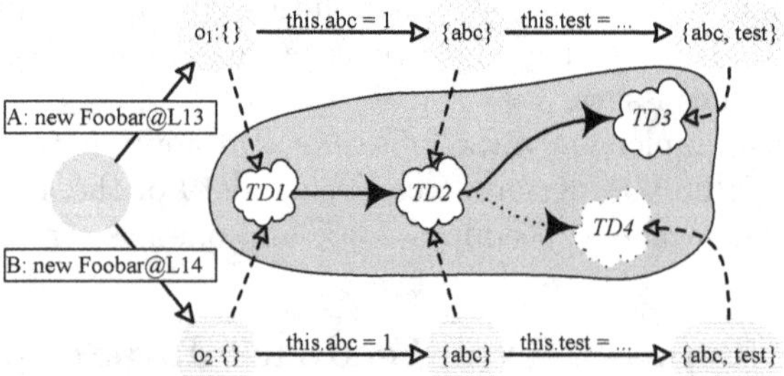

Fig. 4. Type evolution graph. Dashed arrow points to the type descriptor of corresponding object. Shadowed area is the type evolution graph and the type mutation that generates TD4 is highlighted.

Type descriptor should be *immutable* to guarantee the deterministic behavior for the code operated on. Therefore, a *type mutation* operation that changes any information in the descriptor, such as adding a field to an object, derives a new type descriptor. The set of type mutations from the same source type form a *type evolution graph.* Figure 4 shows a type evolution graph for our running example (Fig. 1), where the flows with labels A and B illustrate the "Foobar" objects o_1 and o_2, created at Lines 14 and 15, respectively. From the figure, we observe that o_1 and o_2 share the first type mutation TD1 → TD2, since the statement "this.abc = 1" has the same effect on the type mutations in both executions. Later on, due to the binding of different closure instances to the same field "test", o_1 and o_2 are evolved to different types TD3 and TD4.

2.3 Why Type Mutations Impair Performance

Type mutations create new types. A large volume of types render the JavaScript engine very difficult to generate a unique piece of code that works optimally on all types. As such, programs are falling back to run with conservative runtime strategies, which are summarized as follows.

Trigger Deoptimization. Unnecessary deoptimization is a major source of performance degradation. If a hot function cannot constantly work with optimized code, its performance can be orders of magnitude worse. Moreover, frequent type changes can result in optimization-deoptimization churn and finally disable the optimization opportunity for the type unstable functions.

Trigger IC Fallback. Every IC has limited slots for building fast paths, hence saturating an IC forces some types (perhaps the frequently visited types) to be permanently handled by runtime functions.

Reduce Optimization Strength. PICs are obstacles for JIT optimizers to generate high quality code. For example, function inlining is precluded, which is a very useful optimization to enlarge the scope of intra-procedural analysis and optimizations to cross function boundary. PICs also prevent common sub-expression elimination (CSE) and loop invariant code motion (LICM) to eliminate redundant type guards.

Enter Dictionary Mode. Object and array are often used as a dictionary. JavaScript engines adaptively change the backing storage of object and array to hash table in order to optimize the dictionary usage scenario. However, dictionary is manipulated by runtime functions instead of ICs, thus the fields read, write, and iteration operations slowdown significantly.

Increase GC Pressure. Frequently creating and dropping small objects will increase the garbage collection (GC) frequency. High GC pressure can significantly slowdown the execution of program and increase the latency of each GC invocation, which deteriorates the user experience of interactive programs.

Table 1. Bug patterns that induce type mutations and incur performance issues.

ID		Trigger Deoptimization	Trigger IC Fallback	Reduce Opt. Strength	Enter Dictionary Mode	Increase GC Pressure	
1	Always Use New Closure	✓	✓	✓		✓	V8 2206, 2673 FF 631911, 642001
2	Inconsistent Field Ordering	✓	✓	✓			FF 813425
3	Partially Initialized objects	✓	✓	✓			FF 900849
4	Over-filled Object & Sparse Array	✓	✓		✓		V8 2734, 3313, 2192
5	Prototype Mutation	✓		✓			FF 947048, 1041126
6	Integer Overflow	✓		✓		✓	V8 2306, 2617

3 Type Mutation Code Patterns in Practice

In this section, we present our findings of learning real performance bugs from V8 and Firefox bug repositories incurred by type mutations, denoted as V8 and FF respectively. The results are summarized in Table 1. Each row contains a buggy code pattern and several representative real bug cases labeled as FF *ID* and V8 *ID*, where ID is the bug number in corresponding repository. We identify six code patterns that mutate types and incur performance problems. For each code pattern, we also give one or more refactoring approaches from Table 2 to avoid the performance issues. These refactoring approaches are concluded from the discussion by the programmers in the bug repository.

1. Frequent Closure Creation. Similar to our running example (Fig. 1), real code often creates a new closure instance before calling that function, in order to achieve better code encapsulation. However, these closure instances could result in PICs for call-sites that impair the IC efficiency and preclude inlining (V8 2206), confuse JIT and miss code optimizations opportunities (V8 2673), and increase the pressure of GC (FF 631911).

Table 2. Refactoring approaches and the short descriptions.

Approach Abbr	Interpretation
promFlds(f_1, ..., f_n)	Move the fields f_1, ..., f_n to its prototype
useMixin(o)	Apply mixin pattern to construct object o
ordFlds(f_1, ..., f_n)	Add the fields f_1, ..., f_n in a fixed order
movMap(f_1, ..., f_n)	Move the fields f_1, ..., f_n to an ES6 map
advFlds(f_1, ..., f_n)	Add the fields f_1, ..., f_n before use
initAry(a)	Initialize the array a before use
factorOut($srcL$)	Factor out the code around the code at $srcL$

Refactoring. We can promote the fields that hold closure instances to their prototypes to avoid frequent closure creation, such as we did in Fig. 1. We call this refactoring **promFlds**. If too many fields should be promoted, it is better to use the mixin design pattern to construct objects [22]. We call this way **useMixin** refactoring.

2. Inconsistent Field Ordering. JavaScript programs often have different paths to construct an object (*e.g.* by taking different *if-else* branches), and these paths add fields in different orders. For example, FF 813425 reports a real case in pdf.js: A loop randomly adds fields to the objects created from the same place, and thus, makes a hot function recompile for 11 times.

Refactoring. Guaranteeing the fields that are added in the same order can avoid generating type inconsistent objects. We name this refactoring **ordFlds**. The second suggestion is called **movMap**: Use a specialized ES6 Map [2] if an object is intended to be used as a map.

3. Partially Initialized Objects. It is common that fields are gradually added to an object during its lifetime. If the object is frequently used before fully constructed, every time the object transitioning to a new type always deoptimizes the code generated by the previous types. A dual pattern is that code is optimized against a fully constructed object. However, a partially initialized object is occasionally used and it deoptimizes the code.

Refactoring. A good practice is fully constructing an object before using it, such as adding all the fields in the constructor. We call this refactoring **advFlds**. If a derived object would like to shadow certain fields in the prototype, try to override the shadowed fields as early as possible.

4. Fat Object and Sparse Array. Adding too many fields to an object can change its backing storage to dictionary, especially adding fields via the keyed expression "p[f]" gives stronger hints than the named form "p.f" to enable the dictionary mode (*e.g.* V8 2734). If the dictionary mode is unintended, the subsequent access to the object can slowdown significantly (*e.g.* V8 3313). For arrays, the code such as "a=[]; a[x]=1;" creates a sparse array with a hole $[0, x)$. If the hole is large enough, the array is also changed to a dictionary (*e.g.* V8 2192). Moreover, accessing to a hole element returns a `undefined` value and it can invalidate ICs for operations such as "+" [7].

Refactoring. We can apply **movMap** to eliminate a fat object if most of the fields are added outside constructors. The sparse arrays can be eliminated by initializing the arrays (**initAry**). If writing to an element beyond the current array boundary is needed, try to allocate a large array and initialize it.

5. Prototype Mutation. Prototype of an object can be replaced at runtime. This behavior is popular in web libraries such as JQuery and Zepto. However, changing prototype can disable many JIT optimizations, such as the optimization for `instanceof` operator and inlining the methods in the prototype (*i.e.* FF 1041126). A more thorough discussion on this issue can be found in the bug report FF 642500.

Refactoring. Applying the mixin design pattern (**useMixin**) to construct objects is the best practice if the purpose of changing prototype is to inherit functions from different objects.

6. Integer Overflow. JavaScript only supports `double` data type, but modern JavaScript engines optimize the computations that only involve integer values. When a value exceeds integer range, a much expensive double representation such as boxed double used by V8 [10] is enabled (*i.e.* V8 2306). Moreover, if an array element overflows, the data for all the array elements will be lifted to a more general representations, as described by Bolz *et al.* [5].

Refactoring. If overflow will eventually happen, the best solution is isolating the code that are tainted by the overflowed values to a new function, as suggested by McCutchan [19]. We call this refactoring approach **factorOut**.

4 Finding Unintentional Type Mutations

We adopt a three-step approach based on program execution information to detect the unintended type mutations and infer the refactoring suggestions. First, we capture the type mutations by runtime monitoring and construct type evolution graph. Second, we identify the unintentional type mutations by analyzing the types that incur deoptimizations. Third, we infer the bug pattern of each unintentional type mutation by analyzing the relevant part of the type evolution graph. The refactoring suggestions are naturally derived from the guidelines for refactoring the bug patterns in Sect. 3. More details of these steps are explained in the following sections.

4.1 Modeling Type Evolutions

We instrument the JavaScript engine to collect the *operational log*, which contains the type update operations for objects and deoptimization information. Table 3 defines all the events recorded in the log. Every object event contains the calling context information (***ctxt***) and the source code location (***srcL***) to precisely locate the event triggering code. If the value $\boldsymbol{v}$ recorded in the events *NewField* and *UptField* is a closure instance, we replace $\boldsymbol{v}$ with the unique ID of the definition place of the closure. The most important event is *DeoptCode*, which contains the types $(T_1, \ldots, T_K)$ collected at the deoptimized IC (*id*) and the object (*obj*) that causes the deoptimization.

With the operational log, we build the *type evolution graphs*, one for each *allocation source*, which is defined as follows:

Definition 1. *The allocation source AS_o for object o is:*
- *o = new ctor(...): AS_o is the constructor "ctor".*
- *$o = \{\}$ or o = []: AS_o is the global unique ID that represents this object literal $\{\}$ or [].*

Table 3. Definitions of the events in the operational log.

Event name	Arguments	Interpretation
Object events		
NewObject	*ctxt*, *srcL*, *obj*, *t*	Create an object ***obj*** at line ***srcL*** under calling context ***ctxt*** with initial type ***t***
NewArray	*ctxt*, *srcL*, *ary*, *t*	Create an array ***ary*** at line ***srcL*** under calling context ***ctxt*** with initial type ***t***
ChgProto	*ctxt*, *srcL*, *obj*, *newProto*, *t*	Set the prototype of ***obj*** to ***newProto*** at line ***srcL*** under calling context ***ctxt*** and change type to ***t***
NewField	*ctxt*, *srcL*, *obj*, *f*, *v*, *md*, *t*	Insert field ***f*** to object ***obj*** with value ***v*** at line ***srcL*** under calling context ***ctxt*** ***md***=0: ***f*** is added via ***obj.f*** ***md***=1: ***f*** is added via ***obj***["***f***"]
DelField	*ctxt*, *srcL*, *obj*, *f*, *t*	Delete field ***f*** of object ***obj*** at line ***srcL*** under calling context ***ctxt*** and change type to ***t***
UptField	*ctxt*, *srcL*, *obj*, *f*, *v*, *t*	Assign value ***v*** to field ***f*** of object ***obj*** at line ***srcL*** under calling context ***ctxt*** and change type to ***t***
AryWrite	*ctxt*, *srcL*, *ary*, *inx*, *t*	Writing to array ***ary*** index ***inx*** at line ***srcL*** under calling context ***ctxt*** and change type to ***t***
RepLift	*ctxt*, *srcL*, *obj*, *t*	The representation of the elements or properties in ***obj*** is lifted by executing an operation at line ***srcL*** under calling context ***ctxt*** [5]. The new representation has type ***t***
Function events		
DeoptCode	*func*, *obj*, *t* *id*, $T_1, \ldots, T_K$	The function ***func*** deoptimized at an IC ***id*** because the type ***t*** of object ***obj*** is not previously collected by the IC ***id***. The expected types for the IC are $T_1, \ldots, T_K$.

We aggregate the objects by allocation source because *objects created by the same constructor or from the same literal likely to have the same usage scenarios, and refactoring can be easily performed at the constructor level.* In the rest of this paper, we call the objects created at the same allocation source *sibling* objects. The type evolution graph ψ for an object allocation source is defined as follows:

Definition 2. *A type evolution graph (TEG)* ψ *is a 6-tuple* $(\Omega, S, \theta, \Sigma, \delta, q_0)$*:*

- Ω *is a finite set of types.*
- S *is a finite set of states.*
- θ*:* $S \to \Omega$ *is an injective mapping from a state* $s \in S$ *to a type* $t \in \Omega$*. We name the reversed mapping as* θ^{-1}.
- Σ *is a finite set of events.*
- δ*:* $S \times \Sigma \to S$ *is a type transition function that describes a type update operation.*
- q_0*: the initial state.*

The set of type evolution graphs are collectively represented by Γ. Since the mapping between S and Ω is injective, we abuse the terms type and state in the rest of the paper.

We scan the operational log to generate the type evolution graphs. For every event in the log, we process it with Algorithm 1. The main idea of Algorithm 1 is first calling `GetTEG` to find or build the evolution graph for corresponding

Algorithm 1. UpdateTEG

```
  Input: E = An event in the operational log
1 switch E.type do
2     case Object Event:
3         obj = E.obj;
4         newTy = E.t;
          /* 1. Find or build an TEG          */
5         teg = GetTEG(obj, newTy)
          /* 2: Build type transition         */
6         s = FindState(teg, obj);
7         AddTransition(s, newTy, E);
8         if newTy == Dictionary then
9             hint = ProcessDictObj (o);
10            EmitSuggests (hint);
11        end
12    end
13    case Function Event:
14        CheckDeopt(E.obj, [T_1, T_2, ..., T_K]);
15    end
16 endsw
```

Algorithm 2. ProcessDictObj

```
Input: o: The object in dictionary mode
if o is object then
    if o has more than K_f fields then
        if CountKeyedAddFlds (o) > 0
        then
            SetWatch (o)
    end
else if o is array then
    evt = last event for o;
    if evt == AryWrite And evt.inx >
    o.length then
        if evt.inx ≤ 1,000,000 then
            return initAry(o);
        end
    end
end
```

object. Then, it creates a state transition to reflect the type change. Other sub-procedures appeared in Algorithm 1 are explained in below:

1. `GetTEG(`o, $\boldsymbol{newTy}$`)` : Obtain the TEG for the object $\boldsymbol{o}$. If $\boldsymbol{o}$ is the first object for its allocation source, build a new TEG with initial type $\boldsymbol{newTy}$.
2. `FindState(`ψ`, o)`: Locate the state in the evolution graph ψ that contains the type of the object o at the moment.
3. `AddTransition(`s_1`, t, E)`: Create a labeled transition $s_1 \xrightarrow{E} s_2$ to reflect the type change, where s_2 is the state for type t.

The type evolution graphs created by Algorithm 1 for our running example is similar to that in Fig. 4. The structure of type evolution graph is a *directed acyclic graph* (DAG), because type evolution cannot go back to an old type. However, two different types can evolve to the same type. For example, all dictionary mode objects have the same type.

If an object is changed to dictionary (Line 8), we infer whether or not the dictionary backing storage is intentional with Algorithm 2. First, we only consider an object with more than K_f (*e.g.* $K_f = 15$) fields as a candidate of fat object. Second, if there is at least one field of o added through the keyed expression such as "p[f]" (obtained by `CountKeyedAddFlds`), we mark the object o by `SetWatch`. The reason is adding fields to an object through keyed expression "p[f]" strongly implies that the field name "f" is only known at runtime. Hence, o is very possibly to be a dictionary. However, this heuristic alone is not enough, we need more evidence and hence we make decision in Algorithm 5. If the object is an array, we emit an **initAry** suggestion if the last event is an out-of-bound access and the array size is small enough. Access out-of-bound on a large array is very likely to use the array as a dictionary.

4.2 Checking Type Homogeneity

We define that type t_1 is *homogeneous* to type t_2 if they belong to the same TEG ψ. We use homogeneity to identify the types that are evolved from the same allocation source. In term of graph reachability, two types can be homogeneous in three ways. Suppose R_ψ is the reachability relation on ψ, where $R_\psi(x, y)$ means there is a path $x \rightsquigarrow y$ on ψ. Two types t_1 and t_2 are homogeneous iff:

- $R_\psi(t_1, t_2)$, or
- $R_\psi(t_2, t_1)$, or
- $\exists t_3 \in \Omega_\psi$, $R_\psi(t_3, t_1)$ and $R_\psi(t_3, t_2)$.

We implement the homogeneity testing in Algorithm 3. The high level workflow, excluding the details in the *if ... else* block from Line 11 to Line 21, is checking the relationship between type t_o and type t_c, where t_o is the type of the object o at the time of causing deoptimization and $t_c \in [T_1, T_2, \ldots, T_K]$ is a type needed by the IC at the deoptimization site. To decide how t_o is homogeneous to t_c, we use two auxiliary procedures:

1. `MapToState`: It is exactly the θ^{-1} function (recall Definition 2). If the state for t_c is non-exist, t_c and t_o is not homogeneous.

Algorithm 3. CheckDeopt

Input: o, t_o: object o with the type t_o
Input: id, $[T_1, T_2, \ldots, T_K]$: $T_1, \cdots, T_k$ are the types collected by the IC id
1 $nhomo$ = K;
2 $Q = \emptyset$;
3 s_o = `MapToState` (ψ_o, t_o);
4 **for** $t_c \in [T_1, T_2, \ldots, T_K]$ **do**
5   s_c = `MapToState` (ψ_o, t_c);
6   **if** s_c *is non-exist* **then** // t_o is not homogeneous to t_c
7         $nhomo = nhomo - 1$;
8   **continue** ;
9   **end**
    // Get the path P and the path distance between t_o and t_c on ψ_o
10   P, d = `ComputePath` (t_o, t_c);
11   **if** $d > 0$ **then** // $R_\psi(t_o, t_c)$
12         $Q = Q \cup$ `HandleFutureType` (d, P);
13   **else if** $d < 0$ **then** // $R_\psi(t_c, t_o)$
14         $Q = Q \cup$ `HandlePastType` $(-d, P)$;
15   **else** // $R_\psi(t_s, t_o)$ and $R_\psi(t_s, t_c)$
16   t_s = `FindLCA` (t_o, t_c);
17         $P_o = P_c = \emptyset$;
18   `SplitPaths` (t_s, P, P_o, P_c);
19         $Q = Q \cup$ `HandleSplitType` (t_s, P_o, P_c);
20   **end**
21 **end**
22 **if** *CountDeoptSite(id)* $> K_s$ **then** $Q = Q \cup$ **factorOut**(id);
23 **if** $\frac{nhomo}{K} \geq \pi_h$ **then** `EmitSuggests` (Q);

---

2. `ComputePath`: It computes the shortest path P between t_o and t_c on ψ_o. If multiple paths exist, choose arbitrary one. The choice of the path does not matter, because after the refactoring, we can run the analysis again to study another path. The second return value d is the length of P. The sign of d encodes the path direction: $d > 0$ indicates $R_\psi(t_o, t_c)$. $d < 0$ represents $R_\psi(t_c, t_o)$. $d = 0$ means t_c and t_o are reachable by an intermediate node t_s.

We record how many types cached at the IC are homogeneous to t_o in the variable *nhomo*. If the ratio $\frac{nhomo}{K}$ exceeds the threshold π_h, we decide t_o as an unintentional type and output the refactoring suggestions.

4.3 Inferring the Reason of Deoptimization

The *if ... else* branch from Line 11 to Line 21 in Algorithm 3 infers bug patterns from the path between t_o and t_c on the type evolution graph. Since the path only has three cases, our inference algorithm works in three ways:

Algorithm 4. HandleFutureType

```
Input: P, d: The shortest path P for
       t_o ⇝ t_c with distance d
E = ∅;
if d ≤ K_d then
    foreach evt ∈ P do
        if evt != NewField then
            return
        E = E ∪ evt;
    end
end
return advFlds(E);
```

1. `HandleFutureType(d, P)`: It handles the case where t_c might be a type for object o in future. This case is probably that o is used before fully constructed compared to its sibling objects, which is an instance of *partially initialized objects* bug (pattern 3). If $d \leq K_d$ and all the events between t_c and t_o are *NewField*, we emit an **advFlds** suggestion. We typically choose a small value for K_d (*e.g.* $K_d = 3$), because shorter path is more likely to be exceptional. All events should be *NewField* because advancing the *UptField* and *DelField* events are unsafe.

2. `HandlePastType(d, P)`: This situation is object o or its sibling objects have type t_c in the past. We examine the evolution path $t_c \rightsquigarrow t_o$ to confirm the bug pattern for o. First, if the backing storage of o is dictionary and o is watched at Line 4 of Algorithm 2, we deem the object o has refactoring value and emit a **movMap** suggestion. Second, if there is a *ChgProto* event on the path, we emit a **useMixin** suggestion. Third, if integer overflows and changes the value representation (*e.g.* *int* $\rightarrow$ *double*), we emit a **factorOut** suggestion if the object has more than K_i fields or array elements. The objects with more fields are potentially accessed in more places and thus, incur more IC failures and create higher performance impact. Finally, same to Algorithm 4, if all the events between t_c and t_o are *NewField* and $d \leq K_d$, it could be a *partially initialized objects* case and we emit a **advFlds** suggestion.

3. `HandleSplitType(`t_s`, `P_o`, `P_c`)`: This case states that t_c and t_o deviate to different evolution paths at the state t_s, which is the lowest common ancestor (LCA) for t_c and t_o, computed by `FindLCA`. We first bisect the path into

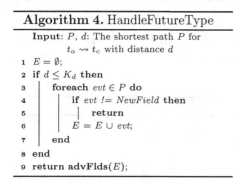

Algorithm 5. HandlePastType

Input: P, d: The shortest path P for $t_c \rightsquigarrow t_o$ with distance d

```
 1  E = ∅, R = ∅;
 2  hasOtherEvents = false;
 3  if IsDictMode (o) And IsWatched (o) then
 4  |     R = R ∪ movMap(o)
 5  end
 6  foreach evt ∈ P do
 7  |     if evt != NewField then
 8  |     |     if evt == ChgProto then R = R ∪ useMixin(o);
 9  |     |     else if evt == RepLift And NumFields (o) > K_i then
10  |     |     |     R = R ∪ factorOut(srcL);
11  |     |     end
12  |     |     hasOtherEvents = true;
13  |     end
14  |     E = E ∪ evt;
15  end
16  if d ≤ K_d And hasOtherEvents == false then R = R ∪ advFlds(E);
17  return R;
```

Algorithm 6. HandleSplitType

Input: t_s, P_o, P_c: The paths P_o: $t_s \rightsquigarrow t_o$ and P_c: $t_s \rightsquigarrow t_c$

```
    // fpos, cls: Mapping from field name to path position and to closure ID
 1  fpos = cls = ∅;
 2  for i ← to len(P_o) do
 3  |     evt = P_o[i] ;                           // Get i^th event on the path P_o
 4  |     if evt == NewField Or evt == UptField then
 5  |     |     v = evt.v;
 6  |     |     if v is closure then cls[evt.f] = v;
 7  |     |     if evt == NewField then fpos[evt.f] = i;
 8  |     end
 9  end
10  proF = ordF = ∅;
11  for i ← to len(P_c) do
12  |     evt = P_o[i] ;                           // Get i^th event on the path P_c
13  |     if evt == NewField Or evt == UptField then
14  |     |     f = evt.f;   v = evt.v;
15  |     |     if v is closure instance And cls[f] == v then proF = proF ∪ f;
16  |     |     if evt == NewField And fpos[f] != i then ordF = ordF ∪ f;
17  |     end
18  end
19  R = ∅;
20  if |proF| > K_p then R = R ∪ useMixin(o);
21  else if |proF| > 0 then R = R ∪ promFlds(proF);
22  if |ordF| > 0 then R = R ∪ ordFlds(ordF);
23  return R;
```

$t_s \rightsquigarrow t_o$ and $t_s \rightsquigarrow t_c$ two segments with `SplitPaths` in Algorithm 6. Then, we scan the two paths and fill and collect the fields that are assigned to different closure instances and the fields that are added in different order in the two paths.

The scan results are stored in *proF* and *ordF*. We emit a refactoring suggestion **useMixin** if *proF* has more than K_p (*e.g.* $K_p = 7$) results, in which case using mixin pattern is better than promoting many fields to the prototype. Otherwise, if *proF* and *ordF* are non-empty, we give the **promFlds** and **ordFlds** refactoring suggestions.

We also count the number of deoptimizations incurred by each deoptimization site via `CountDeoptSite` at Line 22 of Algorithm 3. The counting result tells us which IC is less stable than others. In case the deoptimization is hard to be eliminated, we emit a **factorOut** refactoring suggestion, since factoring the code around the problematic IC site to a new function can limit the performance impact to a smaller scope. This is especially useful for performance problems happened inside a hot loop [19].

5 Evaluation

We implement our algorithm in a tool JSweeter. Operational log collection is performed on a modified version of V8. We apply JSweeter to Octane benchmark suite Version 2. The reason to choose Octane is twofold. First, we only modify V8, which is incapable to execute the JavaScript programs requiring external facilities, such as DOM and AJAX. We did not manage to modify a full functional JavaScript execution tool such as Chrome due to the excessive hacking efforts. Second, compared to other popular JavaScript benchmark suites such as Kraken and SunSpider, Octane has much larger programs modified from real world applications (up to 33,000 LOC for pdfjs) that can prove the effectiveness of our proposed algorithm for real sized programs. Our experiments are conducted on a machine running 32-bit Ubuntu 12.04 with an Intel Core2 3.0GHz CPU and 4GB RAM.

5.1 Overall Results Discussion

Table 4. The benchmark scores before and after fixing the performance issues.

	crypto	splay	box2d	gbemu	typescript	pdfjs
#Total Issues	4	1	8	12	18	3
#Fixed Issues	3	1	3	5	5	2
Score Before fix	18840	9362	20347	38748	19590	13858
Score After fix	19495	11480	21125	40237	20394	14330
Speedup	3.5 %	23.0 %	3.8 %	3.8 %	4.1 %	3.4 %

We empirically choose the parameters $\pi_h = 0.5$, $K_d = 3$, $K_p = 7$, $K_i = 25$ and run JSweeter. Our findings are given in Table 4. The subjects that only have marginal improvements, such as zlib.js, datablue.js, and *etc.*, are omitted. We totally report 46 performance issues, which is surprising since these programs are well tuned. We successfully fix 19 of these issues that are simple enough to fix in one hour following the refactoring suggestions. The remaining 27 issues cannot be fixed in two reasons:

1. We are unable to understand 21 issues. The major reason is JSweeter only records one level calling context information for type update events, which is

insufficient to guide us to trace back to the source of bug introducing place, especially we are not the authors of these programs. The benefit is that our approach incurs low overhead for collecting execution information. A tool such as that described by Feldthaus *et al.* [6] would be helpful and we will explore it in future.
2. We are unable to apply 6 refactoring suggestions (false positives). This is because our algorithm is a pure dynamic analysis without considering the static program semantics. For example, an **advFlds** suggests adding a field in the constructor, but the name of that field is extracted from user input and it is unable to add such fields in advance. Even a field *f* whose name is statically known, blindly adding *f* in the constructor can suppress the field existence testing such as *if (p.f == undefined)* and possibly change the program behaviour. Moreover, the initial value of the field is sometimes hard to determine. In future work, we will consider using static information to weed out infeasible fixes and guide the refactoring.

We measure the benefits of refactoring the programs by Octane score, which is inversely proportional to execution time and the larger the better. The scores are obtained by a fresh checkout of V8 (version 3.29.42). For each program, we run it for five times and obtain its average score. All of the refactored programs gain higher scores, where most of the programs only have 3 % – 4 % speedup and one case splay.js is 23 % faster. The results are indicative and cost benefit, since the JavaScript engine developers often tried hard and achieve the similar results. It is valuable to mention that JSweeter also found the bug reported in FF 813425 bug case. This bug is one of our two findings of *inconsistent field ordering* bugs in pdfjs. By adding the fields before use, we obtain 2.2 % speedup for this single modification, very close to the 2.7 % speedup achieved by the pdfjs developers.

5.2 Case Studies for Octane

We select five issues from three programs for case study. These cases are selected because each of them represents a different bug pattern. Also, these issues are difficult to be observed by programmers, since the bug introducing place and the symptom place are spatially far.

Case 1: splay.js. The splay.js program implements the splay tree data structure, which is primarily designed for testing the performance of memory management. JSweeter finds an obscured performance issue caused by the underscored statements in function `insert` as shown in Fig. 5. There is an instance of the typical *inconsistent field ordering* problem, where the fields "left" and "right" are added to the "SplayTree.Node" objects in different orders. As a consequence, when these "SplayTree.Node" objects are accessed, they would generate PICs and incur additional type checking overhead.

Even worse, these objects would deoptimize the `remove` function through the IC site at Line 16. And the consequent performance degradation incurred by using un-optimized version of `remove` would be prominent, because splay.js frequently inserts and removes nodes from the splay tree. Simply adding the

```
1 SplayTree.prototype.insert =
2 function(key, value) {
3   // ...
4   var node =
5   new SplayTree.Node(key, value);
6   if (key > this.root_.key) {
7     node.left = this.root_;
8     node.right = this.root_.right;
9     this.root_.right = null;
10  } else {
11    node.right = this.root_;
12    node.left = this.root_.left;
13    this.root_.left = null;
14  }
15  this.root_ = node;
16 };
```

```
16 SplayTree.prototype.remove =
17 function(key) {
18   // ...
19   if (!this.root_.left) {
20     this.root_ =
21         this.root_.right;
22   } else {
23     // ...
24   }
25 };
```

Fig. 5. splay.js: The unordered addition of fields "left" and "right" in function `insert` will deoptimize the function `remove` at Line 16.

fields "left" and "right" in the two conditional branches in the same order would fix this problem. A better solution is proactively adding both "left" and "right" in the constructor `SplayTree.Node`, which also avoids the problems caused by the `SplayTree.Node` objects in other places. We obtain 23 % more scores from this simple fix.

Case 2: box2d.js. The box2d.js program is a popular 2D physics engine. It has nearly 9500 lines of deminified code. Since **box2d.js** is compiled from Emscripten[2], a C++ to JavaScript compiler, it is full of simply-named variables such as "a", "Q", and *etc.*. Thus, finding performance issues manually for box2d.js is almost impossible even for an experienced programmer. With the help of JSweeter, we successfully fix three performance bugs.

Among the three bugs, one would incur deoptimizations for seven functions by adding a field "m_toi". This field addition operation is performed in function `h.SolveTOI`. We show a simplified version of `h.SolveTOI` in Fig. 6, where we highlight the two access sites for field "m_toi": Line 7 is a read site and Line 10 is a write site. Line 10 changes the type of the objects referenced by "b", which deoptimize quite a few functions, such as those in Fig. 7.

JSweeter outputs a **addFlds** hint to suggest adding the *m_toi* field in an early stage. In the bug report, JSweeter locates function `Oa` as the constructor of the objects pointed by *b* and the corresponding "Oa" object is in the function `z.Create`. However, our first attempt by directly adding the field *m_toi* followed by the creation of "Oa" object in `z.Create` does not eliminate the performance issue. A further investigation with the calling context information shows that the fields of object "Oa" fields are added in functions `A.Reset` and `A.b2Contact`. At this place, JSweeter cannot offer more help. Based on our human study of functions near to `A.Reset`, we realize `A.Update` is the best place to add the field *m_toi*. With this refactoring, all the seven deoptimizations are eliminated.

[2] https://github.com/kripken/emscripten.

```
h.prototype.SolveTOI =
function(a) {
  // ...
  for ( ; ; ) {
    // ...
    if (b.m_flags & l.
        e_toiFlag)
      c = b.m_toi;
    else {
      // ...
      b.m_toi = c;
    }
  }
};
```

Fig. 6. The simplified code for adding the field "m_toi" in box2d.js.

```
A.prototype.GetNext =
function () {
    return this.m_next
};
A.prototype.GetFixtureA =
function () {
    return this.m_fixtureA
};
A.prototype.GetFixtureB =
function () {
    return this.m_fixtureB
};
```

Fig. 7. Functions that are deoptimized by adding field "m_toi" in `h.SolveTOI`.

```
1 GameBoyCore.prototype.initializeTiming = function () {
2   // ...
3   this.CPUCyclesTotal = (this.baseCPUCyclesPerIteration - this.
        CPUCyclesTotalRoundoff) | 0;
4 }
5 GameBoyCore.prototype.audioUnderrunAdjustment = function () {
6   // ...
7   this.CPUCyclesTotalCurrent += (underrunAmount >> 1)*this.machineOut;
8 }
9 GameBoyCore.prototype.iterationEndRoutine = function () {
10  // ...
11  this.CPUCyclesTotalCurrent += this.CPUCyclesTotalRoundoff;
12 }
13 GameBoyCore.prototype.recalculateIterationClockLimit = function () {
14  // ...
15  this.CPUCyclesTotal = this.CPUCyclesTotalBase + this.
        CPUCyclesTotalCurrent - endModulus;
16  this.CPUCyclesTotalCurrent = endModulus;
17 }
```

Fig. 8. All places that write to "CPUCyclesTotal" and "CPUCyclesTotalCurrent".

Case 3: gbemu.js. The gbemu.js program is a GameBoy emulator. Unlike box2d.js, which allocates many empty objects and incrementally updates them, gbemu.js uses a big monolithic data structure named gameboy to store the virtual machine states. In this flat design, almost all the fields of gameboy are added by the constructor GameBoyCore and most of these fields are integers.

One representative issue is caused by the integer overflow of two fields: *CPUCyclesTotal* and *CPUCyclesTotalCurrent*. From their names, we guess these fields store the number of CPU cycles elapsed on the emulated CPU. There are only four places that write to *CPUCyclesTotal* and *CPUCyclesTotalCurrent* other than the constructor, summarized in Fig. 8.

Taking *CPUCyclesTotal* as an example, its value can exceed 2^{30} at Line 15 of Fig. 8, which is the upper bound for the small integer representation used by V8. The integer overflow triggers a representation change to use double value for *CPUCyclesTotal*. As a consequence, all fields in the object "gameboy" are lifted to double representations [5], and all operations related to these fields are

```
GameBoyCore.prototype.mixerOutputLevelCache = function () {
  this.mixerOutputCache =
  ((((this.channel1currentSampleLeftTrimary +
  this.channel2currentSampleLeftTrimary +
  this.channel3currentSampleLeftSecondary +
  this.channel4currentSampleLeftSecondary) *
  this.VinLeftChannelMasterVolume) << 9) +
  ((this.channel1currentSampleRightTrimary +
  this.channel2currentSampleRightTrimary +
  this.channel3currentSampleRightSecondary +
  this.channel4currentSampleRightSecondary) *
  this.VinRightChannelMasterVolume));
}
```

Fig. 9. The unique place that writes to "mixerOutputCache".

```
1 this.LINECONTROL[line] =
2 function (parentObj) {
3   if (parentObj.LCDTicks<80) {
4     // ...
5   }
6 }
```

Fig. 10. The IC site (highlighted area) that contributes most to the deoptimization of LINECONTROL.

```
function entry0(parentObj) {
  var ticks = parentObj.LCDTicks;
  processLT143(ticks, parentObj);
}
function
processLT143(ticks, parentObj) {
  if (ticks < 80) {
    // ...
  }
}
this.LINECONTROL[line] = entry0;
```

Fig. 11. Isolate the deoptimization site with other parts in LINECONTROL.

impacted. As suggested by the factorOut hint, we use a separate object to place the *CPUCyclesTotal* and *CPUCyclesTotalCurrent* fields. In this way, all fields are not mutually impacted.

The second issue is that the field *mixerOutputCache* occasionally gets **NaN** via the computation as shown in Fig. 9. Since JSweeter does not track the value flows, we cannot understand how *mixerOutputCache* becomes **NaN**. We simply add a **NaN** checking before assigning the computation result to *mixerOutputCache*.

JSweeter also outputs a **factorOut** suggestion for an anonymous closure assigned to array "LINECONTROL", which is responsible for screen rendering. In this case, large volume of closure instances are created and they deoptimize 163 times, where 90.4 % of the deoptimizations are contributed by the field-access site at Line 3 of Fig. 10. To factor out this problematic IC site, we take a two-step solution. We first define function `entry0` that only reads the field *LCDTicks* and keep other statements in function `processLT143`. Second, we add a tail call to `processLT143` in `entry0`, as shown in Fig. 11. By this refactoring, we assign the unique instance of `entry0` to all the elements of array "LINECONTROL", and this *frequent closures creation* problem is solved.

6 Related Work

JavaScript Performance Debugging. The most relevant work to us is Gong *et al.*'s JITProf [9]. This work also performs a pattern matching based dynamic analysis to locate the code that causes JIT failures and results in performance degradation. However, JSweeter is more general and powerful than JITProf in four ways:

1. Our 6 bug patterns are not ad-hoc: Type mutation is their coherent reason to cause performance issues. This deep insight can guide programmers to find new bug patterns easily. Moreover, we also performed an empirical study and showed the pervasiveness of the proposed bug patterns. In contrast, JITProf only lists 7 bug patterns without explaining where these patterns come from.
2. Central to our algorithm is the type evolution graph (TEG), which is a uniform representation for different pattern matching algorithms. In contrast, JITProf designs individual pattern matching algorithm for each bug pattern, which precludes adding new patterns easily.
3. TEG aggregates the type information for sibling objects while JITProf traces the state for each individual object. TEG is superior for bug detection because, by contrasting the behavior of an object to its sibling objects, a deviated type evolution is more likely to be a real bug.
4. JSweeter is running offline and thus have more flexibility to run complicated pattern matching algorithms without incurring runtime overhead. For example, Algorithm 5 retrospects the historic type information to confirm the *partially initialized objects* bug. In contrast, JITProf works totally online and performs limited checks to decide a bug. Nevertheless, JITProf already incurs 18× runtime overhead even with events sampling.

Performance Debugging on Statically Typed Languages. Most of the works still rely on function execution time profiling data and statistical algorithms [3,8, 13,18,20,23–25]. However, as we argued, type mutations cannot be captured by time profiling results. The works Sherlog [26] and G2 [11] share similarity to ours. Sherlog infers a possible control flow from program start to the symptom site. The control flow information is useful for functional bugs, but it is unknown how performance bugs can benefit from it. Instead, JSweeter generates an object centric view of the type update process that only contains the operations pertaining to performance issues. The work G2 also models the log events as a graph and it backwardly and forwardly to search the root cause. Compared to G2, JSweeter goes further to generate refactoring suggestions by pattern matching the objects evolution history to our empirical observations.

Avoid Type Instability with Type Prediction. Instead of preventing type mutations, improving the type prediction successful rate can also speed up JavaScript execution. Hackett *et al.* are the first to design a type-inference algorithm that works for full JavaScript features [12], by performing type inference online with the help of type-feedback. In contrast, Kedlaya *et al.* use the type-inference to aid type-feedback to intelligently place type profiling hooks [17]. Santos *et al.* [21] developed a technique to generate a specialized version of the function for every combination of the parameter values for that function, which significantly enforces the power of constant propagation and other optimizations. All these works are orthogonal to ours, because our aim is involving programmers to address the performance bugs with complex logics.

7 Conclusion and Future Work

In this paper, we propose a dynamic analysis to detect, infer, and refactor six JavaScript performance issues incurred by type mutations. We first empirically study the performance bug patterns common in real world programs. Based on the study, we design a technique that analyzes the type evolution graph to infer the occurrence of the predefined code smells and synthesize refactoring suggestions. We implement a tool JSweeter and find nineteen performance bugs in Octane benchmark suite. These bugs can be effectively fixed by following JSweeter's refactoring suggestions and the benchmark scores for bug fixed programs can increase up to 23 %.

References

1. https://asmjs.org
2. https://people.mozilla.org/jorendorff/es6-draft.html
3. Aguilera, M.K., Mogul, J.C., Wiener, J.L., Reynolds, P., Muthitacharoen, A.: Performance debugging for distributed systems of black boxes. In: SOSP (2003)
4. Ahn, W., Choi, J., Shull, T., Garzarán, M.J., Torrellas, J.: Improving javascript performance by deconstructing the type system. In: PLDI (2014)
5. Bolz, C.F., Diekmann, L., Tratt, L.: Storage strategies for collections in dynamically typed languages. In: OOPSLA (2013)
6. Feldthaus, A., Millstein, T., Møller, A., Schäfer, M., Tip, F.: Tool-supported refactoring for javascript. In: OOPSLA (2011)
7. Flückiger, O.: Compiled Compiler Templates for V8. Master's thesis (2014)
8. Fu, Q., Lou, J.G., Wang, Y., Li, J.: Execution anomaly detection in distributed systems through unstructured log analysis. In: ICDM (2009)
9. Gong, L., Pradel, M., Sen, K.: JITprof: pinpointing JIT-unfriendly javascript code. In: Proceedings of ESEC/FSE, pp. 357–368. ACM (2015)
10. Gudeman, D.: Representing type information in dynamically typed languages (1993)
11. Guo, Z., Zhou, D., Lin, H., Yang, M., Long, F., Deng, C., Liu, C., Zhou, L.: G2: a graph processing system for diagnosing distributed systems. In: USENIXATC (2011)
12. Hackett, B., Guo, S.Y.: Fast and precise hybrid type inference for javascript. In: PLDI (2012)
13. Han, S., Dang, Y., Ge, S., Zhang, D., Xie, T.: Performance debugging in the large via mining millions of stack traces. In: ICSE (2012)
14. Hölzle, U., Chambers, C., Ungar, D.: Optimizing dynamically-typed object-oriented languages with polymorphic inline caches. In: ECOOP (1991)
15. Hölzle, U., Ungar, D.: Optimizing dynamically-dispatched calls with run-time type feedback. In: PLDI (1994)

16. Hölzle, U., Ungar, D.: A third-generation self implementation: reconciling responsiveness with performance. In: OOPSLA (1994)
17. Kedlaya, M.N., Roesch, J., Robatmili, B., Reshadi, M., Hardekopf, B.: Improved type specialization for dynamic scripting languages. In: DLS (2013)
18. Liu, X., Mellor-Crummey, J.: Pinpointing data locality problems using data-centric analysis. In: CGO (2011)
19. McCutchan, J.: Accelerating oz with v8: follow the yellow brick road to javascript performance. In: Google I/O Conference (2013)
20. Nistor, A., Song, L., Marinov, D., Lu, S.: Toddler: detecting performance problems via similar memory-access patterns. In: ICSE (2013)
21. Santos, H.N., Alves, P., Costa, I., Pereira, F.M.Q.: Just-in-time value specialization. In: CGO (2013)
22. Van Cutsem, T., Miller, M.S.: Traits.js: robust object composition and high-integrity objects for ecmascript 5. In: PLASTIC (2011)
23. Xu, G., Arnold, M., Mitchell, N., Rountev, A., Sevitsky, G.: Go with the flow: profiling copies to find runtime bloat. In: PLDI (2009)
24. Xu, W., Huang, L., Fox, A., Patterson, D., Jordan, M.I.: Detecting large-scale system problems by mining console logs. In: SOSP (2009)
25. Yan, D., Xu, G., Rountev, A.: Uncovering performance problems in java applications with reference propagation profiling. In: ICSE (2012)
26. Yuan, D., Mai, H., Xiong, W., Tan, L., Zhou, Y., Pasupathy, S.: Sherlog: error diagnosis by connecting clues from run-time logs. In: ASPLOS XV (2010)

Analyzing Distributed Multi-platform Java and Android Applications with ShadowVM

Haiyang Sun[1(✉)], Yudi Zheng[1], Lubomír Bulej[1], Stephen Kell[2], and Walter Binder[1]

[1] Faculty of Informatics, Università Della Svizzera Italiana (USI), Lugano, Switzerland
{haiyang.sun,yudi.zheng,lubomir.bulej,walter.binder}@usi.ch
[2] Computer Laboratory, University of Cambridge, Cambridge, UK
stephen.kell@cl.cam.ac.uk

Abstract. In this tool demonstration, we present ShadowVM, a dynamic program analysis framework for Java and Android applications. ShadowVM offers a high-level programming model for expressing analyses, ensures complete bytecode coverage, and isolates the analysis from the observed application to avoid unwanted interference. An analysis implemented on top of ShadowVM can handle both Java and Android applications. First, we present and evaluate a simple code-coverage analysis implemented with ShadowVM. Second, we demonstrate the use of ShadowVM to analyze a distributed application comprising a Java server backend and an Android client frontend.

Keywords: Dynamic program analysis · Java · Android

1 Introduction

Dynamic program analyses, such as profiling, tracing and bug-finding tools, are essential for software development. However, despite this importance, the Java platform currently provides very limited support for creating these tools. Shortcomings common both to existing Java Virtual Machines (JVMs) and Android's Dalvik Virtual Machine (DVM) include lack of high-level abstractions for expressing analyses, lack of support for complete code coverage, and difficulty of avoiding interference between analysis and the underlying program. Instead, dynamic program analysis tools must be implemented using low-level mechanisms, such as the JVM Tool Interface (JVMTI) [19]—making for code that is error-prone and difficult to maintain, and often supporting only a particular virtual machine. Bytecode instrumentation presents fundamental interference and coverage difficulties, meaning that many analysis tools necessarily produce output that is unsound or incomplete, in order to avoid crashing or corrupting the application [11].

In this tool paper, we present our dynamic program analysis framework ShadowVM, which offers a high-level programming model for comprehensive,

X. Feng and S. Park (Eds.): APLAS 2015, LNCS 9458, pp. 356–365, 2015.
DOI: 10.1007/978-3-319-26529-2_19

multi-platform analysis. ShadowVM ensures complete bytecode coverage and isolates the execution of the analysis code from the observed program. With our framework, the same implementation of an analysis can be applied to programs running on the JVM and on the DVM. ShadowVM offers dedicated support for analyzing distributed applications comprising multiple communicating processes—fundamental for the analysis of Android applications, which are typically split into multiple components running in separate DVM processes.

This tool demonstration complements our previous publications on Shadow VM. In [14] we presented our initial design of ShadowVM, which only supported the JVM. In [20] we described the challenges of enabling dynamic program analysis on Android and presented an updated design of ShadowVM suited for Android applications running in DVM processes. The corresponding software release of ShadowVM for Android supported only Android SDK ARM emulator, resulting in extremely slow analysis. This tool demonstration provides the first complete presentation of the multi-platform analysis framework that has evolved from these two pieces of work. Additionally, our framework now offers two new deployment options: Android SDK x86 emulator and Android devices.

Section 2 gives an overview of the ShadowVM architecture. Section 3 illustrates how to implement a simple code-coverage analysis with ShadowVM and evaluates its performance on Android. Section 4 shows a new demonstration scenario, where we use ShadowVM to analyze a distributed application comprised of a Java server backend and an Android client frontend. Section 5 discusses related work and Sect. 6 summarizes the strengths and limitations of our framework.

2 ShadowVM Overview

Dynamic program analysis can be regarded as the processing of *events* that are produced within an observed application. Depending on the purpose of the analysis, different kinds of events are relevant, such as e.g. method call, method entry/exit, field access, or object allocation and reclamation. Most of them correspond to the execution of a specific location in the bytecode of the observed application; such events can be produced using bytecode instrumentation, and we call them *instrumentation events*. Other *lifecycle events*, such as e.g. object reclamation or virtual machine termination, do not correspond to any specific code location; they are produced by the framework using some internal mechanism of the virtual machine (such as the JVMTI [19] on the JVM) [14]. Similarly, special *communication events* are produced by the framework in the case of inter-process communication in an Android application [20]. Events may carry various *context information*, such e.g. an object reference or the name of an accessed field.

An analysis implemented on top of ShadowVM consists of two parts, the *event producer* and the *event consumer*. ShadowVM offers high-level programming abstractions for implementing the event-producing and event-consuming logic. Instrumentation events are expressed in the domain-specific aspect language DiSL (DSL for Instrumentation) [13,15,24], whereas lifecycle and communication events are automatically generated by the framework. ShadowVM

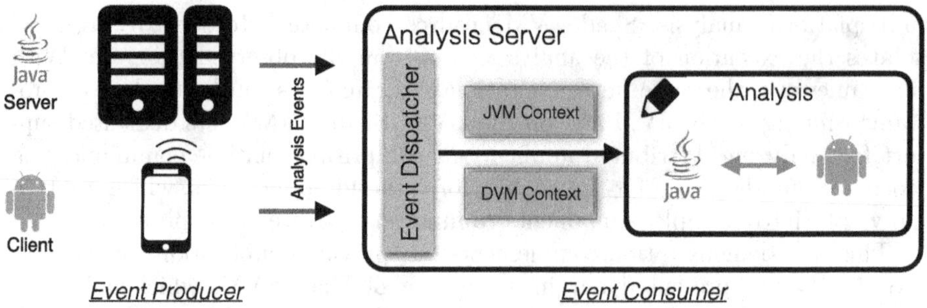

Fig. 1. Overview of an analysis receiving events from multiple observed Java and Android application components.

also includes a library of DiSL code for commonly used instrumentation events. The event-consuming logic is expressed as Java methods that handle the required events.

The deployment of an analysis consists of three components: the observed application (running with instrumentation), an instrumentation server, and an analysis server. The instrumentation server and the analysis server may be deployed within the same JVM process. The observed application is always running in one (or in a set of) separate JVM or DVM processes to avoid unwanted interferences between the observed application and the instrumentation/analysis code [14]. Instrumentation is performed at class load time; any method that has a bytecode representation can be instrumented (including those in the class library and in dynamically generated classes). For the DVM, a conversion between dex files and JVM class files occurs before and after instrumentation, which allows the instrumentation server (running DiSL) to only deal with Java class files.

The events produced in the observed application are sent to the analysis server through sockets. For each received event, a corresponding method (defined in an analysis class) is invoked by the framework's event dispatcher. The payload of the event can include primitives (passed by value) and object references; the latter are exposed to the analysis as *shadow objects*. These preserve the identity of the objects from the original program, and expose reflective metadata mirroring the class hierarchy of the observed application. Shadow objects allow attaching and accessing arbitrary analysis state—perhaps analysis-specific data (e.g. timestamps) or perhaps the real object's contents (by observing field writes). For convenience, shadow strings replicate the real strings' contents.

Figure 1 illustrates multiple observed components of a distributed application, all sending events to the same analysis server. The server-side components of the application are running in JVM processes, whereas the client-side frontend components are executing in DVM processes. The origin of a received event is represented by a JVM/DVM context object. Thanks to ShadowVM, a single implementation of the event-producing and event-consuming parts can observe the entire distributed multi-platform deployment. For example, the analysis may trace all communication between the distributed components. Section 4 demonstrates such an analysis.

```
@SyntheticLocal
static boolean encounterBranch = false;

@Before (marker = BranchMarker.class)
static void beforeBranchInstruction () {
  encounterBranch = true;
}

@AfterReturning (marker = IfThenBranchMarker.class)
static void thenBranch (final CodeCoverageContext c) {
  if (encounterBranch) {
    CodeCoverageAnalysisProxy.branchTaken(
      c.classIdentifier(), c.methodIdentifier(), c.branchIndex());
    encounterBranch = false;
  }
}

@AfterReturning (marker = IfElseBranchMarker.class)
static void elseBranch (final CodeCoverageContext c) {
  if (encounterBranch) {
    CodeCoverageAnalysisProxy.branchTaken(
      c.classIdentifier(), c.methodIdentifier(), c.branchIndex());
    encounterBranch = false;
  }
}
```

(a) Event producer (DiSL code)

```
public class CodeCoverageAnalysis implements VmExitListener {

  public void branchTaken(Context context, ShadowString classID,
          ShadowString methodID, int branchIndex) {
    ... // update coverage profile of corresponding method
  }

  @Override
  public void onVMExit(Context context) {
    ... // dump coverage profile of the process
  }

}
```

(b) Event consumer (plain Java)

Fig. 2. Event producer and consumer of JaCoCo recast for ShadowVM.

3 Code Coverage Analysis with ShadowVM

To illustrate how to implement a simple analysis with ShadowVM, we recast the popular code coverage tool JaCoCo [7].

Figure 2a shows the DiSL [13,15] instrumentation code producing branch events. Figure 2b shows the plain Java analysis code which consumes these branch events. The instrumentation assigns each branch a dedicated number for indexing, and emits an event indicating which branch is taken (the event marshalling code not shown here is in class *CodeCoverageAnalysisProxy*). In DiSL, Java annotations mark a snippet (a static method) with places where it should be inserted (here before and after branches). The extra "synthetic" local boolean is inserted into each method body and used to select only the taken branches. Although snippets appear as static methods within a Java class, along with auxiliary definitions (like the synthetic local), this is simply a convenient container; it is never loaded nor instantiated, and is used only by the instrumentation server. The snippet produces an event consisting of two strings and an integer, uniquely identifying the branch. The analysis maintains a simple data structure tracking taken branches, updated in reaction to the events received.

In [20] we compared the analysis results produced by our analysis and by the original JaCoCo. Both tools support JVM and DVM, and produce equivalent results for application classes. In contrast to the original JaCoCo, our tool is also capable of analyzing code coverage in the class library.

Below we report some new results on source-code metrics and on performance. The original JaCoCo (excluding report generation features) has 1959 logical lines of code (LOC), whereas our recast has only 363 LOC for the same functionality (including event producing and consuming logic). That is, with ShadowVM we can express the same analysis in less than 19 % of the LOC of the original tool.

Our current version of ShadowVM supports three deployment options for Android 4.4: (a) Android SDK ARM emulator; (b) Android SDK x86 emulator; (c) Android devices. Options (b) and (c) are new. Table 1 compares the performance of JaCoCo and our recast for the three Android deployment options.[1] We use GrinderBench[2] for the analysis. The reported metric is the elapsed wall time from the start of a benchmark until completion of the analysis.

In general, our ShadowVM recast introduces more overhead than JaCoCo. The slowdown is explained by event transmission overheads, whereas JaCoCo collects the coverage data within the observed process. The ShadowVM recast of JaCoCo offers greater flexibility—we can switch to different metrics, such as basic block profiling, without redeploying the profiler onto the device, since the instrumentation server runs separately. The option of deploying on the Android x86 emulator greatly reduces overhead (down to a factor of 2, instead of 8.3) by eliminating the cost of emulating a non-native instruction set architecture. We note that even the higher overhead need not be prohibitive; tools with overheads a factor of 10 or greater have gained acceptance among developers [17].

4 Fuzzing a Distributed Multi-platform Application

We will demonstrate ShadowVM with a trace validation tool for fuzzing a distributed application comprising a Java server and an Android device as frontend. Fuzzing is an automatic testing technique that feeds random inputs to a program to trigger exceptional behavior [3]. Monkey is a fuzzing tool generating Android user-interface events; it has been applied to finding security bugs [12]. As Android applications increasingly rely on server-side components, they increasingly suffer

[1] We evaluated the emulator settings with 2GB RAM on a quadcore Intel Core i7 (2.5GHz, 16GB RAM), and the real device setting on a Nexus 5 with 2GB RAM. The analysis and instrumentation servers were deployed on the same type of machine as the emulator and ran under Java8.

[2] http://www.grinderbench.com/.

Table 1. Execution time (in seconds) of the Grinder benchmarks on ARM emulator, x86 emulator or real device. Each deployment option is evaluated without instrumentation (baseline), with JaCoCo, or with our ShadowVM recast.

	ARM emulator			*x86 emulator*			*Nexus 5*		
	Baseline	JaCoCo	Recast	Baseline	JaCoCo	Recast	Baseline	JaCoCo	Recast
Parallel	2.25	2.42	16.67	1.32	1.39	1.93	1.42	1.51	3.25
kXML	2.64	3.00	22.58	1.34	1.43	2.70	1.55	1.55	2.96
PNG	2.28	2.67	19.42	1.34	1.40	2.37	1.42	1.49	2.59
Chess	2.20	2.49	30.75	1.32	1.41	2.88	1.39	1.45	3.48
Crypto	2.38	2.64	7.97	1.31	1.34	1.64	1.39	1.42	1.76
Sum	11.75	13.22	97.39	6.63	6.97	11.52	7.17	7.42	14.04

difficult-to-find bugs triggered only by proper coordination of the client and the server. ShadowVM enables fuzzing these distributed multi-platform applications, by analyzing the whole distributed application's state at once. For example, we can validate traces against a whole-application state machine; on failure, we report to the developer the unexpected next state, the current state, and the triggering input stream.

Figure 3 illustrates the state machine of a login routine. The login credentials are collected by an Android application and validated by a Java server. To avoid brute-force attacks, only three successive login attempts are allowed: the server counts the number of unsuccessful attempts, and will block the account once it exceeds three. During login, the user may also reset the password; the "Reset Password" sub-routine should not change the "Login Attempts" state.

Suppose the implementation of the server-side component violates this specification, by accidentally resetting the "Login Attempts" state after resetting the password. This would permit brute-force attacks by resetting the password every two login attempts. Such a bug is difficult to detect when fuzzing only client or server code in isolation. One must either "mock up" the remote party's interactions in a testing harness usable by the fuzzer or deal with the state-space explosion that can result from overapproximating this behaviour. By contrast, with ShadowVM we can easily fuzz the whole ensemble.

We will demonstrate fuzzing of the aforementioned distributed application (driven by Monkey) using a ShadowVM-based trace validation tool. In the observed virtual machines, events are produced for the login-related actions of both client (DVM) and server (JVM). In the analysis server, a state machine validates the event trace. The specification of the state machine is configurable such that the trace validation tool can analyze different applications.

5 Related Work

The baseline approach on which ShadowVM improves is explicit bytecode instrumentation. Various systems offering services and simple abstractions for this have

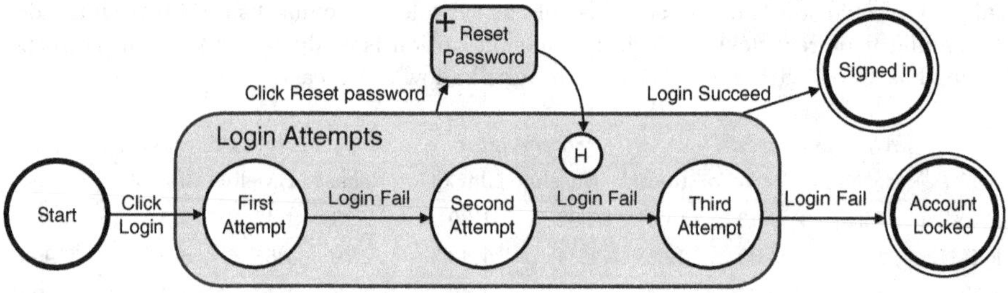

Fig. 3. State machine illustrating all possible login sequences.

been described in the literature [4,6,9,23], but in all cases direct manipulation of instructions, much lower-level than the aspect-oriented primitives proposed in DiSL [15], on which ShadowVM is based, and lack our framework's multi-platform capability. RoadRunner [8] offers a pipeline abstraction, but is specialized to the specific analysis domain of dynamic data-race detection.

Other research addresses the dynamic analysis of distributed systems. Pinpoint [5] aims to identify components correlated with failed requests in multi-tier JavaEE server systems, by tracking incoming requests using a unique identifier propagated along a request execution path. ARM [22] (Application Response Measurement) defines a standardized infrastructure for monitoring multi-tier enterprise applications, using tags to associate system behavior with individual requests. Magpie [2] allows analyzing server workloads and resource consumption of individual requests, enabling the construction of workload models for clusters of canonicalized requests. Aguilera et al. [1] use statistical methods to infer dominant causal paths in a distributed system, using only message-level traces.

The common denominator of these approaches is their use of events for the analysis of the system behavior. None of them focuses on the task of instrumentation and event production. In contrast, ShadowVM is primarily a framework providing easy-to-use event-producer and event-consumer programming models which can be used for implementing cross-platform distributed program analyses.

ShadowVM also relates to distributed aspect-oriented programming [16,18,21], which introduces the concept of a remote pointcut and allows deploying aspects on a set of hosts. In contrast, ShadowVM is primarily tailored for the development of dynamic analyses deployed on a single host, correlating events from potentially many observed hosts.

Existing fuzzing or active testing systems such as CalFuzzer [10] have tackled scenarios similar to our demonstration, with some degree of extensibility, but stop short of being general-purpose dynamic analysis frameworks. For example, CalFuzzer provides a fixed set of instrumentation callbacks that cover only synchronization and shared-memory operations.

6 Conclusions

We gave the first demonstration of our multi-platform dynamic program analysis framework ShadowVM, which reconciles a high-level programming model, expressiveness, complete bytecode coverage, and isolation of the analysis from the observed application. ShadowVM offers seamless support for both the JVM and the DVM; an analysis written for Java applications also supports Android applications out-of-the-box. As demonstrated before, one analysis server can handle the events of multiple observed JVM and DVM processes, enabling centralized analysis of distributed systems. Because the event consumer executes in a separate analysis server, ShadowVM implicitly parallelizes the execution of the observed application and the analysis. This approach also minimizes the extra memory requirements on the observed virtual machine, crucial for deploying heavyweight analyses on resource-constrained Android devices.

The design of ShadowVM also has some drawbacks. As shown in our performance evaluation, the analysis overhead is often higher than with straightforward analysis within the observed virtual machine. In particular, using Android SDK's ARM emulator results in excessive overhead. The newly supported deployment options (Android SDK x86 emulator and Android devices) mitigate this overhead. For the analysis of Android applications, a version-specific patch needs to be applied to the DVM first. The implicit conversion between JVM and DVM bytecode may introduce some bias in metrics related to individual bytecodes or basic blocks of code. As events are processed remotely and asynchronously by the analysis, ShadowVM is not suited for interactive debugging. Finally, our system cannot observe execution in native code.

ShadowVM is available as part of the DiSL 2.1 open-source release (http://disl.ow2.org/). DVM support is currently available as a prototype (http://dag.inf.usi.ch/downloads/); it will be part of the forthcoming DiSL 3.0 open-source release.

Acknowledgments. The research presented in this paper was supported by Oracle (ERO project 1332), by the Swiss National Science Foundation (project CRSII2_136225 and project 200021_141002), and by the European Commission (contract ACP2-GA-2013-605442).

References

1. Aguilera, M.K., Mogul, J.C., Wiener, J.L., Reynolds, P., Muthitacharoen, A.: Performance debugging for distributed systems of black boxes. In: Proceedings of the Nineteenth ACM Symposium on Operating Systems Principles. pp. 74–89. SOSP '03 (2003)
2. Barham, P., Donnelly, A., Isaacs, R., Mortier, R.: Using Magpie for request extraction and workload modelling. In: Proceedings of the 6th Conference on Symposium on Opearting Systems Design & Implementation. OSDI'04, vol. 6, p. 18 (2004)
3. Bird, D., Munoz, C.: Automatic generation of random self-checking test cases. IBM Syst. J. **22**(3), 229–245 (1983)
4. Bruneton, E., Lenglet, R., Coupaye, T.: Asm: a code manipulation tool to implement adaptable systems. In: Systémes á composants adaptables et extensibles (2002)

5. Chen, M.Y., Kiciman, E., Fratkin, E., Fox, A., Brewer, E.: Pinpoint: problem determination in large, dynamic internet services. In: Proceedings of the 2002 International Conference on Dependable Systems and Networks. DSN '02 (2002)
6. Chiba, S.: Load-time structural reflection in java. In: Bertino, E. (ed.) ECOOP 2000. LNCS, vol. 1850, pp. 313–336. Springer, Heidelberg (2000)
7. EclEmma: JaCoCo Java Code Coverage Library. http://www.eclemma.org/jacoco/
8. Flanagan, C., Freund, S.N.: The RoadRunner dynamic analysis framework for concurrent programs. In: Proceedings of 9th Workshop on Program Analysis for Software Tools and Engineering, pp. 1–8. ACM (2010)
9. IBM: Shrike Bytecode Instrumentation Library. http://wala.sourceforge.net/wiki/index.php/Shrike_technical_overview
10. Joshi, P., Naik, M., Park, C.-S., Sen, K.: CalFuzzer: an extensible active testing framework for concurrent programs. In: Bouajjani, A., Maler, O. (eds.) CAV 2009. LNCS, vol. 5643, pp. 675–681. Springer, Heidelberg (2009)
11. Kell, S., Ansaloni, D., Binder, W., Marek, L.: The JVM is not observable enough (and what to do about it). In: Proceedings of the Sixth ACM Workshop on Virtual Machines and Intermediate Languages. VMIL '12, pp. 33–38 (2012)
12. Radu, V.: Application. In: Radu, V. (ed.) Stochastic Modeling of Thermal Fatigue Crack Growth. ACM, vol. 1, pp. 63–70. Springer, Heidelberg (2015)
13. Marek, L., Zheng, Y., Ansaloni, D., Sarimbekov, A., Binder, W., Tůma, P., Qi, Z.: Java bytecode instrumentation made easy: the DiSL framework for dynamic program analysis. In: Jhala, R., Igarashi, A. (eds.) APLAS 2012. LNCS, vol. 7705, pp. 256–263. Springer, Heidelberg (2012)
14. Marek, L., Kell, S., Zheng, Y., Bulej, L., Binder, W., Tůma, P., Ansaloni, D., Sarimbekov, A., Sewe, A.: ShadowVM: robust and comprehensive dynamic program analysis for the java platform. In: Proceedings of the 12th International Conference on Generative Programming: Concepts and Experiences. GPCE '13, pp. 105–114 (2013)
15. Marek, L., Villazón, A., Zheng, Y., Ansaloni, D., Binder, W., Qi, Z.: DiSL: a domain-specific language for bytecode instrumentation. In: Proceedings of the 11th Annual International Conference on Aspect-oriented Software Development. AOSD '12, pp. 239–250 (2012)
16. Navarro, L.D.B., Südholt, M., Vanderperren, W., De Fraine, B., Suvée, D.: Explicitly distributed AOP using AWED. In: Proceedings of the 5th International Conference on Aspect-oriented Software Development. AOSD '06, pp. 51–62 (2006)
17. Nethercote, N., Seward, J.: Valgrind: a framework for heavyweight dynamic binary instrumentation. In: Proceedings of the 28th ACM SIGPLAN Conference on Programming Language Design and Implementation, pp. 89–100. ACM, New York, NY, USA (2007)
18. Nishizawa, M., Chiba, S., Tatsubori, M.: Remote pointcut: a language construct for distributed AOP. In: Proceedings of the 3rd International Conference on Aspect-oriented Software Development. AOSD '04, pp. 7–15 (2004)
19. Oracle: JVM Tool Interface (JVMTI) Version 1.2. http://docs.oracle.com/javase/8/docs/platform/jvmti/jvmti.html
20. Sun, H., Zheng, Y., Bulej, L., Villazón, A., Qi, Z., Tůma, P., Binder, W.: A programming model and framework for comprehensive dynamic analysis on Android. In: Proceedings of the 14th International Conference on Modularity. MODULARITY '15, pp. 133–145 (2015)

21. Tanter, É., Toledo, R.: A Versatile kernel for distributed AOP. In: Eliassen, F., Montresor, A. (eds.) DAIS 2006. LNCS, vol. 4025, pp. 316–331. Springer, Heidelberg (2006)
22. The open group: Application Response Measurement (ARM), Issue 4.1 Version 1. https://collaboration.opengroup.org/tech/management/arm/
23. Vallée-Rai, R. Co, P., Gagnon, E., Hendren, L., Lam, P., Sundaresan, V.: Soot: a java bytecode optimization framework. In: Proceedings of the 1999 Conference of the Centre for Advanced Studies on Collaborative Research. CASCON '99. IBM Press (1999)
24. Zheng, Y., Bulej, L., Binder, W.: Accurate profiling in the presence of dynamic compilation. In: Object-Oriented Programming, Systems, Languages & Applications. OOPSLA '15 (2015)

Medley

Quasi-Linearizability is Undecidable

Chao Wang[1,2(✉)], Yi Lv[1], Gaoang Liu[1,2], and Peng Wu[1]

[1] State Key Laboratory of Computer Science, Institute of Software, Chinese Academy of Sciences, Beijing, China
{wangch,lvyi,gaoang,wp}@ios.ac.cn
[2] University of Chinese Academy of Sciences, Beijing, China

Abstract. *Quasi-linearizability* is a quantitative relaxation of linearizability. It preserves the intuition of the standard notion of linearizability and permits more flexibility. The decidability of quasi-linearizability has been remaining open in general for a bounded number of processes. In this paper we show that the problem of whether a library is *quasi-linearizable* with respect to a regular sequential specification is undecidable for a bounded number of processes. This is proved by reduction from the k-Z decision problem of a k-counter machine, a known undecidable problem. The key idea of the proof is to establish a correspondence between the quasi-sequential specification of quasi-linearizability and the set of all unadmitted runs of the k-counter machines.

1 Introduction

A concurrent library provides a collection of methods for accessing a concurrent object. These methods can be invoked by multiple client processes concurrently. Linearizability [11] is a *de facto* correctness condition for concurrent libraries. A concurrent library is linearizable with respect to its sequential specification, if during any of its executions, each method appears to take effect instantaneously at some point between the invocation and the response of the method.

The standard notion of linearizability imposes a strong synchronization requirement that, in many cases, leads to performance and scalability bottlenecks and hence prevents effective utilization of increasingly parallel hardware. A remedy to this problem is to relax this consistency condition. Although there already exist other consistency conditions for concurrent libraries, such as sequential consistency [12] and quiescent consistency [4], these consistency conditions are less intuitive and allow unexpected behaviors. New relaxed consistency conditions have been proposed recently, including *quasi-linearizability* [2] and a quantitative relaxation framework [9]. These relaxed consistency conditions are essentially based on linearizability, therefore preserving the intuition of the standard linearizability while permitting more flexibility.

This work is partially supported by the National Natural Science Foundation of China under Grants No.60721061, No.60833001, No.61272135, No.61700073, No.61100069, No.61472405, and No.61161130530.

X. Feng and S. Park (Eds.): APLAS 2015, LNCS 9458, pp. 369–386, 2015.
DOI: 10.1007/978-3-319-26529-2_20

Quasi-linearizability is the first quantitative relaxation of linearizability. It extends the standard linearizability by relaxing the sequential specification to a *Q-quasi-sequential specification*. Such quantitative relaxation is guided by a *quasi-linearization factor* Q. Each element in the Q-quasi-sequential specification is a bounded distance away from a legal one. Therefore, the verification of quasi-linearizability needs to deal with not only the subtle difficulty of linearizability, but also that of the relaxed sequential specification.

It is well known that the problem of whether a library is linearizable with respect to its regular sequential specification is decidable for a bounded number of processes [3], but undecidable for an unbounded number of processes [5]. Since the standard linearizability is a special case of quasi-linearizability, it can be easily seen that the problem of whether a library is quasi-linearizable with respect to its regular sequential specification is also undecidable for an unbounded number of processes. For the case with a bounded number of processes, [1,13] have presented model-checking algorithm and runtime tool respectively to check quasi-linearizability with specific quasi-linearization factors. However, the problem of whether a library is quasi-linearizable with respect to a regular sequential specification still remains open in general for a bounded number of processes.

The main result of this paper is to show that the problem of whether a library is quasi-linearizable with respect to a regular sequential specification (quasi-linearizability problem) is undecidable for a bounded number of processes. Our proof can be divided into two parts.

In the first part we reduce the k-Z decision problem of a k-counter machine [3] to the problem of whether a specific concurrent library is linearizable with respect to its sequential specification (linearizability problem) for just one process. The k-Z problem is to decide whether a k-counter machine has an admitted run. This problem is known to be undecidable for $k \geq 3$ [3]. As inspired by the proof of Lemma 5 in [3], the k-Z decision problem can be reduced to a language inclusion problem between two language R and S. R is a prefix-closed regular language constructed from the k-counter machine. S is a non-regular language and it contains all the unadmitted runs of k-counter machine, together with their prefixes. A specific library $\mathcal{L}_R$ can then be constructed to simulate sequentially each sequence of R. Thus, the language inclusion problem can be reduced to the linearizability problem of $\mathcal{L}_R$ for just one process with respect to a non-regular sequential specification constructed from S.

In the second part we prove that the above linearizability problem can then be reduced to a quasi-linearizability problem of the same library for just one process. The quasi-linearizability problem uses a regular sequential specification and a proper quasi-linearization factor. Since the quasi-linearizability problem of the specific library $\mathcal{L}_R$ for one process is equivalent to that for a bounded number of processes, the k-Z decision problem is further reduced to quasi-linearizability problem with respect to a regular sequential specification for a bounded number of processes.

Related Work. There are already several publications on the decidability of linearizability and other consistency conditions [3,5,6,8], two of which are related to our work.

Bouajjani *et al.* [5] proved that the problem of whether a library is linearizable with respect to its regular sequential specification is undecidable for an unbounded number of processes. This was proved through a reduction from an undecidable problem of a counter machine.

The closer work to ours is [3] by Alur *et al.*, which proves that the linearizability of a regular history set with respect to a regular sequential specification is decidable for a bounded number of processes, but its sequential consistency is not. The proofs in [3] rely on the notion of the language closure over a dependency relation. Given a binary dependency relation D over an alphabet Σ, the closure of a language $L \subseteq \Sigma^*$ is the set of all sequences that are obtained from a sequence $l \in L$ by shuffling any adjacent symbols a and b in l such that $(a, b) \notin D$. It may sound possible to encode a dependency relation directly by a quasi-linearization factor Q, which allows shuffling of adjacent independent symbols within certain bound. In this way, the undecidability of quasi-linearizability could be regarded as a corollary of Lemma 5 in [3].

However, unfortunately, there exists a dependency relation that can not be characterized by any quasi-linearization factor, e.g., a dependency relation for sequential consistency. This is because that sequential consistency permits shuffling only symbols of different processes and hence does not allow any shuffling when a history contains only one process. In contrast, relaxations of quasi-linearizability are irrelevant to the number of processes a history may contain. Thus, if a quasi-linearization factor Q permits shuffling symbols of more than one process, it should also permit shuffling symbols of a single process. Based on this observation, the undecidable result of Lemma 5 in [3] can not be directly applied to establish the undecidability of quasi-linearizability.

Adhikari *et al.* [1] proposed a model-checking algorithm for verification of the quasi-linearizability that uses a specific quasi-linearization factor. Zhang *et al.* [13] developed a runtime tool to verify quasi-linearizability with respect to the relaxed sequential specifications that are based on the *strict out-of-order semantics* defined in [2,9]. Both works consider only decidable subclasses of the quasi-linearizability problem.

2 Concurrent Systems

In this section, we present the notations of libraries, the most general clients and concurrent systems. We then introduce their operational semantics.

2.1 Notations

A finite sequence on an alphabet Σ is denoted as $l = \alpha_1 \cdot \alpha_2 \cdot \ldots \cdot \alpha_k$, where $\cdot$ is the concatenation symbol and $\alpha_i \in \Sigma$ for each $1 \leq i \leq k$. For an alphabet Σ', let $l \uparrow_{\Sigma'}$ denote the projection of l to Σ'. Given a set S of sequences, we use $\mathit{Prefix}(S) = \{a_1 \cdot \ldots \cdot a_m | \exists u \text{ and } a_{m+1}, \ldots, a_{m+u}, \text{ such that } a_1 \cdot \ldots \cdot a_{m+u} \in S\}$ to denote the set of prefixes of sequences in S. Given a function f, let $f[x : y]$ be the function that shares the same value as f everywhere, except for x, where it has the value y. Given a function $f : \mathcal{A} \rightarrow \mathcal{B}$, we use $domain(f)$ to denote the domain of f, which is $\mathcal{A}$. We use $\_$ for an item, of which the value is irrelevant.

A *labelled transition system* (LTS) is a tuple $\mathcal{A} = (Q, \Sigma, \rightarrow, q_{init})$, where Q is a set of states, Σ is a set of transition labels, $\rightarrow \subseteq Q \times \Sigma \times Q$ is a transition relation and q_{init} is the initial state. A state of the LTS $\mathcal{A}$ can be refer to as a *configuration* in the rest of the paper. A path of $\mathcal{A}$ is a finite transition sequence $q_{init} \xrightarrow{\beta_1} q_1 \xrightarrow{\beta_2} \ldots \xrightarrow{\beta_k} q_k$ for $k \geq 0$ from the initial state q_{init}. A trace of $\mathcal{A}$ is a finite sequence $t = \beta_1 \cdot \beta_2 \cdot \ldots \cdot \beta_k$, where $k \geq 0$ if there exists a path $q_{init} \xrightarrow{\beta_1} q_1 \xrightarrow{\beta_2} \ldots \xrightarrow{\beta_k} q_k$ of $\mathcal{A}$.

2.2 Libraries and the Most General Clients

A library implementing a concurrent object that provides a set of methods for external users to access the data structure. It may contain private memory locations for its own use. A client program is a program that interacts with libraries. For simplicity, we assume that each method has just one parameter and one return value if it returns. Furthermore, all the parameters and the return values are passed via a specific register r_f.

For a library, let $\mathcal{X}$ be a finite set of its memory locations, $\mathcal{M}$ be a finite set of its method names, $\mathcal{D}$ be its finite data domain, $\mathcal{R}$ be a finite set of its register names and $\mathcal{RE}$ be a finite set of its register expressions over $\mathcal{R}$. Then, a set $PCom$ of primitive commands of the library includes:

- Register assign commands in the form of $r = re$;
- Register reset commands in the form of *havoc*;
- Read commands in the form of $read\ (x, r)$;
- Write commands in the form of $write(r, x)$;
- *Cas* commands in the form of $r_1 = cas(x, r_2, r_3)$;
- Assume commands in the form of $assume(r)$;
- Call commands in the form of $call(m)$;

where $r, r_1, r_2, r_3 \in \mathcal{R}$, $re \in \mathcal{RE}, x \in \mathcal{X}$. Herein, the notations of registers and register expressions are similar to those used in [7]. A *cas* command compresses a read and a write commands into a single one, which is meant to be executed atomically. It is often implemented with the compare-and-swap or load-linked/store-conditional primitive at the level of multiprocessors. This type of commands is widely used in concurrent libraries. A *havoc* command [7] assigns arbitrary values to all registers in $\mathcal{R}$.

A control-flow graph is a tuple $CFG = (N, L, T, q_i, q_f)$, where N is a finite set of program positions, L is a set of primitive commands, $T \subseteq N \times L \times N$ is a control-flow transition relation, q_i is the initial position and q_f is the final position.

A library $\mathcal{L}$ can then be defined as a tuple $\mathcal{L} = (Q_{\mathcal{L}}, \rightarrow_{\mathcal{L}}, InitV_{\mathcal{L}})$, such that $Q_{\mathcal{L}} = \bigcup_{m \in \mathcal{M}} Q_m$ is a finite set of program positions, where Q_m is the program positions of a method m of this library; $\rightarrow_{\mathcal{L}} = \bigcup_{m \in \mathcal{M}} \rightarrow_m$ is a control-flow transition relation, where for each $m \in \mathcal{M}$, $(Q_m, PCom, \rightarrow_m, i_m, f_m)$ is a control-flow graph with a unique initial position i_m and a unique final position f_m; $InitV_{\mathcal{L}} : \mathcal{X} \rightarrow \mathcal{D}$ is an initial valuation for its memory locations.

The most general client of a library is a special client program that is used to exhibit all possible behavior of the library. Formally, the most general client $\mathcal{MGC}$ of library $\mathcal{L}$ is defined as a tuple $(\{q_c, q_c'\}, \rightarrow_c)$, where q_c and q_c' are two program positions, $\rightarrow_c = \{(q_c, havoc, q_c')\} \cup \{(q_c', call(m), q_c) | m \in \mathcal{M}\}$ is a control-flow transition relation and $(\{q_c, q_c'\}, PCom, \rightarrow_c, q_c, q_c)$ is a control-flow graph. Intuitively, the most general client repeatedly calls an arbitrary method with an arbitrary argument for arbitrarily many times.

2.3 Operational Semantics of Concurrent Systems

In this paper we consider a concurrent system consists of a bounded number of processes, each of which runs the most general client program of a library on a separate processor. Then, the operational semantics of a library can be defined in the context of the concurrent system.

For a library $\mathcal{L}=(Q_{\mathcal{L}}, \rightarrow_{\mathcal{L}}, InitV_{\mathcal{L}})$ and a positive integer n, its operational semantics is defined as an LTS $[\![\mathcal{L}, n]\!]_{cs} = (Conf_{cs}, \Sigma_{cs}, \rightarrow_{cs}, InitConf_{cs})$, where '$cs$' represents concurrent system, and $Conf_{cs}, \Sigma_{cs}, \rightarrow_{cs}, InitConf_{cs}$ are defined as follows.

Each configuration of $Conf_{cs}$ is a tuple (p, d, r), where

- $p : \{1, \ldots, n\} \rightarrow \{q_c, q_c'\} \cup Q_{\mathcal{L}}$ represents control states of each process;
- $d : \mathcal{X} \rightarrow \mathcal{D}$ represents values at each memory location;
- $r : \{1, \ldots, n\} \rightarrow (\mathcal{R} \rightarrow \mathcal{D})$ represents values of the registers of each process.

Σ_{cs} consists of the following subsets of actions as transition labels.

- Internal actions: $\{\tau(i) | 1 \leq i \leq n\}$;
- Read actions: $\{read(i, x, a) | 1 \leq i \leq n, x \in \mathcal{X}, a \in \mathcal{D}\}$;
- Write actions: $\{write(i, x, a) | 1 \leq i \leq n, x \in \mathcal{X}, a \in \mathcal{D}\}$;
- *Cas* actions: $\{cas(i, x, a, b) |\ 1 \leq i \leq n, x \in \mathcal{X}, a, b \in \mathcal{D}\}$;
- Call actions: $\{call(i, m, a) | 1 \leq i \leq n, m \in \mathcal{M}, a \in \mathcal{D}\}$;
- Return actions: $\{return(i, m, a) | 1 \leq i \leq n, m \in \mathcal{M}, a \in \mathcal{D}\}$;

The initial configuration $InitConf_{cs} \in Conf_{cs}$ is a tuple $(p_{init}, InitV_{\mathcal{L}}, r_{init})$, where $p_{init}(i) = q_c$ and $r_{init}(i)(r) = regV_{init}$ (a specific initial value of register) for $1 \leq i \leq n$, $r \in \mathcal{R}$;

The transition relation $\rightarrow_{cs}$ is the least relation satisfying the transition rules shown in Fig. 1.

- *Register-Assign* rule: A function $f_{re} : (\mathcal{R} \rightarrow \mathcal{D}) \times \mathcal{RE} \rightarrow \mathcal{D}$ is used to evaluate register expression re under register valuation rv of current process, and its value is assigned to register r_1.
- *Library-Havoc* and *$\mathcal{MGC}$-Havoc* rules: *havoc* commands are executed for libraries and the most general clients respectively.
- *Assume* rule: If the value of register r_1 is *true*, current process can execute *assume* command. Otherwise, it must wait.

- *Read* and *Write* rules: A read action to memory location x will take the value of x in memory, and a write action to memory location x will change the value of x in memory directly.
- *Cas-Success* and *Cas-Fail* rules: A successful *cas* command will change the value of memory location x immediately. The result of whether this *cas* command succeeds is stored in register r_1.
- *Call* and *Return* rules: To deal with *call* command, current process starts to execute the initial position of method m. When the process comes to the final position of method m it can launch a return action and start to execute the most general client.

$$\frac{p(i) = q_1, q_1 \xrightarrow{r_1 = re}_{\mathcal{L}} q_2, r(i) = rv, f_{re}(rv, re) = a}{(p, d, r) \xrightarrow{\tau(i)}_{cs} (p[i : q_2], d, r[i : rv[r_1 : a]])} \textit{Register-Assign}$$

$$\frac{p(i) = q_1, q_1 \xrightarrow{havoc}_{\mathcal{L}} q_2, rv \in \mathcal{R} \rightarrow \mathcal{D}}{(p, d, r) \xrightarrow{\tau(i)}_{cs} (p[i : q_2], d, r[i : rv])} \textit{Library-Havoc}$$

$$\frac{p(i) = q_c, rv \in \mathcal{R} \rightarrow \mathcal{D}}{(p, d, r) \xrightarrow{\tau(i)}_{cs} (p[i : q_c'], d, r[i : rv])} \mathcal{MGC}\textit{-Havoc}$$

$$\frac{p(i) = q_1, q_1 \xrightarrow{assume(r_1)}_{\mathcal{L}} q_2, r(i)(r_1) = true}{(p, d, r) \xrightarrow{\tau(i)}_{cs} (p[i : q_2], d, r)} \textit{Assume}$$

$$\frac{p(i) = q_1, q_1 \xrightarrow{read(x, r_1)}_{\mathcal{L}} q_2, r(i) = rv, d(x) = a}{(p, d, r) \xrightarrow{read(i, x, a)}_{cs} (p[i : q_2], d, r[i : rv[r_1 : a]])} \textit{Read}$$

$$\frac{p(i) = q_1, q_1 \xrightarrow{write(r_1, x)}_{\mathcal{L}} q_2, r(i)(r_1) = a}{(p, d, r) \xrightarrow{write(i, x, a)}_{cs} (p[i : q_2], d[x : a], r)} \textit{Write}$$

$$\frac{p(i) = q_1, q_1 \xrightarrow{r_1 = cas(x, r_2, r_3)}_{\mathcal{L}} q_2, r(i) = rv, rv(r_2) = d(x) = a, rv(r_3) = b}{(p, d, r) \xrightarrow{cas(i, x, a, b)}_{cs} (p[i : q_2], d[x : b], r[i : rv[r_1 : true]])} \textit{Cas-Success}$$

$$\frac{p(i) = q_1, q_1 \xrightarrow{r_1 = cas(x, r_2, r_3)}_{\mathcal{L}} q_2, r(i) = rv, rv(r_2) = a, rv(r_3) = b, rv(r_2) \neq d(x)}{(p, d, r) \xrightarrow{cas(i, x, a, b)}_{cs} (p[i : q_2], d, r[i : rv[r_1 : false]])} \textit{Cas-Fail}$$

$$\frac{p(i) = q_c', r(i)(r_f) = a}{(p, d, r) \xrightarrow{call(i, m, a)}_{cs} (p[i : i_m], d, r)} \textit{Call}$$

$$\frac{p(i) = f_m, r(i)(r_f) = a}{(p, d, r) \xrightarrow{return(i, m, a)}_{cs} (p[i : q_c], d, r)} \textit{Return}$$

Fig. 1. Transition rules of $\rightarrow_{cs}$

3 Linearizability and Quasi-Linearizability

In this section, we introduce the definitions of linearizability and quasi-linearizability.

3.1 Linearizability

Linearizability is a standard correctness condition for concurrent libraries. According to [11], linearizability is a local property in the sense that a concurrent program that contains multiple concurrent libraries and client processes does not violate linearizability if each individual library does not violate linearizability. Therefore, it is safe for us to introduce the definition of linearizability using the operational semantics $[\![\mathcal{L}, n]\!]_{cs}$, which consider the behavior of only one library.

The behavior of a library is typically represented by histories of interactions between library and the clients calling it (through call and return actions). Let Σ_{cal} and Σ_{ret} represent the sets of all call and return actions, respectively. Given an *LTS* $\mathcal{A} = (Q_{\mathcal{A}}, \Sigma_{\mathcal{A}}, \rightarrow_{\mathcal{A}}, q_{\mathcal{A}})$, a finite sequence $h \in (\Sigma_{cal} \cup \Sigma_{ret})^*$ is a history of $\mathcal{A}$ if there exists a trace t of $\mathcal{A}$ such that $t \uparrow_{(\Sigma_{cal} \cup \Sigma_{ret})} = h$. Let *history*($\mathcal{A}$) denote all the histories of $\mathcal{A}$.

In a history, a return action $return(i_1, m_1, a_1)$ matches a call action $call(i_2, m_2, a_2)$, if $i_1 = i_2 \wedge m_1 = m_2$. A history is sequential if it starts with a call action and each call (respectively, return) action is immediately followed by a matching return (respectively, a call) action unless it is the last action. A process subhistory $h|_i$ is a history consisting of all and only the actions of process i. A history h is *well-formed*, if each process subhistory $h|_i$ of h is sequential. All histories considered in this paper are assumed to be well-formed. Two histories h_1 and h_2 are equivalent, if for each process i, $h_1|_i = h_2|_i$. Given a history h, *complete*(h) is the maximal subsequence of h consisting of all matching call and return actions. An operation e in a history is a pair consisting of a call action, *inv*(e), and the next matching return action, *res*(e).

A sequential specification of a library is a prefix closed set of sequential histories. A history h is *linearizable* with respect to a sequential specification S, if h can be extended (by appending zero or more return actions) to a history h', and there exists a sequential history $s \in S$, such that

- *complete*(h') is equivalent to s.
- For each operations e_1, e_2 of h, if *res*(e_1) precedes *inv*(e_2) in h, then this also holds in s.

Definition 1 (Linearizability [11]**).** *A library $\mathcal{L}$ is linearizable with respect to a sequential specification S for n processes, if each history of $[\![\mathcal{L}, n]\!]_{cs}$ is linearizable with respect to S.*

It is natural to assume that for a sequential history $call(i_1, m_1, a_1) \cdot return(i_1, m_1, b_1) \cdot \ldots \cdot call(i_u, m_u, a_u) \cdot return(i_u, m_u, b_u)$ in a sequential specification, each process id i_j ($1 \leq j \leq u$) is actually irrelevant. Thus we can substitute each pair of a call action $call(i, m, a)$ and its matching return action $return(i, m, b)$ with $m(a, b)$. For a library $\mathcal{L}$, let $\Sigma_{spec} = \{m(a, b) | \ m \in \mathcal{M}, a, b \in \mathcal{D}\}$, a sequential specification for $\mathcal{L}$ can also be given as a prefix closed subset of Σ^*_{spec}, as shown in [2].

Then, the notion of linearizability can be accordingly redefined over Σ^*_{spec}. A history h is linearizable with respect to a sequential specification $S \subseteq \Sigma^*_{spec}$, if there exists $m_1(a_1, b_1) \cdot \ldots \cdot m_u(a_u, b_u) \in S$, h can be extended (by appending zero or more return actions) to a history h', and there is a sequential history $s = call(i_1, m_1, a_1) \cdot return(i_1, m_1, b_1) \cdot \ldots \cdot call(i_u, m_u, a_u) \cdot return(i_u, m_u, b_u)$, such that

- $complete(h')$ is equivalent to s.
- For each operation e_1, e_2 of h, if $res(e_1)$ precedes $inv(e_2)$ in h, then this also holds in s.

A library $\mathcal{L}$ is *linearizable* with respect to a sequential specification $S \subseteq \Sigma^*_{spec}$ for n processes, if each history of $[\![\mathcal{L}, n]\!]_{cs}$ is linearizable with respect to S. To comply with the definitions in [2], all the sequential specifications in the rest of this paper are prefix closed subsets of Σ^*_{spec}. Given a library $\mathcal{L}$, a sequential specification S and a positive integer n, the decision problem of linearizability is to determine whether $\mathcal{L}$ is linearizable with respect to S for n processes.

3.2 Quasi-Linearizability

Quasi-Linearizability [2] is a quantitative relaxation of linearizability. Quasi-linearizablity is also a local property [2]. Hence, as in the previous subsection, it is safe for us to introduce the definition of quasi-linearizability using the operational semantics $[\![\mathcal{L}, n]\!]_{cs}$.

For each element α in a sequence l, we use $l[\alpha]$ to denote its index. Given two sequences $l_1, l_2 \in \Sigma^*_{spec}$, where l_1 is a permutation of l_2, we use $distance(l_1, l_2) = max\{l_1[\alpha] - l_2[\alpha] | \ \alpha \text{ is in } l_1\}$ to represent the distance between l_1 and l_2. A *quasi-linearization factor* Q is a function defined as $Q : D \rightarrow \mathcal{N}$, where D is a subset of the power set of Σ_{spec}. A quasi-linearization factor is used to guide the relaxation of quasi-linearizability. Given a sequential specification $S \subseteq \Sigma^*_{spec}$ and a quasi-linearization factor Q, the *Q-quasi-sequential specification* $Q\text{-}spec(S) \subseteq \Sigma^*_{spec}$ is the relaxation of S guided by Q. A sequence h is in $Q\text{-}spec(S)$, if there exists a sequence $s \in S$ and h', such that h is a prefix of h' and for any $d \in domain(Q)$, $distance(h' \uparrow_d, s \uparrow_d) \leq Q(d)$. Each Q-quasi sequential specification $Q\text{-}spec(S)$ is also prefix closed. Given a quasi-linearization factor Q, a history h is *Q-quasi-linearizable* with respect to a sequential specification S, if there exists a sequential history $s = call(i_1, m_1, a_1) \cdot return(i_1, m_1, b_1) \cdot \ldots \cdot call(i_u, m_u, a_u) \cdot return(i_u, m_u, b_u)$ (referred to as *the quasi-linearization of* h), such that $m_1(a_1, b_1) \cdot \ldots \cdot m_u(a_u, b_u) \in Q\text{-}spec(S)$, h can be extended (by appending zero or more return actions) to a history h', and

- *complete*(h') is equivalent to s.
- For each operation e_1, e_2 of h, if *res*(e_1) precedes *inv*(e_2) in h, then this also holds in s.

Definition 2 (***Q-quasi-linearizability*** [2]). *A library $\mathcal{L}$ is Q-quasi-linearizable with respect to a sequential specification S for n processes, if each history of $[\![\mathcal{L}, n]\!]_{cs}$ is Q-quasi-linearizable with respect to S.*

Let Q_{lin} be a quasi-linearization factor, whose domain contains only the element Σ_{spec}. Specially, it maps Σ_{spec} to 0. It is easy to see that Q_{lin}-quasi-linearizability is equivalent to the standard notion of linearizability. One feature of Q-quasi-linearizability is that it allows specifying different deviations to different subsets of Σ_{spec}. For example, a Q-quasi-linearizable queue may have accurate dequeue operations but inaccurate enqueue operations that can bypass at most k preceding enqueue operations [2]. This feature captures the flexibility of possible relaxations, but it also leads to the undecidability result that will be proved in the later section. In the rest of this paper, Q-quasi-linearizability and a Q-quasi-sequential specification are abbreviated as quasi-linearizability and a quasi-sequential specification, respectively, if the context is clear. Given a library $\mathcal{L}$, a sequential specification S, a quasi-linearization factor Q and a positive integer n, the decision problem of quasi-linearizability is to determine whether $\mathcal{L}$ is Q-quasi-linearizable with respect to S for n processes.

4 Undecidability of Quasi-Linearizability

As the main result of this paper, we show in this section that the quasi-linearizability problem is undecidable with respect to a regular sequential specification for a bounded number of processes. We first reduce the k-Z decision problem of a k-counter machine to a linearizability problem of a specific concurrent library for one process. Then, our main undecidability result follows from the correspondence between the linearizability problem and the quasi-linearizability problem of the same library for one process. Since the quasi-linearizability problem of the specific library for one process is equivalent to that for multiple processes, the k-Z decision problem is finally reduced to the quasi-linearizability problem for a bounded number of processes.

4.1 *k*-Counter Machine

The control of a k-counter machine is a finite state automaton, whose alphabet is made up of increment, decrement and test operations to each counter [3]. Let $\Sigma_{ck} = \{I_j, D_j, Z_j | 1 \leq j \leq k\}$ be the set of operations for each counter, where I_j, D_j and Z_j respectively represent the operations for increasing the value of counter j by 1, decreasing the value of counter j by 1 and testing whether the value of counter j is 0. A k-counter machine is a finite state automaton $CM = (Q_{cm}, q_{icm}, F_{cm}, \Sigma_{cm}, \rightarrow_{cm})$, where Q_{cm} is a set of control states, q_{icm} is the initial state, F_{cm} is a set of final states, $\Sigma_{cm} = \Sigma_{ck}$ is a set of transition labels and $\rightarrow_{cm} \subseteq Q_{cm} \times \Sigma_{cm} \times Q_{cm}$ is a transition relation.

Given a finite sequence $l \in \Sigma_{ck}^*$, we use $c_{l,j} = |l \uparrow_{\{I_j\}}| - |l \uparrow_{\{D_j\}}|$ to denote the difference between the numbers of increments and decrements to counter j. We say that a sequence $l \in \Sigma_{ck}^*$ is *admitted*, if for each j and each prefix $l' \cdot Z_j$ $(1 \leq j \leq k)$ of l, $c_{l',j} = 0$. Otherwise, this sequence is *unadmitted*. A k-counter machine *CM* accepts a finite sequence $\alpha_1 \cdot \ldots \cdot \alpha_m$, if there exists states $q_1, \ldots, q_m$, such that $q_m \in F_{cm}$ and $q_{icm} \xrightarrow{\alpha_1}_{cm} q_1 \xrightarrow{\alpha_2}_{cm} \ldots \xrightarrow{\alpha_m}_{cm} q_m$. Let *lang*(*CM*) denotes the language of *CM*, that is, *lang*(*CM*) contains exactly all the sequences that are accepted by *CM*. The *k*-*Z* decision problem is to determine, for a given k-counter machine *CM*, whether there exists an admitted sequence $l \in$ *lang*(*CM*). According to [3], the *k*-*Z* decision problem is undecidable, as stated in the following lemma.

Lemma 1 (Undecidability [3]**).** *The k-Z decision problem is undecidable for* $k \geq 3$.

4.2 Libraries for Prefix Closed Regular Languages

For a finite state automaton R that accepts a prefix closed regular language and whose states are all final states, we can simulate R by the behavior of a specific library $\mathcal{L}_R$ that is constructed based on R.

Formally, given a finite state automaton $R = (Q_r, q_{ir}, F_r, \Sigma_r, \rightarrow_r)$, where Q_r is a set of states, q_{ir} is the initial state, $F_r = Q_r$ is a set of final states, Σ_r is a set of transition labels and $\rightarrow_r$ is a transition relation, the library $\mathcal{L}_R$ is constructed as follows:

- the data domain of $\mathcal{L}_R$ is $Q_r \cup \Sigma_r \cup \{0, 1, \mathit{true}, \mathit{false}, \mathit{regV}_{\mathit{init}}\}$;
- $\mathcal{L}_R$ has two private memory locations *curState* and *flag*. *curState* is used to record the current control state of R, while *flag* is used to ensure mutual exclusion accesses. The initial value of *curState* is q_{ir} and the initial value of *flag* is 0;
- $\mathcal{L}_R$ has one method M, of which the pseudo-code is shown in Method 1. The *if* and *while* statements used in the pseudo-code can be easily implemented with the *assume* commands and other commands in $\mathcal{L}_R$.

The critical section of method M is the region from a successful *cas* command at Line 1 to the *flag* $= 0$ command at Line 5. M first waits until it enters the critical section (Lines 1–2). If there exists one step of transition in R starting from *curState* (Line 3), M changes the value of *curState* according to this transition, leaves the critical section and returns the transition label (Lines 4–6). Otherwise, M is blocked (Lines 7–9).

The pseudo-code in Lines 1–2, where a *cas* operation is used, together with the pseudo-code at Line 5, ensure the mutual exclusion between invocations of this method.[1] We use *lang*(R) to denote the language of R.

[1] Except the *cas* operation, other operations, such as filter lock [10] can also be used herein to ensure mutual exclusion.

Method 1. M

Input: an arbitrary argument
Output: transition label for one step in R

```
while cas(flag, 0, 1) fails do
    ;
if there exists some q, α, such that curState —α→_r q then
    curState = q;
    flag = 0;
    return α;
else
    while true do
        ;
```

4.3 Reducing a k-Z Decision Problem to a Linearizability Problem

In this subsection we show that the k-Z decision problem of a k-counter machine can be reduced to the linearizability problem of a specific library for one process with respect to a non-regular sequential specification. This reduction is achieved with the aid of a language inclusion problem.

It is not hard to see that the set of all unadmitted sequences is far beyond the scope of regular languages. Fortunately, according to [3], there is a regular set of "templates" corresponding to the set of all unadmitted sequences. For instance, the unadmitted sequence $l = I_1 \cdot I_2 \cdot I_1 \cdot I_1 \cdot D_1 \cdot D_1 \cdot Z_1 \cdot D_2 \cdot Z_2$ contains a minimal unadmitted prefix $l' = I_1 \cdot I_2 \cdot I_1 \cdot I_1 \cdot D_1 \cdot D_1 \cdot Z_1$. Let l'' be the projection of l' to counter 1, i.e., $l'' = I_1 \cdot I_1 \cdot I_1 \cdot D_1 \cdot D_1 \cdot Z_1$. It can be seen that l'' is also unadmitted. The template for l can be constructed as the concatenation of two parts. The first part, $I_1 \cdot D_1 \cdot I_1 \cdot D_1 \cdot I_1 \cdot Z_1$, is constructed from l'' by swapping the locations of I_1 and D_1. Such swapping tries to pair as many matching I_1 and D_1 as possible in the beginning of the sequence, while ensuring that $I_1 s$ and $D_1 s$ do not cross Z_1. The second part, $I_2 \cdot D_2 \cdot Z_2$, is the rest contents of l.

Formally, the regular set of templates for the set of all unadmitted sequences of k-counter machines is

$$\bigcup_{j=1}^{k}(((I_j \cdot D_j)^* \cdot Z_j^*)^* \cdot (I_j \cdot D_j)^* \cdot (I_j^+ + D_j^+) \cdot Z_j \cdot \Sigma_{ck}^*)$$

where $\bigcup_{j=1}^{k} \mathcal{A}_j = \mathcal{A}_1 + \ldots + \mathcal{A}_k$. Since this template set will be used later to construct prefix closed sequential specifications, we further extended it to a prefix closed regular language

$$k\text{-}US = \Sigma_{ck}^* + \bigcup_{j=1}^{k}(((I_j \cdot D_j)^* \cdot Z_j^*)^* \cdot (I_j \cdot D_j)^* \cdot (I_j^+ + D_j^+) \cdot Z_j \cdot \Sigma_{ck}^* \cdot end)$$

where '*US*' represents that this set can be considered as the specification for all unadmitted sequences.

The set $Q_k = \{\{I_j, Z_j\}, \{D_j, Z_j\} | 1 \leq j \leq k\} \cup \{\{end, act\} | act \in \Sigma_{ck}\}$ will be used to guide the relaxation to k-*US*, which ensures that each increment and decrement operation can not cross a test operation to the same counter, and each operation in Σ_{ck} can not cross the *end* symbol. The relaxation to k-*US* guided by Q_k is the set Q_k-*set*(k-*US*) $= \{l | \exists l' \in k\text{-}US, \forall d \in Q_k, l \uparrow_d = l' \uparrow_d\}$. Each element l of Q_k-*set*(k-*US*) is either a sequence in Σ_{ck}^* or the concatenation of an unadmitted sequence and the *end* symbol. Moreover, for each unadmitted sequence l, $l \cdot end$ is a member of Q_k-*set*(k-*US*).

Although the language of a k-counter machine may not be prefix closed, we can construct a prefix closed regular language for a k-counter machine. Later, a specific library will be constructed from this language (automaton) and used as a bridge to connect a language inclusion problem and a linearizability problem. Given a k-counter machine $CM = (Q_{cm}, q_{icm}, F_{cm}, \Sigma_{cm}, \rightarrow_{cm})$, we construct the finite state automaton $R_{CM} = (Q, q_i, F, \Sigma, \rightarrow)$ as follows:

- $Q = Q_{cm} \cup \{q_{end}\}$ is the set of states, where q_{end} is a new state not in Q_{cm}.
- $q_i = q_{icm}$ is the initial state.
- $F = Q$ is the set of final states.
- $\Sigma = \Sigma_{cm} \cup \{end\}$ is the set of transition labels, where *end* is a new transition label not in Σ_{cm}.
- $\rightarrow = \rightarrow_{cm} \cup \{(q_f, end, q_{end}) | q_f \in F_{cm}\}$ is the transition relation.

Given a set S of sequences, let $S \cdot a = \{l | \exists l' \in S, l = l' \cdot a\}$ denote the set of concatenations of sequences in S and a symbol a. It is not hard to see that the language of R_{CM}, denoted as *lang*(R_{CM}), is the union of

- *lang*(*CM*) $\cdot$ *end*,
- $\{\alpha_1 \cdot \ldots \cdot \alpha_m | \exists q_1, \ldots, q_m, q_{icm} \xrightarrow{\alpha_1}_{cm} q_1 \xrightarrow{\alpha_2}_{cm} q_2 \cdots \xrightarrow{\alpha_m}_{cm} q_m\}$.

It can be seen that *lang*(R_{CM}) is a prefix closed language.

Figure 2 shows an example R_{CM} that is generated from a k-counter machine *CM*. The counter machine *CM* has four states: q_1, q_2, q_3, and q_4, the last two of which are final states. During the construction of this R_{CM}, we add a new state q_{end} and two additional transitions from q_3 and q_4 to q_{end}, and make all states as final states.

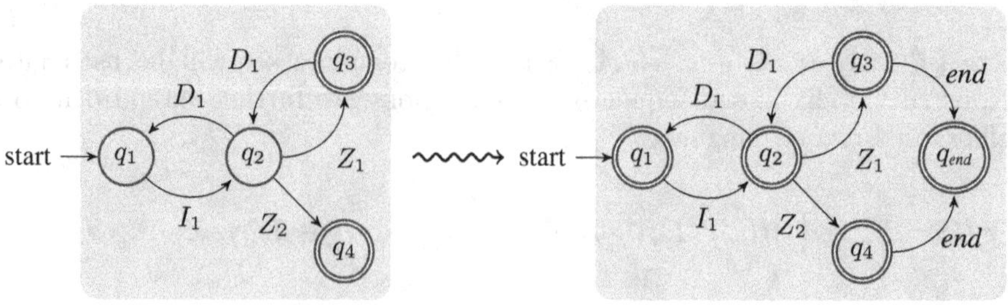

Fig. 2. Generation of R_{CM} from a counter machine *CM*

The following lemma reduces the k-Z decision problem of a k-counter machine CM to the language inclusion problem between $lang(R_{CM})$ and Q_k-$set(k$-$US)$.

Lemma 2. *Given a k-counter machine CM, all the sequences in lang(CM) are not admitted if and only if* $lang(R_{CM}) \subseteq Q_k$-$set(k$-$US)$.

Proof. To prove the *if* direction, for each sequence $l \in lang(CM)$, it is easy to find that $l \cdot end$ is in $lang(R_{CM})$. By assumption, $l \cdot end$ also belongs to Q_k-$set(k$-$US)$. It is obvious that each sequence ending with an *end* symbol in Q_k-$set(k$-$US)$ is a concatenation of an unadmitted sequence and an *end* symbol, so l is not admitted.

To prove the *only if* direction, given a counter machine $CM = (Q_{cm}, q_{icm}, F_{cm}, \Sigma_{cm}, \rightarrow_{cm})$, then for each sequence $l = \alpha_1 \cdot \ldots \cdot \alpha_m \in lang(R_{CM})$, we can observe that

- If $\alpha_m \neq end$ and there exists $q_1, \ldots, q_m$, such that $q_{icm} \xrightarrow{\alpha_1}_{cm} q_1 \xrightarrow{\alpha_2}_{cm} \ldots \xrightarrow{\alpha_m}_{cm} q_m$, then $l \in \Sigma_{ck}^*$. Thus it is an element of k-US, and furthermore an element of Q_k-$set(k$-$US)$.
- If $l \in lang(CM) \cdot end$, then $\alpha_1 \cdot \ldots \cdot \alpha_{m-1} \in lang(CM)$ and $\alpha_m = end$. By assumption $\alpha_1 \cdot \ldots \cdot \alpha_{m-1}$ is an unadmitted sequence, and it is easy to see that $l \in Q_k$-$set(k$-$US)$.

In both situations, $l \in Q_k$-$set(k$-$US)$. This completes the proof. □

Given a set T of sequences over $\mathcal{D}$, we can lift it to a sequential specification $MSeqSpec(T) = \{M(\_, b_1) \cdot \ldots \cdot M(\_, b_u) | b_1 \cdot \ldots \cdot b_u \in T\}$ for the libraries constructed in Subsect. 4.2. Given a set $S \subseteq \Sigma_{spec}^*$, we use $seqHis(S, n)$ to denote all the sequential histories that are generated from a sequence in S by substituting each $m(a, b)$ in the sequence with a pair of a call action $call(i, m, a)$ and its matching return action $return(i, m, b)$ for some i, where $1 \leq i \leq n$. The following lemma reduces a language inclusion problem to a linearizability problem for one process.

Lemma 3. *Given a sequential specification S and a finite state automaton R that accepts a prefix closed language,* $\mathcal{L}_R$ *is linearizable with respect to S for one process if and only if* $MSeqSpec(lang(R)) \subseteq S$.

Proof. The *if* direction is proved as follows. For each history $h \in history([\![\mathcal{L}_R, 1]\!]_{cs})$, since the critical sections of h are constructed according to transitions of R, as well as the fact that each return action returns a transition label of a critical section, we have that $h \in SeqHis(MSeqSpec(lang(R)), 1)$. By assumption, it can be seen that $h \in SeqHis(S, 1)$. Because h itself is a sequential history, it is obvious that h is linearizable with respect to S.

The *only if* direction is proved by contradiction. Assume that L_R is linearizable with respect to S for one process but $MSeqSpec(lang(R))$ is not a subset of S. Therefore there exists a sequence $l = M(a_1, b_1) \cdot \ldots \cdot M(a_m, b_m) \in MSeqSpec(lang(R)) - S$. Let sequential history $h' = call(1, M, a_1) \cdot return(1, M, b_1) \cdot \ldots \cdot call(1, M, a_m) \cdot return(1, M, b_m)$. Because $b_1 \cdot \ldots \cdot b_m \in lang(R)$ and each return value of M is the transition label of one step transition of R, sequential history h' is a history of $[\![\mathcal{L}_R, 1]\!]_{cs}$ and h' can not be linearizable with respect to S. But this contradicts the fact that $\mathcal{L}_R$ is linearizable with respect to S. □

Given a k-counter machine *CM*, with Lemmas 2 and 3, we can reduce the problem of whether all the sequences in *lang*(*CM*) are unadmitted to that of whether the specific library $\mathcal{L}_{R_{CM}}$ is linearizable with respect to the sequential specification *MSeqSpec*(Q_k-*set*(k-*US*)) for one process.

4.4 Undecidability of Quasi-Linearizability

In this subsection we reduce the problem of whether $\mathcal{L}_{R_{CM}}$ is linearizable with respect to the sequential specification *MSeqSpec*(Q_k-*set*(k-*US*)) to the problem of whether $\mathcal{L}_{R_{CM}}$ is quasi-linearizable with respect to a regular sequential specification.

Recall that Q_k-*set*(k-*US*) is the relaxation of k-*US* guided by Q_k, and such relaxation does not permit I_j and D_j to go across Z_j for each counter j, and does not permit operations in Σ_{ck} to cross *end*. Correspondingly, a relaxed specification can be obtained by relaxing *MSeqSpec*(k-*US*) in a similar way as the Q_k relaxation does to k-*US*. The following lemma shows that the sequential specification of the above linearizability problem can be precisely reproduced by certain Q'_k-quasi-sequential specification, which is generated by relaxing *MSeqSpec*(k-*US*) with the quasi-linearization factor Q'_k. In this way, the above linearizability problem can be reduced to a quasi-linearizability problem. The Quasi-linearization factor Q'_k maps every element in D_k to 0, where D_k is the union of the following sets:

- $\{M(a, I_j), M(b, Z_j) | a, b \in \mathcal{D}\}$, where $1 \leq j \leq k$.
- $\{M(a, D_j), M(b, Z_j) |\ a, b \in \mathcal{D}\}$, where $1 \leq j \leq k$.
- $\{M(a, end), M(b, act) | a, b \in \mathcal{D}\}$, where $act \in \Sigma_{ck}$.

Lemma 4. *A library $\mathcal{L}$ is linearizable with respect to MSeqSpec(Q_k-set(k-US)) for one process if and only if $\mathcal{L}$ is Q'_k-quasi-linearizable with respect to MSeqSpec(k- US) for one process.*

Proof. The *if* direction is proved as follows. For each history $h \in$ *history* ($[\![\mathcal{L}, 1]\!]_{cs}$), assume its quasi-linearization $s = call(1, M, a_1) \cdot return(1, M, b_1) \cdot \ldots \cdot call(1, M, a_m) \cdot return(1, M, b_m)$. We can construct a sequence $l_1 = M(a_1, b_1) \cdot \ldots \cdot M(a_m, b_m)$ from s. By definition of quasi-linearizability, $l_1 \in Q'_k$-*spec*(*MSeqSpec*(k-*US*)). There exist sequences $l_2 = M(a_{m+1}, b_{m+1}) \cdot \ldots \cdot M(a_{m+u}, b_{m+u})$ and $l_3 = M(a'_1, b'_1) \cdot \ldots \cdot M(a'_{m+u}, b'_{m+u})$.

- $l_3 \in$ *MSeqSpec*(k-*US*).
- $\forall d \in D_k$, $distance((l_1 \cdot l_2) \uparrow_d, l_3 \uparrow_d) = 0$.

Thus we can find that $\forall d' \in Q_k$, $(b_1 \cdot \ldots \cdot b_m \cdot b_{m+1} \cdot \ldots \cdot b_{m+u}) \uparrow_{d'} = (b'_1 \cdot \ldots \cdot b'_m \cdot b'_{m+1} \cdot \ldots \cdot b'_{m+u}) \uparrow_{d'}$. Based on this fact, we immediately obtain that $b_1 \cdot \ldots \cdot b_m \cdot b_{m+1} \cdot \ldots \cdot b_{m+u} \in Q_k$-*set*($k$-*US*), thus the sequence $b_1 \cdot \ldots \cdot b_m \in$ *Prefix*(Q_k-*set*(k-*US*)). Because Q_k-*set*(k-*US*) is prefix closed, $b_1 \cdot \ldots \cdot b_m \in Q_k$-*set*($k$-*US*). Therefore, s belongs to *SeqHis*(*MSeqSpec*(Q_k-*set*(k-*US*)), 1). It is obvious that h is linearizable with respect to *MSeqSpec*(Q_k-*set*(k-*US*)).

The *only if* direction can be proved in a similar way. □

The following theorem shows that the quasi-linearizability problem is undecidable with respect to a regular sequential specification for one process.

Theorem 1. *Given a library $\mathcal{L}$, a regular sequential specification S and a quasi-linearization factor Q, it is undecidable whether $\mathcal{L}$ is Q-quasi-linearizable with respect to S for one process.*

Proof. Given a k-counter machine *CM*, by Lemma 2, the problem of whether all sequences in *lang*(*CM*) are unadmitted can be reduced to the language inclusion problem between *lang*(R_{CM}) and Q_k-*set*(k-*US*). It can be seen that the latter problem is equivalent to the language inclusion problem between *MSeqSpec*(*lang*(R_{CM})) and *MSeqSpec*(Q_k-*set*(k-*US*)). By Lemma 3, it can be reduced to the problem of whether $\mathcal{L}_{R_{CM}}$ is linearizable with respect to *MSeqSpec*(Q_k-*set*(k-*US*)) for one process. By Lemma 4, it can be further reduced to the problem of whether $\mathcal{L}_{R_{CM}}$ is Q'_k-quasi-linearizable with respect to *MSeqSpec*(k-*US*) for one process. It is easy to see that *MSeqSpec*(k-*US*) is regular. Recall that by Lemma 1 the k-Z decision problem is undecidable for $k \geq 3$. This completes the proof of this theorem. □

The specific library $\mathcal{L}_R$ has the following property: for each positive integer n and history $h \in history(\llbracket \mathcal{L}_R, n \rrbracket_{cs})$, we can construct a sequential history of $history(\llbracket \mathcal{L}_R, 1 \rrbracket_{cs})$ according to the critical section accesses in h, in the way as shown in Fig. 3. Assume history $h \in history(\llbracket \mathcal{L}_R, n \rrbracket)$ contains call actions c_i and return actions r_i, where $1 \leq i \leq 3$. In Fig. 3, the time axes run from left to right, while each method is associated with a line interval. Additionally, the time intervals of the critical section accesses are marked with the shadow regions in Fig. 3. It is not hard to see that if we change the positions of each pair of a call action and its matching return action to the nearest time point before and after the corresponding critical section accesses, we get a sequential history $h' \in history(\llbracket \mathcal{L}_R, n \rrbracket_{cs})$. Since h' is sequential, we can construct another sequential history $h'' \in history(\llbracket \mathcal{L}_R, 1 \rrbracket_{cs})$ of a single process by moving all actions of h' to this process. It is obvious that h'' contains exactly all the actions of h' and preserves exactly the sequential order of all the actions of h'.

Since the specific library $\mathcal{L}_R$ runs in a sequential way, the following lemma shows that the quasi-linearizability problem of $\mathcal{L}_R$ for one process can be reduced to the quasi-linearizability problem of the same library for more than one process.

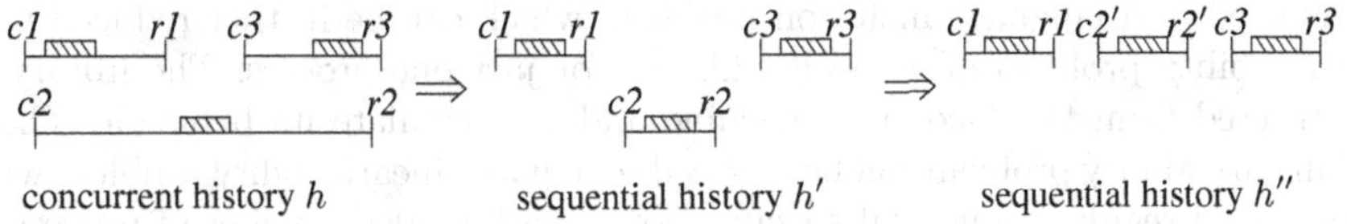

Fig. 3. Construction of a sequential history of a unique process

Lemma 5. *Given a sequential specification S, a finite state automaton R that accepts a prefix closed language, a quasi-linearization factor Q and a positive*

integer $n > 1$, $\mathcal{L}_R$ is Q-quasi-linearizable with respect to S for n processes if and only if $\mathcal{L}_R$ is Q-quasi-linearizable with respect to S for one process.

Proof. The *only if* direction is obvious since $history(\llbracket \mathcal{L}_R, 1 \rrbracket_{cs}) \subseteq history(\llbracket \mathcal{L}_R, n \rrbracket_{cs})$.

The *if* direction is proved by contradiction. Assume that $\mathcal{L}_R$ is Q-quasi-linearizable with respect to S for one process, but not for n processes. Then there must be a history $h \in history(\llbracket \mathcal{L}_R, n \rrbracket_{cs})$ such that h is not Q-quasi-linearizable with respect to S.

As shown in Fig. 3, we can construct a sequential history h' of $\llbracket \mathcal{L}_R, n \rrbracket_{cs}$ from h by changing the positions of each pair of call and return actions to the nearest time point before and after the corresponding critical section. During this process, it is necessary to add some return actions for the case when a method has completed its critical section but not returned yet, it is also necessary to remove some call actions for the case when a method has not entered its critical section. By assumption, it can be seen that h' is not Q-quasi-linearizable with respect to S.

Similarly, we can also construct a sequential history h'' of $\llbracket \mathcal{L}_R, 1 \rrbracket_{cs}$ from h' by moving all actions of h' to the unique process. By assumption, it can be seen that h'' is not Q-quasi-linearizable with respect to S. But this contradicts the assumption that $\mathcal{L}_R$ is Q-quasi-linearizable with respect to S for one process. □

The following theorem states that the quasi-linearizability problem is undecidable with respect to a regular sequential specification for a bounded number $n \geq 1$ of processes. This is a direct consequence of Theorem 1 and Lemma 5.

Theorem 2. *Given a library $\mathcal{L}$, a regular sequential specification S, a quasi-linearization factor Q and a positive integer $n \geq 1$, it is undecidable whether $\mathcal{L}$ is Q-quasi-linearizable with respect to S for n processes.*

5 Conclusion and Future Work

We show in this paper that the quasi-linearizability problem with respect to a regular sequential specification is undecidable for a bounded number of processes. This is essentially proved by reduction from the k-Z problem of a k-counter machine, a known undecidable problem. We prove that the k-Z problem can be reduced to a language inclusion problem, which can be further reduced to a linearizability problem of a specific library for just one process. The library is constructed from the k-counter machine and can simulate its behavior. Then, this linearizability problem can be reduced to a quasi-linearizability problem with respect to a regular sequential specification for a bounded number of processes.

Note that although the sequential specification of the quasi-linearizability problem is regular, its quasi-sequential counterpart is non-regular and rather complex. Thus, a quasi-linearizability problem with respect to a regular sequential specification is equivalent to a linearizability problem with respect to a non-regular sequential specification. Since quasi-linearizability is undecidable for just one process with respect to a regular sequential specification, the undecidability of quasi-linearizability is not resulted from the interactions between processes, but from the fact that no element in D_k is equal to Σ_{spec}. Actually, if the domain of quasi-linearization factor contains only one element Σ_{spec}, then quasi-linearizability problem with respect to regular sequential specification is decidable for a bounded number of processes, as shown in [1]. Therefore, we can conclude that the undecidability of quasi-linearizability is inherent from its flexibility in quantitative relaxation.

Quasi-linearizability has been deprecated since its syntactic distance definition has been demonstrated broken [9]. Compared to the syntactic relaxation in [2], the relaxation in [9] is based on library semantics, and it offers an accurate and efficient way to relax linearizability. We conjecture that quasi-linearizability is a special case of the quantitative relaxation framework presented in [9], of which the decidability is still unknown. Thus, our undecidability work for quasi-linearizability can be used as a gateway to this open problem. As future work we would like to investigate the decision problem of this quantitative relaxation framework for a bounded number of processes.

Acknowledgments. The authors of this paper would like to thank anonymous reviewers for pointing out the connection between dependence relations in [3] and quasi-linearization factors in [2].

References

1. Adhikari, K., Street, J., Wang, C., Liu, Y., Zhang, S.J.: Verifying a quantitative relaxation of linearizability via refinement. In: Bartocci, E., Ramakrishnan, C.R. (eds.) SPIN 2013. LNCS, vol. 7976, pp. 24–42. Springer, Heidelberg (2013)
2. Afek, Y., Korland, G., Yanovsky, E.: Quasi-linearizability: relaxed consistency for improved concurrency. In: Lu, C., Masuzawa, T., Mosbah, M. (eds.) OPODIS 2010. LNCS, vol. 6490, pp. 395–410. Springer, Heidelberg (2010)
3. Alur, R., McMillan, K., Peled, D.: Model-checking of correctness conditions for concurrent objects. In: LICS 1996, pp. 219–228. IEEE Computer Society (1996)
4. Aspnes, J., Herlihy, M., Shavit, N.: Counting networks. J. ACM **41**(5), 1020–1048 (1994)
5. Bouajjani, A., Emmi, M., Enea, C., Hamza, J.: Verifying concurrent programs against sequential specifications. In: Felleisen, M., Gardner, P. (eds.) ESOP 2013. LNCS, vol. 7792, pp. 290–309. Springer, Heidelberg (2013)
6. Bouajjani, A., Emmi, M., Enea, C., Hamza, J.: Tractable refinement checking for concurrent objects. In: Rajamani, S.K., Walker, D. (eds.) POPL 2015, pp. 651–662. ACM (2015)
7. Burckhardt, S., Gotsman, A., Musuvathi, M., Yang, H.: Concurrent library correctness on the TSO memory model. In: Seidl, H. (ed.) Programming Languages and Systems. LNCS, vol. 7211, pp. 87–107. Springer, Heidelberg (2012)
8. Černý, P., Radhakrishna, A., Zufferey, D., Chaudhuri, S., Alur, R.: Model checking of linearizability of concurrent list implementations. In: Touili, T., Cook, B., Jackson, P. (eds.) CAV 2010. LNCS, vol. 6174, pp. 465–479. Springer, Heidelberg (2010)

9. Henzinger, T.A., Kirsch, C.M., Payer, H., Sezgin, A., Sokolova, A.: Quantitative relaxation of concurrent data structures. In: Giacobazzi, R., Cousot, R. (eds.) POPL 2013, pp. 317–328. ACM (2013)
10. Herlihy, M., Shavit, N.: The Art of Multiprocessor Programming. Morgan Kaufmann, San Francisco (2008)
11. Herlihy, M.P., Wing, J.M.: Linearizability: a correctness condition for concurrent objects. ACM Trans. Program. Lang. Syst. **12**(3), 463–492 (1990)
12. Lamport, L.: How to make a multiprocessor computer that correctly executes multiprocess program. IEEE Trans. Comput. **28**(9), 690–691 (1979)
13. Zhang, L., Chattopadhyay, A., Wang, C.: Round-up: Runtime checking quasi linearizability of concurrent data structures. In: Denney, E., Bultan, T., Zeller, A. (eds.) ASE 2013, pp. 4–14. IEEE (2013)

Objects in Polynomial Time

Emmanuel Hainry[1,2,3(✉)] and Romain Péchoux[1,2,3]

[1] Université de Lorraine, LORIA, UMR 7503, 54506 Vandœuvre-lès-Nancy, France
{hainry,pechoux}@loria.fr
[2] Inria, 54600 Villers-lès-Nancy, France
[3] CNRS, LORIA, UMR 7503, 54506 Vandœuvre-lès-Nancy, France

Abstract. A type system based on non-interference and data ramification principles is introduced in order to capture the set of functions computable in polynomial time on OO programs. The studied language is general enough to capture most OO constructs and our characterization is quite expressive as it allows the analysis of a combination of imperative loops and of data ramification scheme based on Bellantoni and Cook's safe recursion using function algebra.

Introduction

Motivations. This paper presents a first characterization of polynomial time computable functions on the Object Oriented paradigm. This characterization is obtained by mixing non-interference techniques à la Volpano et al. [16], for secure flow analysis, with tiering [13] or safe recursion on notation [3] based approaches, in order to capture complexity classes over function algebra.

The main idea is very simple: program data is divided in two classes (called tier **0** and tier **1**); while tier **0** data store computations that may increase, tier **1** data are used for the control flow and never increase. This is ensured by a type system based on non-interference precluding data flows from **0** to **1** and allowing only specific flows from **1** to **0** (when data are cloned). The type system also ensures that data of tier **1** is never modified once initialized and voilà ! As the control flow is only based on tier **1**, then either the program does not terminate or it terminates in polynomial time as tier **1** variables may only point to a number of distinct memory references bounded by the input size.

Though the idea is simple, its implementation is not. Analyzing the complexity of OO programs faces a lot of hardships (complex object data structure, side effects, recursive methods, ...) and one mistake in the application can make the whole system collapse in a dominolike effect. This is the reason why the type system presented in this paper is an original non-straightforward contribution.

There are plenty of works analyzing the complexity of OO programs from a practical perspective in the literature. These works are interesting and sometimes better than the present paper wrt program expressivity. However they

This work was partially supported by ANR-14-CE25-0005 Elica: Expanding Logical Ideas for Complexity Analysis.

X. Feng and S. Park (Eds.): APLAS 2015, LNCS 9458, pp. 387–404, 2015.
DOI: 10.1007/978-3-319-26529-2_21

suffer from some of the following gaps that our contribution tries to tackle: first, the theoretical part can be lacking as some works focus on having effective proofs of concept rather than providing characterizations; second, they usually do not provide any completeness result; finally, many works analyze a bytecode rather than the sourcecode itself, thus avoiding the treatment of complex constructs. This makes the analysis more precise but clearly less portable. Though this choice may be better from a practical perspective, it is constrained by one language implementation. In contrast, our work is more conceptual and forges ties between various programming paradigms: the tiering methodology works for functional programming [3], imperative programs [15], fork processes [10], graph-based language [14]. We show in this paper that it also works in the object paradigm.

The analysis presented in this paper is based on an abstract OO language. Consequently, it can be applied both to impure OO languages (*e.g.* Java) and to pure ones (*e.g.* SmallTalk or Ruby). It just suffices to forget rules about primitive data types in the type system. Moreover, it does not depend on the implementation of the language being compiled (ObjectiveC, OCaml, Scala, ...) or interpreted (Python standard implementation, OCaml, ...). The only restriction is that it does not handle pointer arithmetics. Hence languages such as C++ cannot be handled. However, it merges elegantly with the functional world as it captures Safe Recursion on Notation by Bellantoni and Cook [3]. Consequently, we can expect to handle OO higher-order (as in Scala or Java 1.8). A combination with type discipline for studying complexity for HO functional program such as the ones based Light Linear Logics [2] would then be required.

Related Works. This main idea of combining tiering and non-interference does not appear *ex nihilo*: safe recursion was already a non-interference based result (though the connection was not easy to see in the nineties as both domains were emerging research topics). Two decades later Marion has presented a type system [15] using this idea in order to capture polynomial time computable functions on an imperative language. This idea was adapted to a graph based language in [14]. The current paper tries to pursue this objective but on a distinct paradigm: Object. Thus our results strictly extend the ones of [15] while they are applied on a more concrete language than the ones in [14].

The works [1,5,12] are based on the analysis of heap-space and time consumption of Java bytecode. The results from [1,12] make use of abstract interpretations to infer efficiently symbolic upper bounds on resource consumption of Java programs. A constraint-based static analysis is used in [5] and focuses on certifying memory bounds for Java Card. Current analysis can be seen as a complementary approach that is more expressive on the purely OO fragment as it handles while loops guarded by a variable of reference type whereas most of the aforementioned studies are based on invariants generation for primitive types only.

In a similar vein, characterizing complexity classes below polynomial time is studied in [11], which relies on a programming language, PURPLE, combining imperative statements together with pointers on a fixed graph structure. Although not directly related, our type system was strongly inspired by this work.

Outline. In a first section, we present the syntax and semantics of an abstract generic OO language. We also define the notion of input, input size and computation of a program in this language. In Sect. 2, we introduce a type system based on tiering techniques for controlling program complexity. This is the main contribution of the paper. In Sect. 3, we define a *Safety* condition based on tiers in order to restrict the allowed forms of recursion in a typed program. In Sect. 5, we show that safe and terminating programs characterize the class of functions computable in polynomial time. For the soundness, Theorem 1 shows that such a program terminates in time (number of executed base instructions) polynomial in the input size. For the completeness, Theorem 2 shows that any Turing Machine running in polynomial time can be simulated by a safe and terminating program. Section 4 is devoted to examples illustrating the methodology. Finally, we provide extensions and a conclusion in the last section.

1 Object Oriented Programs

In this section we define the syntax and semantics of an abstract OO programming language. We claim that this language is generic enough so that the complexity analysis performed by the type system presented in the next section can be adapted to most of the well-known OO programs. We also provide a notion of input and a notion of size of the heap and the stack in order to be able to discuss the complexity of such programs.

1.1 Abstract Syntax

Expressions, instructions, methods and classes are defined by the following grammar:

$$\begin{aligned}
\text{Expressions} \ni \mathtt{e} ::= {} & \mathtt{x} \mid \mathtt{n} \mid \mathtt{null} \mid \mathtt{this} \mid \mathtt{true} \mid \mathtt{false} \mid \mathtt{op}(\overline{\mathtt{e}}) \\
& \mid \mathtt{new\ C}(\overline{\mathtt{e}}) \mid \mathtt{e.m}(\overline{\mathtt{e}}) \mid \mathtt{e.clone}() \\
\text{Instructions} \ni \mathtt{I} ::= {} & ; \mid [\tau]\ \mathtt{x{:=}e;} \mid \mathtt{x{+}{+};} \mid \mathtt{x{-}{-};} \mid \mathtt{I}_1\ \mathtt{I}_2 \mid \mathtt{while(e)\{I\}} \\
& \mid \mathtt{if(e)\{I_1\}else\{I_2\}} \mid \mathtt{e.m}(\overline{\mathtt{e}}); \mid \mathtt{break;} \\
\text{Methods} \ni \mathtt{m_C} ::= {} & \tau\ \mathtt{m}(\overline{\tau\ \mathtt{x}})\{\mathtt{I}[\mathtt{return\ x;}]\} \\
\text{Classes} \ni \mathtt{C} ::= {} & \mathtt{C}\ [\mathtt{extends\ D}]\ \{\overline{\tau\ \mathtt{x};}\ \mathtt{C}(\overline{\tau\ \mathtt{x}})\{\overline{\mathtt{x{:=}x}}\}\ \overline{\mathtt{m_C}}\}
\end{aligned}$$

with $\mathtt{n} \in \mathbb{N}$, the set of integers, $\mathtt{x} \in \mathbb{V}$, the set of variables, $\mathtt{op} \in \mathbb{O}$, the set of operators, $\mathtt{C} \in \mathbb{C}$, the set of class names and $\mathtt{m} \in \mathbb{M}$, the set of method names. $[e]$ denotes some optional syntactic element e and $\overline{e}$ denotes a sequence of syntactic elements $e_1, \ldots, e_n$. The τs are type annotations ranging over $\mathbb{C} \cup \{\mathtt{void}, \mathtt{boolean}, \mathtt{int}\}$. Each operator comes equipped with a signature of the shape $\texttt{op} :: \tau_1 \times \cdots \times \tau_n \to \texttt{boolean}$. For simplicity, the signature is restricted to operators with boolean outputs. It can be extended to general operators but in this case a restricted typing discipline as in [10] is required for operators as their computations might increase the data size. The abstract syntax does not include a `for` instruction based on the premise that, as in Java, a for statement can be simulated by a while statement. Let $\texttt{C}.\mathcal{F} = \{\overline{\texttt{x}}\}$ to be the set of fields in a class $\texttt{C}\ \{\overline{\tau\ \texttt{x;}}\ \texttt{C}(\overline{\tau\ \texttt{y}})\{\overline{\texttt{x:=y}}\}\ \overline{\texttt{m}_\texttt{C}}\}$ and $\mathcal{F} = \cup_{\texttt{C}\in\mathbb{C}}\texttt{C}.\mathcal{F} \subseteq \mathbb{V}$ be the set of all fields. In a method or constructor, the arguments are called parameters. Each variable declared in an assignment of the shape τ `x:=e;` is called a local variable. Given a method $\tau\ \texttt{m}(\tau_1\ \texttt{x}_1, \ldots, \tau_n\ \texttt{x}_n)\{\texttt{I}\ [\texttt{return x;}]\}$ of C, its signature is $\tau\ \texttt{m}^\texttt{C}(\tau_1, \ldots, \tau_n)$, the notation $\texttt{m}^\texttt{C}$ denoting that m is declared in C. Also notice that there is no field access in our syntax using the "." operator. Consequently, all fields are implicitly `private`. In contrast, methods and classes are all `public`. This is not a huge restriction for an OO programmer since any field can be accessed and updated in an outer class by writing the corresponding getter and setter. In the particular case where `C extends D`, $\texttt{C}(\overline{\tau\ \texttt{y}})\{\overline{\texttt{x:=y}}\}$ is a constructor initializing both the fields of C and the fields of D. Inheritance defines a partial order on classes denoted by $\texttt{C} \trianglelefteq \texttt{D}$. For readability, classes are assumed to have exactly one constructor initializing all the class fields. The only considered primitive data are boolean values `true` and `false` and integer constants. Other primitive data types such as floats, doubles and characters could be considered and typed as integer values are by the type system provided in Sect. 2. Notice that overload and override are both allowed by our Syntax.

OO Programs. A *program* is a collection of classes together with exactly one executable `Exe{void main(){Init Comp}}` with $\texttt{Init}, \texttt{Comp} \in$ Instructions. The instruction `Init` is called the *initialization instruction*. Its purpose is to compute the program input, which is strongly needed in order to define the complexity of an OO program (if there is no input, all terminating programs are constant time programs). The instruction `Comp` is called the *computational instruction*. The type system presented in this paper will analyze the complexity of this latter instruction.

An important point to stress is that, given a program, the choice of initialization and computational instructions is left to the analyzer. This choice is crucial for this analysis to be relevant. There are two particular cases:

- In the particular case where the initialization instruction is empty, there will be no computation on reference type variables apart from constant time or non-terminating ones, as we will see shortly. This behavior is highly expected as it means that the program has no input. As there is no input, it means that either the program does not terminate or it terminates in constant time.
- In the particular case where the computational instruction is empty (that is ";") then the program will trivially pass the complexity analysis.

Well-Formed Programs. Throughout the paper, only well-formed programs satisfying the following conditions will be considered:

(i) For each class name C, there is exactly one class within the collection. Multiple inheritance and inner classes are prohibited.
(ii) A variable appearing in the collection of classes is either a local variable, a field or a parameter. In order to prevent name clashes, programs are assumed to be statically transformed up-to α-conversion. Each local variable x is both declared and initialized exactly once by a τ x := e; instruction before its first use.
(iii) Each method signature is unique. A method output type is `void` iff the method has no `return` statement.

1.2 Informal Semantics

In this section, we provide an informal semantics of OO programs and introduce data structures for representing the heap and the stack.

The *heap* $\mathcal{H}$ is represented by a a directed multigraph (V, A). The nodes in V are references labeled by class names and the arrows in A are labeled by field names. Given a heap $\mathcal{H} = (V, A)$, a *stack frame* $s_{\mathcal{H}} = \langle s, p\rangle$ is a pair composed by a method signature s and a partial mapping $p : \mathbb{V} \cup \{\mathtt{this}\} \mapsto V \cup \mathbb{N} \cup \{\mathtt{true}, \mathtt{false}\}$ associating, either a reference in V to some variable in $\mathbb{V}$ of reference type in $\mathbb{C}$ or to the current object `this`, or a primitive value in $\mathbb{N}$ (resp. $\{\mathtt{true}, \mathtt{false}\}$) to some variable of primitive type `int` (resp. `boolean`). Let *dom(p)* to be domain of p. By abuse of notation, given an expression e of reference type, let $p(\mathtt{e})$ be the reference of the object corresponding to e.

The *stack* $\mathcal{S}_{\mathcal{H}}$ is a LIFO structure of stack frames corresponding to the same heap $\mathcal{H}$.

The mappings of the stack frames map method's parameters, current object and local variables to the references of the arguments on which they are applied.

A *memory configuration* $\mathcal{C}$ is a pair $\langle \mathcal{H}, \mathcal{S}_{\mathcal{H}}\rangle$ consisting in a heap $\mathcal{H}$ and a stack $\mathcal{S}_{\mathcal{H}}$. The *initial configuration* $\mathcal{C}_0$ is a configuration whose heap only consists in the null reference node `null` and whose stack only contains the stack frame $\langle \mathtt{void\ main}^{\mathtt{Exe}}(), p_0\rangle$; p_0 being a mapping associating each local variable in the main method to the null reference, whether it is of reference type, and to the basic primitive value otherwise (`true` for `boolean` and 0 for `int`). The evaluation of a `new` operator consists in adding a new node to the heap with arrows pointing to its fields; thus implementing the dynamic binding principle. Calling a method $\mathtt{e.m}(\overline{\mathtt{e}})$ of the class C and shape $\tau\ \mathtt{m}(\overline{\tau\ \mathtt{x}})\{\ldots\}$ consists in pushing a new stack frame $\langle \tau\ \mathtt{m}^{\mathtt{C}}(\overline{\tau}), p\rangle$ on the stack with p such that $p(\mathtt{this}) = p(\mathtt{e})$ and $p(\mathtt{x}_i) = p(\mathtt{e}_i)$. A call to e.clone() consists in duplicating the subgraph of source $p(\mathtt{e})$ in $\mathcal{H}$. For simplicity, we assume `clone` to be evaluated in constant time. Though it is a deep-copy, this assumption is reasonable as it makes the analysis easier at a small cost: the polynomial degree of Theorem 1 just differs by one constant as this method is usually evaluated in linear time.

Example 1. Consider the code in Fig. 1. At line 1, the program starts on the initial configuration $\mathcal{C}_0$. After executing line 4, it ends in a configuration $\mathcal{C} = \langle \mathcal{H}, \mathcal{S}_{\mathcal{H}}\rangle$ with a heap $\mathcal{H} = (V, A)$ represented by nodes and arrows and with a stack $\mathcal{S}$ consisting in only one stack frame $\langle$`void main`$^{\text{Exe}}(), p\rangle$; the mapping p being represented by boxed nodes and snake arrows.

```
main(){
    B b := new B(null, new A());
    C c := new C(b);
    D d := new D(c);
    B e := new B(c, c);
}
```

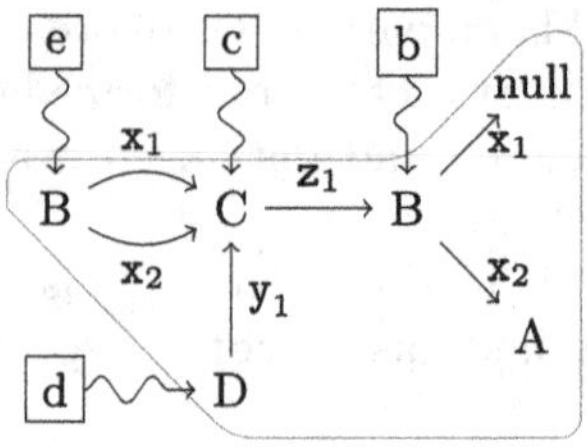

Fig. 1. Example of a pointer graph

1.3 Input and Size

Given a program of executable `Exe{void main(){Init Comp}}`, the *input* is the memory configuration $\mathcal{C}$ obtained after executing the initialization instruction `Init` on the initial memory configuration $\mathcal{C}_0$. Consequently, `Init` is assumed to be a terminating instruction.

Definition 1 (Sizes). *The size $|\mathcal{H}|$ of a heap $\mathcal{H} = (V, A)$ is defined to be the number of nodes in V. The size of a mapping p is defined by $|p| = \sum_{\mathtt{x} \in dom(p)} |p(\mathtt{x})|$ where the size of a boolean value is 1, the size of an integer value is the value itself and the size of a memory reference is 1. The size of a stack frame $s_{\mathcal{H}} = \langle s, p\rangle$ is defined by: $|s_{\mathcal{H}}| = 1 + |p|$. The size of a stack $S_{\mathcal{H}}$ is defined by $|S_{\mathcal{H}}| = \sum_{s_{\mathcal{H}} \in S_{\mathcal{H}}} |s_{\mathcal{H}}|$. Finally, the size of a memory configuration $\mathcal{C} = \langle \mathcal{H}, S_{\mathcal{H}}\rangle$ is defined by $|\mathcal{C}| = |\mathcal{H}| + |S_{\mathcal{H}}|$.*

The above definition is robust if we consider boolean values to be 8 (bits) values, integer values to be 32 (bits) values, ... Indeed, in such a case integers will be considered as constants so that the upper bounds presented in Theorem 1 remain valid. Notice that the out-degree of a node is bounded by a constant of the program (the maximum number of fields in a class) and, consequently, bounding the number of nodes is sufficient to obtain a big O bound on the heap size. The size of a pointer stack is very close to the size of the usual OO Virtual Machine stack since it counts the number of nested method calls (i.e. the number of stack frames in the stack) and the size of primitive data in each frame (that are duplicated during the pass-by-value evaluation).

2 Type System

The main contribution of the paper, a tier based type system for ensuring polynomial time and polynomial space upper bounds on the size of a memory configuration, is introduced in this section. We first define the notion of tiered types inspired by tiering on function algebra and we define the notions of typing environments and judgments. Then we present and explain the type system rules and the notion of well-typedness. Finally, we exhibit the main properties of a well-typed program.

2.1 Tiered Types

A *tiered type* is a pair $\tau(\alpha)$ consisting of a type $\tau \in \{\texttt{void}, \texttt{boolean}, \texttt{int}\} \cup \mathbb{C}$ together with a tier $\alpha \in \{\mathbf{0}, \mathbf{1}\}$. Given a tiered type, the two projections π_1 and π_2 are defined by $\pi_1(\tau(\alpha)) = \tau$ and $\pi_2(\tau(\alpha)) = \alpha$. The order $\preceq$ on tiers is such that $\mathbf{0} \preceq \mathbf{1}$. Let $\wedge$ and $\vee$ be the induced min and max operators on set of tiers and let $\alpha, \beta, \ldots$ denote tier variables.

Given two sequences of types $\overline{\tau} = \tau_1, \ldots, \tau_n$ and tiers $\overline{\alpha} = \alpha_1, \ldots, \alpha_n$ and a tier α, let $\overline{\tau}(\overline{\alpha})$ denote $\tau_1(\alpha_1), \ldots, \tau_n(\alpha_n)$, $\overline{\tau}(\alpha)$ denote $\tau_1(\alpha), \ldots, \tau_n(\alpha)$ and $\langle\overline{\tau}\rangle$ (resp. $\langle\overline{\tau}(\overline{\alpha})\rangle$) denote the cartesian product of types (resp. tiered types).

Intuition: Tiers will be used to separate data in two kinds as in Bellantoni and Cook's safe recursion scheme [3] where data are divided into "safe" and "normal" data kinds. Referring to Danner and Royer [7], "normal data [are the data] that drive recursions and safe data [are the data] over which recursions compute". In our setting, tier **1** will be an equivalent for normal data type, as it consists in data that drive recursion and while loops. Tier **0** will be equivalent for safe data type, as it consists in computational data storages.

2.2 Typing Environments and Judgments

For a given program, a *method typing environment* δ maps each variable $v \in \mathbb{V}$ to a tiered type. For a given program, a *typing environment* Δ maps each method signature $\tau\ \texttt{m}^{\texttt{C}}(\overline{\tau})$ to a method typing environment δ, i.e. $\Delta(\tau\ \texttt{m}^{\texttt{C}}(\overline{\tau})) = \delta$.

A *contextual typing environment* $\Gamma = (s, \Delta)$ is a pair consisting of a method signature and a typing environment. The method signature s in the contextual typing environment (s, Δ) indicates under which context the fields should be typed. $\forall \texttt{x} \in \mathbb{V}$, define $\Gamma(\texttt{x}) = \Delta(s)(\texttt{x})$. Also define $\Gamma\{\texttt{x} \leftarrow \tau(\alpha)\}$ to be the contextual typing environment Γ' such that $\forall \texttt{y} \neq \texttt{x}$, $\Gamma'(\texttt{y}) = \Gamma(\texttt{y})$ and $\Gamma'(\texttt{x}) = \tau(\alpha)$.

Intuition: The main reason for defining typing environments this way is to allow the programmer to type a field with distinct tiers depending on the considered method. This is the reason why the presented type system has to keep information on the context.

Given a contextual typing environment Γ, there are three kinds of typing judgments:

- $\Gamma \vdash \texttt{e} : \tau(\alpha)$ for expressions, meaning that the expression $\texttt{e}$ is of tier type $\tau(\alpha)$ under the environment Γ,
- $\Gamma \vdash \texttt{I} : \texttt{void}(\alpha)$ for instructions, meaning that the instruction $\texttt{I}$ is of tier type $\texttt{void}(\alpha)$ under the environment Γ,
- $\Gamma \vdash s : \texttt{C}(\beta) \times \langle\overline{\tau}(\overline{\alpha})\rangle \to \tau(\alpha)$ for method signatures, meaning that the method $\texttt{m}$ of signature s belongs to the class $\texttt{C}$ ($\texttt{C}(\beta)$ is the tiered type of the current object $\texttt{this}$), has parameters of type $\langle\overline{\tau}(\overline{\alpha})\rangle$ and a return variable of type $\tau(\alpha)$, with $\tau = \texttt{void}$ in the particular case where there is no return statement.

Given a sequence $\overline{\texttt{e}} = \texttt{e}_1, \ldots, \texttt{e}_n$ of expressions, a sequence of types $\overline{\tau} = \tau_1, \ldots, \tau_n$ and a sequence of tiers $\overline{\alpha} = \alpha_1, \ldots, \alpha_n$, the notation $\Gamma \vdash \overline{\texttt{e}} : \overline{\tau}(\overline{\alpha})$ means that $\Gamma \vdash \texttt{e}_i : \tau_i(\alpha_i)$ holds, for all $i \in [1, n]$.

2.3 Typing Rules

The typing rules for expressions, instructions and methods are provided in Figs. 2, 3 and 4, respectively.

The intuition is as follows: keeping in mind, that tier **1** corresponds to while loop guards data and that tier **0** corresponds to data storages (thus possibly increasing data), the type system precludes flows from tier **0** data to tier **1** data.

$$\frac{\mathtt{n} \in \mathbb{N}}{\Gamma \vdash \mathtt{n} : \mathtt{int}(\alpha)}\,(Int) \qquad \frac{w \in \{\mathtt{true}, \mathtt{false}\}}{\Gamma \vdash w : \mathtt{boolean}(\alpha)}\,(Bool) \qquad \frac{}{\Gamma \vdash \mathtt{null} : \mathtt{C}(\alpha)}\,(Null)$$

$$\frac{\Gamma(\mathtt{x}) = \tau(\alpha)}{\Gamma \vdash \mathtt{x} : \tau(\alpha)}\,(Var) \qquad \frac{\forall i,\ \Gamma \vdash \overline{\mathtt{e}} : \overline{\tau}(\alpha) \quad \mathtt{op} :: \langle \overline{\tau} \rangle \to \mathtt{boolean}}{\Gamma \vdash \mathtt{op}(\overline{\mathtt{e}}) : \mathtt{boolean}(\alpha)}\,(Op)$$

$$\frac{\forall \mathtt{x} \in \mathtt{C}.\mathcal{F}, \pi_2(\Gamma(\mathtt{x})) = \alpha}{\Gamma \vdash \mathtt{this} : \mathtt{C}(\alpha)}\,(Self) \qquad \frac{\Gamma \vdash \mathtt{e} : \mathtt{D}(\alpha) \quad \mathtt{D} \trianglelefteq \mathtt{C}}{\Gamma \vdash \mathtt{e} : \mathtt{C}(\alpha)}\,(Pol)$$

$$\frac{\Gamma \vdash \overline{\mathtt{e}} : \overline{\tau}(\mathbf{0}) \quad \mathtt{C}.\mathcal{F} = \{\overline{\mathtt{x}}\} \quad \Gamma \vdash \overline{\mathtt{x}} : \overline{\tau}(\mathbf{0})}{\Gamma \vdash \mathtt{new}\ \mathtt{C}(\overline{\mathtt{e}}) : \mathtt{C}(\mathbf{0})}\,(New) \qquad \frac{\Gamma \vdash \mathtt{e} : \mathtt{C}(\mathbf{1})}{\Gamma \vdash \mathtt{e.clone}() : \mathtt{C}(\mathbf{0})}\,(Cln)$$

$$\frac{(s, \Delta) \vdash \mathtt{e} : \mathtt{C}(\beta) \quad (s, \Delta) \vdash \overline{\mathtt{e}} : \overline{\tau}(\overline{\alpha}) \quad (\tau\ \mathtt{m}^{\mathtt{C}}(\overline{\tau}), \Delta) \vdash \tau\ \mathtt{m}^{\mathtt{C}}(\overline{\tau}) : \mathtt{C}(\beta) \times \langle \overline{\tau}(\overline{\alpha}) \rangle \to \tau(\alpha)}{(s, \Delta) \vdash \mathtt{e.m}(\overline{\mathtt{e}}) : \tau(\alpha)}\,(Call)$$

Fig. 2. Type system for expressions

$$\frac{}{\Gamma \vdash\ ;\ : \mathtt{void}(\alpha)}\,(Skip) \qquad \frac{\Gamma \vdash \mathtt{I} : \mathtt{void}(\mathbf{0})}{\Gamma \vdash \mathtt{I} : \mathtt{void}(\mathbf{1})}\,(ISub) \qquad \frac{\mathtt{x} \notin \mathcal{F} \quad \Gamma \vdash \mathtt{x} : \tau(\alpha) \quad \Gamma \vdash \mathtt{e} : \tau(\alpha)}{\Gamma \vdash [\tau]\ \mathtt{x}{:=}\mathtt{e};: \mathtt{void}(\alpha)}\,(VA)$$

$$\frac{\mathtt{x} \in \mathcal{F} \quad \Gamma \vdash \mathtt{x} : \tau(\mathbf{0}) \quad \Gamma \vdash \mathtt{e} : \tau(\mathbf{0})}{\Gamma \vdash \mathtt{x}{:=}\mathtt{e};: \mathtt{void}(\mathbf{0})}\,(FA) \qquad \frac{\Gamma \vdash \mathtt{x} : \mathtt{int}(\mathbf{0})}{\Gamma \vdash \mathtt{x{+}{+}};: \mathtt{void}(\mathbf{0})}\,(Inc) \qquad \frac{\Gamma \vdash \mathtt{x} : \mathtt{int}(\alpha)}{\Gamma \vdash \mathtt{x{-}{-}};: \mathtt{void}(\alpha)}\,(Dec)$$

$$\frac{}{\Gamma \vdash \mathtt{break};: \mathtt{void}(\mathbf{1})}\,(Brk) \qquad \frac{\forall i,\ \Gamma \vdash \mathtt{I}_i : \mathtt{void}(\alpha_i)}{\Gamma \vdash \mathtt{I}_1\ \mathtt{I}_2 : \mathtt{void}(\alpha_1 \vee \alpha_2)}\,(Seq)$$

$$\frac{\Gamma \vdash \mathtt{e} : \mathtt{boolean}(\alpha) \quad \forall i,\ \Gamma \vdash \mathtt{I}_i : \mathtt{void}(\alpha)}{\Gamma \vdash \mathtt{if(e)\{I_1\}else\{I_2\}} : \mathtt{void}(\alpha)}\,(If) \qquad \frac{\Gamma \vdash \mathtt{e} : \mathtt{boolean}(\mathbf{1}) \quad \Gamma \vdash \mathtt{I} : \mathtt{void}(\mathbf{1})}{\Gamma \vdash \mathtt{while(e)\{I\}} : \mathtt{void}(\mathbf{1})}\,(Wh)$$

Fig. 3. Type system for instructions

$$\frac{\Gamma\{\mathtt{this} \leftarrow \mathtt{C}(\beta), \overline{\mathtt{x}} \leftarrow \overline{\tau}(\overline{\alpha}), [\mathtt{x} \leftarrow \tau(\alpha)]\} \vdash I : \mathtt{void}(\alpha) \quad \tau\ \mathtt{m}(\overline{\tau\ \mathtt{x}})\{\mathtt{I}\ [\mathtt{return}\ \mathtt{x};]\} \in \mathtt{C}}{\Gamma \vdash \tau\ \mathtt{m}^{\mathtt{C}}(\overline{\tau}) : \mathtt{C}(\beta) \times \langle \overline{\tau}(\overline{\alpha}) \rangle \to \tau(\alpha)}\,(Body)$$

$$\frac{\mathtt{C} \trianglelefteq \mathtt{D} \qquad \Gamma \vdash \tau\ \mathtt{m}^{\mathtt{D}}(\overline{\tau}) : \mathtt{D}(\beta) \times \langle \overline{\tau}(\overline{\alpha}) \rangle \to \tau(\alpha) \quad \tau\ \mathtt{m}(\overline{\tau\ \mathtt{x}})\{\mathtt{I}\ [\mathtt{return}\ \mathtt{x};]\} \in \mathtt{D}}{\Gamma \vdash \tau\ \mathtt{m}^{\mathtt{C}}(\overline{\tau}) : \mathtt{C}(\beta) \times \langle \overline{\tau}(\overline{\alpha}) \rangle \to \tau(\alpha)}\,(OverR)$$

Fig. 4. Type system for methods

Most of the rules are basic non-interference typing rules following Volpano et al. type discipline: tiers in the rule premises (when there is one) are equal to the tier in the rule conclusion so that there can be no information flow (in both directions) using these rules. These rules can be divided into two categories:

- The unconstrained rules *(Int)*, *(Bool)*, *(Null)*, *(Var)*, *(Op)*, *(Self)*, *(Pol)*, *(VA)*, *(Skip)*, *(Dec)*, *(If)*, for which the tier is not constrained by the rule. They are fairly standard and only a few of them need some deeper explanations:
  - Primitive constants and the null reference can be given any tier as they have no computational power (Rules *(Int)*, *(Bool)* and *(Null)*). As in Java and for polymorphic reasons, `null` can be considered of any class `C`.
  - The rule *(Self)* makes explicit that the self reference `this` is of type `C` and enforces the tier of the fields to be equal to the field of the current object, thus preventing "flows by references" in the heap.
  - The rule *(VA)* is the main non-interference rule. It forbids information flows from a tier to another: it is only possible to assign an expression `e` of tier α to a variable `x` of tier α.
  - The rule *(If)* constrains the tier of the conditional guard `e` to match the tiers of the branching instructions $\mathtt{I}_1$ and $\mathtt{I}_2$. Hence, it prevents assignments of tier **1** variables to be controlled by a tier **0** expression.
- The constrained rules *(New)*, *(FA)*, *(Inc)*, *(Brk)* and *(Wh)* for which the tier is fixed by the rule, for some precise "complexity" purpose:
  - The rule *(New)* checks that the constructor arguments and output all have tier **0**. The new instance has to be of tier **0** since its creation makes the memory grow (a new reference node is added in the heap). The constructor arguments have also to be of tier **0**. Otherwise a flow from tier **0**, the new instance, to tier **1**, one of its fields, might occur.
  - In the case of a field assignment (Rule *(FA)*), all tiers are constrained to be **0** in order to avoid changes inside the tier **1** graph.
  - In rule *(Inc)*, the tier is constrained to be **0** as the integer value increases.
  - Rule *(Brk)* enforces the tier of a break instruction to be **1**. This prevents the programmer from writing conditionals of the shape:

$$\mathtt{while(}\underbrace{\mathtt{x}}_{\mathbf{1}}\mathtt{)\{I_1\ if(}\underbrace{\mathtt{y}}_{\mathbf{0}}\mathtt{)}\underbrace{\mathtt{\{break;\}}}_{\mathbf{0}}\ \mathtt{else\{I_2\}\ I_3\}}$$

    that would break the non-interference property of tiers (see Rule *(If)* above). Indeed, in the above example the number of iterations in the while loop might depend on the value of the tier **0** variable `y`.
  - Rule *(Wh)* constrains the guard of the loop `e` to be a boolean expression of tier **1**, thus preventing while loops from being controlled by tier **0** expressions.

Now there only remain some particular rules to discuss:

- The rule *(Seq)* shows that the tier of the sequence $\mathtt{I}_1\ \mathtt{I}_2$ will be the maximum of the tiers of $\mathtt{I}_1$ and $\mathtt{I}_2$. It can be read as "a sequence of instructions including at least one instruction that cannot be controlled by tier **0** cannot be controlled by tier **0**" and it preserves non-interference as it is a weakly monotonic typing rule wrt tiers.

- The recovery is performed thanks to the Rule *(ISub)* that makes possible to type an instruction of tier **0** by **1** (as tier **0** instruction use is less constrained than tier **1** instruction use) without breaking the system non-interference properties. Notice also that there is no counterpart for expressions as a subtyping rule from **1** to **0** would allow us to type $\texttt{x}++;$ with $\texttt{x}$ of tier **1** while a subtyping rule from **0** to **1** would allow the programmer to type programs with tier **0** variables in the guards of while loops.
- Consequently, only a restricted form of subtyping is allowed for expressions. This is the purpose of Rule *(Cln)* allowing the programmer to declassify information from a tier **1** expression to a **0** expression through the use of the `clone` method. Consequently, the tier **0** modifications on the copy will not affect the original tier **1** object. Notice that the choice to include the `clone` method as a primitive construct of the language has been made to make this subtyping explicit. An alternative would have been to program this method as usual in any class `C` and to check in a straightforward manner that the following judgment can be derived $\Gamma \vdash \texttt{C clone()} : \texttt{C}(\mathbf{1}) \to \texttt{C}(\mathbf{0})$.
- Methods typing and polymorphism is handled by rules *(Call)*, *(Body)* and *(OverR)*. Rule *(Call)* just checks a direct type correspondence between the arguments types and the method type when a method is called. However this rule is very important as it allows a polymorphic type discipline for fields. Indeed the contextual environment is updated so that a field can be typed wrt to the considered method. Rule *(Body)* shows how to type method definitions. It updates the environment wrt to the parameters, current object and return type in order to allow a polymorphic typing discipline for methods: while typing a program, a method can be given distinct types depending on where and how it is called. Rule *(OverR)* deals with overridden method, keeping tiers preserved, thus allowing standard OO polymorphism.

2.4 Well-Typedness

Given a program of executable $\texttt{Exe\{main()\{Init Comp\}\}}$ and a typing environment Δ, the judgment $\Delta \vdash \texttt{Exe} : \diamond$ means that the program is well-typed wrt Δ and is defined by:

$$\frac{(\texttt{void main}^{\texttt{Exe}}(), \Delta) \vDash \texttt{Init} : \texttt{void} \quad (\texttt{void main}^{\texttt{Exe}}(), \Delta) \vdash \texttt{Comp} : \texttt{void}(\mathbf{1})}{\Delta \vdash \texttt{Exe} : \diamond}$$

where $\vDash$ is a judgment derived from the type system by removing all tiers and tier based constraints in the typing rules. Since no tier constraint is checked in the initialization instruction `Init`, the complexity of this latter instruction is not under control ; as explained previously the main reason for this choice is that this instruction is considered to be building the program input. In contrast, the computational instruction `Comp` is considered to be the computational part of the program and has to respect the tiering discipline.

2.5 Type System Non-Interference Properties

Now we sum up some of the most crucial properties of the presented type system:

Property 1. There is no information flows from tier **0** data to tier **1**. The only flows from tier **1** data to tier **0** is through cloning.

This is due to the non-interference nature of the type system (see Volpano et al. [16] for more details). The only change imposed by the OO paradigm being that the current object has the same tier as its fields (rule *(Self)* of Fig. 2). By looking carefully at the rules of Fig. 2, we can check that Rule *(Cln)* is the only rule allowing flows from **1** to **0**. It does not break the property as the data flow is on a freshly cloned part of the heap.

Property 2. Tier **1** data cannot be altered.

Object creation is restricted to tier **0** by rule *(New)* of Fig. 2. Moreover, tier **1** references cannot change as field assignments are restricted to tier **0** by rule *(FA)* of Fig. 2.

Property 3. Given a program with no recursive method, execution time does not depend on tier **0** data.

This is straightforward if we do not consider recursive methods as while loop guards are restricted to be of tier **1** by rule *(Wh)* of Fig. 3. The next section will be devoted to putting a restriction on recursive methods in order to extend this property. Carefully notice that it does not prevent a tier **0** variable to appear in the guard of a while loop but still the control flow will not depend on it.

3 Safe Recursion

In this section, a safety criterion is provided in order to allow the programmer to use an admissible but restricted form of recursion. Indeed, Property 3 is valid under the hypothesis that there is no recursive call. At the present time, a recursive method might make a recursive call to be controlled by tier **0** data. This is a highly unwanted behavior. Moreover, even assuming such a Property to be satisfied, one would still be able to program a multiply recursive method with an exponential number of recursive calls. The safety criterion eliminates these two issues.

3.1 Level and Intricacy

Given two methods of signatures s and s' and names `m` and `m'`, define the relation $\sqsubset$ on method signatures by $s \sqsubset s'$ if `m'` is called in the body of `m`. This relation is extended to inheritance by considering that overriding methods are called by the overridden method. Let $\sqsubset^+$ be its transitive closure. A method of signature s is *recursive* if $s \sqsubset^+ s$ holds. Given two method signatures s and s', $s \equiv s'$

holds if both $s \sqsubset^+ s'$ and $s' \sqsubset^+ s$ hold. Given a signature s, the class $[s]$ is defined as usual by $[s] = \{s' \mid s' \equiv s\}$. Finally, we write $s \sqsubsetneq^+ s'$ if $s \sqsubset^+ s'$ holds but not $s' \sqsubset^+ s$.

We introduce the level and intricacy of instructions and extend them to programs. The level bounds the number of recursive calls while the intricacy corresponds to the number of nested while loops.

Definition 2 (Level). *The level λ of a method signature is defined by:*

- $\lambda(s) = 0$ *if* $s \notin [s]$ *(i.e. the method is not recursive),*
- $\lambda(s) = 1 + \max\{\lambda(s') \mid s \sqsubsetneq^+ s'\}$ *otherwise, setting* $\max(\emptyset) = 0$.

Let λ be the maximal level of a method in a given program.

Definition 3 (Intricacy). *The intricacy ν of an instruction is defined by:*

- $\nu([[\tau]\ \mathtt{x{:=}e}];) = 0$
- $\nu(\mathtt{x{+}{+}};) = 0$
- $\nu(\mathtt{x{-}{-}};) = 0$
- $\nu(\mathtt{break};) = 0$
- $\nu(\mathtt{I_1\ I_2}) = \max(\nu(\mathtt{I_1}), \nu(\mathtt{I_2}))$
- $\nu(\mathtt{if(x)\{I_1\}else\{I_2\}}) = \max(\nu(\mathtt{I_1}), \nu(\mathtt{I_2}))$
- $\nu(\mathtt{while(x)\{I\}}) = 1 + \nu(\mathtt{I})$

Let ν be the maximal intricacy of an instruction within a given program.

Both intricacy and level are bounded by the size of their program.

3.2 Safety Restriction

Now some side restrictions on recursive methods are provided to ensure that their flow is only controlled by tier **1** variables and to prevent exponential growth rate.

Definition 4 (Safety). *A well-typed program wrt a typing environment Δ is* safe *if for each recursive method $\tau\ \mathtt{m}(\overline{\tau\ \mathtt{x}})\{\mathtt{I}\ [\mathtt{return\ x};]\}$:*

1. *there is at most one call to some* $\mathtt{m}' \in [\mathtt{m}]$ *in the evaluation of* $\mathtt{I}$,
2. *there is no while loop inside* $\mathtt{I}$, *i.e.* $\nu(\mathtt{I}) = 0$,
3. *and* $(s, \Delta) \vdash \tau\ \mathtt{m}^{\mathtt{C}}(\overline{\tau\ \mathtt{x}}) : \mathtt{C}(\mathbf{1}) \times \langle\overline{\tau}(\mathbf{1})\rangle \to \tau(\alpha)$ *can be derived and the call to* $\mathtt{m}$ *is a* **1** *instruction.*

Remark 1. Notice that safety is a generalization of the safe recursion on notation (SRN) scheme by Bellantoni and Cook [3]. Indeed a function SRN function can be defined (and typed) in our setting:

```
f(int x, τ y){
        int res := 0 ;
        if(x == 0){res := g(y;)}
        else{if(x%2 == i){res := hᵢ(f(x/2,y)); }}
        return res;
}
```

If f output is of tier **0** (i.e. computes something) then $\mathtt{h}_i$ will not be able to recurse on it. Clearly, the above program fullfills the above Definition for some typing context Γ such that $\Gamma(\mathtt{x}) = \Gamma(\mathtt{y}) = \mathtt{int}(\mathbf{1})$.

4 Boolean Lists as an Illustrating Example

Consider the class BList encoding integers as linked lists of bits and including a field value of type boolean and a field tail of type BList. Suppose that this class comes with a getter and a setter:

```
BList getTail(){return tail;}
void setTail(BList q){tail := q;}
```

They can be typed by:

- $\Gamma \vdash$ BListgetTail() : BList(α) $\to$ Blist(α), $\alpha \in \{\mathbf{0}, \mathbf{1}\}$, by Rules *(Body)* and *(Self)*. The tier of the current object has to match the tier of the tail because of Rule *(Self)*. However it still can be **0** or **1** depending on the object on which the method is called. Recall that methods are polymorphic in our typing discipline and two distinct calls can be sometimes given distinct tiers.
- $\Gamma \vdash$ void setTail(BListq) : BList(**0**) $\times$ Blist(**0**) $\to$ void(**0**) by Rules *(Body)*, *(Self)* and *(FA)*. Here the tiers of the field and the parameter are forced to be **0** by Rule *(FA)* and, consequently, the tier of the current object is enforced to be the same by Rule *(Body)*.

We can then type the methods concat and length below. We write $\mathtt{e}^\alpha$ (resp. $\mathtt{I}:\ \alpha$) to denote that e (resp. I) is of tier α w.r.t. the environment Γ.

```
void concat(BList other) {
    BList o¹ := this¹;
    BList t⁰ := this.clone()⁰;
    while (o.getTail()¹ != null) {
        o¹ := o.getTail()¹;
        t⁰ := t.getTail()⁰;
    }
    t.setTail(other⁰);
}

int length() {
    int res⁰ := 0;
    if (tail¹ != null) {
        res⁰ := tail.length()⁰; : 1 //using (Isub)
        res++; :0
    } :1 //using (ISub)
    else {;}
    return res⁰;
}
```

$\Gamma \vdash$ voidconcat(BListother) : BList(**1**) $\times$ BList(**0**) $\to$ void(**1**).
$\Gamma \vdash$ intlength() : BList(**1**) $\to$ int(**0**).

The recursive method length satisfies conditions 1 and 2 of Definition 4. It can be typed by BList(**1**) $\to$ int(**0**) and it is called in a tier **1** instruction. Consequently, the program is safe. Moreover, the program obtained is clearly terminating. Its intricacy ν is equal to 0, since there is no nested while loops in its methods, and its level λ is equal to 1, since there is one level of recursion in the method **length**. Consequently, it terminates in time $O(|\mathcal{C}|)$ on input $\mathcal{C}$ by Theorem 1 (see the next section).

5 Characterization of Polynomial Time

In this section, we show the main result of our paper: a characterization of the class of functions computable in polynomial time by a Turing Machine, known as *FPtime*, with respect to safe and terminating OO programs. We first show the soundness by providing a polynomial upper bound on the time of such kind of programs. Then we prove the completeness by simulating polynomial time Turing Machines by safe and terminating programs. We conclude by showing that type inference can performed in polynomial time.

5.1 Polynomial Time Soundness

Let n_1 be the number of tier **1** variables in the whole program wrt the typing environment under consideration.

Theorem 1 (Soundness). *If a program is safe and terminates on input* $\mathcal{C}$ *then it does terminate in time* $O(|\mathcal{C}|^{n_1(\nu+\lambda)})$.

Proof. By Property 1 there is no information flow from tier **0** to tier **1**. Control flow in while loops and recursive calls only depends on tier **1** variables by Property 3 and by definition of safety. Moreover tier **1** variables cannot point out of the initial pointer subgraph by Property 2. Consequently, if the program terminates such a variable has at most $|\mathcal{C}|$ possible distinct values during the program execution. Otherwise it contradicts the termination assumption. Indeed if the same program pointer instruction is encountered during the execution of one program with the same tier **1** values in the heap then an infinite loop is reached as programs are deterministic. Consequently, there can be only $|\mathcal{C}|^{n_1}$ distinct configurations restricted to tier **1** variable (by restricted we mean that two configurations only differing on tier **0** variables are supposed to be equal). Finally, the level λ, intricacy ν and constant n_1 are used to compute the global upper bound. Indeed, the unfolding of while and recursive calls can generate a complexity in $O((|\mathcal{C}|^{n_1})^{(\nu+\lambda)})$.

5.2 Polynomial Time Completeness

We start to show that any polynomial can be computed by a safe and terminating program. By abuse of notation, we will use the notation $\Delta(\mathtt{m}^{\mathtt{C}})$ in all the examples when the method signature is clear from the context. Consider the following method of some class C computing addition:

```
add(int x, int y){
  while(x¹>0){
    x¹--; :1
    y⁰++; :0
  }
  return y⁰;
}
```

It can be typed by $\texttt{C}(\beta) \times \texttt{int}(\mathbf{1}) \times \texttt{int}(\mathbf{0}) \to \texttt{int}(\mathbf{0})$, for any tier β, under the typing environment Δ such that $\Delta(\texttt{add}^{\texttt{C}})(\texttt{x}) = \texttt{int}(\mathbf{1})$ and $\Delta(\texttt{add}^{\texttt{C}})(\texttt{y}) = \texttt{int}(\mathbf{0})$. Notice that x is enforced to be of tier **1**, by typing rules *(Wh)* and *(Op)* as it appears in the guard of a while loop (the operator > keeping the tier unchanged in rule *(Op)*). Moreover y is enforced to be of tier **0**, by typing rule *(Inc)*.

Consider the below method encoding multiplication:

```
mult(int x, int y){
  int z⁰ := 0;
  while(x¹>0){
    x¹--;
    int u¹ := y¹;
    while(u¹>0){
      u¹--;
      z⁰++;
    }
  }
  return z⁰;
}
```

It can be typed by $\texttt{C}(\beta) \times \texttt{int}(\mathbf{1}) \times \texttt{int}(\mathbf{1}) \to \texttt{int}(\mathbf{0})$, for any tier β, under the typing environment Δ such that $\Delta(\texttt{mult}^{\texttt{C}})(\texttt{x}) = \Delta(\texttt{mult}^{\texttt{C}})(\texttt{y}) = \Delta(\texttt{mult}^{\texttt{C}})(\texttt{u}) = \texttt{int}(\mathbf{1})$ and $\Delta(\texttt{mult}^{\texttt{C}})(\texttt{z}) = \texttt{int}(\mathbf{0})$. Notice that x and u are enforced to be of tier **1**, by typing rules *(Wh)* and *(Op)*. Moreover y is enforced to be of tier **1**, by typing rule *(VA)* applied to instruction intu = y;, u being of tier **1**. Finally, z is enforced to be of tier **0**, by typing rule *(Inc)*, as its stored value increases in z++;.

Consequently, any polynomial can be computed by using a composition of the two above methods.

Theorem 2 (Completeness). *Each function computable in polynomial time by a Turing Machine can be computed by a safe and terminating program.*

Proof. We show that every polynomial time function over binary words, encoded using the class BList, can be computed by a safe and terminating program. Consider a Turing Machine TM, with one tape and one head, which computes within n^k steps for some constant k and where n is the input size. The tape of TM is represented by two variables x and y which contain respectively the reversed left side of the tape and the right side of the tape. States are encoded by integer constants and the current state is stored in the variable state. We assign to each of these three variables that hold a configuration of TM the tier **0**. A one step transition is simulated by a finite cascade of if-commands of the form:

```
if (y.getHead()⁰){
        if (state⁰ == 8⁰){
                state⁰ = 3⁰;:0
                x⁰ =new BList(false,x⁰);:0
                y⁰ = y.getTail()⁰);:0
        }else{...:0}
}
```

The above command expresses that if the current read symbol is **true** and the state is 8, then the next state is 3, the head moves to the right and the read symbol is replaced by false. The methods getTail() and getHead() can be given the types (see the Example of Sect. 4 for more details) $\texttt{BList}(\mathbf{0}) \rightarrow \texttt{BList}(\mathbf{0})$ and $\texttt{BList}(\mathbf{0}) \rightarrow \texttt{boolean}(\mathbf{0})$, respectively. Since each variable inside the above command is of tier $\mathbf{0}$, the tier of the if-command is also $\mathbf{0}$. As shown above, any polynomial can be computed by a safe and terminating program: we have already provided the programs for addition and multiplication and we let the reader check that it can be generalized to any polynomial.

5.3 Decidability of Type Inference

Theorem 3 (Decidability of type inference). *Deciding if there exists a typing environment s.t. a program is well-typed can be done in polynomial time in the size of the program.*

Proof. The type inference problem can, be reduced to 2-SAT. Notice that the number of distinct tiered types that can be given to a method is bounded by the number of calls in the program and thus bounded by the program size. Indeed the type checking is a static analysis performed on the code. Consequently, this problem can be solved in linear time. Types can be checked in linear time in the size of the program as typing mainly consists in checking type annotations with respect to method signatures, operator signatures and attributes declarations. We encode the tier of each attribute x within the method m of class C by a boolean variable $x^{\mathtt{m}^{\mathtt{C}}}$ that will be true if the variable is of tier $\mathbf{1}$, false if it is of tier $\mathbf{0}$ in the context of $\mathtt{m}^{\mathtt{C}}$. All local variables and parameters can be encoded by a single variable as their tier is independent from the context. Each instruction generates some constraints. For example, in the case of an assignment $\mathtt{x} := \mathtt{y};$ in the context $\mathtt{m}^{\mathtt{C}}$, we have to check $\pi_2(\Delta(\mathtt{m}^{\mathtt{C}})(\mathtt{x})) \preceq \pi_2(\Delta(\mathtt{m}^{\mathtt{C}})(\mathtt{y})))$, which can be represented as $(y^{\mathtt{m}^{\mathtt{C}}} \vee \neg x^{\mathtt{m}^{\mathtt{C}}})$. All these constraints generate a conjunction of such clauses which are in number linear in the size of the program. As a result, the type inference problem is reduced to 2-SAT and can be solved in polynomial time.

6 Methodology of the Presented Analysis

The OO program complexity analysis presented in this paper can be summed up by the above figure. In a first step, given a program P of a given OO programming language, we first apply a transformation step in order to obtain the program $\tilde{P}$ of our abstract language. This transformation contains the following steps:

- convert syntactical constructs of the source language in P to constructs in the abstract OO language. In particular, transform `for` into `while`.
- for all public fields of P, write the corresponding getter and setter in $\tilde{P}$
- for each constructor in P, write a corresponding factory in $\tilde{P}$ (and just keep the basic constructor for object instantiation)
- α-rename the variables so that there is no name clashes in $\tilde{P}$.

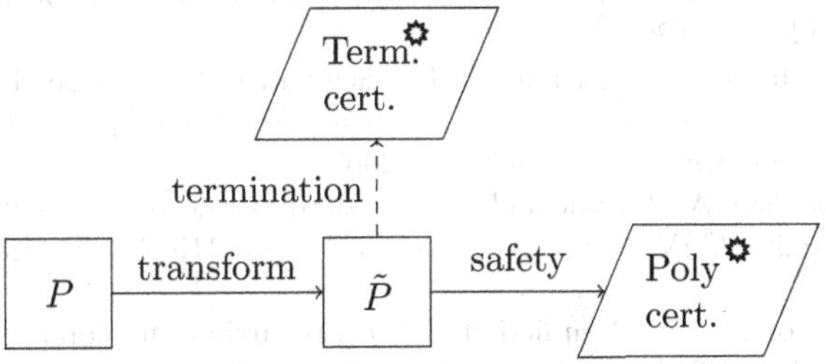

All these steps can be performed in polynomial time and the program abstract semantics is preserved. Consequently, P terminates iff $\tilde{P}$ terminates.

In a second step, we can perform in parallel a termination check and a safety check. The termination certificate can be obtained using existing tools such as [4,6,8,9] (as the semantics is preserved, the check can also be performed on the original program P or on the compiled bytecode). If both succeed, Theorem 1 ensures polynomial time termination. In the safety check, a polynomial time type inference (Theorem 3) is performed together with a criterion check on recursive methods. This latter check is generally undecidable because of condition 1 of Definition 4. However it is very easy to restrict syntactically this condition so that the check becomes decidable (*e.g.* restrict a recursive call to appear at most once in a conditional branching).

7 Expressivity and Open Issues

The expressivity of the presented analysis is good. Most polynomial programs over inductive data types such as linked lists and trees are captured (in particular BC's Safe recursion on notation). It also handles while loops guarded by objects and circular data structure. This is new.

Let us highlight that the expressivity of the method can be improved by a compositional type check: even if an instruction $\texttt{I} = \texttt{I}_1 \ \ldots \ \texttt{I}_n$ fails the safety check, if each of the $\texttt{I}_i$ passes the safety check then we can consider that $\texttt{I}$ succeeds. Indeed, a bounded composition of polynomials remains polynomial.

We could also add operators with outputs distinct from booleans. In such a case, a restriction on the size of their computations is required (see [10] for more details).

A characterization of polynomial space based on the same methodology and OO threads is expected to be highly plausible.

References

1. Albert, E., Arenas, P., Genaim, S., Puebla, G., Zanardini, D.: Cost analysis of object-oriented bytecode programs. Theoret. Comput. Sci. **413**(1), 142–159 (2012)
2. Baillot, P., Terui, K.: Light types for polynomial time computation in lambda-calculus. In: Logic in Computer Science, LICS, pp. 266–275 (2004)
3. Bellantoni, S., Cook, S.: A new recursion-theoretic characterization of the poly-time functions. Comput. Complex. **2**, 97–110 (1992)
4. Ben-Amram, A.M., Genaim, S., Masud, A.N.: On the termination of integer loops. In: Kuncak, V., Rybalchenko, A. (eds.) VMCAI 2012. LNCS, vol. 7148, pp. 72–87. Springer, Heidelberg (2012)
5. Cachera, D., Jensen, T., Pichardie, D., Schneider, G.: Certified memory usage analysis. In: Fitzgerald, J.S., Hayes, I.J., Tarlecki, A. (eds.) FM 2005. LNCS, vol. 3582, pp. 91–106. Springer, Heidelberg (2005)
6. Cook, B., Podelski, A., Rybalchenko, A.: Terminator: beyond safety. In: Ball, T., Jones, R.B. (eds.) CAV 2006. LNCS, vol. 4144, pp. 415–418. Springer, Heidelberg (2006)
7. Danner, N., Royer, J.S.: Ramified structural recursion and corecursion. In: CoRR abs/1201.4567 (2012). http://arxiv.org/abs/1201.4567
8. Gulwani, S.: SPEED: symbolic complexity bound analysis. In: Bouajjani, A., Maler, O. (eds.) CAV 2009. LNCS, vol. 5643, pp. 51–62. Springer, Heidelberg (2009)
9. Gulwani, S., Mehra, K.K., Chilimbi, T.M.: Speed: precise and efficient static estimation of program computational complexity. In: POPL 2009, pp. 127–139. ACM (2009)
10. Hainry, E., Marion, J.-Y., Péchoux, R.: Type-based complexity analysis for fork processes. In: Pfenning, F. (ed.) FOSSACS 2013 (ETAPS 2013). LNCS, vol. 7794, pp. 305–320. Springer, Heidelberg (2013)
11. Hofmann, M., Schöpp, U.: Pure pointer programs with iteration. ACM Trans. Comput. Log. **11**(4), 26 (2010)
12. Kersten, R., Shkaravska, O., van Gastel, B., Montenegro, M., van Eekelen, M.C.J.D.: Making resource analysis practical for real-time Java. In: JTRES, pp. 135–144 (2012)
13. Leivant, D., Marion, J.Y.: Lambda calculus characterizations of poly-time. Fundam. Inf. **19**(1/2), 167–184 (1993)
14. Leivant, D., Marion, J.-Y.: Evolving graph-structures and their implicit computational complexity. In: Fomin, F.V., Freivalds, R.U., Kwiatkowska, M., Peleg, D. (eds.) ICALP 2013, Part II. LNCS, vol. 7966, pp. 349–360. Springer, Heidelberg (2013)
15. Marion, J.Y.: A type system for complexity flow analysis. In: Logic in Computer Science, LICS, pp. 123–132 (2011)
16. Volpano, D., Irvine, C., Smith, G.: A sound type system for secure flow analysis. J. Comput. Secur. **4**(2/3), 167–188 (1996)

Programming Models

Programming Techniques for Reversible Comparison Sorts

Holger Bock Axelsen[1(✉)] and Tetsuo Yokoyama[2]

[1] DIKU, Department of Computer Science, University of Copenhagen, Copenhagen, Denmark
funkstar@di.ku.dk

[2] Department of Software Engineering, Nanzan University, Nagoya, Japan
tyokoyama@acm.org

Abstract. A common approach to reversible programming is to reversibly simulate an irreversible program with the desired functionality, which in general puts additional pressure on the computational resources (time, space.) If the same running time is required, ensuring a minimal space overhead is a significant programming challenge.

We introduce criteria for the optimality of reversible simulation: A reversible simulation is *faithful* if it incurs no asymptotic time overhead and bounds the space overhead (the *garbage*) by some function $g(n)$, and *hygienic* if g is (asymptotically) optimal for faithful simulation.

We demonstrate the programming techniques used to develop faithful and hygienic reversible simulations of several well-known comparison sorts, *e.g.* insertion sort and quicksort, using representations of permutations in both the output and intermediate additional space required.

1 Introduction

Reversible computing studies computation models that exhibit both forward and backward determinism. This field has a long history, and although usually motivated by the promise of lower energy consumption *qua* the thermodynamics of computation, is now increasingly seen to be important in connection with quantum computing, which *e.g.* relies on reversible computing methods for significant parts of quantum circuit synthesis and design (*e.g.* as subroutines.)

A general task in reversible computation models is the simulation of irreversible functionality, and the key problem for simulation is dealing with *erasure*. Any data erased in a simulated irreversible program must be collected and assembled to preserve reversibility. This assembled *garbage data* takes up extra space both during and after the computation, and minimizing garbage has been a significant goal for reversible computation. General reversible simulation methods have been extensively studied, especially in terms of time/space tradeoffs (see *e.g.* [12] and references therein.) However, very little has been done in the field of *reversible programming*, not even for specific algorithm families, despite the importance of finding reversible algorithms that do not significantly deteriorate the asymptotics (*i.e.* use excessive time or space) compared to the irreversible

X. Feng and S. Park (Eds.): APLAS 2015, LNCS 9458, pp. 407–426, 2015.
DOI: 10.1007/978-3-319-26529-2_22

versions. The problem is well-recognized in other subfields, *e.g.* in reversible and quantum logic synthesis and design, where minimizing the number of (output) garbage lines and ancillae (temporary) lines is a central challenge [2,13].

In this paper we focus on developing a family of efficient reversible comparison sorts with asymptotically optimal (minimal) garbage, while also keeping the running times of the irreversible counterparts. Reversible sorts have numerous applications, and analysis and programming techniques for reversible sorts are effectively reusable elsewhere. A key point is that we want the auxiliary garbage to be *reusable* between the various algorithms, to make the solutions as modular as possible. Now, for sorting of an array of length n, it is not difficult to see that $\Theta(n \log n)$ bits (encoding a permutation) will suffice for the output garbage (see *e.g.* [12, Chap. 15]), but the central problem is how to achieve, in practice, efficient information storage and retrieval from minimized garbage at runtime. Using a general reversible simulation method (*history embedding*, or the input-copying *compute-copy-uncompute* method [3], see also below) will not work, as the garbage size will often exceed the lower bound: these methods always use a trace of the size of the running time, even when the optimal garbage is smaller.

Some prior work on reversible sorting exists: In $\mathcal{MOQA}$ quicksort uses *rank* (a number in the range $[0, n! - 1]$ representing the permutation) to ensure injectivity, although not actual reversibility [6]. Yokoyama *et al.* used ranks for generating a reversible insertion and merge sort [15]. Lutz and Derby used direct representations of permutations for a pioneer attempt at reversible bubble sort [9], although unfortunately their program does not work correctly. Hall used factorial representation (also in array form) in an *input-copying* out-of-place reversible insertion sort. Despite the worst case number of comparisons being quadratic, the garbage size is in this way reduced to $n\lceil\log_2 n\rceil$ $(= \Theta(n \log n))$ [7]. The Reverse C compiler [12, Chap. 10] generates reversible simulations of (a subset of) C programs, and is applicable to sorting programs. However, this tool defaults to using a history embedding in nearly all cases.

Based on this, we propose to use direct and factorial (factoradic) representations of permutations for both the intermediate and output garbage of reversible comparison sorts, and show how this facilitates their programming. The techniques apply to many different sorts, and the representations can be efficiently converted into each other (or into ranks) if needed. Our main contributions are:

- The notions of *faithful* and *hygienic* reversible simulation are introduced: A faithful simulation incurs no asymptotic time overhead, and bounds the space overhead by some given function $g(n)$. If $g(n)$ cannot be lowered asymptotically, the simulation is called *hygienic* (Sect. 2.)
- New hygienic reversible versions of sorting programs are developed for in-place insertion sort, bubble sort, and selection sort using factorial representation; and merge sort and quicksort using direct representation (Sect. 3.)
- We uncover several unconventional relations among reversible sorts, where garbage and code are shared in novel ways, including an *identity permutation trick* that yields a two-pass reversible simulation (with optimal *output* garbage), for any comparison sort (Sect. 3.)

Programs can be run on the online interpreter at `topps.diku.dk/pirc/sorts`.

2 Preliminaries

In ordinary programming languages, we usually write programs that lose information during computation, and we have to do so when implementing many-to-one functions. However, in reversible programming languages (*e.g.* [9,14]) the information is preserved in each computation step, and so only injective functions can be implemented. A language is said to be r-Turing-complete if *all* injective computable functions are in range [1,3].

For any function $f : X \rightarrow Y$, there exists injective functions $f' : X \rightarrow Y \times G$ for some G such that for all $x \in X$, $\mathit{fst}(f'(x)) = f(x)$, where *fst* is the projection $\mathit{fst}(x, y) = x$. We say that f' is an *injectivization* of f. The G output is only used to make f' injective, and is in this sense irrelevant to the original Y output. In reversible computing terms G is called *output garbage*.

2.1 Reversible Simulations

Let IR be an (irreversible) language and R be a reversible language. A reversible R-program q is a *reversible simulation of* IR-program p iff $\mathit{fst}([\![\mathtt{q}]\!]^{\mathtt{R}}(x)) = [\![\mathtt{p}]\!]^{\mathtt{IR}}(x)$ for all x, *i.e.* $[\![\mathtt{q}]\!]^{\mathtt{R}}$ is an injectivization of $[\![\mathtt{p}]\!]^{\mathtt{IR}}$. A reversible simulation q of p is called *clean* if it produces *only* the original output of p, but no garbage, *i.e.* $[\![\mathtt{q}]\!]^{\mathtt{R}} : X \rightarrow Y \times \mathbb{1}$ where $\mathbb{1}$ is the unit type.

Clearly, we can only have clean reversible simulations of programs that compute injective functions. For non-injective functions, we need a concept to describe that some reversible simulations behave better in terms of garbage than others. We say that q is a *faithful* reversible simulation of p *with garbage bound* $g : \mathbb{N} \rightarrow \mathbb{N}$, if there is a constant c, which may depend on p (and R), but *not* on the program input x, such that the following three conditions hold:

- bounded garbage output: $|\mathit{snd}([\![\mathtt{q}]\!]^{\mathtt{R}}(x))| \leq c \cdot g(|x|)$ for all x,
- no asymptotic time overhead: $\mathit{time}^{\mathtt{R}}_{\mathtt{q}}(x) \leq c \cdot \mathit{time}^{\mathtt{IR}}_{\mathtt{p}}(x)$ for all x,
- at most g extra space: $\mathit{space}^{\mathtt{R}}_{\mathtt{q}}(x) \leq c \cdot (\mathit{space}^{\mathtt{IR}}_{\mathtt{p}}(x) + g(|x|))$ for all x,

where $|z|$ is the size of data z in the binary representation. Here, $\mathit{time}^{\mathtt{L}}_{\mathtt{p}}(\mathtt{d})$ represents the number of execution steps (or application of semantic rules or some other reasonable measure of time) of a program p for an input d in a language L, and $\mathit{space}^{\mathtt{L}}_{\mathtt{p}}(\mathtt{d})$ represents the maximum space usage (*e.g.* the size of the heap and stack) during the execution of a program p for an input d in a language L.

The first condition states that the garbage size is bounded by $g(|x|)$. What we want to emphasize here is that g depends only on the size of x but not the content of x. The second condition states that the reversible simulation q has the same time complexity as the irreversible counterpart p. The intuition of the third condition is that any extra space is dedicated to garbage manipulation.

A faithful reversible simulation q of p is called *hygienic* with garbage bound g if there is *no* q' and $h(n) = o(g(n))$ such that q' is a faithful reversible simulation of p with garbage bound h. That is, a hygienic simulation is time-wise the best we can hope for: it is (asymptotically) optimal in its garbage usage and it does not violate the time complexity of the program it simulates.

2.2 The Janus Reversible Programming Language

The reversible algorithms in this paper are implemented in an extended version [14] of the reversible programming language Janus developed in 1982 [9]. Janus is a simple imperative language, essentially C-style syntax with a few key differences to ensure reversibility. To make the text as self-contained as possible, we here provide a brief introduction to the language.

As a concrete example, below is a Janus procedure to compute the factorial function. Given a natural number `n` (≥ 0) and zero-cleared `res` (meaning `res` is 0), the procedure `factorial` sets `res` to $n!$ with `n` left unchanged:

```
1  procedure factorial(int n, int res)
2    res += 1
3    local int i = 0                   // { res = 0! }
4      from  i = 0 loop                // After one loop { i ≠ 0 }
5        i += 1                        // { res = (i − 1)! }
6        local int tmp = res * i       // { res = (i − 1)!, tmp = i! }
7          res <=> tmp                 // { res = i!, tmp = (i − 1)! }
8        delocal int tmp = res / i     // { res = i! }
9      until i = n                     // Exit with { res = n! }
10   delocal int i = n
```

The base types of Janus variables are integers, and arrays and stacks of integers. The atomic statements (e.g. lines 2, 5, 7 above) are *reversible updates* of variables relative to their existing content, rather than absolute assignment. For this, C's shorthand for compound assignment `+=`, `-=`, and `^=` is used. As an example, the compound assignment `x += y*3` is allowed, but the simple assignment `x := 3` is not. We require that the left-hand assignment target does not occur in the right-hand expression (or in the index expression if the left-hand side is an array cell), to avoid otherwise irreversible updates like `x -= x`. The `<=>` statement swaps variable values. Control flow operators in Janus use runtime *assertions* to orthogonalize join points, and ensure reversibility. Thus, the conditional statement `if` e_1 `then` s_1 `else` s_2 `fi` e_2 works almost like an ordinary `if-then-else`, but the expression e_2 *must* evaluate to true when exiting the `then` branch, and false when exiting the `else` branch, and this is enforced at run-time. Similarly, the reversible loop statement `from` e_1 `do` s_1 `loop` s_2 `until` e_2 requires the entry assertion e_1 to be true at the first entry to the loop, and false in every subsequent iteration. The `do`-statement s_1 is executed between testing the entry and exit expressions, and the `loop`-statement s_2 between exit and entry. Local variables are declared using the `local` statement initializing a (fresh) variable to the value of given expression. For reversibility, these are paired with `delocal` (un)declarations, which remove variables from scope by zero-clearing them using programmer-given expressions, the correctness of which is enforced at run-time (see lines 3 & 10, and 4 & 6.) A `call` statement can be used for procedure calls using pass-by-reference parameters. An unconventional feature of Janus is the possibility of inverse procedure invocation with the `uncall` statement, which runs the called procedure body *backward*.

Assume that `factorial` is invoked by a `call`. The initially zero-cleared `res` is set to one at line 2. Each loop updates the value of `res` to $res \times i$ by using temporary variable `tmp`, satisfying the invariant $\{res = i!\}$. The loop repeats until the index `i` reaches n. Then `res` is $n!$, and the local variable `i` is removed. Input and output of procedures (the values of the parameters) are related by the semantic function. For example, $[\![\texttt{factorial}]\!]^{\texttt{Janus}}(5,0) = (5,120)$, although keep in mind that parameters are still pass-by-reference.

For brevity, we shall employ a fair amount of syntactic sugar in this paper: this includes declaring/removing multiple local variables simultaneously (*e.g.* `local int x = 0, int y = 1, ...`). When the meaning of any further sugar is not intuitively obvious, this will be explained in the text.

Since we are dealing with reversible simulations of irreversible programs, for the base irreversible language we shall also use Janus, but with two small modifications: we add the irreversible statement `emit(`x`)` which erases (zero-clears) x and elide the `uncall` statement (as `emits` cannot be rolled back.) A central difficulty when writing reversible Janus procedures is to invent the proper assertions for conditionals and loops to specify which direction the control comes from, and to find proper expressions to deallocate local variables. Generally, the invention of assertions is known to be challenging (see [11], and references therein.) However, if we can `emit` data, it is straightforward to implement irreversible programs. An absolute assignment can be mimicked by initially zero-clearing the target with `emit`. For control flow, a fresh variable can be used to temporarily store where the control came from, and subsequently emitted afterwards. For example, to implement an irreversible conditional `if` e_1 `then` s_1 `else` s_2, we allocate a fresh variable `t` before the reversible conditional, add the assignment `t += 1` to the `then` branch and use the assertion `t = 1` to reversibly merge the branches. Afterwards, we discard `t`'s value with `emit(t)` and deallocate. In similar fashion, one can implement ordinary irreversible loops, deletion of variables, and other irreversible behavior fairly easily by vigorous use of `emit`.

Code is written in `typewriter font`. Mathematical objects, semantic values and metavariables are written in *italic fonts*. We use `a[m..n]` to indicate the subarray of `a[]` with the $n-m+1$ elements between the m-th to n-th elements (inclusive), if $m \leq n$, and an empty array, otherwise. Array values are denoted as *italic fonts* with subscripts; the value of `a[i]` is denoted as a_i.

3 Comparison Sorts

We shall consider reversible comparison sorts that take an unordered array of length n (≥ 1) and return an ordered array (together with garbage.) Our aim is in all cases to implement reversible versions of existing comparison sorts such that the reversible programs perform the same number of comparison/exchange operations, on the same elements, and in the same order, as the irreversible comparison sort would on the same input.

Sorting for an array of length two or greater is generally irreversible, in the sense that multiple input arrays are transformed into the same ordered array. If we have an array of distinct elements, the number of possible starting permutations is $n!$. To distinguish $n!$ cases, in binary representation we need garbage of at least $\lceil \log_2(n!) \rceil$ bits ($= \Theta(n \log n)$.)

In this section we iteratively construct reversible simulations of major comparison sorts. We optimize intermediate and output garbage as low as the asymptotically optimal hygienic bound[1] $g(n) = \Theta(n \log n)$.

3.1 Bubble Sort

Bubble sort rearranges the array `a[0..n-1]` in place to be in order. First, it compares the rear two values a_{n-1} and a_{n-2} and exchanges the content of `a[n-1]` and `a[n-2]` if they are out of order. This continues with the preceding entries `a[n-2]` and `a[n-3]`, `a[n-3]` and `a[n-4]`, and so on. In the process, the smallest element is moved sequentially to the front, until it is placed in `a[0]`. This whole process is repeated on the (unordered) subarrays `a[`i`..n-1]` for $i = 0, 1, \ldots, n-1$. Each repetition moves the proper minimal element to the first entry of the subarray `a[`i`..n-1]` so eventually all the elements are ordered.

Table 1. The operation of bubble sort for $\{2, 5, 4, 0, 3, 1\}$. The right table gives the factorial representation used in `bsort4`.

Unsorted array	Zero cleared array
2 5 4 0 3 1	0 0 0 0 0 0
0 2 5 4 1 3	1 1 1 0 1 0
0 1 2 5 4 3	2 2 2 0 1 0
0 1 2 3 5 4	2 3 3 0 1 0
0 1 2 3 4 5	2 4 3 0 1 0
0 1 2 3 4 5	2 4 3 0 1 0
Sorted array	Factorial representation

The left table of Table 1 shows how bubble sort works on a six element array. The unsorted array at the top becomes a sorted one at the bottom. The underlined elements are slided to the right by one element in each loop iteration. The elements under the jagged line are known to be at the final position in the array.

A straightforward program for (irreversible) bubble sort is obtained by adding, to the ordinary bubble sort, assertions of reversible loops, reversible conditionals, reversible deallocation of variables using emits as outlined in Sect. 2.

```
procedure bsort_irev(int a[], int n)
  local int i = 0, int t1 = 1
    from  t1 = 1
    do    emit(t1)
    loop  local int j = n - 1, int t2 = 1, int t3 = 0
            from  t2 = 1
            do    emit(t2)
            loop  if a[j-1] > a[j] then
                     a[j-1] <=> a[j]; t3 ^= 1
                  fi t3 = 1
                  emit(t3); j -= 1
            until j = i  // { a[0..i] is ordered }
            emit(j)
          delocal int j = 0, int t2 = 0, int t3 = 0
          i += 1
    until i = n
    emit(i)
  delocal int i = 0, int t1 = 0
```

[1] This bound can depend significantly on the data structures used. For list sorting, which returns a redundant representation of the sorted array, no garbage is needed.

The temporary variables `t1`–`t3` are at least of size one, and `i` and `j` are at least of size $\lceil \log_2 n \rceil$ and $\lceil \log_2 (n-1) \rceil$. In the outer loop, `t1` and `j` are emitted $n+1$ and n times. In the inner loop, `t2` and `t3` are emitted $\frac{1}{2}(n^2+n)$ and $\frac{1}{2}(n^2-n)$ times. Variable `i` is emitted once. The amount of emitted bits is $\Omega(n^2)$ and is thus greater than asymptotic minimum $\Theta(n \log n)$ discussed above.

Many of the **emit** statements and the use of local variables can be removed by observations on the counter variables `i` and `j`. The outer loop increments counter `i` from 0 to n, and the inner loop decrements counter `j` from $n-1$ to i. Therefore, the assertions on the entries of the outer and inner loops can be replaced with `i=0` and `j=n-1`, respectively, and the final values of the counter variables at the end of the loop execution can be used to deallocate the counter variables. This obviates the preceding **emit** statements and the use of local variables `t1` and `t2`, but does not change the asymptotic complexity of the amount of emitted bits because of the emission of the contents of `t3`. In what follows we shall use such simple refinements without further explanation.

History Embedding. In comparison sorts we compare and, if necessary, swap a pair of elements a, b. Since two precursor states (either a, b or b, a) are merged into a single state (unless $a = b$), one bit of information is lost. Specifically, in , the use of local variable `t3` and the emission of its content cannot be obviated by local analysis. A simple method to reversibly compensate for the lost information is to add this bit to garbage data. If we collect the information from each comparison as garbage, then garbage (and space) use of the reversible simulation are of size $\frac{1}{2}(n^2-n)$. Using a stack **gb** for this yields the following code:

```
procedure bsort1(int a[], int n, stack gb)
  local int i = 0
    from  i = 0
    loop  local int j = n - 1
            from  j = n - 1
            loop  if a[j] < a[j-1]
                  then a[j-1] <=> a[j]
                       push(1,gb)   // push control garbage
                  else push(0,gb)   // push control garbage
                  fi top(gb) = 1
                  j -= 1
            until j = i   // { a[0..i] is ordered }
          delocal int j = i
          i += 1
    until i = n
  delocal int i = n
```

such that `bsort1` is a reversible simulation of , *i.e.*, for all a and n, $\mathit{fst}(\llbracket \texttt{bsort1} \rrbracket^{\text{Janus}}(a,n)) = \llbracket\ \rrbracket^{\text{Janus+Emit}}(a,n)$. The number of garbage bits accumulated by `bsort1` is $\frac{1}{2}(n^2-n)$, provided that **push** only pushes one bit at a time to stack **gb**. Note that the comparisons performed are exactly the same (and in the same order) as that of , so the time complexity is unaffected, and thus `bsort1` is a faithful reversible simulation of with garbage $\Theta(n^2)$. This technique can be regarded as an instance of the Landauer embedding, *cf.* [1,3].

Call-Uncall Convention. Such garbage can be reversibly canceled and replaced with the original input by what is known as the *Bennett trick* [3]. In Janus, the uncomputation (or *Lecerf reversal*) of a procedure call is realized by its inverse invocation (using an `uncall`) with the same parameters as the original call [14]:

```
procedure bsort2(int a[], int n, int b[])
  local stack gb = nil
    call bsort1(a,n,gb)
    call xcopyArray(a,b,n) // Copy a[] to zero cleared b[]
    uncall bsort1(b,n,gb)  // Clear gb and set original a[] to b[]
  delocal stack gb = nil
```

Let k be the bit size of elements of the array `a[]`. The size of the output garbage for `bsort2` is always nk. Note that this does *not* produce a faithful simulation with $O(nk)$ garbage, as the *intermediate* space usage by `gb` is still $\Theta(n^2)$.

The Identity Permutation Trick. A variant of the call-uncall convention can return a (direct) permutation as garbage if it uncalls bubble sort `bsort1` with an identity permutation `p[]`:

```
procedure bsort3(int a[], int n, int p[]) // {p_k = k for all k}
  local stack gb = nil
    call bsort1(a,n,gb)
    uncall bsort1(p,n,gb)
  delocal stack gb = nil
```

Since the sorted `a[]` and identity permutation `p[]` have the i-th smallest element at index i the invocation of `bsort1(p,n,gb)` takes exactly the same path as the inverse invocation of `bsort1(a,n,gb)` in the opposite direction. The size of the elements in `p[]` need not be larger than $\lceil \log_2 n \rceil$, so the permutation can be simply represented in $n\lceil \log_2 n \rceil$ bits ($= \Theta(n \log n)$), which is asymptotically optimal. We refer this programming technique as the *identity permutation trick*.

This observation provides a free source of a useful theorem: For any irreversible comparison sort, there is a reversible comparison sort that returns garbage in the form of a permutation of the same length as the input, with the same (asymptotic) running time for each input array.

Even though the garbage size at the end of this reversible simulation is asymptotically optimal, `bsort3` has two shortcomings. First, `bsort3` as well as `bsort2` is a two pass program; `bsort1` is both called and uncalled in the body, and counting up and down of counter variables in `bsort1` is performed twice, which adds to the time overhead. Second, the reversible simulation is not hygienic. The intermediate garbage size $\Theta(n^2)$ is still asymptotically greater than the optimal garbage size $\Theta(n \log n)$. Still, this trick transforms *intensional* garbage related explicitly to the inner workings of bubble sort into *extensional* garbage related only to the functionality of sorting in general.

Strictly speaking, before calling `bsort3(a,n,p)` we need to prepare an identity permutation of length n to zero cleared `p[]`. However, this only requires time $\Theta(n)$ and does not affect the asymptotic behavior of the reversible simulation. Thus, in the following discussion on complexity we can ignore the process.

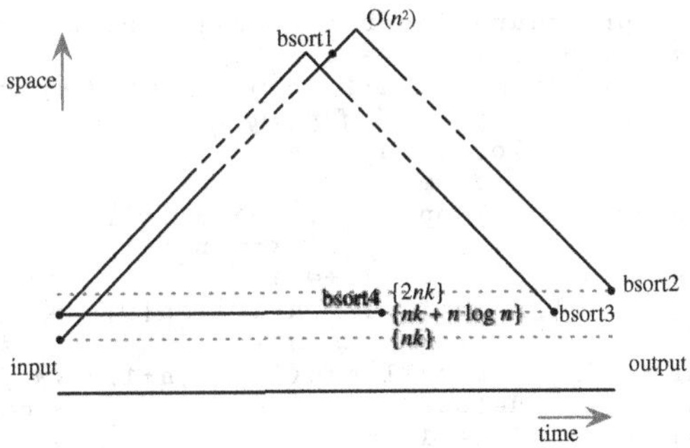

Fig. 1. Time/space of reversible bubble sorts.

Figure 1 provides a conceptual view of the intermediate garbage behavior of the reversible bubble sorts in this paper. The maximum space used by `bsort1`–`bsort3` is proportional to the execution time. Procedures `bsort2` and `bsort3` have slightly different peaks and different garbage size at the end. This is because they use different garbage representation; in this particular diagram we assume that $\log_2 n$ is smaller than the bitsize k of the elements we sort. During the latter half of computation `bsort2` keeps an extra array of size nk for the output garbage, while `bsort3` keeps a permutation of size $n\lceil\log_2 n\rceil$. Later we shall see `bsort4`, which has output garbage of same size as `bsort3`, but is a single-pass hygienic algorithm with (intermediate) garbage $\Theta(n \log n)$.

3.2 Insertion Sort

(Back-to-front) insertion sort maintains the ordered subarray `a[`$j+1$`..n-1]` and in each iteration (for $j = n-1, \ldots, 0$) adds `a[`j`]` to the subarray, by comparing and exchanging a_j with $a_{j+1}, a_{j+2}, \ldots$, until `a[`j`..n-1]` are ordered. In the worst case insertion sort performs $\frac{1}{2}(n^2 - n)$ comparisons, but in the best case just $n-1$. If we naively add a garbage bit for each comparison, *i.e.*, apply the history embedding, then the (garbage) space complexity of the resulting reversible simulation is $O(n^2)$ and $\Omega(n)$. We can then further apply the techniques of the call-uncall convention, and the identity permutation trick (as described above for bubble sort) to transform this reversible simulation into a program with a more useful output garbage representation. (We omit the concrete programs from this paper.) These reversible simulations are all faithful, but with (intermediate) garbage bound $g(n) = n^2$, so they are not hygienic.

To further optimize the intermediate garbage of reversible comparison sorts, and in particular in order to obtain a hygienic solution, it appears that we have to use both problem and algorithm specific knowledge.

Permutations as Intermediate Garbage. Our first attempt at a hygienic insertion sort is to use permutations not just as output, but also for the intermediate garbage data structure. Let `p[]` be initialized to the identity permutation. Every time we swap two elements in the input array `a[]`, we swap the corresponding entries with the same indices in the permutation array `p[]`:

```
1  procedure isort1(int a[], int n, int p[]) //{p_k = k for all k}
2    local int j = n-1
3      from j = n-1 loop // insert a_j into the ordered subarray a[j+1..n-1],
         { p_k = k for any k = 0,...,j }
4        local int i = j
5          from  i = j
6          loop  a[i] <=> a[i+1]
7                p[i] <=> p[i+1]
8                i += 1                          // { p_i = j }
9          until i = n-1 || a[i] <= a[i+1]  //{a[j..n-1] is ordered}
10         // zero clear i              // isort2 diff:
11         uncall min(i,p,j,n-1)  //+ from p[i]=j loop i-=1 until i=j
12       delocal int i = 0          //+ delocal int i=j
13       j -= 1
14     until j = -1
15   delocal int j = -1
```

After each iteration of the inner loop[2] of line 5–9, the element initially stored at the j-th position is inserted at the index i of the ordered subarray `a[`$j+1$`..n-1]` where the elements of `a[`$j+1$`..`i`]` has been shifted to the left by one element. The auxiliary procedure `min(i,p,l,r)` sets (initially zero cleared) `i` to the index k such that p_k is the minimum in $p_l, \ldots, p_r$, using $O(r-l)$ time and $O(r-l)$ space. Therefore, the inverse invocation of `min(i,p,l,r)` zero clears `i` if p_i is the smallest element in $p_l, \ldots, p_r$. Since `min(i,p,j,n-1)` traverses all the elements in `p[`j`..n-1]` for any j, unfortunately `isort1` takes $\Theta(n^2)$ time.[3] Because insertion sort can be sub-quadratic for some inputs, `isort1` is not a faithful reversible simulation of . Here again, we ignore the preprocess setting an identity permutation to `p[]`. This is an example that manipulation of garbage can affect the asymptotic behavior of reversible simulation.

However, we can improve on this by the following observation. Because the inserted element is originally stored at the j-th position in `a[]` and $p_j = j$, p_i must be j after the insertion. Without changing the meaning, we can replace lines 11–12 with the statements in the comments. Call the resulting procedure `isort2`. Then, for each outer loop iteration, the two inner loops have exactly the same number of iterations. Therefore, `isort2` takes $\Theta(n)$ time at best.

The intermediate and output garbage of the bubble sort, the permutation `p[]` of length n, can be represented in $\Theta(n \log n)$ space (which is the hygienic bound.) Since the asymptotic time complexity of `isort2` and is the same for each input (a, n), there is some constant c such that $time^{\texttt{Janus}}_{\texttt{isort2}}(a,n) \leq c \cdot time^{\texttt{Janus+Emit}}_{\texttt{isort\_irev}}(a,n)$ for any a and n. Therefore, reversible program `isort2` is a *hygienic reversible simulation of* . It should be noted that the notion of faithfulness is quite sensitive to the time behaviour of the program it is a reversible simulation of. For instance, although `bsort3` is a faithful bubble sort, it is not a faithful reversible simulation of insertion sort: even though both are $O(n^2)$, on some inputs insertion sort will be linear, which breaks the condition that a faithful simulation must conserve the time complexity on all inputs.

---

[2] If `i=n` holds at line 9, the loop terminates without evaluating expression `a[i-1] <= a[i]` with the out-of-bounds index n, by using *short-circuit evaluation.*

[3] The non-variable actual argument `n-1` is syntactic sugar for a fresh variable allocated with value $n-1$ before the call, and deallocated with value $n-1$ afterwards.

Unfortunately, we see that `isort2` uses two inner loops to simulate a single inner loop of in two passes. Next, we shall change the permutation representation which leads to a one-pass inner loop.

Factorial Representation as Garbage. Hall observed that although the worst-case number of comparisons is $\Theta(n^2)$, the intermediate garbage size of an *input-copying* reversible[4] insertion sort can be reduced down to $\Theta(n \log n)$, since the outcome of the comparisons uniquely define a permutation in factorial representation [7]. We apply this idea to an *in-place* reversible insertion sort:

```
1   procedure isort3(int a[], int n, int d[])
2     local int j = n - 1
3       from j = n - 1 do
4         local int i = j
5           from i = j
6           loop a[i-1] <=> a[i]; i += 1
7           until i = n || a[i-1] <= a[i]  // {a[j-1..n-1] is ordered}
8           d[j-1] += i - j
9         delocal int i = d[j-1] + j
10        j -= 1
11      until j = 0
12    delocal int j = 0
```

Given an unordered array a and an initially zero cleared array d, procedure `isort3` returns an ordered array a together with garbage array d. For each i, array element d_i represents how many times the element initially placed at the index i of array a is moved to the right when it is inserted into the ordered array `a[`i`+1..n-1]` (when $i = n-1$ the ordered subarray is empty and therefore d_{n-1} is always zero). That is, d_i is equal to the number of elements that are smaller than a_i in the initial subarray `a[`$i+1$`..n-1]`. By this construction array d is a *(decreasing) factorial representation* of the sorting permutation, with $0 \leq d_i \leq n-i-1$ for $0 \leq i \leq n-1$ [4], and has $n!$ distinct values. If each element of d is of size $\lceil \log_2 n \rceil$, the garbage size is the asymptotically optimal $\Theta(n \log n)$. A factorial representation can be efficiently transformed into an integer or *rank* of the permutation, with the same number of bits [4].

Table 2 shows how insertion sort `isort3` works on a six element array. In the left table, the unordered array a at the top becomes an ordered array at the bottom. The elements under the diagonal line are already known to be sorted. In the right table, the zero cleared array d at the top becomes a factorial representation at the bottom. The elements under the diagonal are known to be the final values. Thus, in insertion sort, each element of d is set only once and never changed. In the left table, the element just left of the line is inserted into the ordered subarray on the right, where the underlined elements have been moved once to the left by the previous insertion. Note how this corresponds directly to the value to the right of the diagonal in d: at the m-th iteration, the number of interchanged elements is stored in d`[`$n-m-1$`]`. This value d_{n-m-1} is used to directly deallocate the counter variable `i` of the inner loop at line 9 in

[4] We remark that Hall's instruction set is only reversible when programmer discipline is employed, and in fact contains a number of irreversible instructions.

`isort3`. Intuitively, if we know how deep an element is inserted, we can uniquely determine which element it is and what the previous ordered subarray was.

Thus, with optimal garbage, and only constant overhead in each loop iteration, the reversible program `isort3` is a *hygienic reversible simulation of* the irreversible insertion sort.

Table 2. The intermediate arrays and decreasing factorial representation of insertion sort `isort3` for a sample array $\{2, 5, 4, 0, 3, 1\}$.

Unsorted array a	Zero cleared array d
2 5 4 0 3 1	0 0 0 0 0 0
2 5 4 0 1 3	0 0 0 0 1 0
2 5 4 0 1 3	0 0 0 0 1 0
2 5 0 1 3 4	0 0 3 0 1 0
2 0 1 3 4 5	0 4 3 0 1 0
0 1 2 3 4 5	2 4 3 0 1 0
Sorted array a	Factorial representation d

A dual to the decreasing factorial representation we use is known as the *inversion table*, whose i-th element contains the number of elements to the left of i that are greater than i in the original array. Inversion tables can be used for analyzing properties of (conventional) sorting algorithms [8, Chap. 5].

3.3 Hygienic Bubble Sort

Building on the hygienic reversible insertion sort development we shall now define a hygienic reversible bubble sort. The key to this is to consider the relation between the two algorithms as sorting networks.

Insertion sort and bubble sort are identical when considered as parallel sorting networks [8, Sect. 5.3.4]. Each vertical line in such a network contains an array element, and each horizontal edge is a comparison/swap operation. An unordered array is input at the top and a sorted result is obtained at the bottom. Figure 2 shows the network (twice) in action on a sample array; horizontal edges with arrowheads indicates that elements on the lines were swapped, and edges without arrows indicates that they were not swapped. In Fig. 2(b) traversing the (beige) boxes from the upper left to the lower right, and in each box from upper right to lower left, gives the order of comparison/swap operations exactly as done in a bubble sort. In Fig. 2(a) traversing the (gray) boxes from the upper right to the lower left, and each box from upper left to lower right, leads to an insertion sort. Our hygienic reversible insertion sorts count the number of exchanges for each gray box in Fig. 2(a), and stores this in array d, which is exactly the factorial representation at the end.

The factorial representation used in insertion sort contains exactly enough information to compensate for the information lost by each comparison/swap operation of bubble sort. In particular, note that the value of the *intermediate* factorial representation for some specific comparison, will be the same, regardless of whether we build the representation in the order of the gray boxes in Fig. 2(a) or the beige boxes in Fig. 2(b). Thus, we can build the *same* factorial representation as in insertion sort, but in the order of the bubble sort comparisons, and use this for the assertions we need.

We show the solution in form of the reversible program `bsort4`:

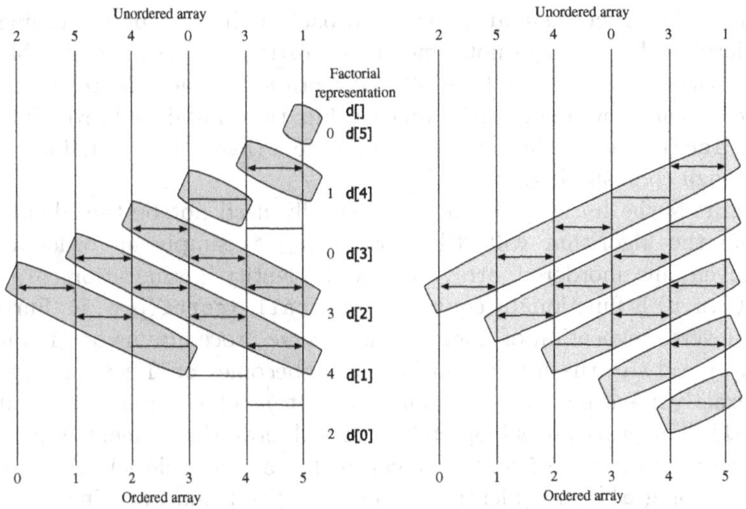

(a) Insertion sort (b) Bubble sort

Fig. 2. A parallel sorting network in action as both insertion sort and bubble sort.

```
procedure bsort4(int a[], int n, int d[])
  local int i = 0
    from i = 0
    loop local int j = n-1
           from j = n-1
           loop  if a[j] < a[j-1] then
                    a[j-1] <=> a[j]; d[j-i-1] += 1
                 fi d[j-i-1] = i + 1
                 j -= 1
           until j = i   // { a[0..i] is ordered }
         delocal int j = i
         i += 1
    until i = n
  delocal int i = n
```

Let us return to Table 1, which shows how `bsort4` behaves. The underlined elements in the left table are those slided to the right in each iteration, *i.e.* those for which the horizontal edges in Fig. 2 have arrows. In the right table we see how the corresponding factorial representation is iteratively built in the order of the bubble sort comparisons, *cf.* the beige boxes in Fig. 2(b). As a subsidiary result, this means that `call isort1(a,n,d); uncall bsort4(a,n,d)` will be the identity, as the procedures generate exactly the same output garbage.

While it was not obvious how to compress the run-time space usage of a reversible bubble sort, the connection to insertion sort provided the key insight of using the factorial representation for this as well. The reversible program `bsort4` is a *hygienic reversible simulation of* .

3.4 Selection Sort

Another closely related sorting algorithm is *selection sort*. Selection sort repeatedly finds the greatest element of the remaining unordered subarray and lines them up in the ordered subarray, front to back. Using the programming techniques developed above, it is not difficult to construct a hygienic reversible selection sort with garbage in the form of a permutation or factorial representation. Here, we instead show a non-trivial relationship: the non-faithful reversible insertion sort `isort1` can be directly used to realize a (hygienic) reversible selection sort, through code sharing.

In `isort1`, the initial `p[]` does not actually need not be the identity permutation; the algorithm will still work if `p[]` is simply an ordered array. Thus, given an unordered array `a[]` and identity permutation `p[]`, `call isort1(a,n,p)` is functionally equivalent to `uncall isort1(p,n,a)`. Further, in such an inverse invocation of `isort1`, the *inverse* procedure invocation `uncall min(i,p,j,n-1)` in the inner loop in line 11 becomes `call min(i,p,j,n-1)`, which exactly identifies the minimum element p_i of the remaining subarray `p[j..n-1]`. The other inner loop of `isort1` will move this element to p_j. Therefore, given the procedure `isort1`, we can realize a reversible selection sort simply by swapping `a[]` and (identity permutation) `p[]` and inverting the sorting process:

```
procedure ssort(int a[], int n, int p[])
  uncall isort1(p,n,a)
```

Thus, although `isort1` was not even a faithful reversible insertion sort, this is a hygienic reversible simulation of the corresponding irreversible selection sort.

Note that the intermediate garbage data of `isort1` and `ssort` in forwards direction are different, as procedure `isort1` generates its ordered subarray from back to front while `ssort` does this front to back. Moreover, if `call ssort(a,n,p)` is stable, so is `uncall ssort(p,n,a)`, and vice versa (where `min(i,p,j,n-1)` sets `i` to the index of the leftmost minimum element.) This is because elements of the same value are not interchanged by the loop in lines 5–9 in `isort1`.

3.5 Merge Sort

Merge sort follows the divide-and-conquer approach. It recursively divides the array in the middle until we have arrays of length zero or one. Such subarrays are already ordered and thus conquered. Then, it recursively merges two ordered arrays into a single ordered array, until, eventually, the entire array is ordered.

Since merge sort is $\Theta(n \log n)$ time, its history embedding reversible simulation becomes hygienic. However, such garbage will depend on the algorithm (and implementation), preventing us from reusing garbage across algorithms. Further, the hidden constant of such a history embedding may be quite large. In this subsection, we therefore construct a reversible (stable) merge sort, with minimal garbage in the form of a permutation in direct representation.

The reversible procedure `merge` in Fig. 3 merges the ordered subarrays `a[l..m]` and `a[m+1..r]` into ordered subarray `a[l..r]`. It takes `a[l..r]`, permutation `p[l..r]`, and the middle index `m` between `l` and `r` as parameters. We

```
1  procedure merge(int a[], int
     l, int m, int r, int p[])
2    local int b[r+1]={0},
           int c[r+1]={0},
           int p_b[r+1]={0},
           int p_c[r+1]={0}
3      local int k = l
4        from  k = l loop
5          b[k-l] <=> a[k]
6          p_b[k-l] <=> p[k]
7          k += 1
8        until k = m + 1
9        from  k = m + 1 loop
10         c[k-m-1] <=> a[k]
11         p_c[k-m-1] <=> p[k]
12         k += 1
13       until k = r + 1
14     delocal int k = r + 1
15
16     b[m-l+1] ^= INF;
       c[r-m] ^= INF // sentinel
17
18     local int i=0, int j=0,
             int k = l
19       from  k = l loop
20         if c[j] < b[i]
21         then a[k] <=> c[j]
22              p[k] <=> p_c[j]
23              j += 1
24         else a[k] <=> b[i]
25              p[k] <=> p_b[i]
26              i += 1
27         fi p[k] > m
28         k += 1
29       until k = r + 1
30     delocal int i = m-l+1,
               int j = r-m,
               int k = r+1
31
32     b[m-l+1] ^= INF;
       c[r-m] ^= INF
33   delocal int b[r+1]={0},
             int c[r+1]={0},
             int p_b[r+1]={0},
             int p_c[r+1]={0}
```

Fig. 3. Merging two sorted subarrays.

allocate zero-cleared temporary arrays b[], c[], , and of length $r+1$ at line 2,[5] and deallocate them at line 33. The first and second loops moves the elements with index $l, \ldots, m$ in the data array a[] and permutation p[] to b[] and , and those with index $m+1, \ldots, r$ to c[] and . Line 16 sets sentinels (used to avoid considering empty arrays) at the end of subarrays b[] and c[]; we assume INF is greater than any other element in a[]. The loop in lines 19–29 iteratively compares the heads of subarrays b[] and c[], and moves the smaller element back to array a[]. Accordingly, the elements of permutations in and are moved back to the original array p[]. Now, before the procedure call p[l..m] will contain the (distinct) values $\{l, \ldots, m\}$ and p[m+1..r] will contain $\{m+1, \ldots, r\}$, although not necessarily in order. Thus, it is straightforward that line 27 is able to disambiguate the incoming control flow correctly. Furthermore, after the procedure call p[l..r] contains the values $\{l, \ldots, r\}$. When all the elements are moved back to the original array a[l..r], now in order, the sentinels are zero cleared at line 32.

We use the procedure to sort the elements in subarray a[l..r]:

```
procedure msort_sub(int a[], int l, int r, int p[])
  if l < r then
    call msort_sub(a,l,(l+r)/2,p)
    call msort_sub(a,(l+r)/2+1,r,p)
    call merge(a,l,(l+r)/2,r,p)
  fi l < r
```

[5] The size of the auxiliary arrays in merge is not optimized, in order to make the indexing clearer in the presentation.

If $l < r$, *i.e.*, the subarray `a[l..r]` has two or more elements, the former half and the latter half elemens are independently sorted by two procedure calls of . The results are merged by procedure `merge`.

Finally, procedure `msort` is a wrapper procedure that passes the index of the first element 0 and the last element $n-1$ of arrays `a[]` and `p[]`:

```
procedure msort(int a[], int n, int p[])
  call msort_sub(a,0,n-1,p)
```

where `p[]` is initially an identity permutation. (This means that the assertion at line 27 of `merge` never fails.) `msort` is a *hygienic reversible simulation* of the corresponding conventional irreversible merge sort.

3.6 Quicksort

Like merge sort, quicksort uses the divide-and-conquer method. We construct a stable reversible quicksort based on simple pivot selection.

Procedure `partition` processes subarray `a[l..r]`. It uses the rightmost element `a[r]` as a pivot, rearranges the subarray `a[l..r]` into `a[l..q-1]` whose elements are smaller than or equal to the pivot and `a[q+1..r]` whose elements are greater than the pivot, and moves the pivot to `a[q]`. The permutation array `p[]` preserves the lost information of the division; during the dividing process, it moves the elements of array `p[]`, such that whenever `a[i]` is set, `p[i]` contains the original position of the element placed there. `p[l..r]` is assumed to hold an increasing subsequence on entry to `partition`, so in particular, the permutation element `p[r]` corresponding to the pivot element `a[r]` will be the *maximum* value in `p[l..r]`. This will be important below. The procedure uses two auxiliary arrays for manipulating data `t[]` and . The original position of `t[i]` should be equal to whenever `t[i]` is set.

```
procedure partition(int a[], int l, int r, int q, int p[])
  local int t[r-l] = {0}, int p_t[r-l] = {0}
    local int j = l
      from  j = l
      loop  if a[j] <= a[r] then    // a[r] is the pivot
              q += 1
              a[q] <=> a[j]          // move a[j] to a[q]
              p[q] <=> p[j]          // move p[j] to p[q]
            else
              t[j-q-1] <=> a[j]      // move a[j] to t[j-q-1]
              p_t[j-q-1] <=> p[j]    // move p[j] to p_t[j-q-1]
            fi (q >= l) && (j-q-1 = -1 || p[q] > p_t[j-q-1])
            j += 1
      until j = r + 1
    delocal int j = r + 1

    local int k = 0
      from  k = 0                   // move t[0..r-q-1] to a[q+1..r]
      loop  a[q+1+k] <=> t[k]        // move t[k] to a[q+1+k]
            p[q+1+k] <=> p_t[k]      // move p_t[k] to p[q+1+k]
            k += 1
      until k = r - q
    delocal int k = r - q
  delocal int t[r-l] = {0}, int p_t[r-l] = {0}
```

The assertion at line 12 relies on short-circuit evaluation: If `q >= l` does not hold (in case no element in the subarray turned out to be greater than pivot `a[r]`), then `j-q-1 = -1` and `p[q] > p_t[j-q-1]` are never evaluated. Dually, if `j-q-1 = -1` holds, `p[q] > p_t[j-q-1]` is never evaluated. Finally, in case we did swap elements, then this is reflected in whether `p[]` or holds the larger index.

To guarantee that assertion at line 12 always holds, we rely on the assumption that `p[l..r]` is in increasing order before the procedure call of `partition`. Note that in particular then `p[l..q]` and `p[q+1..r]` will be increasing subarrays *after* the procedure call, which we exploit recursively in the `qsort` procedure.

Procedure `partition` uses auxiliary arrays `t[]` and of size $r-l+1$, and runs in $\Theta(r-l)$ time. Unfortunately, `partition` is not in-place, contrary to conventional irreversible quicksort programs. Still, because `p[q]` holds the maximum we can erase the pivot pointer `q` after each partition.

The following procedure implements reversible quicksort:

```
procedure qsort(int a[], int l, int r, int p[])
  if l < r then
    local int q = l - 1
      call partition(a,l,r,q,p) // ends with pivot at a[q]
      call qsort(a,l,q-1,p)
      call qsort(a,q+1,r,p)
      uncall max(q,p,l,r)       // zero clear q
    delocal int q = 0
  fi l < r
```

The top-level call to quicksort is `qsort(a,0,n-1,p)` where `p[]` is an identity permutation. Because of this and the pre- and post-condition of `p[l..r]` of `partition`, the recursive calls to `qsort` each consider a subarray `p[l..r]` in increasing order. Therefore, the assertions in `partition` never fail. The only remainder after the recursive calls is the pivot pointer `q`, but by construction this points to the *largest* permutation element (initially in `p[r]`), and is thus easily identified and removed. For this we use the procedure `max`, which is completely analogous to the `min` procedure used in `isort1`. This provides us with a hygienic faithful reversible simulation (although not in-place) of the corresponding conventional irreversible quicksort (using the same choice of pivots.)

4 Concluding Remarks

In this paper we showed reversible programming techniques to enable reversible comparison sort programs to be more efficient, in terms of both time and space usage, than ones generated by general reversible simulation [3], even by asymptotic orders of magnitude. This was facilitated by unique reversible programming techniques such as efficient garbage representation and unconventional code sharing. We developed a family of reversible comparison sorts with better performance than previously known reversible sorts in terms of space usage, number of passes, and/or garbage representation. The resulting programs include several *hygienic faithful* reversible simulations of comparison sorts, *i.e.* reversible implementations which have the same time complexity as their irreversible counterparts, and optimal (minimal) space overhead.

It turns out that certain garbage representations are more suitable for programming some types of sorts than others; factorial permutation representation is suitable for reversible bubble sort and direct permutation representation is suitable for reversible quicksort, but the converse does not appear to be the case. Furthermore, the direct and factorial representations can be easily interpreted, which aids modularity between sorts, while other forms, such as rank, usually cannot. Still, these garbage representations can be efficiently and reversibly transformed to each other by clean reversible simulations of existing translations (e.g. [4,5,10], see Appendix A.) Choosing between these garbage representations is thus not essential from the viewpoint of asymptotic efficiency.

We believe the concepts identified here are also useful in other domains than comparison sorts. The notion of faithfulness and hygienicity can be used as criteria both for judging the efficiency of reversibilized programs, and using appropriate garbage representations can facilitate and guide reversible programming in general. However, this study also shows that reversible algorithmics cannot rely on simply combining generic reversible computing techniques with irreversible algorithms; domain analyses are required to get efficient solutions.

Acknowledgements. H.B. Axelsen was supported by the Danish Council for Independent Research | Natural Sciences under the *Foundations of Reversible Computing* project. T. Yokoyama was supported by MEXT KAKENHI 25730049.

A Converting Between Permutation Representations

Factorial Representation to Rank. Procedure `decfac2rank` takes a decreasing factorial representation `d[]`, its length `n`, and zero-cleared `rank` as arguments, and returns the lexicographic rank (in `rank`) of the decreasing factorial representation, with `d[]` zero-cleared (`n` is preserved):

```
procedure decfac2rank(int d[], int n, int rank)
  local int fac = 1
    local int i = n
      from  i = n
      do    i -= 1
            rank += d[i] * fac
            d[i] -= rank / fac                 // zero clear d[i]
      loop  local int t = fac * (n-i)          // fac *= n-i
              t <=> fac
            delocal int t = fac / (n-i)
      until i = 0
    delocal int i = 0
    uncall factorial(n-1,fac)                  // zero clear fac
  delocal int fac = 0
```

Direct to Factorial Representation. Procedure `perm2decfac` is based on an irreversible unranking algorithm by Bonet [4]. The procedure converts from the direct permutation `p[]` of length `n` to decreasing factorial representation `d[]` using an intermediate tree data structure (here in the form of the array t[] which is initially and finally zero cleared). The key idea of the algorithm is to use the tree t[] to perform the count of how many elements in p[i+1..n-1] are smaller than p[i] in a logarithmic number of updates:

```
1  procedure perm2decfac(int p[], int d[], int n)
2    local int t[n*2-1] = {0}
3      local int i = n
4        from i = n do
5          local int node = p[i-1] + 2 ** log2_ceil(n)
6            p[i-1] -= node - 2 ** log2_ceil(n)  // zero clear p[]
7            t[node-1] += 1
8            local int j = log2_ceil(n)
9              from j = log2_ceil(n) do
10               if node % 2 = 1 then
11                 node -= 1 // zero clear the least significant bit
12                 d[i-1] += t[node-1]
13               fi d[i-1] >= t[node-1]
14               uncall double(node)       // halve node, node >>= 1
15               t[node-1] += 1
16               j -= 1
17             until j = 0
18           delocal int j = 0
19         delocal int node = 1
20         i -= 1
21       until i = 0
22     delocal int i = 0
23     uncall make_tree(t,n)                          // zero clear t[]
24   delocal int t[n*2-1] = {0}
```

We use syntactic sugar in the expressions: the power operator **, which we assume to run in constant time for powers of two (*e.g.* as realized by left rotation), and the function , which evaluates to $\lceil \log_2 n \rceil$. Executable versions are available at topps.diku.dk/pirc/sorts.

The tree t[] has root t[1] and the left and right children of node t[i] are t[$2i$] and t[$2i+1$] for any i (≥ 1). The call to (code not shown) at line 23 sets each node in the tree to two to the power of its height (how many times it is visited.) reversibly simulates the irreversible codelet [4]:

for i = 0 to $\lceil \log_2 n \rceil$ do

  for j = 1 to 2^i do t[2^i + j - 1] := 1 << ($\lceil \log_2 n \rceil$ - i)

Rank to Direct Representation. The implementations decfac2rank and perm2decfac above are reversible and in particular garbage-free, so each procedure can cover conversion in both directions. For instance, the inverse invocation uncall decfac2rank(d,n,r) converts the rank r to the length n factorial representation d[] (initially zero-cleared), clearing r in the process. Further, we can implement the remaining conversions between permutation and rank by subsequent calls to perm2decfac and decfac2rank.

References

1. Axelsen, H.B., Glück, R.: What do reversible programs compute? In: Hofmann, M. (ed.) FOSSACS 2011. LNCS, vol. 6604, pp. 42–56. Springer, Heidelberg (2011)

2. Axelsen, H.B., Thomsen, M.K.: Garbage-free reversible integer multiplication with constants of the form $2^k \pm 2^l \pm 1$. In: Glück, R., Yokoyama, T. (eds.) RC 2012. LNCS, vol. 7581, pp. 171–182. Springer, Heidelberg (2013)
3. Bennett, C.H.: Time/space trade-offs for reversible computation. SIAM J. Comput. **18**(4), 766–776 (1989)
4. Bonet, B.: Efficient algorithms to rank and unrank permutations in lexicographic order. In: Workshop on Search in Artificial Intelligence and Robotics. AAAI (2008)
5. Dijkstra, E.W.: Program inversion. In: Bauer, F.L., Broy, M. (eds.) Program Construction: International Summer School. LNCS, vol. 69, pp. 54–57. Springer, Heidelberg (1979)
6. Early, D., Gao, A., Schellekens, M.: Frugal encoding in reversible $\mathcal{MOQA}$: a case study for quicksort. In: Glück, R., Yokoyama, T. (eds.) RC 2012. LNCS, vol. 7581, pp. 85–96. Springer, Heidelberg (2013)
7. Hall, J.S.: A reversible instruction set architecture and algorithms. In: Proceedings of Physics and Computation, pp. 128–134. IEEE Press, New York (1994)
8. Knuth, D.E.: The Art of Computer Programming, Volume 3: Sorting and Searching, 2nd edn. Addison Wesley Longman Publishing Co. Inc., Boston (1998)
9. Lutz, C.: Janus: A time-reversible language. Letter to R. Landauer (1986)
10. Myrvold, W., Ruskey, F.: Ranking and unranking permutations in linear time. Inf. Proc. Let. **79**(6), 281–284 (2001)
11. Nishida, N., Vidal, G.: Program inversion for tail recursive functions. In: Schmidt-Schauß, M. (ed.) RTA. LIPIcs, vol. 10, pp. 283–298. Schloss Dagstuhl–Leibniz-Zentrum für Informatik, Dagstuhl (2011)
12. Perumalla, K.S.: Introduction to Reversible Computing. CRC Press, Boca Raton (2013)
13. Wille, R., Drechsler, R.: Towards a Design Flow for Reversible Logic. Springer, Heidelberg (2010)
14. Yokoyama, T., Axelsen, H.B., Glück, R.: Principles of a reversible programming language. In: Proceedings of Computing Frontiers, pp. 43–54. ACM Press, New York (2008)
15. Yokoyama, T., Axelsen, H.B., Glück, R.: Minimizing garbage size by generating reversible simulations. In: Proceedings of Networking and Computing, pp. 379–387. IEEE Press, New York (2012)

Transactions on Mergeable Objects

Deepthi Devaki Akkoorath(✉) and Annette Bieniusa

University of Kaiserslautern, Kaiserslautern, Germany
{akkoorath,bieniusa}@cs.uni-kl.de

Abstract. Destructible updates on shared objects require careful handling of concurrent accesses in multi-threaded programs. Paradigms such as Transactional Memory support the programmer in correctly synchronizing access to mutable shared data by serializing the transactional reads and writes. But under high contention, serializable transactions incur frequent aborts and limit parallelism. This can lead to a severe performance degradation.

In this paper, we propose *mergeable transactions* which provide a consistency semantics that allows for more scalability even under contention. Instead of aborting and re-executing, object versions from conflicting updates on shared objects are merged using data-type specific semantics. The evaluation of our prototype implementation in Haskell shows that mergeable transactions outperform serializable transactions even under low contention while providing a structured and type-safe interface.

Keywords: Concurrent programming · Transactional memory · Mergeable objects · Relaxed consistency

1 Introduction

In imperative programming languages, data structures are in general mutable, and updates are executed in-place. Therefore, the effect of an update is immediately reflected on the data structure. If the data structure is shared between multiple threads, the programmer must synchronize potential concurrent accesses to shared state to prevent memory corruption and often ensure progress by rendering updates visible to all threads.

Data structures that implement an abstract data type are often called objects (akin to objects in object-oriented programming). The correctness condition that is traditionally applied to shared concurrent objects is linearizability [12]. An object is linearizable if the result of concurrent operations is equivalent to some legal sequential execution of these operations. For example, concurrent increments of a linearizable counter have to be executed in a sequential order to prevent the loss of updates. This limits the inherent parallelism of an application and imposes high cost due to synchronization.

In contrast, (purely) functional programming languages, such as Haskell's core language, employ referential transparency. Pure functions do not update destructively. Thus, data structures are immutable by default. Though

X. Feng and S. Park (Eds.): APLAS 2015, LNCS 9458, pp. 427–444, 2015.
DOI: 10.1007/978-3-319-26529-2_23

immutability implies thread-safety, it limits how concurrently running threads can exchange information. To overcome this restriction, Haskell offers different monadic interfaces supporting in-place updates and shared memory synchronization, the most prominent being: IO references (`IORef`), mutable references (`MVars`), and transactional variables (`TVars`).

For example, shared references to an (immutable) data item of type `a` can be encapsulated as IO references `IORef a`. IO references are intialized when created, and can be operated on using the following functions:

```
newIORef   :: a -> IO (IORef a)
readIORef  :: IORef a -> IO a
writeIORef :: IORef a -> a -> IO ()
```

In addition, the function `atomicModifyIORef` allows to atomically apply a function on the referenced object in a thread-safe way:

```
atomicModifyIORef :: IORef a -> (a -> (a,b)) -> IO b
```

All calls to `atomicModifyIORef` need to be serialized to achieve atomicity for reading and modifiying the value. Haskell's `MVars` impose even more synchronization by blocking access to objects between calls to `takeMVar` and `putMVar`.

Transactional variables (`TVars`) provide a very similar interface, though their access is restricted to memory transactions. Transactions in this context are sequences of reads and writes that are transparently synchronized by the Software Transactional Memory (STM) system [9]. All operations on `TVars` within a transaction are executed atomically, and isolated from concurrent threads, thus providing a consistent view of the state. Yet again, when transactions concurrently operate on the same `TVar`, with at least one thread updating the variable, the operations conflict. Transactions thus fail their serializability certification check and have to re-execute [21].

Semantically, serializability is unnecessarily strict for a multitude of applications. For example, Fig. 1 shows the code snippet for kmeans clustering from the STAMP benchmark suite [16]. The K-means algorithm partitions n data points into k clusters such that the total distance for the data point to their respective cluster centre is minimized. Classical TMs serialize all transactions that access the same cluster center. However, the only requirement for correctness of the algorithm is that after all points are processed `newcenter` and `numElems` must contain the sum of all points and the number of points that belong to that cluster, respectively. Even with relaxed transactions [5,18,19], conflicts and hence aborts can still arise when updates cannot be serialized.

To optimize the synchronization on shared mutable data structures, we introduce *mergeable objects*. Instead of blocking or aborting updates to objects for serializability, updates are first applied to thread-local object versions. Instead of a get/set interface, mergeable objects therefore implement abstract data types with type-specific read and update operations. When committing the locally performed changes to shared memory, the different versions of an object are merged based on the object's semantics. Updates become visible to other threads only after the `merge` operation is called.

```
assign clusters (x,y) = do
  let cluster = nearestPoint clusters (x,y)
  let center = newcentre cluster
  atomically $ do
    x' <- readTVar (xcord center)
    writeTVar (xcord center) (x' + x)
    y' <- readTVar (ycord center)
    writeTVar (ycord center) (y' + y)
    n <- readTVar (numElems cluster)
    writeTVar (numElems cluster) (n+1) .

thread clusters points = mapM_ (assign clusters) points
```

Fig. 1. Kmeans: Computations by a thread using serializable transactions.

We propose Mergeable Transactional Memory (MTM) based on *mergeable objects* with relaxed consistency semantics (Sect. 3). Similar to snapshot isolation, MTM transactions read from a consistent snapshot and operate concurrently on shared objects. Instead of aborting and re-executing in case of conflicts, transactions commit their changes by *merging* states of concurrently updated objects. All updates from a transaction become visible together. An efficient merge operation enables MTM to execute multiple updates in parallel to other threads and execute the merge inside the critical section.

If `newcenter` and `numElems` in Fig. 1 are represented using *mergeable counters* (Sect. 2) instead of raw integers, transaction can commit by merging the values, thus eliminating aborts. Moreover, we can rewrite the algorithm from Fig. 1 to Fig. 2 where a transaction (represented by `eventually`) process all points. MTM then executes it without synchronisation with other threads, thus allowing more parallelism. With serializable transactions, this would result in more conflicts and sequential execution of transactions.

```
thread clusters points = eventually $ mapM_ (assign clusters) points

assign clusters (x,y) = do
  let cluster = nearestPoint clusters (x,y)
  let center = newcentre cluster
  x' <- readCVar (xcord center)
  writeCVar (xcord center) (incrBy x' x))
  Y' <- readCVar (ycord center)
  writeCVar (ycord center) (incrBy y' y)
  c' <- readCVar (numElems cluster)
  writeCVar (numElems cluster) (incrBy c' 1)
```

Fig. 2. Kmeans: Larger transactions using MTM

The paper makes the following contributions:

- We introduce the notion of *mergeable objects* and propose a classification of mergeability (Sect. 2).
- We introduce a programming model, MTM based on mergeable objects and transactions, and describe an algorithm for implementing the model (Sect. 3).

– We present a prototype implementation of MTM in Haskell (Sect. 4) and evaluate several use cases (Sect. 5).

2 Mergeable Objects

Instead of a get/set interface, mergeable objects implement abstract data types with type-specific operations. The update operations on mergeable object thus differ from that of linearizable objects in imperative programming; the latter provides in-place updates while operations on mergeable objects conceptually modify a local copy of the object. The result of updates on mergeable objects is visible to other threads only after the `merge` operation is called. Depending on the actual data types, mergeability of objects can be achieved in two ways, *semantic mergeability* and *structural mergeability*.

Semantic Mergeability: Exploiting object semantics to define the merge function has been successfully applied in Conflict-free Replicated Data Types (CRDTs) [23] in the context of distributed database systems. State-based CRDTs rely on lattice-based monotonic data values where the merge computes the least upper bound. Operation-based CRDTs re-execute updates that were issued on the local object instance against the global object, therefore requiring commutativity of concurrent updates to achieve consistency despite different orders of update application at the different replicas.

```
class Counter {
 int x = 0;
 synchronized void inc() {
  x = x+1;
 }
}
```

```
type Counter = IORef Int
inc :: Counter -> IO ()
inc c = atomicModifyIORef (\x -> x+1,
      ()) c
```

Fig. 3. Linearizable Counter in (a) Java and (b) Haskell.

```
data Counter = Counter (IORef Int) Int
inc :: Counter -> Counter
inc (Counter g v) = Counter g (v+1)
read :: Counter -> Int
read (Counter g v) = do
  x <- readIORef g
  return (x+v)
merge :: Counter -> IO ()
merge (Counter g v) = do
  atomicModifyIORef (\x.x+v, ()) g
  return Counter g 0
```

Fig. 4. Mergeable counter in Haskell.

As an example, consider a shared counter that can be incremented concurrently by different threads. Figure 3 shows implementations with explicit synchronization in Java and in Haskell. For the mergeable counter in Fig. 4, the increment operations are collected and combined locally into a variable v, while a separate merge operation integrates the results of the local operations into the global state.

The merge operation for the counter in this case is trivial as all update operations commute. In general, CRDTs employ a number of mechanisms to achieve deterministic results for objects with non-commutative operations, e.g. maintaining tombstones for sets where elements can be added and removed. While CRDTs have been successful in avoiding costly synchronization in replicated data stores, employing the known specifications of CRDTs in multi-/many-core programs seems prohibitively expensive. In our work, we therefore focus on variants of CRDTs that are optimized for multi-/many-core programs.

Structural Mergeability: While the merge operation for the counter can be implemented in a simple and efficient way, we have to employ different strategies for larger, composed data structures such as lists and sets. We adopt techniques that have been developed in the context of persistent data structure [7]. A persistent data structure is a mutable data structure that offers accessibility to multiple versions. This technique is widely used to implement purely functional data structures efficiently, in particular linked data structures such as lists, trees etc. When multiple threads modify the data structure, each thread executes updates on a thread-local version of the object, without the need for copying the entire data structure into thread-local storage. The *merge* operation is then reduced to adjust pointers in the local and global version to incorporate the updates in the global version; hence the name *structural* mergeability. The merge operation must preserve the semantics of the abstract data type by resolving potential semantic conflicts due to concurrent updates.

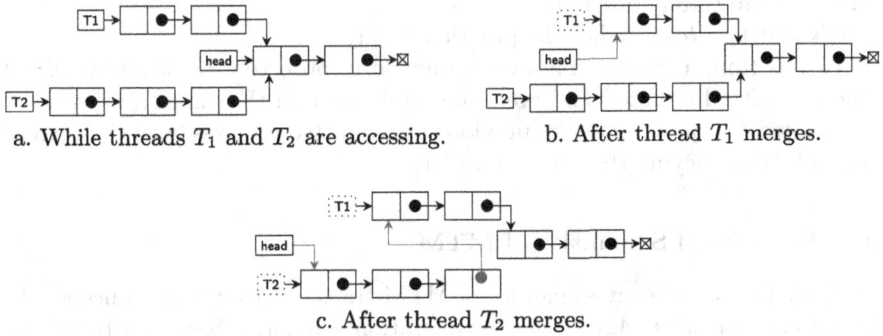

Fig. 5. Structural mergeability of bags.

As an example for structural mergeability, consider an add-only bag implemented as a persistent linked list. A bag is a *set* data structure allowing duplicate elements to be added. Here, threads can concurrently add elements without violating its semantical correctness. An implementation of a mergeable version of the bag is illustrated in Fig. 5. The `head` points to the first node of the global version accessible to all threads. Adding an element to the bag adds a new node at the head of the linked list local to the thread. This results in a multi-headed list. Figure 5a shows the bag after threads T_1 and T_2 have added two and three elements, respectively, and before merging. The list pointed to by `T1` represents the view of the bag to thread T_1, similarly for `T2`. Both versions share the nodes of the elements that have been added before the threads started. When merging `T1`, it updates the global head to point to `T1` (Fig. 5b). When merging `T2`, it has to update both the global head and the local tail of `T2` to include changes of `T1` in the merge (Fig. 5c). The `merge` of an add-only bag is efficient because it requires manipulation of only two pointers.

3 Mergeable Transactions

To leave the triggering of the merge to the programmer poses a number of issues. For example, the programmer might forget to call the function at all. Merging updates to different objects is not atomic, thus possibly violating invariants. We therefore enhance the programming model for mergeable objects with a weak form of transactions.

Mergeable Transactional Memory (MTM) allows to compose operations on shared objects. Akin to STM, MTM guarantees atomicity, isolation and (weak) consistency for dynamic transactions. In contrast to STM, conflicting updates from concurrently executed transactions do not lead to aborts, but are merged during commit.

MTM does not provide serializability. Instead it provides a weak consistency described by the following properties:

- *commits* are totally ordered.
- *reads* and *updates* satisfies the program order.
- All *reads* from a transaction are guaranteed to observe a *consistent prefix* of the committed updates, and preceding updates from the same transaction.
- The *consistent prefix* includes previously committed updates from the current thread, thus obeying the program order.

3.1 Operational Semantics of MTM

To specify the consistency semantics of MTM transactions, we introduce a call-by-need core calculus, Λ_{MTM}, with an operation semantics based on transition rules. Figure 6 shows the syntax of Λ_{MTM}. It relies on disjoint sets of variables (Var) and references (Ref). A value is either a reference r, a mergeable value m, a function, a monadic return, an integer i or unit $()$.

Expressions are given as values, variables, function application, monadic bind, thread fork, MTM transactions, and arithmetic expressions. The expressions marked in gray do not appear in source programs, but represent dynamically generated locations and intermediate system states arising during commits.

$$
\begin{aligned}
&x \in \text{Var},\ r \in \text{Ref}\\
&v \in \text{Val}\ ::=\ \texttt{r} \mid m \mid \lambda x.e \mid \texttt{return}\ e \mid i \mid ()\\
&e \in \text{Exp} ::= v \mid x \mid e\ e \mid e \gg\!= e \mid \texttt{forkIO}\ e \mid \texttt{eventually}\ e \mid \texttt{commit}\ \Theta\ e \mid \texttt{new}\ e \mid\\
&\qquad \texttt{read}\ e \mid \texttt{write}\ e \mid e + e \mid e * e \mid \ldots
\end{aligned}
$$

Fig. 6. Syntax of Λ_{MTM}.

$$
\begin{aligned}
&t \in \text{ThreadId}\\
&\Theta \in \text{Heap} = \text{Ref} \rightharpoonup \text{Exp}\\
&P \in \text{ThreadPool} = \text{ThreadId} \rightharpoonup \text{Exp}
\end{aligned}
$$

Fig. 7. State-related definitions.

A program state $P; \Theta$ is a pair consisting of a thread pool P (partial mapping of thread identifiers to expressions) and a heap Θ (Fig. 7). A reference l corresponds to an object allocated on the heap Θ. Dereferencing $\Theta(l)$ yields the associated object, while a heap update $\Theta[l \mapsto e]$ returns a heap that is identical to Θ, but maps l to e. Similarly, we denote updates in the thread pool P by $P\{t \mapsto e\}$.

The evaluation of a program starts in an initial state $\{t_0 \mapsto e\}; \emptyset$ with an empty heap and a main thread t_0. The evaluation stops when the program reaches a final state of the form $\{t_0 \mapsto v_0, \ldots, t_n \mapsto v_n\}; \Theta$. The reduction rules in Fig. 8 define the semantics of the language constructs. Each global reduction step $\rightarrowtail$ nondeterministically selects a thread from P, thus modeling an arbitrary thread scheduling.

The IO Monad is the top-level evaluation context. Rule IO-MONAD enables the execution of reductions within the current context. Spawning a thread (rule SPAWN) adds a new entry with a fresh thread identifier to the thread pool and returns unit to the parent thread. A transactional expression is evaluated against a copy of the current heap (rule TXN), possibly using multiple transactional transitions denoted by $\Rightarrow$.

Within a transaction, reading an object returns the value referenced in the heap (rule READ). Similarly, after applying the updates the resulting value is written back to the heap (rule WRITE), replacing the previous value. When allocating a new object, rule NEW ensures that the heap is extended using a fresh reference (i.e. one that has not been used in the heap or in concurrently running threads). The initial value of the object is then added to the transaction-local heap instance under the new reference.

Finally, an evaluated transaction is represented as a commit record consisting of the local heap copy, containing possible modifications, and the expression to be returned. Rule COMMIT then applies atomically the heap modifications to the globally shared heap and returns. The changes from the local heap copy Θ' are propagated to the current globally shared heap Θ by merging the individual entries with the thread-local ones. The function $\uplus :: \text{Heap} \times \text{Heap} \rightarrow \text{Heap}$ defines the heap merge:

$$(\Theta \uplus \Theta')(r) = \begin{cases} \text{merge } m\ n & \text{if } \Theta(r) = m, \Theta'(r) = n \\ m & \text{if } r \notin dom(\Theta), \Theta'(r) = m \\ n & \text{if } r \notin dom(\Theta'), \Theta(r) = n \end{cases}$$

Evaluation contexts:

$$\mathbb{E} ::= [\,]\ e \mid [\,] \gg\!= e \mid [\,] + e \mid v + [\,] \mid [\,] * e \mid \ldots$$

Expression evaluation $\rightarrow$:

$$(\lambda x.e)\ e' \rightarrow e[e'/x] \qquad \frac{e \rightarrow e'}{\mathbb{E}[e] \rightarrow \mathbb{E}[e']} \qquad i + j \rightarrow i \oplus j \qquad i * j \rightarrow i \otimes j$$

$$\mathbf{return}\ e' \gg\!= e \rightarrow e\ e'$$

Thread evaluation $\rightarrowtail$:

$$\frac{t' \text{ fresh}}{P\{t \mapsto \mathbb{E}[\mathtt{forkIO}\ m]\}; \Theta \rightarrowtail P\{t \mapsto \mathbb{E}[\mathbf{return}\ ()], t' \mapsto m\}; \Theta} \quad \textsc{Spawn}$$

$$\frac{e; \Theta \Rightarrow \mathbf{return}\ e'; \Theta'}{P\{t \mapsto \mathbb{E}[\mathtt{eventually}\ e]\}; \Theta \rightarrowtail P\{t \mapsto \mathbb{E}[\mathtt{commit}\ \Theta'\ e']\}; \Theta} \quad \textsc{Txn}$$

$$P\{t \mapsto \mathbb{E}[\mathtt{commit}\ \Theta'\ e]\}; \Theta \rightarrowtail P\{t \mapsto \mathbb{E}[\mathbf{return}\ e]\}; \Theta \uplus \Theta' \quad \textsc{Commit}$$

$$\frac{e \rightarrow e'}{P\{t \mapsto \mathbb{E}[e]\}; \Theta \rightarrowtail P\{t \mapsto \mathbb{E}[e']\}; \Theta} \quad \textsc{IO-Monad}$$

Evaluation steps in transaction $\Rightarrow$:

$$\frac{\Theta(r) = m}{\mathbb{E}[\mathbf{read}\ r]; \Theta \Rightarrow \mathbb{E}[\mathbf{return}\ m]; \Theta} \quad \textsc{Read}$$

$$\frac{\Theta(r) = m}{\mathbb{E}[\mathbf{write}\ r]; \Theta \Rightarrow \mathbb{E}[\mathbf{return}\ ()]; \Theta[r \mapsto m]} \quad \textsc{Write}$$

$$\frac{r \text{ fresh}}{\mathbb{E}[\mathbf{new}\ m]; \Theta \Rightarrow \mathbb{E}[\mathbf{return}\ r]; \Theta[r \mapsto m]} \quad \textsc{New}$$

$$\frac{e \rightarrow e'}{\mathbb{E}[e]; \Theta \Rightarrow \mathbb{E}[e']; \Theta} \quad \textsc{MTM-Monad}$$

Fig. 8. Operational semantics for Λ_{MTM}.

3.2 Properties of MTM

Based on the operational semantics for Λ_{MTM}, we can now further characterize MTM transactions.

MTM Allows Non-Serializable Transactions. By rule TXN, the heap-modifying side-effects of a transaction `eventually` e are not immediately applied to the shared global state, but deferred to another reduction step under rule COMMIT. Depending on the scheduling, other transactions may also execute without committing their changes yet. If there are read-write dependencies between the transactions, it is not possible to construct a reduction sequence yielding the same final state.

All Updates are Eventually Applied to the Shared State. The type specific merge during the commit ensures that concurrent updates are merged deterministically into a consistent state of the object.

All Updates Performed by a Transaction are Made Visible Atomically. By rule COMMIT, all updates from a transaction are merged to the globally shared heap in one step, which guarantees atomicity.

All Reads Performed by a Transaction Appear to be Executed at a Single Point of Time. In addition to publishing the updates atomically, transactions are executed on a consistent snapshot; i.e. a snapshot in which either all updates from some transaction that committed before the snapshot time are visible or none. All read operations within a transaction are guaranteed to see the state of objects from a consistent snapshot taken at the time when the transaction started. Rule TXN shows that all operations inside a transaction are executed against the same state Θ. Although there could be concurrently executing transactions, their updates are not globally visible.

3.3 Algorithm

An algorithm for implementing the semantics of MTM transactions is given in Fig. 9. To guarantee that a transaction never tries to read an object that has been modified by another transaction while executing (leading to a read-write conflict), we apply a multi-versioning scheme for mergeable objects. As previous studies have shown [5,18,19], multi-versioning of objects can be efficiently employed to achieve permissive transactions.

A shared mutable reference to a mergeable object which can be accessed in a MTM transaction is represented by *var*. A *var* references a list of versions. Each version contains a value of the object and its version identifier.

A transaction *txn* maintains a snapshot id *sid* in addition to a read and write sets which are represented as maps. When the transaction starts, its *sid* is assigned to be the current value of a *globalclock*. The operations of the transaction are executed on the snapshot identified by this *sid* which includes updates from all transactions committed before this time.

A *var* is accessed using the READ and WRITE methods. When reading, if the write set or read set contains a local copy of *var*, it is returned. Otherwise, the version corresponding to the transaction's *sid* is obtained and inserted in the read set. A new value of the object is written back to *var* using method WRITE, which inserts the value in the write set. Reading an object does not

```
txn: {sid, Map writeset, Map readset}
var: {versions, lock}
versions : [{val, versionid}]
function BEGINTRANSACTION(txn)
    txn.sid ← globalclock
    txn.writeset ← ∅
    txn.readset ← ∅
end function

function READ(var,txn)
    if txn.writeset.contains(var) then
        val ← txn.writeset.lookup(var)                ▷ read your own writes
    else if txn.readset.contains(var) then
        val ← txn.readset.lookup(var)
    else
        val ← READVERSION(var, txn.sid)
        txn.readset.add(var,val)
    end if
    return val
end function

function WRITE(var, val, txn)
    txn.writeset.insert(var,val)
end function

function COMMIT(txn)
    lockAll(txn.writeset)
    versionid ← globalclock++
    for all (var,val) ∈ txn.writeset do
        v' ← READLATESTVERSION(var)
        newval ← merge(v',val)
        WRITENEWVERSION(var, newval, versionid)
    end for
    unlockAll(txn.writeset)
end function
```

Fig. 9. MTM algorithm

necessarily pass over the entire object. Depending on the actual representation of the object, a read might only be reading a reference.

When committing, the transaction acquires a lock on all objects in its write set. This ensures atomicity when two transactions tries to commit to same object. To prevent deadlocks, locks are obtained in a predefined order. Next, a new version id is generated from the current global clock value. The objects updated in the transaction are then merged with the latest version available, using the objects' merge method, hereby creating new versions.

Figure 10 shows the versioned read and write functions. The function WRITENEWVERSION adds the new value with its *vid* to the head of list of versions.

Since *globalclock* is incremented during commit, the *sid* of a transaction always denotes the version id of a committed transaction or a concurrently committing transaction. When reading from the list of versions of a *var*, if the required version is not available, a concurrent transaction might be committing that version. Hence, it waits for the lock to be released before retrieving a version with an id equal or smaller than its *sid*. If the lock is released, it means that there is no other transaction which could potentially commit a version required by this transaction. This guarantees that a transaction always reads from a consistent snapshot identified by its *sid*.

4 MTM in Haskell

We implemented a prototype of MTM in Haskell. Harris et al. [9] have highlighted the benefits of Haskell's monadic type system for composing STM actions and restricting access to transactional variables to the STM monad. MTM is implemented analogously to the STM monad, though with different semantics.

```
 1: function READVERSION(var, vid)
 2:     v ← var.versions
 3:     if v.head.versionid ≥ vid then
 4:         vr ← v.head
 5:     else
 6:         waituntil (not locked(var))        ▷ Wait for a concurrent committer to write
        required version
 7:         vr ← var.versions.head
 8:     end if
 9:     while vr.versionid > vid do
10:         vr ← vr.next
11:     end while
12:     return vr.val
13: end function
14:
15: function READLATESTVERSION(var)
16:     return var.versions.head.val
17: end function
18:
19: function WRITENEWVERSION(var, val, vid)
20:     v ← newVersion(val, vid)
21:     var.versions.addHead(v)
22: end function
```

Fig. 10. Versioned read and write operations in MTM.

For the MTM programming model, we provide an MTM monad (Fig. 11). The shared mergeable objects used in MTM transactions are of type CVar; CVar[1]

---

[1] The name MVar for mergeable variables is already used in Haskell.

stands for convergent variables indicating that concurrent versions converge into a consistent state. Every operation executed on a `CVar` must be an MTM action. These actions can be sequentially combined using monadic bind. The function

```
eventually :: MTM a -> IO a
```

takes an MTM action, executes it, and returns the result. Using function `modifyCVar` to update a `CVar` guarantees that the mergeable values does not escape a transaction's scope.

The type specification ensures that mergeable objects are accessed only inside a MTM transaction. These objects must be of `class Mergeable` and define a `merge` function. Figure 12 shows the implementation of two mergeable objects. The `Counter` contains two integers, one representing the global value and the other the thread-local increments. The `merge` adds the local increments to the global value g and resets the local increments to 0. The `LWWRegister` implements a last-writer-wins register, where the last merge overwrites the previous value.

```
data MTM a  = ...
data CVar a = ...

-- MTM Functions
eventually :: MTM a -> IO a
newCVar    :: Mergeable a => a -> MTM (CVar a)
readCVar   :: Mergeable a => CVar a -> MTM a
modifyCVar :: Mergeable a => CVar a -> (a -> a) -> MTM a

-- Mergeable Objects
class Mergeable a where
   merge :: a -> a -> a
```

Fig. 11. Interface for MTM in Haskell.

```
-- Mergeable Counter
data Counter = Counter Int Int
instance Mergeable Counter where
 merge (Counter g _) (Counter _ i) =
      Counter (g+i) 0

newCounter::Counter
newCounter = Counter 0 0
value :: Counter -> Int
value Counter g l = g+l
incrBy :: Int -> Counter -> Counter
incrBy i (Counter g l) =
 Counter g (l+i)
```

```
-- LWWRegister
type LWWReg = Int
instance Mergeable LWWReg where
    merge g l = l

-- Mergeable Bag
data Bag a = Bag [[a]] [a]
instance CRDT (Bag a) where
 merge (Bag g _) (Bag _ i) =
  Bag (i:g) []
newIntBag :: Bag Int
newIntBag = Bag [[]] []
add :: a -> Bag a -> Bag a
add e (Bag g l) = Bag g (e:l)
```

Fig. 12. Mergeable objects in Haskell.

Example. The following example shows how to program with `CVar`s and the MTM monad in Haskell.

```
addToBag :: Int -> CVar (Bag Int) -> CVar (Counter) -> MTM [Int]
addToBag e bag size = do {
  ; b <- modifyCVar bag  (add e)
```

```
      ; s <- modifyCVar size (incrBy 1)
      ; return (toList b)
   }
```

The function `addToBag` inserts an element to some bag and increments a counter representing the size of the bag. It returns then the elements from the bag in a list, including the added element `e`, but excluding elements that have been concurrently added. When calling the function using `eventually addToBag x b s` with some bag `b` and size counter `s`, the library guarantees that both shared objects are atomically updated and have consistent values.

5 Evaluation

To evaluate the applicability of MTM we ran microbenchmarks, comparing our MTM implementation as Haskell library with a library implementation of a STM algorithm based on 2-phase-commit (2PC) (similar to TL2 [6]) and GHC's STM implementation. GHC's STM is tightly integrated with the runtime system and employs a number of optimization techniques with respect to GC interaction and scheduling. To approximate the runtime overhead incurred by implementing MTM as a library, we use the 2PC implemenation as another point of comparison. All experiments were run on a Quad-core 2.4 GHz Intel Xeon processor with two-way hyperthreading, under Linux 2.6.32-64-server Ubuntu x86_64 and GHC version 7.8.3. The results given are the averages taken over 10 runs for each benchmark.

Microbenchmarks: Counter and Bag In a first experiment, we compared the performance of a shared counter and bag under high contention. The STM variants implement the counter as a `TVar Int` and `TVar [Int]`, while MTM relies on a mergeable counter and bag, as introduced in Sect. 3. For the experiment, each thread repeatedly increments the same shared counter. In total, there were 2×10^6 increments distributed over the available number of threads.

As Fig. 13 shows, the performance of the library version of STM degrades quickly while both MTM and GHC's STM handle the contention more gracefully.

To evaluate the throughput, we chose a workload where each transaction updates m randomly selected objects from a pool of n objects: the larger the pool (n), the lower the probability of contention; the larger the transaction size (m), the higher the probability of conflicts as it is more likely that transaction executions overlap. For $n = 8$ and various transaction size, MTM yields better performance than the STM implementations, even under low contention (Fig. 14).

Application: K-means: To see how actual applications benefit from the MTM programming model, we reimplemented the K-means benchmark from the STAMP benchmark suite [16] in Haskell described in Sect. 1.

For the version running GHC's STM and MTM a cluster centre is updated inside a transaction after processing every data point (here: 10^6 points). We also

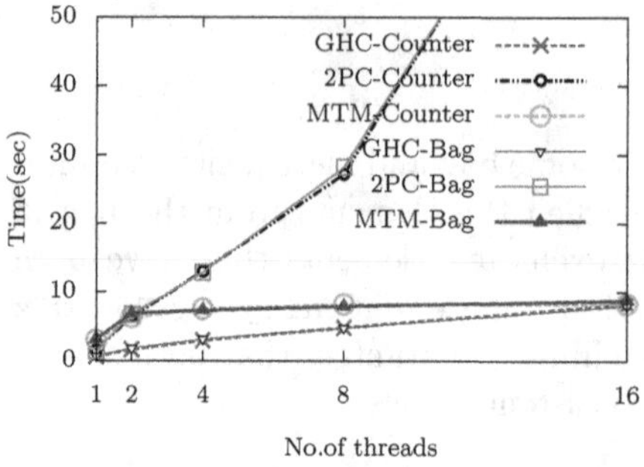

Fig. 13. Every thread updates once the same shared object in a transaction.

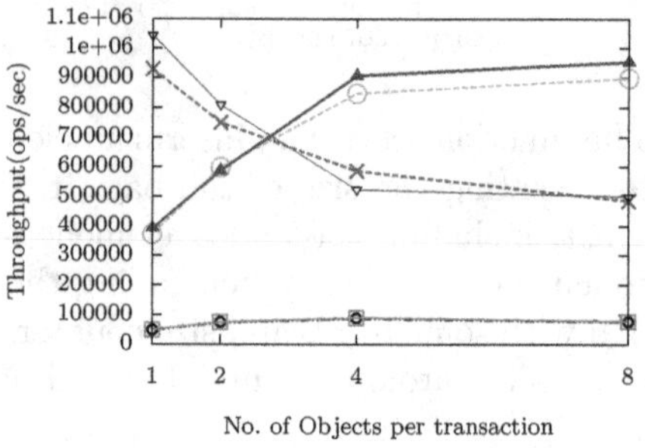

Fig. 14. Every thread updates M objects in a transaction

derived an alternative implementation to exploit the semantics of MTM, MTM-Opt, where all points assigned to some thread are processed together, and cluster centers are updated atomically. This version runs longer transactions, but has less frequent updates to cluster centers.

Both under high contention (Fig. 15) and low contention (Fig. 16), MTM-Opt outperforms GHC and MTM. In particular, MTM-Opt is scalable even under high contention in contrast to the other versions. The reason is that GHC's STM and MTM are blocking during commit, which prohibits scalability when the number of concurrent transactions is high. In the optimized version, commits are less frequent and transactions can run in parallel without the need for serializing the updates to shared memory.

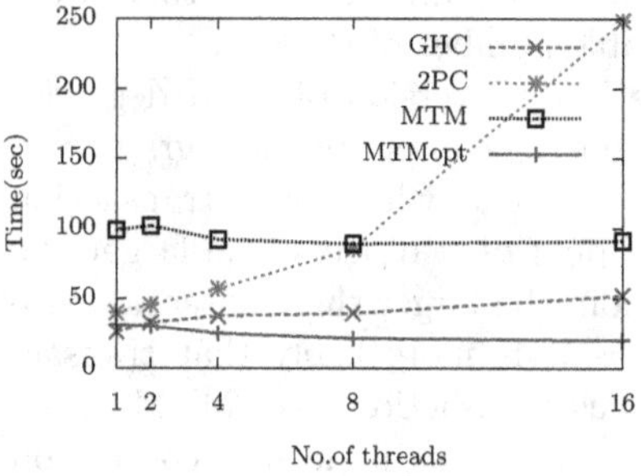

Fig. 15. K-means: High contention.

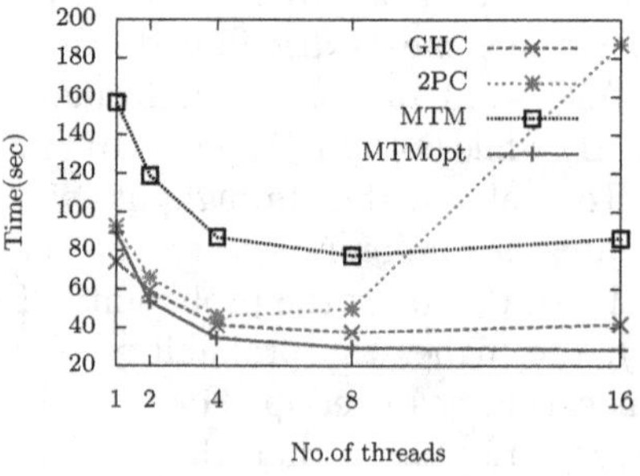

Fig. 16. K-means: Low Contention.

6 Related Work

Software Transactional Memory: Relaxing strong guarantees such as serializability has been considered by different STMs. Multi-versioned STMs [5] and Snapshot Isolation in STMs [19] allow read-only transactions to proceed without any conflicts. However, there may be aborts in case of write-write conflicts. Different apporaches have been proposed to avoid abort or restarting of whole transactions by delaying some computations [20] to commit time and re-executing parts of transaction [5]. Twilight STM [1] allows transaction-specific conflict handling when inconsistencies are detected in commit phase. MTM focuses on introducing the conflict handling mechanisms at the object level.

Composable Memory Transactions [9] provide primitives for making serializable transactions composable in Haskell. The authors describe the benefits of Haskell's type system and monads to achieve safety and composability of transactions. We have adopted these techniques to implement the MTM monad. However, as MTM transactions do never abort, we restrain from providing additional operations that support composability such as `retry` and `orElse`.

Transactional Boosting [11] is a method which allows operations on highly concurrent linearizable objects to execute using concurrent transactions, without the need for acquiring an exclusive lock on the object. A method's abstract lock issues a conflict only if two concurrent method invocations are non-commutative; therefore, concurrent commutative operation on an object can execute without aborting the transaction. Transactional boosting is a pessimistic approach by eagerly acquiring locks on the objects. Optimistic Transactional Boosting [10] is yet another methodology for transforming concurrent data structures to transactional objects. Both approaches take commutativity of operations as the base for detecting conflicts and thus achieving serializability. In contrast, MTM relies on object specific conflict resolution which may allow non-commutative operations to occur in parallel.

Burckhardt et al. [2,15] propose a programming model for concurrent programs using revisions and isolation types. Each revision is considered a unit of concurrency. It executes operations on its local copy of the shared data concurrently to other threads. The modified data is visible to the main thread only after the revision is explicitly joined. The conflicts occurring due to concurrent updates are resolved using custom merge operation for cumulative types and joinee-wins strategy for versioned types. Though MTM and the revisions model share similar semantics in executing operations on consistent snapshots and merging conflicting updates, they target different settings. The revisions programming model is a fork-join model and is suitable for short-running threads that operate mostly in isolation. MTM targets long running threads which need to periodically share data with other threads using transactional semantics.

The Phase Reconciliation mechanism [17] detects high contention on data items in in-memory databases. It then switches to a split phase where the transactions update a local per-core copy of the contended data in parallel. After the split phase, the per-core copies are merged and the transactions proceed to execute using classical concurrency control techniques. Whether transactions can be executed in the split phase, is decided based on the commutativity of operations, thus preserving sequential consistency.

Monotonic and Mergeable Data Structures: Conflict Free Replicated Data Types (CRDT) [22,23] are replicated data types with mergeable semantics used in distributed database systems with eventual consistency. A state-based CRDT takes its values from a semi-lattice. Two states of the same objects are merged by taking the least upper bound in the semi-lattice. Op-based CRDTs, on the other hand, exploit commutativity of updates to deterministically converge the states of two replicas.

LVars [13,14] are lattice-based data structures used for deterministic parallel programming in Haskell. The put operation changes an LVar's state in such a way that it monotonically increases in the lattice structure. Updates from concurrent threads on an LVar result in the same state, irrespective in which order they occur, thus guaranteeing determinism. The merge function computes always the least upper bound according to the lattice. LVars focus on deterministic and efficient execution for parallel programming models to support producer/consumer like application.

We believe that lattice-based data structures such as LVars and CRDTs are beneficial for deterministic merging and verifying the correctness of applications. However, it is not trivial how to construct efficient merge operation in order to be useful in an optimistic transactional model to improve performance. In this paper, we have discussed mergeable data structures which are not lattice structures.

Confluent persistent data structures [7,8] allow operations on multiple versions of a data structure. These operations (e.g. concatenation, union) are constructed in a way such that previous versions are still accessible. Confluent persistent data structures are designed to perform these operations efficiently, in space and time. The applicability of these techniques in mergeable objects is an interesting topic for future work.

Distributed Systems: Weak consistency models such as eventual consistency and causal consistency are being widely researched and used in distributed systems. SwiftCloud [24] is a system that supports client-side replication and uses CRDTs to deterministically merge conflicting updates, while supporting Transactional causal+ consistency. Burckhardt et al. [3] present the idea of eventually consistent transactions and an implementation technique which provides these semantics. Global Sequence Protocol [4] provides a programming model for replicated data stores and a weak consistency model relying on a global total order of updates. Though many recent works have studied eventual consistency in distributed database systems, few have addressed its applicability in multi-core programs. In this paper, we have discussed a way to achieve weak consistency in software transactions.

7 Conclusion

We have presented mergeable transactions as an alternative to the often too strict semantics of serializable transactions. Using abstract data type specifications, mergeable objects provide type-specific merge functions. We discussed semantic and structural mergeability as design alternatives for efficient merge functions and showed how to apply them to counters and bags. Our evaluation results on a prototype implementation in Haskell underline that for many workloads, especially on long running transactions, MTM outperforms standard STM, by eliminating the necessity for rollback.

In future work, we plan to extend MTM with a broader variety of mergeable objects and efficient implementation techniques. We also want to investigate the applicability of the concept in other programming paradigms, where more optimizations regarding the space and time complexity of mergeable objects are possible than in Haskell. It will be further interesting to study the possibility of co-existence of mergeable objects with non-mergeable objects in transaction, where aborts should be only induced when non-mergeable objects conflict.

Acknowledgments. This research is supported in part by the European FP7 project 609 551 SyncFree.

References

1. Bieniusa, A., Middelkoop, A., Thiemann, P.: Brief announcement: actions in the twilight - concurrent irrevocable transactions and inconsistency repair. In: Proceedings of the 29th Annual ACM Symposium on Principles of Distributed Computing, PODC 2010, 25–28 July, 2010, Zurich, Switzerland, pp. 71–72 (2010)
2. Burckhardt, S., Baldassin, A., Leijen, D.: Concurrent programming with revisions and isolation types. In: Proceedings of the ACM International Conference on Object Oriented Programming Systems Languages and Applications, OOPSLA 2010, pp. 691–707 (2010)
3. Burckhardt, S., Leijen, D., Fähndrich, M., Sagiv, M.: Eventually consistent transactions. In: Seidl, H. (ed.) Programming Languages and Systems. LNCS, vol. 7211, pp. 67–86. Springer, Heidelberg (2012)
4. Burckhardt, S., Leijen, D., Protzenko, J., Fähndrich, M.: Global sequence protocol: a robust abstraction for replicated shared state. In: Boyland, J.T. (ed.) 29th European Conference on Object-Oriented Programming (ECOOP 2015), Leibniz International Proceedings in Informatics (LIPIcs), vol. 37, pp. 568–590. Schloss Dagstuhl-Leibniz-Zentrum fuer Informatik, Dagstuhl (2015). http://drops.dagstuhl.de/opus/volltexte/2015/5238
5. Cachopo, J., Rito-Silva, A.: Versioned boxes as the basis for memory transactions. Sci. Comput. Program. **63**(2), 172–185 (2006). special issue on synchronization and concurrency in object-oriented languages
6. Dice, D., Shalev, O., Shavit, N.N.: Transactional locking II. In: Dolev, S. (ed.) DISC 2006. LNCS, vol. 4167, pp. 194–208. Springer, Heidelberg (2006)
7. Driscoll, J.R., Sarnak, N., Sleator, D.D., Tarjan, R.E.: Making data structures persistent. J. Comput. Syst. Sci. **38**(1), 86–124 (1989)
8. Fiat, A., Kaplan, H.: Making data structures confluently persistent. In: Proceedings of the Twelfth Annual ACM-SIAM Symposium on Discrete Algorithms, SODA 2001, pp. 537–546. Society for Industrial and Applied Mathematics (2001)

9. Harris, T., Marlow, S., Peyton-Jones, S., Herlihy, M.: Composable memory transactions. In: Proceedings of the Tenth ACM SIGPLAN Symposium on Principles and Practice of Parallel Programming, PPoPP 2005, pp. 48–60 (2005)
10. Hassan, A., Palmieri, R., Ravindran, B.: Optimistic transactional boosting. In: Proceedings of the 19th ACM SIGPLAN Symposium on Principles and Practice of Parallel Programming, pp. 387–388. ACM (2014)
11. Herlihy, M., Koskinen, E.: Transactional boosting: A methodology for highly-concurrent transactional objects. In: Proceedings of the 13th ACM SIGPLAN Symposium on Principles and Practice of Parallel Programming, PPoPP 2008, pp. 207–216 (2008)
12. Herlihy, M.P., Wing, J.M.: Linearizability: A correctness condition for concurrent objects. ACM Trans. Program. Lang. Syst. **12**(3), 463–492 (1990)
13. Kuper, L., Newton, R.R.: Lvars: Lattice-based data structures for deterministic parallelism. In: Proceedings of the 2nd ACM SIGPLAN Workshop on Functional High-Performance Computing, FHPC 2013, pp. 71–84 (2013)
14. Kuper, L., Turon, A., Krishnaswami, N.R., Newton, R.R.: Freeze after writing: Quasi-deterministic parallel programming with lvars. In: Proceedings of the 41st ACM SIGPLAN-SIGACT Symposium on Principles of Programming Languages, POPL 2014, pp. 257–270 (2014)
15. Leijen, D., Fahndrich, M., Burckhardt, S.: Prettier concurrency: Purely functional concurrent revisions. In: Proceedings of the 4th ACM Symposium on Haskell, Haskell 2011, pp. 83–94. ACM, New York (2011). http://doi.acm.org/10.1145/2034675.2034686
16. Minh, C.C., Chung, J., Kozyrakis, C., Olukotun, K.: Stamp: Stanford transactional applications for multi-processing. In: IEEE International Symposium on Workload Characterization, IISWC 2008, pp. 35–46, September 2008
17. Narula, N., Cutler, C., Kohler, E., Morris, R.: Phase reconciliation for contended in-memory transactions. In: Proceedings of the 11th USENIX Conference on Operating Systems Design and Implementation, OSDI 2014, pp. 511–524 (2014)
18. Perelman, D., Fan, R., Keidar, I.: On maintaining multiple versions in stm. In: Proceedings of the 29th ACM SIGACT-SIGOPS Symposium on Principles of Distributed Computing, PODC 2010, pp. 16–25 (2010)
19. Riegel, T.: Snapshot isolation for software transactional memory. In: Proceedings of the First ACM SIGPLAN Workshop on Languages, Compilers, and Hardware Support for Transactional Computing, TRANSACT 2006 (2006)
20. Ruan, W., Liu, Y., Spear, M.: Transactional read-modify-write without aborts. ACM Trans. Archit. Code Optim. 11(4), 63:1–63:24 (2015). http://doi.acm.org/10.1145/2688904
21. Scott, M.L.: Sequential specification of transactional memory semantics. In: Proceedings of the First ACM SIGPLAN Workshop on Languages, Compilers, and Hardware Support for Transactional Computing, June 2006
22. Shapiro, M., Preguiça, N., Baquero, C., Zawirski, M.: A comprehensive study of Convergent and Commutative Replicated Data Types. Rapport de recherche RR-7506, INRIA, January 2011
23. Shapiro, M., Preguiça, N., Baquero, C., Zawirski, M.: Conflict-free replicated data types. In: Défago, X., Petit, F., Villain, V. (eds.) SSS 2011. LNCS, vol. 6976, pp. 386–400. Springer, Heidelberg (2011)
24. Zawirski, M., Bieniusa, A., Balegas, V., Duarte, S., Baquero, C., Shapiro, M., Preguiça, N.: SwiftCloud: Fault-Tolerant Geo-Replication Integrated all the Way to the Client Machine. Research Report RR-8347, October 2013

A Sound Type System for Layer Subtyping and Dynamically Activated First-Class Layers

Hiroaki Inoue(✉) and Atsushi Igarashi

Graduate School of Informatics, Kyoto University, Kyoto, Japan
hinoue@fos.kuis.kyoto-u.ac.jp

Abstract. Key features of context-oriented programming (COP) are *layers*—modules to describe context-dependent behavioral variations of a software system—and their *dynamic activation*, which can modify the behavior of multiple objects that have already been instantiated. Typechecking programs written in a COP language is difficult because the activation of a layer can even change objects' interfaces. We formalize a small COP language called ContextFJ$_{<:}$ with its operational semantics and type system and show its soundness. The language features (1) dynamically activated *first-class* layers, (2) *inheritance* of layer definitions, and (3) layer *subtyping*.

1 Introduction

Software is much more interactive than it used to be: it interacts with not only users but also external resources such as network and sensors and changes its behavior according to inputs from these resources. For example, an e-mail reader may switch to a text-based mode when network throughput is low. Such external information that affects the behavior of software is often referred to as *contexts*. However, such context-dependent software is hard to develop and maintain, because the description of context-dependent behavior, which we desire to be modularized, often crosscuts with the dominating module structure. To address such a problem from a programming-language perspective, Context-Oriented Programming (COP) [9] has been proposed by Hirschfeld et al.

The main language constructs for COP are *layers*, which are modules to specify context-dependent behavior, and their *dynamic layer activation*. A layer is basically a collection of what are called *partial methods*, which add new behavior to existing objects or override existing methods. When a layer is activated at run time by a designated construct, the partial methods defined in it become effective, changing the behavior of objects until the activation ends. Roughly speaking, a layer abstracts a context and dynamic layer activation abstracts change of contexts.

JCop language [1] is an extension of Java with language constructs for COP. It not only supports basic COP constructs described above, but also introduces many advanced features such as inheritance of layer implementations and first-class layers. However, typechecking implemented in the JCop compiler does not take into account the fact that layer activation can change objects' interface

X. Feng and S. Park (Eds.): APLAS 2015, LNCS 9458, pp. 445–462, 2015.
DOI: 10.1007/978-3-319-26529-2_24

by partial methods that add new methods and, as a result, not all "method not found" errors are prevented statically. In our previous work [14], we have studied this problem, proposed a type-safe version of JCop (we call Safe JCop in this paper) with informal discussions on how JCop can be made type-safe.

In this paper, we formalize most of the ideas proposed in the previous work and show they really make the language sound. More concretely, we develop a small COP language called ContextFJ$_{<:}$, which extends ContextFJ by Igarashi, Hirschfeld, and Masuhara [10,11] to layer inheritance, subtyping of layer types, first-class layers and layer swapping; and we show type soundness of ContextFJ$_{<:}$. Main issues we have to deal with are (1) the semantics of layer inheritance, which adds another "dimension" to method lookup, (2) sound subtyping for first-class layers, which led us to two kinds of subtyping relation, and (3) (a limited form of) type-safe deactivation, which we realize by layer swapping, first proposed in the previous work [14]. We also have implemented a prototype of the proposed type system by extending the JCop compiler.

The rest of the paper is organized as follows. After informally reviewing features of Safe JCop in Sect. 2, we develop ContextFJ$_{<:}$ in Sect. 3 and state type soundness. In Sect. 4, we discuss related work and then conclude in Sect. 5. We omit some rules of ContextFJ$_{<:}$ and proofs for brevity; the full definitions and proofs can be found in the full version of the paper. The implementation of the type system and the full version are available at http://www.fos.kuis.kyoto-u.ac.jp/~hinoue/.

2 Language Constructs of Safe JCop

In this section, we review language constructs of Safe JCop, first described in [14], including first-class layers, layer inheritance/subtyping, and layer swapping along informal discussions about the type system.

As a running example, we consider programming a graphical computer game called *RetroAdventure* [2]. In this game, a player has a character "hero" that wanders around the game world. Here, we introduce class `Hero` that represents the hero, which has method `move` to walk around, and class `World` that represents the game world.

```
public class Hero {
  Position pos;
  public void move(Direction dir){
    pos = /* changes pos according to dir */;
  }
}
public class World { ... }
```

2.1 Layers and Partial Methods

As mentioned already, a first distinctive feature of COP is *layers*—collections of *partial methods* to modify the behavior of existing objects. A partial method is syntactically similar to an ordinary method declared in a class, except that the name is given in a qualified form `Hero.move()`; this means the partial method is going to override method `move` defined in `Hero` or (if it does not exist) add to `Hero`. A layer can contain partial methods for different classes, so, when it is activated, it can affect objects from various classes at once. Similarly to `super` calls in Java, the body of a partial method can contain `proceed` calls to invoke the original method overridden by this partial method.

Here, suppose that the hero's behavior is influenced by weather conditions in the game world. For example, in a rainy weather, the hero gets slow and, in a stormy weather, the hero cannot move as he likes. Here are layers that denote weathers of the game world.

```
public layer Rainy {
  /* partial method */
  public void Hero.move(Direction dir){
    pos = /* the distance of move is smaller */;
  }
}
public layer Stormy {
  /* partial method */
  public void Hero.move(Direction dir){
    proceed(randomDirection(dir));
  }
  /* baseless partial method */
  public Direction Hero.randomDirection(Direction dir){
    return /* add randomness to dir */;
  }
}
public layer Sunny { ... }
```

`Rainy` and `Stormy` have the definitions of `Hero.move`, which change the behavior of the original definition in different ways. In particular, `Hero.move` in `Stormy` uses `proceed`, replacing the arguments to calls to `move`. It also has `Hero.randomDirection`, used to determine a new randomized direction to which the hero is going to move.

Methods defined in classes are often referred to as *base methods* and partial methods without corresponding base methods as *baseless partial methods*. Notice that activating a layer with baseless partial methods extends object interfaces and `proceed` in a baseless method is unsafe unless another layer activation provides a baseless method of the same signature.

2.2 Layer Activation and First-Class Layers

In Safe JCop, a layer can be activated by using a layer instance (created by a `new` expression, just as an ordinary Java object, from a layer definition) in a `with` statement. The following code snippet shows how `Rainy` can be activated.

```
with(new Rainy()){
  hero.move(); /* The hero will get slow by Rainy weather. */
}
```

Inside the body of `with`, dynamic method dispatch is affected by the activated layers so that partial methods are looked up first. So, `movement` of the `hero` will be slow.

Layer activation has a dynamic extent in the sense that the behavior of objects changes even in methods called from inside `with`. If more than one layer is activated, a more recent activation has precedence and a `proceed` call in a more recently activated layer may call another partial method (of the same name) in another layer.

In Safe JCop, a layer instance is a first-class citizen and can be stored in a variable, passed to, or returned from a method. A layer name can be used as a type. Combining with layer subtyping discussed later, we can switch layers to activate by a run-time condition. For example, suppose that the game has *difficulty* levels, determined at run time according to some parameters, and each level is represented by an instance of a sublayer of `Difficulty`. Then, we can set the initial difficulty level by code like this:

```
Difficulty dif = /* an expression to compute difficulty */ ;
with(dif){...}
```

Moreover, a layer can declare fields (although we do not model fields in layers in this paper). So, first-class layers significantly enhances expressiveness of the language.

2.3 Dependencies Between Layers

Baseless partial methods and layer activation that has dynamic extent pose a challenge on typechecking because activation of a layer including baseless partial methods can change object interfaces. So, a method invocation, including a `proceed` call, may or may not be safe depending on what layers are activated at the program point. Safe JCop adopts `requires` clauses [11] for layer definitions to express which layers should have been activated before activating each layer (instance). The type system checks whether each activation satisfies the `requires` clause associated to the activated layer and also uses `requires` clauses to estimate interfaces of objects at every program point.

For example, consider another layer `ThunderStorm`, which expresses an event in a game. It affects the way how the hero's direction is randomized during a storm and includes a baseless partial method with a `proceed` call. To prevent `ThunderStorm` from being activated in a weather other than a storm, the layer `requires Stormy` as follows:

```
public layer ThunderStorm requires Stormy {
  public Direction Hero.randomDirection(Direction dir){
    Direction tmpd = proceed(dir);
    ... /* change tmpd to speed up */
    return tmpd;
  }
}
```

An attempt at activating ThunderStorm without activating Stormy will be rejected by the type system (unless the activation appears in a layer requiring Stormy). Thanks to the requires clause, the type system knows the proceed call will not fail. (It will call the partial method in Stormy or some other depending on what layers are activated at run time.)

In general, a layer can require any number of layers.

2.4 Layer Inheritance

In Safe JCop, a layer can inherit definitions from another layer by using the keyword extends and the extends relation between layers yields subtyping, just like Java classes. If weather layers have many definitions in common, it is a good idea to define a superlayer Weather and concrete weather layers as its sublayers.

```
public abstract layer Weather {
  public String World.getWorldText(){
    ..... + this.getWeatherInfo() + ....;
  }
  public abstract String World.getWeatherInfo();
}
public layer Rainy extends Weather {
  public String World.getWeatherInfo(){
    return "rain";
  }
}
public layer Stormy extends Weather {
  public String World.getWeatherInfo(){
    return "storm";
  }
}
```

Here, Weather provides partial method getWorldText to retrieve the status of the world. Although the implementation of World.getWeatherInfo is not given here, concrete weather layers provide it by overriding.

Naturally, we expect an instance of a sublayer can be substituted for that of its super-layer. However, substitutability is more subtle that one might expect and we are led to distinguishing two kinds of substitutability and introducing two kinds of subtyping relation, called weak and normal subtyping.

Since a sublayer defines more partial methods than its superlayer, an instance of a sublayer can be used where a superlayer is required. For example, to activate the following layer called Thunder, which requires Weather, it suffices to activate Rainy, a sublayer of Weather, beforehand.

```
public layer Thunder requires Weather {
  public String World.getWeatherInfo(){
    return "thunder and " + proceed();
  }
}
```

```
...
with(new Rainy()){
  with(new Thunder()){...}
}
```

We will formalize substitutability about `requires` as *weak subtyping*, which is the reflexive transitive closure of the `extends` relation between layer types. For the weak subtyping to work, we require a sublayer declare what its superlayer `requires` because partial methods inherited from the superlayer may depend on them. We could relax this condition when a sublayer overrides all the partial methods but such a case is expected to be rare.[1] Therefore, we do not consider the case.

This notion of subtyping is called weak because it does *not* guarantee safe substitutability for *first-class* layers. Consider layer `Difficulty` again and assume that it requires no other layers and has sublayers `Easy` and `Hard`. In the following code snippet

```
Difficulty dif = someCondition() ? new Easy() : new Hard();
with(dif){...}
```

activation of `dif` appears safe because its static type `Difficulty` does not require any layer to have been activated. However, the case where `Easy` or `Hard` requires some layers breaks the expected invariant that `requires` is satisfied at run time. So, for assignments and parameter passing, we need one more condition for subtyping, namely, `requires` of a sublayer must be the same as that of its superlayer. We call this strong notion of subtyping *normal subtyping*.

Just like `Object` in Java, there is `Base`, which is a superlayer of all layers, in Safe JCop. If a layer omits the `extends` clause, it is implicitly assumed that the layer `extends Base`.

2.5 Layer Swapping and Deactivation

The original JCop provides constructs to *de*activate layers. However, only with `requires`, it is not easy to guarantee that layer deactivation does not lead to an error. For safe deactivation, it has to be checked that there is no layer that `requires` the deactivated layer, but the type system is not designed to keep track of *absence* of certain layers. Instead of general-purpose layer deactivation mechanisms, Safe JCop introduces a special construct to express one important idiom that uses deactivation, namely *layer swapping* to deactivate some layers and activate a layer at once.

In Safe JCop, we can define a layer as *swappable*, which means that all its sublayers can be swapped with each other, by adding the modifier `swappable`. The `swap` statement for layer swapping is of the following form:

`swap(`*activation_layer*, *deactivation_layer_type*`){ ... }`

[1] Re-typechecking inherited methods under the new `requires` clause would be another way to relax this condition but this is against modular checking.

The *activation_layer* is an expression whose static type must be a sublayer of *deactivation_layer_type*, which in turn has to be swappable. It deactivates *all* instances of *deactivation_layer_type* (and its sublayers), and activates the *activation_layer*.

Let's consider `Difficulty` once again. We could define `Difficulty` as a `swappable` layer and use `swap` to switch to another mode temporarily.

```
swappable layer Difficulty {...}
...
Difficulty dif = someCondition() ? new Easy() : new Hard();
with(dif){
  ...
  swap(new Hard(), Difficulty){
    // Enforce hard mode
  }
}
```

As discussed in the previous work [14], the layer swapping mechanism also requires no sublayers of a swappable layer to be `required` by other layers.

3 ContextFJ$_{<:}$

In this section, we formalize a core functional subset of Safe JCop as ContextFJ$_{<:}$, give its syntax, operational semantics and type system, and show type soundness. ContextFJ$_{<:}$, a descendant of Featherweight Java (FJ) [13], extends ContextFJ [10,11] with layer inheritance, layer subtyping, first-class layers, and swappable layers. Note that we omit some rules (especially when they are similar to those in ContextFJ [11]). The whole calculus is in the full version of this paper. We also recommend that readers consult [11].

3.1 Syntax

Let metavariables `C`, `D` and `E` range over class names; `L` over layer names; `f` and `g` over field names; `m` over method names; `x` and `y` over variables, which contains special variable `this`. The abstract syntax of ContextFJ$_{<:}$ is given in Fig. 1.

Following FJ, we use overlines to denote sequences: so, $\overline{\mathtt{f}}$ stands for a possibly empty sequence $\mathtt{f}_1, \cdots, \mathtt{f}_n$ and similarly for $\overline{\mathtt{T}}$, $\overline{\mathtt{x}}$, $\overline{\mathtt{e}}$, and so on. The empty sequence is denoted by $\bullet$. Concatenation of sequences is often denoted by a comma except for layer names, for which we use a semicolon. We also abbreviate pairs of sequences, writing "$\overline{\mathtt{T}}\ \overline{\mathtt{f}}$" for "$\mathtt{T}_1\ \mathtt{f}_1, \cdots, \mathtt{T}_n\ \mathtt{f}_n$", where n is the length of $\overline{\mathtt{T}}$ and $\overline{\mathtt{f}}$, and similarly "$\overline{\mathtt{T}}\ \overline{\mathtt{f}}$;" as shorthand for the sequence of declarations "$\mathtt{T}_1\ \mathtt{f}_1;\ldots\mathtt{T}_n\ \mathtt{f}_n;$" and "$\mathtt{this}.\overline{\mathtt{f}}=\overline{\mathtt{f}};$" for "$\mathtt{this}.\mathtt{f}_1=\mathtt{f}_1;\ldots;\mathtt{this}.\mathtt{f}_n=\mathtt{f}_n;$". Sequences of field declarations, parameter names, layer names, and method declarations are assumed to contain no duplicate names.

We briefly explain the syntax, focusing on COP-related constructs. A layer definition `LA` consists of optional modifier `swappable`, its name, its superlayer name, layers that it `requires`, and partial methods. A partial method is similar

$$
\begin{array}{lll}
\texttt{T,S} & ::= \texttt{C} \mid \texttt{L} & (\textit{types}) \\
\texttt{CL} & ::= \texttt{class C} \lhd \texttt{C \{ } \overline{\texttt{T}}\ \overline{\texttt{f}}\texttt{; K } \overline{\texttt{M}} \texttt{ \}} & (\textit{classes}) \\
\texttt{LA} & ::= [\texttt{swappable}]\ \texttt{layer L} \lhd \texttt{L req } \overline{\texttt{L}} \texttt{ \{ } \overline{\texttt{PM}} \texttt{ \}} & (\textit{layers}) \\
\texttt{K} & ::= \texttt{C(}\overline{\texttt{T}}\ \overline{\texttt{f}}\texttt{)\{ super(}\overline{\texttt{f}}\texttt{); this.}\overline{\texttt{f}} = \overline{\texttt{f}}\texttt{; \}} & (\textit{constructors}) \\
\texttt{M} & ::= \texttt{T m(}\overline{\texttt{T}}\ \overline{\texttt{x}}\texttt{)\{ return e; \}} & (\textit{methods}) \\
\texttt{PM} & ::= \texttt{T C.m(}\overline{\texttt{T}}\ \overline{\texttt{x}}\texttt{)\{ return e; \}} & (\textit{partial methods}) \\
\texttt{e,d} & ::= \texttt{x} \mid \texttt{e.f} \mid \texttt{e.m(}\overline{\texttt{e}}\texttt{)} \mid \texttt{new T(}\overline{\texttt{e}}\texttt{)} \mid \texttt{with e e} \mid \texttt{swap (e,L) e} & (\textit{expressions}) \\
 & \quad \mid \texttt{proceed(}\overline{\texttt{e}}\texttt{)} \mid \texttt{super.m(}\overline{\texttt{e}}\texttt{)} \mid \texttt{new C(}\overline{\texttt{v}}\texttt{)<C,}\overline{\texttt{L}}\texttt{,}\overline{\texttt{L}}\texttt{>.m(}\overline{\texttt{e}}\texttt{)} & \\
\texttt{v,w} & ::= \texttt{new C(}\overline{\texttt{v}}\texttt{)} \mid \texttt{new L()} & (\textit{values})
\end{array}
$$

Fig. 1. Syntax of ContextFJ$_{<:}$. A phrase enclosed by [] is optional.

to a method but the former specifies which m to modify by qualifying the simple method name with its class C. Instantiation can be a layer instance new L(). Note that arguments to the constructor are always empty because a layer has no fields. In the expression with $\texttt{e}_1$ $\texttt{e}_2$, $\texttt{e}_1$ stands for the layer to be activated and $\texttt{e}_2$ the body of with. In the expression swap ($\texttt{e}_1$, L) $\texttt{e}_2$, $\texttt{e}_1$ means the layer to be activated, L layers to deactivate, $\texttt{e}_2$ the body. All instances of L and its subclasses are deactivated. The expression $\texttt{new C(}\overline{\texttt{v}}\texttt{)<D,}\overline{\texttt{L}}'\texttt{,}\overline{\texttt{L}}\texttt{>.m(}\overline{\texttt{e}}\texttt{)}$ is a special run-time expression that is related to method invocation mechanism of COP, and not supposed to appear in classes and layers. It basically means that m is going to be invoked on $\texttt{new C(}\overline{\texttt{v}}\texttt{)}$. The annotation $\texttt{<D,}\overline{\texttt{L}}'\texttt{,}\overline{\texttt{L}}\texttt{>}$ is used to model super and proceed. $\overline{\texttt{L}}$ means activated layers in the method lookup and D and $\overline{\texttt{L}}'$ (which is assumed to be a prefix of $\overline{\texttt{L}}$) stand for the location of a "cursor" where the method lookup starts from.

Program. A ContextFJ$_{<:}$ program $(CT, LT, \texttt{e})$ consists of a class table CT, a layer table LT and an expression e, which stands for the body of the main function. CT maps a class name to a class definition and LT a layer name to a layer definition. A layer definition can be regarded as a function that maps a partial method name C.m to a partial method definition. So, we can view LT as a Curried function, so we often write $LT(\texttt{L})(\texttt{C.m})$ for the partial method C.m in L in a program. We assume that the domains of CT and LT are finite. Precisely speaking, the semantics and type system are parameterized over CT and LT but, to lighten the notation, we assume them to be fixed and omit from judgments.

Given CT and LT, extends and requires clauses are considered relations, written $\lhd$ and req, respectively, over class/layer names. As usual, we write $\mathcal{R}^+$ for the transitive closure of relation $\mathcal{R}$; similarly for $\mathcal{R}^*$ for the reflexive transitive closure of $\mathcal{R}$. We write L swappable if $LT(\texttt{L})$ is defined with the swappable modifier.

We assume the following sanity conditions are satisfied by a given program:

1. $CT(\texttt{C}) = \texttt{class C} \ldots$ for any $\texttt{C} \in dom(CT)$.
2. $\texttt{Object} \notin dom(CT)$.
3. For every class name C (except Object) appearing anywhere in CT, $\texttt{C} \in dom(CT)$.

4. $LT(\mathtt{L}) = \ldots\ \mathtt{layer\ L}\ \ldots$ for any $\mathtt{L} \in dom(LT)$.
5. $\mathtt{Base} \notin dom(LT)$.
6. For every layer name L (except Base) appearing anywhere in LT, $\mathtt{L} \in dom(LT)$.
7. Both for classes and layers, there are no cycles in the transitive closure of the extends clauses.
8. $LT(\mathtt{L})(\mathtt{C.m}) = \ldots\ \mathtt{C.m(\ldots)\{\ldots\}}$ for any $\mathtt{L} \in dom(LT)$ and $(\mathtt{C.m}) \in dom(LT(\mathtt{L}))$.
9. There are no cycles in $\mathtt{req}^{+}$.
10. A layer cannot require any superlayer of it, that is, $\mathtt{L}_1 \triangleleft^{+} \mathtt{L}_2 \rightarrow \neg(\mathtt{L}_1\ \mathtt{req}^{+}\ \mathtt{L}_2)$.
11. $\mathtt{L}_1 \triangleleft^{+} \mathtt{L}_2 \land \mathtt{L}_2\ \mathtt{swappable} \rightarrow \neg(\exists \mathtt{L}_3 . \mathtt{L}_3\ \mathtt{req}^{+}\ \mathtt{L}_1)$

In the condition 6, like Object of classes, Base layer is defined as the root of layer sub-typing tree. Conditions 7, 9 and 10 are very important for our formal system, because they are used to ensure that proceed and super calls will not fail. The final condition means that no sublayers of a swappable layer can be required by other layers, as we mentioned earlier.

3.2 Operational Semantics

Lookup Functions. We need a few auxiliary lookup functions to define operational semantics. The function *fields*(C) (whose definition is omitted) returns a sequence $\overline{\mathtt{T}}\ \overline{\mathtt{f}}$ of pairs of a field name and its type by collecting all field declarations from C and its superclasses. Other lookup functions are defined in Fig. 2. The function $pmbody(\mathtt{m}, \mathtt{C}, \mathtt{L})$ returns the parameters and body $\overline{\mathtt{x}}.\mathtt{e}$ of the partial method C.m defined in layer L. If C.m is not found in L, the superlayer of L is searched and so on. The function $mbody(\mathtt{m}, \mathtt{C}, \overline{\mathtt{L}}_1, \overline{\mathtt{L}}_2)$ returns the parameters and body $\overline{\mathtt{x}}.\mathtt{e}$ of method m in class C when the search starts from $\overline{\mathtt{L}}_1$; the other sequence $\overline{\mathtt{L}}_2$ keeps track of the layers that are activated when the search initially started. It also returns D and $\overline{\mathtt{L}}''$ (which will be a prefix of $\overline{\mathtt{L}}_2$), information on where the method has been found. For example, since the rule MB-LAYER means that the method is found in class C and layer $\mathtt{L}_0$ (or its superlayers), which is the rightmost layer of $\overline{\mathtt{L}}_1 = (\overline{\mathtt{L}}'; \mathtt{L}_0)$, *mbody* returns C and $(\overline{\mathtt{L}}'; \mathtt{L}_0)$. Such information will be used in reduction rules to deal with proceed and super. Readers familiar with ContextFJ will notice that the rules for *mbody* are mostly the same as those in ContextFJ, except that $pmbody(\mathtt{m}, \mathtt{C}, \mathtt{L})$ is substituted for $PT(\mathtt{m}, \mathtt{C}, \mathtt{L})$ to take layer inheritance into account.

Operational Semantics. The operational semantics of ContextFJ$_{<:}$ is given by a reduction relation of the form $\overline{\mathtt{L}} \vdash \mathtt{e} \longrightarrow \mathtt{e}'$, read "expression e reduces to e′ under the activated layers $\overline{\mathtt{L}}$". The sequence $\overline{\mathtt{L}}$ of layer names stands for nesting of with and the rightmost name stands for the most recently activated layer. $\overline{\mathtt{L}}$ do not contain duplicate names. Note that we put a sequence of layer names $\overline{\mathtt{L}}$ rather than layer instances because layer instances have no fields and new L() and L can be identified. If we modelled fields in layer instances, we would have to put instances for layer names.

$\boxed{pmbody(\mathtt{m}, \mathtt{C}, \overline{\mathtt{L}}) = \overline{\mathtt{x}}.\mathtt{e}}$

$$\frac{LT(\mathtt{L})(\mathtt{C.m}) = \mathtt{T_0\ C.m(\overline{T}\ \overline{x})\{\ return\ e;\ \}}}{pmbody(\mathtt{m}, \mathtt{C}, \mathtt{L}) = \overline{\mathtt{x}}.\mathtt{e}} \quad \text{(PMB-LAYER)}$$

$$\frac{LT(\mathtt{L})(\mathtt{C.m})\ \text{undefined} \qquad \mathtt{L} \lhd \mathtt{L}_S \qquad pmbody(\mathtt{m}, \mathtt{C}, \mathtt{L}_s) = \overline{\mathtt{x}}.\mathtt{e}}{pmbody(\mathtt{m}, \mathtt{C}, \mathtt{L}) = \overline{\mathtt{x}}.\mathtt{e}} \quad \text{(PMB-SUPER)}$$

$\boxed{mbody(\mathtt{m}, \mathtt{C}, \overline{\mathtt{L}}', \overline{\mathtt{L}}) = \overline{\mathtt{x}}.\mathtt{e}\ \text{in}\ \mathtt{D}, \overline{\mathtt{L}}''}$

$$\frac{\mathtt{class\ C} \lhd \mathtt{D\ \{\ \ldots\ T_0\ m(\overline{T}\ \overline{x})\{\ return\ e;\ \}\ \ldots\}}}{mbody(\mathtt{m}, \mathtt{C}, \bullet, \overline{\mathtt{L}}) = \overline{\mathtt{x}}.\mathtt{e}\ \text{in}\ \mathtt{C}, \bullet} \quad \text{(MB-CLASS)}$$

$$\frac{pmbody(\mathtt{m}, \mathtt{C}, \mathtt{L_0}) = \overline{\mathtt{x}}.\mathtt{e}}{mbody(\mathtt{m}, \mathtt{C}, (\overline{\mathtt{L}}'; \mathtt{L_0}), \overline{\mathtt{L}}) = \overline{\mathtt{x}}.\mathtt{e}\ \text{in}\ \mathtt{C}, (\overline{\mathtt{L}}'; \mathtt{L_0})} \quad \text{(MB-LAYER)}$$

$$\frac{\mathtt{class\ C} \lhd \mathtt{D\ \{\ ..\ \overline{M}\ \}} \qquad \mathtt{m} \notin \overline{\mathtt{M}} \qquad mbody(\mathtt{m}, \mathtt{D}, \overline{\mathtt{L}}, \overline{\mathtt{L}}) = \overline{\mathtt{x}}.\mathtt{e}\ \text{in}\ \mathtt{E}, \overline{\mathtt{L}}'}{mbody(\mathtt{m}, \mathtt{C}, \bullet, \overline{\mathtt{L}}) = \overline{\mathtt{x}}.\mathtt{e}\ \text{in}\ \mathtt{E}, \overline{\mathtt{L}}'} \quad \text{(MB-SUPER)}$$

$$\frac{pmbody(\mathtt{m}, \mathtt{C}, \mathtt{L_0})\ \text{undefined} \qquad mbody(\mathtt{m}, \mathtt{C}, \overline{\mathtt{L}}', \overline{\mathtt{L}}) = \overline{\mathtt{x}}.\mathtt{e}\ \text{in}\ \mathtt{D}, \overline{\mathtt{L}}''}{mbody(\mathtt{m}, \mathtt{C}, (\overline{\mathtt{L}}'; \mathtt{L_0}), \overline{\mathtt{L}}) = \overline{\mathtt{x}}.\mathtt{e}\ \text{in}\ \mathtt{D}, \overline{\mathtt{L}}''} \quad \text{(MB-NEXTLAYER)}$$

Fig. 2. ContextFJ$_{<:}$: Lookup functions.

Before giving reduction rules, we have to define two auxiliary functions, $with(\mathtt{L}, \overline{\mathtt{L}})$ and $swap(\mathtt{L}, \mathtt{L}_{sw}, \overline{\mathtt{L}})$ to manipulate activated layers.

$$with(\mathtt{L}, \overline{\mathtt{L}}) = (\overline{\mathtt{L}} \setminus \{\mathtt{L}\}); \mathtt{L} \qquad swap(\mathtt{L}, \mathtt{L}_{sw}, \overline{\mathtt{L}}) = (\overline{\mathtt{L}} \setminus \{\mathtt{L}' \mid \mathtt{L}' \lhd^* \mathtt{L}_{sw}\}); \mathtt{L}$$

The function *with* removes L (if exists) from layer sequence $\overline{\mathtt{L}}$ and adds L to the end of $\overline{\mathtt{L}}$ and *swap* removes $\mathtt{L}_{sw}$ and all sublayers of $\mathtt{L}_{sw}$ from $\overline{\mathtt{L}}$, and adds L to the end of $\overline{\mathtt{L}}$.

Main reduction rules are found in Fig. 3. The rules R-INVK and R-INVKP for method invocation are essentially the same as ones in ContextFJ. R-INVK initializes the cursor according to the currently activated layers $\overline{\mathtt{L}}$ and R-INVKP represents invocation of a partial method (the rule for base method invocation is omitted). Note how `this`, `proceed` and `super` are replaced with the receiver with different cursor locations. For `proceed`, the cursor moves one layer to the left and, for `super`, the cursor moves one level up. The rules RC-WITH and RC-SWAP are related to layer activation and swapping, respectively. The rule RC-WITH means that `with (new L()) e` executes `e` with L activated (as the first layer). The rule RC-SWAP is similar; it means that `swap (new L(),` $\mathtt{L}_{sw}$`) e` executes by deactivating all sublayers of $\mathtt{L}_{sw}$ and activating a layer L.

$$\boxed{\overline{\mathtt{L}} \vdash \mathtt{e} \longrightarrow \mathtt{e}'}$$

$$\frac{\overline{\mathtt{L}} \vdash \mathtt{new\ C(\overline{v})<C,\overline{L},\overline{L}>.m(\overline{w})} \longrightarrow \mathtt{e}'}{\overline{\mathtt{L}} \vdash \mathtt{new\ C(\overline{v}).m(\overline{w})} \longrightarrow \mathtt{e}'} \quad \text{(R-INVK)}$$

$$\frac{\begin{array}{c} \mathit{mbody}(\mathtt{m}, \mathtt{C}', \overline{\mathtt{L}}'', \overline{\mathtt{L}}') = \overline{\mathtt{x}}.\mathtt{e}_0 \ \mathtt{in}\ \mathtt{C}'', (\overline{\mathtt{L}}'''; \mathtt{L}_0) \\ \mathtt{class}\ \mathtt{C}'' \triangleleft \mathtt{D\{...\}} \end{array}}{\overline{\mathtt{L}} \vdash \mathtt{new\ C(\overline{v})<C',\overline{L}'',\overline{L}'>.m(\overline{w})} \longrightarrow \left[\begin{array}{ll} \mathtt{new\ C(\overline{v})} & \mathtt{/this}, \\ \overline{\mathtt{w}} & /\overline{\mathtt{x}}, \\ \mathtt{new\ C(\overline{v})<C'',\overline{L}''',\overline{L}'>.m} & \mathtt{/proceed}, \\ \mathtt{new\ C(\overline{v})<D,\overline{L}',\overline{L}'>} & \mathtt{/super} \end{array}\right] \mathtt{e}_0} \quad \text{(R-INVKP)}$$

$$\frac{\mathit{with}(\mathtt{L}, \overline{\mathtt{L}}) = \overline{\mathtt{L}}' \qquad \overline{\mathtt{L}}' \vdash \mathtt{e} \longrightarrow \mathtt{e}'}{\overline{\mathtt{L}} \vdash \mathtt{with\ new\ L()\ e} \longrightarrow \mathtt{with\ new\ L()\ e}'} \quad \text{(RC-WITH)}$$

$$\frac{\mathit{swap}(\mathtt{L}, \mathtt{L}_{sw}, \overline{\mathtt{L}}) = \overline{\mathtt{L}}' \qquad \overline{\mathtt{L}}' \vdash \mathtt{e} \longrightarrow \mathtt{e}'}{\overline{\mathtt{L}} \vdash \mathtt{swap\ (new\ L(),L_{\mathit{sw}})\ e} \longrightarrow \mathtt{swap\ (new\ L(),L_{\mathit{sw}})\ e}'} \quad \text{(RC-SWAP)}$$

Fig. 3. ContextFJ$_{<:}$: Reduction rules.

3.3 Type System

As usual, the role of a type system is to ensure the absence of a certain class of run-time errors. Here, they are "field-not-found" and "method-not-found" errors, including the failure of `proceed` or `super` calls.

As discussed in the last section, the type system takes information on activated layers at every program point into account. We approximate such information by a set Λ of layer names, which mean that, for any element in Λ, an instance of one of its sublayers has to be activated at run time. This set gives underapproximation in the sense that other layers might be activated. Activated layers are approximated by sets rather than sequences because the type system is mainly concerned about access to fields and methods and the order of activated layers does not influence which fields and methods are accessible.

In our type system, a type judgment for an expression is of the form $\mathcal{L}; \Lambda; \Gamma \vdash \mathtt{e} : \mathtt{T}$, where Γ is a type environment, which records types of variables, and $\mathcal{L}$ stands for where `e` appears, namely, a method in a class or a partial method in a layer. For example, the body of the partial method `World.getWeatherInfo()` in layer `Thunder` is typed as follows:

$$\mathtt{Thunder.World.getWeatherInfo}; \{\mathtt{Weather}, \mathtt{Thunder}\}; \bullet$$
$$\vdash \mathtt{"thunder\ and\ "\ +\ proceed()} : \mathtt{String}$$

where $\bullet$ stands for the empty type environment. The layer name set {`Weather`, `Thunder`} comes from the fact that `Thunder requires Weather`. `Thunder` is also included because `Thunder` is obviously activated when a partial method defined in this very layer is executed.

We start with the definitions of two kinds of layer subtyping discussed in the last section and proceed to functions to look up method types and typing rules.

Subtyping. We define subtyping $\mathtt{C} <: \mathtt{D}$ for class types, weak subtyping $\mathtt{L}_1 <:_w \mathtt{L}_2$ and normal subtyping $\mathtt{L}_1 <: \mathtt{L}_2$ for layer types by the rules in Fig. 4. Class subtyping $\mathtt{C} <: \mathtt{D}$ (whose rules are omitted) is defined as the reflexive and transitive closure of $\triangleleft$, just as FJ. Weak layer subtyping is also the reflexive and transitive closure of $\triangleleft$. We extend it to the relation $\Lambda_1 <:_w \Lambda_2$ between layer name sets by LSS-Intro. It is used to check activated layers Λ_1 satisfy requirement Λ_2 given by a `requires` clause in typechecking a layer activation. So, for every element in Λ_2, there must exist a sublayer of it in Λ_1. Normal subtyping is almost the reflexive and transitive closure of $\triangleleft$ but there is one additional condition: for $\mathtt{L}_1$ to be a normal subtype of $\mathtt{L}_2$, the layers they `require` must be the same (LS-Extends). The notation $\mathtt{L}\ \mathtt{req}\ \Lambda$ means that $\mathtt{L}\ \mathtt{req}\ \mathtt{L}'$ for any $\mathtt{L}' \in \Lambda$.

layer subtyping <:

$$\frac{}{\mathtt{L} <: \mathtt{L}} \quad \text{(LS-Refl)}$$

$$\frac{\mathtt{L}_1 <: \mathtt{L}_2 \qquad \mathtt{L}_2 <: \mathtt{L}_3}{\mathtt{L}_1 <: \mathtt{L}_3} \quad \text{(LS-Trans)}$$

$$\frac{\mathtt{L} \triangleleft \mathtt{Base} \qquad \mathtt{L}\ \mathtt{req}\ \emptyset}{\mathtt{L} <: \mathtt{Base}} \quad \text{(LS-Base)}$$

$$\frac{\mathtt{L}_1 \triangleleft \mathtt{L}_2 \qquad \mathtt{L}_1\ \mathtt{req}\ \Lambda \qquad \mathtt{L}_2\ \mathtt{req}\ \Lambda}{\mathtt{L}_1 <: \mathtt{L}_2} \quad \text{(LS-Extends)}$$

weak layer subtyping $<:_w$

$$\frac{}{\mathtt{L} <:_w \mathtt{L}} \quad \text{(LSw-Refl)}$$

$$\frac{\mathtt{L}_1 <:_w \mathtt{L}_2 \qquad \mathtt{L}_2 <:_w \mathtt{L}_3}{\mathtt{L}_1 <:_w \mathtt{L}_3} \quad \text{(LSw-Trans)}$$

$$\frac{\mathtt{L}_1 \triangleleft \mathtt{L}_2}{\mathtt{L}_1 <:_w \mathtt{L}_2} \quad \text{(LSw-Extends)}$$

layer set subtyping

$$\frac{\forall \mathtt{L}_2 \in \Lambda_2 . \exists \mathtt{L}_1 \in \Lambda_1 \text{ s.t. } \mathtt{L}_1 <:_w \mathtt{L}_2}{\Lambda_1 <:_w \Lambda_0} \quad \text{(LSS-Intro)}$$

Fig. 4. ContextFJ$_{<:}$: Subtyping relations.

Method Type Lookup. Similarly to *pmbody* and *mbody*, we define two auxiliary functions *pmtype* and *mtype* to look up the signature $\overline{\mathtt{T}} \rightarrow \mathtt{T}_0$ (consisting of argument type $\overline{\mathtt{T}}$ and a return type $\mathtt{T}_0$) of a (partial) method. *pmtype*$(\mathtt{m}, \mathtt{C}, \mathtt{L})$ returns the signature of `C.m` in `L` (or one of its superlayers); we omit its definition, which is similar to *pmbody*. *mtype*$(\mathtt{m}, \mathtt{C}, \Lambda_1, \Lambda_2)$, whose definition is essentially the same (save layer inheritance) as that in ContextFJ but shown in Fig. 5, returns the type of `m` in `C` under the assumption that Λ_1 is activated. The other layer set Λ_2 ($\supseteq \Lambda_1$) is used when the lookup goes to a superclass. If Λ_1 and Λ_2 are the same, which is mostly the case, we write *mtype*$(\mathtt{m}, \mathtt{C}, \Lambda_1)$.

These rules by themselves do not define *mtype* as a function, because different layers may contain partial methods of the same name with different signatures. So, precisely speaking, it should rather be understood as a relation; in a well-typed program, it will behave as a function, though.

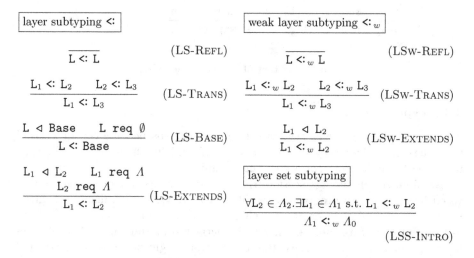

$\boxed{mtype(\mathtt{m},\mathtt{C},\Lambda_1,\Lambda_2) = \overline{\mathtt{T}}\rightarrow\mathtt{T_0}}$

$$\frac{\mathtt{class\ C \lhd D\ \{...\ T_0\ m(\overline{T}\ \overline{x})\{\ return\ e;\ \}\ ...\}}}{mtype(\mathtt{m},\mathtt{C},\Lambda_1,\Lambda_2) = \overline{\mathtt{T}}\rightarrow\mathtt{T_0}} \quad \text{(MT-CLASS)}$$

$$\frac{\mathtt{L} \in \Lambda_1 \qquad pmtype(\mathtt{m},\mathtt{C},\mathtt{L}) = \overline{\mathtt{T}}\rightarrow\mathtt{T_0}}{mtype(\mathtt{m},\mathtt{C},\Lambda_1,\Lambda_2) = \overline{\mathtt{T}}\rightarrow\mathtt{T_0}} \quad \text{(MT-PMETHOD)}$$

$$\frac{\begin{array}{c}\mathtt{class\ C \lhd D\ \{...\ \overline{M}\ \}} \qquad \mathtt{m} \notin \overline{\mathtt{M}} \\ \forall \mathtt{L} \in \Lambda_1.LT(\mathtt{L})(\mathtt{C.m}) \text{ undefined} \qquad mtype(\mathtt{m},\mathtt{D},\Lambda_2,\Lambda_2) = \overline{\mathtt{T}}\rightarrow\mathtt{T_0}\end{array}}{mtype(\mathtt{m},\mathtt{C},\Lambda_1,\Lambda_2) = \overline{\mathtt{T}}\rightarrow\mathtt{T_0}} \quad \text{(MT-SUPER)}$$

Fig. 5. ContextFJ$_{<:}$: Method type lookup functions.

Expression Typing. As mentioned already, the type judgment for expressions is of the form $\mathcal{L};\Lambda;\Gamma \vdash \mathtt{e} : \mathtt{T}$, read "e is given type T under context Γ, location $\mathcal{L}$ and layer set Λ". In addition to C.m and L.C.m, $\mathcal{L}$ can be $\bullet$, which means the top-level (i.e., under execution). Main typing rules are given in Fig. 6.

The rule T-INVK is straightforward: for the method signature $\overline{\mathtt{T}}\rightarrow\mathtt{T_0}$, retrieved from the receiver type $\mathtt{C_0}$, the types of the actual arguments must be their subtypes. The whole expression is given the method return type. The rule T-PROCEED is similar, but the activated layer set Λ' is taken from the `requires` clause of the layer L in which this expression appears. The last argument to *mtype* is $\Lambda \cup \{\mathtt{L}\}$ because a `proceed` call can proceed to a partial method D.m (where D is a superclass of C) defined in the same layer L. The rule T-WITH checks, by $\Lambda <:_w \Lambda'$, that the layers `required` by L—the layer type to be activated—are already activated and that the body $\mathtt{e_0}$ is well typed under the assumption that

$\boxed{\mathcal{L};\Lambda;\Gamma \vdash \mathtt{e} : \mathtt{T}}$

$$\frac{\mathcal{L};\Lambda;\Gamma \vdash \mathtt{e_0} : \mathtt{C_0} \qquad mtype(\mathtt{m},\mathtt{C_0},\Lambda) = \overline{\mathtt{T}}\rightarrow\mathtt{T_0} \qquad \mathcal{L};\Lambda;\Gamma \vdash \overline{\mathtt{e}} : \overline{\mathtt{S}} \qquad \overline{\mathtt{S}} <: \overline{\mathtt{T}}}{\mathcal{L};\Lambda;\Gamma \vdash \mathtt{e_0.m(\overline{e})} : \mathtt{T_0}} \quad \text{(T-INVK)}$$

$$\frac{\mathcal{L};\Lambda;\Gamma \vdash \mathtt{e}_l : \mathtt{L} \qquad \mathtt{L\ req}\ \Lambda' \qquad \Lambda <:_w \Lambda' \qquad \mathcal{L};\Lambda \cup \{\mathtt{L}\};\Gamma \vdash \mathtt{e_0} : \mathtt{T_0}}{\mathcal{L};\Lambda;\Gamma \vdash \mathtt{with}\ \mathtt{e}_l\ \mathtt{e_0} : \mathtt{T_0}} \quad \text{(T-WITH)}$$

$$\frac{\begin{array}{c}\mathcal{L};\Lambda;\Gamma \vdash \mathtt{e}_l : \mathtt{L} \qquad \mathtt{L}_{sw}\ \mathtt{swappable} \qquad \mathtt{L} <:_w \mathtt{L}_{sw} \qquad \mathtt{L\ req}\ \Lambda' \\ \Lambda_{rm} = \Lambda \setminus \{\mathtt{L'} \mid \mathtt{L'} <:_w \mathtt{L}_{sw}\} \qquad \Lambda_{rm} <:_w \Lambda' \qquad \mathcal{L};\Lambda_{rm} \cup \{\mathtt{L}\};\Gamma \vdash \mathtt{e_0} : \mathtt{T_0}\end{array}}{\mathcal{L};\Lambda;\Gamma \vdash \mathtt{swap}\ (\mathtt{e}_l,\mathtt{L}_{sw})\mathtt{e_0} : \mathtt{T_0}} \quad \text{(T-SWAP)}$$

$$\frac{\mathtt{L\ req}\ \Lambda' \qquad mtype(\mathtt{m},\mathtt{C},\Lambda',\Lambda' \cup \{\mathtt{L}\}) = \overline{\mathtt{T}}\rightarrow\mathtt{T_0} \qquad \mathtt{L.C.m};\Lambda;\Gamma \vdash \overline{\mathtt{e}} : \overline{\mathtt{S}} \qquad \overline{\mathtt{S}} <: \overline{\mathtt{T}}}{\mathtt{L.C.m};\Lambda;\Gamma \vdash \mathtt{proceed(\overline{e})} : \mathtt{T_0}} \quad \text{(T-PROCEED)}$$

Fig. 6. ContextFJ$_{<:}$: Expression typing.

L is additionally activated. T-SWAP is similar; the set Λ_{rm} stands for the set of layers after deactivation and must be a weak subtype of the required set Λ'.

Other Typing Rules. For typing other entities, such as (partial) methods and layers, we use the following judgments:

`PM ok in L`	partial method `PM` is well formed in layer `L`
`M ok in C`	base method `M` is well formed in class `C`
`LA ok`	layer definition `LA` is well formed
`CL ok`	class definition `CL` is well formed
override(*CT*, *LT*)	method override is valid in *CT* and *LT*
$\vdash (CT, LT, \mathtt{e}) : \mathtt{T}$	program $(CT, LT, \mathtt{e})$ is given type `T`

Representative typing rules are given in Fig. 7. The rule T-PMETHOD for a partial method means that the method body `e` is typed under the layer set `required` by this layer. The rule T-LAYER demands that the requires clause of the layer be *covariant* and all partial methods are well formed. A program is typed if all classes and layers in *CT* and *LT* are well formed, the main expression `e` is typed (at the top-level •), and *override*(*CT*, *LT*) holds.

The most involved is the rule to check valid method overriding. Note that, unlike Java, checking valid method overriding requires a whole program (except for the main expression) because a layer may add a new method to a base class, one of whose subclass may accidentally define a method of the same name without knowing of that layer. The first premise means that for two partial methods of the same (qualified) name must have the same signature. The second premise means that, for any partial method, the overridden method (base method in `C` or partial methods for `C`'s superclass) must have the same signature. Finally, the third premise means that a base method can override a (partial) method in its superclass (or layers modifying it) with a covariant return type.

3.4 Type Soundness

We prove type soundness of ContextFJ$_{<:}$ via subject reduction and progress [17]. To prove subject reduction, we have to give a typing rule for run-time expressions of the form `new` $\mathtt{C}(\overline{\mathtt{v}})\mathtt{<D},\overline{\mathtt{L}}',\overline{\mathtt{L}}\mathtt{>.m}(\overline{\mathtt{e}})$, which are not supposed to appear in a class/layer table. The typing rule is given as follows:

$$\frac{\begin{array}{ccc} \mathit{fields}(\mathtt{C}_0) = \overline{\mathtt{T}}\ \overline{\mathtt{f}} & \mathcal{L};\Lambda;\Gamma \vdash \overline{\mathtt{v}} : \overline{\mathtt{S}} & \overline{\mathtt{S}} <: \overline{\mathtt{T}} \\ \mathtt{C}_0 <: \mathtt{D}_0 & \mathit{mtype}(\mathtt{m}, \mathtt{D}_0, \{\overline{\mathtt{L}}'\}, \{\overline{\mathtt{L}}\}) = \overline{\mathtt{T}}' \rightarrow \mathtt{T}_0 & \\ \mathcal{L};\Lambda;\Gamma \vdash \overline{\mathtt{e}} : \overline{\mathtt{S}}' \quad \overline{\mathtt{S}}' <: \overline{\mathtt{T}}' & \{\overline{\mathtt{L}}\}\ \mathit{wf} & \mathit{WP}(\mathtt{m}, \mathtt{D}_0, \overline{\mathtt{L}}', \overline{\mathtt{L}}) \end{array}}{\mathcal{L};\Lambda;\Gamma \vdash \mathtt{new}\ \mathtt{C}_0(\overline{\mathtt{v}})\mathtt{<}\mathtt{D}_0,\overline{\mathtt{L}}',\overline{\mathtt{L}}\mathtt{>.m}(\overline{\mathtt{e}}) : \mathtt{T}_0} \quad \text{(T-INVKA)}$$

Basically, it combines the typing rules for `new` and method invocation with a few additional complications. The first three premises mean that the types of the values $\overline{\mathtt{v}}$ for fields $\overline{\mathtt{f}}$ are subtypes of the declared. The method signature is taken from the current location $\mathtt{<}\overline{\mathtt{D}}_0,\overline{\mathtt{L}}',\overline{\mathtt{L}}\mathtt{>}$ of the cursor and the types of the actual arguments $\overline{\mathtt{e}}$ have to be subtypes of the formal argument types. We detail the last two conditions below.

PM ok in L

$$\frac{\texttt{L req } \Lambda \qquad \texttt{L.C.m}; \Lambda \cup \{\texttt{L}\}; \overline{\texttt{x}} : \overline{\texttt{T}}, \texttt{this} : \texttt{C} \vdash \texttt{e}_0 : \texttt{S}_0 \qquad \texttt{S}_0 <: \texttt{T}_0}{\texttt{T}_0\ \texttt{C.m(}\overline{\texttt{T}}\ \overline{\texttt{x}}\texttt{) \{ return e}_0\texttt{; \} ok in L}} \quad \text{(T-PMethod)}$$

LA ok

$$\frac{\texttt{L}' \texttt{ req } \Lambda' \qquad \{\overline{\texttt{L}}\} <:_w \Lambda' \qquad \overline{\texttt{PM}} \texttt{ ok in L}}{\texttt{layer L req } \overline{\texttt{L}} \lhd \texttt{L}' \texttt{ \{ } \overline{\texttt{PM}} \texttt{ \} ok}} \quad \text{(T-Layer)}$$

override(*CT*, *LT*)

$$\frac{\begin{array}{c} \forall \texttt{m}, \texttt{C}, \texttt{L}_1, \texttt{L}_2, \overline{\texttt{T}}, \overline{\texttt{T}}', \texttt{T}_0, \texttt{T}'_0, \text{ if } LT(\texttt{L}_1)(\texttt{C.m}) = \texttt{T}_0\ \texttt{m(}\overline{\texttt{T}}\ \overline{\texttt{x}}\texttt{)\{...\}} \text{ and} \\ LT(\texttt{L}_2)(\texttt{C.m}) = \texttt{T}'_0\ \texttt{m(}\overline{\texttt{T}'}\ \overline{\texttt{y}}\texttt{)\{...\}}, \text{ then } \overline{\texttt{T}}, \texttt{T}_0 = \overline{\texttt{T}}', \texttt{T}'_0 \\ \forall \texttt{m}, \texttt{C}, \texttt{L}, \overline{\texttt{T}}, \overline{\texttt{T}}', \texttt{T}_0, \texttt{T}'_0, \text{ if } LT(\texttt{L})(\texttt{C.m}) = \texttt{T}_0\ \texttt{C.m(}\overline{\texttt{T}}\ \overline{\texttt{x}}\texttt{)\{ return e; \}} \text{ and} \\ mtype(\texttt{m}, \texttt{C}, \bullet, dom(LT)) = \overline{\texttt{T}}' \to \texttt{T}'_0, \text{ then } \overline{\texttt{T}} = \overline{\texttt{T}}' \text{ and } \texttt{T}_0 = \texttt{T}'_0 \\ \forall \texttt{m}, \texttt{C}, \texttt{D}, \overline{\texttt{T}}, \overline{\texttt{T}}', \texttt{T}_0, \texttt{T}'_0, \text{ if } \texttt{class C} \lhd \texttt{D \{... T}_0\ \texttt{m(}\overline{\texttt{T}}\ \overline{\texttt{x}}\texttt{)\{ ... \} ...\}} \text{ and} \\ mtype(\texttt{m}, \texttt{D}, dom(LT), dom(LT)) = \overline{\texttt{T}}' \to \texttt{T}'_0, \text{ then } \overline{\texttt{T}} = \overline{\texttt{T}}' \text{ and } \texttt{T}_0 <: \texttt{T}'_0 \end{array}}{override(CT, LT)}$$

$\vdash (CT, LT, \texttt{e}) : \texttt{T}$

$$\frac{\begin{array}{c} \forall \texttt{C} \in dom(CT).CT(\texttt{C}) \texttt{ ok} \qquad \forall \texttt{L} \in dom(LT).LT(\texttt{L}) \texttt{ ok} \\ \bullet; \emptyset; \bullet \vdash \texttt{e} : \texttt{T} \qquad override(CT, LT) \end{array}}{\vdash (CT, LT, \texttt{e}) : \texttt{T}} \quad \text{(T-Prog)}$$

Fig. 7. ContextFJ$_{<:}$: Method/class/layer/program typing.

The following two predicates Λ *wf* and $WP(\texttt{m}, \texttt{C}, \overline{\texttt{L}}', \overline{\texttt{L}})$ are crucial to ensure successful `proceed` and `super` calls in the presence of `with`.[2] The condition $\{\overline{\texttt{L}}\}$ *wf*, read "layer set $\{\overline{\texttt{L}}\}$ is well formed," means that for every layer in the set, there are layers that it `requires` in the same set. Formally, it is defined by the following rule:

$$\frac{\forall \texttt{L} \in \Lambda, \forall \texttt{L}' \text{ s.t, } \texttt{L req+ L}', \exists \texttt{L}'' \in \Lambda \text{ s.t, } \texttt{L}'' <:_w \texttt{L}'}{\Lambda\ wf} \quad \text{(LS-wf)}$$

The last premise $WP(\texttt{m}, \texttt{D}_0, \overline{\texttt{L}}', \overline{\texttt{L}})$ intuitively means "a chain of `proceed` calls from the given cursor location eventually reaches a (partial) method that does *not* call `proceed`" and is defined by the following rules:

$$\frac{(\exists \texttt{L}_0 \in \overline{\texttt{L}}_1.\texttt{proceed} \notin pmbody(\texttt{m}, \texttt{C}, \texttt{L}_0)) \text{ or } \texttt{class C \{.. C}_0\ \texttt{m(..)\{..\} ..\}}}{WP(\texttt{m}, \texttt{C}, \overline{\texttt{L}}_1, (\overline{\texttt{L}}_1;\overline{\texttt{L}}_2))} \quad \text{(WP-Layer)}$$

[2] The previous type system for ContextFJ [11] deals with `ensure`, an activation mechanism with a semantics slightly different from `with`, and T-InvkA is simpler. Further discussions on making `proceed` and `with` typesafe can be found in [12].

$$\frac{\texttt{C} \lhd \texttt{D} \qquad \mathit{WP}(\texttt{m}, \texttt{D}, (\overline{\texttt{L}_1}\,;\overline{\texttt{L}_2}), (\overline{\texttt{L}_1}\,;\overline{\texttt{L}_2}))}{\mathit{WP}(\texttt{m}, \texttt{C}, \overline{\texttt{L}_1}, (\overline{\texttt{L}_1}\,;\overline{\texttt{L}_2}))} \qquad \text{(WP-SUPER)}$$

Given the typing rule for run-time expressions, we can state the type soundness theorem below.

Theorem 1 (Subject Reduction). *Suppose given CT and LT are well-formed. If* $\bullet; \{\overline{\texttt{L}}\}; \Gamma \vdash \texttt{e} : \texttt{T}$ *and* $\{\overline{\texttt{L}}\}$ *wf and* $\overline{\texttt{L}} \vdash \texttt{e} \longrightarrow \texttt{e}'$, *then* $\bullet; \{\overline{\texttt{L}}\}; \Gamma \vdash \texttt{e}' : \texttt{S}$ *for some* S *such that* $\texttt{S} <: \texttt{T}$.

Theorem 2 (Progress). *Suppose given CT and LT are well-formed. If* $\bullet; \{\overline{\texttt{L}}\}; \bullet \vdash \texttt{e} : \texttt{T}$ *and* $\{\overline{\texttt{L}}\}$ *wf, then* e *is a value or* $\overline{\texttt{L}} \vdash \texttt{e} \longrightarrow \texttt{e}'$ *for some* $\texttt{e}'$.

Theorem 3 (Type Soundness). *If* $\vdash (CT, LT, \texttt{e}) : \texttt{T}$ *and* e *reduces to a normal form under the empty set of layers, then the normal form is* `new` $\texttt{S}(\overline{\texttt{v}})$ *for some* $\overline{\texttt{v}}$ *and* S *such that* $\texttt{S} <: \texttt{T}$.

4 Related Work

Our work is a direct descendant of Igarashi, Hirschfeld, and Masuhara [10,11], where a tiny COP language ContextFJ is developed and its type system is proved to be sound. ContextFJ is not equipped with layer inheritance, layer subtyping, or first-class layers but allows baseless methods to be declared in the second type system [11], in which `requires` declarations are first introduced into COP.

There are many type systems proposed for advanced composition mechanisms such as mixins [4,8], traits [16], open classes (a.k.a. inter-type declarations) [6], and revisers [5]. A common idea is to let programmers declare dependency between modules as required interfaces; our `requires` declarations basically follow it. In most work, however, composition is done at compile or link time unlike COP languages. So, it is interesting that the same idea works even for dynamic composition found in COP languages.

Kamina and Tamai [15] propose McJava, in which mixin-based composition can be deferred to object instantiation. In fact, `new` expressions can specify a class and mixins to instantiate an object. So, the type of an object also consists of a class name and a sequence of mixin names. Whereas composition is per-instance basis in McJava, it is global in ContextFJ$_{<:}$. However, in McJava, composition cannot be changed once an object is instantiated.

Drossopoulou et al. [7] proposed *Fickle*$_{\text{II}}$, a class-based object-oriented language with *dynamic reclassification*, which allows an object to change its class at run time. Their idea of root classes, which serve as interface, is similar to our swappable layers; their restriction that state classes cannot be used as type for fields is similar to ours that a sublayer of a swappable cannot be `required` by any other layer.

Bettini et al. [3] developed a type system for *dynamic trait replacement*, which allows methods in an object to be exchanged at run time. They introduce the notion of *replaceable* to describe the signatures of replaceable methods; a replaceable appears as part of the type of an object and the trait to replace methods of the object has to provide the methods in that replaceable. The roles of replaceables and traits are somewhat similar to those of swappable layers, which provide interfaces common to swapped layers, and sublayers of swappable.

5 Concluding Remarks

We have developed a formal type system for a small COP language with layer inheritance, layer subtyping, swappable layers, and first-class layers, and shown that the type system is sound with respect to the operational semantics. As in previous work, `requires` declarations are important to guarantee safety in the presence of baseless methods. Subtyping for first-class layers is subtle because there are two kinds of substitutability. We have introduced weak subtyping for checking whether a `requires` clause is satisfied and normal subtyping for usual substitutability.

We are working on implementing the type system on top of the existing JCop compiler but there are many other features that are not modelled in our calculus. We briefly discuss how our type system can be extended to these features.

In JCop, a layer definition can contain field and (ordinary) method declarations so that a layer instance can act just like an ordinary object. Typechecking accesses to these members of layer instances is the same as ordinary objects. If we model fields of layer instances, we will have to modify the reduction relation so that the sequence of activated layers consists of layer instances (with their field values) rather than layer names.

JCop provides special variable `thislayer`, which can be used in partial methods and is similar to `this` of classes. It represents the layer instance in which the invoked partial method is found at run time and can be used to access fields and methods of that layer instance. In operational semantics, the layer instance would be substituted for `thislayer`, similarly to `this`. Typing `thislayer` is also similar to `this` in the sense that it is given the name of the layer in which it appears but `thislayer` cannot be used for layer activation because, at run time, it may be bound to an instance of a *weak* subtype.

JCop also introduces `superproceed()` call, which can be used in a partial method and invokes a superlayer's partial method that is overridden by the partial method. Similarly to `super` calls in Java, the destination of `superproceed()` is known statically, so it is easy to typecheck.

We have not fully investigated the interaction between our type system with other features in Java, such as concurrency, generics, and lambda, although we expect most of them are orthogonal.

Acknowledgments. We thank Tomoyuki Aotani, Malte Appeltauer, Robert Hirschfeld, and Tetsuo Kamina for valuable discussions on the subject. We appreciate valuable comments and suggestions from the anonymous reviewers. This work was supported in part by Kyoto University Design School (Inoue) and MEXT KAKENHI Grant Number 23220001 (Igarashi).

References

1. Appeltauer, M., Hirschfeld, R.: The JCop language specification: Version 1.0, April 2012. Number 59. Universitätsverlag Potsdam (2012)
2. Appeltauer, M., Hirschfeld, R., Lincke, J.: Declarative layer composition with the JCop programming language. J. Object Technol. **12** (2013)
3. Bettini, L., Capecchi, S., Damiani, F.: On flexible dynamic trait replacement for Java-like languages. Sci. Comput. Program. **78**(7), 907–932 (2013)
4. Bono, V., Patel, A., Shmatikov, V.: A core calculus of classes and mixins. In: Guerraoui, R. (ed.) ECOOP 1999. LNCS, vol. 1628, pp. 43–66. Springer, Heidelberg (1999)
5. Chiba, S., Igarashi, A., Zakirov, S.: Mostly modular compilation of crosscutting concerns by contextual predicate dispatch. In: Proceedings of the ACM OOPSLA, pp. 539–554 (2010)
6. Clifton, C., Millstein, T., Leavens, G.T., Chambers, C.: MultiJava: design rationale, compiler implementation, and applications. ACM Trans. Prog. Lang. Syst. **28**(3), 517–575 (2006)
7. Drossopoulou, S., Damiani, F., Dezani-Ciancaglini, M., Giannini, P.: More dynamic object reclassification: $\text{Fickle}_{\text{II}}$. ACM Trans. Prog. Lang. Syst. **24**(2), 153–191 (2002)
8. Flatt, M., Krishnamurthi, S., Felleisen, M.: Classes and mixins. In: Proceedings of the ACM POPL, pp. 171–183. ACM (1998)
9. Hirschfeld, R., Costanza, P., Nierstrasz, O.: Context-oriented programming. J. Object Technol. **7**(3), 125–151 (2008)
10. Hirschfeld, R., Igarashi, A., Masuhara, H.: ContextFJ: a minimal core calculus for context-oriented programming. In: Proceedings of Foundations of Aspect-Oriented Languages (FOAL), March 2011
11. Igarashi, A., Hirschfeld, R., Masuhara, H.: A type system for dynamic layer composition. In: Proceedings of FOOL, October 2012
12. Igarashi, A., Inoue, H., Hirschfeld, R., Masuhara, H.: ContextFJ: a minimal calculus for context-oriented programming (2015) (in preparation for submission)
13. Igarashi, A., Pierce, B.C., Wadler, P.: Featherweight Java: a minimal core calculus for Java and GJ. ACM TOPLAS **23**(3), 396–450 (2001)
14. Inoue, H., Igarashi, A., Appeltauer, M., Hirschfeld, R.: Towards type-safe JCop: a type system for layer inheritance and first-class layers. In: Proceedings of the Workshop on Context-Oriented Programming, pp. 7:1–7:6. ACM (2014)
15. Kamina, T., Tamai, T.: McJava – a design and implementation of Java with mixin-types. In: Chin, W.-N. (ed.) APLAS 2004. LNCS, vol. 3302, pp. 398–414. Springer, Heidelberg (2004)
16. Liquori, L., Spiwack, A.: FeatherTrait: a modest extension of Featherweight Java. ACM Trans. Prog. Lang. Syst. **30**(2), 11 (2008)
17. Wright, A.K., Felleisen, M.: A syntactic approach to type soundness. Inf. Comput. **115**(1), 38–94 (1994)

Program Analysis - II

Bottom-Up Context-Sensitive Pointer Analysis for Java

Yu Feng(✉), Xinyu Wang, Isil Dillig, and Thomas Dillig

UT Austin, Austin, USA
yufeng@cs.utexas.edu

Abstract. This paper describes a new bottom-up, subset-based, and context-sensitive pointer analysis for Java. The main novelty of our technique is the constraint-based handling of virtual method calls and instantiation of method summaries. Since our approach generates polymorphic method summaries, it can be context-sensitive without reanalyzing the same method multiple times. We have implemented this algorithm in a tool called SCUBA, and we compare it with k-CFA and k-obj algorithms on Java applications from the DaCapo and Ashes benchmarks. Our results show that the new algorithm achieves better or comparable precision to k-CFA and k-obj analyses at only a fraction of the cost.

1 Introduction

Pointer analysis is a key enabling technology underlying many program analysis, software engineering, and compiler optimization tasks. Given a pointer variable p, pointer analysis statically determines the set of all heap objects that p may point to. The result of such an analysis can be used to resolve important program analysis questions, such as whether two pointers can be aliases or whether a heap location may be referenced in a given piece of code.

While existing pointer analysis algorithms differ along many dimensions, a key feature that determines the precision of an algorithm is *context-sensitivity*. In particular, a context-sensitive analysis respects the call/return semantics of procedure calls and does not yield spurious points-to facts that arise from inter-procedurally unrealizable paths. Furthermore, a context-sensitive analysis distinguishes heap objects that are allocated at the same program location, but due to different invocations of the same method. While more precise than context-insensitive ones, context-sensitive algorithms are much harder to scale to real programs, and many existing techniques use approximations of full context-sensitivity. For instance, *object-sensitive* analyses [14,15,23] only distinguish callsites where the receiver objects are different, and *k-CFA* analyses [12,22] differentiate contexts by tracking callstrings up to some fixed length k.

This work is supported in part by the Air Force Research Laboratory under agreement numbers FA8750-14-2-0270 and FA8750-15-2-0096 and in part by NSF Awards #1453386.

X. Feng and S. Park (Eds.): APLAS 2015, LNCS 9458, pp. 465–484, 2015.
DOI: 10.1007/978-3-319-26529-2_25

```
class X {
   Z f; Z g;
   void bar(Z z) {
      this.f = z;
   }
}

class Y extends X {
   void bar (Z z) {
      this.g = z;
   }
}

class A {
   X x; X y;

   void a1() {
      y = new Y();
      x = y;
      Z z = new Z();
      foo(z);
   }

   void a2() {
      x = new X();
      y = x;
      Z z = new Z();
      foo(z);
   }

   void foo(Z a) {
      x.bar(a);
      y.bar(a);
   }
}
```

Fig. 1. Code example to illustrate our approach

Context-sensitivity can be achieved either by performing a *top-down* or *bottom-up* interprocedural analysis. Top-down analyses start ethods of a program and analyze callers before callees. In contrast, bottom-up analyses start at leaf methods of the callgraph and analyze callees before callers. Since top-down algorithms analyze every method in a known calling context, they are simpler to design and implement, but they need to re-analyze the same method multiple times under different contexts. In contrast, bottom-up analyses generate a *polymorphic* method summary that may be used in *any* calling context to get context-sensitive results. While generating a polymorphic points-to summary is trickier than determining points-to information at a particular call site, bottom-up analyses do not need to reanalyze the same method several times[1] and have the potential to scale better. In addition, the results of a bottom-up pointer analysis are *reusable*: For instance, using a bottom-up pointer analysis, we can analyze a library just once and reuse its summary for many different clients.

In this paper, we present a bottom-up context- and field-sensitive pointer analysis algorithm for Java. A key novel feature of our approach is the constraint-based treatment of virtual method calls. Similar to many other approaches, our method starts with an imprecise callgraph and refines the callgraph as points-to facts are discovered. However, we construct the callgraph in a purely bottom-up fashion by predicating points-to facts on the possible dynamic types of the receiver object. As method summaries are propagated up the call chain, these dynamic types are resolved, thereby allowing the refutation of infeasible call targets and spurious points-to facts in a context-sensitive manner.

Another salient feature of our approach is that it can generate polymorphic method summaries without performing expensive case splits on possible aliasing patterns at call sites. In particular, a key challenge in bottom-up pointer analysis is how to generate method summaries that soundly capture the aggregate effect of a call to method m under *any* possible aliasing relation at m's call sites. Most previous techniques deal with this difficulty either by performing case splits on all possible aliasing patterns [3,6] (which can cause exponential blow-up) or by

[1] Bottom-up algorithms only re-analyze methods that belong to SCCs in the callgraph.

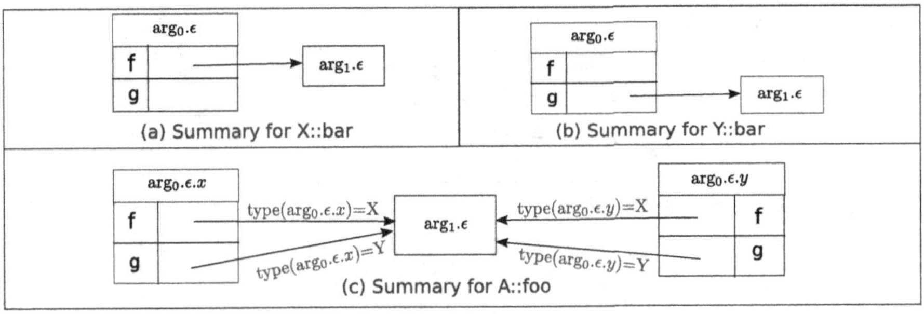

Fig. 2. Method summaries computed by our algorithm

using unification-based methods [10,13,27,28] (which are imprecise compared to subset-based methods). A main advantage of our technique is that it is as precise as subset-based methods despite modeling the unknown state of the heap in a simple and uniform way. In particular, since our technique does not perform *strong updates*[2] to heap locations, it can soundly account for the callee's side effects by performing a fixed-point computation during summary instantiation.

We have implemented our algorithm in a tool called SCUBA, and we compare its scalability and precision with top-down pointer analysis algorithms implemented in CHORD [16]. Our experimental results on programs from the DaCapo and Ashes benchmark suites indicate that SCUBA achieves better or comparable precision to k-CFA and k-object-sensitive algorithm at a fraction of the cost.

To summarize, this paper makes the following contributions:

- We present a bottom-up, subset-based, and context-sensitive pointer analysis for Java. A key novelty of our approach is the handling of virtual method calls using constraint-based techniques.
- We describe a new method for summarizing and instantiating points-to facts. Unlike previous techniques, our approach does not case-split on aliasing patterns and guarantees soundness by performing fixed-point computation during summary instantiation.
- We describe an implementation of our algorithm and compare it with k-CFA and k-obj algorithms on the DaCapo and Ashes benchmarks.

2 Example

This section illustrates our approach on an example that showcases virtual method calls and the need for context-sensitivity. Consider the code shown in Fig. 1, which defines classes `X`, `Y`, and `A`. Here, `Y` is a subclass of `X` and overrides `X`'s `bar` method. Class `A` has two instance variables `x` and `y` of type `X`. For concreteness, suppose we want to know whether `x.f` and `y.g` can be aliases at the end of `a1` and `a2`.

[2] A strong update to memory location o kills the existing points-to facts for o, while a *weak update* does not.

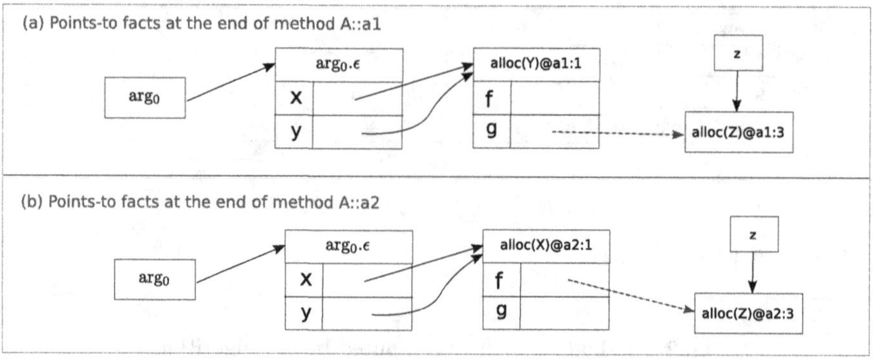

Fig. 3. Dashed lines indicate points-to edges added after the `foo` call.

Our algorithm starts by analyzing `X::bar` and `Y::bar`, which are leaf procedures in the callgraph. The summaries for `X::bar` and `Y::bar` are shown in Fig. 2(a) and (b). We depict both method summaries as well as local points-to facts in the form of a graph, where nodes correspond to abstract heap objects and directed edges denote may-point-to relations. Our method summaries only include points-to edges that may be *added* due to an invocation of the summarized method. In particular, method summaries do not include points-to relations that already exist on method entry, and since our analysis does not apply strong updates, no points-to edges can be removed as a result of analyzing a method. Hence, the summary for a method `m` can be thought of as a bag of (symbolic) points-to edges that are introduced due to an invocation of `m`.

Now, consider the summary for `X::bar` shown in Fig. 2(a). We use $\texttt{arg}_0$ to denote the `this` pointer, and $\texttt{arg}_1$, $\texttt{arg}_2$ to denote the first and second formal parameters. For parameter i, we use $\texttt{arg}_i.\epsilon$ to denote the heap object pointed to by $\texttt{arg}_i$ on method entry. Hence, according to the summary in Fig. 2(a), `X::bar` adds a points-to edge via field `f` from the object pointed to by the `this` pointer to the object pointed to by `X::bar`'s first parameter. Note that, at a call site of `X::bar`, parameter `z` may have multiple points-to targets, hence, the single edge in `X::bar`'s summary may introduce multiple points-to edges at a call site. The summary for `Y::bar`, which is shown in Fig. 2(b), is very similar.

Now consider method `A::foo`, whose summary is shown in Fig. 2(c). Since `x` has type `X`, the call `x.bar(a)` could either invoke `X::bar` or `Y::bar`. Hence, to analyze the method call, we instantiate the summaries of both `X::bar` and `Y::bar`, but the points-to edges induced by instantiating method `T::bar` are qualified by a constraint that stipulates that the dynamic type of `x` is `T`.

As an example, consider the potential target `X::bar` of the call `x.bar(a)`. Here, the only points-to edge in the summary for `X::bar` is from the `f` field of $\texttt{arg}_0.\epsilon$ to $\texttt{arg}_1.\epsilon$. Since $\texttt{arg}_0$ of `X::bar` corresponds to `this.x` at the call site, $\texttt{arg}_0.\epsilon$ instantiates to $\texttt{arg}_0.\epsilon.x$, which denotes the memory location *pointed to* by `this.x`. On the other hand, $\texttt{arg}_1$ in `X::bar` corresponds to parameter `z` at the call site, hence $\texttt{arg}_1.\epsilon$ translates to a location with the same name, i.e., $\texttt{arg}_1.\epsilon$.

Therefore, as shown in Fig. 2(c), instantiating the summary of `X::bar` for this call site induces an edge from $\mathtt{arg}_0.\epsilon.x$ to $\mathtt{arg}_1.\epsilon$, but this edge is qualified by the constraint $\text{type}(\text{arg}_0.\epsilon.x) = \text{X}$.

Continuing with the method invocation `y.bar(a)` in the second line of `A::foo`, we again instantiate the summaries of `X::bar` and `Y::bar`, since the type of `y` is `X`. However, this time, the location named $\mathtt{arg}_1.\epsilon$ used in the summaries of `X::bar` and `Y::bar` correspond to the location pointed to by `this.y`, which is denoted by $\mathtt{arg}_0.\epsilon.y$ in method `foo`. Hence, as shown in Fig. 2(c), the summary for `foo` includes points-to edges from the `f` and `g` fields of $\mathtt{arg}_0.\epsilon.y$ to $\mathtt{arg}_1.\epsilon$, again qualified by the appropriate type constraints. Observe that our approach is context-sensitive because two different invocations of `bar` induce different points-to relations. Also, even though `this.x` and `this.y` may alias at a call site of `foo`, we represent their points-to targets on method entry using two *separate* locations called $\mathtt{arg}_0.\epsilon.x$ and $\mathtt{arg}_0.\epsilon.y$. As we explain shortly, this approach is sound as long as we do not perform strong updates.

Now consider method `a1` defined in `A`. The *solid* black edges in Fig. 3(a) denote points-to facts that hold right before the call to `foo`. In particular, the location named $\mathtt{arg}_0.\epsilon$ denotes the object pointed to by the `this` pointer, and both the `x` and `y` fields of $\mathtt{arg}_0.\epsilon$ point to a location called alloc(Y)@a1 : 1, which corresponds to the memory allocated at the first line of method `a1`. Throughout the paper, we use the notation alloc(T)@Ctx to denote heap objects of type `T` that are allocated in context Ctx.

We now turn to the method invocation `foo(z)` in `a1`. Here, $\mathtt{arg}_1.\epsilon$ in `foo`'s summary corresponds to the location pointed to by `z` in `a1`, which is alloc(Z)@a1 : 3. On the other hand, the locations named $\mathtt{arg}_0.\epsilon.x$ and $\mathtt{arg}_0.\epsilon.y$ in `foo` represent the locations pointed to by `this.x` and `this.y` in `a1` respectively. Following the chain of points-to edges in Fig. 3(a), we see that $\mathtt{arg}_0.\epsilon.x$ and $\mathtt{arg}_0.\epsilon.y$ both correspond to the location alloc(Y)@a1 : 1. Since this allocation is tagged with type `Y`, the constraints $\text{type}(\text{arg}_0.\epsilon.x) = \text{X}$ and $\text{type}(\text{arg}_0.\epsilon.y) = \text{X}$ evaluate to false, while $\text{type}(\text{arg}_0.\epsilon.x) = \text{Y}$ and $\text{type}(\text{arg}_0.\epsilon.y) = \text{Y}$ evaluate to true. Hence, instantiating `foo`'s summary induces a single points-to edge from the `g` field of alloc(Y)@a1 : 1 to alloc(Z)@a1 : 3, which is shown with the dotted edge in Fig. 3(a). A similar chain of reasoning allows us to obtain the points-to facts shown in Fig. 3(b) for method `a2`.

As we can see from Fig. 3, the analysis determines that `x.f` and `y.g` are not aliases in either `a1` or `a2`. Observe that an analysis that is either context-insensitive or based on an imprecise callgraph would conclude otherwise. Also, even though there are two different calls to `foo` and four different calls to `bar`, observe that our algorithm analyzes each method only once.

3 Conceptual Foundations

Before describing our analysis in detail, we first describe a conceptual framework that lays the foundations of our algorithm. We describe the main ideas using a may-points-to graph, which we refer to as an *abstract heap*:

Definition 1 (Abstract heap). *An abstract heap H is a graph (N, E) where N is a set of nodes corresponding to abstract memory locations, and E is a set of directed edges between nodes labeled with field names or ϵ. An edge (o_1, o_2, f) indicates that the f field of o_1* may *point to o_2.*

Here, an abstract memory location represents either the stack location of a variable or a set of heap objects. The edge label ϵ is used to model points-to relations from stack locations to heap objects. The root nodes of an abstract heap denote locations of variables, and we write *root*(H) to indicate the set of root nodes of H. Given two abstract heaps H_1 and H_2, $H_1 \cup H_2$ represents the abstract heap containing nodes and edges from both H_1 and H_2. Given a heap H and edges E, we write $H \backslash E$ to denote the heap that contains all nodes and edges in H except the set of edges E.

3.1 Normalization of Abstract Heaps

Given an abstract heap H, we define a *normalization operation* $\mathbb{N}(H)$, which yields a *normalized heap* H^* and a mapping ζ from nodes in H to nodes in H^*.

Definition 2 (Normal form). *Given heap $H = (N, E)$, $\mathbb{N}(H)$ yields* normalized heap $H^* = (N^*, E^*)$ *and mapping $\zeta : N \to 2^{N^*}$ such that:*

1. *If $x \in \text{root}(H)$, then $x \in N^*$ and $\zeta(x) = \{x\}$.*
2. *If $(o, o', f) \in E$ and $o^* \in \zeta(o)$, then $o^*.f \in N^*$, $o^*.f \in \zeta(o')$, and $(o^*, o^*.f, f) \in E^*$.*

We use the notation $\mathbb{N}(H) = H^*$ to indicate that H^* is in normal form, and we write *Map*$(H, H^*) = \zeta$ to indicate that ζ maps nodes of H to nodes in H^*.

Example 1. Consider the abstract heap H shown in Fig. 4(a) and its normal form H^* in Fig. 4(b). Here, *Map*(H, H^*) yields the following mapping ζ:

$$\begin{array}{lll} \zeta(x) = \{x\} & \zeta(y) = \{y\} & \zeta(A) = \{x.\epsilon\} \\ \zeta(B) = \{x.\epsilon, y.\epsilon\} & \zeta(C) = \{y.\epsilon\} & \zeta(D) = \{x.\epsilon.f\} \\ \zeta(E) = \{x.\epsilon.f, y.\epsilon.f\} & & \zeta(F) = \{x.\epsilon.f, y.\epsilon.f\} \end{array}$$

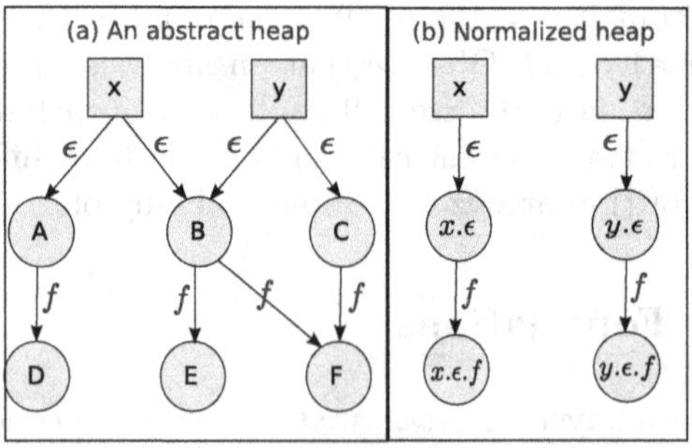

Fig. 4. An abstract heap and its normal form

We use heap normal forms to model the heap on entry to a method. In particular, H^* corresponds to a "generic" heap representing the unknown points-to targets of object o's f field as $o.f$. While the mapping ζ from abstract heap H to its normal form H^* differs for each call site, the normalized heap for a method m is the same irrespective of calling context. Observe that no pair of abstract memory locations alias each other in a normalized heap, and every location has exactly one points-to target for a given field.

Given an abstract heap $H = (N, E)$ and its normal form $H^* = (N^*, E^*)$ such that $Map(H, H^*) = \zeta$, we define ζ^{-1} to be a mapping from N^* to 2^N such that $n \in \zeta^{-1}(n^*)$ iff $n^* \in \zeta(n)$. In general, there is a many-to-many relationship between the nodes of an abstract heap and its corresponding normal form.

Example 2. Consider the heap from Example 1. We have:

$$\zeta^{-1}(x) = \{x\} \qquad \zeta^{-1}(y) = \{y\} \qquad \zeta^{-1}(x.\epsilon) = \{A, B\}$$
$$\zeta^{-1}(y.\epsilon) = \{B, C\} \quad \zeta^{-1}(x.\epsilon.f) = \{D, E, F\} \quad \zeta^{-1}(y.\epsilon.f) = \{E, F\}$$

The mapping ζ^{-1} is important in summary-based analysis because it allows us to instantiate a method summary to a particular abstract heap at a call site. We use the notation $\overline{\zeta^{-1}}$ to denote the extension of ζ^{-1} that maps any element that is not in the domain of ζ^{-1} to itself. Given heap $H^* = (N^*, E^*)$, we also write $\zeta^{-1}(H^*)$ to denote a heap $H = (N, E)$ where $(o_1, o_2, f) \in E$ iff there exists an edge $(o_1^*, o_2^*, f) \in E^*$ such that $o_1 \in \zeta^{-1}(o_1^*)$ and $o_2 \in \zeta^{-1}(o_2^*)$.

Definition 3 (Default Edge). *We say an edge* (n, n', f) *is a* default edge *of an abstract heap if* $n' = n.f$.

Given a heap H, we write $default(H)$ to denote the set of default edges in H.

SUMANALYZE(H, S, A):
    input: abstract heap H, code S, intraprocedural analysis A
    output: abstract heap H'

  (1)   let $H^* = \text{NormalForm}(H)$
  (2)   let $H'^* = \text{Analyze}(H^*, S, A)$
  (3)   let $\Delta = H'^* \backslash default(H'^*)$
  (4)   let $\zeta_0 = Map(H, H^*)$
  (5)   let $H' = H$;   let $\zeta = \zeta_0$
  (6)   do {
  (7) $\zeta_0 = \zeta$
  (8) $H' = \overline{\zeta^{-1}}(\Delta) \cup H'$
  (9) $\zeta = Map(H', H^*)$
 (10) }
 (11) while($\zeta \neq \zeta_0$)
 (12) return H'

Fig. 5. Basic structure of summary-based analysis

3.2 Summary-Based Pointer Analysis

We now explain the basic idea underlying our summary-based analysis, assuming a family of pointer analyses that are sound and weakly-updating. Given code snippet S, an abstract heap H, and pointer analysis A, we write $H' = \mathit{Analyze}(H, S, A)$ to indicate that, if statement S is executed in an environment that satisfies abstract heap H, then analyzing code S using pointer analysis A yields a heap H' which conservatively models the concrete heap after S.

The basic structure of our summary-based pointer analysis is shown in Fig. 5. The algorithm SUMANALYZE takes as input an abstract heap H, a code snippet S, and a weakly-updating pointer analysis A, and works as follows. Line (1) constructs the normalized heap H^* representing the unknown state of the heap before executing S, and line (2) analyzes S without making any assumptions about points-to facts that hold before S. Line (3) generates a polymorphic points-to summary Δ which characterizes side effects of code S. Lines (4)–(11) instantiate the summary Δ by performing a fixed-point computation. Finally, H' at line (12) models the state of the heap after S when S is executed in an environment satisfying H.

Before discussing details, let us first understand in what way this algorithm is "summary-based". Since H^* can be constructed in a context-independent manner, we can analyze S in isolation and compute its side effects without knowing the points-to facts that hold before S. Hence, lines (1)–(3) in Fig. 5 correspond to *summary generation*. On the other hand, lines (4)–(11) perform *summary instantiation* by computing the context-specific mapping ζ_0 and by adding all points-to edges that represent S's side effects.

The most involved part of the above algorithm is the fixed-point computation at lines (4)–(11). Intuitively, the algorithm maps each edge in the summary to a set of edges at the callsite by using the mapping $\overline{\zeta^{-1}}$ and adds these edges to the initial abstract heap H. However, as new edges are added to H, the mapping ζ must to be recomputed since locations used in the summary may map to new additional locations after the summary has been applied. Hence, H' is recomputed until the mapping ζ from H' to H^* stabilizes. It is easy to see that SUMANALYZE is sound because (i) the underlying pointer analysis does not apply strong updates to memory locations, and (ii) the summary is applied to a

$$
\begin{array}{ll}
\text{Program } P & := C^+ \\
\text{ClassDecl } C & := \text{class } T_1 \text{ [extends } T_2\text{]? } \{F^*; M^*\} \\
\text{FieldDecl } F & := T \text{ fld\_name;} \\
\text{MethodDecl } M & := m(T_0\ v_0,\ \ldots,\ T_k\ v_k) = \{V^*; I;\} \\
\text{VarDecl } V & := T \text{ var\_name;} \\
\text{Instruction } I & := v_1 = v_2 \mid v_1 = v_2.f \mid v_1.f = v_2 \mid v = \text{new}^{\rho}\ T \\
& \quad \mid \text{if}(*)\ I_1 \text{ else } I_2 \mid I_1; I_2 \mid m^{\rho}@T(v_1, \ldots, v_n) \mid v_0.m^{\rho}(v_1, \ldots, v_n)
\end{array}
$$

Fig. 6. Core language used for our formalization

fixed-point. In particular, observe that H' overapproximates H and $\{H'\}S\{H'\}$ is a valid Hoare triple [8].

The reader may wonder why it is necessary to re-apply the summary until the mapping ζ reaches a fixed point in Fig. 5. This is necessary because our summary Δ encodes all possible side effects of code snippet S, but not the *order* in which they happen. Hence, while the fixed point computation is required for soundness, an immediate corollary is that the procedure SumAnalyze can be less precise than *Analyze* if the underlying pointer analysis A is flow-sensitive.

4 Formalization of Algorithm

While the previous section describes core ideas of the analysis, it omits many important details. In this section, we describe our full algorithm using the core object-oriented language of Fig. 6. Here, a program consists of one or more class declarations C, which defines a class T_1 with optional superclass T_2. Instructions include assignments, loads, stores, heap allocations (marked with a unique program point ρ), non-deterministic conditionals, sequences, static method calls $m^{\rho}@T(...)$ (also marked with program point ρ), and virtual method calls $v_0.m^{\rho}(\ldots)$. We assume that the first argument of a method is always the `this` pointer, and if a class T inherits a method m from its superclass T', then T' also contains a definition of m with the same implementation.

4.1 Abstract Domains

Figure 7 shows the abstract domains that we need for describing our algorithm. Since our analysis is bottom-up, we differentiate between two kinds of heap objects o: *Access paths* of the form $a_i.\eta$ represent (caller-allocated) unknown heap objects reachable through the i'th argument, whereas objects named alloc(T)@$\boldsymbol{\rho}$ represent heap objects of type T that are allocated either in the currently analyzed method or in a transitive callee. Specifically, $a_i.f_1...f_n$ denotes the unknown locations reachable on method entry through a series of field accesses $f_1...f_n$ from the i'th argument. We use the notation $a_i.(f_1...f_n)^{\star}$ to denote all unknown locations reachable from a_i through any combination of field selectors $f_1, ..., f_n$. For instance, $a_0.(f.g)^{\star}$ represents the infinite set of access paths $a_0.f$, $a_0.g$, $a_0.f.f$, $a_0.g.f$ and so on. As we will see in Sect. 4.3, access paths in our analysis correspond to node labels of the normalized heap from Sect. 3.

Abstract memory locations π are either heap objects o or stack locations. In particular, a_i denotes the stack location of the i'th argument, and $v_i@\boldsymbol{\rho}$ denotes the location of local variable v_i under *context* $\boldsymbol{\rho}$. We represent calling contexts using a sequence of program points $\rho_1, \ldots, \rho_n$, where each ρ_i corresponds to some call or allocation site. For instance, a memory location named alloc(T)@$\rho_1\rho_2$ corresponds to a heap object allocated at program point ρ_2 of some method m which is invoked at call site ρ_1. Similarly, $v@\rho_1$ denotes the local variable v of some method m when m is invoked at callsite ρ_1. Since our analysis builds contexts in a bottom-up way, local variables declared in the currently analyzed method

$$\begin{array}{ll}
\text{(Field selector)} & \eta : f \mid \eta.f \mid \eta^\star \\
\text{(Heap obj)} & o : a_i.\eta \mid \text{alloc}(T)@\boldsymbol{\rho} \\
\text{(Abstract loc)} & \pi : o \mid a_i \mid v_i@\boldsymbol{\rho} \\
\text{(Pts set)} & \theta : o \rightarrow \phi \\
\text{(Abstract heap)} & \Gamma : (\pi \times f) \rightarrow \theta \\
\text{(Summaries)} & \Upsilon : (T \times M) \rightarrow \Gamma
\end{array}$$

Fig. 7. Abstract domains used in our analysis

m do not have any context information; hence, we abbreviate the locations of locals in the current method as v_i.

Definition 4 (Argument-Derived Location). *We say location* π *is* derived from an argument, *written* $\text{arg}(\pi)$, *if it is either (i)* a_i *representing the location of the i'th argument or (ii) a heap object represented with an access path* $a_i.\eta$.

An *abstract heap* Γ maps each field f of location π to a points-to set. A (guarded) points-to set θ is a set of pairs (o, ϕ) where o is a heap object and ϕ is a constraint. As discussed in Sect. 2, we use constraints to predicate points-to facts on dynamic types of receivers. Constraints ϕ belong to the theory of equality with uninterpreted functions, defined according to the following grammar:

$$\begin{array}{ll}
\text{Function } f & := \text{pts} \mid \text{alloc} \mid \varsigma_i \\
\text{Term } t & := c \mid v \mid f(\boldsymbol{t}) \\
\text{Formula } \phi & := \top \mid \bot \mid \text{type}(t) = T \mid \phi_1 \wedge \phi_2 \mid \phi_1 \vee \phi_2
\end{array}$$

Here, terms include constants c, variables v, and function applications $f(\boldsymbol{v})$ where f is either the binary function pts, alloc, or an n-ary function drawn from $\varsigma_1, \ldots, \varsigma_k$. Formulas are composed of $\top$ (true), $\bot$ (false), and conjunctions and disjunctions of equality constraints of the form $\text{type}(t) = T$, where T is a type constant. In addition to the usual function and equality axioms, the alloc and type functions obey the additional axiom $\forall x.\ \text{type}(\text{alloc}(T, \boldsymbol{\rho})) = T$, which states that the type of an allocation of type T is T.

Since we will convert heap objects to terms, we define an operation called *lift*(π), abbreviated $\overline{\pi}$, as follows:

$$\overline{a_i} = a_i \quad \overline{\text{alloc}(T)@\boldsymbol{\rho}} = \text{alloc}(T, \boldsymbol{\rho}) \quad \overline{\pi.f} = \text{pts}(\overline{\pi}, f) \quad \overline{\pi.(\boldsymbol{f})^\star} = \varsigma_i(\overline{\pi}, \boldsymbol{f}) \ (\varsigma_i \text{ fresh})$$

We also assume an operation *lift*$^{-1}(t)$ which is the inverse of *lift*(π). Given a term t, *lift*$^{-1}(t)$ yields an abstract memory location representation of that term.

Example 3. The constraint $\text{type}(\overline{a.\epsilon.f}) = A \wedge \text{type}(\overline{a.\epsilon.f}) = B$ is unsatisfiable since the dynamic type of $a.\epsilon.f$ cannot simultaneously be A and B. But the constraint $\text{type}(\overline{a.\epsilon.g^\star}) = A \wedge \text{type}(\overline{a.\epsilon.g^\star}) = B$, which translates to $\text{type}(\varsigma_1(\text{pts}(a, \epsilon), g)) = A \wedge \text{type}(\varsigma_2(\text{pts}(a, \epsilon), g)) = B$, is satisfiable because two distinct occurrences of $a.\epsilon.g^\star$ may correspond to different objects (e.g., $a.\epsilon.g$ and $a.\epsilon.g.g$).

We now define a function *has_type(θ, T)* which generates a constraint that evaluates to true if *some* element in points-to set θ can have dynamic type T:

Definition 5 has_type(θ, T). *Given a points-to set* θ, *the function* has_type(θ, T) *yields the following constraint:*

$$\bigvee_{(\pi_i,\phi_i)\in\theta} (((\text{type})(\overline{\pi_i}) = T) \wedge \phi_i)$$

Now, going back to Fig. 7, an environment Υ maps each method M in class T to its corresponding summary, which is an abstract heap Γ summarizing M's side effects. Applying the summary at a call site allows us to determine points-to relations of the caller without having to reanalyze the callee. In addition, our method summaries include points-to information for locals in the summarized method. In particular, this design choice allows us to determine points-to sets for *all* program variables without employing a separate top-down pass.

4.2 Operations on Abstract Domains

In this section, we describe some operations on abstract domains that simplify the description of our algorithm. Since our algorithm constructs the initial heap on method entry in a demand-driven way, we first define *default targets* for argument-derived locations:

Definition 6 (Default Target). *Given an argument-derived location* π *and a field* f, *the* default target *of the* f *field of* π, *written* $\text{def}(\pi, f)$, *is given as follows:*

$$\text{def}(\pi, f) = \begin{cases} \pi & \text{if } \pi = \pi'.(\boldsymbol{f})^\star \text{ and } f \in \boldsymbol{f} \quad (1) \\ \pi'.(f.\boldsymbol{g})^\star & \text{if } \pi = \pi'.f.\boldsymbol{g} \quad (2) \\ \pi.f & \text{otherwise} \quad (3) \end{cases}$$

In other words, if field f is *not* part of a recursive field cycle (line 3), then the default target for field f of an argument derived location π is $\pi.f$, just like the normal form heaps from Sect. 3. However, if f is part of a recursive field cycle, then our analysis collapses this cycle into a single abstract memory location (lines 1–2). For example, $\text{def}(a.\text{next}, \text{next}) = a.\text{next}^\star$ (line 2), and $\text{def}(a.\text{next}^\star, \text{next}) = a.\text{next}^\star$ (line 1). The summarization of recursive field cycles into access paths of the form $a.\boldsymbol{f}^\star$ is needed to ensure termination of the fixed-point computation performed by our algorithm.

Next, we define a *field lookup* operation on abstract heaps Γ:

Definition 7 (Field Look-up). *Given heap* Γ, *field* f, *and location* π, *the* field lookup *operation* $\Gamma[\pi, f]$ *retrieves the points-to target for* π*'s* f *field:*

$$\Gamma[\pi, f] = \begin{cases} \Gamma(\pi, f) \cup \{(\text{def}(\pi, f), \top)\} & \text{if } \arg(\pi) \\ \Gamma(\pi, f) & \text{otherwise} \end{cases}$$

Since our algorithm does not explicitly add default edges to the abstract heap, $\Gamma[\pi, f]$ always yields x $def(\pi, f)$ as part of the points-to set of $\pi.f$ if π is an argument derived location. Now, since our analysis performs weak updates, we need to merge two points-to sets using the following join operator:

Definition 8 (Join $\sqcup$ of points-to sets θ_1, θ_2)

$$(\theta_1 \sqcup \theta_2)(o) = \begin{cases} \theta_1(o) \vee \theta_2(o) & \text{if } o \in \mathit{dom}(\theta_1) \cap \mathit{dom}(\theta_2) \\ \theta_1(o) & \text{if } o \in \mathit{dom}(\theta_1) \text{ and } o \notin \mathit{dom}(\theta_2) \\ \theta_2(o) & \text{if } o \in \mathit{dom}(\theta_2) \text{ and } o \notin \mathit{dom}(\theta_1) \end{cases}$$

Observe that if an object o is in both points to sets θ_1 and θ_2, we take the disjunction of the constraints associated with o. We also extend this join operator to abstract heaps in the expected way. That is, for a location π and field f, $(\Gamma_1 \sqcup \Gamma_2)(\pi, f)$ yields $\Gamma_1(\pi, f) \sqcup \Gamma_2(\pi, f)$. In our analysis, we sometimes need to predicate points-to information on constraints. For this purpose, an operation $\theta \downarrow \phi$ conjoins ϕ with every constraint in θ:

Definition 9 (Projection of θ on ϕ). $\theta \downarrow \phi = \{(\pi_i, \phi_i \wedge \phi) \mid (\pi_i, \phi_i) \in \theta\}$

Finally, we extend the field lookup operation on points-to sets as follows:

Definition 10 (Field lookup for pts-to set). $\Gamma[\theta, f] = \bigsqcup_{(\pi_i, \phi_i) \in \theta} \Gamma[\pi_i, f] \downarrow \phi_i$

That is, $\Gamma[\theta, f]$ includes the points-to target of every element in θ under the appropriate constraints.

4.3 Intraprocedural Analysis

Figure 8 describes the intraprocedural analysis using judgements of the form $\Upsilon, \Gamma \vdash I : \Gamma'$. which indicates that, if statement I is executed in an environment that satisfies summary environment Υ and abstract heap Γ, we obtain a new heap Γ'. Since the analysis is (partially) flow-sensitive, we distinguish between heaps Γ, Γ' before and after executing I.

Rule (1) in Fig. 8 describes the analysis of assignments. Although our analysis only performs weak updates to heap objects, it does apply strong updates to variables. Hence, rule (1) updates the points-to set for (v_1, ϵ) to be $\Gamma[v_2, \epsilon]$, where the lookup operation is defined in Sect. 4.2. Rule (2) for memory allocations $v = \text{new}^\rho\ T$ introduces a new abstract location named alloc(T)@ρ and assigns v_1 to this singleton.

Rule (3) concerns loads of the form $v_1 = v_2.f$. Here, we first look up the points-to set θ of v_2 and then use $\Gamma[\theta, f]$ to retrieve the targets of memory locations in θ. Finally, since our analysis applies strong updates to variables, we override v_1's existing targets and change its points-to set to $\Gamma[\theta, f]$.

Rule (4) analyzes stores $v_1.f = v_2$. First, we look up the points-to sets θ_1 and θ_2 of v_1 and v_2. Now, the store operation will update every location o_i such that $(o_i, \phi_i) \in \theta_1$. However, since we apply only weak updates to heap objects, we preserve the existing points-to targets $\Gamma(o_i, f)$ for each o_i. Furthermore, since v_1

$$(1)\ \frac{\Gamma' = \Gamma[(v_1, \epsilon) \leftarrow \Gamma[v_2, \epsilon]]}{\Upsilon, \Gamma \vdash v_1 = v_2 : \Gamma'} \qquad (2)\ \frac{\Gamma' = \Gamma[v \leftarrow \{(\text{alloc}(T)@\rho, \top)\}]}{\Upsilon, \Gamma \vdash v = \text{new}^{\rho}\ T : \Gamma'}$$

$$(3)\ \frac{\begin{array}{c}\theta = \Gamma[v_2, \epsilon] \\ \Gamma' = \Gamma[(v_1, \epsilon) \leftarrow \Gamma[\theta, f]]\end{array}}{\Upsilon, \Gamma \vdash v_1 = v_2.f : \Gamma'}$$

$$(4)\ \frac{\begin{array}{c}\theta_1 = \Gamma[v_1, \epsilon] \quad \theta_2 = \Gamma[v_2, \epsilon] \\ \Gamma' = \Gamma[(o_i, f) \leftarrow (\Gamma(o_i, f) \sqcup (\theta_2 \downarrow \phi_i)) \mid (o_i, \phi_i) \in \theta_1]\end{array}}{\Upsilon, \Gamma \vdash v_1.f = v_2 : \Gamma'}$$

$$(5)\ \frac{\begin{array}{c}\Upsilon, \Gamma \vdash I_1 : \Gamma_1 \\ \Upsilon, \Gamma \vdash I_2 : \Gamma_2\end{array}}{\Upsilon, \Gamma \vdash \text{if}(*)\ I_1 \text{ else } I_2 : \Gamma_1 \sqcup \Gamma_2} \qquad (6)\ \frac{\begin{array}{c}\Upsilon, \Gamma \vdash I_1 : \Gamma_1 \\ \Upsilon, \Gamma_1 \vdash I_2 : \Gamma_2\end{array}}{\Upsilon, \Gamma \vdash I_1; I_2 : \Gamma_2}$$

Fig. 8. Rules for intraprocedural analysis

$$\frac{}{\mathcal{M}, \Gamma, \rho \vdash \textit{inst\_loc}(a_i) : \{\mathcal{M}(a_i), \top\}} \qquad \frac{\mathcal{M}, \Gamma, \rho \vdash \textit{inst\_loc}(\pi) : \theta}{\mathcal{M}, \Gamma, \rho \vdash \textit{inst\_loc}(\pi.f) : \Gamma[\theta, f]}$$

$$\frac{\begin{array}{c}\mathcal{M}, \Gamma, \rho \vdash \textit{inst\_loc}(\pi) : \theta_0 \\ \theta_i = \bigsqcup_{1 \le j \le n} \Gamma[\theta_{i-1}, f_j]\end{array}}{\mathcal{M}, \Gamma, \rho \vdash \textit{inst\_loc}(\pi.(f_1 ... f_n)^* : \bigsqcup_{i \ge 0} \theta_i)} \qquad \frac{\boldsymbol{\rho}_{\text{new}} = \text{new\_ctx}(\rho, \boldsymbol{\rho})}{\mathcal{M}, \Gamma, \rho \vdash \textit{inst\_loc}(v@\boldsymbol{\rho}) : \{(v@\boldsymbol{\rho}_{\text{new}}, \top)\}}$$

$$\frac{\boldsymbol{\rho}_{\text{new}} = \text{new\_ctx}(\rho, \boldsymbol{\rho})}{\mathcal{M}, \Gamma, \rho \vdash \textit{inst\_loc}(\text{alloc}(T)@\boldsymbol{\rho}) : \{(\text{alloc}(T)@\boldsymbol{\rho}_{\text{new}}, \top)\}}$$

Fig. 9. Rules for instantiating memory locations

points to o_i under constraint ϕ_i, o_i points to elements in θ_2 only when ϕ_i holds. Hence, the new points-to set for o_i is given by $(\theta_2 \downarrow \phi_i) \sqcup \Gamma(o_i, f)$ where the $\downarrow$ operation is given by Definition 9. Since rules (5) and (6) for if statements and sequencing and are fairly standard, we do not describe them in detail.

4.4 Interprocedural Analysis

We now describe the instantiation of summaries at call sites. Since a key part of summary instantiation is constructing the mapping from locations in the summary to those at the call site, we first start with the rules in Fig. 9 which describe the instantiation of memory locations. Informally, the rules of Fig. 9 construct the mapping ζ^{-1} from Sect. 3. More formally, they produce judgements of the form $\mathcal{M}, \Gamma, \rho \vdash \textit{inst\_loc}(\pi) : \theta$ where $\mathcal{M}$ maps formals to actuals, and Γ and ρ are the abstract heap and program point associated with a call site respectively. The meaning of the judgement is that, under $\mathcal{M}, \Gamma, \rho$, location π used in the summary maps to (guarded) location set θ.

The first rule Fig. 9 maps formal parameter a_i to the actual $\mathcal{M}(a_i)$. The second rule instantiates argument-derived locations of the form $\pi.f$. For this purpose, we first instantiate prefix π to location set θ, then retrieve the points-to targets of the f field of locations in θ. The third rule instantiates access paths of the form $\pi.(f_1 \ldots f_n)^\star$. As in the previous rule, we first instantiate prefix π, which yields θ_0. Now, recall that the access path $\pi.(f_1 \ldots f_n)^\star$ describes the infinite set of access paths given by the regular expression $\pi.(f_1 + \ldots + f_n)^*$. Hence, to instantiate $\pi.(f_1 \ldots f_n)^\star$, we need to compute all locations that are reachable from θ_0 using any combination of field selectors $f_1, \ldots, f_n$. The resulting set $\bigsqcup_{i \geq 0} \theta_i$ is the reflexive transitive closure of θ_0 with respect to fields $f_1, \ldots, f_n$.

The last two rules in Fig. 9 describe the instantiation of allocations and local variables. Both rules use a helper new_ctx method defined as follows:

$$\text{new\_ctx}(\rho, \boldsymbol{\rho}) = \begin{cases} \rho, \boldsymbol{\rho} \text{ if } |\boldsymbol{\rho}| \leq k \\ \boldsymbol{\rho} \quad \text{otherwise} \end{cases}$$

In other words, new_ctx appends call site ρ to context $\boldsymbol{\rho}$ if the length of $\boldsymbol{\rho}$ is less than some pre-determined threshold k. Hence, our analysis uses a k-CFA style context-sensitive heap abstraction where the value of k is configurable.

We now turn to the instantiation of constraints, summarized in Fig. 10. To translate a constraint $\text{type}(t) = T$, we map t to its corresponding location set θ by using *inst_loc*. The function $\textit{has\_type}(\theta, T)$ then yields the condition under which some element in θ has dynamic type T (recall Definition 5).

Using these ingredients, Fig. 11 shows how to instantiate an abstract heap Δ. Given location π_i and field f_j from the callee heap, *inst_partial_heap* instantiates all points-to edges from π_i labeled with f_j and yields instantiated partial heap Δ_{ij}. The instantiation of Δ is obtained by taking the join over all Δ_{ij}'s.

$$\frac{\mathcal{M}, \Gamma, \boldsymbol{\rho} \vdash \textit{inst\_loc}(\textit{lift}^{-1}(t)) : \theta \qquad \phi = \textit{has\_type}(\theta, T)}{\mathcal{M}, \Gamma, \boldsymbol{\rho} \vdash \textit{inst}_\phi(\text{type}(t) = T) : \phi} \qquad \frac{\star \in \{\wedge, \vee\} \qquad \mathcal{M}, \Gamma, \boldsymbol{\rho} \vdash \textit{inst}_\phi(\phi_1) : \phi_1' \qquad \mathcal{M}, \Gamma, \boldsymbol{\rho} \vdash \textit{inst}_\phi(\phi_2) : \phi_2'}{\mathcal{M}, \Gamma, \boldsymbol{\rho} \vdash \textit{inst}_\phi(\phi_1 \star \phi_2) : \phi_1' \star \phi_2'}$$

Fig. 10. Rules for instantiating constraints

$$\frac{\mathcal{M}, \Gamma, \boldsymbol{\rho} \vdash \textit{inst\_loc}(\pi_1) : \theta_1 \ldots \textit{inst\_loc}(\pi_n) : \theta_n \qquad \mathcal{M}, \Gamma, \boldsymbol{\rho} \vdash \textit{inst}_\phi(\phi_1) : \phi_1' \ldots \textit{inst}_\phi(\pi_n) : \phi_n'}{\mathcal{M}, \Gamma, \boldsymbol{\rho} \vdash \textit{inst\_pts}(\{(\pi_1, \phi_1), \ldots, (\pi_n, \phi_n)\}) : \sqcup_i (\theta_i \downarrow \phi_i)}$$

$$\frac{\mathcal{M}, \Gamma, \boldsymbol{\rho} \vdash \textit{inst\_loc}(\pi) : \theta' \qquad \mathcal{M}, \Gamma, \boldsymbol{\rho} \vdash \textit{inst\_pts}(\theta) : \theta'' \qquad \Delta = [(\pi_i, f) \leftarrow (\theta'' \downarrow \phi_i) \mid (\pi_i, \phi_i) \in \theta']}{\mathcal{M}, \Gamma, \boldsymbol{\rho} \vdash \textit{inst\_partial\_heap}(\pi, f, \theta) : \Delta}$$

$$\frac{\Delta = \{(\pi_1, f_{11}) \mapsto \theta_{11}, \ldots, (\pi_n, f_{nk}) \mapsto \theta_{nk}\} \qquad \mathcal{M}, \Gamma, \boldsymbol{\rho} \vdash \textit{inst\_partial\_heap}(\pi_1, f_{11}, \theta_{11}) : \Delta_{11} \quad \ldots \quad \mathcal{M}, \Gamma, \boldsymbol{\rho} \vdash \textit{inst\_partial\_heap}(\pi_n, f_{nk}, \theta_{nk}) : \Delta_{nk}}{\mathcal{M}, \Gamma, \boldsymbol{\rho} \vdash \textit{inst\_heap}(\Delta) : \sqcup_{ij} \Delta_{ij}}$$

Fig. 11. Rules for instantiating summaries

Finally, Fig. 12 describes the analysis of method calls. First, consider a static call to m with corresponding summary Δ (rule (1)). To analyze it, we construct the formal-to-actual mapping $\mathcal{M}$ and perform a least fixed-point computation that instantiates the summarized heap Δ until we obtain an overapproximation of the set Δ' of m's side effects. The abstract heap after the method call is obtained by taking the union of the existing heap Γ and the new "edges" Δ'.

The second rule of Fig. 12 describes the analysis of virtual calls. Here, we first overapproximate the call's targets and then use the previous rule for analyzing static method calls to obtain heap Γ_i assuming the called method is $T_i :: m$. Now, since the target of the virtual call is $T_i :: m$ under the assumption that v_0 has dynamic type T_i, we generate the constraint $\phi_i = \text{has\_type}(\Gamma(v_0), T_i)$. Then, the final abstract heap after the call is obtained as $\sqcup_i(\Gamma_i \downarrow \phi_i)$.

$$(1)\ \frac{\Upsilon(T,m) = \Delta \quad \mathcal{M} = [a_1 \mapsto v_1, \ldots, a_n \mapsto v_n] \quad \mathcal{M}, \Gamma \sqcup \Delta', \rho \vdash \mathit{inst\_heap}(\Delta) : \Delta'}{\Upsilon, \Gamma \vdash m^{\rho}@T(v_1, \ldots, v_n) : \Gamma \sqcup \Delta'}$$

$$(2)\ \frac{\text{static\_type}(v_0) = T \quad T_1 <: T, \ldots, T_n <: T \quad \phi_i = \text{has\_type}(\Gamma(v_0), T_i) \quad \Upsilon, \Gamma \vdash m^{\rho}@T_1(v_0, \ldots, v_k) : \Gamma_1 \quad \cdots \quad \Upsilon, \Gamma \vdash m^{\rho}@T_n(v_0, \ldots, v_k) : \Gamma_n}{\Upsilon, \Gamma \vdash v_0.m^{\rho}(v_1, \ldots, v_k) : \sqcup_i(\Gamma_i \downarrow \phi_i)}$$

Fig. 12. Analysis of method calls

5 Implementation and Extensions

We implemented the proposed algorithm in a tool called Scuba (http://www.cs.utexas.edu/~yufeng/scuba.html) which is built on top of Chord [16]. Scuba performs analysis on the Quad representation of Joeq [25] and obtains an initial callgraph by running the context-insensitive pointer analysis implemented in Chord. It also uses the Z3 SMT solver [5] for checking satisfiability of constraints.

Our implementation performs several optimizations over the core algorithm described here. One optimization is memoizing instantiation results. For example, consider an access path $a_0.\epsilon.f.g.h$ used in m's summary. Since this access path may be instantiated many times when analyzing a call site of m, our analysis maintains a cache per callsite that records instantiation results. A second optimization concerns constraint generation for virtual method calls. Consider a call $v.m(...)$ where the static type of v is T_0. Further, suppose T_0 has a large number of subclasses $T_1, \ldots, T_n$ all of which inherit T_0's m method except T_n. Assuming v points to heap object o, we need to introduce constraints of the form $\bigvee_{0 \leq i < n} \text{type}(o) = T_i$. Since such constraints can be very large, our implementation allows subtyping constraints and translates them to linear inequalities by assigning integer identifiers to types in reverse topological order.

6 Evaluation

We evaluated SCUBA on ten large Java applications from the DaCapo and Ashes benchmark suites [1,2]. These applications range between 92615 and 227507 lines of statements in the Quad IR and contain between 4634 and 9653 reachable methods. To evaluate our algorithm, we compared SCUBA against the k-CFA and k-object-sensitive algorithms implemented in Chord [16]. All analyses are Anderson-style flow-insensitive pointer analyses that allow customizing the value of k. Chord also allows customizing the context-sensitivity associated with heap objects using a value h. For example, a 2-obj-1-h analysis uses the abstract allocation site of the receiver as a context up to depth 2, and it also differentiates heap allocations with different contexts up to depth 2.

Table 1. Analysis time in seconds. Runs exceeding the time-limit of 3600 s are labeled T/O.

Benchmark	# methods	# statements	CIPA	2-CFA	2-obj	SCUBA-2	SCUBA-3	SCUBA-4
antlr	5411	112831	29	1380	355	30	37	50
hedc	4967	103066	25	1337	446	25	28	31
avrora	5230	104948	24	1328	336	53	55	59
polyglot	4634	92615	21	608	284	14	17	16
toba-s	4702	101501	24	930	299	15	18	17
weblech	5816	115937	27	1657	506	41	35	39
xalan	6405	131332	27	1100	3600	173	180	211
hsqldb	6767	137947	33	2474	1348	63	65	77
luindex	6157	127451	28	2525	532	93	147	315
sunflow	9653	227507	66	T/O	T/O	411	405	521

Before describing the results, we first explain how our algorithm relates to k-CFA and k-obj-sensitive analyses. Similar to k-CFA, SCUBA uses *call sites* rather than *receiver objects* as contexts. However, unlike k-CFA, we do not impose a fixed value of k since our algorithm instantiates method summaries differently for each call site. On the other hand, we can customize the context-sensitivity associated with heap objects by varying the parameter k used in the new_ctx function from Sect. 4.4. Hence, for a given value of k in the new_ctx function, SCUBA is *roughly* comparable to a ∞-CFA-k-h analysis. In what follows, we write SCUBA-k to refer to different configurations of SCUBA for different values of parameter k used in the new_ctx function from Sect. 4.4.

Table 1 compares the running times of SCUBA-k (for $2 \leq k \leq 4$) against the context-insensitive(CIPA), 2-CFA, and 2-obj-sensitive analyses using h value of 1. While we also tried comparing SCUBA against k-CFA and k-obj-sensitive analyses for $k = 3$ and $k = 4$, these analyses did not complete within an hour for most of the benchmarks; hence, we do not include these results in Table 1.

Table 2. May-alias results. The bigger the better.

Benchmark	Alias pairs	CIPA	2-CFA	2-obj	SCUBA-2	SCUBA-3	SCUBA-4
antlr	6839	0	1082	2785	3219	3231	3231
hedc	1728	0	725	962	1025	1055	1055
avrora	1182	0	406	687	738	741	745
polyglot	165	0	59	103	128	128	128
toba-s	5118	0	3354	3350	3589	3589	3595
weblech	1417	0	662	654	656	681	763
xalan	124	0	24	24	24	24	24
hsqldb	5254	0	2746	2724	3318	3318	3426
luindex	4649	0	1326	1420	1353	1400	1400
sunflow	4303	0	N/A	N/A	339	339	339

We also note that the running times shown in Fig. 1 include the analysis time for libraries (e.g., JDK, Swing, Sun Security) as well as the application code (i.e., we did not use manually provided stub methods for analyzing libraries). As the results in Table 1 show, SCUBA-k is significantly faster compared to k-CFA and k-obj analyses.

To compare the precision of SCUBA against k-CFA and k-obj analyses, we used two typical pointer analysis clients, namely *may-alias* and *downcast* analyses. Table 2 compares the precision of different analysis configurations in the context of the may-alias client. The column labeled "Alias pairs" shows the number of variable pairs that are queried by the may-alias client. To generate these pairs, we first ran a context-insensitive pointer analysis to identify potential may-alias in the application code. From these variables, we further filtered those pairs that are "obviously" aliases (e.g., due to a direct assignment). Columns 3–11 in Table 2 show the number of variables proven not to be aliases according to each analysis configuration. Hence, a higher number indicates better precision. Observe that every configuration of SCUBA-k yields better precision *on average* compared to 2-CFA and 2-obj analyses[3].

Table 3 shows the precision of each analysis in the context of the downcast client. Here, the second column labeled "# downcasts" shows the total number of downcasts in the application, and the subsequent columns show the number of downcasts that can be proven safe. The number of downcasts shown in Table 3 only include the downcasts performed in the application code rather than in external libraries[4]. According to the results shown in Table 3, SCUBA-k has better precision on average compared to both 2-CFA and 2-obj.

[3] We manually inspected a randomly selected subset of the may-alias queries that could only be discharged by SCUBA and confirmed that these are not false negatives.

[4] Since most benchmarks use the same libraries, this strategy avoids double counting. Furthermore, clients are typically interested in finding defects in the application.

Table 3. Downcast results. Bigger numbers indicate higher precision.

Benchmark	# downcasts	CIPA	2-CFA	2-obj	SCUBA-2	SCUBA-3	SCUBA-4
antlr	76	18	21	48	45	52	52
hedc	28	5	6	23	23	23	23
avrora	21	0	0	8	15	18	18
polyglot	13	2	3	9	13	13	13
toba-s	59	23	23	34	37	37	37
weblech	48	16	23	33	38	38	38
xalan	14	7	10	13	13	13	13
hsqldb	45	22	24	32	28	28	35
luindex	213	104	106	180	177	177	177
sunflow	81	19	N/A	N/A	25	52	52

7 Related Work

Top-Down Pointer Analysis. Most existing context-sensitive pointer analysis algorithms are top-down [7,12,14,24,26]. Generally speaking, top-down context-sensitivity comes in two flavors: *call-site sensitivity* [22] (k-CFA) and k-*object-sensitivity* [14]. Specifically, CFA-based algorithms use method call sites as the context, while object-sensitive approaches use the receiver's abstract allocation site. The recent work described in [9] has proposed selectively combining k-CFA and k-object sensitivity to achieve better precision. Several papers have used BDD-based methods for top-down context-sensitive pointer analysis [11,26,31]. The use of BDDs exposes commonalities between different contexts and allows the technique to scale better. The Chord framework [16] used in our experimental evaluation also uses BDDs to exploit equivalences between calling contexts.

Bottom-Up Pointer Analysis. While not as widely-studied as top-down algorithms, several papers propose bottom-up pointer analysis. However, many of these approaches are unification-based [10,13,18]. The algorithm proposed in [28] is also bottom-up but uses a combined equality- and subset-based approach. By contrast, our algorithm is subset-based and therefore more precise.

The algorithm described in [4] presents a subset-based, partially bottom-up pointer analysis for C. Unlike our approach, it incorporates both top-down and bottom-up phases where the top-down phase is used for precise handling of function pointers. Also unlike our approach, it tracks alias pairs as opposed to an explicit heap model and is meant for C rather than Java. Another subset-based pointer analysis for C that combines top-down and bottom-up phases is based on the observation that context-insensitivity does not result in a loss of precision if function side effects are accounted for [17]. In contrast to our approach, that technique handles SCCs in a context-insensitive way and employs a top-down phase that removes callee side effects. The algorithms described in [3,6] perform bottom-up pointer analysis for C++ programs. Unlike the method presented in this paper, they perform case splits on possible aliasing patterns. Since the approach of [6] performs strong updates, it is more precise but less scalable compared to our technique.

Another related work is the algorithm described in [27], which describes a compositional pointer and escape analysis for Java. While this analysis is flow-sensitive and applies strong updates, it assumes that parameters do not alias and generates a summary that is valid under this assumption. However, if this assumption is violated at a call site, the analysis corrects the summary through a complex mechanism that involves merging of memory locations. Another difference is that [27] does not precisely handle virtual method calls.

Summarization. Many papers describe general frameworks for interprocedural analysis [19–21]. The work described in [29,30] compute polymorphic summaries for dataflow problems but both rely on global points-to sets.

8 Conclusion

We described a new bottom-up, summary-based pointer analysis for Java. The experimental evaluation demonstrates that our algorithm runs significantly faster than top-down pointer analyses with comparable precision. We believe that SCUBA is able to scale better because the cost of instantiating a method summary is smaller compared to the cost of re-analyzing the function.

References

1. Ashes benchmark suite. http://www.sable.mcgill.ca/software/#ashessuitecollection
2. Dacapo benchmarks. http://www.dacapobench.org/
3. Chatterjee, R., Ryder, B.G., Landi, W.A.: Relevant context inference (1999)
4. Cheng, B.-C., Hwu, W.-M.W.: Modular interprocedural pointer analysis using access paths: design, implementation, and evaluation. In: PLDI (2000)
5. de Moura, L., Bjørner, N.S.: Z3: an efficient SMT solver. In: Ramakrishnan, C.R., Rehof, J. (eds.) TACAS 2008. LNCS, vol. 4963, pp. 337–340. Springer, Heidelberg (2008)
6. Dillig, I., Dillig, T., Aiken, A., Sagiv, M.: Precise and compact modular procedure summaries for heap manipulating programs. In: PLDI (2011)
7. Fähndrich, M., Rehof, J., Das, M.: Scalable context-sensitive flow analysis using instantiation constraints. In: PLDI 2000 (2000)
8. Hoare, C.A.R.: An axiomatic basis for computer programming. Commun. ACM **12**(10), 576–580 (1969)
9. Kastrinis, G., Smaragdakis, Y.: Hybrid context-sensitivity for points-to analysis. In: PLDI, pp. 423–434 (2013)
10. Lattner, C., Lenharth, A., Adve, V.: Making context-sensitive points-to analysis with heap cloning practical for the real world. In: PLDI (2007)
11. Lhoták, O.: Program analysis using binary decision diagrams. Ph.D. thesis, McGill University (2006)

12. Lhoták, O., Hendren, L.: Context-sensitive points-to analysis: is it worth it? In: Mycroft, A., Zeller, A. (eds.) CC 2006. LNCS, vol. 3923, pp. 47–64. Springer, Heidelberg (2006)
13. Liang, D., Harrold, M.J.: Efficient points-to analysis for whole-program analysis. In: Wang, J., Lemoine, M. (eds.) ESEC 1999 and ESEC-FSE 1999. LNCS, vol. 1687, p. 199. Springer, Heidelberg (1999)
14. Milanova, A., Rountev, A., Ryder, B.G.: Parameterized object sensitivity for points-to and side-effect analyses for Java. In: ISSTA (2002)
15. Milanova, A., Rountev, A., Ryder, B.G.: Parameterized object sensitivity for points-to analysis for Java. TOSEM **4**, 1–41 (2005)
16. Naik, M.: Chord framework. http://pag.gatech.edu/chord
17. Nystrom, E.M., Kim, H.-S., Hwu, W.W.: Bottom-up and top-down context-sensitive summary-based pointer analysis. In: Giacobazzi, R. (ed.) SAS 2004. LNCS, vol. 3148, pp. 165–180. Springer, Heidelberg (2004)
18. O'Callahan, R.: Generalized aliasing as a basis for program analysis tools. Ph.D. thesis, Carnegie Mellon University (2001)
19. Reps, T., Horwitz, S., Sagiv, M.: Precise interprocedural dataflow analysis via graph reachability. In: POPL, pp. 49–61 (1995)
20. Sagiv, S., Reps, T.W., Horwitz, S.: Precise interprocedural dataflow analysis with applications to constant propagation. In: TAPSOFT 1995 (1996)
21. Sharir, M., Pnueli, A.: Two Approaches to Interprocedural Data Flow Analysis, Chap. 7, pp. 189–234. Prentice-Hall, Englewood Cliffs (1981)
22. Shivers, O.: Control-flow analysis of higher-order languages. Technical report (1991)
23. Smaragdakis, Y., Bravenboer, M., Lhoták, O.: Pick your contexts well: understanding object-sensitivity. In POPL (2011)
24. Sridharan, M., Bodík, R.: Refinement-based context-sensitive points-to analysis for Java. In: PLDI, pp. 387–400 (2006)
25. Whaley, J.: Joeq: a virtual machine and compiler infrastructure. In: IVME, pp. 58–66. ACM (2003)
26. Whaley, J., Lam, M.S.: Cloning-based context-sensitive pointer alias analysis using binary decision diagrams. In: PLDI, pp. 131–144 (2004)
27. Whaley, J., Rinard, M.: Compositional pointer and escape analysis for Java programs. In: OOPSLA, pp. 187–206 (1999)
28. Xu, G., Rountev, A.: Merging equivalent contexts for scalable heap-cloning-based context-sensitive points-to analysis. In ISSTA (2008)
29. Yorsh, G., Yahav, E., Chandra, S.: Generating precise and concise procedure summaries. In: POPL, pp. 221–234 (2008)
30. Zhang, X., Mangal, R., Naik, M., Yang, H.: Hybrid top-down and bottom-up interprocedural analysis. In: PLDI, p. 28 (2014)
31. Zhu, J., Calman, S.: Symbolic pointer analysis revisited. In: PLDI (2004)

More Sound Static Handling of Java Reflection

Yannis Smaragdakis[1(✉)], George Balatsouras[1], George Kastrinis[1], and Martin Bravenboer[2]

[1] University of Athens, Athens, Greece
smaragd@di.uoa.gr
[2] LogicBlox Inc., Atlanta, GA, USA

Abstract. Reflection is a highly dynamic language feature that poses grave problems for static analyses. In the Java setting, reflection is ubiquitous in large programs. Any handling of reflection will be approximate, and overestimating its reach in a large codebase can be catastrophic for precision and scalability. We present an approach for handling reflection with improved empirical soundness (as measured against prior approaches and dynamic information) in the context of a points-to analysis. Our approach is based on the combination of string-flow and points-to analysis from past literature augmented with (a) substring analysis and modeling of partial string flow through string builder classes; (b) new techniques for analyzing reflective entities based on information available at their use-sites. In experimental comparisons with prior approaches, we demonstrate a combination of both improved soundness (recovering the majority of missing call-graph edges) and increased performance.

1 Introduction

Whole-program static analysis is the engine behind several modern programming facilities for program development and understanding. Compilers, bug detectors, security checkers, modern development environments (with automated refactorings, slicing facilities, and auto-complete functionality), and a myriad other tools routinely employ static analysis machinery. Even the seemingly simple effort of computing a program's call-graph (i.e., which program function can call which other) requires sophisticated analysis in order to achieve precision.

Yet, static whole-program analysis suffers in the presence of common dynamic features, especially reflection. When a Java program accesses a class by supplying its name as a run-time string, via the `Class.forName` library call, the static analysis needs to either conservatively over-approximate (e.g., assume that *any* class can be accessed), or to perform a string analysis that will allow it to infer the contents of the `forName` string argument. Both options can be detrimental to the scalability of the analysis: the conservative over-approximation may never become constrained enough by further instructions to be feasible in practice; precise string analysis is impractical for programs of realistic size. It is telling

X. Feng and S. Park (Eds.): APLAS 2015, LNCS 9458, pp. 485–503, 2015.
DOI: 10.1007/978-3-319-26529-2_26

that *no practical Java program analysis framework in existence handles reflection soundly* [19], although other language features are modeled soundly.[1]

Full soundness is not practically achievable, but it can still be approximated for the well-behaved reflection patterns encountered in regular, non-adversarial programs. Therefore, it makes sense to treat soundness as a continuous quantity: something to improve on, even though we cannot perfectly reach. To avoid confusion, we use the term *empirical soundness* for the quantification of how much of the dynamic behavior the static analysis covers. Computable metrics of empirical soundness can help quantify how close an analysis is to the fully sound result. Based on such metrics, one can make comparisons (e.g., "more sound") to describe soundness improvements.

The second challenge of handling reflection in a static analysis is *scalability*. The online documentation of the IBM WALA library [8] concisely summarizes the current state of the practice, for *points-to analysis* in the Java setting.

> *Reflection usage and the size of modern libraries/frameworks make it very difficult to scale flow-insensitive points-to analysis to modern Java programs. For example, with default settings,* WALA*'s pointer analyses cannot handle any program linked against the Java 6 standard libraries, due to extensive reflection in the libraries.*

In this paper, we describe an approach to analyzing reflection in the Java points-to analysis setting. Our approach requires no manual configuration and achieves significantly higher empirical soundness without sacrificing scalability, for realistic benchmarks and libraries (DaCapo Bach and Java 7). In experimental comparisons with the recent ELF system [16] (itself improving over the reflection analysis of the DOOP framework [6]), our algorithm discovers most of the call-graph edges missing (relative to a dynamic analysis) from ELF's reflection analysis. This improvement in empirical soundness is accompanied by *increased* performance relative to ELF, demonstrating that near-sound handling of reflection is often practically possible. Concretely, our work:

- introduces key techniques in static reflection handling that contribute greatly to empirical soundness. The techniques generalize past work from an intra-procedural to an inter-procedural setting and combine it with a string analysis;
- shows how scalability can be addressed with appropriate tuning of the above generalized techniques;
- thoroughly quantifies the empirical soundness of a static points-to analysis, compared to past approaches and to a dynamic analysis;
- is implemented and evaluated on top of an existing open framework (DOOP [6]).

2 Background: Joint Reflection and Points-To Analysis

As necessary background, we next present an abstracted model of the inter-related reflection and points-to analysis upon which our approach builds. The

[1] In our context, *sound* = over-approximate, i.e., guaranteeing that all possible behaviors of reflection operations are modeled.

model is a light reformulation of the analysis introduced by Livshits et al. [18,20]. The main insight of the Livshits et al. approach is that reflection analysis relies on points-to information, because the different key elements of a reflective activity may be dispersed throughout the program. A typical pattern of reflection usage is with code such as:

```
String className = ... ;
Class c = Class.forName(className);
Object o = c.newInstance();
String methodName = ... ;
Method m = c.getMethod(methodName, ...);
m.invoke(o, ...);
```

All of the above statements can occur in distant program locations, across different methods, invoked through virtual calls from multiple sites, etc. Thus, a whole-program analysis with an understanding of heap objects is required to track reflection with any amount of precision. This suggest the idea that reflection analysis can leverage points-to analysis—it is a client for points-to information. At the same time, points-to analysis needs the results of reflection analysis—e.g., to determine which method gets invoked in the last line of the above example, or what objects each of the example's local variables point to. Thus, under the Livshits et al. approach, reflection analysis and points-to analysis become mutually recursive, or effectively a single analysis.

This mutual recursion introduces significant complexity. Fortunately, a large amount of research in points-to analysis has focused on specifying analyses declaratively [5,6,10,13–15,17,22,23,25,26], in the Datalog programming language. Datalog is ideal for encoding mutually recursive logic—recursion is the backbone of the language. Computation in Datalog consists of monotonic logical inferences that apply to produce more facts until fixpoint. A Datalog rule "$\mathbf{C}(z,x) \leftarrow \mathbf{A}(x,y),\ \mathbf{B}(y,z)$." means that if $\mathbf{A}(x,y)$ and $\mathbf{B}(y,z)$ are both true, then $\mathbf{C}(z,x)$ can be inferred. Livshits et al. expressed their joint reflection and points-to analysis declaratively in Datalog, which is also a good vehicle for our illustration and further changes.

We consider the core of the analysis algorithm, which is representative and handles the most common features, illustrated in our above example: creating a reflective object representing a class (a *class object*) given a name string (library method `Class.forName`), creating a new object given a class object (library method `Class.newInstance`), retrieving a reflective method object given a class object and a signature (library method `Class.getMethod`), and reflectively calling a virtual method on an object (library method `Method.invoke`). This treatment ignores several other APIs, which are handled similarly. These include, for instance, fields, constructors, other kinds of method invocations (static, special), reflective access to arrays, other ways to get class objects, and more.

The domains of the analysis include: invocation sites, I; variables, V; heap object abstractions (i.e., allocation sites), H; method signatures, S; types, T; methods, M; natural numbers, N, and strings. The analysis takes as input the relations (i.e., tables filled with information from the program text) shown in Fig. 1. Using these inputs, the Livshits et al. reflection analysis can be expressed

Call($i : I, s : string$): instruction i is an invocation to a method with signature s.
ActualArg($i : I, n : N, v : V$): at invocation i, the n-th parameter is local var v.
AssignRetValue($i : I, v : V$): at invocation i, the value returned is assigned to local variable v.
HeapType($h : H, t : T$): object h has type t.
Lookup($sig : S, t : T, m : M$): in type t there exists method m with signature sig.
ConstantForClass($h : H, t : T$): class/type t has a name represented by the constant string object h in the program text.
ConstantForMethod($h : H, sig : S$): method signature sig has a name represented by the constant string object h in the program text.
ReifiedClass($t : T, h : H$): special object h represents the class object of type t. Such special objects are created up-front and are part of the input.
ReifiedHeapAllocation($i : I, t : T, h : H$): special object h represents objects of type t that are allocated with a `newInstance` call at invocation site i.
ReifiedMethod($sig : S, h : H$): special object h represents the reflection object for method signature sig.

Fig. 1. Relations representing the input program and their informal meaning.

as a five-rule addition to any points-to analysis. The rest of the points-to analysis (not shown here—see e.g., [10,14,25]) supplies more rules for computing a relation **VarPointsTo**($v : V, h : H$) and a relation **CallGraphEdge**($i : I, m : M$). Intuitively, the traditional points-to part of the joint analysis is responsible for computing how heap objects flow intra- and inter-procedurally through the program, while the added rules contribute only the reflection handling. We explain the rules below.

ClassObject$(i, t) \leftarrow$
  Call$(i,$ `"Class.forName"`$)$, **ActualArg**$(i, 0, p)$,
  VarPointsTo(p, c), **ConstantForClass**(c, t)
VarPointsTo$(r, h) \leftarrow$
  ClassObject(i, t), **ReifiedClass**(t, h), **AssignRetValue**(i, r).

The first two rules, above, work jointly: they model a `forName` call, which returns a class object given a string representing the class name. The first rule says that if the first argument (0-th parameter, since `forName` is a static method) of a `forName` call points to an object that is a string constant, then the type corresponding to that constant is retrieved and associated with the invocation site in computed relation **ClassObject**. The second rule then uses **ClassObject**: if the result of the `forName` call at instruction i is assigned to a local variable r, and the reflection object for the type associated with i is h, then r is inferred to point to h.

VarPointsTo$(r, h) \leftarrow$
  Call$(i,$ `"Class.newInstance"`$)$, **ActualArg**$(i, 0, v)$, **VarPointsTo**(v, h_c),
  ReifiedClass(t, h_c), **AssignRetValue**(i, r), **ReifiedHeapAllocation**(i, t, h).

The above rules could easily be combined into one. However, their split form is more flexible. In later sections we will add more rules for producing **ClassObject** facts—for instance, instead of constant strings we will have expressions that still get inferred to resolve to an actual type.

The above rule reads: if the receiver object, h_c, of a `newInstance` call is a class object for class t, and the `newInstance` call is assigned to variable r, then make r point to the special (i.e., invented) allocation site h that designates objects of type t allocated at the `newInstance` call site.

VarPointsTo$(r, h_m) \leftarrow$
  Call$(i,$ `"Class.getMethod"`$)$, **ActualArg**$(i, 0, b)$, **ActualArg**$(i, 1, p)$,
  AssignRetValue(i, r), **VarPointsTo**(b, h_c), **ReifiedClass**(t, h_c),
  VarPointsTo(p, c), **ConstantForMethod**(c, s),
  Lookup$(t, s, \_)$, **ReifiedMethod**(s, h_m).

The above rule gives semantics to `getMethod` calls. It states that if such a call is made with receiver b (for "base") and first argument p (the string encoding the desired method's signature), and if the analysis has already determined the objects that b and p may point to, then, assuming p points to a string constant encoding a signature, s, that exists inside the type that b points to ("_" stands for "any" value), the variable r holding the result of the `getMethod` call points to the reflective object, h_m, for this method signature.

CallGraphEdge$(i, m) \leftarrow$
  Call$(i,$ `"Method.invoke"`$)$, **ActualArg**$(i, 0, b)$, **ActualArg**$(i, 1, p)$,
  VarPointsTo(b, h_m), **ReifiedMethod**(s, h_m),
  VarPointsTo(p, h), **HeapType**(h, t), **Lookup**(t, s, m).

Finally, all reflection information can contribute to inferring more call-graph edges. The last rule encodes that a new edge can be inferred from the invocation site, i, of a reflective `invoke` call to a method m, if the receiver, b, of the `invoke` (0th parameter) points to a reflective object encoding a method signature, and the argument, p, of the `invoke` (1st parameter) points to an object, h, of a class in which the lookup of the signature produces the method m.

3 Techniques for Empirical Soundness

We next present our main techniques for higher empirical soundness.

3.1 Generalizing Reflection Inference via Substring Analysis

An important way of enhancing the empirical soundness of our analysis is via richer string flow. The logic discussed in Sect. 2 only captures the case of entire string constants used as parameters to a `forName` call. The parameter of `forName` could be any string expression, however. It is interesting to attempt to deduce whether such an expression can refer to a class name. Similarly, strings representing field and method names are used in reflective calls—we already encountered the `getMethod` call in Sect. 2.

In order to estimate what classes, fields, or methods a string expression may represent, we implement *substring matching*: all string constants in the program text are tested for prefix and suffix matching against known class, method, and field names. (We use tunable thresholds to limit the matches: e.g., member prefixes, resp. suffixes, need to be at least 3, resp. 5, characters long.)

The strings that may refer to such entities are handled with more precision than others during analysis. For instance, a points-to analysis (e.g., in the DOOP or WALA frameworks) will typically merge most strings into a single abstract object—otherwise the analysis will incur an overwhelmingly high cost because of tracking numerous string constants. Strings that may represent class/interface, method, or field names are prevented from such merging. Furthermore, the flow of such strings through factory objects is tracked.

String concatenation in Java is typically done through `StringBuffer` or `StringBuilder` objects. The common concatenation operator, `+`, reduces to calls over such factory objects. To evaluate whether reflection-related substrings may flow into factory objects, we leverage the points-to analysis itself, pretending that an object flow into an `append` method and out of a `toString` method is tantamount to an assignment. A simplified version of the logic is in the rule below. (The rule assumes we have already computed relation **ReflectionObject**($h : H$), which lists the string constants that partially match method, field, or class names, as described above. It also takes an extra input relation **StringFactoryVar**($v_f : V$) that captures which variables are of a string factory type.)

VarPointsTo(r, h) $\leftarrow$
 Call(i_a, `"append"`), **ActualArg**($i_a, 0, v_f$), **ActualArg**($i_a, 1, v$),
 StringFactoryVar(v_f), **Call**(i_t, `"toString"`), **AssignRetValue**(i_t, r),
 ActualArg($i_t, 0, u_f$), **VarPointsTo**(v_f, h_f), **VarPointsTo**(u_f, h_f),
 VarPointsTo(v, h), **ReflectionObject**(h).

In words: if a call to `append` and a call to `toString` are over the same factory object, h_f, (accessed by different vars, v_f and u_f, at possibly disparate parts of the program) then all the potentially reflection-related objects that are pointed to by the parameter, v, of `append` are inferred to be pointed by the variable r that accepts the result of the `toString` call.

In this way, the flow of partial string expressions through the program is tracked. By then appropriately adjusting the **ConstantForClass** and **ConstantForMethod** predicates of Sect. 2 (to also map from partial strings to their matching types) we can estimate which reflective entities can be returned at the site of a `forName` or `getMethod` call. In this way, the joint points-to and reflection analysis is enhanced with substring reasoning without requiring any changes to the base logic of Sect. 2. String flow through buffers becomes just an enhancement of the points-to logic, which is already leveraged by reflection analysis.

An interesting aspect of the above approach is that it is easily configurable, in commonly desirable ways. Our above rule for handling partial string flow through string factory objects does not concern itself with how string factory objects (h_f) are represented inside the analysis. Indeed, string factory objects are often as numerous as strings themselves, since they are implicitly allocated on every use of the `+` operator over strings in a Java program. Therefore, a pointer analysis will often merge string factory objects, with the appropriate user-selectable flag.[2] The rule for string flow through factories is unaffected by this treatment. Although precision is lost if all string factory objects are merged into one abstract object, the joint points-to and reflection analysis still computes a fairly precise outcome: "does a partial string that matches some class/method-/field name flow into some string factory's `append` method, and does some string factory's `toString` result flow into a reflection operation?" If both conditions are satisfied, the class/method/field name matched by the partial string is considered to flow into the reflection operation.

3.2 Use-Based Reflection Analysis

Our second technique for statically analyzing reflection calls is called *use-based reflection analysis* and it integrates two sub-techniques: a *back-propagation* mechanism and a (forward) *object invention* mechanism.

Inter-Procedural Back-Propagation. An important observation regarding reflection handling is that it is one of the few parts of a static analysis that are typically *under-approximate* rather than *over-approximate* [19]. Our first use-based reflection analysis technique back-propagates information from the use-site of a reflective result *to the original reflection call that got under-approximated.* Such an under-approximated call can be a `Class.forName`, `Class.get[Declared]Method`, `Class.get[Declared]Field`, etc. call, which returns a dynamic representation of a class, method, or field, given a string name.

The example below, which we will refer to repeatedly in later sections, shows how the use of a non-reflection object can inform a reflection call's analysis:

```
Class c1 = Class.forName(className);
...       // c2 aliases c1
Object o1 = c2.newInstance();
...       // o2 aliases o1
e = (Event) o2;
```

Typically (e.g., when `className` does not point to a known constant) the `forName` call will be under-approximated (rather than, e.g., assuming it will

[2] E.g., `SMUSH_STRINGS` in WALA [8] and `MERGE_STRING_BUFFERS` in DOOP.

return any class in the system). The idea is to then treat the cast as a hint: it suggests that the earlier `forName` call should have returned a class object for `Event`. This reasoning, however, should be *inter-procedural* with an understanding of heap behavior. The above statements could be in distant parts of the program (separate methods) and aliasing is part of the conditions in the above pattern. Further, note that the related objects are twice-removed: we see a cast on an *instance* object and need to infer something about the `forName` site that *may* have been used to create the class that got used to allocate that object. This propagation should be as precise as possible: lack of precision will lead to too many class objects returned at the `forName` call site, affecting scalability.

Therefore, we see again the need to employ points-to analysis, this time in order to detect the relationship between cast sites and `forName` sites, so that the latter can be better resolved and we can improve the points-to analysis itself—a mutual recursion pattern. The high-level structure of our technique (for this pattern) is as follows:

- At the site of a `forName` call, create a marker object (of type `java.lang.Class`), to stand for all unknown objects that the invocation may return.
- The special object flows freely through the points-to analysis, taking full advantage of inter-procedural reasoning facilities.
- At the site of a `newInstance` invocation, if the receiver is our special object, the result of `newInstance` is also a special object (of type `java.lang.Object` this time) that remembers its `forName` origins.
- This second special object also flows freely through the points-to analysis, taking full advantage of inter-procedural reasoning facilities.
- If the second special object (of type `java.lang.Object`) reaches the site of a cast, then the original `forName` invocation is retrieved and augmented to return the cast type or its subtypes as class objects.

The algorithm for the above treatment can be elegantly expressed via rules that are mutually recursive with the base points-to analysis. The rules for the `forName`-`newInstance`-cast pattern are representative. We use extra input relations **ReifiedForName**$(i : I, h : H)$, and **ReifiedNewInstance**$(i : I, h : H)$, analogous to our earlier "**Reified...**" relations. The first relation gives, for each `forName` invocation site, i, a special object, h, that identifies the invocation site. The second relation gives a special object, h, that stands for all unknown objects returned by a `newInstance` call, which was, in turn, performed on the special object returned by a `forName` call, at invocation site i. The rules then become:

VarPointsTo$(v, h) \leftarrow$
  Call$(i,$ `"Class.forName"`$)$, **AssignRetValue**(i, v), **ReifiedForName**(i, h).

In words: the variable that was assigned the result of a `forName` invocation points to the special object representing all missing objects from this invocation site. In this way, the special object can then propagate through the points-to analysis.

VarPointsTo$(r, h_n) \leftarrow$
  Call$(i_n,$ `"Class.newInstance"`$)$, **ActualArg**$(i_n, 0, v)$, **VarPointsTo**(v, h),
  AssignRetValue(i_n, r), **ReifiedForName**(i, h), **ReifiedNewInstance**(i, h_n).

According to this rule, when analyzing a `newInstance` call, if the receiver is a special object that was produced by a `forName` invocation, i, then the result of the `newInstance` will be another special object (of appropriate type—determined by the contents of `ReifiedNewInstance`) that will identify the `forName` call.

The final rule uses input relation **Cast**$(v' : V, v : V, t : T)$ (with v' being the variable to which the cast result is stored and v the variable being cast) and **Subtype**$(t : T, u : T)$ with its expected meaning:

ClassObject$(i, t') \leftarrow$
  Cast$(\_, v, t)$, **Subtype**(t', t), **VarPointsTo**(v, h_n), **ReifiedNewInstance**(i, h_n).

The rule ties the logic together: if a cast to type t is found, where the cast variable points to a special object, h_n, then retrieve the object's `forName` invocation site, i, and infer that this invocation site returns a class object of type t', where t' is a subtype of t.

Other Use-Cases. As seen above, the back-propagation logic involves the result of several inter-procedural queries (e.g., points-to information at possibly distant call sites). In fact, there are use-based back-propagation patterns with even longer chains of reasoning. In the case below, the cast of `o2` informs the return value of `forName`, three reflection calls back!

```
Class c1 = Class.forName(className);
...        // c2 aliases c1
Constructor[] cons1 = c2.getConstructors(types);
...        // cons2 aliases cons1
Object o1 = cons2[i].newInstance(args);
...        // o2 aliases o1
e = (Event) o2;
```

Interestingly, the back-propagation analysis can exploit not just cast information but also strings (including partial strings, transparently, per our substring/ string-flow analysis of Sect. 3.1). When retrieving a member from a reflectively discovered class, the string name supplied may contain enough information to disambiguate what this class may be. Consider the pattern:

```
Class c1 = Class.forName(className);
...        // c2 aliases c1
Field f = c2.getField(fieldName);
```

In this case, the value of the `fieldName` string can inform the analysis result for the earlier `forName` call. We apply this idea to the 4 API calls `Class.get[Declared]Method` and `Class.get[Declared]Field`.

Contrasting Approaches. Our back-propagating reflection analysis has some close relatives in the literature. Livshits et al. [18,20] also examined using future casts as hints for `forName` calls, as an alternative to regular string inference. Li et al. [16] generalize the Livshits approach to many more reflection calls. There are, however, important ways in which our techniques differ:

- Our analysis generalizes the pattern significantly. In our earlier example, from the beginning of this section, both the Li et al. and the Livshits et al. approaches require for the cast to not only occur in the same method as the `newInstance` call but also to post-dominate it! This restricts the pattern to an intra-procedural and fairly specific setting, reducing its generality:

```
Class c1 = Class.forName(className);
...       // c2 aliases c1
e = (Event) c2.newInstance();
```

The result of such a restriction is that the potential for imprecision is diminished, yet the ability to achieve empirical soundness is also scaled back. There are several cases where the cast will not post-dominate the intermediate reflection call, yet could yield useful information. This is precisely what Livshits et al. encountered experimentally—a direct quote illustrates:

> *The high number of unresolved calls in the JDK is due to the fact that reflection use in libraries tends to be highly generic and it is common to have '`Class.newInstance` wrappers'—methods that accept a class name as a string and return an object of that class, which is later cast to an appropriate type in the caller method. Since we rely on intraprocedural post-dominance, resolving these calls is beyond our scope* [20].

- We generalize back-propagation to string information and not just cast information (i.e., we exploit the use of `get[Declared]{Method,Field}` calls to resolve earlier `forName` calls). This feature also benefits from other elements of our overall analysis, namely substring matching and substring flow analysis (Sect. 3.1). For instance, by having more information on what are the possible strings passed to a `getMethod` call, we are more likely to determine the return value of a `getClass`, on which the `getMethod` was called.

Inventing Objects. Our approach introduces an alternative use-based reflection analysis technique, which works as a *forward propagation* technique (in contrast to the earlier back-propagation). It consists of inventing objects of the appropriate type at the point of a cast operation that has received the result of a reflection call. Consider again our usual `forName-newInstance`-cast example:

```
Class c1 = Class.forName(className);
...       // c2 aliases c1
Object o1 = c2.newInstance();
...       // o2 aliases o1
e = (Event) o2;
```

A major issue with our earlier back-propagation technique is that its results may adversely affect precision. The information will flow back to the site of the `forName` call, and from there to multiple other program points—not just to the point of the cast operation (line 5), or even to the point of the `newInstance` operation (line 3) in the example.

The object invention technique offers the converse compromise. Whenever a special, unknown reflective object flows to the point of a cast, instead of informing the result of `forName`, the technique invents a new, regular object of the right type (`Event`, in this case) that starts its existence at the cast site. The "invented" object does not necessarily abstract actual run-time objects. Instead, it exploits the fact that a points-to analysis is fundamentally a may-analysis: it is designed to possibly yield over-approximate results, in addition to those arising in real executions. Thus, an invented value does not impact the correctness of the analysis (since having extra values in points-to sets is acceptable), yet it will enable it to explore possibilities that might not exist without the invented value. These possibilities are, however, strongly hinted by the existence of a cast in the code, over an object derived from reflection operations.

The algorithm for object invention in the analysis is again recursive with the main points-to logic. We illustrate for the case of `Class.newInstance`, although similar logic applies to reflection calls such as `Constructor.newInstance`, as well as `Method.invoke` and `Field.get`.

As in the back-propagating analysis, we use special marker objects. These are represented by input relations **ReifiedMarkerNewInstance**($i : I, h : H$), and **ReifiedInventedObject**($i : I, t : T, h : H$). The first relation gives, for each `newInstance` invocation site, i, a special object, h, that identifies the invocation site. The second relation gives an invented object, h of type t, for each `newInstance` invocation site, i, and type t that appears in a cast. The algorithm is captured by two rules:

VarPointsTo(v, h) ←
  Call(i, `"Class.newInstance"`), **AssignRetValue**(i, v),
  ReifiedMarkerNewInstance(i, h).

That is, the variable assigned the result of a `newInstance` invocation points to a special object marking that it was produced by a reflection call. The marker object can then propagate through the points-to analysis.

The key part of the algorithm is to then invent an object at a cast site.

VarPointsTo(r, h) ←
  Cast(r, v, t), **VarPointsTo**(v, h_m),
  ReifiedMarkerNewInstance(i, h_m), **ReifiedInventedObject**(i, t, h).

In words, if a variable, v, is cast to a type t and points to a marker object that was produced by a `newInstance` call, then the variable, r, storing the result of the cast, points to a newly invented object, with the right type, t.

Note that in terms of empirical soundness the object invention approach is weaker than the back-propagation analysis: if a type is inferred to be produced by an earlier `forName` call, it will flow down to the point of the cast, removing the need for object invention. (Conversely, inventing objects at the cast site will not catch all cases covered by back-propagation, since the special object of the back-propagation analysis may never flow to a cast.) Nevertheless, back-propagation is often less scalable. Thus, the benefit of object invention is that it allows to selectively turn off back-propagation while still taking advantage of information from a cast.

3.3 Balancing for Scalability

Consider again our inter-procedural back-propagating analysis technique relative to prior, intra-procedural techniques. Our approach explicitly aims for empirical soundness (i.e., to infer all potential results of a reflection call). At the same time, however, the technique may suffer in precision, since the result of a reflection call is deduced from far-away information, which may be highly over-approximate. Conversely, our object invention technique is more precise (since the invented object only starts existing at the point of the cast) but may suffer in terms of soundness. Thus, it can be used to supplement back-propagation when the latter is applied selectively.

To balance the soundness/precision tradeoff of the back-propagating analysis, we employ precision thresholds. Namely, back-propagation is applied only when it is reasonably precise in terms of type information. For instance, if a cast is found, it is used to back-propagate reflective information only when there are up to a constant, c, class types that can satisfy the cast (i.e., at most c subtypes of the cast type). Intuitively, a cast of the form "`(Event)`" is much more informative when `Event` is a class with only a few subclasses, rather than when `Event` is an interface that many tens of classes implement. Similarly, if string information (e.g., a method name) is used to determine what class object could have been returned by a `Class.forName`, the back-propagation takes place only when the string name matches methods of at most d different types. This threshold approach minimizes the potential for noise back-propagating and polluting all subsequent program paths that depend on the original reflection call.

A second technique for employing back-propagation without sacrificing precision and scalability adjusts the flow of special objects (i.e., objects in **ReifiedForName** or **ReifiedNewInstance**). Although we want such objects to flow inter-procedurally, we can disallow their tracking through the heap (i.e., through objects or arrays), allowing only their flow through local variables. This is consistent with expected inter-procedural usage patterns of reflection results: although such results will likely be returned from methods (cf. the quote from [20] in Sect. 3.2), they are less likely to be stored in heap objects.

We employ both of the above techniques by default in our analysis (with $c = d = 5$). The user can configure their application through input options.

4 Evaluation

We implemented our techniques in the DOOP framework [6], together with numerous improvements (i.e., complete API support) to DOOP's reflection handling. Following the ELF study [16], we perform the default joint points-to and call-graph analysis of DOOP, which is an Andersen-style context-insensitive analysis, with full support for complex Java language features, such as class initialization, exceptions, etc. Our techniques are orthogonal to the context-sensitivity used, and can be applied to all analyses in the DOOP framework. In general, nothing in our modeling of reflection limits either context- or flow-sensitivity.

Experimental Setup. Our evaluation setting uses the LogicBlox Datalog engine, v.3.9.0, on a Xeon X5650 2.67 GHz machine with only one thread running at a time and 24GB of RAM. We have used a JVMTI agent to construct a dynamic call-graph for each analyzed program.

We analyze 10 benchmark programs from the DaCapo 9.12-Bach suite [3], with their default inputs (for the purposes of the dynamic analysis). Other benchmarks could not be executed or analyzed: *tradebeans*/*tradesoap* from 9.12-Bach do not run with our instrumentation agent, hence no dynamic call-graphs can be extracted for comparison. This is a known, independently documented, issue (see http://sourceforge.net/p/dacapobench/bugs/70/). We have been unable to meaningfully analyze *fop* and *tomcat*—significant entry points were missed. This suggests either a packaging error (no application-library boundaries are provided by the DaCapo suite), or the extensive use of dynamic loading, which needs further special handling.

We use Oracle JDK 1.7.0_25 for the analysis. (For comparison, consider the quote from [8] in the Introduction, refers to the smaller JDK 1.6.)

Empirical Soundness Metric. We quantify the empirical unsoundness of the static analysis in terms of missing call-graph edges, compared to the dynamic call-graph. Call-graph construction is one of the best-known clients of points-to analysis [1,2,16] and has the added benefit of quantifying how much code the analysis truly reaches. We compare the call-graph edges found by our static analysis to a dynamic call-graph—a comparison also found in other recent work [24]. For a sound static analysis, no edge should occur dynamically but not predicted statically. However, this is not the case in practice, due to the unsound handling of dynamic features, as discussed in the Introduction.

Results. Figure 2 plots the results of our experiments, combining both analysis time and empirical unsoundness (in call-graph edges). Each chart plots the missing dynamic call-graph edges that are not discovered by the corresponding static analysis. We use separate bars for the *application-to-application* and

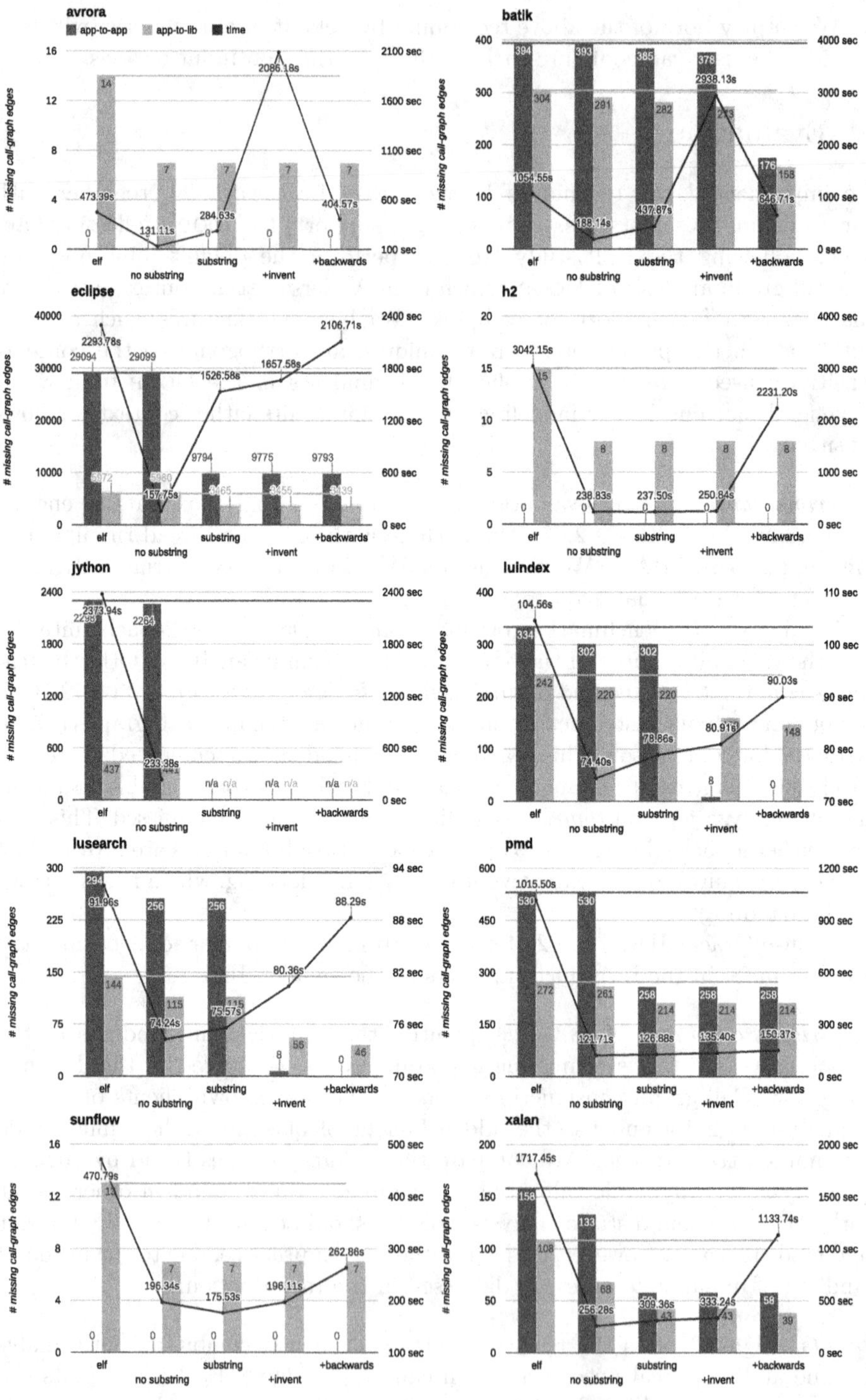

Fig. 2. Unsoundness metrics (two bars: missing call-graph edges app-to-app and app-to-lib) and analysis time (line) over the DaCapo benchmarks. *Lower is better for all.* For missing bars ("n/a"), the analysis did not terminate in 90 mins.

Total Edges		Settings				
Benchmark	*dynamic*	elf	no substring	substring	+invent	+backwards
avrora	4165	19355	19379	20591	26586	20677
batik	8329	31602	31708	35314	47303	37013
eclipse	40026	10191	9032	115967	116635	117576
h2	4901	38252	35538	38107	38162	43952
jython	13583	19709	20537	n/a	n/a	n/a
luindex	3027	4547	4676	4682	5773	6115
lusearch	1845	4209	4352	4362	5266	5587
pmd	4874	8544	8592	9533	9557	9577
sunflow	2215	4223	4251	4285	4319	4407
xalan	6128	35918	35221	45160	45343	63746

Fig. 3. Total static and dynamic call-graph edges for the DaCapo 9.12-Bach benchmarks. These include only *application-to-application* and *application-to-library* edges.

application-to-library edges. Library-to-library edges are also computed but they are not comparable in static vs. dynamic analysis due to native calls. We filter out edges to implicit methods (static initializers, `loadClass()`) that are not statically modeled. We show five techniques:

1. *Elf.* This is the ELF reflection analysis [16], which also attempts to improve reflection analysis for Java.
2. *No substring.* Our reflection analysis, with engineering enhancements over the original DOOP framework, but no analysis of partial strings or their flow.
3. *Substring.* The analysis integrates the substring and substring flow analysis of Sect. 3.1.
4. *+Invent.* This analysis integrates substring analysis as well as the object invention technique of Sect. 3.2.
5. *+Backwards.*[3] This analysis integrates substring analysis as well as the back-propagation technique of Sect. 3.2.

It is important to note that, by design, our techniques do not enhance the precision of an analysis, only its empirical soundness. Thus, the techniques only find *more* edges: they cover more of the program. This improvement appears as a reduction in the figures ("lower is better") only because the number plotted is the *difference* in the missing edges compared to the dynamic analysis.

As can be seen, our techniques substantially increase the soundness of the analysis. In most benchmarks, more than half (to nearly all) of the missing *application-to-application* edges are recovered by at least one technique. The *application-to-library* missing edges also decreased, although not as much. In fact,

[3] The *+Backwards* and *+Invent* techniques are both additions to the substring analysis, but neither includes the other.

the *eclipse* benchmark was hardly being analyzed in the past, since most of the dynamic call-graph was missing.

Furthermore, although our approach emphasizes empirical soundness, it does not sacrifice scalability. All four of our settings are faster than ELF for almost all benchmarks. Aside from *jython*, for which only the ELF and *no substring* techniques are able to terminate before timeout, in all other cases *substring* and at least one of *+invent* or *+backwards* outperformed ELF, while in 7-of-10 benchmarks *all* our techniques outperformed ELF. This is due to achieving scalability using the threshold techniques of Sect. 3.3 instead of by sacrificing some empirical soundness, as ELF does. (A major design feature of ELF is that it explicitly avoids inferring reflection call targets when it cannot fully disambiguate them.)

For completeness, we also show a sanity-checking metric over our analyses. Empirical soundness could increase by computing a vastly imprecise call-graph. This is not the case for our techniques. Figure 3 lists the total static and dynamic edges being computed. On average, *+backwards* computes the most static edges (about 4.5 times the number of dynamic edges). On the lower end of the spectrum lies *no substring*, with a minimum of 3.4 times the number of dynamic edges being computed.

In pragmatic terms, a user of our analysis should use flags to pick the technique that yields more soundness without sacrificing scalability, for the given input program. This is a familiar approach—e.g., it also applies to picking the exact flavor and depth of context-sensitivity.

5 Related Work

The traditional handling of reflection in static analysis has been through integration of user input or dynamic information. The Tamiflex tool [4] exemplifies the state of the art. The tool observes the reflective calls in an actual execution of the program and rewrites the original code to produce a version without reflection calls. Instead, all original reflection calls become calls that perform identically to the observed execution. This is a practical approach, but results in a blend of dynamic and static analysis. It is unrealistic to expect that uses of reflection will always yield the same results in different dynamic executions—or there would be little reason to have the reflection (as opposed to static code) in the first place. Our approach attempts to restore the benefits of static analysis, with reasonable empirical soundness.

An alternative approach is that of Hirzel et al. [11,12], where an online pointer analysis is used to deal with reflection and dynamic loading by monitoring their run-time occurrence, recording their results, and running the analysis again, incrementally. This approach is quite interesting when applicable. However, maintaining and running a precise static analysis during program run time is often not realistic (e.g., for expensive context-sensitive analyses). Furthermore, the approach does not offer the off-line soundness guarantees one may expect from static analysis: it is not possible to ask questions regarding all methods that may ever be called via reflection, only the ones that have been called so far.

Interesting work on static treatments of reflection is often in the context of dynamic languages, where resolving reflective invocations is a necessity. Furr et al. [9] offer an analysis of how dynamic features are used in the Ruby language. Their observations are similar to ours: dynamic features (reflection in our case) are often used either with sets of constant arguments or with known prefixes/suffixes (e.g., to re-locate within the file system).

Madsen et al. [21] employ a use-based analysis technique in the context of Javascript. When objects are retrieved from unknown code (typically libraries) the analysis infers the object's properties from the way it is used in the client. In principle, this is a similar approach to our use-based techniques (both object invention and back-propagation) although the technical specifics differ. The conceptual precursor to both approaches is the work on reflection by Livshits et al. [18,20], which has been extensively discussed and contrasted throughout the paper (see Sects. 2 and 3.2).

Advanced techniques for string analysis have been presented by Christensen et al. [7]. They analyze complex string expressions and abstract them via a context-free grammar that is then widened to a regular language. Reflection is one of their examples but they only apply it to small benchmarks.

Stancu et al. [24] empirically compare profiling data with a points-to static analysis. However, they target only the most reflection-light benchmarks of the DaCapo 9.12-Bach suite and patch the code to avoid reflection entirely.

6 Conclusions

Highly dynamic features, such as reflection and dynamic loading, are the bane of static analysis. These features are not only hard to analyze well, but also ubiquitous in practice, thus limiting the practical impact of static analysis. We presented techniques for static reflection handling in Java program analysis. Our techniques build on top of state-of-the-art handling of reflection in Java, by elegantly extending declarative reasoning over reflection calls and inter-procedural object flow. Our main emphasis has been in achieving higher empirical soundness, i.e., in having the static analysis truly model observed dynamic behaviors. Although full soundness is infeasible for a realistic analysis, it is possible to produce general techniques that enhance the ability to analyze reflection calls.

Although our techniques improve on the problem of handling reflection, further work is necessary to achieve good scalability and empirical soundness for complex programs. Furthermore, our work has not addressed another major and commonly used dynamic feature: dynamic loading. Continued work will hopefully make such language features a lot more feasible to analyze statically.

Acknowledgments. We gratefully acknowledge funding by the European Research Council under grant 307334 (SPADE).

References

1. Ali, K., Lhoták, O.: Application-only call graph construction. In: Noble, J. (ed.) ECOOP 2012. LNCS, vol. 7313, pp. 688–712. Springer, Heidelberg (2012)
2. Ali, K., Lhoták, O.: AVERROES: whole-program analysis without the whole program. In: Castagna, G. (ed.) ECOOP 2013. LNCS, vol. 7920, pp. 378–400. Springer, Heidelberg (2013)
3. Blackburn, S.M., et al.: The DaCapo benchmarks: Java benchmarking development and analysis. In: Proceedings of the 21st Annual ACM SIGPLAN Conference on Object Oriented Programming, Systems, Languages, and Applications, OOPSLA 2006, pp. 169–190. ACM, New York (2006)
4. Bodden, E., Sewe, A., Sinschek, J., Oueslati, H., Mezini, M.: Taming reflection: Aiding static analysis in the presence of reflection and custom class loaders. In: Proceedings of the 33rd International Conference on Software Engineering, ICSE 2011, pp. 241–250. ACM, New York (2011)
5. Bravenboer, M., Smaragdakis, Y.: Exception analysis and points-to analysis: Better together. In: Proceedings of the 18th International Symposium on Software Testing and Analysis, ISSTA 2009, pp. 1–12. ACM, New York (2009)
6. Bravenboer, M., Smaragdakis, Y.: Strictly declarative specification of sophisticated points-to analyses. In: Proceedings of the 24th Annual ACM SIGPLAN Conference on Object Oriented Programming, Systems, Languages, and Applications, OOPSLA 2009. ACM, New York (2009)
7. Christensen, A.S., Møller, A., Schwartzbach, M.I.: Precise analysis of string expressions. In: Proceedings of the 10th International Symposium on Static Analysis, SAS 2003, pp. 1–18. Springer (2003)
8. Fink, S.J., et al.: WALA UserGuide: PointerAnalysis. http://wala.sourceforge.net/wiki/index.php/UserGuide:PointerAnalysis
9. Furr, M., An, J.D., Foster, J.S.: Profile-guided static typing for dynamic scripting languages. In: Proceedings of the 24th Annual ACM SIGPLAN Conference on Object Oriented Programming, Systems, Languages, and Applications, OOPSLA 2009, pp. 283–300. ACM, New York (2009)
10. Guarnieri, S., Livshits, B.: GateKeeper: mostly static enforcement of security and reliability policies for Javascript code. In: Proceedings of the 18th USENIX Security Symposium, SSYM 2009, pp. 151–168. USENIX Association, Berkeley (2009)
11. Hirzel, M., von Dincklage, D., Diwan, A., Hind, M.: Fast online pointer analysis. ACM Trans. Program. Lang. Syst. **29**(2), 11 (2007)
12. Hirzel, M., Diwan, A., Hind, M.: Pointer analysis in the presence of dynamic class loading. In: Odersky, M. (ed.) ECOOP 2004. LNCS, vol. 3086, pp. 96–122. Springer, Heidelberg (2004)
13. Kastrinis, G., Smaragdakis, Y.: Efficient and effective handling of exceptions in java points-to analysis. In: Jhala, R., De Bosschere, K. (eds.) Compiler Construction. LNCS, vol. 7791, pp. 41–60. Springer, Heidelberg (2013)
14. Kastrinis, G., Smaragdakis, Y.: Hybrid context-sensitivity for points-to analysis. In: Proceedings of the 2013 ACM SIGPLAN Conference on Programming Language Design and Implementation, PLDI 2013. ACM, New York (2013)
15. Lam, M.S., Whaley, J., Livshits, V.B., Martin, M.C., Avots, D., Carbin, M., Unkel, C.: Context-sensitive program analysis as database queries. In: Proceedings of the 24th Symposium on Principles of Database Systems, PODS 2005, pp. 1–12. ACM, New York (2005)

16. Li, Y., Tan, T., Sui, Y., Xue, J.: Self-inferencing reflection resolution for Java. In: Jones, R. (ed.) ECOOP 2014. LNCS, vol. 8586, pp. 27–53. Springer, Heidelberg (2014)
17. Liang, P., Naik, M.: Scaling abstraction refinement via pruning. In: Proceedings of the 2011 ACM SIGPLAN Conference on Programming Language Design and Implementation, PLDI 2011, pp. 590–601. ACM, New York (2011)
18. Livshits, B.: Improving Software Security with Precise Static and Runtime Analysis. Ph.D. thesis, Stanford University, December 2006
19. Livshits, B., et al.: In defense of soundiness: A manifesto. Commun. ACM **58**(2), 44–46 (2015)
20. Livshits, B., Whaley, J., Lam, M.S.: Reflection analysis for Java. In: Yi, K. (ed.) APLAS 2005. LNCS, vol. 3780, pp. 139–160. Springer, Heidelberg (2005)
21. Madsen, M., Livshits, B., Fanning, M.: Practical static analysis of JavaScript applications in the presence of frameworks and libraries. In: Proceedings of the ACM SIGSOFT International Symposium on the Foundations of Software Engineering, FSE 2013, pp. 499–509. ACM (2013)
22. Naik, M., Aiken, A., Whaley, J.: Effective static race detection for java. In: Proceedings of the 2006 ACM SIGPLAN Conference on Programming Language Design and Implementation, PLDI 2006, pp. 308–319. ACM, New York (2006)
23. Reps, T.W.: Demand interprocedural program analysis using logic databases. In: Ramakrishnan, R. (ed.) Applications of Logic Databases, pp. 163–196. Kluwer Academic Publishers, Boston (1994)
24. Stancu, C., Wimmer, C., Brunthaler, S., Larsen, P., Franz, M.: Comparing points-to static analysis with runtime recorded profiling data. In: Proceedings of the 2014 International Conference on Principles and Practices of Programming on the Java Platform Virtual Machines, Languages and Tools, PPPJ 2014, pp. 157–168. ACM (2014)
25. Whaley, J., Avots, D., Carbin, M., Lam, M.S.: Using datalog with binary decision diagrams for program analysis. In: Yi, K. (ed.) APLAS 2005. LNCS, vol. 3780, pp. 97–118. Springer, Heidelberg (2005)
26. Whaley, J., Lam, M.S.: Cloning-based context-sensitive pointer alias analysis using binary decision diagrams. In: Proceedings of the 2004 ACM SIGPLAN Conference on Programming Language Design and Implementation, PLDI 2004, pp. 131–144. ACM, New York (2004)

Author Index

Printed in the United States
By Bookmasters